G·L·O·B·A·L S·T

WESTERN EUROPE

SIXTH EDITION

Dr. Henri J. Warmenhoven

Virginia Commonwealth University

OTHER BOOKS IN THE GLOBAL STUDIES SERIES

- Africa
- China
- India and South Asia
- Japan and the Pacific Rim
- Latin America
- The Middle East
- Russia, the Eurasian Republics,
  and Central/Eastern Europe

Dushkin/McGraw-Hill
Sluice Dock, Guilford, Connecticut 06437
Visit us on the Internet—http://www.dushkin.com

STAFF

Ian A. Nielsen	Publisher
Brenda S. Filley	Production Manager
Lisa M. Clyde	Developmental Editor
Roberta Monaco	Editor
Charles Vitelli	Designer
Cheryl Greenleaf	Permissions Coordinator
Lisa Holmes-Doebrick	Administrative Coordinator
Lara M. Johnson	Design/Advertising Coordinator
Laura Levine	Graphics
Michael Campbell	Graphics
Tom Goddard	Graphics
Eldis Lima	Graphics
Juliana Arbo	Typesetting Supervisor

Cataloging in Publication Data
Main Entry under title: Global Studies: Western Europe.
  1. Europe—History—1945–. 2. Europe—Politics and government—1945–. 3. Europe—
Civilization—1945–. I. Title: Western Europe. II. Warmenhoven, Henri J., *comp.*
ISBN 0–07-024995-4

Sixth Edition

We would like to thank Digital Wisdom Incorporated for allowing us to use their Mountain High Maps cartography software. This software was used to create the relief maps in this edition.

Printed in the United States of America   1234567890BAHBAH5432109   Printed on Recycled Paper

Western Europe

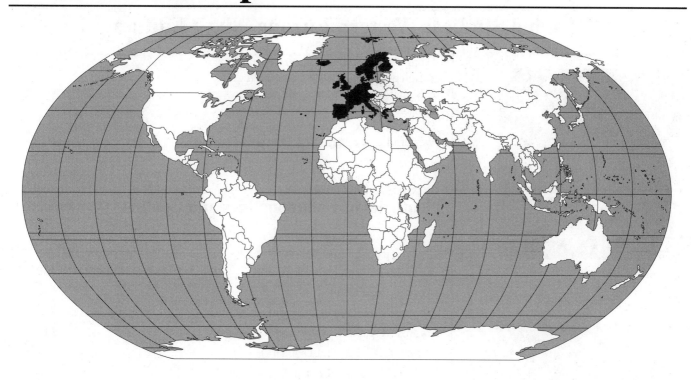

AUTHOR/EDITOR

Dr. Henri J. Warmenhoven

Born and raised in Southeast Asia, the author/editor of *Global Studies: Western Europe* studied law at the Law School of Leyden University in the Netherlands. Having earned the Bachelor's and Master's degrees, he served for some years in a legal capacity with the Secretariat of Netherlands New Guinea. Rather than returning to the Netherlands, Dr. Warmenhoven enrolled in graduate studies in the Political Science Department of Melbourne University in Australia. The primary foci of his Master's and Ph.D. studies there were Comparative and International Politics. Having lived in Australia for 5 years, Dr. Warmenhoven accepted a position with the Virginia Commonwealth University. There he taught for 25 years, a period punctuated by frequent research trips to Western Europe. Dr. Warmenhoven also participated in a faculty exchange with a French university. Recently accorded the Emeritus status, he teaches occasional courses in International Relations and European Politics.

CONTRIBUTORS
Paul M. Cole
Center for Strategic and International Studies

Dr. David Gress
The Hoover Institution

Professor Martin O. Heisler
Department of Government and Politics
University of Maryland

Contents

Global Studies: Western Europe, Sixth Edition

Western Europe Politics   *Page 43*

Belgium   *Page 56*

Germany   *Page 82*

Italy   *Page105*

Spain   *Page 136*

United Kingdom   *Page 161*

Using Global Studies: Western Europe

THE GLOBAL STUDIES SERIES

The Global Studies series was created to help readers acquire a basic knowledge and understanding of the regions and countries in the world. Each volume provides a foundation of information—geographic, cultural, economic, political, historical, artistic, and religious—that will allow readers to better assess the current and future problems within these countries and regions and to comprehend how events there might affect their own well-being. In short, these volumes present the background information necessary to respond to the realities of our global age.

Each of the volumes in the Global Studies series is crafted under the careful direction of an author/editor—an expert in the area under study. The author/editors teach and conduct research and have traveled extensively through the regions about which they are writing.

In this *Global Studies: Western Europe* edition, the author/editor has written a regional essay and country reports for each of the countries included.

MAJOR FEATURES OF
THE GLOBAL STUDIES SERIES

The Global Studies volumes are organized to provide concise information on the regions and countries within those areas under study. The major sections and features of the books are described here.

Regional Essay

For *Global Studies: Western Europe,* the author/editor has written an essay focusing on the history and current characteristics of Western Europe. A regional map accompanies the essay.

Country Reports

Concise reports are written for each of the countries within the region under study. These reports are the heart of each Global Studies volume. *Global Studies: Western Europe, Sixth Edition,* contains 25 country reports.

The country reports are composed of five standard elements. Each report contains a detailed map visually positioning the country among its neighboring states; a summary of statistical information; a current essay providing important historical, geographical, political, cultural, and economic information; a historical timeline, offering a convenient visual survey of a few key historical events; and four "graphic indicators," with summary statements about the country in terms of development, freedom, health/welfare, and achievements.

A Note on the Statistical Reports

The statistical information provided for each country has been drawn from a wide range of sources. (The most frequently referenced are listed on page 246.) Every effort has been made to provide the most current and accurate information available. However, sometimes the information cited by these sources differs to some extent; and, all too often, the most current information available for some countries is somewhat dated. Aside from these occasional difficulties, the statistical summary of each country is generally quite complete and up to date. Care should be taken, however, in using these statistics (or, for that matter, any published statistics) in making hard comparisons among countries. We have also provided comparable statistics for the United States and Canada, which can be found on pages viii and ix.

World Press Articles

Within each Global Studies volume is reprinted a number of articles carefully selected by our editorial staff and the author/editor from a broad range of international periodicals and newspapers. The articles have been chosen for currency, interest, and their differing perspectives on the subject countries. There are 17 articles in *Global Studies: Western Europe, Sixth Edition.*

The articles section is preceded by an annotated table of contents as well as a topic guide. The annotated table of contents offers a brief summary of each article, while the topic guide indicates the main theme(s) of each article. Thus, readers desiring to focus on articles dealing with a particular theme, say, the environment, may refer to the topic guide to find those articles.

WWW Sites

An extensive annotated list of selected World Wide Web sites can be found on the facing page (vii) in this edition of *Global Studies: Western Europe.* In addition, the URL addresses for country-specific Web sites are provided on the statistics page of most countries. All of the Web site addresses were correct and operational at press time. Instructors and students alike are urged to refer to those sites often to enhance their understanding of the region and to keep up with current events.

Glossary, Bibliography, Index

At the back of each Global Studies volume, readers will find a glossary of terms and abbreviations, which provides a quick reference to the specialized vocabulary of the area under study and to the standard abbreviations used throughout the volume.

Following the glossary is a bibliography, which lists general works, national histories, and current-events publications and periodicals that provide regular coverage on Western Europe.

The index at the end of the volume is an accurate reference to the contents of the volume. Readers seeking specific information and citations should consult this standard index.

Currency and Usefulness

Global Studies: Western Europe, like the other Global Studies volumes, is intended to provide the most current and useful information available necessary to understand the events that are shaping the cultures of the region today.

This volume is revised on a regular basis. The statistics are updated, regional essays and country reports revised, and world press articles replaced. In order to accomplish this task, we turn to our author/editor, our advisory boards, and—hopefully—to you, the users of this volume. Your comments are more than welcome. If you have an idea that you think will make the next edition more useful, an article or bit of information that will make it more current, or a general comment on its organization, content, or features that you would like to share with us, please send it in for serious consideration.

Selected World Wide Web Sites for *Global Studies: Western Europe*

GENERAL SITES

BBC World Service—**http://www.bbc.co.uk/worldservice/europe/**—The BBC, one of the world's most successful radio networks, provides the latest news from around the world and in Western Europe at this site. It is possible to access the news in several languages.

CNN Online Page—**http://www.cnn.com**—U.S. 24-hour video news channel. News, updated every few hours, includes text, pictures, and film. Good external links.

C-SPAN ONLINE—**http://www.c-span.org**—See especially C-SPAN International on the Web for International Programming Highlights and archived C-SPAN programs.

International Network Information Center at University of Texas—**http://inic.utexas.edu**—Links to international sites, including United Kingdom and Western Europe.

Penn Library: Resources by Subject—**http://www.library. upenn.edu/resources/subject/subject.html**—This vast site is rich in links to information about the United Kingdom and Western Europe.

Political Science RESOURCES—**http://www.psr.keele.ac. uk**—A dynamic gateway to sources available via European addresses. Listed by country name.

ReliefWeb—**http://wwwnotes.reliefweb.int**—UN's Department of Humanitarian Affairs clearinghouse for international humanitarian emergencies.

Social Science Information Gateway [SOSIG]—**http:// sosig.esrc.bris.ac.uk**—Project of the Economic and Social Research Council [ESRC]. It catalogs 22 subjects and lists countries' URL addresses.

Speech and Transcript Center—**http://gwis2.circ.gwu.edu/~ gprice/speech.htm**—This unusual site is the repository of transcripts of every kind, from radio and television, of speeches by world government leaders, and the proceedings of groups like the United Nations, NATO, and the World Bank.

United Nations System—**http://www.unsystem.org**—This is the official Web site for the United Nations system of organizations. Everything is listed alphabetically.

U.S. Central Intelligence Agency—**http://www.odci.gov/cia**—This site includes information about the CIA and its publications: *The World Factbook, Factbook on Intelligence, Handbook of International Economic Statistics,* and CIA maps. The *World Factbook* contains extensive statistics on all the countries of the world.

U.S. Department of State—**http://www.state.gov/index. html**—Organized alphabetically: Country Reports, Human Rights, International Organizations, etc.

World Bank Group—**http://www.worldbank.org/html/Welcome. html**—News [i.e., press releases, summary of new projects, speeches], publications, topics in development, countries, and regions. Links to other financial organizations.

World Trade Organization [WTO]—**http://www.wto.org**—Topics include foundation of world trade systems, data on textiles, intellectual property rights, legal frameworks, trade and environmental policies, recent agreements, and others.

GENERAL EUROPEAN SITES

Europa—**http://europa.eu.int**—This site provides information on the European Union's goals and policies, history, institutions, publications, and statistics.

IM-Europe—**http://www2.echo.lu**—This site lists the European Union's programs and activities; it also offers the context of official texts, as well as current relevant news.

NATO—**http://www.nato.int**—This is the official site of the North Atlantic Treaty Organization. The site includes information on members, current programs, policy statements, and current relevant news.

SELECTED COUNTRIES

Austria: General—**http://www.austria.org**—This site outlines the history, government, and statistics of Austria, and presents solid general information about the country.

Denmark: Royal Danish Embassy in Washington—**http:// www.denmarkemb.org**—Offers interesting background on the Vikings, an extensive profile of Queen Margrethe II, and a guide for tracing Danish ancestry.

Finland: Virtual Finland—**http://virtual.finland.fi**—This site has background on government institutions, recent political events, and some information on Finnish culture.

France: French Embassy in Washington—**http://www.info-france-usa.org**—This site offers a profile of the French government and culture, and allows the visitor to select a region of France for specific information.

Germany: German Embassy and German Information Center—**http://www.germany-info.org**—This site offers many links to German topics such as facts, figures, statistics, news, history, and government. It also includes current information about German life today.

Greece: The Greek Embassy in Washington—**http://www. greekembassy.org**—This large site offers information on Greek culture, history, and links to many Greek ministries and U.S.–Greek organizations.

Information on the Irish State—**http://www.irlgov.ie/frmain. htm**—Information about all aspects of the government of the Republic of Ireland can be found at this Web site.

Italy: Windows on Italy—**http://www.mi.cnr.it/WOI/**—This site delves deep into Italian history, and includes links to pages on some 100 Italian cities and towns.

Luxembourg: Survey of Luxembourg—**http://www.restena. lu/luxembourg/**—This site outlines the history of the grand duchy as well as its geography, culture, language, and cuisine.

Netherlands: Netherlands Board of Tourism—**http://www. NBT.nl**—The links on this site include information on culture, history, geography, and politics.

Sweden: The Swedish Embassy—**http://www.sweden.nw. dc.us/sweden/**—This site offers information on geography, politics, culture, and current events.

United Kingdom: Britain in the U.S.—**http://www.britain-info.org**—This site highlights top stories of the British press, and also links to information on politics, geography, and history.

Most individual country report pages have additional Web sites.

The United States (United States of America)

GEOGRAPHY

Area in Square Miles (Kilometers):
3,618,770 (9,578,626) (slightly larger than China)

Capital (Population): Washington, D.C. (567,100)

Environmental Concerns: air pollution resulting in acid rain; water pollution from runoff of pesticides and fertilizers; desertification; habitat loss; other concerns

Geographical Features: vast central plain, mountains in the west; hills and low mountains in the east; rugged mountains and broad river valleys in Alaska; volcanic topography in Hawaii

Climate: mostly temperate; wide regional variations

PEOPLE

Population

Total: 270,312,000

Annual Growth Rate: 0.87%

Rural/Urban Population Ratio: 24/76

Major Languages: predominantly English; a sizable Spanish-speaking minority; many others

Ethnic Makeup: 83% white; 12% black; 5% Asian, Amerindian, and others

Religions: 56% Protestant; 28% Roman Catholic; 2% Jewish; 14% others or no affiliation

Health

Life Expectancy at Birth: 73 years (male); 80 years (female)

Infant Mortality Rate (Ratio): 6.44/1,000

Average Caloric Intake: 138% of FAO minimum

Physicians Available (Ratio): 1/381

Education

Adult Literacy Rate: 97.9% (official) (estimates vary widely)

Compulsory (Ages): 7–16; free

COMMUNICATION

Telephones: 1 per 1.6 people

Daily Newspaper Circulation: 228 per 1,000 people; approximately 63,000,000 circulation

Televisions: 1 per 1.2 people

TRANSPORTATION

Highways in Miles (Kilometers): 3,906,960 (6,261,154)

Railroads in Miles (Kilometers): 149,161 (240,000)

Usable Airfields: 13,387

Motor Vehicles in Use: 200,500,000

GOVERNMENT

Type: federal republic

Independence Date: July 4, 1776 (from United Kingdom)

Head of State: President William ("Bill") Jefferson Clinton

Political Parties: Democratic Party; Republican Party; others of minor political significance

Suffrage: universal at 18

MILITARY

Military Expenditures (% of GDP): 3.8%

Current Disputes: none

ECONOMY

Per Capita Income/GDP: $30,200/$8.08 trillion

GDP Growth Rate: 3.8%

Inflation Rate: 2%

Unemployment Rate: 4.9%

Labor Force: 136,300,000

Natural Resources: metallic and nonmetallic minerals; petroleum; natural gas; timber

Agriculture: food grains; feed crops; oil-bearing crops; livestock; dairy products

Industry: diversified in both capital- and consumer-goods industries

Exports: $625.1 billion (primary partners Canada, Western Europe, Japan, Mexico)

Imports: $822 billion (primary partners Canada, Western Europe, Japan, Mexico)

Canada*

GEOGRAPHY

Area in Square Miles (Kilometers):
3,850,790 (9,976,140) (slightly larger than the United States)

Capital (Population): Ottawa (1,000,000)

Environmental Concerns: air pollution and resulting acid rain severely affecting lakes and damaging forests; water pollution

Geographical Features: permafrost in the north; mountains in the west; central plains

Climate: from temperate in south to subarctic and arctic in north

PEOPLE

Population

Total: 30,676,000

Annual Growth Rate: 1.09%

Rural/Urban Population Ratio: 23/77

Major Languages: both English and French are official

Ethnic Makeup: 40% British Isles origin; 27% French origin; 20% other European; 1.5% indigenous Indian and Eskimo; 11.5% others, mostly Asian

Religions: 46% Roman Catholic; 16% United Church; 10% Anglican; 28% others

Health

Life Expectancy at Birth: 76 years (male); 83 years (female)

Infant Mortality Rate (Ratio): 5.59/1,000

Average Caloric Intake: 127% of FAO minimum

Physicians Available (Ratio): 1/464

Education

Adult Literacy Rate: 97%

Compulsory (Ages): primary school

COMMUNICATION

Telephones: 1 per 1.7 people

Daily Newspaper Circulation: 189 per 1,000 people

Televisions: 1 per 1.5 people

TRANSPORTATION

Highways in Miles (Kilometers): 637,104 (1,021,000)

Railroads in Miles (Kilometers): 48,764 (78,148)

Usable Airfields: 1,139

Motor Vehicles in Use: 16,700,000

GOVERNMENT

Type: confederation with parliamentary democracy

Independence Date: July 1, 1867 (from United Kingdom)

Head of State/Government: Queen Elizabeth II; Prime Minister Jean Chrétien

Political Parties: Progressive Conservative Party; Liberal Party; New Democratic Party; Reform Party; Bloc Québécois

Suffrage: universal at 18

MILITARY

Military Expenditures (% of GDP): 1.53%

Current Disputes: none

ECONOMY

Currency ($U.S. Equivalent): 1.53 Canadian dollars = $1

Per Capita Income/GDP: $21,700/$658 billion

GDP Growth Rate: 3.5%

Inflation Rate: 1.8%

Unemployment Rate: 8.6%

Labor Force: 15,300,000

Natural Resources: petroleum; coal; natural gas; fish and other wildlife; minerals; cement; forestry products

Agriculture: grains; livestock; dairy products; potatoes; hogs; poultry and eggs; tobacco

Industry: oil production and refining; natural-gas development; fish products; wood and paper products; chemicals; transportation equipment

Exports: $208.6 billion (primary partners United States, Japan, United Kingdom)

Imports: $194.4 billion (primary partners United States, Japan, United Kingdom)

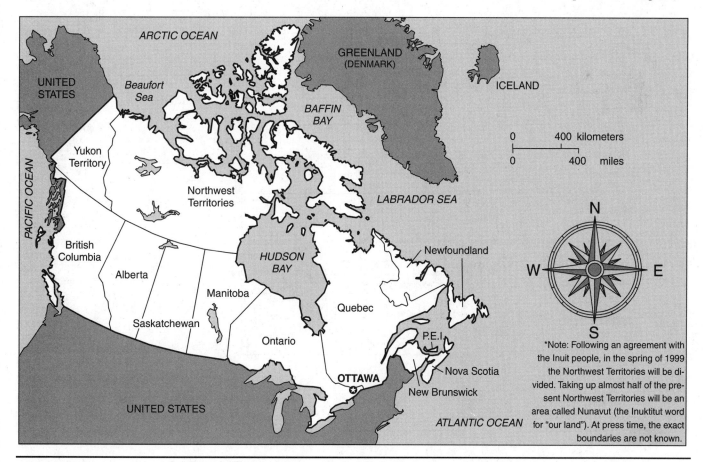

*Note: Following an agreement with the Inuit people, in the spring of 1999 the Northwest Territories will be divided. Taking up almost half of the present Northwest Territories will be an area called Nunavut (the Inuktitut word for "our land"). At press time, the exact boundaries are not known.

This map is provided to give you a graphic picture of where the countries of the world are located, the relationships they have with their region and neighbors, and their positions relative to the superpowers and power blocs. We have focused on certain areas to illustrate these crowded regions more clearly.

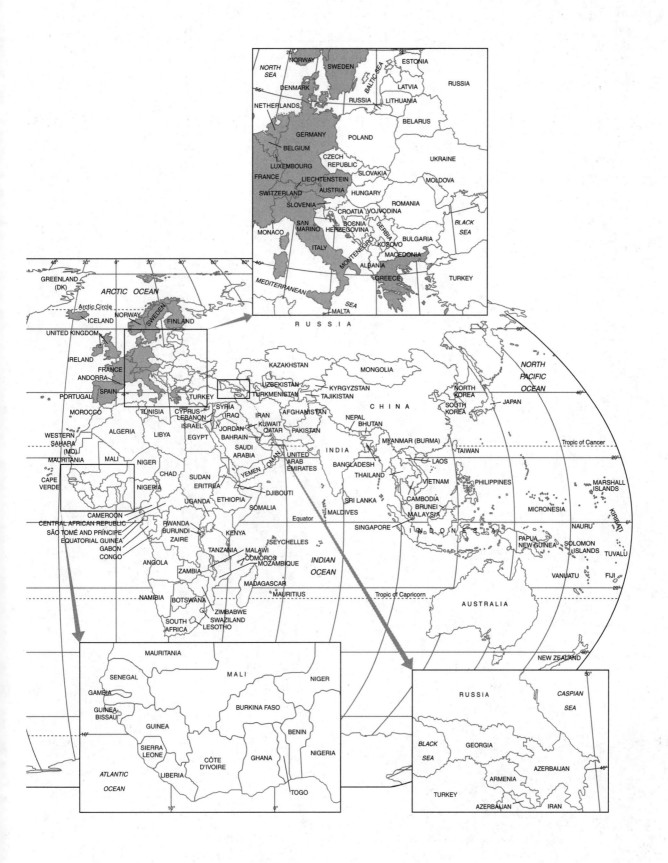

Western Europe

Western Europe:
Centuries of Commonalities and Conflict

British historian Arnold Toynbee compared civilizations to living organisms. Civilizations, he said, are born, grow, flourish, and, after several centuries, die—that is, they fail to exert political or economic influence.

The European continent has spawned a variety of civilizations over the course of time. For many centuries, Europe was the equivalent of the known world, and its impact on global events has been truly formidable. World history was long defined from strictly European perspectives, a tendency that has been labeled *Eurocentrism.* (Indeed, many people argue that Eurocentrism persists to this day.) However, two world wars (1914–1918 and 1939–1945) were to a large extent fought in the European theater, and the devastation that they wrought reduced the continent's prestige and influence. Europe's leading position in the world rapidly faded as a result, becoming in effect a phenomenon of the past.

In recent years, however, Europe has proven to be a reservoir, stronger and more durable than most analysts and observers had deemed possible.

EUROPE AND THE NEW WORLD ORDER
Although death and destruction during World War II were not confined to Europe, the continent took a thorough beating during those years. No wonder, then, that shortly afterward, disgust and revulsion with war emerged. These sentiments, in combination with observation of the stunning success of the United States' economic aid program for Europe known as the Marshall Plan, led a Frenchman named Jean Monnet to envision a European economic and political federation. His vision was translated by Robert Schuman, another Frenchman, into a declaration that aimed at Europe's eventual political and economic unification. The Schuman Declaration (1950) heralded the European Communities; and, although that term started to be used by the late 1980s in the singular (that is, the *European Community,* or EC), it gained spectacularly in substance. In the early 1990s, the EC entered one of its most critical phases, that of political union, a concept that would grant Europe a powerful impetus in world affairs. Indeed, it has since come to be called the *European Union,* or EU. (*Note:* The European Union is discussed at various points later in this essay as well as in the individual country reports and the articles section.)

There is no certainty yet whether a new political system, in the nation-state sense, is in the making as a result of centripetal forces. But a most remarkable coincidence is taking place: The "renaissance of Europe" (a phrase that in this context has political and economic overtones in contrast to its fifteenth-century meaning) coincides with the disappearance of the rivalry between the states and the confrontation of the two cold war superpowers, the Soviet Union and the United States.

It is true that these superpowers emerged as a by-product of World War II and that some 40 years later, in the late 1980s, one of them, the Soviet Union, crumbled and disintegrated.

By the same token the United States often appears to have lost its appetite for superpowership. The United States seems more eager to leave global issues and conflicts to international organizations, notably to the United Nations, which, now that the competition for superpowership has ended, has become a somewhat more workable instrument in conflict management. There can thus be no doubt that a new world order is emerging and that Western Europe is to play a large role in that construct.

The world as a whole still bristles with Western European concepts and ideas. This is well illustrated by the struggle for economic advancement and greater political autonomy in many countries in Asia, Africa, and Latin America—often called the *Third World* or the *developing world.* The belief in prosperity and the belief in self-government both derive from the European treasury of ideas (although their transplantation to the United States boosted them substantially).

Another major change in world politics that illustrates the enduring influence of European ideas is the rise of Japan as a global economic power. Japan's current democratic system of government as well as its technology derive from Western, if not solely European, foundations, although both have also been influenced by indigenous traditions. Japan has started to be included in definitions of what is conceived of as "the West." It is no longer only the Trilateral Commission, the Organization of European Cooperation and Development (OECD), and the so-called Group of Seven (G-7) that include Japan as a part of the West.

WHY STUDY WESTERN EUROPE?
Two major sets of reasons explain why the study of Western Europe is critical. The first is cultural or philosophical and has to do with the significance of European ideas. The second is political and strategic and concerns the economic and political importance of Western Europe today as a group of countries that, even though they no longer control the world, nevertheless exercise considerable economic and diplomatic power and influence.

The cultural or philosophical reason for studying Western Europe focuses on the dominant role of European ideas around the world. The U.S. Constitution, to cite one example, is one of the finest expressions of European ideas about the limitation of power, freedom, and human rights; and the legal and political arguments in the United States concerning civil rights—what they are, and how they are best protected—are based on European ideas about society, citizenship, and freedom. In addition, there are the concepts of the "just war," the justification of self-defense, and peace, all issues that have been perennial questions in the American (and European) debate. Religious pluralism, arguments over the separation of church and state, and the relationship of religion to politics are also issues paramount in the United States that sprouted in Europe and still have significance there.

(United Nations/Nagata)

A harmonious blend of cultures and historical eras characterizes the Western Europe of today, as this view of Genoa, Italy, illustrates.

There are also important political and strategic reasons to study Europe: For half a century, Canada and the United States have been militarily allied with 14 Western European countries. The North Atlantic Treaty Organization (NATO, or the *Atlantic Alliance*) was founded in 1949, primarily as a military association against possible expansion on the part of the Soviet Union. It has experienced a great many ups and downs. In addition to some intra-NATO quarrels, there has been recurring friction concerning the very superior position that the United States has taken in NATO as well as frequent squabbles about the relative contributions that members should give to the total effort. Until recently, this effort was, as NATO's Charter stated, in large part dedicated to the containment of communism in the European theater. For decades, the alliance was far and away the most important foreign-policy commitment to which the United States was bound.

Interestingly, when the Soviet or Eastern bloc (a term referring to the Soviet Union and the majority of Central/Eastern European countries) collapsed beginning in 1989—an eventuality that few analysts had foreseen or predicted—the Warsaw Treaty Organization (NATO's opposite number, also known as the Warsaw Pact) disintegrated as well. NATO itself, however, was left intact, although its future role has become uncertain, and the organization's dismal record in containing the various nationalist crises in the former Yugoslavia, in the 1990s has given rise to considerable skepticism about its purpose and effectiveness. As of yet,

however, no plans have been made to abolish or dissolve the Atlantic Alliance; on the contrary, it has been enlarged by new partnerships, including, in 1999, three countries from the former Eastern bloc: Hungary, the Czech Republic, and Poland.

For many North Americans, Europe conjures stereotypical biases. An example is the perception that Europe is fragmented and, in fact, irreversibly divided. Until recently, the main fault line was the so-called Iron Curtain, which divided Communist Central/Eastern Europe on the one hand and democratic Western Europe on the other. But even that basic division, which is now grossly obsolete, was surrounded by erroneous notions. Other North American ideas concerning Europe have reference to an abundance of internal continental differences, such as ethnicity, varieties of beliefs, and lifestyle and linguistic differences. One may also point to class distinctions, believed to be more endemic to Europe than to the supposedly egalitarian societies of Canada and the United States.

Thus, the notion persists that people in Europe generally favor democratic ideals but that their societies have on the whole remained stagnant. As a contrast, in the United States, democracy materialized, coming to expression in the 1787 Constitution. Even Thomas Jefferson, one of the most sophisticated Americans of his day—a man, moreover, who had lived and traveled in Europe—at one point exclaimed, "We are ahead of Europe in political science." By this he meant that while the science of government might have originated in Europe, the United States had started to apply it, testing democratic tenets by putting them into practice. In Europe, on the other hand, much of the theory and philosophy of government had an aura of unreality, consisting of distant ideals.

Since North American values are closely related to those nursed and fostered in Europe, many Americans and Canadians assume that Western Europeans are just like them and certainly less different or interesting than Russians, Arabs, Japanese, or any other powerful but non-Western European group whose activities *appear* to be more dramatic or *seem* to affect North America more immediately. During the first few decades after World War II, Europe certainly diminished in political and economic importance. But it has clearly risen again, another major reason for studying the region.

Finally, study of Western Europe is valuable if only because it is an intrinsically interesting part of the world. Nowhere else is found such a combination and variety of political and economic traditions and practices, cultural and social pluralism, and artistic and intellectual heritage, based on a rich and thoroughly documented record of great achievements as well as great disasters.

Should "Western Europe" Be Redefined?
The question could be raised as to what extent the qualification "Western" in the phrase "Western Europe" is still relevant, now that the Berlin Wall has been dismantled and the Iron Curtain has fallen. It should be remembered that "Western" in this context has never been applied as a geographical qualification per se. In a strictly geographical sense, for example, Finland, Greece, and Cyprus fall outside Western Europe. The term thus has a distinctly ideological ring, conveying notions and ideals of democracy (often explicitly excluding communism). It also fosters impressions of political and economic predictability as well as social and technological advancement. It is possible that in the not-too-distant future, the differences between Western and Central/Eastern Europe will have been reduced to the extent that treatment of Western and Central/Eastern Europe as separate entities may no longer be justified or meaningful. For the moment, however, strong contrasts still exist.

HOW TO STUDY WESTERN EUROPE
The variety of political, economic, and social arrangements in Western Europe is such that there is no best single way of looking at this region. It is thus necessary to combine elements of four approaches. The first three approaches concern various levels of political and economic organization, starting at the broadest and most comprehensive level. The fourth approach relates to issues and policies. We utilize all of these approaches in this volume.

The First Approach: Country Studies
The first approach to studying Western Europe concerns the level of individual countries, which has been the traditional method of historical and area studies. The concept of the nation-state emerged when the Peace of Westphalia was concluded in 1648. That same era also gave birth to international law. As a result, Western Europe was rarely viewed as a consistent entity but, rather, as a conglomeration of countries, internally fragmented and competing for power among themselves.

Two questions may thus be raised. First, why is Europe not more integrated? (One of the answers would undoubtedly be because ethnicity and culture have proven to be such strong variables.) Second, is it possible to speak of a Western European system? (Here the answer should be no, or not yet, except in a purely political sense.) For a full elaboration of both questions and answers, the individual-country approach lends itself well, especially since it by no means ignores the multiple interactions between the nation-states.

The Second Approach: Supranational Networks
The second approach focuses on the supranational economic and security networks, such as the European Union and NATO, respectively. At this level, we learn of the broad limits of policy, how Western European leaders perceive their common interests, and how these countries relate diplomatically, economically, and militarily as a group to other actors on the world scene, the most important or dominant being the United States and Russia (generally accepted as the successor state of the Soviet Union). Russia, of course, is no longer considered a superpower and, in that sense, cannot be compared to the United States. But in terms of geography, it is for all intents and purposes a large, neighboring power—and, what is more, a large, neighboring power with a nuclear arsenal.

Several things should be kept in mind when examining Europe at this level. First, a lot more is going on in Western Europe than merely the activities of organizations like NATO and the EU. Second, the memberships of these organizations do not include all the countries of Western Europe. (And, in the case of NATO, it includes non-European members.) Finally, ideologies and religions in Western Europe operate most distinctively at this level. Examples are the peace and disarmament movements of the 1970s and 1980s, respectively; the international youth culture; and a great variety of religious activities and currents.

The Third Approach: Regionalism
The third approach focuses on regions within countries or across borders. *Regionalism* is a term that has come up in the EU vocabulary, where it refers to some of the more outlying regions (such as Sicily and Scotland) among its members. These usually have been poor or less developed and, as such, deserving of special policies for economic activity. One has to bear in mind that regional issues more often than not are ethnic issues—that is, on the fringes of nation-states, one will often find ethnically divergent peoples.

Nation-states endeavor to control their borders and enforce compliance from their subjects. National governments make economic, social, and military policy; but nationality, language, and cultural or ethnic affiliation do not always coincide. In recent years, many ethnic groups have rediscovered their roots (such as the Welsh) and cross-border connections (such as German-speaking Italians), often the result of conquests and wars. This has given rise to a range of activities, mostly cultural, but some political. In the future, these areas are bound to merit increasing attention.

The Fourth Approach: Comparative
The fourth approach to the study of Western Europe is truly comparative, concentrating on government institutions, policy formation, issues, and the all-important linkage mechanisms such as party systems and interest groups. This approach endeavors to find how governmental and nongovernmental institutions compare in several or all countries. Among the many issues that need to be studied and compared are defense, the environment, welfare policy, and unemployment.

Utilizing the Approaches
It is possible to construct a time frame that employs all four approaches. This time frame has six sections: 1) the pre-1945 background; 2) reconstruction, 1945–1951; 3) the consolidation of Western Europe and the cold war, 1951–1963; 4) prosperity and détente, 1963–1973; 5) stagflation and insecurity, 1973–1989; and 6) since the end of the cold war, 1989–present.

While such a division is practicable and useful, one must bear in mind that the dates are somewhat tentative and that the periods overlap to some extent. There can, for example, be no doubt that both the consolidation of Western Europe and the cold war started earlier than 1951, while détente was an intermittent phenomenon at best, punctuating an extended phase, much longer than the years specified.

PRE-1945 BACKGROUND
Western Europe owes part of its political organization to the Romans, whose empire started to dissolve between the fifth and ninth centuries A.D. This protracted dissolution was marked by a great deal of political fragmentation and instability, which in turn produced massive migrations, occasionally on the part of small groups of extended families but also by larger tribes across Western Asia, Northern Africa, and Europe. As these movements gradually stabilized, the main centers of economic and cultural activity of Western civilization moved from the Mediterranean littoral to the river valleys of Western Europe, between the North Sea, the Alps, and the Western Mediterranean.

From the ninth to the thirteenth centuries, the settled, cultivated parts of Europe comprised roughly the same territory as Western Europe today. The major nationalities—including French, German, Italian, and English—emerged. Most Western European countries came into being as recognizable political entities during the Middle Ages. The most fundamental political conflict in Western Europe before 1945—that between French- and German-speaking peoples for control of Northwestern Europe and control of the political and cultural legacy of the Roman Empire—began in that period, with the breakup of the Carolingian Empire in the mid-ninth century. This empire had included the ancestors of both the French and the German nations and was in effect the only successful attempt to unite these two ethnically different societies under one government. The eleventh century produced a landmark, in that the Normandic invasion led by William the Conqueror changed England both demographically and linguistically.

In the fourteenth century, England, which was already a centralized monarchy under a single ruler, held large parts of France under its dominion. For a considerable period, England replaced a variety of Middle European principalities (most of whose people spoke Teutonic dialects) as France's main opponent. In that time, England reigned supreme in various parts of western France. In the fifteenth century, the French drove out the English, an effort that led to national unity and centralized political organization.

Early Modern Western Europe
Although feudalism and prefeudal conditions (e.g., the Roman Empire) greatly influenced the growth and development of Western Europe, the Peace of Westphalia, concluded in 1648, usually serves as an important historical watershed. It was then that the nation-state emerged as a form of political organization. Between the middle of the seventeenth century and the outbreak of the French Revolution in 1789, Western Europe developed its modern identity: a system of sovereign states. A number of countries, such as England, France, Spain, and the Scandinavian countries (Norway, Sweden, Finland, and Denmark, also called the *Nordic Countries*), assumed the size and adopted the character they have today. Germany, the Netherlands, the Alpine and Danubian lands, and Italy were divided politically into territories belonging to a loose federation that covered most of Central/Eastern Europe and, since the twelfth century, included the Holy Roman Empire on the one hand and a number of smaller nations on the other.

The Protestant Reformation, initiated in 1517, started to have a profound political impact after 1530. It divided Europe into hostile religious camps, each claiming the right to subject and convert the other. The old dichotomy of church and state, which had been strictly observed throughout the centuries of the Holy Roman Empire, now started to come apart. In addition, the old conflict between France and the diverse German states revived.

The combination of these and other religious, ideological, territorial, and dynastic struggles led to the cataclysm of the Thirty Years' War (1618–1648). This was the greatest disaster

The Reformation had its seeds in the 1520 excommunication of Martin Luther by Pope Leo X. This illustration portrays some of the notable events of the Reformation era.

in European history occurring between the Black Death of 1348–1349 and World War I. More than half the population of Germany, where almost all the action took place, perished as a result of the Thirty Years' War. It ended in the Peace of Westphalia, which more or less defined the nation-state and laid down precise rules for international relations. This drastically reduced the frequency and severity of wars in the period between the middle of the seventeenth century and the end of the eighteenth century.

The largest and most prosperous country for most of that period was France, which had 20 million inhabitants. The 12 million Germans had not found a home in a single state; rather, they were organized politically in a number of states, most of which in one way or another were affiliated with the Holy Roman Empire, an entity that dissolved in 1806. England, which, after annexing Scotland in 1707, had started to be called Great Britain, remained a much smaller and less important country until about 1800. However, as a result of the British victory over Napoleon Bonaparte, the enormous growth of its colonial empire, and its vanguard position in the Industrial Revolution, the nineteenth century was to become the "Century of Britain."

Political Development (1789–1914)

The term *sovereignty,* a product of international law, originally derived from the word *sovereign*—that is, the monarch. The French Revolution had no difficulty discarding the monarchy but apparently did not want to relinquish the idea of sovereignty. Thus, the world witnessed the emergence of popular sovereignty as a joint product of the American experience and the French Revolution. Following John Locke, an English philosopher, the idea took hold in Europe that kings were to rule at the mercy of the people—the people were to set the parameters of royal power. The republican and democratic concept of rule by the people through their chosen representatives turned out to be the first of four major and related factors that shaped European history in the nineteenth century.

(The Bettmann Archive)

A depiction of the storming of the Bastille, July 14, 1789, the event that sparked the French Revolution.

A second strong force was *nationalism,* the belief that people who belonged to one ethnic strain, who spoke one language, and who fostered one culture were to cherish and maintain a common identity and that they ideally should live under one government. Nationalism, either in a democratic or an authoritarian format, held a particular appeal for politically divided minorities, such as could be found in what was to become Germany and Italy.

A third factor was *industrialism.* From about 1770, British inventors and entrepreneurs were discovering and organizing modern, industrial methods of production. The Industrial Revolution that resulted spread to the continent in the second half of the nineteenth century and was accompanied by rapid population growth. The population of Western Europe expanded from 72 million in 1680, to 115 million in 1820, and to 200 million in 1900.

This was followed by the emergence of *socialism* as a powerful force. Initially, this new ideology represented little more than a response to the often unscrupulous methods increasingly applied in the latter stages of the Industrial Revolution. A number of thinkers found that government was not the only evil against which people had to be protected. One had also to watch against the economically powerful— the capitalists, as they had started to be called in the late nineteenth century. They too could cause oppression, depriv-

ing people of a full life. At the end of the nineteenth century, first trade unions and subsequently political parties arose in all countries where the Industrial Revolution made life miserable for the toiling masses. It was a matter of course that the platforms of these emerging political parties were geared toward a social transformation that would benefit the workers. Still, it proved hard to oppose and defeat the established order, which was based only nominally on democracy. Opportunities for input through voting were very limited (indeed, in nearly all of Europe, the average person was excluded from the vote). As a result, the new political parties did not achieve a great deal. Until World War I, progress was erratic at best, proceeding in waves, and none of the parties were able to gain decisive political power.

Last but not least, another wave of democratic revolutions, which involved both nationalist and socialist factions, made itself felt across much of Western and Central/Eastern Europe in 1848 and 1849. The revolutions failed, and the result was to strengthen rather than weaken the power of established governments. The unification under a single monarch of Italy in 1861 and of most German-speaking areas outside of Austria in 1871 marked the high point of the centuries-long process of political consolidation in Western Europe and of the more recent nationalist movement. Most educated people in the second half of the nineteenth century thought that the European political system was stable and set for permanent, if gradual, progress in the struggle against poverty, sickness, illiteracy, and political repression. Indeed, that part of the nineteenth century has often been nicknamed the "Age of Optimism."

World War I (1914–1918)

In the period from 1848 to 1918, Europe reigned supreme in the world. Its major powers were Britain and France. However, Germany and Austria were also being formed during that era, and Russia, which had hardly counted as a European power before the Napoleonic Wars, had gradually extended its diplomatic influence and strategic grasp after the Vienna Congress in 1815. By 1700, no Western European power had taken much notice of Russia; by 1900, circumstances had changed to the extent that no European power could afford *not* to take Russian interests or policies into account in its own foreign policy. This Russian influence in the West turned out to be a permanent fact of twentieth-century European politics and was ultimately strengthened, not weakened, by the Communist Revolution, which, starting in 1917, transformed Russia and many other nations in the general area into the Soviet Union.

There is no permanence in history, however. Some nations gradually lose power; others rise quickly. By 1914, the constellation of forces had changed to the extent that a major war, which would come to be known as World War I, could no longer be avoided. This "Great War" was to be a long and protracted struggle. (Some historians have adopted the view that there are so many connections between the two world wars that they should be jointly viewed as one longer struggle, the "Second Thirty Years' War." In brutality and gruesomeness, that conflict easily compares to the Thirty Years' War of the seventeenth century.)

The leading cause of World War I was the growing power of Germany and the fear that this inspired in Germany's main rivals—namely, France, Russia, and Britain. After 1897, the rulers of united Germany moved from a policy of domestic consolidation and economic growth to a continental and ultimately global strategy aimed at giving Germany what they regarded as its rightful place as a world power, on a par with Britain. To some, that would include having an overseas empire as well. None of the other European powers could tolerate this ambition.

Furthermore, the old antagonisms, particularly the conflict between Germany and France, had not disappeared. Germany's defeat of France in 1870–1871 spurred the French governments of the Third Republic (1871–1940) to seek allies for a future war of revenge. Otto von Bismarck, the German chancellor from 1871 to 1890, knew that Germany would lose a general European war and sought to preserve peace through a pact among Germany, the Austrian Empire, and Russia. This fell apart due to Austro–Russian disagreements, however, and in 1894, Russia formed an anti-German pact with France. In turn, Great Britain, alarmed by Germany's growing military and economic power, broke with its long-standing policy of noninvolvement in Europe and

(The Bettmann Archive)

World War I: A German gun company is shown in battle at Darkehmen.

(The Bettmann Archive)

Otto von Bismarck, the "Iron Chancellor," founded the German Empire in 1871, thus introducing new equations into the European political and social arenas.

signed colonial agreements with France in 1904 and Russia in 1907, thus creating what became known as the Triple Entente. On the other side, Germany remained allied with Austria. In 1882, Italy joined this pact, which was called the Triple Alliance.

On June 28, 1914, one of the most fateful days in history, an assassin killed the heir to the thrones of Austria and Hungary in Sarajevo, part of the Bosnian province of Austria-Hungary. During the next 5 weeks, threats and counterthreats escalated and triggered the mutual-support provisions of the Triple Entente and the Triple Alliance, with merciless automatism. By mid-August, Germany and Austria were at war with France, Great Britain, and Russia. At first, Italy was neutral, but in 1915 it decided to enter the war as an ally of the Entente.

Although the rulers of Germany in 1914 lacked Bismarck's foresight, they knew that Germany's only chance was to defeat France quickly, before the United Kingdom could send strong forces to the European continent, and then to rush its forces east and defeat Russia in alliance with Austria. The plan failed. The war in the west became a war of attrition between entrenched armies, wherein the side with the most men and the best supplies of food and ammunition ultimately prevailed. In the east, Germany finally defeated Russia in 1917–1918, thanks in large part to the Russian Revolutions of

February and October 1917, which temporarily destroyed Russia's military power. After a final German offensive in the west, in the early summer of 1918, the Entente (now supported by the United States, which had entered the war in April 1917) drove the German armies back almost to the German frontier. Revolution broke out in Germany and Austria, and the emperors of the two countries abdicated. The government of the new German republic, composed of leaders of the Liberal and Socialist Parties, requested an armistice, which the Entente granted on November 11, 1918.

The fighting, which had cost more than 10 million lives, was over. The economic situation in Germany rapidly deteriorated after the armistice had been signed; and, when peace was concluded in the following year, the conditions were by no means commensurate with German power at the time of the armistice.

The Interwar Years (1918–1939)

The impact of the war on politics, technology, religion, philosophy, social life, ideology, and the European and world economies culminated in the Great Depression of the 1930s. This was followed by World War II, the last act of the "Second European Thirty Years' War." In Germany and Italy, the seemingly continuous crises brought dictators to power; in Britain, Scandinavia, and the Low Countries (the Netherlands, Belgium, and Luxembourg), Democrats remained in control and responded to the problems by instituting social-welfare programs and accepting that government had a responsibility for employment and living standards. In France, a strong right-wing movement threatened—but did not destroy—democracy.

The fundamental reason for the emergence of anti-Democratic sentiment in Western Europe in the 1920s and 1930s was that a large and, in some countries, decisive proportion of the politically active population simply did not believe that democracy was adequate to deal with the economic, technological, and social problems of the time. They believed that the modern world demanded a new way of political life, a way involving national mobilization, paramilitary regimentation, and a leadership free to do what was necessary for national security and survival without being accountable to sectional interests.

Some of these anti-Democrats went to the far right and joined nationalistic movements, of which the most important were the Nazi movement in Germany and the Fascist movement in Italy. The leaders of these movements, insisting that terrible dangers threatened their peoples, promised glory and renewal for their nations. These dangers, the Nazis and Fascists said, could be defeated only if the people shook off the shackles of democracy and did what was necessary to discard them completely. Others, including many intellectuals, drifted to the left and joined or supported Communist parties, whose adherents promised equality and justice in a perfect future society. Like the Nazis, they said that terrible dangers threatened this promise, which could be overcome only if Communists subjected themselves to the iron discipline of each country's Communist party, which was in turn controlled completely by the Soviet Union, the world's first Communist state. Both Nazis and Communists absolutely insisted that the only criterion of morality was that which served the movement. Any thought or action (including murder and betrayal) that served the movement was good; any thought or action that might hinder it was bad and was to be ruthlessly suppressed.

The Great Depression

The Wall Street stock-market crash of 1929 in the United States caused a worldwide depression. Unemployment soared in all Western European countries, regardless of their political format and structure. World trade came to an end, in large part because of U.S. protectionism and fiscal policies. In the period 1930–1933, world manufacturing production outside the Soviet Union shrank by more than one third; the volume of international trade fell by two thirds; and more than one third of all laborers in Great Britain, Germany, Denmark, Norway, and France were unemployed.

In Germany, the situation was aggravated by the restrictions imposed by the Versailles Treaty. This allowed Adolf Hitler, who in the 1920s founded the Nazi Party after a failed coup, to make rapid gains. In 1933, his Nazi government was installed and the first contours of the Third Reich appeared. It could claim a measure of success by having built a road system such as Germany had never had and by having launched a rapid rearmament program, which clearly violated the terms of the Versailles Treaty.

In fact, unemployment began falling on its own in 1934, because world trade and business investment were picking up throughout Western Europe. In the Scandinavian countries, alliances of Socialist and Liberal parties introduced social-security programs, which protected against unemployment and favored health insurance, and finally initiated programs of public works. The British government did not introduce major social policy reforms until 1945, but it succeeded in reducing unemployment somewhat in the 1930s by modest programs of public investment and other measures.

Unemployment and underinvestment were not the only problems facing Western European economies in this era. Most countries were also completing the transition from an economy based on agricultural employment and production to one based overwhelmingly on industry. Britain and Germany were furthest along in this process; the Scandinavian countries, Italy, and France did not become fully industrialized until after World War II. Spain finally shed its largely agricultural image after dictator General Francisco Franco's death in 1975.

Unlike Central/Eastern Europe, where the landed aristocracy and a small middle class dominated society, politics, and culture until World War II, Western and Northern Europen society had started to generate a middle class by 1920. The aristocracy was losing ground as a cultural and political factor of influence, but this retreat was gradual and continued into the post–World War II period. Most workers abandoned revolutionary ideology in 1917–1920 and followed reformist leaders of the Socialist parties, who wanted to work for social change and redistribution of income and wealth by demo-

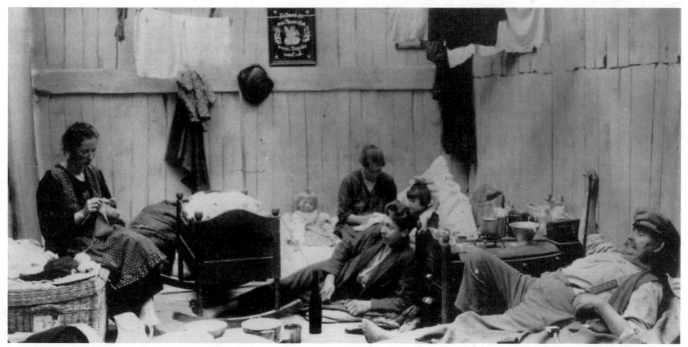

(The Bettmann Archive)

The Great Depression of the 1930s devastated the world economy, as illustrated by these unemployed refugees in a temporary workhouse in Germany.

cratic means rather than through the revolution that communism advocated.

France, Italy, and Spain, in that order, had fewer industrial workers and proportionally more peasants. Italy and Spain were also restrained by a powerful Roman Catholic Church establishment that was arch-conservative, if not reactionary. Many Church leaders regarded liberal democracy as permissive and anti-Christian and thus lent their support to authoritarian movements. The main cause of their fears was the virulent anticlericalism of some liberal or left-wing movements in these countries. The net effect of mutual distrust of liberal democrats and Catholics was to permit authoritarian groups to gain support. These groups, like Mussolini's Fascists, promised to protect the Church from leftist anticlericals, while in reality they exploited its social power and influence for their own ends.

The Spanish Prelude to World War II

In the early and mid-1930s, Spain experienced a high degree of instability, which was capped by the assumption of power on the part of a left-wing government based on the middle class and workers. The new government provoked a right-wing rebellion, which generated a civil war of extraordinary brutality, lasting from 1936 to 1939. Many governments in Europe took sides, though refraining from involving themselves officially.

Some political analysts view the conflict as the "dress rehearsal for World War II." Since the leaders of the rebels, Francisco Franco and his Falange movement, had a strong Fascist orientation or at least represented right-wing dictatorship, they were able to count on active support from Germany and Italy. The republican (or Communist) side, however, gathered a measure of sympathy, but it did not receive much active support. It lost, and, for nearly 40 years, General Franco exercised unbridled power in Spain. One might have expected some gratitude on the part of the Spanish dictator for the German and Italian help, but Franco refused to join the Axis forces when World War II started, shortly after the end of the Spanish Civil War. Once France had fallen, Hitler and Franco met somewhere in the Pyrenees, on the French–Spanish border. The meeting generated an instant mutual dislike, which may have caused Franco to deny the German forces passage through Spain in order to capture Gibraltar.

Fascism and Nazism

The two basic antidemocratic movements, fascism and nazism, had a great deal in common. However, they are often erroneously identified as one and the same belief system. It may, therefore, be useful to compare and contrast them.

Fascism was the first to arrive on the scene. Benito Mussolini, a journalist who had often published his work in *Avanti,* a socialist periodical, and who had been a leader of the Italian Socialist Party, suddenly switched from the left to the far right of the political spectrum. Organizing bands of fighters and terrorists (these bands were called *fasci,* a Latin

(National Archives)

Adolf Hitler was named chancellor of Germany in January 1933. This was one of the most disastrous events of the twentieth century. Within just a few months, Hitler removed all restraints on his power through the issuance of emergency decrees.

term for a bundle of wooden staves, which was the symbol of the office of Roman magistrates), Mussolini directed his speeches and addresses against communism in general and the Russian Communist Revolution in particular. In 1921, that broad movement, which by now was commonly identified as fascism, was reconstructed into a political party. The next year, Mussolini organized the historic March on Rome. In this huge protest rally, thousands and thousands of Fascist Party members marched hundreds of miles in order to assemble, finally, in front of the main government institution in Rome. (Mussolini himself joined the marchers in the Italian capital.) The March on Rome was attended by a great deal of publicity, and Mussolini and his party made headlines. As a result of the media exposure and his increased influence, Mussolini was able to manipulate the king into naming him prime minister; soon, Mussolini developed a dislike of this "bourgeois" term and took to calling himself *Il Duce* (Italian for "The Leader"). In the mid-1920s, Mussolini seized full dictatorial powers. His effort to gain a power monopoly was attended by laws and decrees banning all other parties. As a matter of course, dissidents were tried and sentenced. Those who were lucky were given internal exile; others, such as

Thousands of Adolf Hitler's troops are shown here massed in Germany at a Nazi rally in November 1934.

Antonio Gramsci, the leader of the Italian Communist Party, languished, and eventually died, in prison.

Hitler and Mussolini met several times before World War II began, concluding the Axis Pact, so named because the two dictators expected their joint forces to steamroll through Europe. However, Mussolini did not immediately join Hitler once the war started in September 1939, preferring to sit on the fence for nearly a year. Only after the German forces had defeated Poland, Denmark, Norway, the Low Countries, and France did Il Duce think fit to declare war on the one remaining European country that stood up to Hitler: England.

Nazism and fascism differed considerably in ideological respect. Although Mussolini and the Fascist Party in general lauded and glorified Italy's past and forged an ancestral connection with the great Roman Empire, racial discrimination, highlighted by the Nazis' persecution of Jews, was conspicuously absent in Fascist thinking. Only in a much later stage—that is, during the war, when German forces had several times rescued Italy's military—did Mussolini oblige his Axis partner by rounding up Jews in Italy.

If the foundation of fascism in Italy had depended on the March on Rome and Mussolini's subsequent coup, the Nazis owed their success to circumstance, in particular the fragility of the governmental system. Shortly after the German emperor had fled, the so-called Weimar Republic was established. This system of government suffered from a number of intrinsic weaknesses. Most of the political parties of its multiparty system attempted to represent their constituents in Parliament, and, as a consequence, the government was always based on coalitions—alliances of political parties that from time to time were able to work together.

The various parties that were not in power frequently voted down government proposals or programs; in many cases, the government was forced to resign as a result. Party leaders then came together to deliberate on a new government, which, of course, would soon be ousted in turn. Two parties in particular conspired to maintain this gridlock: the *Nazi Party* (short for National Socialist German Workers' Party) and the Communist Party. It was said that they held a "negative majority," which implied that, although neither of them had the numbers to be an effective vehicle for government, jointly they could prevent all the other parties from gaining government power. Finally, on January 30, 1933, Field Marshal Paul von Hindenburg was persuaded to resolve the deadlock by allowing Hitler, whose Nazis held a plurality but not a majority, to form a government. Von Hindenburg was aged and tired and no longer seemed to care.

Hitler also disliked his official title of chancellor (the German term for prime minister), and, just like Mussolini, he had himself called "Leader" (in German, *Führer*). He almost immediately consolidated his power. Just a few months after the Nazis gained office, the *Reichstag* (Parliament) building burned down. Arson was suspected, and a Communist (who had most probably been planted in the building) was tried,

sentenced, and executed. Hitler then assumed emergency powers, an action that enabled him to shunt aside all the relics of democracy—freedom of the press, freedom of assembly, freedom of speech, and so on. These emergency powers were never revoked and, in fact, lasted throughout the entire lifespan of the Third Reich (1933–1945). The German Communist Party, the Socialist Party, and all other parties were banned, their leadership mercilessly persecuted. In less than 3 months' time, Germany became a totalitarian state.

It may be of interest to note that Hitler's rise to power, with the exception of the *putsch* (coup) he attempted in 1923, was completely constitutional. Article 48 of the Weimar Constitution gave the chief executive the power to declare an emergency, and the burning down of the Reichstag building could seem a legitimate opportunity to do so. Of course, Hitler did violate international agreements and treaties—first and foremost, the peace treaty that had been concluded in 1919 (which Hitler nicknamed the *Versailles Diktat*).

The Road to the Holocaust

Hitler's regime was far more oppressive and violent than that of the Italian Fascists. One very important difference was the role of anti-Semitism in Nazi ideology. To the Nazis, the Jews were irredeemably evil, like germs infecting an otherwise healthy body; Hitler and his government therefore considered it necessary to destroy all of European Jewry. They first took away the civil rights and liberties of Jews in Germany. In 1938, they started to confiscate what was left of Jewish property. By the outbreak of war, in September 1939, more than half of over 500,000 Jews who had lived in Germany in 1925 had left the country. Almost all those who remained perished in concentration and extermination camps in the period 1941–1945. Many who had fled Germany in the late 1930s were caught in countries that Hitler subsequently conquered.

World War II

Hitler's regime had not been in power for long when it began a program of armaments and expansion that destabilized European security and led to World War II. World War II essentially began as a European war between Great Britain, France, and Germany. The war was a result not only of Nazi policies but also of the weakness of the French and British response, which failed to deter Hitler and instead allowed him to think that there was nothing for which the French and British would fight.

Hitler had a secret as well as a public agenda in his foreign policy. His secret agenda was to make Germany all-powerful in Europe by destroying all rivals and to remove all Jews from Germany and occupied countries. His public agenda was to give Germany equal status with the other major powers. The first steps in this public agenda were to re-arm and to bring all ethnic Germans into a single state. Many Western politicians thought these wishes were reasonable enough, despite the aggressive ways in which Hitler presented them. Few objected, therefore, when, in 1938, Germany annexed Aus-

Jewish women with crosses painted on their backs by Nazis. These women spent at least part of the war in forced labor at the German ammunition factory in Kaunitz.

tria, which had existed as an independent country since 1920. Most Austrians, including Hitler himself, had wanted to join Germany in 1920, but the Allies had made that impossible. Later in 1938, Hitler annexed Sudetenland, the border areas of Czechoslovakia where the population happened to be German. The British and the French accepted even this. Indeed, the British prime minister, Neville Chamberlain, went to Germany to conduct negotiations with Hitler. This Munich agreement has come to stand for a policy of appeasement.

In March 1939, Adolf Hitler's armies occupied most of what remained of Czechoslovakia, where there were no Germans to speak of. Finally, the Western powers realized that Hitler intended to dominate the whole of Europe. When Germany invaded Poland, in September, an immediate reaction followed: The Allies issued an ultimatum that made it clear that if the German forces did not leave Poland within 3 days, a state of war would exist, between England and France on the one hand and Germany on the other. Hitler simply ignored the ultimatum.

The war that followed lasted almost 6 years and cost 55 million lives. More than half the casualties were civilians, whereas in World War I, about 10 percent of casualties were civilians.

In order not to be fighting wars on two fronts, shortly before he invaded Poland, Hitler had concluded a "non-aggression"

pact with the Soviet dictator Joseph Stalin. This treaty also made provisions for a division of Central/Eastern Europe. After the Germans defeated Poland, the Soviets occupied the eastern part of that country. Late in 1939, the Soviet Union attacked Finland, which had always been in its sphere of influence, as was agreed to in the pact. (In early 1940, the Finns were forced to cede the eastern part of their country to the Soviet Union.) Also late in 1939, the Soviets invaded and annexed the three small Baltic countries of Estonia, Latvia, and Lithuania, which had gained independence from Russia in 1918, when the latter was in the process of becoming the Soviet Union.

Starting in 1940, Hitler conquered Denmark, Norway, the Low Countries, and France, and he threatened Britain with invasion. The Battle of Britain in August and September 1940 turned out to be an air war of unprecedented proportions. (However, it was not a prelude to an invasion of Great Britain.) In April 1941, Germans suddenly turned toward Yugoslavia and Greece, conquering both countries after fierce battles. Shortly thereafter, on June 22, 1941, Hitler's Third Reich embarked upon "Operation Barbarossa," which was meant to liquidate the Soviet Union while England was still too weak to attack on the other side. Here Hitler committed the same fatal mistake that Napoleon Bonaparte had made about 130 years earlier. The Soviet territory turned out to be too vast, its winters too grueling, its people too determined. After some initial successes, the German war machine was driven back, slowly and steadily. The United States had up to this point remained neutral; but once Japan, Hitler's ally, attacked Pearl Harbor on December 7, 1941, the United States declared war on Japan, and Germany and Italy declared war on the United States 3 days later. Thus the European war became a true world war.

Switzerland, Sweden, Spain, Ireland, and Portugal remained neutral throughout the war. The first two were democracies and remained so, although both restricted civil liberties and free expression, in deference first to the Germans and later to the Western Allies and the Soviets. The rest of the European continent endured various degrees of oppression and arbitrary violence under German occupation. Although many British cities were bombed to rubble by German planes, the Third Reich never succeeded in invading Britain, where democratic government and civil liberties continued in force throughout the war.

Resistance Movements

Resistance movements arose in all occupied countries, which had come to include Italy, most of which the Germans occupied in September 1943, after the Italian government had surrendered to the Allies. In many cases, notably in France and Italy, the resistance had a Communist as well as a Democratic wing, with radically opposed ideas for postwar politics. In Denmark, Norway, the Netherlands, and Belgium, the Communist movements had been much weaker before the war, and the democratic resistance was accordingly stronger. Its members regarded the old politicians as discredited. They aimed at a general reconstruction of political life that would take power away from the old business and aristocratic elites, institute a welfare state, and equalize income. In Britain, similarly, a broad consensus of the political elite insisted that the people deserved a "New Britain" after the war, to include socialized medicine, vastly increased welfare provisions, subsidized housing, nationalization of heavy industry, and more equality of income and wealth. Few understood how impoverished the country actually was due to the war and how difficult it would be to pay for these reforms.

The Nazis' Final Solution: Genocide

In 1941, after launching the attack on the Soviet Union, Hitler ordered his "Final Solution"—that is, the deliberate extermination, as opposed to physical deportation, of all Jews. Most European Jews lived in Poland, Czechoslovakia, Hungary, and the Soviet Union, and the Nazis killed more than 4 million Jews from these territories. In total, approximately 6 million Jews were murdered during the Holocaust (1933–1945). Nearly 5 million other people were also killed by the Nazis.

By late 1942, the tide was turning against the German armies, which had suffered major defeats in Russia and in North Africa. The "Big Three"—U.S. president Franklin D. Roosevelt, British prime minister Winston Churchill, and the Soviet dictator Joseph Stalin—met on various occasions to plan the postwar shape of the world: for example, at Teheran, Iran, in November 1943; and at Yalta, on the Crimean Peninsula in the Soviet Union, in February 1945.

Their agreement on establishing a United Nations Organization to secure world peace through mutual security concealed irreconcilable differences in interests and aspirations. Stalin wished to extend communism as far westward into Europe as possible; Roosevelt and Churchill believed that Stalin would forgo an expansionist policy if they invited him to join in peaceful world leadership. All three claimed to promote democracy and peace; but whereas the Western statesmen understood "democracy" to mean rule by the people and "peace" to mean rejection of policies of violence and expansionism, Stalin, an orthodox Communist, understood democracy to mean Communist rule and peace to mean Soviet global hegemony. The conflict that was later to grow into the cold war thus loomed ominously before the real war ended.

The most important bone of contention in Europe was how to deal with Germany. In 1944, the Soviets, the Americans, and the British decided to divide Germany. The Soviet Union, which had taken nearly 70,000 square miles from eastern Poland, wanted to compensate the latter by granting it 40,000 square miles of eastern Germany. Stalin also incorporated a much smaller part of eastern Germany into the Soviet Union. (These drastic territorial changes were officially recognized by the Helsinki Accords some 30 years later, in 1975.) The remainder of Germany was divided into Soviet, U.S., British, and French zones of occupation. These zones closely corresponded with the military conquests at the end of the war.

In 1945, the Soviet, American, and British armies invaded Germany from the east and the west, crushing all resistance and forcing the unconditional surrender of the German armed forces on May 8. The Soviets, who had suffered far more than the other belligerents from Nazi atrocities, unleashed furious vengeance on the German civilians—mostly old men, women, and children—in their path. Almost the entire population of the part of Germany given to Poland—15 million people—fled westward in an attempt to escape the invaders. More than 2 million died as a result.

RECONSTRUCTION (1945–1951)

Western Europe recovered from the material destruction wrought by the war far more quickly and completely than could have been expected in 1945. Living standards had fallen drastically throughout the continent during the war, the greatest drop being in Central/Eastern Europe. Shortly after the hostilities had ended, people all over Europe braced themselves for the task of removing the rubble of the war and rebuilding their countries. This impulse was reinforced by the European Recovery Program—popularly known as the Marshall Plan—which was proposed and initiated by the United States in 1947. Within a few years, the levels of production and living standards in all of Western Europe, except Ger-

(National Archives)

The cordiality apparent in this picture of Joseph Stalin, Franklin D. Roosevelt, and Winston Churchill (from left to right), meeting at Teheran in November 1943, soon dissolved into the mutual suspicion of the cold war.

many, were at or slightly above prewar rates. The recovery marked the beginning of more than 20 years of economic growth, spreading affluence, and a resulting sense of optimism, which were the underlying reasons for an equally remarkable political revival.

Political Effects of World War II

World War II had two fundamental effects, one negative and one positive, that are still being felt today. The negative effect was the political division of Europe into West and Central/East. Western Europe was mostly democratic, whereas the countries of what people now began calling Central or Eastern Europe were ruled by Communist dictatorships imposed by Soviet power and control. The dividing line between the two parts of Europe ran right through one country, Germany, and separated others, such as Austria and Hungary, that in the past had been united under a common government and in a common culture. Physically, the line was marked by a fortified border erected by the Communist regimes, ostensibly to prevent their citizens from escaping to the West. This demarcation emerged as soon as hostilities ended; by July 1945, it was fixed. In 1947, the wartime British prime minister Winston Churchill coined the phrase "Iron Curtain." The metaphor stuck, since what had been established divided Europeans from one another more ruthlessly and sharply than any

earlier division in history, including the division into Catholic and Protestant camps following the Reformation of the sixteenth century.

One effect of the war was to discredit the belief of the interwar years that democracy was inefficient and inadequate, a belief that had led so many to turn to nazism, fascism, or communism in their search for solutions to problems of politics and government in the modern world. After 1945, most Western Europeans, including almost all Germans and most Italians, came to regard the former contempt for democracy as the main indirect cause of World War II. Now, far from seeing democracy as inadequate, they now saw it as the only proper way of conducting political life and as the greatest guarantor of peace and prosperity.

This revitalization of democracy did not occur everywhere to the same degree. It was strongest in Germany, where defeat in war and the revelations of Nazi atrocities against Jews and other peoples permanently prejudiced the people against totalitarianism; and in the countries of Northwestern Europe that had never surrendered voluntarily to antidemocratic ideologies—Britain, Scandinavia, and the Low Countries. In France and Italy, the antidemocratic right lost its credibility; but the antidemocratic left—that is, the Communist parties—remained influential. This occurred not only because they took the credit for defeating nazism and fascism, but also because many on the left continued to believe that democracy without socialism was politically and morally inadequate. In both France and Italy, Communist movements commanded the support of up to a third of the voters and presented a clear challenge to democracy, at least until the 1970s.

The Cold War

The Big Three met for the last time, at Potsdam, in the middle of defeated Germany, in July–August 1945, to decide what to do about the future of the world. (By that time, Harry Truman had replaced Franklin Roosevelt, who had died in April.) Although the United States, Britain, and the Soviet Union agreed on a number of details, their differences in broader objectives and methods were now too clear to be papered over. Even so, however, many politicians in the West continued to hope for a period of peaceful collaboration with Stalin.

By late 1946, few people in the United States and Britain shared that hope. East of the dividing line in Europe, Communist parties were seizing absolute power in ways that were not very different from Nazi German tactics. Many feared that Stalin and his henchmen were determined not only to crush democratic movements in Central/Eastern Europe but that they wanted to extend their control into Western Europe as well. The Soviet Army was much stronger than the skeleton U.S. and British forces remaining on the continent, and the French and Italian Communist Parties, with their millions of supporters, were a formidable threat to the weak democratic institutions in those countries.

Countries in Western Europe faced two different, yet related, threats in the late 1940s: economic crisis, which might have led to civil war; and a Soviet attack to support a Communist bid for power. True, economic recovery had begun in 1945; but the entire region badly needed raw materials and investment if this were to continue and not to end in inflation and unemployment, as had happened after World War I. Such an eventuality would present great opportunities to the Communist parties. Furthermore, economic growth was absolutely necessary if Western Europe were to re-arm sufficiently to deter Soviet military aggression. Finally, the Europeans would have to convince the United States to maintain and extend the military and economic ties to Europe that had developed during the war. One of the causes of World War II may have been that the United States had withdrawn from involvement in Europe after 1919. U.S. isolationism may well have contributed to the success of Hitler, who did not believe that the United States was interested in protecting democracy in Europe. Most Western Europeans understood in 1945 that this should not be allowed to happen again; for Western Europe by itself, in its impoverished condition, was no match for the Soviet Union.

Like the threat, the response had to be a double one, involving both the reorganization of the Western European economies to promote prosperity as well as a defense pact between the major countries of Western Europe and the United States. The Western European nations, especially France and Germany, would have to discard their old rivalries and understand that close economic, diplomatic, and military cooperation was the only way to save their newly regained liberty. Close collaboration between German chancellor Konrad Adenauer and French president Charles de Gaulle become the axis of a broader harmony in Europe. That cooperation took the form of a series of policies and institutions, established in 1947–1951, that have formed the framework of Western European politics ever since.

The Economic Framework

Immediately after the war, a number of European statesmen, ideologues, and writers expressed their hope that the European nations would join together in a political federation, a "United States of Europe." Even Winston Churchill, Britain's wartime leader who as a rule held extremely conservative views, mentioned this eventuality in speeches presented in the Netherlands and Switzerland. Indeed, it could seem that such a political structure was less distant at that time than 50 years later. Such a federation would have three advantages: a coordinated economic policy, permitting faster recovery; sufficient resources to defend such a union against any threat; and freedom from political control by either the United States, the Soviet Union, or a revanchist Germany, which would be an integral part of the federation and thus unable to become a threat to its neighbors. By early 1947, it seemed clear that Europe was already permanently divided and that the Communist regimes would never agree to joining such a political construction.

That left the option of a federation of Western Europe alone. One leading spokesperson for a Western European federation involving a common economic market and united armed forces was Jean Monnet. From 1947 to 1954, Monnet and others worked toward this goal, but it continued to be beyond their reach. Western Europe remained divided into national states. Nevertheless, Monnet's ideas materialized in various supranational bodies for economic development as well as, to some extent, in the European contribution to Western defense.

In early 1947, all of Western Europe, including the western zones of occupied Germany, faced a serious shortage of dollar reserves. They needed these funds to pay for imports from the United States that were essential to their continued recovery. Indeed, severe shortages of food in nearly all Western European countries made it necessary to retain rationing systems.

In June of that year, U.S. secretary of state George C. Marshall (who as a general had participated in defeating Germany) announced the European Recovery Program. Responding to this offer of help, representatives of all the Western European nations except Spain, but including Sweden and Switzerland (which had kept out of the war), met in Paris to discuss the coordination of their economic policies. As a first step, in October they signed the General Agreement on Tariffs and Trade (GATT), an undertaking to remove duties and other restrictions on free trade. The various European governments had concluded that one of the main causes of economic depressions had been protectionism—that is, a set of policies designed to protect domestic employment within individual countries. Protectionist measures provoke retaliation and, by reducing international trade, tend to dampen rather than protect domestic employment. GATT was a clear signal that the Western Europeans were prepared to keep their economies open in the future, thus inviting investment and stimulating trade.

After a winter of talks between the United States and Europe, the Marshall Plan came into effect in the spring of 1948. It provided financial aid to all Western European governments (including West Germany, which did not possess a government of its own until late 1949) for a period of 5 years (1948–1953). The U.S. government had insisted that, in the execution of the European Recovery Plan, it would not deal with the various European countries individually. Western European governments had accordingly met in Paris in 1947 in order to create the Organization for European Economic Cooperation (OEEC), which was to receive all aid coming from the United States and to manage and distribute it among themselves. When Marshall Plan aid ended, in 1953, the OEEC was not disbanded but was maintained as a monitoring agency for the economic policies and prospects of member countries. It later came to include the United States and, in 1960, was renamed the Organization for Economic Cooperation and Development (OECD).

France and Germany

The French were afraid of Germany's potential economic power even after 1945. Before the war, Germany had produced almost half of the entire steel production in Europe and more than the other four major producers (France, Belgium, Italy, and Luxembourg) combined. Moreover, the German methods were more efficient, and their labor costs were lower. These conditions revived after the war.

If Germany were allowed to produce freely again, the French worried, the Germans would soon regain their economic, if not political, dominance in Europe. To avoid that eventuality, the French wanted to exploit German coal and steel production for their own economic reconstruction while preventing German producers from becoming a future competitive threat.

In January 1947, the American and British occupation authorities granted some autonomy in economic policy to the Germans under their control. The French interpreted this measure as a first step toward establishing an independent West German government. They also noted that German steel production, while still far below prewar levels, more than doubled in 1947–1948, and that there was a huge pent-up demand for steel both in West Germany and in Western Europe as a whole. They therefore insisted that the Ruhr—a German coal-mining and steel-producing area that was in the British zone of occupation—should either be removed altogether from Germany or at least be put under an international authority that would control production and distribution. The French were still thinking in terms of their ancient rivalry with Germany and believed that any German recovery could become a threat to them. Since Germany under Hitler had tried to conquer Europe and crush all other nations, the French believed that they had a right to exploit German industrial power for themselves, if only to prevent it from becoming a danger in the future.

The Atlantic Alliance

The interest that the Americans and the British had in Germany in 1946–1948 was entirely different from that of other Western European nations. The United States and Great Britain wanted West Germany to recover economically so that the Germans could support themselves and help the rest of Western Europe in its economic recovery and resistance to the threat of Soviet attack. Only a prosperous Western Europe would have the domestic stability and the resources to remain free, which is why economic recovery and re-armament were two sides of the same coin. Discussions between the United States and Western Europe began at the same time as the Marshall Plan (they were, in fact, both cold war phenomena).

Since 1944, the British had been involved in a brutal civil war in Greece, where an army supported mainly by the Yugoslav Communists was trying to seize power. In the winter of 1947, the British told Truman that they could no longer afford the commitment and would have to withdraw. By then, the cold war had started to dominate American foreign policy, and Truman not only took over from the British but also indicated explicitly that the United States would come to the rescue of foreign governments, resisting an overthrow by armed minorities if the latter were assisted from the outside. This spelled out what came to be known as the Truman Doctrine, specifically directed against communism's more subtle methods of aggression. Its promulgation heartened Western Europeans, who interpreted it as the first sign that the United States would help defend Western Europe against an increasingly aggressive Soviet Union.

In early 1948, Britain, the United States, France, and the Benelux countries agreed to permit the Germans to form a democratic, national government in the western zones of occupation. There was no chance of establishing a democratic government in all of Germany, because the Soviets would not accept a united Germany that was not communist. In March of that year, France, Britain, and the Benelux countries signed the Brussels Pact, which was an agreement for mutual cooperation and defense. It was an important step, because it showed American political leaders that the Western Europeans had the will to defend themselves and needed help only with resources—which had to come primarily from the United States but secondarily from a reorganized and inde-

(Harry S. Truman Library)

U.S. president Harry S. Truman signed the anti-Communist Truman Doctrine on May 23, 1947.

pendent West Germany. In June 1948, the United States, Britain, and France—the occupying powers in West Germany—gave the green light to the Germans to start instituting a government.

When the Soviets realized that the Western Allies were going to stimulate the formation of a West German government, they retaliated by cutting off the land connections between West Germany and West Berlin. The former German capital city had been divided into four sectors, just as Germany as a whole had been; but, since Berlin was located deep inside the Soviet zone of occupation, the Western allies had to cross that zone to get to their sectors in Berlin. The Soviets hoped to drive the Western Allies out of Berlin. However, they had left the existing air corridors intact, not expecting that the United States would ever be able to supply the millions of civilians as well as the Allied troops by air. The United States took up the challenge, and, for about a year, large planes provided West Berlin with all it needed. In May 1949, the siege was lifted.

Planning the new democratic government in West Germany took place in the shadow of the Berlin crisis, which many feared would lead to war between the Western Allies and the Soviet Union. The new government, the Federal Republic of Germany, came into being in 1949. It held its first free elections in August; and, on September 21, 1949, the American, British, and French military occupation authorities surrendered most of their powers to the new government, whose seat became Bonn, a somewhat sleepy but centrally located German city on the Rhine. Konrad Adenauer, who had resigned from his post of mayor of Cologne when Hitler came

to power, became West Germany's first chancellor. Until 1955, the Western powers retained ultimate authority through their occupation forces and their civilian High Commission, which was in charge of West Germany's defense and foreign relations. In fact, the West German government assumed control of its foreign policy well before the occupation formally ended.

The Berlin crisis also tended to accelerate the dialogue between the Western Europeans and the Americans on defense. In early 1949, the United States, Canada, and the Brussels Pact countries (Britain, France, and the Benelux countries) invited Italy, Portugal, Denmark, Norway, and Iceland to join the proposed Western defense pact, which was signed on April 4, 1949, in Washington. It was named the North Atlantic Treaty, and the organization to which it gave rise was the North Atlantic Treaty Organization. The original treaty ran for 20 years and was renewable by each country for periods of 10 years thereafter. No country has ever failed to renew, although France left the military organization in 1966 while remaining a treaty member. For reasons unknown, France also had the organization's headquarters moved from Paris to Brussels. (Of late, however, France has shown signs of wishing to return to the fold.)

The Schuman Plan

In 1948–1949, the French government realized that its attempt to control German economic recovery was harming common Western European interests and that a prosperous Germany was a better partner than a poor and resentful one. France's foreign minister, Robert Schuman, who hailed from the Alsace, a French area bordering on Germany, established a close relationship with West Germany's first head of government, Konrad Adenauer, who had come from a part of Germany close to the French border. Adenauer himself was determined to make French–German reconciliation the cornerstone of his policy vis-à-vis Western Europe. In 1950, Jean Monnet put to Schuman a plan to begin the unification of Western Europe by pooling French and German coal and steel resources in a "common market" open to other countries in Europe. Schuman, in presenting the proposal publicly on May 9, 1950, expressed the hope that it would "create the first concrete foundation for a European federation which is so indispensable for the preservation of peace."

Italy and the Benelux countries joined the talks, which resulted in April 1951 in the establishment of the European Coal and Steel Community (ECSC). Not surprisingly, the first chairperson of the High Authority (the original name of the ECSC governing body) was Monnet.

The founding of this Community proved to be of great importance. Subsequent Communities came to include the same members. Although these nations were by no means integrated politically, people started to refer to "Little Europe" when discussing their joint ventures.

On April 4, 1949, NATO was formed by nations pledged to the common defense of Western Europe.

CONSOLIDATION (1951–1963)

NATO, the ECSC, and the new democratic government in West Germany were the three pillars of Western European economic growth and political stability in the 1950s. Spain and Portugal did not participate in the consolidation process, not only because they had not been involved in World War II but also because their right-wing dictatorships were still holdovers from the war period. They had, in effect, become outcasts.

Great Britain, Scandinavia, the Benelux countries, and, to a lesser extent, West Germany soon developed into modern welfare states, with high taxation and redistribution of income. France, Italy, and the rest of Southern Europe were poorer and tolerated more economic inequality among their populations.

Although all countries in Western Europe adhered to democratic tenets in varying degrees, there were differences in their party systems and in the ideologies that were their moving force. The party systems of Britain and West Germany were somewhat similar, in that they both had two large parties (in Britain, the Conservative Party and the Labour Party; in West Germany, the Christian Democratic Union and the Social Democratic Party) plus a considerably smaller party that sometimes acted as balancer (in Britain, the Liberal Party; in Germany, the Free Democratic Party, also a liberal party). The party systems of the Benelux resembled those of Scandinavia, in that the countries in both areas had multiparty systems that required coalitions.

(In both cases, center-left governments prevailed for many years; but Sweden, for decades in the vanguard of welfarism, adopted a center-right government in the early 1990s. In all Western European countries, with the exception of Italy, Communist parties had become quite small even before the collapse of the Soviet Union in 1991. In the 1986 elections in the Netherlands, for example, the Communists failed even to secure representation in Parliament. Another big change in this country was that most of the religious parties merged into the Christian Democratic Appeal, which was the mainstay of the government for many years but which in recent years has lost its plurality. Indeed, a 1994 coalition, the Christian Democratic Appeal, was left out of the government and thus entered the opposition. As far as political parties are concerned in Western Europe, the biggest change is not so much that the leftist parties have receded but that socialist doctrine itself has changed. It has moved to the right, and it has accordingly become difficult to tell the revised Socialist parties from the traditionally conservative parties.)

In the 1950s, Socialist parties called for nationalization of heavy industry, increased employee rights, participation by trade unions in business decisions, and broad equality of income and wealth. Christian Democratic parties supported private property and free enterprise but also believed that Christian doctrine demanded that the owners of industry use their wealth for the common good. Thus they supported the welfare state while ignoring the specific redistributionist aims of the Socialists.

NATO and the prospect of a common economic market produced a favorable climate for investment and production, so most Western European countries enjoyed high economic growth rates, low unemployment, and low inflation during

(UPI/Bettmann Newsphotos)

In a ceremony in Rome's Campidoglio Palace, statesmen of Belgium, France, West Germany, Italy, the Netherlands, and Luxembourg sign treaties for a European Common Market and European Atomic Energy Community, March 25, 1957.

the 1950s. Living standards differed greatly between north and south, but, even in the more well-to-do north, they were substantially lower than for most Americans. Single-family homes, electric appliances, and automobiles were luxuries in most countries until the 1960s. Even indoor plumbing was by no means widely prevalent in the Mediterranean countries and in rural or inner-city pockets elsewhere in Europe.

Contrary to a common impression, Western European culture during the consolidation years was anything but dull. Many writers and artists who had fled from the Nazis or kept silent enjoyed new popularity, while the younger generation of those who had actually fought in the war emerged with impulses and experiences of its own. The French and Italian Communist Parties exercised a great deal of control over culture—not by overt political force, as in Central/Eastern Europe, but through a sort of moral ascendancy that they held over many intellectuals who continued to regard the Soviet Union as a bastion of liberation and freedom from capitalism. Thus, people such as the philosopher Jean-Paul Sartre, the author Simone de Beauvoir, and the painter Pablo Picasso became avowed Communists. Indeed, many intellectuals became members of Communist parties.

Defense
The North Atlantic Treaty was only the first step in securing the defense of Europe. Major problems included how much Europe could afford for its defense and how German re-

sources might be used without allowing a German army—a reality that most people in areas occupied by Nazi Germany during the war (particularly in France) would find hard to swallow and that would in addition be unduly irritating to the Soviets. Even at the height of the cold war, the vast majority of Western politicians favored détente and therefore tried to avoid actions that the Soviets might regard as provocative.

In June 1950, Communist North Korea, supported by the Soviet Union and China, invaded South Korea. The United States decided to respond in kind, which meant that it could not devote as many of its scarce military resources to Europe, where the threat of a Soviet invasion seemed acute.

The problem of Europe's defense had been only partially solved by establishing NATO the year before. The Atlantic Alliance, after all, was there largely as a result of an American initiative and, to a great extent, at U.S. expense. Jean Monnet, chairman of the governing body of the European Coal and Steel Community, at that point wanted to kill two birds with one stone. On the one hand, he was very satisfied with the way in which the first Community (the ECSC) had developed, believing that the time had come to form other Communities. On the other hand, he felt that a European defense community could more conclusively solve the question of Europe's defense.

A New Community Emerges . . . and Fails
Thus, in February 1952, the six nations participating in the ECSC decided that, in view of its success and the apparent

progress that was being made in the preparation of a new community, the European Defense Community (EDC) could now be formed. In May 1952, the design of the EDC was formally launched. It was at that point that the Soviet Union became alarmed. The prospect of having Europe's defense in the immediate neighborhood, not 3,000 or 4,000 miles farther west, proved enough to bias Moscow against the plan. The Soviets therefore started to apply pressure on the ECSC membership, notably on France. They realized that, although the plan had been proposed and sponsored by the French government, many French people were against it, since the EDC was also to include German contingents. While the plan was discussed in the Assemblée Nationale (the French lower house), a large proportion of the French public communicated with their representatives, imploring them to reject the EDC. This indeed happened, and the EDC, which had been a brainchild of France, died as a result of French opposition.

The European Economic Community

When the EDC failed, the plans for the European Political Community appeared similarly doomed. Western Europeans who viewed political integration as the way to peace and prosperity were dismayed. However, Monnet, who had attempted to translate the concept of political integration into action, was not. He realized that the prospects were dead for an EDC and hence for the ultimate supranational government that he originally had had in mind. Instead, he now proposed to work piecemeal toward integration, by means of a permanent dialogue between the leading ministers of the countries already in the ECSC and possibly others in the future. Realizing that politics and economics are closely related, he trusted that a gradual harmonization of economic and social policies in various widening spheres would eventually lead to political integration.

At their meeting in Messina, Italy, in June 1955, the ECSC foreign ministers accepted a six-point proposal for the further integration of member countries' economies in the areas of traffic, energy, social policy, and a common market for goods and services. Shortly thereafter, Monnet set up a committee of representatives from all the non-Communist political parties in Western Europe, except the French Gaullists, who were opposed to any surrender of national sovereignty. This Action Committee for the United States of Europe led the so-called *Rélance*—the "relaunching" of Europe.

This relaunching culminated in the Rome Treaties of March 1957, which established the European Economic Community (EEC) and the European Community for Atomic Energy (Euratom). The purpose of the EEC was to put into practice the Messina proposals in all possible areas. The purpose of Euratom was to promote nuclear energy rather than oil as a replacement for coal as the main source of electric power. Oil, after all, had to be imported, a fact that rendered Europe vulnerable to the vagaries of the Middle East.

West Germany

In May 1952, just before it joined in the discussion of the EDC, West Germany performed its first important foreign-policy act when it signed the Paris Accords with Great Britain, France, and the United States. These accords established and defined the relations between West Germany and the countries that had occupied it. They included provisions for West German participation in Western defense, but the delay and final defeat of the EDC prevented the provisions from coming into force as planned. In September 1954, at a conference seeking alternatives to the failed EDC, participating countries decided to admit West Germany to NATO and thus to permit West German armed forces under German officers. The Paris Accords were revised, and the formal end of the occupation of West Germany was determined in the following month. On May 8, 1955, 10 years to the day after the final surrender of Germany, the democratic government of Konrad Adenauer received virtually full sovereignty in its domestic and foreign affairs, including the right to raise armed forces. West Germany was accepted into NATO.

The Second Berlin Crisis

In 1958, Berlin was still divided into a Soviet and three Western sectors. Access to West Berlin was either over land, through the territory of the former Soviet zone of occupation, now the Soviet satellite state of the German Democratic Republic (East Germany), or by air, along certain air corridors. Movement among the sectors within Berlin was free, which meant that East Germans who came to East Berlin could easily move to the Western sectors and thence fly out to West Germany. More than 3 million East Germans escaped to the West this way from 1945 to 1961. They represented the best and the brightest of the workforce. Both the Soviets and the East German Communist regime wanted to stop the flow, but to do so would have violated standing agreements. The Soviets therefore had to produce a crisis in East–West relations so serious that the West would accept closing off access to West Berlin from East Berlin as a lesser evil.

The Soviet leader, Nikita Khrushchev, saw his chance to solve the Berlin problem while at the same time causing confusion in the camp and undermining European faith in the United States. In November 1958, he launched the first of a series of diplomatic offensives designed to accomplish these purposes. He demanded that the Western Allies leave Berlin within 6 months; failure to do so would cause him to transfer the control of the access routes between West Germany and West Berlin to the government of East Germany. Had this ultimatum been successful, there is no doubt that the East German regime would have quickly swallowed West Berlin. The Western Allies would have lost all their prestige in West Germany, and the Germans would have been very tempted to leave NATO and try to make a deal with the Soviets.

Although the execution of Khrushchev's bold plans did not achieve their primary purpose of neutralizing Berlin, they did wreak confusion and disarray in the Western camp. Indeed, in 1959–1960, the Soviet leader almost succeeded in splitting the ranks of the NATO countries. British prime minister Harold Macmillan went to Moscow, without consulting the United States, to try to reach a settlement with Khrushchev. Like many Europeans, Macmillan had come to believe that the East–West confrontation was largely artificial and could be solved by negotiations and concessions. Adenauer regarded this as a betrayal of common interests, but by now he was very old and increasingly isolated, both in West Germany and in the Western alliance as a whole. And the new American president, John F. Kennedy, was not prepared to risk war to preserve Allied rights in Berlin or to maintain the principle that the government of the German Democratic Republic had no jurisdiction in the Soviet sector of the city, as the Four-Power Agreement had stipulated. Instead, the East German government declared East Berlin its capital. Khrushchev, encouraged by this provocation, gave the East German satellite government the green light to erect a barrier between the eastern and western sectors of Berlin: the Berlin Wall. The East German authorities began erecting the barrier on August 13, 1961. Until the Berlin Wall was finally dismantled, in 1989, escape from East Germany across the wall or across the even more imposing land frontier to West Germany was nearly impossible, and most of those trying it paid with their lives.

European Repercussions

The second Berlin crisis pulled the French and the Germans closer together and caused the United States and Great Britain to become somewhat uncertain allies. In 1958, Charles de Gaulle returned to power in France with the promise of ending the civil war in Algeria, a French possession in North Africa. In Europe, he wanted to keep Britain out of the European Economic Community while wooing the Germans away from what he considered their excessively close alignment with the United States. This strategy culminated in the Franco–German Non-Aggression Pact and Friendship Treaty of January 16, 1963. The treaty prescribed semiannual consultations between the heads of government of the two countries and listed a range of economic and political issues for future collaboration.

The treaty had great symbolic importance. To conclude and celebrate it, Adenauer went to Reims, a city in northeastern France where kings had been crowned when France was still a monarchy. In the medieval cathedral, Adenauer and de Gaulle knelt together to receive communion, a gesture that was reminiscent of the ancient unity of the French- and German-speaking peoples in the Carolingian Empire of the eighth and ninth centuries. The old enmity, both statesmen said, was dead forever.

De Gaulle hoped that the treaty would not only be the beginning of a political and economic relationship but also forge a military relationship between France and Germany that would gradually supersede NATO and reduce U.S. influ-

(The Bettmann Archive)

French president Charles de Gaulle, December 1958.

ence in Western Europe. The German Bundestag (the lower house of the national Legislature), however, unilaterally added a provision to the treaty saying that nothing in it would affect the Federal Republic's alliance and other ties to the United States. This effectively took away the substance of the treaty. Much later, in the late 1970s and 1980s, German and French leaders revitalized the treaty, and it began to take on the shape envisaged by de Gaulle: an alternative structure for Western European military cooperation.

Great Britain

Great Britain did not join the ECSC in 1951, and it took no part in the process of European economic integration during the 1950s. The British had a centuries-old tradition of noninvolvement on the European continent except as a response to a direct threat to Britain, and this tradition was still dominant in British foreign policy. The country preferred to rely on the "special relationship" with the United States and on the Commonwealth, its worldwide network of dominions and colonies that all had free access to the British market. If Britain joined the European Economic Community, an organization that had done away with tariffs, it would have granted all those countries, most of them developing-world countries with cheap labor, a tremendous competitive advantage in Europe. Neither the ECSC nor Great Britain, therefore, was interested in British membership under the circumstances.

Toward the end of the decade, the British government decided to dissolve what remained of the British Empire. That entailed also the gradual termination of "imperial preference," as the trade relations with the Commonwealth were called. Britain then decided to move slowly toward involvement in European politics. Its first step was to organize the smaller European countries, which were not members of the EEC, into a free trade area. In 1959, Britain, Portugal, Austria, Switzerland, Sweden, Denmark, and Norway concluded a treaty in Stockholm that established the European Free Trade Association (EFTA).

The Failure of Political Integration

Monnet's hope that the "relaunching" of Europe in 1955–1957 would lead to political integration turned out to be illusory. A significant dilemma that faced the EEC's founders was summarized in the phrase *élargissement ou profondissement* ("widening or deepening"): Should the organization increase its membership, or should it enhance the quality of its integration? In 1961, the heads of government of the six EEC countries decided to restart the process of political integration. They began developing a European Political Statute, a kind of basic constitution, albeit a more modest one than the European Political Community had envisaged in 1952–1954. The statute would have strengthened the supranational institutions of the EEC, the European Commission, and the Council of Ministers, at the expense of national sovereignties. Although it could seem that the French were behind the plans for the statute, Charles de Gaulle was not interested in any proposal that would reduce national sovereignty; thus, its failure in August 1962 proved no great disappointment to him. There was no further significant attempt to extend the integration process to the political area until the early 1980s.

In August 1961, Britain officially applied for admission to the European Economic Community, while Austria, Sweden, and Switzerland applied for associate status. In January 1963, de Gaulle vetoed the British application, arguing that the British industrial equipment and output were backward and obsolete. British membership would, in his opinion, drag down the performance level of the existing Community. (It is possible that de Gaulle's real aim was to hurt the United States.) A renewed British application did not meet success until 1972, after de Gaulle had died.

PROSPERITY AND DÉTENTE (1963–1973)

The early 1960s marked a number of important turning points in postwar European development. First, the series of crises concerning Berlin ebbed after the Berlin Wall was built. Most people thought that Khrushchev and the East German Communists had achieved what they wanted in closing off access to West Berlin and that there was now reason to hope for some stability in East–West relations in Germany. Since that had hitherto been the main potential flashpoint of the cold war, the achievement of stability was a momentous development, promising to turn the political division of Germany into a condition of, rather than a threat to, peace and stability in Europe.

Second, de Gaulle's veto of British membership in the EEC confirmed the existence of "two Europes" within Western Europe: a core consisting of the original six ECSC members; and a periphery of unconnected, less dynamic, and less integration-minded outsiders. Even after Britain and other countries joined in the 1970s and 1980s, the European Economic Community remained unofficially a two-tier institution, consisting of a core of original members far more integrated psychologically as well as economically than the latecomers, and with a different and more positive attitude to the whole matter of European integration.

Third, the European economy witnessed a dramatic rise. This was particularly the case in West Germany, where the phenomenon was labeled *Wirtschaftswunder* ("Economic Miracle"), but other countries both within and outside the EEC also enjoyed unprecedented prosperity.

Finally, a new generation had grown up in Europe, a generation that was not automatically hostile to communism and consequently less cold war–minded. This generation, moreover, had lost sight of the American achievements of winning the war and promoting European recovery. Indeed, the new generation that had started to people the universities, that prevailed in the media and in society at large, appeared suspicious of American motives, particularly where Europe was concerned. Many European intellectuals ridiculed the often obsessive forms of American anticommunism (such as the McCarthy era had displayed). Anti-American sentiment as a rule expressed itself in large rallies and demonstrations in front of American embassies. It was concerned with the U.S. involvement in Vietnam, with everything that unambiguously revealed American imperialism in general, and with the U.S. nuclear arsenal and the world's armament race. In sum, this emerging generation had accumulated a long list of grievances.

But the 1960s also changed Europe in general. A different set of mores developed, and it is possible to speak of a cultural revolution (although one should of course steer clear of analogies with China's Cultural Revolution of 1966–1976).

Defense and Security

The Berlin Wall reminded the democratic majority of Western Europeans that there was little that they could do directly to change the existing division of Europe into democracy and dictatorship. Accepting that Communist rule in Central/Eastern Europe might be a permanent fact of life, they began in the mid-1960s to view their relations with the Soviet bloc in a different way. Instead of supposing either that the Soviets were poised to attack Western Europe or that Western Europe and the United States should try to undermine Communist power, they asked whether it was possible to combine deterrence of the Soviets with an increase in economic and diplomatic ties that might give the Soviets a stake in peaceful relations and the Central/Eastern Europeans the means to regain some autonomy vis-à-vis Moscow.

By 1970, the major Western European governments had adopted the view that the way to preserve peace and their own

(Photo No. ST-C230-37-63, in the John F. Kennedy Library)

U.S. president John F. Kennedy in Berlin, June 26, 1963.

independence was not primarily through a stronger defense but through closer relations with the Soviets and the Central/Eastern European regimes. In other words, Western European politicians came to believe that the Soviet leaders had given up their hostility to democracy and now shared the Europeans' own goals and values concerning peace in Europe. These assumptions continued to be the foundation of Western European policy toward the East until the breakdown of the Soviet Union in the early 1990s. U.S. administrations did not always share them, at least to the same degree, and these attitudes have been the source of numerous misunderstandings and quarrels within the Atlantic Alliance.

The British, Germans, and Italians were the most committed to the new view of security. The French government under de Gaulle shared it but also believed that Western Europe must in any case develop its own policy toward the Soviet Union, because the United States could not be expected permanently to guarantee the defense of Western Europe. The French president, in fact, wanted Europe to be a "third force," headed by France. He therefore concentrated on the development of an independent French nuclear force and, in 1966, withdrew France from the integrated military structure of NATO. France has ever since been proud of its nuclear weaponry, which enabled it to rely less on the Atlantic Alliance. In doing so, de Gaulle weakened NATO in the short term but gave France greater autonomy and self-confidence, which strengthened Western Europe in the long term.

The last obstacle on the road to East–West stability in this period was the Cuban missile crisis of 1962. Ironically, that incident also made Western Europeans realize that the United

States no longer had clear superiority over the Soviets in intercontinental nuclear forces (often identified as strategic weapons). This was one reason why most people in Western Europe believed so strongly in East–West stability from the 1960s onward. If the United States could no longer threaten to destroy the Soviet Union in response to a Soviet threat or attack in Europe without the risk of being destroyed itself, then the old NATO doctrine of massive retaliation was no longer credible. Instead, the NATO governments, in December 1967, declared a new doctrine, which contained two elements. The first was "flexible response," which meant that NATO would respond to a threat or an attack at any level, nuclear or conventional, without declaring beforehand to which level it would resort. The idea was that this uncertainty would itself be a sufficient deterrent. The second element was the principle that deterrence and détente—as long as they were based on negotiations with the Soviet Union for arms-control and true peaceful coexistence—were two sides of the same coin. Neither could be pursued without the other. These two elements were official policy for more than a quarter of a century. They naturally became irrelevant when Soviet communism and the cold war faded away.

The second principle, the mutual dependence of deterrence and détente, signaled the beginning of the era of arms-control negotiations in Europe. After 1968, talks almost continuously took place between the two chief protagonists, the Soviets and the Americans, concerning military forces in Europe. The Western Europeans were not directly involved in most of these talks. Nevertheless, arms control became a solid part of Western European political orientation, regardless of their actual effect on the numbers of Soviet troops and nuclear forces, which was negligible.

The first major arms-control agreement was the Nuclear Nonproliferation Treaty of 1968 (in force from 1970), whereby the United States, the Soviet Union, Great Britain, West Germany, and certain other countries undertook not to supply to third parties any nuclear technology that might be used for weapons. Some countries, such as France and the People's Republic of China, delayed their participation. India was indignant, arguing that the Nuclear Nonproliferation Treaty was highly discriminatory, or at least biased toward the status quo. In the course of 1992, rumors—occasionally corroborated by press reports—circulated to the effect that certain countries and China had violated the treaty as well as other international laws by selling nuclear materials to Iraq. And in 1994, a new rebel emerged: North Korea. That country's position, however, became very confused when its dictator, Kim Il-Sung, died in 1994.

Germany's Ostpolitik (Eastern Policy)

The German term *Ostpolitik* originated in Otto von Bismarck's days (the early 1870s). The "Iron Chancellor" did not want to embark upon colonialism, believing that an overseas empire would be exceedingly vulnerable in times of war.

Instead, he drew attention to the vast, almost vacant, spaces to the east of Germany. Ostpolitik in those days referred to policies that would enable Germany to acquire those lands as *Lebensraum* ("living space" for its population).

Shortly after the 1969 elections put the Social Democratic Party of Germany into office, Willy Brandt, the new West German chancellor, revived the term in an entirely different context. Now Ostpolitik started to refer to attempts at reconciliation by West Germany with all its eastern neighbors, with the exception of East Germany. These countries had greatly suffered in World War II from the German onslaught eastward at the time of Operation Barbarossa. Brandt visited most of them, gave away large sums of money by way of compensation, and negotiated diplomatic relations with all of them. The so-called Eastern Treaties (which specifically referred to the Soviet Union, Poland, Czechoslovakia, and East Germany) became part of the permanent legal and diplomatic framework of West European politics as regards Central/Eastern Europe. In doing so, West Germany naturally had to recognize the status quo, which implied the acceptance of Soviet control of Central/Eastern Europe and, more important, Communist rule in East Germany. However, what Brandt and West Germany received in return was incalculable: A great deal of prestige accrued to the young republic, while the condition of the German nation was henceforth described in the formula "one nation, two states."

As far as the compensation program was concerned, those countries that had suffered at the hands of Nazi Germany received large-scale compensations. This program, which was named *Wiedergutmachung,* was even extended to Israel—which, of course, did not exist in Hitler's time.

EEC Problems

As has been mentioned, the EEC was faced with the dilemma *élargissement ou profondissement* (enlargement by having more members or deepening by becoming better integrated). During the 1960s, the Community failed on both scores. Two major problems emerged that became worse as time went on.

The first was that, even though the EEC was supposed to be a common market in goods and services with no internal tariffs, member countries were able to protect their national economic interests, as they perceived them, in ways other than by outright tariffs. There were two main methods. One was to introduce complicated national rules for the approval of industrial products of all kinds, which, in accordance with EEC rules, made it necessary for producers elsewhere to adjust their products to each country's specifications. Such technical-approval rules were not legally equivalent to tariffs, but they had the same effect of making it difficult for foreign producers to enter a domestic market. An example of this may be the West German set of laws specifying the exact ingredients and regulating other requirements for brewing beer. Other European beers followed a variety of very different regulations or specifications. As a result, West Germany,

referring to its beer-brewing laws, was able to prevent potential competition; foreign beers made with different specifications and procedures were not permitted to enter the country.

The other method of protecting national economic interests was taxation. The EEC was a customs, not a tax, union. Each government levied taxes in whatever way it chose. High indirect taxes on business transactions or on imported consumer durables were an effective means of discouraging importation and consumption.

In the early 1960s, the governments of the ECSC introduced another kind of tax, one that had been in use in Great Britain and which has since been adopted by all Western European governments. This value-added tax (VAT) works like U.S. sales taxes, but the difference is that it is levied at each stage of the process of production and distribution. The producer as well as all intermediaries must collect the tax from the next person down the chain; they are then entitled to a refund of the tax that they themselves have paid. Only the final consumer, who actually uses the product, gets no refund.

Rates of VAT varied from product to product and from country to country, as did the list of products or services liable to it. Gradually, all governments raised the tax rates and extended the scope of VAT. In the beginning, rates were typically around 5 percent; and many items, such as food, educational materials, and legal fees, were exempt. But by the 1970s, rates in some countries were as high as 33 percent for some products, and there were very few exemptions.

A second major stumbling bloc for the EEC in the 1960s was agriculture. By 1965, it had established a common market in agricultural products with common prices. The member governments discovered that the inevitable effect of this common market would be to drive farmers in most of France and much of West Germany out of business, since their costs of production were far higher than those of poorer or more productive farmers in Italy or the Netherlands. Consequently, they instituted a system of price supports and payments from country to country to maintain agricultural employment and farmers' income at specified levels. This Common Agricultural Policy (CAP) soon became enormously expensive; by the mid-1970s, it was consuming more than 80 percent of the EEC budget as well as most of the administrators' time, thus effectively blocking any movement on substantive issues of common interest. The main beneficiary of the CAP was France; its main victim was West Germany.

In 1965, the ECSC, the EEC, and Euratom were united in a single administrative entity, governed in common by the Council of Ministers (one cabinet member from each country, depending on the subject that is being discussed), the European Commission (composed of 13 top civil servants answerable to the Council), and the European Parliament (delegates originally appointed by the parliaments of the various member states, and subsequently directly elected). In 1972, shortly after de Gaulle retired as president of France, formal membership applications were accepted from Great Britain, Den-

THE EUROPEAN UNION: A CONFUSING NOMENCLATURE

To many people, the names as well as the abbreviations relative to the European Union (EU) have become more than a little confusing. It should be borne in mind that, in fact, three Communities were established in the 1950s and based on agreements among European countries for spending Marshall Plan funds. The first was the European Coal and Steel Community (ECSC), which was founded in 1951 by the Treaty of Paris. The original ECSC included six countries: France, the Federal Republic of Germany (West Germany), Italy, Belgium, the Netherlands, and Luxembourg. The intent was to pool the coal and steel resources of these countries—that is, to entrust these resources to some supranational agency.

The second and third Communities came into being through the Treaties of Rome, which were both signed at the Italian capital on March 25, 1957. These Communities were the European Economic Community (EEC), an economic-integrative entity and by far the most important Community, and the European Atomic Energy Community (Euratom). Euratom was meant to be a research body that would investigate the peaceful use of atomic energy. But it soon ran into grave difficulties and, as a result, it always remained very much behind the two other Communities. The Treaties of Rome covered the same countries as the Treaty of Paris.

The three Communities operated separately. However, since they had the same membership and were pursuing similar goals, the three Communities were increasingly viewed as a collectivity. In the late 1960s, moreover, Community institutions (the European Commission, the Council of Ministers, the European Parliament, and the Court of Justice) were, for the sake of economy, applied to all three of the Communities. This measure naturally enhanced the collective notion, and the term *European Community* (EC)

started to be used for all of them. With the Maastricht Treaty of 1991, that term was replaced by the *European Union*. (*Note:* To avoid confusion, we generally use the term *European Union* in this volume.)

Another term that may require some explanation is *Common Market*. It was used for the first time in the Treaty of Paris, where it meant putting together all the coal and steel resources for the common use of the six member states. The term also came to be used as a synonym of the European Economic Community. In recent years, it has fallen into disuse.

European Integration

The European experience has demonstrated clearly that politics and economics are closely intertwined. Although the economic aspects of the old EEC remain important, many authorities believe that the political aspects of the EU may gain significance to the point where they may overshadow the economic ramifications—a contingency foreseen as early as 1957. The Single European Act, which came into force on July 1, 1987, to all intents and purposes constitutes a comprehensive amendment to the Treaties of Paris and Rome. It too underscores the politicization of European integration, and it therefore is no longer possible to view the Communities as vehicles solely of economic integration. An interesting side effect of the momentous changes that they have brought about is that, in the United States, the word *Europe* has almost become synonymous with what the EU has come to stand for, although Europe as such is much larger in area and is composed of a host of countries that are not—at least, not yet—member states of the Union.

INTEGRATIVE PROPOSALS AND PROCESSES

1947   The Marshall Plan is announced; Jean Monnet begins working for a common European economic market and defense

1950   The Schuman Declaration, aimed at supranationalism

1951   The Treaty of Paris establishes the ECSC

1957   The Treaties of Rome establish the EEC and Euratom

1960s Adoption of the Common Agricultural Policy

1962   The Fouchet Plan coordinates foreign and defense policies

1969   The first summit in The Hague comes to be known as the "relaunching" of Europe

1970s The Lomé Conventions render many developing-world countries associate members; the Communities become known as the European Community

1979   The first direct election of the European Parliament

1980   The Mansholt Plan for Agriculture

1981   The Genscher-Colombo Plan is considered

1983   The Solemn Declaration of European Union

1984   An initiative concerning the Draft Treaty on European Union

1985   The Schengen Agreement, concerning the removal of border controls, initially not extending to all members

1985   The Single European Act is passed

1986   The Single European Act is ratified

1987   Completion of the Cecchini Report on the costs of non-Europe; the Single Act revises the founding treaties

1988   Bruges speech by British prime minister Margaret Thatcher

1990   Britain enters the European Exchange Rate Mechanism

1991   The European Council adopts the Maastricht Treaty for a closer union; the EC becomes the European Union

1992   An Irish referendum endorses Maastricht; a Danish referendum rejects it; a French referendum approves it—barely; the Treaty on European Union further revises the founding treaties

1995   The EU pledges to start looking for membership candidates in Central/Eastern Europe

1997   The draft Treaty of Amsterdam proposes further revisions to the founding treaties; Agenda 2000 aims to strengthen the EU and prepare for enlargement

1999   Europe's currency union (EMU) is launched with issue of the Euro

mark, Norway, and the Irish Republic. The Norwegian voters rejected membership in a referendum, but the other three countries formally joined the EEC on January 1, 1973. Gradually, this more integrated entity became commonly known, simply, as the European Community, or EC. (In the 1990s it became known as the European Union, or EU.)

A Cultural Revolution

The generation of statesmen who had lived as adults through Europe's "Second Thirty Years' War" of 1914–1945 and who survived to build democracy in Western Europe after World War II had to a great extent faded from the political scene by the mid-1960s. Some of the leaders of that generation were men remarkable for their stamina and longevity. Konrad Adenauer was finally forced out of office by his own party in 1963. Four years later, he died, at age 91. Charles de Gaulle, leader of the Free French in 1940–1944, of France in 1944–1946, the first president of the Fifth Republic in 1958–1969, and advocate of an *Europe des Patries* (an autonomous Europe composed of sovereign national states), died a year after leaving the presidency, at age 79. Alcide de Gasperi was another giant on the European scene who actively participated in European integration. And finally, Harold Macmillan, who as British prime minister became known for his "Winds of Change" speech (which referred to the liquidation of the empire rather than to East–West relations), having held the office from 1957 to 1963, died in 1986, at age 92. These men regarded the outbreak of World War I in 1914 as the major disaster in modern European and world history from which all the other subsequent disorders stemmed: totalitarianism, genocides, the attacks on democracy, economic disruption, and chaos. They did their best, as they understood it, to prevent a repetition of these events.

Their departure from power symbolized a broader shift in Western European politics and culture—from concern with defense and peace in the most elementary sense, to concern with social issues, domestic politics, and new revolutionary ideologies. In many countries, left-wing parties came to power for the first time, with new agendas for extending the welfare state, cutting down military spending, giving more power to the common person, and redistributing income, wealth, and authority. Since these agendas required more, not less, government, their outcome usually was to expand bureaucracy and to centralize power. Also, with the advances in technology, government tended to be more specialized. This produced disillusionment and cynicism, two tendencies that would strongly characterize European politics in coming years.

The most dramatic expression of the shift in European attitudes and culture in the 1960s was in the area of higher education. The number of university students had been growing explosively since the late 1950s. A university education was no longer an elite luxury in Western Europe but something that almost everyone who qualified might expect to have. A great many of the new students rejected orthodox communism but were oriented toward new forms of revolutionary ideology, directed against the existing social and political authorities.

French education, at all levels, has always been extremely centralized and rigid. The university curricula provoked the indignation of university students all over France, but particularly in Paris. These curricula had become old-fashioned, if not obsolete. Emphasizing the classics and the humanities, they in no way met the requirements of the times—that is, they had not adapted to the emerging postindustrial world. Those shortcomings were clearly reflected in massive graduate unemployment. In 1968, the situation came to a head. Paris then presented a most revolutionary picture: Students established barricades on the Left Bank, close to the Sorbonne and Nanterre University. From these somewhat dubious fortifications they hurled cobblestones and Molotov cocktails at the police. Although no one was killed, these scenes made a deep impression on French society, which has continued to refer to these raucous activities by the euphemism *les événements* ("the events"). Unfortunately, their outcome was extremely disappointing. After temporary adaptations and adjustments, the education system suffered a retrenchment of obsolescence. In fact, in France and some other European countries, education has become encapsuled in bureaucracy, eroding the centuries-old self-government status of universities.

STAGFLATION AND INSECURITY (1973–1989)

Although economic growth had slowed down by the early 1970s and many Western European countries had significant budget or trade deficits, no one expected the sudden crisis of 1973–1974, which put a final end to what the French called "the thirty glorious years" (1944–1973) of increasing prosperity and even more rapidly rising expectations. The crisis began with oil-price increases imposed by the Organization of Petroleum Exporting Countries (OPEC). These increases triggered equally dramatic increases in the costs of many other commodities essential to the European economies. The result was an unprecedented combination of inflation and unemployment, which economists gave the ugly name of "stagflation." One of its most remarkable aspects was that unemployment and inflation no longer responded to traditional laws. In the past, they had related conversely—that is, if one went up, the other went down. But since the early 1970s, unemployment and inflation may both rise or both fall simultaneously.

Barely had the Western Europeans dealt, with varying success, with the first wave of stagflation than a further crisis developed. In 1979, the Islamic Revolution in Iran produced a new round of oil-price increases, which hit Western Europe as hard as the first had done. Still, it seemed that Europeans had become more accustomed to these stresses. At the gas stations, there were no long lines of cars waiting to be filled;

(Mobil Oil Corporation)

North Sea oil was a boon to several Western European countries during the 1970s and early 1980s, but the bonanza was not so sweet after oil prices dropped dramatically in the mid-1980s.

no country instituted "carless Sundays" (as the Netherlands had done during the first oil squeeze). Nevertheless, the period did generate some friction in the Allied camp. The Soviet Union in the early 1980s offered to supply Western Europe with natural gas from Siberia. To that end, a pipeline had to be built across the Republic of Russia (then still a constituent state of the Soviet Union), Poland, and what was then East Germany. U.S. president Ronald Reagan feared that such a supply of energy would render Western Europe politically vulnerable, since the supplier, the Soviet Union, could always threaten to cut the supplies if Western Europe went against its wishes. However, Western Europe's internal energy sources were extremely limited, a fact that was bound to create a dependency anyway. Such a dependency could as a matter of course be translated into a cold war weapon. The acrimonious debates that ensued between the United States and its Western European allies with reference to the Soviet offer have been named "pipeline politics."

At the same time, the major NATO countries, believing that their security was threatened by new nuclear weapons, decided to update their own weaponry, at the instigation of the United States. The most controversial element of that mod-

ernization was a plan to deploy new U.S. intermediate-range nuclear missiles in Western Europe. This category of weapons posed the danger that Europe itself could be destroyed by nuclear bombs (in the past, the so-called strategic missiles were mainly intended to hit the two adversaries, the United States and the Soviet Union). The plan provoked a large wave of pacifist movements in Western Europe, which for centuries has been a battlefield for wars. Pacifism rocked the political systems of various Western European countries.

Economic Slowdown
In Western Europe, oil provided all the fuel for transportation as well as most of the energy needed for generating electricity. In 1973, Western Europe imported 90 percent of its oil. The import price of crude oil in September 1973 was $2.50 a barrel; by January 1974, it had jumped to $12.00.

The effect of the OPEC price increases was to transfer about 2 percent of the value of Western Europe's total annual production of goods and services to the oil-producing states. This meant that the Western Europeans had that much less to spend on their own goods and services, a factor that as a matter of course led to unemployment. At the same time, labor was politically strong enough in most countries to prevent employed workers from suffering any loss of real income. Instead, the net loss of wealth fell disproportionately on the young or unemployed. Unemployment, which had been virtually unknown in many countries since the early 1950s, rose in 1974–1975 to about 10 percent of the labor force in all the major countries, where it has largely remained ever since.

The impact of the oil shock, as it was called, varied. The surplus countries, above all West Germany, absorbed the increases far more easily than the deficit countries like Italy. Norway and Great Britain had an advantage. In the 1960s, explorers had found petroleum underneath the North Sea, but, at the price level that prevailed at the time, it had not been economical to extract this oil. After the oil shock, extracting the continental-shelf oil between Britain and Norway proved competitive, and, by the late 1970s, Britain itself had become an oil-exporting country.

In the second oil shock, in 1979–1980, prices rose to about $40.00 a barrel. This hit Western Europe especially hard, since the value of the U.S. dollar was rising against European currencies. Again, the surplus countries did better than the deficit countries. More important, all countries had been improving energy efficiency in transportation, industrial processes, and domestic heating, so that much less oil was needed for the same effect. In addition, France and West Germany expanded their nuclear-energy programs. In the 1980s, nuclear fission produced about 70 percent of all the electricity used in France. Only in the early 1990s did France begin to face some difficulties in its reliance on nuclear energy.

Terrorism and Military Security

Western Europeans had not thought a great deal about security matters since the early 1960s. The student demonstrations

UPI/Bettmann Newsphotos)

West German chancellor Helmut Schmidt (1974–1982), addressing a UN session on disarmament.

of 1968 had been confined to France. Most Western Europeans were too young to remember the last time that domestic violence had been a factor in politics—namely, in the 1940s. They were all the more taken aback—indeed, aghast—when gangs of terrorists began to kill civilians arbitrarily, to blow up public buildings in West Germany and Italy, to hijack airplanes, and to disrupt the Olympic Games in Munich in 1972 by the selective massacre of Israeli athletes. Some of these terrorists were Europeans themselves, young radicals who had started out as student activists in the 1960s and who had formed or joined gangs such as the Red Army Faction in West Germany and the Red Brigade in Italy. Others hailed from the Middle East. It took some time for the Western European governments and police forces to coordinate an effective response to them, but, in a series of dramatic actions in 1977–1979, most of the gang members were captured or dispersed. In West Germany, the government of Chancellor Helmut Schmidt had a number of antiterrorist laws passed that to many appeared too drastic, in that they went very much against the spirit of democracy.

Toward the end of the 1970s, some Western European leaders, notably Schmidt, concluded that the 1960s view that détente policies in the West would encourage the Soviets to reduce their own vast military strength was mistaken. The Soviets were building up both their conventional and their nuclear forces in Central/Eastern Europe, far beyond what they needed to suppress dissidence or maintain their own security. In 1977, Schmidt suggested that the United States either obtain a reliable arms-control agreement with the Soviets for disarmament in Europe or install new nuclear missiles in Western Europe to achieve a balance with the Soviet buildup. In 1978, NATO decided on its own to begin a long-term process of modernizing all its forces to maintain the credibility of the flexible-response strategy in the 1980s.

In December 1979, NATO decided to pursue arms-control talks with the Soviets regarding European nuclear forces—but those talks failed, and the United States deployed 572 new missiles. This measure was dubbed "double-track," since it involved both nuclear diplomacy and a material escalation of sorts. It provoked the opposition of hundreds of thousands of Western Europeans, mostly young persons under age 35 who had no memory of the 1940s and 1950s, when many people feared a Soviet attack and were determined to defend democracy by force if necessary. The members of these new peace movements did not believe that the Soviet Union was a military or political threat. In the early 1980s, they demonstrated against the projected deployments in many cities of West Germany, Britain, and the Netherlands. There were no peace movements to speak of in France and Italy, however. Both countries had large Communist parties that had used peace slogans for their own purposes in the past. Many remembered this and regarded the new peace movements as witting or unwitting tools of Soviet expansionism.

The American negotiators failed to persuade the Soviets to reduce their superiority in nuclear arms in Europe. Therefore,

(Reuters/Bettmann Newsphotos)

A demonstrator attaches an antinuclear banner at a war memorial in Munich, Germany.

starting in late 1983, NATO deployed the U.S. missiles. The peace movements had failed in their immediate objective. In the longer term, though, they had changed the terms of debate on defense and security, above all by questioning the moral and political value of the NATO doctrine of flexible response, including the threat of a nuclear response to attack.

Strengthening the Core

One important result of the economic problems and the common Western European concerns over defense in the later 1970s was the revitalization of the French–German dialogue. The Friendship Treaty of 1963 prescribed such a dialogue, to take place chiefly in the semiannual meetings of the heads of government of the two countries; but, until the mid-1970s, the talks concerned mainly economic and trade issues. In 1974, the French elected as president the conservative Valéry Giscard d'Estaing. Much to the surprise of many observers, he formed a close friendship with Chancellor Schmidt. Giscard and Schmidt turned the semiannual talks into mini-summits, where they discussed issues of general European significance, including security. Both felt that Western Europe needed to establish its own position in international politics rather than remain dependent on or react to U.S. or Soviet actions. They also believed that the United States no longer had the resources, the interest, or the ability to conduct a consistent worldwide foreign policy. Finally, they believed that if Western Europe was to have a voice of its own, that voice should come from two core countries—namely, France and West Germany.

Peace Movements: A New Credo

The peace movements of the early 1980s convinced a sizable number of people in Western Europe that even the *threat* of

using nuclear weapons in response to a Soviet attack was immoral. A factor that gave the peace movement added legitimacy was that it was in large part based on religion. Often it seemed that churches were trying to win back the young among their flocks by endorsing their causes. In addition, most Western Europeans had over 20 years come to believe that there was probably no Soviet military threat and that any East–West problems could be solved by negotiations and concessions. A popular phrase of the 1980s had it that Western Europe and the Soviet Union (with Central/Eastern Europe) were bound together in a "security partnership," a notion that implied that each side's security depended on that of the other. A corollary of security partnership was that Western Europe should do nothing that might provoke the Soviets or that might cause them to think that the West was planning to undermine Soviet rule in Central/Eastern Europe.

Most of the peace movements operated in Northern Europe, but throughout the democratic part of the continent, many politicians, mostly but not exclusively from Socialist parties, began calling for the United States to withdraw its troops. The United States then maintained naval, ground, and air forces in West Germany, Italy, Turkey, Greece, Spain, Portugal, and Great Britain. Greece and Spain had right-of-center governments, which were particularly insistent that the United States should either close its military bases or offer significantly more in return for the right to use them. In these countries, irritation over U.S. bases stemmed from a complex mixture of feelings of national inferiority and anti-Americanism, and these tendencies promised to grow stronger in the future.

Even among West Germans, who, although many might sympathize with the pacifists, had been overwhelmingly pro-American since the 1950s, there was more than a little apprehension about the U.S. troop presence. It had become customary to claim that peace in Europe would be better served if the United States abandoned its provocative attitude and withdrew its forces. In Great Britain, the British Labour Party (BLP) took a strong stand against the U.S. presence and the country's own independent nuclear force, but the party was too factionalized to stand a chance of gaining power in the 1980s.

In 1986, the Americans and the Soviets began a new round of arms-control talks aimed at reducing nuclear missiles in Europe. Most Western Europeans considered these talks promising and worthwhile; others, notably the French, wondered whether the Soviets could be trusted to fulfill their part of the bargain or whether they were merely negotiating to remove weapons that they no longer wanted anyway.

The Beginning of Change

Many in Western Europe put great faith in the Soviet leader who took power in 1985, Mikhail Gorbachev. They believed that he was sincere in wanting to reform the Soviet economic system; that, in fact, he must do so if the Soviet Union were to remain a superpower; and that it was in Western Europe's

(UPI/Bettmann Newsphotos)

Soviet president Mikhail Gorbachev.

One of the early admirers of Gorbachev was British prime minister Margaret Thatcher, who, even before Gorbachev had made it to the top leadership post, observed that here was a man with whom the West could do business. In time, the West Germans became enthusiastic admirers of the Soviet leader, who, according to several public-opinion polls, was found to be "more likeable" than the American president (Ronald Reagan). In the 1980s, West Germany moved to regain some of Germany's historic role as the main trading partner of the Central/Eastern European countries. The German leaders thought that Germany could play a role in moving the Central/Eastern European regimes in the direction of democratization and a greater respect for human rights.

The French were more worried than the Germans about Gorbachev's intentions. Since de Gaulle's tenure in the 1960s, they had adopted their own stance in East–West relations and in Western European political integration. By the 1980s, they had shed most of their anti-Americanism and had emerged as the most anti-Soviet of all European nations. Central in their apprehensions was the fear that Gorbachev simply wanted Western help to streamline the Soviet system and make it a more efficient threat to Western European liberties and prospects. They also feared that the Germans were likely to succumb to Gorbachev's diplomatic blandishments, chiefly because the Soviet Union held 17 million Germans—the populace of East Germany—hostage. For several reasons, therefore, the French continued to push actively

interest to help him by giving him loans and technological assistance. Few thought that a revitalized and more efficient Soviet Union might be a new danger rather than a friendly new partner of the West.

(U.S. Air Force photo)

A Ballistic Missile Early Warning System site in Pylingdales Moore, England.

in the 1980s for a new European security and political system, based on the French–German alliance rather than on the weak institutions of the EU. First, falling back on de Gaulle's Eurocentric vision, they espoused the belief that Western unity would be the best guarantor of peace. In addition, they argued that unity must be based on Europe, asserting that the United States no longer had the will or the skill to maintain its superpower status vis-à-vis the Soviets. And finally, the only two relevant European powers were France and West Germany, with the latter likely to slide toward Gorbachev unless its tendencies in that direction were firmly countered by the French.

The Population Bust

All of Western Europe, but especially Germany, the Scandinavian countries, France, and Great Britain, were confronted by a new and disturbing reality beginning in the early 1980s: declining populations. This unprecedented development has several serious implications. First, since Western Europe is above all a society of skilled, professional people, a population decline is bound to have a disproportionate impact on the global product of valuable goods and services. The whole world, not just Europe, benefits from Western European technology and production. Fewer Western European designers, entrepreneurs, and producers mean fewer high-quality goods for the whole world, and therefore a net decline in global income.

Second, societies progress as a result of the intellectual and economic investments and achievements of young people, whereas older people mostly repeat the tasks they learned when young. Therefore, a decline in the numbers of young people is bound to have a disproportionate effect on inventiveness, productivity, and cultural continuity, with unpredictable but potentially catastrophic effects on the vitality of Western European society as a whole.

Third, all Western European countries had become advanced welfare states by the 1980s. All the welfare systems operated on the assumption that there would be a sufficient number of young, productive people of working age to support the elderly and the disabled, the military forces, and people in education. In the 1980s, there were between three and four people of working age for every one welfare recipient, a ratio that could cause problems. It has been estimated that by the year 2020, that ratio will have deteriorated to perhaps about two to one in Germany. A declining number of working-age people will have to produce the revenue through their taxes to support the many pensioners. In addition, there are two other related factors that tend to jeopardize pension plans and social security systems: To combat unemployment, business and government have come up with early retirement offers. At the same time, life-expectancy rates have also risen in most industrialized countries. This means that pensioners will be dependent on public moneys for a much longer time. Raising taxes to pay for all this will have the effect of discour-

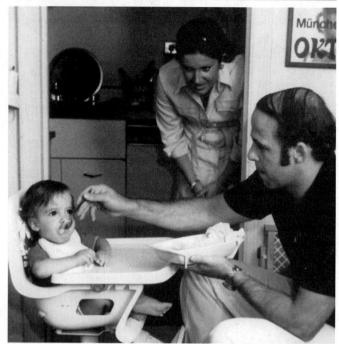

(United Nations/M. Faust)

Western European countries have made a strong commitment to both state-supported child care and paid parental leave.

aging large families. Thus, the problem is bound to get progressively worse, escalating in an upward spiral. Experts predict that the whole welfare system on which political stability in Western Europe has rested since the 1940s is bound to disintegrate at some point.

There is little that any government can do about the population bust, since no one fully understands its causes. There is no single explanation for the problem, but several factors clearly contribute to it. One is the availability of birth control since the mid-1960s. This makes having children a matter of choice, and many people choose not to have them. Another is the welfare system itself, which means that people no longer need to have children to take care of them in old age or when they get sick. In addition, the economic cost of the welfare system is making it difficult for many families to have more than one or two children while simultaneously supporting the system through their taxes. Another reason is the psychological and cultural atmosphere that has prevailed in Western Europe since the mid-1960s, an atmosphere that puts immediate gratification and adult pleasures over family life. To illustrate this, one may point to the fact that nowadays most Europeans enjoy 4 or 5 weeks of paid vacation per year.

THE POST–COLD WAR ERA (1989–PRESENT)

Almost overnight, the cold war, which had haunted world politics for more than 4 decades, came to an end. It is possible to speculate that Gorbachev had unwittingly written the scenario of the cold war's demise. In the mid-1980s, he introduced two new concepts: *glasnost* (Russian for "openness," which implied that the government was willing to lift its censorship and other repressive strictures) and *perestroika* (which referred to economic reform, actually the road to a market economy). It was these two formulas that opened the Soviet Pandora's box, releasing forces that could no longer be contained. There can be no doubt that Gorbachev was sincere. By the same token, he remained a Communist, apparently believing that Marxism (the brand of communism that was instituted in the Soviet Union after World War I) could be purged of all the evil that had amassed over the course of 7 decades. Also, he must have severely underrated the forces of nationalism fueled by the momentous changes that he sponsored in the country. Ethnicity in general and ethnonationalism in particular were virtually invisible, or at least largely academic subjects, in the heyday of the Soviet Union. In hindsight, it appears that they must simply have been dormant and, under Gorbachev's rule, they awoke. Not only the three Baltic nations (Estonia, Latvia, and Lithuania) but several other states, one by one, seceded from what until then had seemed a solid union.

The collapse of the Union of Socialist Soviet Republics may best be compared to an implosion. In some republics, there were skirmishes; in others, serious fighting was attended by bloodshed and destruction. But soon, the Soviet Union was no more.

As far as Central/Eastern Europe was concerned, Gorbachev was instrumental in a much more direct fashion. In the late 1980s, he visited the various heads of state and heads of government in that part of Europe, leaving the message everywhere that the Brezhnev Doctrine was no longer in force. Soviet leader Leonid Brezhnev had in 1969 stated that there was a commonwealth of Socialist nations. If one of its members attempted to get out—that is, to defect—the others had the obligation to prevent it. Since the Soviet Union was the most important member of the Warsaw Treaty Organization, the obvious implication was that the Soviet Union would interfere whenever an East bloc nation tried to get rid of communism or to liberalize its form of government. In fact, such interference had taken place in Hungary in 1956 and in Czechoslovakia in 1968, thus before Brezhnev had come up with his warning. Gorbachev, who feared that, considering its rock-bottom economy, the Soviet Union had far too many commitments, told the Soviet bloc leaders that they would now be on their own, whatever happened.

Soon the Central/Eastern European nations were in an uproar. Massive rallies started to take place, day after day. As a rule, the demonstrators clamored for changes, for better conditions, and for an improved economy. Ultimately, the leadership in these countries was faced with the dilemma to shoot and repress or simply to step down. Since most leaders feared that the military could not be entrusted with the unsavory task of perpetrating a bloodbath, they chose the latter alternative. Surprisingly, there was no bloodbath in any of the countries except Romania. In Czechoslovakia, people prided themselves on the orderliness of their transition; they called it a "velvet revolution." (A few years later, when the Czech Republic and Slovakia ceased to be a national entity, this was referred to as the "velvet divorce.")

The German Reunification

The disintegration of the Soviet system and the unexpected events in Central/Eastern Europe had further repercussions. In East Germany, a strong sentiment surged to rid itself of its Communist leadership. In addition, the season of flight had resumed, but, since the border between East and West Germany was almost hermetically sealed, and heavily guarded, those wishing to leave East Germany took recourse requesting asylum at the various embassies in East Berlin, the capital. Others left on "vacation trips" for Czechoslovakia, Hungary, and Austria in an attempt to enter West Germany.

As soon as neighboring countries allowed "transit tourists" to pass through without proper papers, a veritable stampede commenced that could be stopped, first, only by promises on the part of the East German government that conditions would soon improve, and, subsequently, by unification overtures. On November 9, 1989, the Berlin Wall came down, a day that Germans on both sides identified as the most significant day since the end of World War II. Reunification procedures were set in motion and, less than a year later, the two Germanys were officially united. The entire area is now called the Federal Republic of Germany, so that it is possible to say that, in accordance with the Basic Law (the West German Constitution), the various states of East Germany have simply merged with West Germany.

The unification was not a source of universal joy. The government of the new Germany insisted that STASI files be made accessible to the general public, particularly to those who were under surveillance during the years of repression on the part of the East German government. STASI was East Germany's Secret Service, and its files made it clear that a great many people had been overzealous in submitting reports on friends, family, and acquaintances to the generally hated STASI. The fact that numerous reports appeared to be untrue or exaggerated naturally set bad blood among family members or those who had seemed to be loyal friends.

It is interesting to note that the migration from East to West, which had been partly responsible for the drive toward unification, continued after the two Germanys had reunited. Many people were impatient, or at least unwilling to wait until the conditions in eastern Germany (as the German Democratic Republic had started to be called) improved. The migration slowed to a trickle and then stopped only when Chancellor Helmut Kohl, who feared that the new Germany would be demographically unbalanced, indicated that, henceforth, the new arrivals would no longer receive the treatment that had traditionally been accorded to refugees from eastern Germany.

Changing the Focus of Confrontation

If superpowership has become a phenomenon of the past, the East–West confrontation that was, so to speak, its territorial expression, has also faded away since the fateful days of 1989. The Warsaw Pact was abolished almost immediately after the collapse of communism in Central/Eastern Europe. This was done at the explicit wish of its entire membership, including the former Soviet Union. It is possible that the various Central/Eastern European states feared a comeback of one or more of the *anciens regimes,* which then might make use of the forces of the Warsaw Treaty Organization in order to restore their powers fully.

However that may be, NATO has continued to exist, which renders the Western European situation highly unbalanced from a military point of view. Although NATO is a very expensive organization, it does not appear likely that it will be abolished in the foreseeable future. (Indeed, it expanded in 1999 to include three new members—Hungary, Poland, and the Czech Republic—and further expansion is likely.) Conceivably it could have been used to reintroduce law and order in Yugoslavia when that federation fell apart. Still, the nearby and well-armed NATO forces remained inactive until March 1999, when NATO launched air strikes against Yugoslavia in retaliation for Serb refusals to sign a Kosovo peace plan.

While global attention was riveted on the new Germany and to a lesser extent on the new Europe that appeared to be emerging, Iraq absorbed its oil-rich neighbor, Kuwait, on August 2, 1990. As the United States led coalition forces against Iraq in early 1991, the world's focus moved to the Middle East in general and to the Persian Gulf in particular. The European Union generally declared itself fully behind the United States; to some Europeans, Iraq's aggression against Kuwait may have evoked the specter of Hitler's *Anschluss* of Austria in 1938. Most Western European countries, however, did not go beyond an endorsement of American efforts. Except for Great Britain, and to a smaller extent Italy and France, they provided little in the way of a contribution, either by sending military personnel or materiel or by providing the financial wherewithal to sustain what was officially a UN attempt to restore Kuwait's sovereignty. (Germany and Japan claimed that their Constitutions, put together shortly after World War II by the Allied forces, would not allow them to send troops.)

The North–South as a New Global Concept

The focus of the global confrontation is no longer East–West but, rather, North–South, although one should bear in mind that the latter dichotomy is based on economic premises. The phrase *North–South* has come to stand for the adversarial relationship between countries at opposite ends of the development concept: industrialized countries, with a high degree of economic advancement, versus the developing countries, which until fairly recently were parts of empires whose traditional societies had been left in a prolonged impasse. Once the latter had acquired political independence, they lacked the infrastructure and the know-how to make any headway. These new nation-states remain extremely poor. Most still do not have any industry to speak of. The South is very backward in economic respect; in addition, it is often riddled with corruption and, as a result, is politically highly volatile and unstable. The colonial experience has also rendered most of these new nations very sensitive with regard to Western interference.

A large North–South Conference was held in Cancún, Mexico, in 1981. Some eight leaders of countries that could be said to belong to the "North" and leaders of 14 countries that are part of the "South" convened. A major disappointment for the South and for those who had exerted themselves on behalf of the developing world was that the conference achieved very little, if anything. Before the Cancún Conference started, an agenda had been made that included a thorough discussion of ways to achieve the New International Economic Order (NIEO), a concept that had been recognized by the UN General Assembly as early as 1974. Unfortunately, the General Assembly's adoption of a resolution concerning the NIEO had never been followed by implementation. Since politics and economics are closely intertwined, one may surmise that the NIEO could succeed only if it were preceded by a political overhaul.

A Peaceful Invasion

Rather than discussing this "new deal," the North behaved as if it held all the trump cards. The South has since started to confront the North in more subtle ways—that is, by entering North America and Europe in ever-larger numbers. There can be no doubt that international immigration, whether legal or not, has become one of the more critical issues since the cold war ended, if only because of its sheer numerical force. Among the huge numbers of illegal immigrants are Africans crossing the Strait of Gibraltar in order to get into Spain, a country that may not be very rich but that is at least up and coming as a result of its membership in the European Union; Spain also provides an avenue to other parts of Europe. And indeed, this quiet invasion by illegal immigrants, which in the United States has long been the order of the day, may well be the latest phenomenon within the context of what Günter Grass has called the "Century of Expulsion."

Germany as Core Country for Immigrants

The massive migrations from the South should not be taken lightly or as a phenomenon that is bound to blow over in due time. Originally a trickle, the numbers have soared and now literally run in the millions (official estimates of the total number of refugees all over the world approach 14 million).

In his book *The Call of the Toad,* Grass makes a Bengali rickshaw operator in Gdansk admonish his German audience in the following words:

> Please look upon me as a person with nine hundred and fifty million human beings, soon a round billion, behind him.

The modern *Völkerwänderung* (migration of nations) has come to Germany in three separate drives. The first group consisted of the so-called guest workers of the 1960s, who, like most guests, were supposed to spend a limited time (in this case, 2 or 3 years) with their hosts, in Western Europe. Germany, like most Western European nations, was short of labor. In their desperation, its corporations allowed many of the Turks and other persons from the Mediterranean basin who opted to stay to renew their contracts.

Then the mid-1970s produced, as an epilogue to the wars in Indochina, tragic groups of huddled masses, packed in unseaworthy vessels, who defied the elements in the Indian and Pacific Oceans in search of a new home. Whenever they landed on an island in one of the various archipelagoes in Southeast Asia, they soon found that they were not very welcome. Indeed, on a number of occasions, their boats were unceremoniously pushed back into the sea. Less frequently, they were put into refugee camps, awaiting a further destination. Many Southeast Asians opted for resettlement in European countries, following the official channels. Some countries in Western Europe allowed a few hundred or so to settle.

Hardly had this relatively small flow ended than Southeast Asians adopted yet another modus operandi to enter Western Europe in general and Germany in particular. They boarded planes, with one-way tickets, to East Germany. Even during the cold war, it was not difficult for non-Germans to get from East Berlin to West Berlin and from there to West Germany. Once on West German soil, they destroyed all their identification and traveling documents and asked for asylum. As a rule, it would take the German authorities some 2 years to find out to what extent their claims were genuine.

Over time, the total of *Scheinasylanten* (literally, "fake asylum-seekers") came to exceed 1 million. In October 1992, the press reported that the flow into Germany of asylum-seekers appeared to have stabilized at 60,000 a month, more than to the rest of Europe combined. Many of them were not sent back or deported, even if their quest for asylum was officially rejected. The great majority of *Scheinasylanten* appeared to consist of "economic refugees," persons thus who were not politically persecuted but who believed that they could make a better living elsewhere. This particular ambition is the same one that motivated millions of Europeans in the nineteenth century to leave for the United States.

Critics have argued that the laws in Germany and elsewhere in Europe that govern immigration should be adapted to modern circumstances and thus be made considerably more rigorous. Germany has been very slow in getting to that point, for two reasons. First, the German Basic Law mirrors the immediate postwar years. It was deliberately made very flexible with regard to immigration, a reaction no doubt to the harsh Nazi years. In other words, when Germany rose from its ashes, the founders of the Federal Republic to all intents and purposes suffered from a guilty conscience regarding racism and wanted to make amends. In addition, one should take into account that the only refugees who were expected to ask for asylum at that time (the late 1940s and the 1950s) were the sporadic refugees fleeing from Communist brutality in Central/Eastern Europe, including East Germany. It was certainly not necessary to make the Federal Republic impenetrable through the erection of legal barriers. If this argument harked back to the past, the second point referred to the future: The European Union would have to tackle the immigration issue, since persons and goods would be able to freely cross the borders within the EU. That being the case, there would be little point in having varieties of rules and regulations passed in one member state, since immigrants would be able to enter the Union through a member state with lax provisions, after which they could still move around with impunity. In other words, the immigrants could enter Denmark or the Netherlands, which have not yet erected immigration barriers, and then find their way to Germany.

The Re-migration of Expatriates

To complicate matters even further, Germany in the early 1990s became subject to yet another type of immigration. Hardly had the two Germanys been formally united when references were made to all the Germans who lived in Central/Eastern Europe and thus missed out on the joys of unification. The persons concerned were usually referred to as "ethnic Germans," a somewhat infelicitous phrase, since it could easily have been part of the Nazi lexicon. (One may wonder how these Germans came to be there, and often in such large numbers. The *Drang nach Osten,* or drive toward the East, endemic in Germans concerned about the lack of *Lebensraum,* or living space, caused many of them to settle in eastern territories in the hope, perhaps, that some future German Manifest Destiny would cause them to be part of the Reich again. In that respect, Operation Barbarossa had turned out to be a dismal failure.) A large proportion of these ethnic Germans spoke heavily accented German or no German at all. Tens of thousands of them were repatriated (a term that was used officially), at the expense of the newly reunited Germany's treasury. In Germany, these "ethnic Germans" coming from Russia, Romania, Poland, and many other Central/Eastern European states received red-carpet treatment.

It is difficult to fathom why the chancellor of the Federal Republic made the repatriation scheme a priority while still maintaining that Germany was not a country of immigration. A great many people immediately responded positively to this call—too many. With an economy that had turned sour, a large public debt for the first time in the existence of the Federal Republic, and diminishing resources, the German government was forced to reverse itself in repatriation matters. German consulates were established in or near German settlements in Central/Eastern Europe. These consulates were given the task of making the Germans who qualified for repatriation stay where they were. Thus, the large-scale repatriation slowed to a trickle of emergency cases: sick family members, some very elderly persons who wanted "to die in Germany," and people who had already been promised that they could resettle in their ancestral country.

Public Reactions in France and Germany

Two countries—France and Germany—have been selected here for discussing their reactions to the massive invasion of foreigners, not so much because they happen to be the largest countries in Western Europe but because they are most affected. The political orientation of the societies in both countries has moved to the right, in large part because Socialists and the left in general are supposed to be kindly disposed toward the hordes of immigrants. Both countries too have political parties that make a great deal of political capital out of foreigner issues. It is possible that the French and the Germans share the feeling of *Uberfremdung* ("Overalieniza-tion") that has caused the Swiss, who coined the term, to limit entry into their country severely. But thus far the governments of these two countries have not given in to the increasingly hostile sentiments of xenophobia. For example, Richard von Weizäcker, the previous president of Germany, as well as various other German top authorities were greatly upset by the events in Rostock, in former East Germany, where Neo-Nazis and skinheads set fire to hostels that had been allocated to foreigners. As soon as the foreign women and children fled the fire (most of the men were at work), they were either killed or severely injured and in some cases were thrown back into the flames. What the authorities particularly resented were two ugly and incriminating circumstances: The police arrived very late on the scene and thus left the women and children to fend for themselves, and the large crowd of onlook-ers did nothing to prevent the arson as well as the events that followed. The investigations into the behavior of the police in this instance have thus far proven inconclusive. As far as the passive crowds were concerned, von Weizäcker, addressing the nation, solemnly stated: "We must never forget how the first German republic [the Weimar Republic] failed: not because there were too many Nazis too early but because there were too few democrats for too long . . ."

Von Weizäcker also found that openness toward suffering was a strong tradition in Germany. Since its reunification, Germany thus has been confronted with new challenges: increased migration and asylum-seekers on the one hand, and extremist violence on the other. The violence that von Weizäcker referred to has gradually become endemic. Indeed, at one point, it was the order of the day, with left and right both parading through the streets, constantly provoking and attacking each other, and the police trying in vain to come between them.

It was only to be expected that the Federal Constitutional Court would endeavor to reverse the tide. In May 1996, *Die Zeit* reported: "First the legislators acted, now the Federal Constitutional Court has issued a ruling. What remains of the right to asylum is the memory of a heroic promise." The editorial concluded: "What remains, however, is [the knowl-edge] that we have abandoned part of a culture."

The European Union Expands

The original European Economic Community (the Six), did not expand from 1958 to 1973. It then admitted Great Britain (whose application for admission had been rebuffed by de Gaulle), Denmark, and Ireland. It admitted Greece in 1981, and, in January 1986, Spain and Portugal. In 1988, Morocco's application for accession was rejected, on the grounds that the country's territory fell outside the confines of the European continent. "Associate member" status was granted to Turkey. Sweden, Norway, Switzerland, and Austria had long-standing associate agreements. During the early 1990s, the debate on enlargement was resumed. Norway, Sweden, Finland, and Austria were considered. (All but Norway have since joined the Union.) By 1995, the European Union, including associ-ate members, was more or less co-extensive with Western Europe. Any country in Europe can join the Union—provided it meets certain standards, including a commitment to democ-racy, the market economy, and the rule of law.

The original EEC countries remained the most eager for integration. The last serious attempt before the 1980s to move forward toward political union was in 1962. In the late 1970s, the French–German dialogue provided an alternative forum for political coordination of the policies of the two most important continental countries, but this did not as yet engender the EU. At the same time, however, an institution known as the European Political Co-operation (EPC) was launched. The EPC was a weak reflection of the ambitious plans of the 1950s and 1960s for a "European Political Community." Still, the EPC may be viewed as the first intrusion of politics into what had until now been largely economic concerns: It was intended to harmonize foreign-policy stands, or, at least, to allow the leaders of the various EU countries to formulate common stands and even platforms on political as opposed to purely economic issues.

It revealed three major handicaps. First, the EPC was not binding, in the sense that it had no authority to commit member states. It was soon clear that those who had more recently become members were more reluctant to use it than were the original charter members. The former had joined largely for economic benefits to themselves; they did not like to be reminded that the original purpose of the European Economic Community, as expressed in the Treaty of Rome, included political integration.

Second, the EPC was able to act on its own in areas where the major powers had no conflicts of interest with one another or with the United States or the Soviet Union. Thus, the only major policy initiative of the EPC to date is the so-called Venice Declaration of 1980, accepting the Palestinian Libera-tion Organization (PLO) as the legitimate representative of the Palestinian, that is, Arab, population in Israeli-held terri-tory in the Middle East. The purpose of the Venice Declara-tion, which the EU countries made at a time when oil prices

Western Europe—European Union Members

ICELAND

N
W E
S

0   250 Miles
0   250   500 Kilometers

NORTH
SEA

ATLANTIC
OCEAN

SWEDEN
EU member
1995
(GDP $176.2 billion)

FINLAND
EU member 1995
(GDP $102.1 billion)
Euro

NORWAY

ESTONIA

LATVIA

LITHUANIA

RUSSIA

DENMARK
EU member 1973
(GDP $122.5 billion)

IRELAND
EU member 1973
(GDP $59.9 billion)
Euro

NETHERLANDS
EU member 1954
(GDP $343.9 billion)
Euro

BELARUS

**UNITED
KINGDOM**
EU member 1973
(GDP $1.19 trillion)

POLAND

ENGLISH CHANNEL

GERMANY
EU member
1954
(GDP $1.74 trillion)
Euro

**CZECH
REPUBLIC**

BELGIUM
EU member 1954
(GDP $204.8 billion)
Euro

SLOVAKIA

LUXEMBOURG
EU member 1954
(GDP $13.48 billion)
Euro

LIECHTENSTEIN

MOLDOVA

AUSTRIA
EU member 1995
(GDP $174.1 billion)
Euro

HUNGARY

ROMANIA

BAY OF
BISCAY

FRANCE
EU member 1954
(GDP $1.32 trillion)
Euro

SWITZERLAND

SLOVENIA

CROATIA

VOJVODINA

ITALY
EU member 1954
(GDP $1.24 trillion)
Euro

BOSNIA-
HERZEGOVINA

SERBIA

PORTUGAL
EU member 1986
(GDP $122.1 billion)
Euro

ANDORRA

MONACO

SAN
MARINO

ADRIATIC
SEA

KOSOVO

BULGARIA

SPAIN
EU member 1986
(GDP $642.4 billion)
Euro

MONTENEGRO

MACEDONIA

Vatican
City

ALBANIA

Strait
of
Gibraltar

MEDITERRANEAN SEA

TYRRHENIAN
SEA

AEGEAN
SEA

GREECE
EU member 1981
(GDP $137.4 billion)

MOROCCO

ALGERIA

TUNISIA

MALTA

The European Commission views enlargement of the EU as a long-term process. At the beginning of 1999, the European Union had 15 member states. Eleven of these participated in the implementation of the Euro on January 1, 1999.

were at their peak, was to appease the Arabs by granting an important Arab political claim in the hopes of securing favorable treatment from OPEC, which the Arabs controlled.

Third, distance played a role. When Yugoslavia was torn apart in 1992, it was obvious that Italy and Greece were much more affected than were Ireland and Denmark. It proved difficult to find a common position, not only vis-à-vis the enormous violence that had erupted but also regarding the recognition of the new states that were produced by the implosion. Greece, for example, greatly objected to recognizing Macedonia—one of the offshoots—because there was also a Greek province by that name. Greece got its way, but the incident vividly illustrates that the various Union members were motivated by very different interests and that, as a result, it would frequently be hard to arrive at compromises on foreign-policy positions.

In 1981, the German and Italian foreign ministers, Hans-Dietrich Genscher and Emilio Colombo, proposed a program for moving toward European political unity by 1990. The Genscher–Colombo plan harked back to the ambitions of the 1950s, reminding analysts that even the expanded EEC was supposed to have a purpose other than the making of deals and the transferring of money among member countries. Great Britain and Denmark objected to the plan's political implications, and these objections in fact foreshadowed similarly negative attitudes vis-à-vis the Maastricht Treaty in the early 1990s. The Council of Ministers did not accept the plan in full, but, in 1985–1986, all member countries did adopt various minor reforms designed to make the operations of the Council and the Commission smoother. The most important one was to remove the requirement that all important decisions of the Council be unanimous. This left some hope that there might be renewed progress toward political unification in the 1990s.

One of the stated goals of the Treaty of Rome and the Maastrich Treaty is "an ever closer union among the peoples of Europe." The founders of the Union envisioned that it would eventually become a sort of "United States of Europe." Politically, that goal still seems elusive. The people of Europe are still highly diversified populations, and many of them are "Euroskeptics" who will need more time and evidence before they can be convinced that political integration is a good idea.

Economically, however, the European Union has become a tremendously powerful economic bloc, and protecting that status means pressing on with integration—first toward a single currency, then to standardized tax policies and common economic policymaking, and ultimately to political union. The first of those steps, the single currency, has already been launched.

The Euro

European economic integration began to take off toward the end of the 1980s. The fundamental long-term challenge facing Europe was to establish a strong and stable foundation for job-creating growth.

At the beginning of the 1990s, Europe was faced with deficits in three major areas that held it back from rapid and long-term growth; fiscal, jobs, and investment. Recently, there have been impressive progress made in the fiscal area, but there remain significant problems in both the job and investment sectors. In fact, in 1998 the average unemployment in the European Union countries was approximately twice what it was in 1979.

It became evident that any improvement in employment levels and investment would require a major push toward the private business sector, and the key to both of these areas would be the establishment of basic structural changes that would provide an attractive environment for private investment. Europe, in the aggregate, is an economic superpower, and many Euro-enthusiasts believed that by developing a common monetary system, it would be able to flex this power and influence policymaking in the broad global arena.

The first action toward developing a common currency began in 1994 with the establishment of the European Monetary Institute (EMI), which would become the European Central Bank (ECB). The next phase began in May 1995, when the European Commission adopted what was called the "Green Paper on the Single Currency," which outlined the parameters of how this currency would be implemented. In December 1995, the European Council of Madrid named this new Single Currency the *Euro* and established the date of January 1, 1999, for the single currency policy to become a reality.

When the Euro came into being, eleven EU members participated in the launch: Belgium, Germany, Spain, France, Ireland, Italy, Luxembourg, Finland, the Netherlands, Austria, and Portugal. World markets welcomed it and saw this consolidation of currency as a reflection of Europe's positive economic outlook. Initially, the Euro will be the currency of business and investment; actual Euros as hard cash, both bills and coins, will not be in everyday usage until January 1, 2002. At that time stores, firms, and individuals can choose whether or not to accept them.

With the launch of the Euro, the European Central Bank controls a market second only to that of the United States. Many see the role of the head of the ECB as comparable to that of Alan Greenspan, the head of the U.S. Federal Reserve. This tremendous centralized economic power is unique in history, and it will be the first time that Europe will have had one currency since the Roman Empire ruled nearly 2,000 years ago.

THE WELFARE STATE IN WESTERN EUROPE

Government and its institutions have always generated disputes and dilemmas. Among these, the welfare state ranks as one of the most controversial. Emerging as a human reaction to the excesses of the Industrial Revolution, its growth, particularly in Western Europe, soon assumed spectacular proportions. Al-

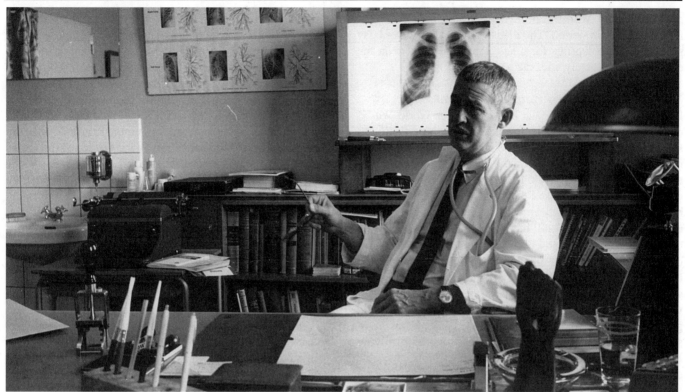

(World Health Organization/T. Farkas)

A physician of the International Health Centre for Seafarers, Göteborg, Sweden.

though welfare states have experienced some decline of late, they are still alive and well, and their major focus still is Europe.

The origins of the welfare state are fairly recent. In 1883, German chancellor Otto von Bismarck, one of the most astute politicians of the nineteenth century, introduced the first social-security measures, a comprehensive system that offered citizens insurance against accident, sickness, and old age. Ironically, the last person who could be suspected of anything that smacked of socialism (a doctrine that is usually associated with having sponsored the welfare state) would have been Bismarck, generally a conservative politician whose policies in the international arena were the first to merit the epithet "realpolitik." Yet establishing a social-security system in 1883 was by no means devoid of opportunism. By that time, it was clear to the whole of Europe that the German unification of the early 1870s (also largely designed and executed by Bismarck) had worked well. But empire building had yielded a counterproductive streak: Bismarck's opponents, the Social Democrats, had grown in number, and Bismarck felt that his political survival was at stake. To preempt their Socialist slate, he came up with the plan of comprehensive social security.

These measures, in spite of the insincerity that attended their introduction, were to become a model for many industrialized nations. The Industrial Revolution and its aftermath gave, on the one hand, undeniable blessings to Europe in general, providing greater comfort and prosperity. On the other hand, however, they tended to divide European society. Karl Marx's dismal prophecy concerning the emergence of a *proletariat*—a large mass that, according to the term's etymology, only had its offspring to offer—appeared to have come true. Laborers in those days were eking out an existence that was devoid of quality; frequently they were unemployed for prolonged periods without any compensation. If they were lucky, they could work long hours (10 to 16 hours a day) for pitiful wages. The wages were so low, in fact, that entire families were obliged to join the workforce in order to earn their keep.

Economic and social justice were virtually nonexistent, and political democracy at that juncture was unable to remedy the situation. Bismarck's social-welfare measures, however slow and piecemeal their expansion over the continent may have been, thus became a beacon and a model to the whole of Europe.

Denmark adopted a plan for state-supported unemployment compensation in 1907. And in Great Britain, which had always been in the vanguard of industrialization, the government embarked upon a pension scheme shortly before World War I. If this could seem promising, most of the fundamental reforms of the so-called Poor Law had to wait until the Great Depression and the mass unemployment of the 1930s, a catastrophe of truly horrendous proportions whose only benefit may have been that it finally did away with the myth that the poor had only themselves to blame. Although greatly preoccupied by World War II, Britain also focused on its future during that period. The British Labour Party was busy preparing the blueprints for a new era. That party won the elections immediately after the war.

Wartime Anxieties Generate New Solutions

In matters of social policy, it is obvious that World War II operated as a catalyst. New attitudes emerged, partly in answer to the question: Why can the government in peacetime not provide a better deal to people who during a war are asked to fight and to risk their lives? It was a question that must have come naturally to the tens of thousands of young people who before the war had not been able to find a job, who consequently were marginal until they were drafted into the army.

By the war's end, a consensus had developed on both sides of the Atlantic that government had to guarantee minimum living standards, not only to reduce individual hardship but also to protect society from internal strife. Some of these aims were embedded in the Atlantic Charter. European countries in general, as soon as the war ended, pursued a dual strategy of seeking economic growth by basing the economy firmly on Keynesian principles and by establishing a more equitable distribution of goods and services through transfer payments and social services.

The Birth of the British Welfare State

The 1942 British victory at El Alamein in North Africa provided a World War II watershed. A total of 25,000 men died there, and British prime minister Winston Churchill commented, "Before El Alamein we had no victories and after El Alamein no defeats." The German Afrika Korps, under Field Marshal Erwin Rommel, was decisively defeated in a series of battles. The British victory coincided with a domestic triumph: the publication of the Beveridge Report, which became the blueprint for the construction of the welfare state in Great Britain once the war would be over. Even before the war had globally come to an end, Churchill, immensely popular as a wartime leader, was ousted by the first election held once the European hostilities had ended. It now was Labour's turn, and that party immediately produced the blueprints on which it had been working. The British welfare state will always be remembered for its core, the National Health Service, which entitles each citizen to completely free medical treatment. Nearly all the physicians in Great Britain were, from that moment, in the service of the government. Upon falling ill, people went to a doctor and/or a pharmacist and the government picked up the tab. Subsequent welfare states in other countries have never been considered to be complete unless they have also included free medical treatment.

Europe and the United States Compared

All welfare states provide unemployment and disability insurance in addition to national pension plans; on top of that,

most provide sickness insurance and national medical care, which in some cases includes dental care and other benefits.

While Europe has witnessed a wide variety in this progress toward the welfare state, the United States has been slow to follow suit, providing only minimal welfare programs. It is possible that, in the United States, too many people harbor suspicions that a welfare system is susceptible to manipulation and abuse. But it is certainly true that welfare states are extremely costly: The money to pay for all the benefits must come from some source and, as a rule, that source is the taxpayer. In countries that have a comprehensive welfare system, taxes are very high, not only because the benefits in question cost a great deal of money, but also because a larger bureaucracy is required to operate and oversee the numerous services provided by the government.

In the United States, taxes are usually low as compared to those in Europe, and Americans appear to prefer that. There are always, of course, potential dangers, such as becoming disabled or unemployed for a long time, but Americans seem to prefer to deal with these contingencies on a personal level by buying insurance against long-term illness, unemployment, and other catastrophes. Often they do not even protect themselves against these risks (in 1998, for instance, more than a quarter of all Americans were not insured against hospitalization).

However that may be, the U.S. government has traditionally ignored poverty and unemployment as administrative concerns. For a long time, it refused to believe that these matters constituted legitimate matters for government consideration. It instructed "the less fortunate" (a somewhat euphemistic phrase referring to the poor and unemployed) to depend on self-help as well as on private charity or similar initiatives. Also, historically, American people, or at least a fairly large proportion of them, have passed through extremely hard times, such as during the frontier period. These too may have helped to breed formative attitudes, notably the so-called work ethic, which insists that work is wholesome and that every acquisition and achievement should be worked for. In sharp contrast, a number of European countries developed government programs that actually redistribute wealth.

Peculiarities of the Modern Welfare State

Denmark, the Netherlands, Norway, Sweden, and, to a somewhat lesser extent, Great Britain have all been in the vanguard of the development of programs characteristic of the welfare state in Western Europe. In many cases, the growth of the welfare state progressed by leaps and bounds—the pace depending on the orientation of the government in power. However, gains were never reversed. Generally, the policies in the above countries may be identified as follows: 1) the provision of social services and transfer payments, which make up the welfare state proper; 2) the management of a capitalist market economy, aimed at maintaining optimal economic growth while minimizing unemployment; and 3) the regulation of the behavior of individuals, groups, and corporations, which reduces the costs of welfare programs by restricting the *need* for welfare. The ultimate aim of such measures is twofold: On the one hand, a decent standard of living is guaranteed to those worst off in society; on the other hand, the target is an increase of equality among socioeconomic groups without undercutting the dynamics of the market economy.

Achieving these ends is complicated by the fact that they harbor a contradiction. The Swedish and British systems have operated under divergent conditions. Not only did Sweden not suffer horrifically from World War II, but its politics can only be characterized as extremely stable ever since. Although governments have changed, the ideological basis on which they were founded has not. In Great Britain, the Conservative and Labour Parties alternated in power for the first 35 years after the war. Although the Conservative Party occasionally attempted to undo measures legislated by Labour, it had to carry the burden of the welfare state designed by the Labour Party; often the former viewed the welfare system as an albatross around its neck. This frequently led to modifying the interpretations given to the regulations inherent in the welfare system. Even before Prime Minister Margaret Thatcher assumed office, in 1979, some retrenchment was noticeable. This came about in part as a result of the abuses that were made. People had been willing to pay high taxes to maintain the welfare system as long as they were convinced the benefits went to the neediest. The media, particularly the print media, shared at least part of the responsibility for the retrenchment, since they so often highlighted cases of abuse or corruption.

Natural gas was found in the Netherlands in the late 1950s, in such large quantities that the country was soon self-sufficient in energy. In addition, part of the natural gas was sold throughout Europe. The proceeds were used to finance the welfare system. This type of economy, often nicknamed "the Dutch disease," was naturally precarious, if not doomed, since the welfare system would be endangered if the revenues from the sale of energy resources were reduced. Indeed, as many people had predicted, the earnings *were* reduced in the early 1980s. When they went down, the government was forced to raise taxes; at the same time, a great many benefits were cut.

Another kind of difficulty can be found in the example of the Irish welfare system, which to some extent is based on that of Great Britain. Irish eligibility standards are not very clearly defined and, as a result, they remain somewhat flexible. Human nature being what it is, these blurred distinctions make it possible for many people to enjoy social-security benefits in one way or another even while they are able to provide fully for themselves. These eligibility errors have constituted a great drain on Ireland's national treasury. Indeed, Ireland has had the highest percentage of people drawing on that treasury. However, that said, it is also true that Ireland, like Belgium and Germany, has cut social spending as a share of gross domestic product since 1985.

(Credit: UN/DPI Photo by Greg Kinch)

The momentum behind the Conservative movement in Western Europe was demonstrated with the 1979 accession of Margaret Thatcher as Britain's prime minister. This Conservative government endorsement continued with the election of John Major. However, in 1997, the swing toward a more liberal perspective was emphasized when the Labour Party, led by Tony Blair (pictured above), took power.

Physicians in France are not required to fill out as many forms as their colleagues in Great Britain to account for the medical treatment they provide. In France, it is the patients who face the administrative burden of filling out all the forms and filing the claims. And it is the patients again who have to advance the money for the bills. Medical bills can of course be very substantial, and occasionally citizens have to obtain loans from a bank to pay them. Ultimately, the patients are reimbursed for 80 percent of all the money paid to doctors and pharmacists. (In France, the pharmacist is often paid a great deal more than the doctor, where lesser treatments are concerned.)

Generally, the European social-welfare system has been going through a period of retrenchment. While the system is still largely intact, it has become somewhat more difficult to obtain benefits in the past few years. Also, there have been

(Sabb–Scania)

Many industrial workers in Western Europe, like these in a Swedish automobile-production facility, are members of labor unions.

cuts—not only in the cash benefits of the welfare system but overall, as in the salaries of all those working for the government.

However, most people feel confident that most wrinkles can be removed from the welfare system, and they support the goals of the system. National statistics indicate a narrowing of income differentials; the rich are still wealthy relative to the poor, but they are less wealthy, and the poor are less poor, than they would be without the transfer payments and social services, and the taxes that pay for them.

Europeans' positions vis-à-vis the welfare state are based on personal as well as national views and convictions. Persons who are right of center on the political spectrum, for instance, often do not want to pay taxes to help support someone else. The influx of aliens has particularly harmed the standing of welfarism. It is known that the *Gastarbeiter* (guest workers) or the *Scheinasylanten* (fake asylum-seekers), if they happen to be unemployed, are entitled to the same unemployment benefits as the country's citizens. In fact, their entitlement derives from sums of money that were withheld from their wages while they were still working. But the cases of aliens are always viewed as very different, because the standards of living in their countries of origin are considerably lower and often these countries do not have a framework of unemployment or disability benefits, or even pensions, to fall back on. As a result, the treatment that these individuals

receive in matters of social policy is more often than not viewed as luxurious, as something they could not possibly enjoy in their own countries. What these critics fail to take into account is that the two societies differ widely and that it has become virtually impossible to live without an income in industrialized society.

The Welfare System and Foreign Workers

Several right-wing parties, such as the National Front in France, have made a great deal of political capital out of the influx of aliens that have taken place into these countries during the last decade. Their respective leaders often assert that the foreign-born workforce will take work away from the national labor reservoir, in so doing causing the unemployment of able-bodied French and Germans, but will in addition necessitate higher taxes, since the unemployed aliens are bound to draw social security for prolonged periods.

There can be little doubt that many foreigners have been motivated by considerations of social welfare when settling in a country in Western Europe. A study that endeavored to find out what moved so many aliens to select Germany as their destination came up with two important reasons: First, the legal framework in the Federal Republic was definitely more congenial to the noncitizen; and second, that country had a reputation for providing a great deal of security—in fact, the welfare state had reached its pinnacle in West Germany. Interestingly, East Germany also was a target of immigration before German reunification was achieved in 1990.

Reforms in the British Welfare System

Great Britain has also arrived at the point where it faces the double problem of too much public spending, while too little reaches those most in need of it. As is the case in most Western industrialized countries, the United Kingdom faces welfare costs that have been going up year after year. The population is aging, people are living longer, and less and less is being undertaken by private charity or through relatives.

The country is, of course, a great deal richer than when William Henry Beveridge released his blueprint of the welfare state in 1945. The majority of families are doing fairly well for themselves: Home ownership has risen to approximately two thirds, for example. Another indicator of affluence: Nine out of 10 manual workers get more than 4 weeks' paid vacation a year.

However, one cannot overlook the lowest levels of the income range. Here it has been found that the real incomes of the poorest 20 percent have expanded little, if at all. On the contrary, Peter Townsend of Bristol University calculated that the real incomes of the poorest 20 percent have dropped. Rendering uniform or universal benefits would thus be unwise and unjust, and the Department of Social Security, which designs and executes British welfare, will target the truly poor and concentrate on the area of pension reform.

Another benefit that is being reassessed is the child's allowance, which may or may not be an encouragement for young couples to start families. For every child in Great Britain, a benefit is paid. The rich and well-to-do currently receive the same amount for a child as do destitute families; although the former do not need it, they tend to accept it. This may well be the opposite of the stigma that "the dole" had in earlier days, when the genteel poor preferred not to apply, pretending that they did not need government handouts. It will be difficult to discriminate between the rich and the poor unless means tests are instituted. But these are as a rule very costly and might in addition provide various loopholes that would be cumbersome to guard.

Other Limitations

It is not easy to reform the welfare state, much less to cut it. In the first place, one has to take into account its size in Europe. Benefits themselves have gradually increased. But more benefits—that is, a larger variety of benefits—have been created, and some of them give one pause. In the Netherlands, for instance, the unemployed once received vacation money over and above their unemployment benefits, the reasoning being that unemployment does not really create leisure. In that same country, it was customary to allow convicts to enjoy a vacation under guard. This usually concerned persons who had received lesser sentences; they were

allowed to go to Spain in order to sunbathe at the beach, where their guards would watch them. Such examples are excessive, but they have existed. In these lean times, however, many of them have been reconsidered and canceled. It will obviously be very hard to arrive at equitable systems that will not drain national treasuries.

THE LABOR MOVEMENT IN WESTERN EUROPE

Samuel Gompers, the founder of the American Federation of Labor, once commented that a country without labor strikes would be a country without liberty. Industrial conflict is a given, a fact of life in society, and the resolution of such conflict in a democratic ambience depends on the rules of the game—that is, the labor laws that have been created specifically to remove grave economic injustices. A major difficulty, of course, is that it is not possible to put a price on the product—to evaluate precisely the price of labor—especially in a fluctuating market.

Labor organizations have emerged in both the United States and in Western Europe, but their origins and evolution have differed. Capitalist exploitation of the worker was at its worst during the Industrial Revolution (a period roughly spanning a century); the first reaction to this exploitation in Western Europe was the formation of *craft unions,* which meant to organize laborers who had the same skill or trade. (In Great Britain, the term *trade union* has persisted, and in fact the largest umbrella organization in that country is the Trades Union Congress, or TUC, comparable to the AFL-CIO in the United States.) Craft unions today typically target skilled construction workers such as bricklayers and carpenters.

Unskilled workers also came to be organized, but their unions experienced an entirely different evolution, which took place in the period between 1890 and 1940. They were organized in either *industrial unions* or *general workers unions.* In the past, some distinction was made, in that the industrial unions organized all workers in an industry, regardless of the type of work they performed. A good example is the modern-day United Auto Workers in the United States. By comparison, in general workers unions, all industrial workers were organized across industrial lines, like today's Transport and General Workers Union in Great Britain.

Recent Developments

Participation in unions tends to be much higher in Western Europe than the United States. Organized labor in Western Europe may be distinguished from American unions in that the former have been greatly influenced by belief systems, either religion or ideology. European countries thus developed *denominational unions.* The influence of belief systems is not surprising if one realizes that political parties, a related linkage mechanism, are similarly affected. Indeed, in many countries, political parties and unions have been and frequently still are closely intertwined. However, one should bear in mind that, as a rule, the union existed first. An example is Great Britain's TUC, which after a time wanted to exert pressure in Parliament; to that end, it established the British Labour Party. In Germany, the Greens existed first and foremost as a large environmental pressure group. At one point, they started to run for seats in the Bundestag (Parliament). However, for a considerable time they did not receive the 5 percent of the total vote that would have qualified them to acquire parliamentary representation. Such hurdles have been put up to prevent extreme political fragmentation.

Structural Similarities

Unions may have originated in craft or industry, but in structure they are remarkably alike on both sides of the Atlantic. Often local unions establish affiliations until they reach national proportions. The latter, in turn, may join national federations. These federations, like the Trades Union Congress in Great Britain, generally are loose, umbrellalike organizations and do not have the right to bargain. That right is jealously guarded by the national unions. The union federations in Scandinavia are the exception; they can, and often do, bargain national contracts.

No Western European country has a mixture of craft and industrial unions like the United States does today. Great Britain, Ireland, and Denmark have craft and general workers unions. Germany, Spain, Sweden, and Norway have almost exclusively industrial unions. Belgium, France, Italy, and the Netherlands have denominational unions. The labor movements in Spain, France, and Italy include three types: communist unions, socialist unions, and unions that trace their origins to the Catholic labor movement.

In Northern Europe, the labor movement is overwhelmingly social democratic. The British Labour Party, for example, has a strong union flavor. Even today it is possible to say that most Labour leaders started their political career in the unions. Neil Kinnock, for example, until recently a leader of the Opposition, hailed from a poor mining district in south Wales. He joined a union, and his organizational and oratorical gifts eventually qualified him for a leadership post in the Labour Party.

The political aspects of unions are much more obvious in Western Europe than in the United States. In Europe, all unions, at least until recently, were oriented toward the left. In the United States, the AFL-CIO is basically a conservative body, and the same may be said of most labor organizations, some of which have been infiltrated by criminal organizations such as the Mafia. But, whatever the basis for union organization, all unions come into conflict with employers (who often are themselves organized into unions—an example of an American employers' union is the National Association of Manufacturers, or NAM).

Industrial relations is the system of rules provided to manage conflict between employers and labor. These rules are not designed to suppress conflict but to keep it within bounds. They generally are laid down by national legislation and prescribe how to conduct collective bargaining between management and labor in the plant, in the company, or on an industry-wide basis. Bargaining typically has to do with wages, hours, and working conditions. But in some Western European countries, such as Sweden, the scope of bargaining has been broadened to include what are called "management prerogatives," such as hiring practices and investment policy. Industry-wide bargaining is far more usual in Western Europe than in the United States; and unions in the Netherlands, Denmark, Norway, and Sweden frequently bargain national contracts that encompass practically all the organized workforce. Indeed, a larger proportion of the workforce in Western Europe is covered by collectively bargained contracts than in the United States.

In many Western European countries, persons working in the public sector are allowed to unionize. This is in stark contrast to the United States, where there is substantial ambivalence regarding the right to unionize for those who have government positions. Indeed, some U.S. states explicitly prohibit this practice.

Unions and Politics

Industrial relations has always been political. Unions have ties to parties of the left; employers' organizations have similar ties to parties of the right. Before World War I, unions were generally social democratic in political orientation. In the Catholic countries, socialist unions generally competed with Catholic unions. After the 1917 Bolshevik Revolution, which created the Soviet state, Communist Party–led unions collectively affiliated their members to the party. In Norway and Sweden, local unions affiliate with the local Social Democratic parties. In Denmark, the executive board of the labor federation interlocks with the executive board of the Social Democratic Party. While the German unions lack similar formal ties, they remain closely linked to the Social Democratic Party.

In Great Britain, unions have tended to be most frequently and intensely in conflict with the government during Tory administrations. Nevertheless, while in office, the Labour Party has also experienced labor unrest. However, when the Conservative Party took over in 1979, the outspokenly hostile attitudes vis-à-vis the unions immediately made clear that the new prime minister was unwilling to put up with them. In fact, in the early 1980s, the unions were weakened and muzzled. Contrary to what Prime Minister Margaret Thatcher had expected, the economy did not improve a great deal; indeed, it took a nosedive toward the end of her tenure. The "New Labour" government of Prime Minister Tony Blair of course has better relations with unions, but it faces a tenuous economy and a need to trim social-welfare benefits, which make clashes with unions seem inevitable.

Not surprisingly, there are certain parallels in the development of organized labor and the development of the welfare state. The latter often features among its achievements the number of weeks of paid vacation that workers must have. In France, for instance, every employee is entitled to 5 weeks' paid vacation annually. Other countries have started to provide similar entitlements. Some of these achievements, however, may be counterproductive to the economy as a whole. It is, for example, doubtful whether a country such as Belgium can afford to let its workers have 5 weeks of paid vacation. A recent goal of both unions and political parties in Western Europe is to reduce the work week, such as from 39 hours to 35, in order to reduce unemployment. However, how this can be achieved without reducing annual wages to individuals is unclear and, despite some enthusiastic politicians' claims to the contrary, probably impossible.

Less universally known are the so-called Collective Labor Contracts, which some Western European countries have developed. These labor contracts are typically produced at a conference at which three groups convene: delegations of workers (as a rule taken from unions), delegations of employers, and government labor experts. These parties, two of which are bound to have opposing, or at least different, interests, convene for months, and in some cases even for years, to work out specific contracts. The United States, in contrast, has always preferred the workings of the free market over some prearranged set of rules.

Codetermination and Industrial Democracy

Since World War II, there has been a dramatic development in Western Europe that has led to direct channels for employee influence in company management. It began with the establishment in 1951 of what the Germans call *Mitbestimmung*—"codetermination"—in the coal and steel industries. Fearing the right-wing inclinations of the coal and steel barons who had backed Adolf Hitler, the Allies encouraged the Germans to build democratic safeguards into the companies themselves. The German model called for employees to select half the members of the company board of directors. That model was broadened to include all large firms in 1976.

France's institution of *autogestion* resembles the German *Mitbestimmung* in many respects; however, it also allows employees to have a voice in the nomination and appointment of company directors. Such rights also exist in Denmark, Luxembourg, the Netherlands, Norway, and Sweden.

Most unions in the countries mentioned tend to view these developments with a measure of apprehension. However, the Industrial Revolution is clearly a phenomenon of the past; all industrial democracies appear to be moving inexorably into a new era: that of postindustrialism. The question may legitimately be raised, therefore, whether or not the confrontational institutions and instruments of the period associated with the Industrial Revolution should be left in place.

Some harmonization in such policies is due before the economies of Western European countries more fully integrate. The Treaty of Rome allows freedom of residence, while the workers of the various European Union (as the European Community has come to be known) member states may also work wherever they want within the confines of the EU. In addition, many countries in Western Europe maintain a basic, or minimum, wage.

Andorra (Principality of Andorra)

GEOGRAPHY
Area in Square Miles (Kilometers): 185 (466) (about 2.5 times the size of Washington, D.C.)
Capital (Population): Andorra la Vella (22,400)
Environmental Concerns: deforestation; overgrazing contributing to soil erosion
Geographical Features: rugged mountains dissected by narrow valleys; landlocked
Climate: temperate

PEOPLE

Population
Total: 64,700
Annual Growth Rate: 1.5%
Rural/Urban Population Ratio: 5/95
Major Languages: Catalán; Spanish; French
Ethnic Makeup: 61% Catalán; 30% Spanish; 6% Andorran; 3% French
Religion: predominantly Roman Catholic

Health
Life Expectancy at Birth: 81 years (male); 87 years (female)
Infant Mortality Rate (Ratio): 4.1/1,000
Physicians Available (Ratio): 1/538

Education
Adult Literacy Rate: 99%
Compulsory (Ages): 6–16; free

COMMUNICATION
Telephones: 1 per 2.3 people
Televisions: 1 per 2.7 people

TRANSPORTATION
Highways in Miles (Kilometers): 161 (269)
Railroads in Miles (Kilometers): none
Usable Airfields: none

GOVERNMENT
Type: parliamentary democracy (since March 1993)
Independence Date: 1278
Head of State/Government: co-principality: the president of France and the Spanish bishop of Urgel; Executive Council President Marc Forne Molne
Political Parties: National Democratic Group; Andorran National Coalition; Andorran Democratic Party; National Democratic Initiative; Liberal Union; Liberal Party of Andorra; others

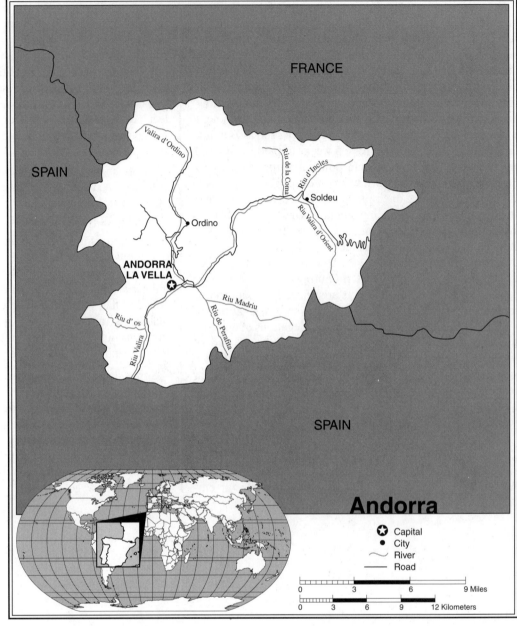

Andorra

- ✪ Capital
- ● City
- ∿ River
- — Road

Suffrage: universal at 18

MILITARY
Military Expenditures (% of GDP): none; defense is the responsibility of Spain and France
Current Disputes: none

ECONOMY
Currency ($ U.S. Equivalent): currently the French franc (5.49 = $1) and the Spanish peseta (134.7 = $1) are both in use
Per Capita Income/GDP: $18,000/$1.2 billion
Unemployment Rate: 0%
Natural Resources: hydropower; mineral water; timber; iron ore; lead

Agriculture: sheep; small quantities of tobacco, rye, barley, oats, and some vegetables
Industry: tourism; banking; sheep (wool); timber; tobacco; small manufacturing
Exports: $47 million (primary partners France, Spain)
Imports: $1 billion (primary partners France, Spain, United States)

 http://www.odci.gov/cia/publications/factbook/country-frame.html

Andorra comes under the joint suzerainty of France and the bishop of Urgel
A.D. **1278**

The Plan of Reform is adopted by the co-princes
1966

Women achieve suffrage
1970

Andorran citizenship is redefined; the PDA is formed
1970s

A referendum calls for proportional representation
1982

1990s

Andorra concludes a trade agreement with the European Union

Andorra becomes a sovereign state and is admitted to the United Nations

ANDORRA

The largest of Europe's micro-states, Andorra is situated high in the Pyrénées Mountains, between France and Spain. Originally home to a pastoral society whose language and culture were intimately intertwined with those of the neighboring Spanish province of Catalonia, Andorra was long sheltered from rapid change by its remote and relatively inaccessible location.

More recently, the region has been opened to tourism. Frenzied economic development has increased Andorra's income but also has threatened its rich cultural heritage. The official language remains Catalán, but today only 6 percent of the country's population are native Andorrans; most of the rest are immigrants from Spain and France. The requirements for becoming a citizen have been somewhat eased in recent years. (Andorran citizenship was relaxed to include second-generation residents in 1971; first-generation Andorrans were enfranchised in 1977.) But that factor has introduced new social strains.

Andorra's six valleys have been inhabitated since prehistoric times. Although the country became an independent sovereign state only in 1993, its political structure dates from the end of the thirteenth century. In 1278, the French count of Foix and the Spanish bishop of the nearby See of Urgel agreed to joint suzerainty (as co-princes) over the region. The feudal arrangement, which was temporarily abrogated during the French Revolution, defined the country's political organization.

Under the terms of the French–Spanish agreement, the co-princes exercised full executive, legislative, and judicial power over Andorra through their designated representatives and magistrates. In 1966, a Plan of Reform was adopted by the co-princes, which provided for the creation of a General Council. Until quite recently, no government or separate executive body

existed, although the Council elected a chairperson and vice chairperson who were charged with implementing Council decisions. The Political Reform Law of 1981, however, granted Andorra a true head of government, elected by the Council for a 4-year term. Until 1970, only male Andorran citizens (legally defined at that time as at least third-generation residents of the principality) over age 25 were entitled to vote in Executive Council and communal elections. In 1970, women were enfranchised and, 3 years later, they were allowed to run for public office.

As a principality, Andorra had no written constitution, and the rights and powers of the co-princes in relation to the country's domestic political institutions were never clearly defined. Andorra's external relations were managed almost exclusively by the French, while both France and Spain provided for the principality's defense. Political parties were officially outlawed, but there was a variety of political groups, some of which were represented in the National Council. In 1976, the Andorran Democratic Association was established through a fusion of the moderate and "Democracy and Progress" groups within the National Council. It consistently challenged the co-princes to press forward with reform of the electoral system; in 1979, it was reorganized as the Andorran Democratic Party (PDA). What will endure of all these arrangements now that Andorra has become more clearly sovereign remains to be seen.

Andorra's economic surge has been fueled primarily by services related to tourism. But other factors have played a role. Andorra has no form of direct taxation on either individual income or company profits. More important, it has no minimum requirements—in fact, there are no restrictions at all—on the purchase of property, which implies that individuals in some types of business might be able to operate perfectly legally from Andorra and avoid

paying any form of income or company taxes. Finally, Andorra has a highly sophisticated and completely confidential banking system, although it is likely that the rules on confidentiality and secrecy are bound to change now that the European Union has strengthened its regulations on finance in general and banking in particular.

The general reluctance to regulate or tax economic activity within its borders has rendered Andorra into a tax haven. Andorra's anything-goes economy has attracted numerous foreign-owned companies and banks, some of which use the unregulated haven to evade taxes and launder foreign currencies. The country's free-port status and permeable borders have made it one of the leading centers of smuggling in Western Europe.

The few products that Andorrans manufacture for foreign consumption enjoy privileged access to Spanish and French markets, thanks to favorable trade agreements with these neighbors. In 1991, a trade agreement with the European Union went into effect. As a member of the EU Customs Union, Andorra is treated as an EU member for trade in manufactured goods and as a non-EU member for agricultural products. Andorra is not an official member of the Union.

DEVELOPMENT

Andorra's economic development has pursued a path that may not prove sturdy over the years. Tourism accounts for roughly 80% of gross domestic product.

FREEDOM

Andorra came under the joint suzerainty of the French authorities and the bishop of Urgel in 1278. The appearance of the long-lasting (715 years) arrangement was feudal, its substance not.

HEALTH/WELFARE

Reliable statistics are difficult to find for Andorra, but indicators point to a healthy, well-educated population with exceptionally high life-expectancy rates.

ACHIEVEMENTS

Although its roots and foundations are not stable or promising for the future, the Andorran economic growth since the end of World War II has contributed tremendously to the well-being of the people.

Austria (Republic of Austria)

GEOGRAPHY

Area in Square Miles (Kilometers): 32,369 (83,835) (about the size of Maine)
Capital (Population): Vienna (2,060,000)
Environmental Concerns: soil and air pollution
Geographical Features: mostly mountains (Alps) in the west and south; mostly flat or gently sloping along the northern and eastern margins; landlocked
Climate: temperate

PEOPLE

Population
Total: 8,133,600
Annual Growth Rate: 0.05%
Rural/Urban Population Ratio: 36/64
Major Language: German
Ethnic Makeup: predominantly German
Religions: 85% Roman Catholic; 6% Protestant; 9% unaffiliated or others

Health
Life Expectancy at Birth: 74 years (male); 81 years (female)
Infant Mortality Rate (Ratio): 5.2/1,000
Physicians Available (Ratio): 1/296

Education
Adult Literacy Rate: 99%
Compulsory (Ages): 6–15; free

COMMUNICATION
Telephones: 1 per 2.1 people
Daily Newspaper Circulation: 472 per 1,000 people
Televisions: 1 per 2.1 people

TRANSPORTATION
Highways in Miles (Kilometers): 77,400 (129,000)
Railroads in Miles (Kilometers): 3,381 (5,636)
Usable Airfields: 55
Motor Vehicles in Use: 4,400,000

GOVERNMENT
Type: federal republic
Independence Date: 1156 from Bavaria; on May 15, 1955, Austria recovered its sovereignty and independence from occupation forces
Head of State/Government: President Thomas Klestil; Chancellor Viktor Klima
Political Parties: Social Democratic Party (previously the Socialist Party); Austrian People's Party; Freedom Party of

Austria; Communist Party; the Greens; Liberal Forum
Suffrage: universal at 18; compulsory for presidential elections

MILITARY
Military Expenditures (% of GDP): 1%
Current Disputes: none

ECONOMY
Currency ($ U.S. Equivalent): 11.3 schillings = $1
Per Capita Income/GDP: $21,400/$174.1 billion
GDP Growth Rate: 2.5% (1998 est.)
Inflation Rate: 1.3%
Unemployment Rate: 7.1%
Labor Force: 3,646,000

Natural Resources: iron ore; petroleum; timber; magnesite; coal; lignite; lead; copper; hydropower
Agriculture: livestock; forest products; cereals; potatoes; sugar beets
Industry: foods; iron and steel; machinery; textiles; chemicals; electrical; paper and pulp; tourism; mining; motor vehicles
Exports: $57.8 billion (primary partners EU countries, Eastern Europe, Japan)
Imports: $67.3 billion (primary partners EU countries, Eastern Europe, Japan)

http://www.odci.gov/cia/publications/
factbook/country-frame.html
http://portal.research.bell-labs.com/
cgi-wald/dbaccess/411?key=18

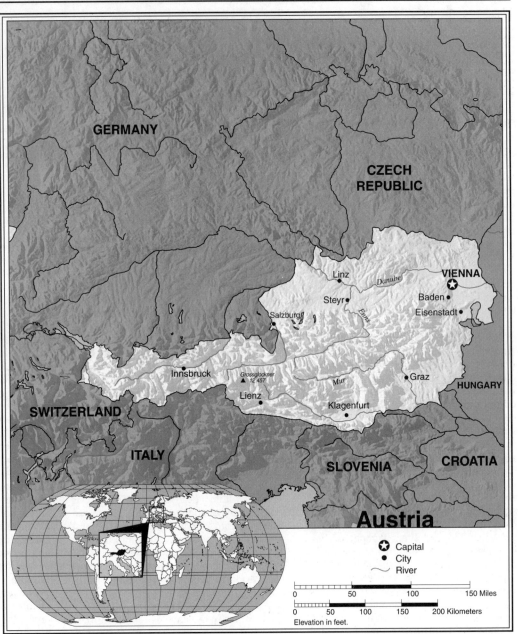

GERMANY

CZECH REPUBLIC

Linz Danube VIENNA
Steyr Baden
Salzburg Eisenstadt
Enns
Innsbruck Grossglockner ▲ 12,457 Graz HUNGARY
Lienz Mur
Klagenfurt
SWITZERLAND

ITALY SLOVENIA CROATIA

Austria

⊛ Capital
• City
〜 River

0   50   100   150 Miles
0   50   100   150   200 Kilometers
Elevation in feet.

THE REPUBLIC OF AUSTRIA

Once the nucleus of a vast multinational governmental entity that ruled most of Eastern and Southeastern Europe, this small Alpine country assumed its current format when the Austro–Hungarian Empire collapsed at the end of World War I. In 1918, the Republic of Austria was established; 2 years later, a democratic Constitution, introducing a federal form of government, came into effect. However, as in neighboring Germany, the transition from an absolutist monarchy to a democratic republic proved extremely difficult in Austria. Loss of territory and the attendant economic disorientation caused by the war and its inflationary aftermath thoroughly destabilized the political and economic systems of the new Austria.

During the Great Depression of the 1930s, socioeconomic and political divisions within Austrian society continued, and the fragile political consensus sustaining the country's democratic order fell apart. In 1933, faced with an impending civil war at home and a growing threat to its national sovereignty from Nazi Germany, the Austrian government abandoned its democratic Constitution and reverted to authoritarian rule, in a futile attempt to stabilize the country and protect its independence.

In the following year, civil war did indeed erupt between the country's *Lager* subcultures. The term *Lager,* meaning "camp," is often used by students of Austrian politics to highlight the confrontational characteristics that the two major political antagonists—that is, Socialists and conservative Catholics—display. In the midst of worsening political violence, an extreme right-wing group of Austrian National Socialists took the maverick Chancellor Engelbert Dollfuss prisoner and murdered him in an aborted coup.

In March 1938, Austria succumbed to the threats and pressures on the part of Germany. Adolf Hitler, who had been an Austrian himself until 6 weeks before he was sworn in as chancellor of Germany in 1933, sent the Third Reich's armed forces into the country. The assorted Nazis (the Austrian ones as well as those from across the border in Germany) had actively prepared for this occasion, and the German troops and Hitler were hailed by much of the citizenry as they entered Vienna and other large cities. Records have revealed that Hitler initially intended to terminate the turbulence and to mold Austria into a National Socialist (Nazi) satellite. Soon, however, the appeal of *Anschluss* ("annexation") won the day, and for 7 years Austria was submerged in the Third Reich as its *Ostmark* ("eastern province"). Before and during the war, there appeared to be little or no resistance among most Austrians to being part of Germany. On the contrary, the *Ostmark* eagerly subscribed to all of Hitler's designs, including the persecution and murder of Jews in what would become known as the Holocaust.

THE POSTWAR YEARS

It was only natural that, once World War II finally came to an end, the all-important question loomed: Was Austria an early *victim* of Nazi expansionism or a willing *belligerent,* and thus an ally of Germany? There was no consensus on this point among the Allied powers, which divided the country into occupation zones just like they had done in Germany. Nevertheless, a greater measure of leniency was applied to the case of Austria than that of Germany in that the former was allowed its first postwar election as early as November 1945. This general election revolved around the two major parties of right and left—the Austrian People's Party (OVP) and the Socialist Party of Austria (SPO). These two blocs, which hailed from the pre-*Anschluss* days, fostered dogmas and philosophies that were highly antithetical to each other. But, in spite of this mutual incompatibility, a grand-coalition government was forged.

It is hard to overstate the role that the Marshall Plan played in Western Europe, particularly in vanquished countries such as Germany and Austria. This large-scale injection into Austria's economy greatly promoted the country's economic reconstruction and political stability.

The political situation was somewhat anomalous, in that Austria was encouraged to engage in the politics of independence while remaining occupied by the Allied powers. (Thus, "independence" implied only separation from Germany.) A breakthrough finally came in early 1955, when the Soviet Union announced that it was prepared to terminate the occupation of its zone, on the condition that the United States, Great Britain, and France would do likewise with their zones. Another condition was that the new Austria would sign a treaty that would commit it to "neutrality in perpetuity."

It is not easy to fathom the Soviet considerations behind this plan. Linkage has been suggested: West Germany was on the verge of joining the North Atlantic Treaty Organization, and the prospect of reunification of the two German zones might persuade it to follow the Austrian example of neutrality (which it did not).

In 1955, the Allied powers withdrew their armies from Austria; signed the Austrian State Treaty, which formally acknowledged Austrian independence; and made Austria commit itself to neutrality in perpetuity. That commitment would prove not a little demanding to Austria, which had a capitalist economic system and close economic relations with its Western neighbors. When at one point the question arose whether or not Austria might become a member of the European Union (at that time known as the European Coal and Steel Community), the Soviet Union immediately vetoed any such plan, on the grounds that Austrian membership would as a matter of course constitute a breach of the neutrality clause in the Austrian State Treaty. (After the Soviet Union crumbled in 1991, Austria became a member of the European Union, in 1995.)

Consensus Politics

During the more than 20 consecutive years that the Socialist Party/People's Party coalition constituted the Austrian government, the gap was bridged that had long separated the country's Socialist and Catholic subcultures. A new, durable political and economic consensus came to be institutionalized. By the time the coalition fell apart, in 1966, the legitimacy of the country's democratic institutions was no longer in question. The single-party rule, initiated in that year through the election of a People's Party government, headed by Chancellor Joseph Klaus, provoked a great deal of confrontation during the campaign. More often than not this was a matter of appearances, for as soon as the election fever subsided, rhetoric and hyperbole were replaced by consultation, if not cooperation, on the part of the OVP and the SPO.

In 1970, the Socialist Party secured some gains in Parliament, which enabled it to defeat the Klaus government and form a minority government of its own, under the leadership of Bruno Kreisky. Minority governments are as a rule precarious and ephemeral, but Kreisky's government fared well; indeed, it gained an absolute majority in Parliament that the party would enjoy for the next 13 years. During the years of his chancellorship, Kreisky gradually achieved international stature. In a sense, he became a spokesperson of the left in Europe.

Political Conflicts

Kreisky's international stature notwithstanding, Austria's domestic problems accumulated. By the early 1980s, the government was no longer able to control the country's trade and budget deficits. In addition, an increasingly powerful environmental movement had started to sap the government party's strength.

In the 1983 general elections, the Socialists were not defeated, but they lost their absolute majority in Parliament. Party leaders were reluctant to form another minority government (as had happened in 1970) and thus entered into a coalition government with the small Freedom Party (FPO). Kreisky refused to lead the new coalition and stepped down. He was succeeded as chancellor by his Socialist vice chancellor, Fred Sinowatz. Major disagreements on economic policy surfaced between the two coalition partners, and a series of political scandals made matters worse.

The situation was compounded by the controversy over presidential candidate Kurt Waldheim's Nazi ties during World War II. The allegations against Waldheim drew headlines all over the world, as he had recently served as secretary general of the United Nations. The presidential election left the country rife with unusually bitter conflict that cut along party divisions. Waldheim won, but Sinowatz refused to serve under him. The SPO–FPO coalition disintegrated in 1986. In the ensuing general elections, Franz Vranitzky, a former minister of finance, led the SPO to victory. But since the party held a slim majority in Parliament, the Socialist government realized that it lacked sufficient votes to rule by itself. Accordingly, in 1987, Vranitzky formed a new coalition government with the Austrian People's Party. In 1990, new elections were held. Against all expectations, the Socialist Party consolidated itself, gaining 43 percent of the vote. However, this victory reintroduced polarization, since the right-wing Liberal Party also made gains. (Note: In European politics, the term *liberal* has a rightist connotation.) In a general election at the end of 1995, Vranitzky retained the chancellorship. (The Socialists were by then called the Social Democrats.) He remained in power until January 1997, when he resigned and handed over the reins of power to his finance minister, Viktor Klima.

FOUNDATIONS OF AUSTRIA'S POSTWAR SUCCESSES

In 1945, Austria resurrected the constitutional framework that it had forged immediately following World War I, which provided for a federal democratic republic made up of nine states (*Laender*), including the capital area of Vienna. Although the political constellation is formally structured as a federation, the division of powers has been such that the national government is by far the stronger. That government follows the traditional parliamentary model, consisting of a cabinet headed by a chancellor, a bicameral Legislature, and a president whose functions are largely ceremonial. The chancellor is appointed by the president from the dominant party within the lower, or more powerful, chamber, the National Council. However, the chancellor must maintain the support of a majority within the National Council in order to govern. The upper house, the Federal Council, representing the *Laender*, has somewhat limited powers, although it may review and delay legislation passed by the National Council.

During the 1920s and 1930s, this parliamentary framework came to be supplemented by corporatist arrangements that brought government officials together with representatives of the country's major economic interest groups in an effort to enlist the latter's cooperation in meeting the political and economic crises of the period. Yet neither the parliamentary system nor its corporatist appendage was capable of containing or defusing the extreme social and political tensions, which polarized Austrian society and wrecked the fledgling republic.

During the interwar period, the forces of the left (the Socialist Party and the trade unions) were effectively disenfranchised by the more powerful groups of the center and far right (the Christian Socialist Party, the Nationalists, and agricultural and industrial interests). The Socialist Party was outlawed in the 1930s. Austrian trade unions were poorly organized and incapable of exercising real power. The adoption of national socialism, as well as the *Anschluss* and its dreadful aftermath, discredited the right, which had generally supported the liquidation of Austria—or, rather, its inclusion in the Third Reich. Conversely, the moral legitimacy and political power of the Socialist Party and of organized labor came out of the war greatly strengthened. The result was a new political and economic order with a leftward tilt. On the whole, however, the two major political forces—the Socialist and People's Parties and their affiliated interest groups—were more evenly balanced.

In contrast, after World War II, Austria's political and economic institutions were remarkably successful in cultivating political stability and economic prosperity. The reasons for this adaptability are complex. To be sure, Hitler's invasion and the *Anschluss,* the war, and the subsequent Allied occupation had been object lessons that clearly revealed to a majority of Austrians the high costs of domestic divisiveness. Furthermore, the immediate goal of restoring their own national sovereignty and independence, not to mention the formidable task of economic reconstruction, demanded a truce between the *Lager* subcultures, which had crystallized in the major political parties and interest groups.

Over the long run, however, two changes wrought by the war turned out to be pillars of domestic tranquillity: the redistribution of power between the country's two major political camps, and the emergence of a new consensus regarding the role of the state in society and the economy.

Consociational Democracy

Interestingly, this parity in strength produced a new consensus concerning the nature of political competition and the relationship between the state, society, and the economy, a consensus clearly reflected in the two-party, grand-coalition government and in its institutional counterpart, proportional democracy. The term *proportional democracy* refers to a system that allows public jobs or appointments from the cabinet level on down to be distributed among representatives of the various political parties or in proportion to their respective strengths in the legislature. The practice, which has permeated all aspects of Austrian public life as well as much of Austrian business and finance, survived the transition to one-party rule in 1966 and continues to prevail today.

More recently, political analysts have discussed Austrian politics in terms of consociationalism. Indeed, political scientist Arend Lijphart argues that Austria (like the Netherlands from 1917 to 1967) has become a *consociational democracy,* a system specifically designed to reduce conflict and promote compromise in highly fragmented societies. In a consociational democracy, the various segments of society—in the case of Austria, the *Lagers*—are vigorously segregated through vertical organization. The actual wheeling and dealing—the very essence of politics—is conducted at the elite level. Thus, consociational democracy does not remove the element of conflict that is always part of politics. It simply confines conflict and its clashes to a less conspicuous place. It is here, out of the glare of the media, that the segments of society are bound together. For this "cartel of elites" (as one political scientist has called it) to operate effectively, these segments must be able to cooperate and compromise without losing the support of their subcultures.

Another point of agreement was the need to create a mixed economy with a large public sector and a generous social welfare state. Not surprisingly, the new political–economic trends were most strongly recommended by the Socialist Party and organized labor. However, the People's Party and its affiliated interest groups also accepted the greatly increased role of the state in the economy, in return for certain concessions. These included state protection and state subsidies for Austrian industry and agriculture as well as noninterference on the part of the state in the general management of state-owned enterprises.

The major organized interest groups also have some input into the policy-making process, and their role is fairly structured. First, there is Chamber government, a system of quasi-governmental institutions that represent the interests of various groups at the national and state levels. The Chambers are consulted by the government as well as the major political parties on policy questions affecting Chamber interests. A second institution is the Joint Commission, an ongoing incomes-policy committee in which representatives from the government, organized labor, and business meet to establish annual wage and price guidelines in accordance with projections of economic growth. Thus the Austrian model reveals a merger of consociationalism and functionalism.

THE SOCIAL PARTNERSHIP

Within the context of the rapidly expanding world economy of the 1950s and 1960s, Austria's social partnership yielded impressive results. By finding new outlets for Austrian exports, the postwar liberalization of world trade accelerated the modernization of Austria's economy. The country's manufacturing sector expanded vigorously as human and capital resources migrated from agriculture to industry, where they could earn a high return.

The Austrian government played an important role in finding new outlets for Austrian exporters. Austria was a charter member of the European Free Trade Association, founded in 1960. It also started to cultivate a special commercial relationship with the European Union.

By the 1960s, in addition to its more traditional exports of timber and minerals, Austria had started to export a wide range of capital and consumer goods, including iron and steel, electrical and transportation equipment, chemicals, and textiles. By 1970, Austria exported nearly 20 percent of its gross national product and employed 30 percent of its workforce in manufacturing.

As long as world demand for Austrian exports and the productivity of the country's industry continued to grow at a reasonable pace, the Austrian economy had little trouble generating the surpluses needed to sustain standard-of-living increases for its citizens, the comprehensive social-security net, and the subsidies for less competitive domestic industries. Low inflation; a large, modern industrial base; a skilled indigenous workforce as well as an abundant supply of less skilled "guest

workers"—all seemed to conspire to an indefinite continuation of the twin phenomena of economic prosperity and political stability.

Negative forces began to intrude, however. There were scandals connected with the Roman Catholic Church; it appeared that seminarians had been sexually abused by some of the nation's highest Church dignitaries. Another important issue was unemployment, which haunted Europe in the early and mid-1970s. It became clear that the subsidized and troubled industries could not stem its rise. The late 1970s brought a brief reprieve, but the fundamental problems facing the Austrian economy were suppressed only temporarily.

It would take the second oil shock of 1979 and the subsequent world recession to reveal clearly the full significance of the 1970s to the world economy and Austria's political–economic equilibrium. The events of the 1970s, which have come to be called the decade of OPEC (the Organization of Petroleum Exporting Countries), did not constitute a random trend in post-

war economic growth. Rather, they marked a watershed in the world economic order. Oil prices went down in the 1980s and were volatile in the 1990s, but world trade continued to grow slowly. A new generation of low-cost competitors emerged in the newly industrialized countries of Asia and Latin America. And most advanced industrialized countries, the General Agreement on Tariffs and Trade notwithstanding, sought to defend their domestic markets and export industries with new forms of protectionism.

Austria can do little to change its external economic environment. At home, however, the government is beginning to explore various less expensive ways of recasting the old social partnership. After assuming power in 1986, the coalition government headed by the Socialist banker and former finance minister Franz Vranitzky cut state spending in an effort to reduce budget deficits. The government also embarked on an ambitious plan to restructure state-owned industries that have been a chronic drain on the public treasury

(Courtesy Austrian Embassy)

Austria has kept up with the evolving world economy, but much of its architecture reflects its long history.

The birth of
Austria, resulting
from the collapse
of the
Austro-Hungarian
Empire
1918

Austria in turmoil:
civil war;
Chancellor
Engelbert
Dollfuss is
murdered
1934

The *Anschluss:*
Hitler's Germany
annexes Austria,
which becomes
Ostmark
1938

Austria is divided
into four
occupation
zones; otherwise
independent
1945

Occupation
forces withdraw;
Austria signs the
Austrian State
Treaty
1955

The question of
Austria's role in
the Nazi cause
resurfaces during
Kurt Waldheim's
successful bid to
become president
1986

Franz Vranitzky
becomes
chancellor; the
government cuts
state spending to
reduce budget
deficits
1986

1990s

Viktor Klima
succeeds
Vranitzky

Austria reapplies
for membership in
the European
Union; Austria is
admitted in 1995

Banking scandals
plague the
government;
Austria joins the
launch of the Euro

during the past decade. Vranitzky's limited austerity program did not revolutionize or destroy the ongoing social partnership, but it may have marked the beginning of a gradual retrenchment, the trend to reduce the state's heavy obligations to the Austrian society and economy. The number and severity of commercial insolvencies reached unprecedented heights in 1995. Vranitzky resigned early in 1997. Thus far, his successor, Chancellor Viktor Klima, has not had resounding success in turning around Austria's economy, although Austria did manage to achieve one of its coveted goals—being among the eleven European Union member countries to join the launch of the Euro in January 1999. Gross domestic product growth has been small, and Austria has been forced to reduce its social-welfare benefits. Klima has been distracted by such events as coping with the growing popular appeal of the post-Fascist Freedom Party, which is opposed to immigration and membership in the European Union; and an ongoing scandal involving charges of price fixing and sleaze in the Austrian banking system. Gerhard Praschak, head of Kontrollbank, the main export-credit provider, shot himself in April 1997 in protest at political cronyism in the banking system. His six-page suicide note described how he had been bullied into accepting a former Social Democrat politician on the bank's board. Questions in Parliament were brushed aside; Praschak, it was said, had been depressed. Chancellor Klima announced that in the future all jobs in the state sector would be allocated "strictly on merit," thus tacitly admitting that past practice had been different. The allegations of political cronyism were taken seriously enough by the European Union that in June 1998 it sent a dozen investigators on surprise visits to seven Austrian banks in search of misbehavior.

FOREIGN RELATIONS

Shortly after the ratification of the Austrian State Treaty of 1955, both houses of Parliament endorsed a constitutional amendment that committed the nation to permanent armed neutrality. Austria's defense forces are severely limited by the Four-Power State Treaty. Its army of approximately 55,000 ground troops is largely made up of draftees, who serve a compulsory 6-month term and from then on may be called up for military exercises or emergencies. Austria is forbidden from possessing nuclear, chemical, and other weapons of mass destruction. Although not prohibited by the treaty to have an air force, Austria has not yet embarked on its development. In essence, the country's military security and autonomy depend on the unspoken guarantees of its former occupying forces.

It is neutral in *military* respect, but Austria, unlike its neighbor Switzerland, has neither declared nor practiced *political* neutrality. The distinction may seem a fine one, but in essence the negation of political neutrality means that Austria is not nonaligned. In general, it sides with the West. It is not only a member of the United Nations but also of the Council of Europe and several Western-oriented international economic organizations. These include the Organization for European Cooperation and Development, the International Monetary Fund, the World Bank, and the European Free Trade Agreement. Numerous international agencies have their headquarters in Vienna, including the International Atomic Energy Agency and the UN Industrial Development Organization. Naturally, the collapse of communism in Europe and the fragmentation of the Soviet Union have in effect released Austria from its commitment to neutrality in perpetuity. The Austrian government, aware of this opportunity, applied again for European Union membership. The country was one of the first to be admitted to the post–Maastricht Treaty EU. It is not yet a member of the North Atlantic Treaty Organization.

Because of its geographical position and an active commitment to promoting global peace and understanding, Austria has been able to play a role in international politics far out of proportion to its size. The country, particularly Vienna, has often been a meeting ground for East–West conferences. And in 1981, Chancellor Bruno Kreisky, forever dedicated to the cause of international socialism, planned the North–South Conference at Cancún, Mexico. On the other hand, Kreisky also alienated the Jewish community and the State of Israel by selling arms to moderate Arab states in the Middle East and by supporting the Palestinian Liberation Organization's calls for a Palestinian homeland. Finally, it has taken a long time to recover from the damage that the revelations concerning Kurt Waldheim did to Austria's international prestige. In the last few years, Austria has also been forced to confront its role in the Holocaust and to respond to pleas for reparations and return of assets of Jews, including money placed in Austrian banks for safekeeping before and during the war, and artworks looted during that period.

DEVELOPMENT

Approximately half of Austria's workers are involved in industrial jobs. Austrians are working hard to retain their footing in world trade.

FREEDOM

Austria has a highly favorable human-rights rating. A special government appointee monitors women's rights.

HEALTH/WELFARE

Austria has a comprehensive welfare system at this time, but the current trend is to reduce the state's role in the Austrian economy and social-welfare sector.

ACHIEVEMENTS

Austrian theorists have reached great heights in economics (Austrian School of Economics). Vienna is internationally regarded as an important cultural capital.

Belgium (Kingdom of Belgium)

GEOGRAPHY
Area in Square Miles (Kilometers): 11,781 (30,513) (about the size of Maryland)
Capital (Population): Brussels (952,000)
Environmental Concerns: water pollution; industrial air pollution
Geographical Features: flat coastal plains in northwest; central rolling hills; rugged mountains of Ardennes Forest in southeast
Climate: temperate

PEOPLE

Population
Total: 10,165,000
Annual Growth Rate: 0.11%
Rural/Urban Population Ratio: 3/97
Major Languages: Flemish; Walloon; German
Ethnic Makeup: 55% Flemish; 33% Walloon; 12% mixed or others
Religions: 75% Roman Catholic; 25% Protestant, others, or no affiliation

Health
Life Expectancy at Birth: 74 years (male); 80 years (female)
Infant Mortality Rate (Ratio): 6.4/1,000
Physicians Available (Ratio): 1/268

Education
Adult Literacy Rate: 99%
Compulsory (Ages): 6–18

COMMUNICATION
Telephones: 1 per 2.2 people
Daily Newspaper Circulation: 321 per 1,000 people
Televisions: 1 per 2.2 people

TRANSPORTATION
Highways in Miles (Kilometers): 85,538 (221,544)
Railroads in Miles (Kilometers): 2,124 (5,501)
Usable Airfields: 42
Motor Vehicles in Use: 4,715,000

GOVERNMENT
Type: federal parliamentary democracy under a constitutional monarch
Independence Date: October 4, 1830
Head of State/Government: King Albert II; Prime Minister Jean-Luc DeHaene
Political Parties: Christian People's Party; Social Christian Party; Flemish Socialist Party; Francophone Socialist Party; Flemish Liberal Democrats; Francophone Democratic Front; Francophone

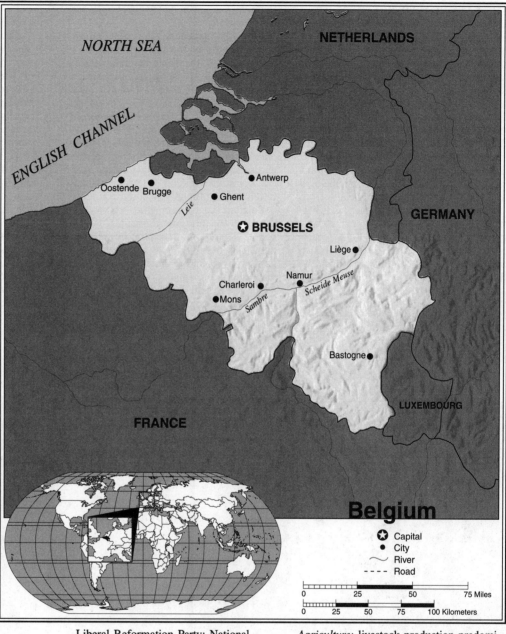

Belgium

- ⬟ Capital
- ● City
- 〰 River
- - - - Road

| 0 | 25 | 50 | 75 Miles |
| 0 | 25 | 50 | 75 | 100 Kilometers |

Liberal Reformation Party; National Front; others
Suffrage: universal and compulsory at 18

MILITARY
Military Expenditures (% of GDP): 1.7%
Current Disputes: none

ECONOMY*
Currency ($ U.S. Equivalent): 33.07 Belgian francs = $1
Per Capita Income/GDP: $20,300/$204.8 billion
GDP Growth Rate: 1.4%.
Inflation Rate: 2.1%
Unemployment Rate: 14%
Labor Force: 4,283,000
Natural Resources: coal; natural gas

Agriculture: livestock production predominates; pork; grains; sugar beets; flax; potatoes; other vegetables; fruits
Industry: engineering and metal products; processed food and beverages; chemicals; basic metals; textiles; glass; petroleum; motor-vehicle assembly; coal
Exports: $108 billion (primary partners EU countries, United States)
Imports: $140 billion (primary partners EU countries, United States)

*Note: Belgium has a customs union with Luxembourg (BLEU) under which trade figures are recorded jointly for the two countries.

 http://www.europeonline.com/bel/index_gb.htm

THE KINGDOM OF BELGIUM

In geographic terms, Belgium is one of the smaller sovereign countries in Western Europe. Apart from the Ardennes, a low-altitude mountain range that covers the southeastern part of the country, the land is fairly flat. However, Belgium, unlike its northern neighbor, the Netherlands, is not significantly below sea level. (Both are often jointly referred to as "the Low Countries," along with Luxembourg.) Belgium is located on the crossroads of more powerful Western European nations, and it has for that reason occasionally been nicknamed "the cockpit of Europe." Tragically, from times immemorial it has served as a battlefield for European wars.

To the west, Belgium's 60-mile coastline adjoins the North Sea. The seacoast, however, does not afford a large port; the only important Belgian port is Antwerp, which is not located on the coast but, rather, at the mouth of the river Scheldt. There are very few harbors for fishing boats. Again contrary to the Netherlands, Belgium has never developed into a seafaring nation.

Flemish, spoken in the western and northern parts of the country, is close to Dutch. Indeed, there is a tendency among Flemish people nowadays to call their language Dutch rather than Flemish. Walloon, however, spoken in the eastern and southern parts of Belgium, differs considerably less from French than Flemish does from Dutch. German, although spoken by only a tiny minority in the southeastern part of Belgium, has been declared one of the country's official languages. Thus, Belgium has officially become trilingual.

Belgium has a temperate climate. Its summers are mild and its winters not too severe. There is a great deal of precipitation. The rivers Scheldt (in the western part of the country) and Meuse (through the center) are major commercial waterways. The Scheldt leads to Antwerp, which is one of the largest ports in Europe.

The country is populous, certainly, considering its size. As a consequence, its population density is one of the highest in the world.

Belgian industry traditionally was found largely in the central and eastern parts of the country; the western and northwestern parts were rural and agricultural. This contrast started to change after World War II, when industries were established west of Brussels. Currently the only distinction that can be made is that the central and eastern parts harbor older industries, some of which have become obsolete and consequently less competitive. Some coal mines, for example, were closed down when Middle East oil started to conquer Western Europe.

ETHNIC DIVERSITY

Belgium is a divided country—so much so that Julien Destrée, a nineteenth-century author, once exclaimed, "There is no Belgian nation!" Of the 10 million citizens, 55 percent are Flemish. Walloons (the French-speaking, or Francophone, Belgian people) constitute 33 percent. Other

The beauty of Belgium is exemplified by this photograph of a canal in Brujes.

Belgium is under Spanish rule A.D. 1555–1713	Austrian rule 1713–1795	Annexation by France 1795	The Treaty of Vienna adds Belgium to the Netherlands 1815	The start of the Belgian Revolution 1830	The Treaty of the 18 Articles regulates the separation of Belgium and the Netherlands 1831

groups make up the remaining 12 percent. In the course of history, Belgium's main battles were fought between the Flemish and the Walloons. In numerical terms, the Walloons were traditionally a minority, but what they lacked in numbers was made up for by the prestige their language carried. Since French was a world language and Dutch was not, for a long time the Walloons believed themselves to be superior in every respect.

A rural exodus, however, had a devastating effect on the Flemish–Walloon ratio. Flemish people tired of life in the countryside left for the cities, learned French, and forgot their native language within a generation. This pattern changed after World War II. With the establishment of industries in Flanders, there was no need to seek fame and fortune in cities that were predominantly Francophone. The Flemish mentality also changed: It became less submissive, less willing to accept the presumed inferiority of Flanders.

In 1971, a new Constitution rendered the country quasi-federal. If Belgium had been officially bilingual, it now became *regionally* monolingual—that is, communities were created in which only French or Flemish was spoken. Communal problems continued to exist, however, and for many years Belgian authorities worked toward further constitutional reform, which was accomplished with the new Constitution in 1993. This time, a real federation was created, with two states, Flanders and Wallonia, and a national capital, Brussels, where both cultures meet and mingle. The late King Baudouin, who was scrupulously bilingual in his monarchical duties, delivering royal addresses and the opening of Parliament speeches in both languages, declared in 1988 wistfully that "to federate means to unite."

HISTORY

Belgian is a very ancient term. Julius Caesar, a Roman general who subsequently became emperor, made mention of Belgians (whom he deemed very valorous) in his famous book *De Bello Gallico* ("On the War in Gaul"). But although Belgians must have existed for many centuries, they did not achieve nationhood before the 1830s—that is, after they seceded from the Netherlands.

The area that is now Belgium (as well as Holland, historically often referred to as the Northern Netherlands) was once ruled by the Spanish King Charles V, a native of Ghent who resided in Brussels. Abdicating in 1555, he left the throne to his son Philip, who preferred to rule from Madrid. The Spanish environment conditioned the new king, who was considerably less tolerant than his father had been. The Reformation was then rife in Western Europe. In the Northern Netherlands, this implied religious warfare (the fight for the new Protestant creed), which invigorated the struggle for political independence. The war was fought along political and religious lines. While it took the Northern Netherlands 80 years (from 1568 until 1648) to achieve independence, the southern part, remaining Catholic, did not rise against Spain. The Southern Netherlands (that is, Belgium) was subsequently transferred to Austrian rule; later, in Napoleonic times, it was incorporated in the French Empire. So was Holland, which by then had been a sovereign state for nearly 2 centuries.

Once the turmoil created by Napoleon Bonaparte had come to an end, rulers and statesmen from all over Europe convened in Vienna in order to reestablish Europe as much as possible in the way it had existed before Napoleon started on his conquests. Prince Clemens von Metternich, an Austrian statesman, presided. Viewing France as a monster that should be kept at bay, he believed that a strong buffer should be created in its immediate vicinity. England was on the other side of the English Channel and consequently was unable to prevent a French resurgence. Germany and Italy did not exist yet as sovereign states. Switzerland was small and divided. But if the Southern Netherlands (which thus far had never been independent) were to be added to the Northern Netherlands, a fairly strong buffer would emerge. The Northern and Southern Netherlands were thus merged by the Treaty of Vienna (1815).

The Congress of Vienna failed to take into account the reality of a centuries-long alienation: The Northern Netherlands (which, after all, had been independent) and its southern counterpart had grown apart, developing into two entirely different cultures. The new Dutch monarch, King William I, did not make things easier: Since France had become unpopular as a result of the Napoleonic conquests,

he saw fit to ban the use of French in public, ignoring the fact that a large number of his new subjects spoke only French. There were other grievances as well. Finally, in 1830, a revolution started. At that point, King William I added stubbornness to prejudice: He had Belgium invaded by a Dutch army. The great powers, oblivious of the original rationale behind Dutch–Belgian unity, soon sided with the underdog—the new state of Belgium. After Belgium recruited a king as its chief of state, Belgium and the Netherlands started their separate destinies.

However, Belgium's self-determination was flawed from the beginning, since it was in effect a bicultural nation. The area of Flanders that had not been part of the Netherlands prior to the Congress of Vienna took up the Belgian cause and joined Belgian independence. The discord, which had never amounted to very much as long as Belgium had been a dependency, now began to be very pronounced. Subsequent interethnic relations in the Belgian state have been extremely troubled. It remains to be seen whether the recent federalization will lead to a measure of harmony.

THE MONARCHY

Belgium emerged very late as a nation-state. In spite of the fact that the revolution had been directed against the power of the Dutch king, the country opted for a monarchy, following the general trend in Europe. Belgium at the time did have an aristocratic class, but the revolutionary leaders preferred to have the new king recruited from other countries.

The Belgian monarchy is just as ceremonial and symbolic as its European counterparts; the Constitution does not grant any real powers to the king. Its royal house has not been spared personal mishaps. World War II produced the real crucible, in that the monarch alienated his people through his behavior. When the Germans were about to occupy the Low Countries, the Dutch queen fled. However, the Belgian king, Leopold II, indicated that he preferred "in these dark times to remain with his people." This could have seemed heroic were it not for some of his wartime activities. For example, he voluntarily paid a visit to Adolf Hitler in Berlin and was photographed with him. In addition, King Leopold, who had lost his wife in a car accident before the war, remarried

Belgium
is invaded by
German troops
on their way to
France
1940
●

The monarchy is
endangered;
Leopold II
abdicates
1947
●

Belgium
becomes a
charter member
of NATO
1949
●

Belgium
becomes a
founding
member of the
European Union
1957
●

Zaire, formerly a
Belgian
possession as the
Belgian Congo,
gains its
independence
1960
●

New Constitution
1971
●

1990s

Prime Minister
Wilfried Martens
is replaced by
Jean-Luc
DeHaene

King Baudouin
dies and is
succeeded by
his brother,
Albert

Another new
Constitution takes
effect; Belgium is
federalized;
Belgium joins the
launch of the Euro

during the occupation, and, considering the austerity of the war years, the wedding was sumptuous and costly. As if this were not enough to enrage the population, the father of the bride appeared to be a prominent Nazi sympathizer.

The immediate postwar years witnessed popular outrage against Leopold, who wanted to resume his royal activities after the war as if nothing had happened. The country was in an uproar. The increasing unrest finally forced the king to resort to a referendum that would decide whether or not he would abdicate. Its outcome appeared to favor the continued role of Leopold as king of the Belgians by a small margin. However, the unrest persisted, and the king finally decided to abdicate in favor of his eldest son, who ruled Belgium for 42 years as King Baudouin I. Those decades were in many ways instrumental to the return of respect for the monarchy, although Baudouin's reign too was not without mishaps.

Although monarchies elsewhere have also witnessed slumps in their prestige as a result of unseemly royal behavior, the fact is that the Belgian royal family has never been as popular as its counterparts in other European countries. One particular difficulty as regards the monarchy in Belgium was that Baudouin and his wife Fabiola did not have any children. The Constitution thus was changed to allow the throne to pass to Baudouin's younger brother Albert, or, alternatively, to Albert's eldest son. Albert now rules Belgium as King Albert II.

THE ECONOMY

The Belgian economy has not always been sound. Socialist governments promoted the welfare state, which caused governmental expenditures to grow. The 1980s witnessed a degree of retrenchment, but the October 1987 U.S. stock-market crash had a devastating effect on Belgium. The Belgian economy appeared to bottom out at that point, however, and there has been

some recovery since. Today, about half of Belgium's entire production is sold abroad.

A Belgian professor recently indicated that the "Belgian economy did not use common sense." He found that the larger part of Belgian products are machine-made, mass-produced items, which can be made anywhere. Some people urge that Belgium concentrate on products that can uniquely be identified as Belgian. Another frequent complaint is the very high level of taxation, particularly on personal income. Labor-intensive projects have shown themselves to be profitable in recent years but businesses have become very apprehensive about hiring more people. The Belgian economy certainly cannot be compared to that of the group of poor (or "marginalized") countries within the European Union, but the recession has clearly harmed it. One effect is a rise in unemployment.

POLITICAL CONDITIONS

Ever since ethnic friction reemerged after World War II, Belgium has been preoccupied with establishing political, cultural, and linguistic units inside its body politic. Before Belgium became a completely federal state in 1993, numerous changes were made to the Constitution causing the country to be divided into regions and cultural communities—a division highly confusing to Belgians and non-Belgians alike. The traditional nine provinces have been left intact, and there are 589 communes—local governments that are, in effect, municipalities. With the exception of Brussels, there are hardly any bilingual communes. Nevertheless, some cities within the Dutch-speaking community have islands of French-speaking people. Antwerp provides an example: It is overwhelmingly Dutch-speaking, but, in a certain area of the city, there are still some French-speaking families who for generations have refused to assimilate.

Belgium has always had a multiparty system, which necessitates coalitions. All

parties have their counterparts in the other linguistic group. Political parties are extremely powerful, even vis-à-vis the government, a factor that is reflected in the use of the term *partitocracy*.

Strangely enough, it is not communalism (the division into two major ethnic groups) that causes political instability but, rather, the party system. Newly established governments are unsure how long they will be in power, a condition that naturally inhibits their planning. One prime minister, Wilfried Martens, has been credited with creating a climate of consensus. He was in power for a long time, surviving numerous cabinet crises. He finally became a victim of the recession. Martens was replaced by Jean-Luc DeHaene, who endeavored to emulate Martens's diplomatic skills.

The current prime minister (since 1992), Jean-Luc DeHaene, is a tremendously popular figure. He has overseen the transition of Belgium to a fully federal state, and in 1996–1997 he cut the budget deficit in order to ensure Belgium's qualification in the EU's nascent monetary union. Whether he will survive the elections scheduled for June 1999, however, is not clear.

Belgium is a charter member of both the North Atlantic Treaty Organization and the European Union. In fact, it houses the headquarters of these important regional organizations, and some of its prime ministers have been instrumental in promoting a supranational government in Europe.

DEVELOPMENT

Belgium is highly developed and has entered the postindustrial phase. In the 1990s, however, its economy has been experiencing difficulties as a result of recession.

FREEDOM

Belgium ranks high as a democracy and in regard to compliance with human rights, at least in its own borders. It granted independence to the Belgian Congo (Zaire) in 1960.

HEALTH/WELFARE

Belgium has an advanced social security system and favorable health statistics, including high life expectancy rates and low birth and death rates.

ACHIEVEMENTS

Belgium has an excellent educational system. It hosts many students from developing-world countries. It also benefits economically and culturally by being the site of many regional and global organizations' headquarters.

Cyprus (Republic of Cyprus)*

GEOGRAPHY

Area in Square Miles (Kilometers): 3,571 (9,250) (about half the size of Connecticut)
Capital (Population): Nicosia (186,400)
Environmental Concerns: water scarcity; water pollution; coastal degradation; loss of wildlife habitats
Geographical Features: central plain with mountains to north and south; scattered but significant plains along the southern coast
Climate: temperate; mediterranean

PEOPLE

Population
Total: 749,000
Annual Growth Rate: 0.69%
Rural/Urban Population Ratio: 45/55
Major Languages: Greek; Turkish; English
Ethnic Makeup: 78% Greek; 18% Turkish; 4% British, Armenian, Maronite, and others
Religions: 78% Greek Orthodox; 18% Muslim; 4% others

Health
Life Expectancy at Birth: 75 years (male); 79 years (female)
Infant Mortality Rate (Ratio): 7.9/1,000
Physicians Available (Ratio): 1/433

Education
Adult Literacy Rate: 94%
Compulsory (Ages): 5½–15; free

COMMUNICATION

Telephones: 1 per 2.1 people
Daily Newspaper Circulation: 110 per 1,000 people
Televisions: 1 per 3.1 people

TRANSPORTATION

Highways in Miles (Kilometers): 7,659 (12,765)
Railroads in Miles (Kilometers): none
Usable Airfields: 15
Motor Vehicles in Use: 324,000

GOVERNMENT

Type: republic
Independence Date: August 16, 1960 (from United Kingdom)
Head of State/Government: President Glafcos Clerides is both head of state and head of government
Political Parties: Greek area: Progressive Party of the Working People; Democratic Rally; Democratic Party; United Democratic Union of the Center; oth-

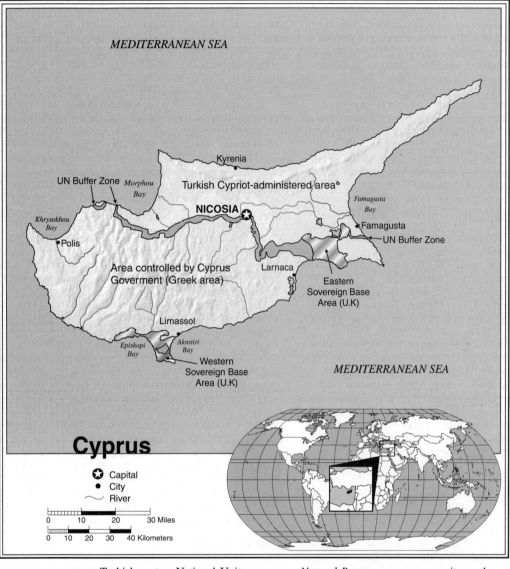

Cyprus

⭐ Capital
● City
〰 River

| 0 | 10 | 20 | 30 Miles |
| 0 | 10 | 20 | 30 | 40 Kilometers |

ers; Turkish sector: National Unity Party; Communal Liberation Party; Republican Turkish Party; others
Suffrage: universal at 18

MILITARY

Military Expenditures (% of GDP): 5.4%
Current Disputes: opposition among the Greek Cypriots to the Turkish occupation of 37% of the island

ECONOMY

Currency ($ U.S. Equivalent): 0.48 Cypriot pound = $1; 112,019 Turkish lira = $1
Per Capita Income/GDP: $11,800/$8.8 billion (Greek); $3,950/$536 million (Turkish)
GDP Growth Rate: 4% (Greek); 0.5% (Turkish)
Inflation Rate: 3.3% (Greek); 86% (Turkish)
Unemployment Rate: 2.3% (Greek); 3.6% (Turkish)
Labor Force: 299,700 (Greek); 76,500 (Turkish)

Natural Resources: copper; pyrites; asbestos; gypsum; timber; salt; marble; clay earth pigment
Agriculture: potatoes; vegetables; grapes; citrus; barley; olives
Industry: food; beverages; textiles; chemicals; metal products; wood products; tourism
Exports: $1.4 billion (Greek); $71 million (Turkish) (primary partners Russia, Bulgaria, Turkey, United Kingdom)
Imports: $4 billion (Greek); $330 million (Turkish) (primary partners United States, Turkey, United Kingdom)

*Note: There are great disparities between the Greek Cypriot area and the Turkish Cypriot area in many of these statistics.

 http://www.kypros.org/Cyprus/root.html
http://www.odci.gov/cia/publications/factbook/country-frame.html

THE REPUBLIC OF CYPRUS

The Republic of Cyprus is situated on an island in the northeastern part of the Mediterranean Sea, south of Turkey. It is the largest independent island in the Mediterranean. Cyprus lies about 50 miles south of Turkey and 260 miles east of Rhodes. Its anomalous position—populated in large part by Greeks but located far from the Greek archipelago—has generated tremendous geopolitical strife.

Cyprus has a long recorded history, and the island has often been a bone of contention. Greeks and Turks have fought for its possession from times immemorial. During the late Bronze Age (1600–1050 B.C.), Greek traders and settlers roaming through the entire Mediterranean area expanded Hellenic (Greek) culture into Cyprus. From 700 B.C. onward, the island was successively dominated by Assyrians, Egyptians, and Persians, until it became part of the Roman Empire in 58 B.C. When, 4 centuries later, the split between the West and East Roman Empires took place, Cyprus fell to the latter. For some 800 years, it remained part of Byzantium (as the East Roman Empire came to be known), during which period it was attacked frequently. Richard the Lionhearted did so during the Crusades, and the English king briefly held the island before it came under Frankish control in the late twelfth century. Cyprus became an outpost of the Venetian Republic in 1489 and finally fell into the hands of the Ottoman Turks in 1571.

The Ottomans applied the *millet* system to Cyprus—a system that incorporated the Islamic belief that "like over like is mercy." This implied that non-Muslim minorities were governed by their own religious authorities. "Like over like" did not just promote the cohesion and internal solidarity of the ethnic Greek community; it also greatly strengthened the position of the Greek Orthodox Church. In fact, the Church became important in secular matters, at least as much as Turkish rule would allow.

Late in the nineteenth century, Great Britain assumed control of the island. Cyprus was formally annexed in 1914 and became a British Crown colony in 1925. The Mediterranean had by then in effect become a British sea—Gibraltar and Suez holding the entrances, with Cyprus and Malta the strongholds in the eastern and western parts.

INDEPENDENCE

Even before the island fell to Britain, some strong ethnonationalism in the Greek community had started to generate unrest. The strife only intensified under the British colonial administration. Most inhabitants of Greek stock identified so strongly with the ancestral land that they came to view *enosis*—the notion that Cyprus should be part and parcel of Greece—as the ideal solution. After a brief lull during World War II, agitation resumed.

The situation in Cyprus was very complicated. It was a colony of Britain; but on the island itself, there was a measure of *internal* colonialism, in that the living conditions of the Turkish Cypriots were definitely inferior to those of the Greek Cypriots. Indeed, the former were as a rule regarded as second-class citizens. Nevertheless, the two ethnic groups lived close to each other, with the Turks more often than not subservient to the Greek Cypriots. The Turkish Cypriots objected strongly to enosis, since such an integration would only enhance their minority position in an expanded context.

Lengthy conferences on the subject took place, some in London, others in Geneva. Finally, the idea of an independent Cyprus appeared to gain strength. On August 16, 1960, sovereignty was transferred from Britain to a Cypriot government in Nicosia, the new capital. But it did not take long for new communal violence to erupt, at which point both the United States and the United Nations started to become involved. These ethnic tensions gradually affected the island's demography, as the Greek and the Turkish peoples began to live in separate enclaves. This segregation augured ill for the island, foreshadowing long-lasting friction and hostility between the two ethnic groups.

THE CRISIS OF 1974

The independent Cypriot government, headed by President (and Archbishop) Michael Makarios, kept the situation under control for some years. Indeed, it made some sincere efforts to lessen the ethnic tensions. However, the government of Greece, which since 1967 had consisted of a military dictatorship (a junta of right-wing colonels), was apprehensive about Makarios, whom it viewed as left-leaning, if not clearly Communist. In July 1974, the junta suddenly announced that it favored enosis as a solution to Cypriot troubles—that is, it wanted to render the island part of Greece. In making this statement, the Greek government in effect reneged on the treaty to which it had been party shortly before Cyprus became independent. The announcement, which amounted to an outright rejection of all that Makarios stood for, triggered an immediate response on the island, where the enosis ideal had simmered for a long time: Makarios and his government were overthrown.

They were replaced by the leader of the revolt, Nicos Sampson, a reputed enosis fanatic. It was only natural, then, that the extremely apprehensive Turkish Cypriot community reacted in turn. Turkey, no longer feeling bound by the treaties it had concluded when Cyprus was about to become independent, launched what it called the "Attila Peace Operation," landing troops on the island. Heavy fighting followed.

The foreign ministers of the guarantor powers (Greece, Turkey, and Great Britain) met in late July 1974. The following month, Turkey renewed its offensive, and by the time hostilities ended, it appeared in control of more than one third of Cyprus. The dissociation of the Greek and Turkish communities now became more pronounced. It seemed like an "iron curtain" descended on the island, in effect severing whatever communication the two groups had been able to maintain.

The northern part (where the Turkish troops had landed and operated) enjoyed a degree of self-rule, if only by default. Turkey also started to transmigrate relatively large numbers of Turks from the mainland into northern Cyprus. A large proportion of these "immigrants" hailed from Anatolia and similarly undeveloped areas of Turkey. This deliberate effort to change the island's demographic composition was viewed with the utmost suspicion by Greek Cypriots; even their Turkish counterparts did not favor this addition to their numbers.

On June 8, 1975, Turkish Cypriots voted overwhelmingly to allow a separate Turkish Cypriot state to emerge. Incumbents were elected for newly established executive and legislative offices. Some 200,000 Greek inhabitants of the Turkish-held area were forcibly removed, and a prolonged impasse followed. The confrontation escalated even further when, on November 15, 1983, northern Cyprus made an effort to secede. Turkish Cypriot leader Rauf Denktash issued a unilateral declaration of independence and proclaimed the new "Turkish Republic of Northern Cyprus."

Thus far, Turkey has been the only country to recognize the new state as a distinct entity. It is conceivable that this lack of success in garnering international recognition has caused Turkish Cypriot leaders to become more amenable to a resolution of the crisis.

THE CHASM ENDURES

The two parts of Cyprus are separated by a buffer zone patrolled by the United Nations Force in Cyprus (UNFICYP). There is little movement of people and essentially no movement of goods or services between the two parts of the island. In 1988,

| Hellenic culture comes to Cyprus **1600–1050 B.C.** | Cyprus is incorporated into the Roman Empire **58 B.C.** | Ottoman Turk influence begins **A.D. 1571** | Cyprus is conquered by Great Britain **1875** | Cyprus becomes a British Crown colony **1925** | Cyprus becomes independent **1960** | Turkey invades northern Cyprus **1974** | Preliminary talks are held between the leaders of the two parts of Cyprus **1988** |

1990s

| Turkey continues its illegal occupation of Cyprus, benefiting from its opposition to Iraq in the Gulf War | The European Union pressures Turkey and Cyprus to resolve their political and ethnic problems | A large forest fire in the Turkish-occupied area is believed to have been set by Kurdish sympathizers |

the two leaders of the estranged areas on Cyprus, President George Vassiliou and Rauf Denktash, met without any preconditions. Turkish Cypriot leaders previously had refused to negotiate before a variety of conditions had been met, whereas the Greek Cypriots were willing to negotiate only once the Turkish troops had left the island.

In meetings in November 1988 with UN secretary general Javier Pérez de Cuellar, the first round of intercommunal talks (begun in September) was critically reviewed. President Vassiliou indicated that a "wide gap" continued to separate the two sides. However, the two Cypriot leaders agreed to hold a second round of talks under the sponsorship of the UN secretary general. This round was to focus on an integrated comprehensive approach to a solution. Vassiliou emphasized that agreement on three basic freedoms—movement, settlement, and property ownership—would be fundamental to any solution. He pointed out that Europe, to which Turkey aspired to belong, had based the whole of its post–World War II policy on those principles.

There is a strong possibility that the nation-state of Cyprus, however small in area as well as in populace, may ultimately receive a federal format, the two subnational entities being ruled by Greek Cypriot and Turkish Cypriot governments, respectively. But even a federation is not a guarantee of peaceful coexistence. And in any case, to date the deep conflict between the Greek Cypriots and Turkish Cypriots remains unresolved.

Generally, Greek Cypriots continue to resent that hundreds of their compatriots are still missing, or at least unaccounted for. (The Cypriot government has submitted a list that identifies 1,619 such persons.) The forced population movements in 1974 and 1975 appear to have been attended by terrorism and, on occasion, massacres.

In the mid-1980s, a new concern emerged among the Greek Cypriots. It came to light

that the Turkish occupation authorities (civilian as well as military) had resorted to looting centuries-old monasteries and churches under their control. If anger and rage initially had caused the Turks to commit large-scale iconoclasm throughout the area they occupied, they soon came to realize that most of these art items and antiques would yield large amounts of money. Their intent was more often than not foiled, since many reputable art dealers immediately recognized these internationally known treasures as having been taken out of Cyprus illegally.

The Cyprus Bulletin reported in 1993 that UNESCO "has decided to send a special mission to Cyprus in a bid to protect the island's 9,000-year-old cultural heritage." The Cyprus government and the Church had repeatedly protested to UNESCO, the World Council of Churches, and other international bodies against the destruction and smuggling abroad of ancient and religious treasures by the Turks.

Apart from the pillage and plunder, the illegal occupation by Turkey has caused international organizations such as the European Union to be highly critical. In November 1993, the EU urged Turkey "to use all its influence to make a contribution." Several weeks later, the EU and Cyprus began talks meant to lead to negotiations for the island's accession to the Union. The European Union may thus ultimately hold the key to the solution of the Cyprus issue. There can be little doubt that the EU will never consider Cypriot membership before the island's political and ethnic divisions have been resolved.

THE PRESENT

In both section of Cyprus, there is a generally strong regard for democratic principles, though occasional instances of police brutality have been reported, and discrimination and violence against women are serious concerns. Glafcos Clerides of the

conservative Democratic Rally Party was elected president of the Republic of Cyprus in 1993 and again in 1998—though, with 50.8 percent of the vote, he just barely won out over rival George Iakovou, with 49.2 percent. (The president of Cyprus is both the chief of state and head of government. The post of vice president—which is reserved for a Turkish Cypriot—is currently vacant.) Following his reflection, he formed a "government of national unity" with open invitations for participation by all political parties. In 1995, Turkish Cypriots reelected Rauf Denktash as their leader.

There are profound economic and quality-of-life disparities between the Greek and Turkish areas of Cyprus. Both are free-market economies, but they have significant administrative controls. The government-controlled (Greek Cypriot) part of the island has a robust, service-oriented economy, highly dependent on tourism and trade. The Turkish Cypriot economy, which relies heavily on subsidies from Turkey, is basically service-oriented, but it has a smaller tourism base and a larger agricultural sector. As long as the deep political chasm between Greek and Turkish Cypriots endures, it is unlikely that the differences in quality of life for people in the two groups will diminish significantly. Although periodic talks between President Clerides and Mr. Denktash have continued, under the auspices of the United Nations, little progress has been made in this regard.

DEVELOPMENT

Cyprus is working with representatives of the World Bank and International Monetary Fund to address problems related to its foreign debt and other economic matters. In 1997, Turkey signed a $250 million economic cooperation accord with the Turkish Cyrpist area to support education, tourism, and industry.

FREEDOM

Freedom has become restricted as a result of the internal hostilities. President Glafkos Clerides, who succeeded George Vassiliou, is working to reunite Cyprus within a federal system of government, which will safeguard the basic rights of all its inhabitants. There are some human rights concerns, especially regarding treatment of women.

HEALTH/WELFARE

Infant mortality is low and adult literacy is very high in Cyprus. In 1988, smoking was banned in all public places. The Turkish Cypriot economy has about ⅓ the per capita GDP of the Greek Cyrpiot economy.

ACHIEVEMENTS

Cyprus was represented at the Seoul Olympics by a 9-member team that included participants in track and field, sailing, judo, and shooting events.

Denmark (Kingdom of Denmark)

GEOGRAPHY

Area in Square Miles (Kilometers): 16,638 (43,076) (about twice the size of Massachusetts)

Capital (Population): Copenhagen (1,326,000)

Environmental Concerns: air pollution; North Sea pollution; drinking- and surface-water pollution

Geographical Features: low and flat to gently rolling plains

Climate: temperate

PEOPLE

Population

Total: 5,334,000

Annual Growth Rate: 0.49%

Rural/Urban Population Ratio: 15/85

Major Languages: Danish; a small German-speaking minority

Ethnic Makeup: Scandinavian; Inuit (Eskimo); Faeroese; German

Religions: 91% Evangelical Lutheran; 2% other Protestant and Roman Catholic; 7% others

Health

Life Expectancy at Birth: 73 years (male); 79 years (female)

Infant Mortality Rate (Ratio): 5.2/1,000

Average Caloric Intake: 133% of FAO minimum

Physicians Available (Ratio): 1/358

Education

Adult Literacy Rate: 99%

Compulsory (Ages): 7–16

COMMUNICATION

Telephones: 1 per 1.6 people

Daily Newspaper Circulation: 365 per 1,000 people

Televisions: 1 per 1.9 people

TRANSPORTATION

Highways in Miles (Kilometers): 42,960 (71,600)

Railroads in Miles (Kilometers): 1,773 (2,838)

Usable Airfields: 118

Motor Vehicles in Use: 2,042,000

GOVERNMENT

Type: constitutional monarchy

Independence Date: became a constitutional monarchy in 1849

Head of State/Government: Queen Margrethe II; Prime Minister Poul Nyrup Rasmussen

Political Parties: Social Democratic Party; Conservative Party; Liberal Party; Socialist People's Party; Progress Party; Center Democratic Party; Social Liberty Party; Unity Party; Danish People's Party

Suffrage: universal at 18

MILITARY

Military Expenditures (% of GDP): 1.6%

Current Disputes: Rockall continental-shelf dispute with Iceland, Ireland, and the United Kingdom

ECONOMY

Currency ($ U.S. Equivalent): 6.11 kroner = $1

Per Capita Income/GDP: $23,200/$122.5 billion

GDP Growth Rate: 3%

Inflation Rate: 2.2%

Unemployment Rate: 7.9%

Labor Force: 2,896,000

Natural Resources: petroleum; natural gas; fish; salt; limestone; stone, gravel, and sand

Agriculture: highly intensive; specializes in dairying and animal husbandry; cereals; root crops

Industry: food processing; machinery and equipment; textiles and clothing; chemical products; electronics; construction; furniture and other wood products; shipbuilding

Exports: $48.8 billion (primary partners Germany, Sweden, United Kingdom)

Imports: $43.2 billion (primary partners Germany, Sweden, Netherlands)

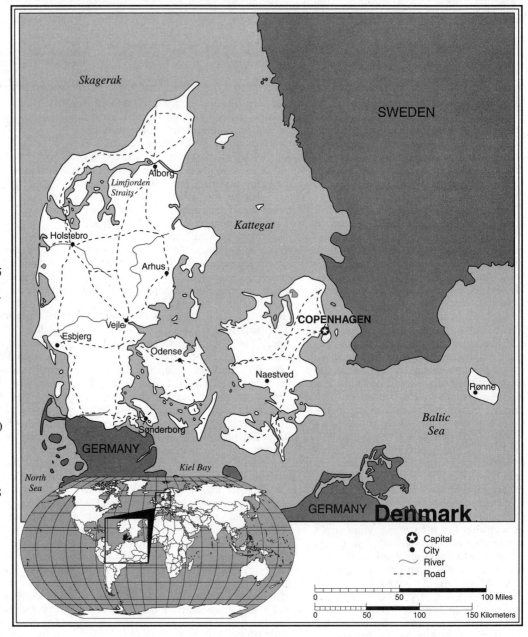

A BLEND OF PAST AND PRESENT

Practically every person who visits Copenhagen will see the "Little Mermaid," a bronze figurine immortalized by Hans Christian Andersen's fairy tale. She sits on a rock in the northern part of Copenhagen's harbor. But on the coastline surrounding the harbor, the fairy tale yields to today's realities, exemplified by the massive construction hall and cranes of the Burmeister and Wain shipyard.

These contrasts of old and new, of a past glittering with royal splendor and a more down-to-earth, democratic present, of a modern industrial society with agrarian roots, are pervasive in Denmark. Tivoli, Copenhagen's famed amusement park, was carved out of what were once the city defense works; the lake there used to be part of the city's moat. The royal hunting grounds north of Copenhagen were converted into a most attractive park. The *Folketing* (the Danish Parliament) meets in the Christiansborg Palace, the magnificent royal residence for 4 centuries. Thus, past and present offer a fascinating balance in the Kingdom of Denmark.

HISTORY

Denmark was once a great world power. In Viking times—that is, in the ninth and tenth centuries A.D.—a Danish kingdom extended to the east of England. This was known as Danelaw. The Danish king, Canute, and his son ruled as kings of England from 1017 to 1050.

Dynastic union with Norway and Sweden in the late fourteenth century, forged by the so-called Union of Kalmar, brought all of Scandinavia under Danish rule, including Finland as well as the North Atlantic islands of the Faeroes (a group of 18 rugged islands), Iceland, and Greenland. The Swedes ultimately revolted; there were adjustments in the balance of power that resulted in a military and diplomatic rivalry between Denmark–Norway and Sweden–Finland that lasted until the early nineteenth century. The Swedes wrested Skane (Norwegian Sweden) from the Danes and annexed Norway in 1814. Defeat at the hands of the Prussians and Austrians half a century later cost Denmark the duchies of Schleswig (in Danish, Slesvig) and Holstein. The Danish recovery of northern Schleswig (now called Southern Jutland) after World War I gave the country its current European borders.

In the Caribbean, the Virgin Islands held by Denmark were sold to the United States during World War I. Americans feared that these islands might be used as a refuge for German submarines. Iceland was another colony, if that term may also be used for an area that does not exactly offer "a place in the sun."

Iceland, which had long-standing ties with Scandinavian countries, appeared to be moving toward independence when World War II broke out. In April 1940, the German Third Reich conquered Denmark and Norway. At this point, Great Britain became apprehensive that the Germans would consider colonies or overseas possessions as nothing more than the spoils of war, in which case the strategically located island would also become part of the growing Nazi German empire. The British thus felt forced to make a preemptive move by taking possession of Iceland. As soon as the United States joined the British war effort (shortly after Pearl Harbor), it assumed its share of Iceland's protection.

The Faeroe Islands, despite an early claim to independence (about a thousand years ago), are nominally still Danish. The 17 *inhabited* islands have a total population of about 50,000; the land area of all the islands is 540 square miles. But although the Danish influence is considerable, the islands have enjoyed a great deal of autonomy for some time. They have, for instance, their own flag and even their own currency, which carries markings in the Faeroe language, which most Danes find hard to understand. Thus it could happen that, in the early 1970s, their popularly elected Assembly, the *Lagting,* decided to remain outside the European Union (then called the European Community), while Denmark negotiated and acquired EU membership. The local government of the Faeroe Islands confined itself to establishing a trade agreement with the European Union some 5 years later. The islands, it turned out, were unhappy with that agreement. Thus the 1990s witnessed attempts to replace it with a broader free-trade treaty. The stumbling block has been EU resistance to a Faeroe demand for free export of fish to the Union. For the Faeroes, such a condition would amount to enjoying the privileges of EU membership without facing its obligations. The rugged islands, which have little to offer beyond fish, fear that their political influence in the Union will be marginal, since they would be represented by Danes from continental Denmark.

GREENLAND

Greenland, which has also been one of Denmark's possessions (as a colony, it might perhaps be qualified as "a place in the midnight sun"), is the world's largest island (840,000 square miles, of which more than 708,000 square miles are covered with ice, a condition that is termed *permafrost*). Located far northwest of Denmark, its population, now numbering approximately 58,000, had enjoyed home rule for some time, expressing its political will through an elected Assembly, the *Landsrad.* However, when Denmark was in the process of becoming a member of the European Union, the Greenlanders (mostly Inuits widely scattered over a vast area) had no objection to being included. Unlike the Faeroe people, they assumed that their fishing grounds would be inaccessible, or at least too remote to be vulnerable to interlopers and poachers from fellow EU members. That assumption soon proved to be erroneous, in that modern trawlers had no difficulty in entering the rich fishing grounds close to Greenland. Soon the island's fishing industry was swamped by competitors. As soon as the Greenlanders realized their error, they started to make preparations to get out of the EU. In a referendum, a fairly large majority voted in favor of this unprecedented step, which was effected on February 1, 1985. It is the only area thus far to secede from the European Union. Ironically, Greenland remains an integral part of Denmark.

DEMOCRATIC INSTITUTIONS AND POLITICAL PARTIES

Democratic political institutions developed relatively late in Denmark. In fact, the Danish monarchy established its absolute supremacy in 1660, at a time when England was gradually embarking on the road toward a constitutional monarchy. Royal absolutism persisted in Denmark until the mid-nineteenth century, when King Frederik VII was forced to issue a liberal Constitution, which extended voting rights to all adult males. This Constitution was adopted on June 5, 1849 (the Danes still celebrate June 5 as Constitution Day). Although it has since been amended four times, its main principles still form the basis of the structure of government in Denmark. But it took another half-century before parliamentary supremacy was fully established, in 1901.

Constitutional reform in 1915 produced changes in the electoral system. Universal suffrage was granted, and from then on, nearly all adult men and women were able to participate in elections. But there were also limitations. The Danes did not want the vote to be fragmented into innumerable splinter parties; as a result, political parties would receive representation in the Folketing only if they had secured at least 2 percent of the total vote. Paradoxically, this same reform introduced the proportional representation system, which typically allows smaller political parties to survive. The system basically implies that each political party will be accorded the same proportion of seats in Parliament that it has secured of the total vote. To illustrate this principle, since the Folketing has 179 seats, a party that secures 10 percent of the total vote must be accorded 18 seats. According to the 2 percent rule, a party cannot have fewer than 4 seats in the lower house.

Constitutional reform in 1953 abolished the upper house, the *Landstinget,* which had been representative of the aristocracy, or at least of the privileged class. (Other countries, particularly in the Scandinavian region, have followed Denmark's lead, rendering their parliaments unicameral.) That same reform made female succession to the throne possible, an addition for which many Danes have been grateful since Margrethe II became queen, in 1972.

The Danish electoral system is further typified by two characteristics that may well be related: first, elections are held with a large degree of frequency (in fact, with 22 elections since the end of World War II, Denmark must have one of the world records); and second, some 10 political parties typically compete in elections. Inevitably, no party will ever receive a majority, which implies that coalitions will have to be formed.

The election of 1973 has gone down in history as the "earthquake election." The number of parties represented in the Folketing was suddenly doubled, to 10. Two of the new parties were antitax parties; a third was a Christian party protesting what it perceived as a decline in moral standards in society. While these protest parties have since become less vehement and less influential, they continue to play a role in Danish party politics.

Since 1982, Danes have referred to their government as "a four-leafed-clover government," as the coalitions have always comprised the Conservative Party, the Liberal Party, and the smaller Center Democratic Party and Christian People's Party. These are not the largest parties, but they are clearly very accommodating toward one another. The Social Democratic Party (a working-class party linked to the trade-union movement) does not belong to this cluster, although it is invariably the main force in government. On the other hand, its former ally, the Liberal Party, representing agrarian interests, has now become part of the semipermanent establishment. The Liberal Party split in 1905, and the Social Democrats then allied themselves with the new Radical Liberals. That alliance lasted for some 6 decades. When it broke, the Social Democratic Party became odd man out again—that is, the largest party but not aligned except in ad hoc

coalitions. However, that party has often constituted the most important and forceful part of the opposition.

One political party that has lost a great deal of influence is the Danish Communist Party. It steadily lost its appeal in the period 1950 to 1990, possibly as a result of its close links to the Soviet model. Its place on the extreme left of the spectrum has been filled by the more independent Socialist People's Party, founded in 1958.

Election campaigns in Denmark are short, generally lasting around 6 weeks. They largely revolve around television programs in which journalists put sharp questions to the candidates. The electorate also watches debates between party leaders, particularly the final debates. No television advertising is permitted. Voter turnout is extremely high. It often scores between 85 and 90 percent (in the United States, it is sometimes as low as 50 percent). Denmark, like most Western European countries, has an excellent registry system. No advance registration is required; all citizens are automatically registered as voters upon becoming 18. People who change residence are obliged to notify the civil registry of the municipality they leave as well as the civil registry of the municipality they enter.

Danish political parties are characterized by mass membership and considerable discipline. Most people interested in politics become dues-paying party members. The Social Democratic and Liberal Parties have close ties to interest groups. Newspapers usually have some party affiliation; only the government-owned electronic media seek to be neutral in partisan disputes. Once elected, party representatives will nearly always vote their party line, on the national as well as local levels. If they do not, they may risk losing their renomination, because the party leadership controls the nominating process.

Danish parliamentary politics has tended to polarize into a two-bloc pattern since 1966. The parties on the left (the Social Democratic Party, the Socialist People's Party, and others) are squared off against the "bourgeois" or "middle-of-the-road" plus right-wing parties (the Conservative, Liberal, and Radical Liberal Parties).

Denmark was governed from 1982 to early 1993 by Conservative prime minister Poul Schluter's coalition of the Conservatives, the Liberals, the Christian People's Party, and the Center Democrats, with support on domestic issues from the Radical Liberals. December 1992 witnessed the election of the center-left coalition, composed of the Social Democrats, the Center Democrats, the Radical Liberals, and the Christian People's Party, along

with two of the four so-called North Atlantic members, from the Faeroes and Greenland, which gained a total of 90 seats, giving them a majority of the 179 seats in the Folketing. This forced Prime Minister Schluter to resign after more than a decade in power. His coalition was able to hold onto only 59 seats. His credibility had suffered because of charges that he misled Parliament over immigration restrictions on Tamil (Sri Lankan) refugees in the late 1980s. Schluter proposed Finance Minister Henning Dyremose, a member of Schluter's Conservative Party, to succeed him. This was not acceptable to the Danish Parliament, however, and on January 25, 1993, Poul Nyrup Rasmussen, the leader of the Social Democratic Party, was appointed prime minister. (He has remained prime minister ever since, even through a period of recession and a shrinking welfare state.)

It so happened that Rasmussen's new government was forced to host (as well as preside over) the European Council in the first half of 1993. This is an obligation that rotates among the European Union members. The deliberations of the European Council, an extremely important body that consists of the prime ministers and other ministers of the EU members, are held in the successive capitals of the Union, and it was Denmark's turn.

Danish EU policy is supported by seven out of a total of eight parties in the Folketing. In a second referendum held on the subject, Danes also accepted the Maastricht Treaty, after certain exceptions had been agreed upon. Danish feelings toward the European Union, while pragmatic, are perhaps best described as skeptical and prickly. It passed on joining the first wave of joining the Euro zone in January 1999, but the government expects that Danes will be ready to take part in the not-too-distant future.

THE ECONOMY
Sixty-two percent of Denmark's land is arable—a very high percentage. The countryside is primarily flat and, unlike much of its Nordic neighbors, not rocky but fertile. Bearing in mind this factor, which predisposes the nation toward agriculture, as well as the absence of raw materials, one need not be surprised that industrialization has not made such vast strides in Denmark as in other Western European countries. Denmark is among the world's foremost agricultural countries. This characteristic still prevails, although industry has overtaken agriculture with respect to exports.

The structure of Danish agriculture has experienced an almost revolutionary transformation over the last few decades. There were more than 200,000 farms only 20 to

| Gorm the Old initiates the Danish royal dynasty **ca. A.D. 900** | The Kalmar Union unites three Scandinavian countries **1397** | The Reformation arrives in Denmark; people almost universally adopt the Lutheran faith **1530s** | Absolute monarchy is introduced in Denmark **1660** | Abolition of serfdom **1788** | Denmark loses Norway to Sweden **1814** | End of royal absolutism; Denmark's first Constitution **1849** |

30 years ago. Today, after a great many closures and mergers, that figure barely exceeds 100,000. Another indicator of the decline in agricultural pursuits is that only about 4 percent of the population are now employed in agriculture; a quarter-century ago, the figure was about 20 percent. But if these figures express quantities, agriculture—or, more generally, farming—has *qualitatively* improved. Farmers are considerably better trained and better informed than they were in the past, thanks to the numerous agricultural colleges. Farmers in Denmark were among the first to experiment with cooperative societies in dairy produce, slaughterhouses, and other communal business ventures, as well as in the field of exports.

Industry is overwhelmingly made up of small- and medium-size companies, most of which have an ability to adapt to market demands and have a penchant for strict quality control. Denmark has concentrated on light industry, another side effect of absence of raw materials. These enterprises are very labor-intensive. Examples are the production and export of furniture, handcrafts, medical goods, automatic cooling and heating devices, and precision instruments. Danish beer has been world-famous since the early 1950s. The export of machinery, textiles, and electronics has also risen, albeit to a lesser extent.

In a highly competitive global market, Danish industry has been able to find niches for particular specialties. For example, in the world of the child, Lego blocks have become well known. And Bang and Olufsen have produced lines of products distinctive enough to be displayed at the Museum of Modern Art in New York.

Nevertheless, journalists describing Denmark's economy often cite Shakespeare's line, "There is something rotten in the state of Denmark." One of the real economic problems is unemployment, which started rising in the 1960s. While unemployment (currently about 8 percent) is not as high as in, for example, Finland, it is persistent in Denmark. Some analysts explain that the unemployment results from the fact that the labor force has continued to grow fairly rapidly despite the shortage of employment, because younger women have not left the labor market after having children. High unemployment, however, may also be a consequence of adjustments to changing conditions in the international market and high labor costs,

which have affected the competitiveness of some Danish exports. Danish businesses have been encouraged to make the necessary adaptations without government intervention, but this has not led to a restoration of full employment. Frequent balance-of-payments deficits also pose problems to Danish industry. Trade deficits have been the order of the day in Denmark, and heavy foreign borrowing has compounded the problem.

Fortunately, the Danish North Sea oil and natural-gas exploitation has started to reduce the country's dependence on imported fuels. The opening of Central/Eastern Europe also bodes well. Denmark does not border on Central/Eastern European nation-states, as do Germany and Austria, but the country does look across the Baltic Sea toward Estonia, Latvia, and Lithuania, with which it has had ties since the fifteenth century. Copenhagen was quick to open the first international air links with the Baltic nations and began ferry services with Riga, Latvia's capital, as soon as Central/Eastern Europe opened up in the 1980s and early 1990s, and this initiative has paid off in economic terms.

THE WELFARE STATE

Denmark is one of the world's best-run and most generous social-welfare states. All working persons are entitled to an annual 5-week paid vacation. Employees temporarily out of work as a result of sickness, disability, unemployment, or maternity/ paternity leaves are accorded up to 80 percent of their wages. Danish workers are entitled to up to 2½ years of unemployment compensation—and the government has to come up with job offers. This system has of course proven to be very expensive during the high unemployment of the last decade.

A variety of special programs benefit children—the so-called family allowance for each child under age 18, day-care facilities, and special housing allowances for low-income families. Public education is free through the university level. And the cornerstone of the welfare state is national health care: All Danish residents are covered by a plan that provides free hospitalization and medical care and covers most dental expenses.

Welfare programs in Denmark enjoy virtually universal support, since ultimately everyone benefits from them. But they require a great deal of money. The

government collects about half the total income in the country in taxes, the bulk of which goes to meet the costs of social services. That not all people approve was shown in the 1973 "earthquake election," when antitax parties jointly secured almost a quarter of the total vote. Income taxes peaked the next year; indirect taxes also witnessed a slow and continuous rise. The unpopularity of these measures caused the government to finance its activity by borrowing abroad. And, like the other Nordic countries, Denmark has been forced to begin trimming its welfare state in order to put a brake on taxation as well as to protect the overall budgetary health of the economy.

FOREIGN RELATIONS

Between the world wars, Denmark was one of the Oslo States, an organization that furthered economic cooperation during the Great Depression. However, this was not a military alliance, and, being a small country, Denmark doubted that it would be able to protect itself against a large aggressor. The Danes therefore decided, on the eve of World War II, to abolish their army and to rely on a small police force for domestic emergencies; Denmark was thus the only country to succumb to Nazi aggression without offering any military resistance at all. After 5 years, the German surrender forced the Nazi forces to withdraw. But the Danes had learned the lesson that proclaiming oneself neutral was not enough to prevent war and occupation.

When the East–West tension rose to a high pitch in the late 1940s, the United States took the initiative to establish a collective security system to deter the Soviet Union from invading and occupying Western Europe. It was not hard to find allies. At that time, Sweden, Norway, and Denmark were trying to establish "bloc neutrality," which implied that the countries concerned would be neutral unless one of them was attacked. However, as soon as the North Atlantic Treaty Organization loomed, Norway abandoned the plan and went over to the Atlantic Alliance.

Rather than joining a truncated Nordic Council, Denmark followed suit. However, it did not join NATO without reservations. The Danish government made it a condition of joining that no nuclear weapons would be stored on Danish territory in peacetime. This reservation caused difficulties when, 30 years later,

Parliamentary supremacy is established 1901	Universal suffrage 1915	The first Social Democratic government 1924	German occupation 1940–1945	A constitutional amendment allowing female succession to the throne 1953	Danish membership in the EU (then the EC) becomes effective; the earthquake election 1973	1990s

A Danish referendum rejects vital parts of the Maastricht Treaty; after adjustments are made, the treaty is approved

Denmark strengthens ties to the Baltics; Denmark battles a few years of recession but begins pulling out of it

A new bridge/tunnel is under construction to link Copenhagen with Malmo, Sweden

NATO decided to install nuclear missiles in each of the European member-states. The Danish government was unable to secure a majority vote in favor of lifting its restrictions concerning the deployment of nuclear arms on Danish soil.

In 1945, Denmark was one of the 50 nations to sign the Charter of the United Nations, and generally the country has been considerably enthusiastic about this world body. Although its importance in the United Nations has been limited by its relatively small economy, Denmark has played a role in the organization out of proportion to its size. Contributions for development aid as a proportion of Denmark's gross national product are among the highest in the world, and the country has contributed to various UN peacekeeping forces. Denmark is also a member of all specialized UN agencies. Throughout General Assembly debates, the Danish delegation, invariably headed by the minister of foreign affairs, has emphasized the promotion of respect for human rights.

THE EUROPEAN UNION
Denmark has always been ambivalent with regard to its membership in the European Union. Initially, its economy was almost exclusively geared toward the Nordic Council. A shift took place in the early 1960s, when Denmark became a member of the European Free Trade Association. But when in 1972 Great Britain, the EFTA's foremost member, started negotiations for EU membership, Denmark felt that the time had come to consider Union membership as well. Both Denmark and Norway were involved in the negotiations that were held in Brussels and that would make the EU membership jump from six to 10. Indeed, on January 22, 1972, all those countries solemnly signed the conditions and requirements for accession. However,

almost as an afterthought, Norway and Denmark suddenly stipulated that their peoples be consulted before they would officially become members. In September 1972, the Norwegian referendum revealed an opposition of 54 percent. It was believed that the Danish vote would be influenced by this rejection, but a few weeks later, the Danish Folketing voted favorably on accession by an overwhelming majority (a surprising 141 versus 34 votes).

It is possible that the Danish public (including its politicians) were after all poorly informed about the advantages and disadvantages that came with EU membership. However that may be, the Danes often felt shortchanged. They repeatedly grumbled and occasionally threatened to withdraw. The real crucible, however, came in the early 1990s during negotiations that led to the so-called Maastricht Treaty. At that time, the British were expressing reservations concerning political integration as well as financial union. They were allowed to opt out—that is, Great Britain was granted more time to think about these important matters before signing the Maastricht accords. The Danish suggestion that this privilege be accorded to other EU members as well was deemed irrelevant, since all other members had already expressed agreement.

Shortly after the Maastricht meeting, Denmark suddenly announced that its ratification of the treaty would be contingent on a referendum to be held in June 1992. From then onward, Danish politics was in a fever pitch. Approval and disapproval of the treaty was not entirely consistent with party lines. There was, nevertheless, an expectation that there would be a majority of people favoring Danish accession to the stipulations concerning the economic and political union. However, it turned out that a slim majority (50.7 versus 49.3 percent)

favored rejection. The outcome left the world stunned and the European Union, to a degree, devastated.

In view of the closeness of the vote, the Danish government proposed another referendum, to be held in June 1993, to focus on similar issues (to have another referendum on exactly the same issues was believed to be offensive to the Danish electorate).

Meanwhile, the European Union recovered from its stunning defeat in Denmark. Ireland and Greece had ratified the treaty, and some other countries took recourse to their normal parliamentary procedures. And although the French referendum in September 1992 turned out to be a cliffhanger, resulting in 51 percent of the electorate being in favor of Maastricht and its ramifications, many analysts believed that extraneous factors had entered that race, such as the popularity or unpopularity of President François Mitterrand. Nevertheless, the outcome of the June 1993 Danish referendum revealed that the Danish referendum of June 1992 had provided only a temporary obstacle on the road to Danish membership in the European Union. But, that said, the fact remains that Denmark is not the EU's biggest booster. Indeed, the government did not join the launch of the Euro in January 1999, though it does expect its people to be more favorably inclined toward monetary union within a couple of years. Observers expect Denmark to be the next Nordic state to join the Euro zone.

DEVELOPMENT

The first few years of Denmark's membership in the EU were disappointing, since that period coincided with a severe recession. Economic recovery has been increasing but not yet complete. Heightened demand has overheated the economy, exerting pressures on the balance of payments.

FREEDOM

Denmark has one of the highest human-rights ratings in the world. The country used to have an extremely liberal policy with respect to political asylum, but the tide of refugees has been stemmed by changes in the law.

HEALTH/WELFARE

Denmark has one of the most comprehensive welfare systems in the world. There have been times when Danes have tired of paying the high taxes required to maintain the system, but when the chips are down, most Danes feel that nobody should be without the assistance he or she needs.

ACHIEVEMENTS

Denmark was one of the first countries in the world to institute the office of ombudsman, in the early 1950s. This office was created to protect the individual citizen against wrongdoing or even indifference on the part of the bureaucracy. Many countries have followed suit, instituting ombudsmen of their own.

Finland (Republic of Finland)

GEOGRAPHY
Area in Square Miles (Kilometers): 130,160 (337,113) (slightly smaller than Montana)
Capital (Population): Helsinki (525,000)
Environmental Concerns: water and air pollution; habitat loss
Geographical Features: mostly low, flat to rolling plains interspersed with lakes and low hills
Climate: cold temperate

PEOPLE

Population
Total: 5,150,000
Annual Growth Rate: 0.2%
Rural/Urban Population Ratio: 36/64
Major Languages: Finnish; Swedish; small Lapp- and Russian-speaking minorities
Ethnic Makeup: 93% Finnish; 6% Swedish; 1% Sami (Lapp) and others
Religions: 89% Evangelical Lutheran; 9% unaffiliated; 2% Greek Orthodox and others

Health
Life Expectancy at Birth: 73 years (male); 81 years (female)
Infant Mortality Rate (Ratio): 3.8/1,000
Average Caloric Intake: 118% of FAO minimum
Physicians Available (Ratio): 1/371

Education
Adult Literacy Rate: 100%
Compulsory (Ages): 7–16; free

COMMUNICATION
Telephones: 1 per 1.8 people
Daily Newspaper Circulation: 473 per 1,000 people
Televisions: 1 per 2 people

TRANSPORTATION
Highways in Miles (Kilometers): 46,669 (77,782)
Railroads in Miles (Kilometers): 3,515 (5,859)
Usable Airfields: 158
Motor Vehicles in Use: 2,180,000

GOVERNMENT
Type: republic
Independence Date: December 6, 1917
Head of State/Government: President Martti Ahtisaari; Prime Minister Paavo Lipponen

Political Parties: Social Democratic Party; Center Party; National Coalition Party; Leftist Alliance People's Democratic League and Democratic Alliance; Swedish People's Party; Finnish Christian League; Green League; Rural Party; others
Suffrage: universal at 18

MILITARY
Military Expenditures (% of GDP): 1.6%
Current Disputes: none

ECONOMY
Currency ($ U.S. Equivalent): 4.77 Finnish marks = $1
Per Capita Income/GDP: $20,000/$102.1 billion
GDP Growth Rate: 4.6%
Inflation Rate: 1.2%
Unemployment Rate: 14.6%
Labor Force: 2,533,000
Natural Resources: timber; copper; zinc; iron ore; silver
Agriculture: animal husbandry, especially dairying; cereals; sugar beets; potatoes; fish
Industry: metal manufacturing; shipbuilding; pulp and paper; copper refining; foodstuffs; chemicals; textiles; clothing
Exports: $38.4 billion (primary partners EU countries, Sweden, United States)
Imports: $29.3 billion (primary partners EU countries, Sweden, United States)

http://www.vtourist.com/Europe/Finland/
http://www.odci.gov/cia/publications/factbook/country-frame.html

THE REPUBLIC OF FINLAND

In some of the frozen parts of North-eastern Europe, artifacts have been found that suggest that humans first made their appearance in what is now known as Finland some 6,000 to 8,000 years ago. However, not before about 100 B.C. did people arrive (probably from the central Russian area) who may properly be identified as Finnish or Karelian. Except in its southern part, Finland remained sparsely populated, with clusters of communities that were nomadic (as were most of the Sami, also known as Lapps) close to the polar circle and seminomadic in the center. Natural conditions may well have prevented more permanent settlements.

Finland's climate is not as arctic as its location would suggest; indeed, it is actually less cold than its neighbors Sweden, Norway, and northern Russia. But nature has left the separation between land and water somewhat indistinct. There are some 55,000 lakes, mostly small, which in total make up more than 10 percent of Finland's area. An additional 20 percent of the country consists of marshland and moors.

In view of these geographical conditions, it is not surprising that during most of its history, Finland was little more than an appendage to one of its politically better-developed neighbors. Indeed, its chief function may have been that of a *cordon sanitaire*, a buffer of sorts that prevented, or at least minimized, wars between Scandinavians on the one hand and Russians

on the other. Surprisingly, neither of these neighbors overwhelmed Finland. (It is true that, after the Winter War, discussed later in this report, the Soviet Union availed itself of the province of Karelia, but it also could have occupied all of Finland, but did not.) And although Finland has always been tolerant of its minorities, there was no assimilation, which may be attributable to the uniqueness of Finnish language and culture. Finns and Karelians descend from the Finno–Ugric group, found nowhere else in Europe. Even so, since they lived scattered over a relatively large area and did not have well-developed political institutions of their own when their country was occupied, nationalism was slow in coming. Sweden could thus rule the Finns for more than 500 years without engendering unrest of any significance, let alone rebellion. And during the days of Russian occupation, the area was converted into a Grand Duchy, headed by Czar Alexander II.

During the last years of Czarist rule, however, some nationalist stirrings could be noted. When World War I broke out, the Finns appeared ready for a change. It was the war that, according to U.S. president Woodrow Wilson, was fought to make the world safe for democracy. The Finns seized the opportunity to declare themselves independent when Russia was in turmoil as a result of the 1917 Russian Revolution. Nevertheless, that independence was hard to realize, since political divisions were also evident in the Finnish area.

Indeed, a civil war developed between the Whites (those who stood for a truly independent Finland) and the Reds (those who wanted Finland to be a part of the emerging Soviet empire).

The political turbulence was to last for several years, since other nations started to intervene on behalf of or against the Finnish cause. That the Whites eventually prevailed was largely due to the single-minded heroism of General Mannerheim, whose exploits have become legendary in Finland. Finnish independence was thus the result of skirmishes between political factions rather than of a revolution against alien usurpers.

Although the Soviet Union had at the Treaty of Tartu (Dorpath) acknowledged Finland's sovereignty, in 1939 it started to make war on the fledgling nation. In this Russo–Finnish war, generally termed the Winter War, the Finns' valor and persistence proved to the world that their independence had not been solely a matter of rhetoric. While Soviet troops moved slowly through the snow in areas alien to them, Finnish ski brigades moved swiftly to their rear, fighting a guerrilla war that in some ways proved disastrous to the Soviet Union. In the end, however, the Finns lost the Winter War and were forced to cede part of Karelia, a province bordering on the Soviet Union.

The settlement of the Winter War was followed closely by Operation Barbarossa, the invasion of the Soviet Union by the

(Sky Foto)

Finland boasts some 55,000 lakes, which make up more than 10 percent of its geographic area. Historically, the Finnish lakes have acted as a buffer between Scandinavia and Russia.

German war machine on June 22, 1941. The carefully planned attack by Adolf Hitler's juggernaut seemed, at least initially, so promising that it posed a dilemma to Finnish nationalism. On the one hand, as a democratic nation, the Finns abhorred Nazi totalitarianism and violence; but on the other, the Soviet Union had clearly been their most recent enemy. Although under the circumstances it might have been possible to maintain a precarious neutrality, it did not take the Finns long to decide in favor of resuming the war against their recent enemy. It is conceivable that the retrieval of the part of Karelia that they had been forced to cede may also have been a consideration. The Finns insisted that there was no question of an alliance with Germany—that theirs was a separate war, unrelated to the general conflagration in the rest of Europe.

However that may be, their choice caused them to become de facto allies of the Third Reich. German troops were allowed to move freely throughout Finland so as to attack the Soviet armies from the north. In part, this might have been achieved by crossing the Norwegian–Russian border, Norway having been occupied a year or so earlier; but using Finland as a base facilitated the German attacks from the north. Also, German victories in the Soviet Union were hailed by the Finns, since these entailed the defeat of their enemy. But reverses came after a time and, in 1944, Finland was forced to sue for a separate armistice.

The armistice was granted on the condition that Finland would rid itself of all German troops. There were still more than 200,000 of them, mostly in the northern part of Finland. Thus Finland started its third war, fighting the German troops on its soil. Some of these escaped along the Norwegian route, but most were killed or taken prisoner and handed to the Soviet armies.

If the Finns had expected that their belated cooperation with the Soviets would have ingratiated them to Moscow, they were mistaken: The Treaty of Paris, which settled the war in 1947, included harsh terms. Karelia was now entirely ceded to the Soviet Union, including the important city of Viborg. The loss of territory amounted to more than 11 percent of the country's total area and, more significantly, an even larger percentage of its arable land. Also, Finland was henceforth supposed to have only token military forces. (This stipulation was amended in 1963, when an agreement granted Finland more leeway in establishing an army commensurate with its size.)

On the positive side, Finland was not occupied by Soviet troops after World War

(Photo Lisa Clyde)

Turku is Finland's oldest city, dating back to the thirteenth century. It was the capital under Swedish and Russian rule until 1812. In 1827, Turku was almost entirely destroyed by fire; after it was rebuilt, it prospered until once again it burned during World War II. Shown above is a view of the courtyards of Turku Castle, dating from the medieval period, which today houses a historical museum, the Swedish Theater, and a Greek Orthodox church.

II, as were numerous countries in Eastern Europe, and no force was applied to convert Finland into a Soviet satellite. Nevertheless, Finns were painfully aware that their country existed in the shadow of its vast Soviet neighbor. Thus, the country signed a mutual-assistance treaty with the Soviet Union in 1948. The treaty was renewed for another 20 years in 1955, the same year that Finland joined the United Nations.

THE ECONOMY

World War II devastated Finland, not only because of the war against the Soviets but even more so by the subsequent fight against the Germans. It proved extraordinarily hard to recover from the destruction that had been wrought, especially since Finland did not receive any reparations, having been classified as a belligerent on the side of the vanquished nations. Although the European Recovery Program (better known as the Marshall Plan) was extended to Finland, the Soviet Union did not allow it to accept the aid.

Since Finland had hardly embarked upon industrialization before the war, it is not surprising that it clung to sources of primary industry for a considerable period. It thus attempted to concentrate on agriculture, timber, and mining. Mining

was insignificant in the 1950s; today, however, mining is an important part of Finland's economy.

Tourism has also increased in importance, although the revenues from this industry are much lower than the amount of money Finns themselves spend as tourists abroad. This imbalance may decrease somewhat now that Western European (mainly German) travel agencies have started to focus on Finland as a tourist destination. In addition, the Finnish airline Finnair has been granted landing facilities in numerous European cities.

A major challenge for Finland emerged with the gradual collapse of the trade markets of the Soviet Union and other Communist neighbors in the late 1980s and early 1990s. Finland's economic well-being will depend on its ability to forge new trade alliances in the coming years, which it expects to achieve through its membership in the European Union and with its enthusiastic participation in the Euro.

THE POLITICAL CULTURE

Although Finland was part of Czarist Russia at the time that it declared itself independent, Swedish influence in Finland's society and culture has been considerably more pronounced and durable. Indeed, the

Finland declares its independence; civil war between the Whites and the Reds A.D. 1917	The Winter War between the Soviet Union and Finland 1939–1940	Finland decides to wage war on the Soviet Union 1942	Finland, suing for a separate armistice, is forced to expel all the German troops on its soil 1944	The Treaty of Paris imposes harsh peace terms on Finland 1947	Marshall Plan aid is extended to Finland, but the Soviet Union does not allow it to accept 1948	Finland gains international prestige when the Olympic Games are held in its capital 1952	The Helsinki Accords are signed 1975	Finland's economic sights shift to Western Europe 1980s

1990s

country still houses a sizable minority (6 percent) of Swedes who actually do not consider themselves expatriates. Swedish is also one of the two official languages.

Finland's political culture also reflects a Swedish background, and in many other ways the country can be clearly identified as Western European. In its anxiety to pass the acid test that Woodrow Wilson proclaimed in matters of national self-determination, the Finns adopted a democracy that rested on pluralism and consensual politics. The dual executive that is institutionally embedded in Western Europe also prevails in Finland: a president who is chief of state and largely ceremonial, and a prime minister who heads a government that is actively engaged in policy making. Finland, like France and several other countries, has a system of *cohabitation,* in that the president and prime minister may belong to different political parties. As in most parliamentary systems, the political power of the executive to a large extent depends on the support it receives from the Legislature. If the government forfeits the confidence of the lower house, it must resign (Finland's Parliament, however, is unicameral).

Democracies as a rule have a great deal of party strife, which is why they are customarily identified as "competitive systems." In Finland, party competition used to be very fierce. However, since World War II, this competition has been noticeably mitigated by two factors. First, as has been the case in other Western European political systems, coalitions are considerably less volatile than they used to be. Indeed, some of these coalitions have been turned into more or less permanent blocs—one bloc of parties to the left, and another composed of parties of the center and the right. Variations are still possible, but they will in effect emerge only under the pressure of highly controversial pro-

grams or policies. A second factor is that the former Soviet Union unambiguously indicated that it did not want Finland's Social Democratic Party ever to become a government party. Finland was not in a position to ignore this mandate, even though it clearly infringed on its sovereignty. Thus, the Social Democrats, who were not only powerful as a political party but also hostile vis-à-vis the Soviet Union, were for many years relegated to the opposition.

THE SHIFT TOWARD EUROPE

Finland, much more so than any other nation in Western Europe, was dumbfounded when its giant neighbor, the Soviet Union, started to experience overwhelming problems in the late 1980s—problems that led to the total collapse of a system that had prevailed for some 7 decades. The Finnish government took a strictly neutral attitude when the nearby Baltic states, particularly Lithuania, began to agitate for independence, although it would have been possible for Finland to encourage Lithuania in its effort. The conditions of Finland and the Baltic states are very different—Finland broke away from Russia when the latter was about to become the Soviet Union, while the Baltic states were independent nations from 1918 until 1940.

In an address that Esko Aho, then the prime minister of Finland, presented in 1992 at the National Press Club in Washington, D.C., he touched on two points of paramount importance. First, he stated, "The world around us has dramatically changed. The Soviet Union is no more, and gone are the last vestiges of the Cold War. The institutional framework of the old world order is gradually adjusting itself to new realities, the exact and final nature of which are not yet known. Even the cozy old world of domestic policies as usual in the Western industrial democracies seems to be on its way out. And

In the late 1990s, the Finnish economy grows about 5% per year, indicating a successful shift from ties with the Soviets to ties with Western Europe

Finland becomes a member of the European Union on January 1, 1995; in 1999, it eagerly joins the Euro zone

In parliamentary elections in March 1999, the Social Democrats retained power

here I do not speak only of my own experience and Finnish experience."

If this could seem part of an international relations textbook, a little later the prime minister introduced a new reality, that is, the subject of Finland becoming part of the European Union (then referred to as the European Community) in the following words: "Finland is an integral part of Western Europe, and the well-being of the Finns hinges on trade with the rest of the pack and increasingly on our ability to keep Finland an attractive place to live and invest in. Less than two months ago Finland submitted her application to join the European Community. Negotiations are expected to start sometime next year, maybe the beginning of next year, and membership may be possible as early as the mid-1990s." The negotiations were eventually concluded, and Finland became an EU member on January 1, 1995. Of all the Nordic countries, Finland is the most enthusiastic supporter of the European Union and its economic and political goals. In January 1999, Finland was one of the 11 EU member nations to participate in the launch of the Euro.

It is interesting to note that Aho described Finland as "an integral part of Western Europe," a fact that is belied by any continental map. Undoubtedly, the Soviet decision not to occupy Finland or to render it into a satellite was instrumental in shaping this evaluation.

DEVELOPMENT

Against all odds, postwar Finland changed from a country based on primary industry (agriculture, forestry, and mining) into a semi-industrial country with modern manufacturing plants. This shift was effected in a relatively short period of time. Economic diversification in recent years has meant greater emphasis on high technology.

FREEDOM

Finland rates very high in the realm of human rights. Its citizens enjoy basic rights to the fullest extent. Finland hosted the ceremonial signing of the Final Act, which led to the Helsinki Accords in 1975.

HEALTH/WELFARE

Finland's health score is very solid (some argue that the Finnish invention of the sauna has contributed to high health levels). The social-welfare system is modeled on that of Sweden. High unemployment, however, clouds the rosy picture.

ACHIEVEMENTS

In the not-too-distant past, Finnish rated low as a language. People "of culture" in Finland spoke Swedish among themselves; books were always published in Swedish. After World War II, however, a linguistic battle concluded in the removal of the stigma that Finnish carried. Finland has become a favorite destination for summer music festivals.

France (French Republic)

GEOGRAPHY

Area in Square Miles (Kilometers): 213,700 (547,026) (about twice the size of Colorado)

Capital (Population): Paris (9,523,000)

Environmental Concerns: acid rain; air and water pollution

Geographical Features: mostly flat plains or gently rolling hills in the north and west; the remainder is mountainous

Climate: temperate

PEOPLE

Population

Total: 58,805,000

Annual Growth Rate: 0.31%

Rural/Urban Population Ratio: 26/74

Major Languages: French, with rapidly declining regional languages (Provençal, Breton, Alsatian, Corsican, Catalán, Basque, and Flemish)

Ethnic Makeup: Celtic and Latin with Teutonic, Slavic, North African, Indochinese, and Basque minorities

Religions: 90% Roman Catholic; 2% Protestant; 1% Jewish; 1% Muslim; 6% unaffiliated

Health

Life Expectancy at Birth: 74 years (male); 82 years (female)

Infant Mortality Rate (Ratio): 5.8/1,000

Average Caloric Intake: 134% of FAO minimum

Physicians Available (Ratio): 1/361

Education

Adult Literacy Rate: 99%

Compulsory (Ages): 6–16; free

COMMUNICATION

Telephones: 1 per 1.8 people

Daily Newspaper Circulation: 237 per 1,000 people

Televisions: 1 per 1.7 people

TRANSPORTATION

Highways in Miles (Kilometers): 535,500 (892,500)

Railroads in Miles (Kilometers): 21,273 (32,027)

Usable Airfields: 473

Motor Vehicles in Use: 29,500,000

GOVERNMENT

Type: unitary republic

Independence: A.D. 486 (unified by Clovis)

Head of State/Government: President Jacques Chirac; Prime Minister Lionel Jospin

Political Parties: Rally for the Republic; Union for French Democracy; Republican Party; Democratic Force; Radical Party; Socialist Party; Communist Party; National Front; others

Suffrage: universal at 18

MILITARY

Military Expenditures (% of Central Government Expenditures): 2.5%

Current Disputes: minor territorial disputes

ECONOMY

Currency ($ U.S. Equivalent): 5.41 francs = $1

Per Capita Income/GDP: $22,700/$1.32 trillion

GDP Growth Rate: 2.3%

Inflation Rate: 2%

Unemployment Rate: 12.4%

Labor Force: 25,500,000

Natural Resources: coal; iron ore; bauxite; fish; timber; zinc; potash

Agriculture: beef; dairy products; wheat; cereals; sugar beets; potatoes; wine grapes; fish

Industry: steel; machinery; textiles; chemicals; automobiles; food processing; metallurgy; aircraft; mining; electronics; tourism

Exports: $275 billion (primary partners Germany, Italy, United Kingdom)

Imports: $256 billion (primary partners Germany, Italy, United States)

http://www.odci.gov/cia/publications/factbook/country-frame.html

http://portal.research.bell-labs.com/cgi-wald/dbaccess/411?key=83

A LENGTHY HISTORY

Until the reunification of the two Germanys, France was the largest country in modern Western Europe. Its history dates back many millennia, although it would be somewhat unrealistic to claim that it started in 40,000 B.C., when people left traces of their culture in stone monuments and on the walls of caves, since there is no clear connection between these rudimentary civilizations and subsequent developments, which rely on records rather than inference. The period around 1200 B.C. seems a more likely starting point for tracing France's history. At that juncture, the Gauls, a large tribe related to the Celts, settled in what is now called France.

One of the oldest sources on Gaul, as the area came to be called, was a Roman general, Julius Caesar, who aimed at extending the Roman Empire to the north between 60 and 50 B.C. Since he also had political ambitions, he recorded his forays and battles in Gaul in his book *de Bello Gallico*. The Gauls—if one goes by Caesar's account—were determined and ferocious fighters, but once they had been decisively beaten, they allowed their area to be incorporated into the Roman Empire. Only after the fall of the West Roman Empire, several centuries later, did the Gauls regain a measure of independence.

MONARCHISM

The history of France was for a long time the history of kingdoms. The French monarchy was, from the sixth century until its final demise in the nineteenth century, the equivalent of absolutism and despotism.

The four best-known monarchs of that era are Charlemagne, Henri IV, Louis XIV, and Napoleon Bonaparte. Charlemagne, solemnly crowned in a cathedral in A.D. 800, ruled an empire that was considerably larger than present-day France. He was, in fact, called the "Emperor of the Western World," a title that expresses the notion of the illusory Holy Roman Empire.

Like many other parts of Europe, France was rocked by religious strife in the sixteenth century. When the French throne was vacated and Henri of Navarre's Protestantism stood in the way of his succession, he simply announced, "*Paris vaut bien une messe*," which implied, "Becoming king is well worth my conversion to Roman Catholicism." In spite of this crass opportunism, the king who came to be known as Henri IV was one of France's most popular kings.

The seventeenth century witnessed the power and the glory of Louis XIV. The so-called Sun King was extremely fond of games. During one of the matches (which, remarkably, he always won), one of his ministers reminded him that they had still to discuss matters of state. Louis XIV, taken aback, retorted, *L'état, c'est moi* ("The state, it is I"), a phrase that has gone down in history as the most concise definition of absolutism.

And then there is perhaps the most illustrious Frenchman of all time. Napoleon Bonaparte wrought havoc in all of Europe. Although he was an offshoot of the French Revolution, which attempted to do away with monarchy and aristocracy, he reestablished monarchical splendor. Indeed, even after Napoleon's defeat, monarchy and republicanism alternated. Monarchism disappeared permanently only after Napoleon III, Bonaparte's nephew, had plunged France into despair and defeat at the hands of the Prussian armies in 1870. Even today, many Frenchmen and -women, while paying lip service to democratic principles, are ready to condone rather than condemn "Bonapartism," the tendency on the part of strong political leaders to be careless when it comes to observing democratic rules. Some consider such negligence a necessity since, in their opinion, it is, at least in France, the only alternative to chaos.

THE SUCCESSIVE REPUBLICS

French history since the watershed year of 1870, when the monarchy disappeared from the scene, has generally been divided into the Third Republic (1870–1940), the Fourth Republic (1946–1958), and the Fifth Republic (1958–present). These ordinal numbers do not reflect random phases; they correspond to the respective Constitutions that obtained in the periods concerned.

The Third Republic ended as it began: as a result of German aggression. It was marked by a high degree of partitocracy, which led to legislative supremacy. Nothing was achieved as a result of the balance between left and right and of the endless disputes between Catholics and anticlericals. Thus, its nickname "the stalemate society" appeared to be well deserved. In fact, the Third Republic exemplified both the need for and the distrust of the strong state that French people so often experience. The centralization that the absolute monarchy had manifested continued not only because the various *départements* ("departments") were governed by prefects who were all appointed by the Ministry of the Interior in the capital, but also because Paris became the hub of the railway network.

During the interwar years (1920–1940), the French population declined, a fact often attributed to the colossal losses suffered during World War I. While France recovered from the German onslaught in 1914, beat the Germans back, and emerged victorious from the Great War, the cost in young male lives had a prolonged effect.

World War II, which ominously loomed behind Adolf Hitler's expansionist tactics, found France poorly prepared and poorly equipped. A little more than a month after the German armies had forced their way through the Low Countries, France surrendered. A small band of French officers and soldiers, headed by General Charles de Gaulle, managed to escape to England, where the Free French Movement was founded. The vanquished France they left behind was divided into two parts. One part was occupied by the German armies, and the other, named *État Français* ("French State," better known as *Vichy*), was rendered a German satellite. Resistance groups soon sprouted in both areas; these illegal forces gradually grew and greatly undermined the German war effort. On the other hand, many French people, mesmerized by the 1940 defeat, and some sympathetic with Nazi Germany's anti-Semitism, sought solace in cooperating with the Germans. This was particularly the case in Vichy. To France, the war ended when the Germans were expelled from its area in the latter half of 1944. A bitter debate remains to this day as to how much responsibility France should assume for the crimes and collaboration of the Vichy regime.

After World War II, a provisional government, semi-military in nature and often referred to as a "constitutional dictatorship," emerged, headed by de Gaulle. During the next 2 years, frequent clashes occurred between those who had helped to liberate France from outside (the so-called Free French) and those who had served the French cause in German-occupied or Nazi-oriented areas (the Resistance). All French people, however, were looking forward to the creation of the Fourth Republic. General de Gaulle expressed his distaste for Third Republic politics on numerous occasions, notably in his celebrated Bayeux Speech, in which he announced his ideas on how France was to be governed.

The Fourth Constitution, however, must have disappointed him, because it was almost a replica of the Third. And although it met with little enthusiasm on the part of the French public, it was nevertheless adopted. De Gaulle decided instantly to retire from political life. The period that followed turned out to be exactly as de Gaulle had predicted, characterized by prolonged party strife and a series of ineffectual governments.

The Fourth Republic was also plagued by great colonial crises. First, successive governments attempted for 8 years (1946–1954) to restore French rule to what used to be French Indochina. In this first Vietnam war, France failed miserably. It ended its involvement after military defeat.

The French hoped to be more successful in an area closer to France—Algeria, which was officially designated as an "overseas department" rather than as a colony. Algeria was the home not only of the native Arab population but also of hundreds and thousands of French settlers. As is the case in colonial societies, discrimination was rampant. Now that Algerian self-determination was in the offing, the French settlers feared that once the tables were turned, the former colonial subjects would seek revenge. First there were skirmishes and then regular battles between the nationalists among the native Arab population and the French Army. Nevertheless, the French settlers found their protection insufficient and established a secret army (the OAS).

The Algerian crisis brought about the demise of the Fourth Republic. De Gaulle, when called back from his self-imposed exile, indicated that he was willing to resolve this crisis but that he should be given powers greater than the Fourth Constitution yielded. In other words, the French political leadership of that time was blackmailed into agreeing to a new Constitution that would carry de Gaulle's imprimatur. Michel Debré, a lawyer and close friend of the general, was entrusted with the task of putting the Fifth Constitution together. Predictably, it closely followed de Gaulle's preferences, doing away with the power of political parties, their coalitions, and, above all, legislative supremacy. It gave considerable powers to the executive branch of government, particularly to the office of the president. As soon as the Fifth Constitution was completed, it was adopted by referendum, after which de Gaulle was, almost automatically, elected the first president of the Fifth Republic.

Government by Referendum
Since the new Constitution rendered the French Legislature very weak—indeed, almost insignificant—there was no reason to bypass it. Still, de Gaulle developed a predilection for government by referendum, a device that bordered on violation of the Fifth Constitution. Rather than have the Legislature discuss legislative proposals, he would couch these in a referendum, which he would submit to the French people. He would explain his proposal to the nation in a televised speech, stressing the importance of voting "yes" to the referendum. Sometimes he would threaten to step down should the proposal not pass. A not-inconsiderable number of people would vote in favor of the referendum, fearing that if they did not, the country might fall

(Photo courtesy Lisa Clyde)

The spires of the Cathedral of Notre-Dame at Chartres, located at the top of a hill in the ancient town, soar above the houses on the small streets. The main part of the cathedral was built in the mid-thirteenth century. This cathedral illustrates the all-encompassing presence of the Roman Catholic Church in the daily lives of citizens in medieval France.

prey to chaos again, as had been the situation in the period preceding de Gaulle's coming to power.

The Evian Accords
One of the first points that de Gaulle addressed was the termination of colonialism and imperialism. The so-called Union Française was abolished, and a global referendum was designed that allowed all dependencies and former dependencies to become members of a new French Community. This new organization resembled the British Commonwealth of Nations.

Contrary to what many people had been led to expect, de Gaulle did not use the sword in order to bring the Algerian rebellion to an end. He appeared to recognize the forces of history and started to negotiate with the nationalist leadership of the former overseas department. It took 4 years to arrive at some agreement, but finally, in 1962, the ac-

cords that declared Algeria completely independent were signed at Evian. A large proportion of the settlers in Algeria were disappointed with the outcome, in which they had had no voice; they left the country in droves and settled in southern France (most of them had never even been in France before).

De Gaulle generally contributed certain biases to the operation of the new Fifth Republic government that were distinctly anti-British and anti-American. If the former surfaced in his repeated refusal to allow Britain into the European Union (then known as the European Community), the latter was clearly evidenced by his objection to and obstruction of American hegemony in the North Atlantic Treaty Organization. Some analysts attribute de Gaulle's hostility vis-à-vis Britain and the United States to the war years, when he felt slighted by Winston Churchill and Franklin Roosevelt, who excluded him from their meetings.

Sometimes it could seem that France simply wanted to go its own way. In de Gaulle's view, it seemed destined to become the leader of the third force—that is, a Europe that would not participate in the deadly confrontation between the United States and the Soviet Union. These notions caused the French president to order the North Atlantic Treaty Organization to move its headquarters out of Paris and to minimize the French contribution to this U.S.–sponsored collective-security pact. Indeed, in 1966, de Gaulle withdrew all French troops from the integrated military command of NATO (although 60,000 remained stationed in West Germany). Paradoxically, France continued to claim the right to attend NATO's political meetings. In 1992, Pierre Joxe, the French defense minister, indicated that, although there was no chance that France would return to NATO's integrated military command, his country would like to "take part more fully than previously in politico-military discussions." Later in the 1990s, President Jacques Chirac initiated discussions with NATO on possible French reintegration into NATO's military structure. France has actively participated in recent peacekeeping operations. In May 1997, Paris hosted the NATO–Russia summit for the Founding Act on Mutual Relations, Cooperation, and Security.

The French–German Rapprochement
As an actor on the world scene, de Gaulle regularly committed gaffes that caused analysts to think that he lacked the diplomatic skills required for the presidency. It was clear that the general was far less interested in diplomatic niceties than in getting his message across. To do him justice, however, it must be noted that his monumental achievement—a French–German rapprochement—has certainly found its place in history. De Gaulle's opposite number in West Germany, Konrad Adenauer, belonged more or less to the same age group. In spite of the language barrier, both statesmen appeared to like each other very much. Without de Gaulle's initiative and without the leaders' mutual sympathy, this unprecedented rapprochement would never have been achieved between the two nations, which had for a long time been hostile toward each other. The French–German rapprochement has to all intents and purposes been a major factor in the emergence of the "new Europe" (which ultimately led to the European Union).

Social Problems
If most French people appeared to like France's increasingly isolationist stance in international politics, other issues produced dissent. Very little had been done to adapt university curricula to modern times. Most learning was still geared toward life as it had been half a century or a century before. It had no relevance to society as it had developed, and as a result, many university graduates remained unemployed for prolonged periods of time. Repeated petitions to the government had no effect, and, in 1968, large-scale student rebellions erupted, mainly in Paris but also in other parts of the country. Street fights were the order of the day, and the police were unable to arrest the rebels, who barricaded themselves on the Left Bank and in the heart of Paris. Although de Gaulle had been forewarned that trouble was brewing, he had left on a scheduled state visit to Romania. Georges Pompidou, the premier at the time, had great difficulty in coping with what came to be known as the "student revolt," especially once Renault automotive workers decided to throw in their lot with the students. De Gaulle thus had to be called back from Bucharest. Yet, even after his television address upon his return to Paris, the rebellious acts did not immediately cease. The combined student and worker revolt, which is often referred to by the euphemism *les événements* ("the events"), made it clear that de Gaulle had lost part of his charisma, if not his grip. Some analysts have concluded that the 1968 events may have caused the president to decide to retire. He did so in 1969, appearing to accept the verdict of the people as expressed in a referendum on constitutional reform. That was the first referendum he lost, and conceivably de Gaulle wanted it that way.

THE POST–DE GAULLE ERA
In the contest that developed as to who would be his successor, François Mitterrand, the leader of the French Socialist Party (PSF), competed for the first time. Interestingly, de Gaulle gave only lukewarm political support to Georges Pompidou, the man who had been his faithful co-pilot (in a press interview, de Gaulle had once argued that, ideally, the premier should serve the president as a "co-pilot").

Pompidou nevertheless won the election, and as president never departed from *Gaullisme*. However, his tenure was fairly brief, since he died in office before his first term had run its course. New elections were held in 1974, and the Socialist Party again made Mitterrand its presidential candidate. The Gaullist contender now was Valéry Giscard d'Estaing, who had been part of de Gaulle's administration. Giscard won. As a former minister of finance, he endeavored to find solutions to the financial and economic problems associated with the changing nature of the French economy. At the end of his term, however, the French economy was still behind those of other European Union (then known as the European Community) members.

A more serious drawback to reelection, however, was Giscard's personality. He was by nature an elitist who made little effort to ingratiate himself with the public at large. In 1981, he again ran against Mitterrand, an outgoing man who radiated bonhomie, and this time he lost.

Mitterrand had intermittently aligned himself with the French Communist Party (PCF). In order to avoid fierce competition between the two leftist parties, the Union of the Left had put together a *Programme Commun*, which in effect served as a joint platform. Mitterrand consequently had to share his victory with Communists. Four ministerial posts were given to the PCF leadership, and the new premier, Pierre Mauroy, belonged to the left wing of the Socialist Party. The four ministerial posts, to be sure, were of lesser importance; but, by the same token, the cabinet was less moderate than many people had anticipated.

The early part of the Mitterrand administration was marked by large-scale nationalization and increased government spending. It soon became obvious that these measures were no remedies to the lingering economic ills and, after 4 years, the president appointed a young economist, Laurent Fabius, to be his premier. The latter was in actuality a technocrat, not given to ideological stands.

The Communists strenuously objected to this move, correctly perceiving Fabius's appointment as a shift toward the center, or at least as a departure from the Programme Commun. When Mitterrand did not yield to their arguments, the Union of the Left collapsed and the Communists left their ministerial posts.

The government was thus entirely in Socialist hands. Fabius, however, was given little time to implement his remedies. Parliamentary elections were held in early 1986, and they clearly evidenced a revulsion with socialism. The major contender on the right was Jacques Chirac, the mayor of Paris, who called himself a "neo-Gaullist." Socialists and Communists saw their support in Parliament reduced to such an extent that a different cabinet, headed by another premier, had to be established. (In the late 1990s, Fabius and two of his former ministers made headlines around the world when they were charged with manslaughter and criminal negligence as part of a long-running scandal about HIV-contaminated blood. Fabius and Georgina Dufoix, who was his social-affairs minister, were acquitted; former health minister Edmond Herve was convicted but not sentenced. The trial was interpreted by many as a reluctance in France to hold those in elected office to account.)

Chirac, who (predictably) accepted the post, initially insisted that Mitterrand step down and that new elections be held for the office of president, as the government might otherwise be unworkable. France's Fifth Constitution, however, lacks clarity on this point. Its founding fathers apparently did not foresee the anomalous situation emerging from elections scheduled at different points in time. As a result, intragovernmental backbiting played a large part in the final years of Mitterrand's first term. The Fifth Constitution was then severely tested, since political conflict was the order of the day in these 2 years of *cohabitation* (as the forced cooperation between two opposing blocs—or, rather, the lack of same—came to be called). So divided was the French government that both the Socialist president and the Conservative premier appeared at international conferences to which France had been invited, occasionally debating each other! And when the presidential elections of 1988 approached, Chirac announced that he would run.

The incumbent remained silent, indicating that he would indeed be a candidate only a few months before the actual election was to take place. Since the Socialist candidate was reelected, one may assume that the period of cohabitation had worked to Mitterrand's advantage. More important, Mitterrand's record had overall been a fairly positive one, in spite of the strident claims by Chirac to the contrary. It is true that the economy left much to be desired, but in France (as in many other countries), the adage prevails that "There is no final victory in economics."

Foreign Relations
On the international scorecard, the Socialist government had done well. The closer bonds with West Germany, established in de Gaulle's time, continued to be emphasized now that both countries had experienced an ideological reversal (France had moved to the left, West Germany to the right). And, most ironically, socialism proved to be less anti-American than might have been expected. The noticeable improvement of the French–American relationship appeared to coincide with France becoming more amenable in NATO matters. Washington was also impressed with the way in which France defended Chad, its former colony, against Libyan aggression. In addition, the country lost 58 men, killed in an Islamic Jihad terrorist suicide attack in Lebanon.

On the other hand, France proved unwilling to conform to nuclear testing standards. To be sure, it had never signed the Nuclear Test Ban Treaty, and its traditional nuclear testing in the South Pacific did incur the anger and annoyance of a great many nations, notably those in the Southern Hemisphere. In the port of Auckland, New Zealand, in July 1985, an explosion caused the sinking of the *Rainbow Warrior*, the flagship of the Greenpeace environmental movement, which had been scheduled to obstruct French nuclear testing farther east. Suspicions were immediately aroused that the French government might be involved. These suspicions were later confirmed, and the French were forced to pay a large compensation. Surprisingly, the incident never became an issue in the election campaign a few years later. More recently, the French government suddenly decided to sign the Nuclear Non-Proliferation Treaty. It is possible that this move was inspired by Iraq's attempts to avail itself of nuclear weaponry.

After Mitterrand was reelected, he dissolved the Parliament and ordered new legislative elections to be held. These did not grant the president's party a majority, but the Socialists were now at least Parliament's largest group. (The Socialists were short of a majority in the 577-seat National Assembly, but they could only be ousted from government if the Communists teamed up with the Conservatives, which appeared unlikely.)

This time Mitterrand's hand was not forced, and he chose Michel Rocard to be his fourth premier. Rocard was a technocrat who preferred practicable policies. The appointment served another function as well, in that it clearly separated the presidential and prime-ministerial fields of concern. Rocard was chiefly interested in domestic policies, whereas Mitterrand had started to move into foreign affairs. Both men worked closely together but did not attempt to influence, let alone override, each other.

The president maintained the firm and amicable relationship with West Germany that had puzzled many American (and European!) observers. He also paid a state visit to the United States, strengthening the bonds with the country that had been the target of snide remarks on the part of de Gaulle. But during the second Mitterrand administration, new foreign policy facets developed. The president's interest in the European Union, which had grown by leaps and bounds, stabilized at a very high level, causing some analysts to believe that France was destined for leadership within the EU. However, the increased French interest should be attributed in part to the fact that the Union had started to be headed by Jacques Delors, an extremely active Frenchman who looked forward to the Union's target—that is, the time when there would be a single European market.

To some extent Mitterrand also reversed the traditional pro-Arab policy that had characterized French attitudes and sentiments vis-à-vis the Middle East. It was not Iraq's 1990 invasion of Kuwait by itself but, rather, the massive hostage-taking and the way in which French citizens were treated in Baghdad and Kuwait that caused France to join those who had organized themselves militarily against Iraq.

Ultimately, Mitterrand was the only president to serve two terms. When he died of cancer in 1995, he was eulogized by members of the political left and right alike.

THE EXECUTIVE
France, like many other Western European democracies, has a dual executive. The position of chief of state is taken by the president. Departing from the tradition of the Third and Fourth Republics, the president under the Fifth Republic does not merely have a ceremonial role but actually exercises a great deal of power. The president is elected for a term of 7 years and, as the 1988 election exemplified, may be reelected. Most analysts believe that with the Fifth Constitution, France has taken a big step in the direction of the presidential system. However, the relationship between president and premier is a delicate one, depending on the degree of forcefulness that emanates from the respective incumbents of these offices. This is evidenced by the responses of the public that the various premiers inspire. The fact that a great deal of criticism erupted around France's first female premier, Edith Cresson, indicates that Mitterrand left her a lot of leeway. The succeeding premier, Pierre Bérégovoy, seemed lackluster, but it is entirely possible that he influenced the political system in a more subtle manner. Ultimately, however, he proved no match for the withering attacks from the opposition, and he committed suicide. The subsequent premier was Edouard Balladur, a former minister of finance.

The president's executive powers are shared with the premier, also known as the chairperson of the Council of Ministers (cabinet). The Fifth Constitution discusses the policy areas of these top executives in broad terms yet establishes no clear demarcation. Yet it is obvious that the premier, who is supposed to "direct the

Louis XIV becomes king of France 1651	Outbreak of the French Revolution 1789	Napoleon is defeated; the Congress of Vienna 1815	The fall of the Second Empire; the founding of the Third Republic 1870

operation of government" and to "ensure the execution of the laws," is in fact subordinate to the president. Thus, the premier's task in effect consists of particularizing the policies that the chief of state has outlined. As was mentioned earlier, de Gaulle considered the relationship between the premier and the president as co-pilotage. But then, de Gaulle actually claimed all policy-making powers for himself and allowed his premier only to implement them. And even during Giscard's presidency, a premier resigned, disgusted with the role of puppet.

The premier is appointed by the president. However, the latter is not completely free in his or her choice, since the premier and the Council of Ministers should reflect the strength of the various political parties in the National Assembly.

THE LEGISLATURE
The French Parliament is bicameral. The more important chamber is the National Assembly, whose 577 members are directly elected. In the 1993 legislative elections, the anti-Socialist forces won 80 percent of the National Assembly's seats. The Senate, which has less important duties, has 274 members, who are indirectly elected for 9-year terms. In the past, it was possible for members of the government to be members of Parliament as well. The Fifth Constitution, however, rules this out, though it allows members of the government to have access to the two assemblies. Parliamentary powers have been greatly reduced in the Fifth Constitution. Gone are the days of legislative supremacy that haunted the Third and Fourth Republics. Not only is it no longer possible for the National Assembly to topple the government, but its tasks are strictly circumscribed. Thus, although Article 34 of the Constitution states blandly that "All laws shall be passed by the Parliament," the Legislature is in fact empowered only to tackle legislation within certain specified policy areas.

An interesting feature, no doubt blown over from England, is the provision that states, "One meeting a week shall be reserved, by priority, for questions asked by members of Parliament and for answers by the Government."

THE ECONOMY
Today, France is among the top Western industrialized economies. Government policy stresses promotion of investment and maintenance of fiscal and monetary discipline. The French economy has traditionally been based on two major strands: *paysantisme* and *dirigisme*. The former concept constitutes the emotional relationship of the French with the soil, the source of all produce, a relationship that has persisted through times of industrialization. Thus President Giscard could, in a 1977 speech, refer to agriculture as *pétrole vert* ("green oil"), a national asset of supreme value.

Dirigisme has in effect been a concurrent theme, instituted as early as the seventeenth century, when Jean-Baptiste Colbert introduced his system of mercantilism to the statecraft of King Louis XIV. Colbert hoped that government intervention, which gradually became entrapped in a host of regulations and bureaucratic devices, would ultimately benefit the country. A century later, mercantilism was attacked by the physiocrats, who combined governmental direction with an emphasis on nature.

In the mid-twentieth century, Keynesianism became a beacon to many French economists, even if in detail they departed from the original conclusions that its founder had established. Upon taking office in 1981, Mitterrand embarked upon more-than-moderate government spending in order to cure the sagging economy. That, too, may have been inspired by the lessons of John Maynard Keynes.

France also offers many contemporary examples of the practice of state involvement in industries. Although de Gaulle paid lip service to laissez-faire principles (it is ironic that this term originated in a country that has persistently preferred statism), he introduced heavy and basic industries that were to be controlled by the bureaucracy. In the context of contemporary examples of government interference, one may also point to nationalizations, which as a matter of course extend state control. Even leading companies such as Thomson and Rhone Poulenc have come to be nationalized (although in the cases cited, the motivation may have differed from the traditional ones—infusions of public capital were made in industries weakened by the oil crises of the 1970s).

It may even be possible to detect institutionalized statism in the establishment of the Economic and Social Council. It was intended as an advisory body, but its foundation is nevertheless symptomatic of governmental interest. A much stronger case may be made for the Planning Commission, which has churned out government plans since the mid-1950s. There is ample evidence that the French economy is thoroughly planned nowadays, even when a centrist or right-wing executive presides in the Elysée Palace. For the past 30 years, planning has been necessitated by France's membership in the European Union. (It is possible that then–British prime minister Margaret Thatcher was subtly referring to France when she argued in 1988 that allowing Great Britain to integrate politically into the EU would be tantamount to "introducing socialism by stealth.") France has coped remarkably well with the changes wrought on its economy in an extraordinarily brief period. It is also true, though, that, overall, the country has lagged behind other industrializing democracies in its march toward postindustrialism.

Statistics reveal that only half a century ago, the country was still basically agrarian. The proportion of the workforce employed in the agricultural sector exceeded that of those working in industry (in 1939, these percentages were 37 and 30 respectively). Currently, the proportion of the workforce engaged in industry is nearly 4 times that of the agricultural workforce (the percentages are approximately 35 and 10).

It is certainly remarkable to find France entering the postindustrial era, if one considers that the rural exodus took place only after World War II. At that time, farm mechanization made itself felt, and literally millions of people left the small rural communities in search of city jobs. The postindustrial era will undoubtedly have sociopolitical implications. The numbers of workers in the old industries are bound to decline. There will probably be a rise of a white-collar, better-educated working class, a trend that will likely further hurt the Communist Party.

While France is currently the largest food producer and food exporter in Western Europe, there can be little doubt that, in the not-too-distant future, it also will be one of the larger industrial powers. French industry is highly advanced in computer science and in telecommunications. France also has the world record as far as nuclear energy consumption is con-

The end of the Third Republic; France is defeated by Germany; World War II
1940–1945

The founding of the Fourth Republic
1946

The Fifth Republic is founded by General De Gaulle
1958

Students and autoworkers revolt
1968

De Gaulle leaves office
1969

François Mitterrand is elected as the first Socialist president under the Fifth Constitution
1981

The Socialist cabinet is phased out and replaced by a right-wing cabinet; cohabitation
1986

Mitterrand is reelected; the right-wing cabinet is replaced by a center-left cabinet
1988

1990s

Jacques Chirac wins the presidency; right-wing extremism gains a boost when Jean-Marie LePen wins 15% of the vote

Alain Juppe and then Lionel Jospin serve as prime minister

Protests mount: thousands of farmers demonstrate against EU agricultural policies; thousands of teenagers demonstrate against the *lycee* system

cerned: More than 70 percent of all its energy derives from nuclear energy.

The overall picture of the French economy would be very rosy if it were not for the high unemployment rate. Like a number of other Western European countries, France has witnessed a veritable invasion of foreign workers. Most of them arrived in the 1960s, when there was a strong need for extra laborers. The majority of guest workers in France came from former French colonies, notably Morocco, Algeria, and Tunisia. To most of the foreign workers, the culture shock was somewhat mitigated by the fact that, as a rule, they had had a foretaste of French culture and often spoke the language. Nevertheless, the ultra right wing, notably the National Front, attempts to make political capital out of their presence. Arousing French ethnocentric and xenophobic sentiments in recent elections, it has argued that the foreign workers increase French unemployment and has recommended that they be sent back to where they came from.

RECENT DEVELOPMENTS
In 1992, the Maastricht Treaty (the Treaty on Political and Economic Union), endangered by a negative referendum outcome in Denmark, was rescued when a similar referendum in France resulted in 51 percent favoring the treaty, with 49 percent opposing it. Certainly this was a very small majority, but the majority in Denmark that rejected large parts of the treaty was even weaker. In subsequent years, France has continued to display ambivalence about the European Union and its goals, though it plays a central role in the organization.

The extent of presidential power in France made the outcome of the 1995 presidential election extremely important, not only to France, but also to the European Union and the world. In the first round of the election process, on April 23,

1995, Socialist Lionel Jospin got the most votes, with 23.3 percent, a surprise even to his own pollsters. In a very close battle for second place, Paris mayor Jacques Chirac edged out Premier Edouard Balladur, with 20.8 percent and 18.6 percent respectively. Among right-wing candidates, National Front leader Jean-Marie Le Pen won 15 percent of the vote, and Philippe de Villiers won 4.7 percent. This showing was the highest for the far right in Europe since the end of World War II. On the left, Communist, Trotskyite, and environmental candidates won a total of 17.2 percent. The run-off election was held on May 7, between the two leaders, Jospin and Chirac. As most polls had predicted, the run-off was won by Chirac.

Although most French people consider the spontaneous and charming Chirac quite likeable (he's called Grand Jacques), the government has appeared rather directionless during his presidency. The economy has improved somewhat during his years in office, but there are many trouble spots. Unemployment is particularly of concern: It runs 27 percent among people under age 25, and more than 12 percent overall. Chirac has had some achievements, including implementing measures to end conscription and streamline the armed forces, overhaul the public-health system, and sell off or deregulate parts of the public sector. But it is not clear whether he or his prime ministers have been responsible for these accomplishments.

During his first two years in office, President Chirac's prime minister was Alain Juppe, the leader of Chirac's party, the neo-Gaullist Rally for the Republic. Chirac and Juppe benefited form a very large majority in the National Assembly (470 out of 577 seats). In order to ensure that France met the Maastricht criteria for the single European currency (to bolster the franc's stability and strength), and

mindful that the government might have to take politically costly decisions in advance of the legislative elections planned for spring 1998, Chirac decided in April 1997 to call early elections. This impulse turned out to be rash. The left, led by Jospin, the Socialist Party's leader, unexpectedly won a solid National Assembly majority (319 seats, with 289 required for an absolute majority) in the two rounds of balloting, which took place May 25 and June 1, 1997. President Chirac named Jospin prime minister on June 2, and Jospin went on to form a government composed primarily of Socialist ministers, along with some ministers from allied parties of the left, such as the Communists and the Greens.

The tradition in periods of cohabitation is for the president to exercise the primary role in foreign and security policy, with the dominant role in domestic policy falling to the prime minister and his or her government. Prime Minister Jospin has stated, however, that he will not leave any domain exclusively to the president, though President Chirac still claims to have the "final word" regarding foreign and security issues.

DEVELOPMENT

Until World War II, France was still largely agrarian, with little industry. This has changed, particularly under de Gaulle, who emphasized heavy and basic industries. France is now entering the postindustrial era.

FREEDOM

France ranks high in Humana's human-rights rating. However, French government has become somewhat arbitrary in matters of asylum of refugees. The strength of several far-right groups that are venomously anti-Semitic and anti-immigrant is disturbing to many observers both within and outside of France

HEALTH/WELFARE

France has a welfare system that includes health care. However, patients have to pay for health services first and subsequently have 80% of charges reimbursed. Under the welfare system, all French people have 5 weeks of paid vacation annually.

ACHIEVEMENTS

France has traditionally been known for its cultural sophistication. Several Nobel Prizes have been won by French scholars and authors. France has also become very advanced in computer, space, and telecommunications technology.

Germany

GEOGRAPHY

Area in Square Miles (Kilometers): 139,412 (356,853) (about the size of Montana)

Capital (Population): Berlin (3,317,000)

Environmental Concerns: air and water pollution; acid rain; hazardous-waste disposal

Geographical Features: lowlands in the north; uplands in the center; Bavarian Alps in the south

Climate: temperate

PEOPLE

Population

Total: 82,079,500

Annual Growth Rate: 0.02%

Rural/Urban Population Ratio: 13/87

Major Language: German

Ethnic Makeup: 92% German; 2% Turkish, 6% others

Religions: 38% Protestant; 34% Roman Catholic; 28% unaffiliated or other

Health

Life Expectancy at Birth: 74 years (male); 80 years (female)

Infant Mortality Rate (Ratio): 5.3/1,000

Physicians Available (Ratio): 1/298

Education

Adult Literacy Rate: 99%

Compulsory (Ages): 6–15

COMMUNICATION

Telephones: 1 per 2 people

Daily Newspaper Circulation: 317 per 1,000 people

Televisions: 1 per 1.8 people

TRANSPORTATION

Highways in Miles (Kilometers): 379,800 (633,000)

Railroads in Miles (Kilometers): 26,380 (43,966)

Usable Airfields: 620

Motor Vehicles in Use: 43,600,000

GOVERNMENT

Type: federal republic

Independence Date: January 18, 1871 (German empire unification)

Head of State/Government: President Roman Herzog; Chancellor (Prime Minister) Gerhard Schroeder

Political Parties: Christian Democratic Union; Christian Social Union; Free Democratic Party; Social Democratic Party; Alliance '90/Greens; Party of Democratic Socialism

Suffrage: universal at 18

MILITARY

Military Expenditures (% of Central Government Expenditures): 1.5%

Current Disputes: none

ECONOMY

Currency ($ U.S. Equivalent): 1.60 marks = $1

Per Capita Income/GDP: $20,800/$1.74 trillion

GDP Growth Rate: 1.4%

Inflation Rate: 1.8%

Unemployment Rate: 12%

Labor Force: 38,700,000

Natural Resources: iron ore; coal; potash; timber, lignite; uranium; natural gas; salt; nickel

Agriculture: grains; potatoes; sugar beets; fruit; meat

Industry: iron; steel; coal; cement; chemicals; machinery; ship building; motor vehicles; food and beverages; machine tools; others

Exports: $521.1 billion (primary partners EU countries)

Imports: $455.7 billion (primary partners EU countries)

 http://www.odci.gov/cia/publications/factbook/country-frame.html
http://portal.research.bell-labs.com/cgi-wald/dbaccess/411?key=91

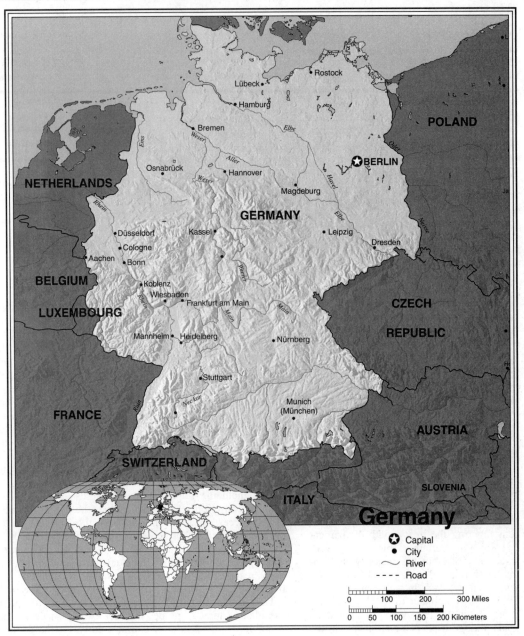

Germany

⭐ Capital
• City
〰 River
- - - Road

THE GERMAN IDENTITY PROBLEM

Of the larger and more important countries in Western Europe, Germany seems to be the one that is most afflicted by identity problems. It is possible that the German psyche has been hampered in its development by two related factors: On the one hand, the German nation (or at least the Germanic communities) is very old; whereas on the other hand, its experience in the nation-state format has been relatively brief.

There was but limited contact between the classical and the Germanic worlds, but some Roman records mention the existence of Germanic tribes living in the general area between the Ems and what is currently known as the Oder–Neisse border. The Roman province of Gaul, created in 51 B.C., extended to the Rhine River, which was regarded as an ethnic frontier. Nevertheless, the general area was extremely turbulent since, in addition to the earlier *Völkerwanderung* ("great migration"), there were other—smaller—population movements as well. The Roman historian Tacitus, who lived from A.D. 55 to 120, ventured some scathing observations. He believed that the Germans had not progressed a great deal in civilization. By way of proof, he noted that they were dressed in skins and armed with clubs. He also noted that the Germans had a penchant for war as well as for gambling. Indeed, so grievous was their addiction to the latter vice that, after losing all their worldly possessions, they would wager their family members.

Conversion to Christianity resulted from the unrelenting efforts of such missionaries as Boniface, an English monk (680–754). By then, German society had come to be politically organized as feudal units, which occasionally were loosely aligned. The tenth century A.D. witnessed further fragmentation, with the so-called rise of the duchies, the direct outcome of the Carolingian decision to leave defense in the hands of those attacked. This organization of defense on a local basis implied a clear decentralization of military command. By itself this could appear to be a usual trend in the Middle Ages, a time when danger, isolation, and the dearth of communications conspired to make every feudal unit fend for itself. However that may be, Germany took much longer to lift these limitations and to arrive at a semblance of unity. Religious warfare possibly played a role (the area currently known as Germany served as a battlefield in the prolonged strife between a variety of Protestant denominations and Roman Catholicism). Certainly the doctrine *cuius regio, eius religio,* which caused the religion of the ruler to be the prime determinant for the religion of the particular area, wrought havoc with whatever unity may have existed shortly after the Peace of Westphalia in 1648. The nation-state format soon became universal in Western Europe. While Germans, from medieval times, rendered significant contributions to the intellectual, cultural, musical, and artistic enrichment of Western Europe, they also suffered from grievous handicaps, in that the political landscape was barren. There were no states; small units were ruled by members of the aristocracy.

There was some dividing line in the past, as the northern set of states, mostly Protestant in religion, exhibited many characteristics that differed from those of the southern set of states, which were predominantly Roman Catholic. Although that line has become too blurred to continue to serve as a watershed, it may still be possible to note certain discrepancies between north and south Germany. Another enduring legacy may well be the preference that many Germans reputedly have for strong state authority—which in fact amounts to a penchant for authoritarianism. Psychologically, such a penchant may well have been a backlash against the powerlessness that the small states experienced over centuries of fragmentation.

But against the *Wille zur Macht,* as philosopher Friedrich Nietzsche called the impulse for power, one must also take into account the German definition of the *Rechtsstaat,* a state bound by laws, a concept that became the continental counterpart of the Anglo-American Rule of Law. It came to be formulated by Prussia, a unit east of the Elbe. Prussia had grown out of the Electorate of Brandenburg around the city of Berlin. Aided by its aristocracy, it became an important military power in the eighteenth century, excelling in such "Prussian virtues" as administrative efficiency (for a long time Prussia served as a model for Western bureaucracy) and governmental legalism. A couple of unification attempts were made in the course of the nineteenth century, possibly as a result of the efforts on the part of the Congress of Vienna to redraw the map of Europe.

Not surprisingly, Prussia, being in the vanguard of political change, started to become more and more insistent on unification. Finally, in 1871, Otto von Bismarck founded the Wilhelmine Empire, putting all the German states under one roof and under one ruler. Bismarck, who held the post of chancellor (the German term for prime minister) of Prussia, became chancellor of the new construction as well.

Typically, one of the first foreign-policy moves of the new Germany related to war. It is possible that Bismarck viewed this as the crucible, that he believed that no state should be standing on its own unless it was able to wage war. France, at that time headed by an emperor, was tricked into a conflict, and very soon the German armies massed against Paris. Napoleon III fled; in fact, the entire French government abandoned the capital. Needless to say, Germany was a clear victor in this war, the first major conflict between these two continental powers. There was more to come; indeed, France and Germany remained on terms of rivalry and occasional hostility for the next 8 decades. A Franco–German alliance came into being only in the 1950s.

In World War I, which France hoped would yield a revanche, England and eventually even the United States became involved. Now the German emperor fled, seeking asylum in the Netherlands, a neutral country. On November 11, 1918, an armistice was proclaimed. Germany had lost the war. (Refer to the regional essay for more information on World War I.)

The German Empire had come down with a bang, and what came in its stead was the Weimar Republic, founded in 1919. (It lasted until 1933.) Germany had been forced to cede territory and had to pay formidable amounts in reparations. As a result, its economy deteriorated even further. Against this backdrop, a little-known Austrian agitator named Adolf Hitler, who in 1923 had attempted a coup that had failed miserably (and for which he spent time in prison, during which he wrote his anti-Semitic manifesto *Mein Kampf*), started his steady ascent to power in Germany. He used to the utmost the bad economic conditions, which in his view derived from the Versailles *Diktat* (the dictated peace of 1919) and from alleged Jewish conspiracies. Gradually his National Socialist (Nazi) Party gained power. It never gained a majority during the Weimar years, but in elections in 1933, it received 34 percent of the vote. With the Communists (the Nazis' arch-enemy) it held a "negative majority"—that is, it could forestall or torpedo any policy designed by the moderate parties that were part of the government. Finally, President Paul von Hindenburg, then 86 years old, had no alternative but to appoint Hitler as chancellor. A new era had begun.

THE NAZI YEARS

Hitler was sworn in as chancellor on January 30, 1933, commencing 12 years that constituted a horrifying period for Germany and for the world. Believing that his aims would be better served through a highly centralized government apparatus,

Hitler immediately put an end to the federal form of government adopted by the Weimar Republic. His lust for power was evidenced by other measures as well. On the pretext that Communists had set fire to the Parliament building, Hitler declared a state of emergency only 2 months after having assumed office. The Weimar Constitution allowed him in that case to rule through emergency decrees, giving him extraordinary powers. This "emergency" was maintained until the very end of Hitler's reign (May 1945).

In foreign-policy matters, Hitler was drastic: He almost immediately tested the Allies' will to maintain and police the conditions of the Versailles Treaty. It soon became clear to him that France and Great Britain, not to mention the United States, were war-weary and reluctant to risk any conflict. While German strength was still below par, Hitler launched his march into the Saar, something the peace treaty had specifically prohibited. Gradually the chancellor (or *führer,* "leader," as his title had become) embarked upon two major strands of policy: 1) the building of a formidable army; and 2) the wholesale, state-sponsored elimination of the Jews of Europe. The first policy led to World War II. The second led to the Holocaust, the horrific period when the Nazis murdered 6 million European Jews and 5 million

other people. This period is discussed in greater detail in the regional essay.

Shortly before World War II began, Hitler concluded a nonaggression treaty with the Soviet Union. He feared that he would be preoccupied in the West and did not want to fight a war on two fronts. The areas that were incorporated into Germany before the war were Austria (which Hitler did not view as a real occupation; he regarded this as an *Anschluss*—a voluntary merger), Sudetenland, and, subsequently, Czechoslovakia in its entirety. After that, an amazing number of countries were invaded and occupied by Germany: Poland (1939, setting off World War II), Denmark and Norway (April 1940), the Low Countries (Belgium, the Netherlands, and Luxembourg, May 1940), and France (June 1940). Then came a pause, since the German armies did not succeed in invading England. But in April 1941, Hitler felt strong enough to fight on another front: Although he had not conquered Great Britain, he directed his attention eastward and invaded the Balkans, notably Yugoslavia and Greece. These countries too were conquered.

Finally, Operation Barbarossa (the name given to the plans for the German invasion of the Soviet Union) was launched, a little later than originally scheduled, that is, in June 1941. This move proved to be Hitler's

downfall, since what he had feared most—to have to fight on two fronts—now became a reality. It is possible that he had hoped that, like the campaign in the Balkans, Barbarossa would be of limited duration.

But it was not, and now two new factors became of prime importance. First, the Russian winter turned out to be considerably fiercer than the German Army leaders had anticipated; it forced the war machine to stop. Second, Japan had launched a war against the United States in December 1941, causing the European war to become a world war. Thus, the United States, which had refused to be dragged into the European theater, now found itself at war first with Japan but by implication also with the Third Reich. The Nazi empire had been at its largest when Japan entered the war, and although the hostilities were still to last more than 3 years, that period was marked by gradual diminution—the Soviet armies driving back the Nazis from the East, and the Anglo–American forces, after an invasion in Normandy had been staged, from the West. For Germany, the drama finally came to an end in May 1945: Hitler committed suicide in a bunker, besieged from all sides, having made not entirely successful attempts to transfer government to others outside Berlin. His ravaged armies, which, in desperation, had started to include youngsters and the

(Photo credit National Archives)

On January 30, 1933, following a steady rise to power in a time of economic turmoil, Adolf Hitler was sworn in as German chancellor. He immediately set about implementing radical domestic and foreign policies that eventually would fuel a world war and bring about the Holocaust, a genocide in which literally millions of Jews and other peoples were murdered.

physically handicapped, continued fighting. Often they were barely armed.

RENEWED DIVISION

Once the European war had become a world war, the Allied leaders, although globally scattered, were in frequent contact with one another, notably through a number of historic "summit" meetings (the term had yet to be coined) held in Cairo, Teheran, Yalta, and Potsdam. These conferences were intended to map out the course of the war. Thus it was soon agreed to concentrate the efforts on the European theater and to tackle Japan more fully later, once the war in Europe would be over.

In addition, these "war councils" fully considered the future—how the postwar world would be constructed. It was decided to establish zones of occupation for the time being. The Soviet armies coming from the East would be responsible for those parts of Germany and Austria that would come under their control when the Third Reich surrendered. Similarly, the armies coming from the West would institute American, British, and French zones of occupation. Berlin, the German capital, which would fall in the Soviet-occupied area, would become a miniature replica of Germany, in that it too would have four occupation zones.

Naturally, these measures would cause Germany to be divided, but they were believed to be only temporary. Little thought was given to the future of the vanquished Germans, although it was generally assumed that the Allies were not to benefit territorially from their victory.

However, within 2 years of the end of the war, the frequent friction between the Soviet Union and the United States had degenerated into what came to be known as the "cold war," a bitter enmity devoid of armed hostilities. This cold war diverted, if not eliminated, some of the vengeance and vindictiveness on the part of the victors vis-à-vis their former enemies. Thus, as early as 1947, the United States decided to include Germany (or at least the parts that were under the control of the United States, Great Britain, and France) among the recipients of Marshall Plan aid. This assistance scheme, the official name of which was the European Recovery Plan, provided goods and money to Western European countries devastated by the war, enabling their economies to recover. The U.S. secretary of state at that time, George Marshall, feared that these countries would otherwise be a ready prey for communism. The aid had initially been offered to some countries behind the Iron Curtain as well. But Moscow did not want any area that fell under its control to participate in the plan.

The Marshall Plan and the intensifying cold war caused growing alienation and disaffection between Central/Eastern and Western Europe, and thus between the two parts of Germany. The western part recovered economically in a remarkably short time. By contrast, the eastern part was plundered, its industry shipped to the Soviet Union. Officially, these acts were labeled "reparations."

The cold war also caused the two Germanys to develop extremely hostile attitudes toward each other. This was particularly the case once separate states had started to take the place of the occupation zones. In 1949, the United States wanted to include the western part of Germany in an alliance that was to prevent the Soviet Union from conquering all of Europe. Since only an independent country could be the buffer that the United States wanted, the U.S., British, and French occupation zones were united and converted into a new state, to be called the Federal Republic of Germany. Moscow followed suit with its eastern part, and soon the western and eastern sections of Germany had become incorporated as states in collective defense organizations (respectively, NATO and the Warsaw Pact).

East Germany—that is, the part that became the German Democratic Republic—was considerably smaller in area and in population than its Western counterpart. In addition, the Soviet Union annexed part of East Germany, and a large slice of eastern Germany was given to Poland in order to compensate that country for a slice of eastern Poland that the Soviet Union had incorporated into its body politic. These border "adjustments" have never been undone; as a consequence, hundreds of thousands of Germans born and raised in the eastern part of their country still find themselves living under the Polish or Russian government.

THE GENESIS OF MINORITY PATTERNS IN GERMANY

The Federal Republic of Germany (West Germany) not only exceeded the German Democratic Republic (East Germany) in prosperity, it soon also outstripped most Western European countries. West Germany's economic strength and prospects were such that it was invited to be a party to the Treaty of Rome in 1957, a pact that was to lead to the European Union. In that context, too, West Germany performed extremely well. In this period—the late 1950s and early 1960s—West Germany experienced its "economic miracle." No wonder that it developed into a magnet for the entire Eastern bloc, but particularly for the German Democratic Republic. After

all, whether one found oneself in the western or eastern part of Germany when the war ended was in effect an accident of war.

Some 3 million people fled from East Germany before the government of that country managed to prevent further flights by strengthening its border controls and shooting at persons who still attempted to flee. One of the favorite escape routes at the time was through Berlin. East Germans went to East Berlin (which had been declared the capital of East Germany) and then found their way to West Berlin; it was very easy to get from West Berlin to West Germany at that time. The population movement from East Germany to West Germany had been fairly gradual, which allowed the West German economy to absorb the newcomers. Indeed, there was still a great demand for labor, and West German industries started to attract workers from the entire Mediterranean basin, notably from Turkey. The so-called *Gastarbeiter* ("guest workers") were hired on a short-term basis, usually for 2 or 3 years. In reality, though, when their contracts expired, they were usually renewed. Many of them did not return to Turkey at all or did so only for a brief leave or vacation. The guest workers started to constitute minorities in West Germany who often failed to integrate into the German culture. Most of the Turks were also Muslim, another source of alienation from the overwhelmingly Christian host country.

Today there is a Turkish minority population of some 2 million, who live in parts of Berlin and other big cities in Germany. Friction between the guest-worker populations and Germans historically has become acute in times of economic stress. These tensions, however, appear minor when compared to the social and economic problems associated with asylum-seekers in the 1980s and 1990s. The "plane people," as they came to be called, hailed from a variety of countries in South Asia. Interflug, a Central/Eastern European airline with a dubious reputation, offered individuals one-way tickets to East Germany, ostensibly for the purpose of vacationing. However, that was not the final destination. The "plane" people proceeded to East Berlin, which yielded easy access to West Berlin for non-Germans. As soon as they found themselves on West German soil, they claimed political persecution in their home countries, trying to achieve refugee status and eventually asylum.

It was up to the German authorities to find out whether these asylum-seekers were covered by Article 16 of the Basic Law (the German Constitution), which declares, "Persons persecuted on political

(Photo courtesy Cornelia Warmenhoven)

In 1937, the Nazis created the Buchenwald concentration camp in Germany. Today the site is a national memorial, helping to teach people about what happened to the millions of Jews and others who were murdered in the Holocaust.

such neighbors as Russia and Poland. In addition, such maneuvers were bound to cause fear in Western Europe and the United States, which would be reminded of Hitler's demands for more *Lebensraum* ("living space") in the prewar days. The situation was very complex, with the right wing asserting that the new Germany was deliberately abandoning its brethren living in bondage in foreign lands, often in conditions of dispossession and deprivation.

Thus far, the call "home" has been answered by more than half a million Germans or former Germans resident in the ex-Soviet Union alone. There are still close to 3 million ethnic Germans in Central/ Eastern and Southeastern Europe, many of whom do not even speak German. In combination with the costs of upgrading the economy of the former German Democratic Republic (now referred to as "eastern Germany"), these repatriation plans have proved to be so colossal that the German government was forced to modify them somewhat. For now, at least, the Federal Republic has stopped encouraging ethnic Germans to repatriate. Instead, the government has begun sponsoring German-language courses and German cultural activities in other European countries and simultaneously encouraging ethnic Germans to stay where they are. However, these efforts may prove futile.

OSTPOLITIK AND DEUTSCHLANDPOLITIK

In the early 1970s, West German chancellor Willy Brandt embarked upon what he called *Ostpolitik* ("Eastern Policy"). In fact, the term was originally part of the German lexicon in the days of Otto Bismarck. Bismarck, the Iron Chancellor, appeared dead-set against letting Germany have "her place in the sun" (the standard expression for a colonial empire). Instead, he cast a favorable eye on countries and areas east of Germany that could easily be annexed to grant the German Empire vital *Lebensraum*. Bismarck's overtures in that direction were thus labeled *Ostpolitik*. They never developed, however, since the chancellor finally gave in and allowed Germany to have overseas colonies.

In Brandt's time, however, the term referred to West Germany's attempts to arrive at some reconciliation with those countries that as stepping stones to Operation Barbarossa had been plundered and pillaged by the German armies. The contemporary Ostpolitik consisted of three major gestures: Brandt, on behalf of his nation, apologized for the atrocities committed; he came up with a compensation program to persons who had particularly suffered at the hands of the Nazis; and he proposed

grounds shall enjoy the right of asylum." That article had left the asylum question simple because, at the time it was written, only persons fleeing from Communist regimes east of Germany were expected to qualify for asylum. (Germans fleeing Communist East Germany did not require asylum, since they already had German citizenship.) It usually took West German authorities 2 to 3 years to find out whether or not the Basic Law had been abused. In the meantime, those aspiring to asylum were housed and fed at German taxpayers' expense. In the vast majority of cases, the claims of political persecution appeared groundless. But, surprisingly, even if refugee status was denied, the *Scheinasylanten* ("fake asylum-seekers") would not be forcibly expelled. Thus, the asylum route was,

and continues to be, the way for certain minorities in Germany to increase in numbers.

Early in the 1990s, the federal government of Germany announced that all residents of Central/Eastern European countries, including the successor states of the former Soviet Union who were able to trace their ancestry to Germany could demand to be brought back to Germany— and fed and sheltered—at the Federal Republic's expense. Needless to say, this type of repatriation was to prove extremely costly to the German treasury.

The Helmut Kohl administration felt cornered by right-wing demands for the reunified Germany to assume the same boundaries that Germany had in 1937. It would have been impossible to give in to those demands without seriously irritating

Beginning of the Protestant Reformation A.D. 1517–1521	The Thirty Years' War ravages most of Germany 1618–1648	The Congress of Vienna 1814–1815	Otto von Bismarck pushes forward the unification of Germany under Prussian leadership 1860s	The unification of Germany; Bismarck becomes chancellor of the German Empire (Second Reich) 1871	Bismarck is dismissed as chancellor by the new emperor, William II 1890	World War I ends in the defeat of Wilhelmine Germany; the Weimar Republic is established 1914–1918	The Weimar Republic 1919–1933	Adolf Hitler is appointed chancellor and proceeds to consolidate power 1933	Annexation of Austria and Sudetenland; increased terror against Jews in Germany 1938

mutual recognition to be followed by the establishment of diplomatic relations.

Brandt was an emotional man, and when, in 1974, it was found that an East German spy had been able to penetrate his inner circle, thereby endangering vital NATO secrets, the chancellor immediately assumed responsibility and resigned. He was succeeded by Helmut Schmidt, a rational Socialist who, in the late 1970s and early 1980s, developed what came to be called the *Deutschlandpolitik*. This policy addressed the relationship between the two Germanys, which had frequently been overtly hostile, especially whenever the cold war flared up. While it did not create a climate of reconciliation, the Deutschlandpolitik provided a measure of communication between the Germanys. Still, it is difficult to see any correlation between the budding but often intermittent dialogue that West Germany and East Germany entertained and the events that started to unfold in the latter half of 1989. Both Germanys were then 40 years old and more often than not victims of, as well as participants in, the cold war. Those 4 decades had witnessed a host of cold war incidents such as the Berlin Airlift, the Hungarian Revolution, the Prague Spring and its bitter aftermath, and repeated crises in Poland. If these events punctuated the period, there was no accumulation of hostility; however, as the years went by, the hopes for a reunification faded. Back in 1949, when the Federal Republic of Germany was established, its Basic Law, describing its genesis, indicated that the German people in some 11 states

had also acted in behalf of those Germans whose cooperation had been made impossible. The entire German nation [as the Preamble puts it] remains invited to complete the unity and freedom of Germany.

REUNIFICATION

It is difficult to point to a single factor or, for that matter, to a combination of factors that were to lead to the reunification. Possibly the armaments race, with its emphasis on high technology, ultimately proved too costly to the Soviet Union, causing its economy to collapse. Perhaps the changing direction of the Soviet Union through Mikhail Gorbachev's glasnost and perestroika policies produced totally unexpected side

effects. However that may be, in early 1989 Gorbachev made the rounds in Central/Eastern Europe, telling its rulers that the Soviet Union would no longer be able to protect them; in other words, they would be on their own. The era of the Brezhnev Doctrine was over.

The factor of relative deprivation may also have played a role. The affluent lifestyle of their Western neighbors was something East Germans were thoroughly aware of: They heard it on radio broadcasts, they watched it on television. It was a lifestyle that they would have preferred for themselves. Instead, their economic lives continued to be grim. With remarkable candor, Central/Eastern Europeans had once made clear that they wanted "socialism with a human face." That had been the stern slogan during the days of the Prague Spring in 1968. One might have hoped the Soviets and the Central/Eastern European Communists would heed the implicit criticism. They did not. Instead, communism (socialism and communism were identical in Central/Eastern Europe) started to be on the defensive. As a result, the daily situation became even grimmer, more rigorous, and less humane. The economy deteriorated and, with it, morale. Corruption became widespread, especially among those who held positions of power.

In a way, it is somewhat surprising that it took 21 years for dissent to ferment into protests, but it should be remembered that, until early 1989, the Soviet presence and pressure were intense. All over Central/Eastern Europe, Soviet troops were in place; the Warsaw Treaty was still in force; and ugly memories of two bloody episodes that had cost many lives (in Budapest and Prague) made it difficult to start thinking about new protests.

But 1989 was the year of the explosion. Shortly after Gorbachev had paid his respects to the heads of state or government in the Eastern bloc, the increasing disenchantment revealed itself in two ways.

East Berliners and East Germans started to take to the streets, day after day, in ever-larger numbers. While these demonstrations, which involved hundreds of thousands of people, were peaceful, they must by the same token have appeared threatening to East German authorities, since many demonstrators had started displaying antigovernment slogans. Others again made attempts to flee East Germany

by asking for asylum at foreign embassies. East Germans occasionally remained the guests of foreign embassies for weeks on end. The Hungarian Embassy was often selected, because Hungary had become a maverick in the Eastern bloc. But Hungary too was only used as a transit country, the goal being to enter West Germany. This massive "voting with their feet" was extremely embarrassing to the East German government, which occasionally made statements, announcements, and promises that things would soon get better.

The Berlin Wall, which cut through Berlin, had since its erection in 1961 been a symbol of the isolation and separation in which East Berliners lived. Suddenly, in November 1989, it proved possible to get across this monument; indeed, people started to stand on the wall, to walk on it, to hack away at it. Thus, freedom of access was achieved by the collective will of thousands and thousands of people. The wall as a containment device had gone. The West German government was so exhilarated that it started donating cash to every German coming from East Germany in order to look around or to shop.

East Germans could now enter the promised land directly; there was no longer any need to make use of detours through Austria and Hungary. East Germans, who had never been regarded as normal, run-of-the-mill refugees, now lost the privileges and prerogatives they had enjoyed for decades in West Germany. The momentum toward reunification started to accelerate, if only because of the unspoken fear that East German authorities, who had more to lose than their subjects, would have second thoughts or that some other backlash might present itself.

Measures were taken step by step. First came the equalization of the two German currencies. Although the Eastmark rated considerably lower, both officially and on the black market, it was granted a state of parity—that is, it was declared to have the same value as the Deutschmark. In addition, in order to arrive at a reunification, both parties agreed to resort to an article of the Basic Law that in fact had reference to the incorporation of states into the body politic of West Germany. The name German Democratic Republic was dropped; the name *Deutschland* (Germany) was given to the new construction in its entirety. And

| World War II begins in Europe with the German attack on Poland 1939 | The defeat of Germany ends World War II in Europe; shortly before the end, Hitler commits suicide in Berlin 1945 | Germany is under Allied military occupation 1945–1949 | The founding of the Federal Republic of Germany and the German Democratic Republic 1949 | West Germany becomes a member of NATO; East Germany joins the Warsaw Pact 1955 | West Germany is one of the charter members of the European Union 1957 | The Berlin Wall is constructed 1961 | Willy Brandt becomes West Germany's first Social Democratic chancellor and initiates *Ostpolitik* 1969 | Helmut Schmidt becomes the second Social Democratic chancellor after Brandt steps down 1974 | Helmut Kohl, a Christian Democrat, is chancellor of an increasingly respected West Germany 1980s |

1990s

| The Berlin Wall topples; reunification; Kohl is named chancellor of reunited Germany | Holocaust survivors accuse Germany's most respected companies of profiting from forced labor during the Nazi era | Gerhard Schroeder receives a clear mandate in legislative elections and unseats Kohl |

naturally, attention was paid to what should become the new capital. The choice was Berlin, which had been the capital before World War II. However, there would be a period of transition, of a decade.

The boundaries of the new state constituted a painful issue. Immediately after World War II, Germany lost territory to Poland and the Soviet Union. It was decided to keep the Oder-Neisse as the eastern boundary. However, persons in the political right wing continue to claim that Germany is territorially short-changed as long as it is not allowed to regain its 1937 boundaries. Helmut Kohl has ignored these claims. (Those had been the boundaries before Nazi Germany started on its expansionist course.)

THE NEW GERMANY
Since reunification in October 1990, the social and economic difficulties associated with merging the two states and their peoples have dampened the initial euphoria of the government and their citizens. Satisfactory resolution of these tremendous problems will likely take many more years to achieve.

Germany has undertaken enormous economic obligations, such as upgrading its eastern part both economically and environmentally and managing its new minorities equitably. At the same time, it has pressing obligations within the European Union. Germany's economy is the most powerful in Europe, and in September 1992, a currency crisis broke out that was caused by the tremendous strength of the German mark. This currency fight, which flared up in anticipation of measures undertaken to arrive at a European monetary union, caused a number of currencies to crumble. Finally, the EU decided in 1993 to make Frankfurt its financial heart. Still,

the country's structural economic weaknesses will take years to fix.

One of the negative points in any evaluation of the new Germany is the hostility that has been directed against members of minority groups. Many rallies and fights have been started by young individuals who call themselves neo-Nazis, and bombs have been thrown into the apartments of Turks and other minorities. While it is hoped that the outrage of the overall German populace against such neo-Nazi groups will lead to a lessening of ethnic-based hostilities in Germany—and indeed outbreaks of related violence have become less frequent in recent years—it is likely that discriminatory attitudes will persist during the difficult social and economic shifts of the coming years.

On September 27, 1998, Germans voted in legislative elections. At stake: the chancellorship, a post that many people view as the most important in all Europe. The incumbent, Christian Democrat Helmut Kohl, who first came to power in West Germany in 1982, was challenged by Gerhard Schroeder, a Social Democrat. Once considered a political outsider, Schroeder was able to draw critical support from various political groups, including the environmentalist, left-leaning Greens. He promised "economic stability, domestic security and continuity in foreign affairs." The voters chose Schroeder by a clear margin, signifying their deep desire for change and dissatisfaction with Germany's high unemployment and other indicators of economic malaise.

It was a watershed for the country that is still haunted by the memories of its Nazi past, as Schroeder is the first German leader too young to remember World War II. It also signified a sea change in political and social climate—an abrupt move away from the conservativism of Kohl's era to the center-left. Said Schroeder in

his inaugural address: "We are going to turn this country into a place on the move again. The only thing we need to fear is getting stuck in blockades of our own making." The latter statement proved uncomfortably close to the mark in his first months in power, as Chancellor Schroeder "hit the ground stumbling," as some wags put it. Within weeks of his inauguration, there were strains within his coalition and questions about who is and will be running Germany. Schroeder, however, showed signs of being a master of compromise. Whether he can maintain the balance remains to be seen.

DEVELOPMENT

Germany has the leading industrial economy in Western Europe. It ranks second in the world in international trade and fourth in economic output. A strong base in some traditional industries, such as heavy goods, autos, and chemical products, is now being supplemented by high-tech development.

FREEDOM

Germany is a representative democracy with civil rights and liberties guaranteed by the Basic Law (Constitution), which will remain in place until the reunited Germany's new constitution is voted upon. There is a vigorous press, and many checks and balances are built into the governmental system. Extensive formal study of the Holocaust is required of all German students.

HEALTH/WELFARE

Germany's economy combines an emphasis on private enterprise with an extensive social network of protection and welfare benefits for the citizenry. A conservative statesman, Otto von Bismarck introduced the rudiments of the welfare state more than 100 years ago.

ACHIEVEMENTS

The emergence of a well-functioning, stable West German democracy after 1949 must be regarded as a political miracle that outranks even the economic miracle of rebuilding a ruined country and becoming one of the world's most prosperous states. The reunification of Germany in 1990 was achieved nonviolently.

Greece (Hellenic Republic)

GEOGRAPHY

Area in Square Miles (Kilometers): 51,146 (131,940) (about the size of Alabama)
Capital (Population): Athens (3,093,000)
Primary Environmental Concerns: air and water pollution
Geographical Features: mostly mountains, with ranges extending into the sea as peninsulas or chains of islands
Climate: temperate

PEOPLE

Population

Total: 10,662,000
Annual Growth Rate: 0.44%
Rural/Urban Population Ratio: 41/59
Major Languages: Greek (mostly Demotiki); English and French widely understood
Ethnic Makeup: 98% Greek; 2% Turkish, Vlach, Slav, and others
Religions: 98% Greek Orthodox; 2% Muslim and others

Health

Life Expectancy at Birth: 76 years (male); 81 years (female)
Infant Mortality Rate (Ratio): 7.6/1,000
Physicians Available (Ratio): 1/259

Education

Adult Literacy Rate: 95%
Compulsory (Ages): 6–15; free

COMMUNICATION

Telephones: 1 per 2 people
Daily Newspaper Circulation: 156 per 1,000 people
Televisions: 1 per 4.9 people

TRANSPORTATION

Highways in Miles (Kilometers): 70,200 (117,000)
Railroads in Miles (Kilometers): 1,484 (2,474)
Usable Airfields: 78
Motor Vehicles in Use: 3,101,000

GOVERNMENT

Type: presidential parliamentary republic
Independence Date: 1829 (from the Ottoman Empire)
Head of State/Government: President Konstandinos Stephanopoulis; Prime Minister Konstandinos Simitis
Political Parties: Panhellenic Socialist Movement; New Democracy; Democratic Social Movement; Political Spring; Coali-

tion of the Left and Progress; Communist Party; Rainbow Coalition
Suffrage: universal and compulsory at 18

MILITARY

Military Expenditures (% of Central Government Expenditures): 4.6%
Current Disputes: constant friction with neighboring Turkey; tensions with Macedonia over name

ECONOMY

Currency ($ U.S. Equivalent): 251.5 drachmas = $1
Per Capita Income/GDP: $13,000/$137.4 billion
GDP Growth Rate: 3.7%
Inflation Rate: .6%

Unemployment Rate: 10%
Labor Force: 4,210,000
Natural Resources: bauxite; lignite; magnesite; petroleum; marble
Agriculture: wheat; olives; tobacco; corn; cotton; fruit; olive oil; wine; meat; dairy products
Industry: food and tobacco processing; textiles; chemicals; metal products; tourism; mining; petroleum
Exports: $9.8 billion (primary partners EC-countries, United States)
Imports: $27 billion (primary partners EU countries, United States)

 http://www.greekembassy.org
http://www.odci.gov/cia/publications/factbook/country-frame.html

- ☆ Capital
- • City
- 〰 River

0   50   100   150 Miles
0   50   100   150   200 Kilometers
Elevation in feet.

THE HELLENIC REPUBLIC

Ancient civilizations have always fascinated and intrigued historians, politicians, and the public in general, particularly those civilizations that left a clearly visible heritage of monuments. It is tempting to assume the existence of direct links between societies currently resident in the same general area and the peoples of past glory. The interval between classical Greece and modern Greece was lengthy—2,000 years between "the cloud rising in the West," a signal that spelled the Roman conquest of ancient Greece, and the time that modern Greece arose. In the interim, the country was part of the Roman Empire, the Byzantine Empire, and the Ottoman Empire. In the early nineteenth century, the Greeks were at last able to liquidate the hated *tourkokratia* (rule by Turks) in areas that were to become the new nation-state of Greece. Modern Greeks nevertheless point with pride to their classical ancestry beyond the chasm of foreign rule, finding the discontinuity

to be of less importance than the large number of historic and linguistic data supporting the existence of a direct link.

Greece lies on the southern tip of the Balkan Peninsula, flanked on the west by Italy, across the Ionian Sea, and on the east by Turkey, across the Aegean Sea. It also shares a common land border with Turkey in Thrace. Many of the country's several hundred islands are within sight of Turkish Anatolia. Crete, another center of an ancient civilization, is the largest of the Greek islands. The country—both the mainland and the islands—is mostly mountainous and dry. Only a quarter of the land is arable.

HISTORY

Only in the early nineteenth century did Greeks regain a measure of independence, after having been under Turkish rule for centuries. Yet even a decade later, they still did not have an exclusive say in such matters as their independence, the boundaries of the new state, and other issues that attend self-determination. A conference held

in London in 1827 established all this, although it was at least left to the Greeks to convene a National Assembly in order to draw up the Constitution.

When apprised of the size of their new home, many Greeks felt acutely unhappy, since one out of every five was destined to live in areas that were not included. Whatever the glorious past of its ancient ancestry, modern Greece started out with a yearning for *enosis*, that typically Greek version of irredentism, which would not be satisfied until all Greek communities had become part of Greece. The fulfillment of these enosis ideals met with occasional disappointments, but it was nevertheless achieved (with a few exceptions) within 1½ centuries. The turmoil that more recently descended on Cyprus and that nearly triggered a war in the Eastern Mediterranean was in effect provoked by a resurgence of the enosis trauma.

The greatest expansion of the Greek national borders took place during the Balkan Wars (1912–1913), fought under the charismatic leader Eleftherios Venizelos. After these wars were concluded, shortly before World War I, Greece's national territory appeared to have expanded by 70 percent and its population by 75 percent. Some of these gains were offset by massacres and murders that Turks perpetrated in Anatolia in 1922 (where, it is believed, some 600,000 ethnic Greeks were killed). In addition, 1½ million Greeks were forcibly expelled from their ancestral lands.

POLITICAL CHARACTERISTICS

Since monarchies were the order of the day in Western Europe until well into the twentieth century, Greece was destined to become a kingdom upon achieving independence. This at least was the conclusion of the big powers that convened in London in 1827. But, as Greece had been part of foreign empires for more than 20 centuries, no aristocracy had been able to develop. This proved no obstacle: Monarchs were, after all, often recruited from the aristocratic elites of other countries. Louis I of Bavaria, who was party to the London convention, accepted the crown on behalf of his 17-year-old son, Otto. Surrounded by Bavarian advisers and troops, Otto made his debut in Nauplia, the provisional capital.

No attempts were made by what was basically a foreign court to assimilate or to bridge the differences in culture, and it consequently did not take long for Bavarian elitism to become an irritant. When Greece seemed on the road to becoming a Bavarian colony, a backlash forced Otto to step down, in 1862. George I, the second son of the heir to the throne of Denmark,

(United Nations/M. Tzovaras)

The Acropolis in Athens, pictured above, has witnessed political and social turmoil since the dawn of Western culture.

was then invited to rule Greece; he managed to stay in power for half a century. During this period, Greece was both a monarchy and a democracy (like the remaining monarchies in Western Europe today). George I was assassinated during the turmoil that the Balkan Wars created, and he was succeeded by Constantine (George II).

The period that followed was one of utter confusion and instability. Kings were on occasion set aside, exiled, and subsequently returned to power. However, this monarchical instability was only a reflection of the overall turbulence that has been Greece's fate since its birth as a modern nation-state.

Since 1831, Greece has experienced seven changes of constitutions, five removals of kings, three republics, seven military dictatorships, and more than a dozen revolutions or attempted coups. More than 150 cabinets have governed Greece since then, one third of these since 1945. Assessing Greek politics with these statistics in mind, one cannot escape the impression that the country is in perpetual turmoil. Yet the overall record is not entirely negative. Greece has enjoyed some form of parliamentary rule with adequate guarantees of individual rights for about 80 percent of the time. One should also take into account that for many years during the period at issue, Greece was at war, a circumstance that is bound to weaken democracy. Indeed, it is possible to conclude that modern Greeks appear to have inherited a natural preference for democracy.

POST–WORLD WAR II DEVELOPMENTS

Greece has experienced war not only on its eastern frontier but also to its west. Shortly after Italy joined World War II on the side of Germany, in June 1940, it sought to expand across the Adriatic Sea. To that end, it attacked first Albania and then Greece. In the latter operation, the Italians met with stiff resistance; in fact, the Greek Army proved in many ways superior to the invading Italians. The situation became embarrassing—so much so that, in April 1941, Adolf Hitler decided to come to the rescue of Italy, its Axis partner, and "clean up the Balkans" before launching Operation Barbarossa—invading the Soviet Union—on June 22, 1941. As a result of this delay, Operation Barbarossa had to forfeit summer months that were essential to its drive. (Operation Barbarossa eventually led to Hitler's defeat.) The Greeks were unable to hold out against the Germans for very long, and their government as well as a significant portion of their army were relocated to the Middle East. (While numerous Western

European governments fled to London, Greece instituted a government-in-exile to its east.)

The German occupation provoked massive armed resistance and shaped Greek political attitudes for the next 4 decades. Greek resistance mainly operated in the mountains, and it was there that it became increasingly infiltrated by Communist partisans. It was only natural that the resistance troops would attempt to fill the power vacuum once the German armies retreated. Thus, when the government-in-exile returned to Greece, now headed by George Papandreou, it found a country dominated by Communists. However, it was obvious that obstacles to the return to normalcy had been foreseen, since the returning government was accompanied by no fewer than 15,000 British troops. In December 1944, their leader was forced to put down a revolt in Athens that had been instigated by the Communist-led National Liberation Army (ELAS). This military group, which had been extremely courageous in its resistance against the Germans, now attempted to capitalize on its popularity by seizing power, as its counterparts in such neighboring countries as Yugoslavia, Albania, and Bulgaria had done, with greater success.

The monarch still had not returned, and Archbishop Damaskinos, who had been appointed regent, organized the first postwar elections, to which some 2,000 foreign observers were invited through the intermediary of the United Nations. The elections strongly favored bourgeois conservative parties, which received more than 70 percent of the popular vote. The Greek Communist Party (KKE), still very strong in the mountains, boycotted the process.

Having more or less settled what government would rule Greece, the time had come to make a decision regarding the monarchy. A referendum revealed that 64 percent of the participants wanted the return of the king.

By that time, however, the KKE had commenced a civil war, which was to last for 4 years. The Greek Civil War was one of the specific situations to which the Truman Doctrine referred, and the United States offered a great deal of material assistance to the Greek government. The war was won by the nationalist forces, but it left scars on Greek society. The KKE was outlawed between 1946 and 1974. The war influenced the political orientation of Greek governments for 35 years. Between 1946 and 1981, Greece was under conservative government for a total of 28 years, whereas liberal–center parties were in power for less than 7 years.

In practice, some of the conservative governments turned out to be far less than democratic; the "regime of the colonels," as the (conservative) military dictatorship has often been called, represented a clear departure from democracy. One of the most surprising facts of modern Greek political history is that this highly authoritarian phase ended not with a bang but with a whimper. In the seventh year of their rule, the military dictators (who were not completely united) were preoccupied with the possibility of the long-awaited enosis, or integration, of Cyprus. To render Cyprus, which had been independent for 14 years, a part of Greece would naturally have amounted to a gross violation of international law. The general ineffectiveness of the United Nations with respect to sudden changes in the status quo, as well as the supposed silent support of the United States (which had continued its full recognition of the junta), may have caused the regime to assume that the politics of *fait accompli* would work as it so often does. Domestically, of course, the enosis of Cyprus would have put a feather in an otherwise featherless cap.

The Greek government, however, had apparently not anticipated a Turkish response. The Turkish government tried to safeguard itself against encirclement by preempting enosis. Its troops landed on the north side of Cyprus and soon held more than one third of the island. It was obvious that an attempt to remove Turkish troops would cause a full-scale war between the two neighbors, who had been mutually hostile for a long time. Not only did the gamble not work, but it actually proved counterproductive. The public turned even more against the military dictatorship, which, without further ado, abandoned power.

There was no immediate backlash; the first post-junta government proved conservative and centrist (but democratic!). The royal house, having left the country at the military takeover, returned. However, there was some uncertainty about their political future, and it was decided to let the people determine that in a referendum. A strong preference for a republican form of government resulted.

VAGARIES OF A SYSTEM

But it was not only the somewhat anticlimactic eclipse of the monarchy, which had headed Greece for 1½ centuries without ever being very popular, that generated the urge for a new constitution. The military junta, coming into power in 1967, had never paid any attention to the existing Constitution, a charter that dated from 1952. Only after it had been dusted off and briefly revived did the new civilian government realize that it had become outdated and that Greece needed a completely new one. Put together in a surprisingly brief time and promulgated in June 1975, the new Constitution contained a number of innovations. It identified the Greek political system as a "presidential parliamentary system," an unusual designation, since democracies are customarily classified as either presidential *or* parliamentary. It is possible that the new Constitution's founders wanted the world to know that Greece had become a republic. Indeed, Greece is often classified as a unitary multiparty republic.

The office of the chief of state now fell to a president, to be elected for 5-year terms. If the old charter had granted the king little more than ceremonial powers, the new Constitution gave the president a balancing role in politics. The president would thus moderate, and occasionally reconcile, extreme views. Such a task could only be performed if the office were granted some power.

Meanwhile, a leftist party, the Panhellenic Socialist Party (PASOK), which had been created by Andreas Papandreou shortly after the demise of the rule of the colonels, gained in strength. Papandreou had lived in the United States for a number of years and had even become an American citizen. Yet his dislike of American imperialism was obvious. In 1981, PASOK won the elections and Papandreou became prime minister. He immediately made clear that he did not like the power-sharing that the new Constitution implied. He managed to get adopted a constitutional revision that took away the large majority of presidential powers, granting them to the prime minister. The designation "presidential parliamentary system" as a consequence became less appropriate, the Greek system of government having become, like many other democracies in Western Europe, a republican monarchy.

The new Constitution also converted the bicameral Legislature into a unicameral Parliament with 300 members. If nominally there was a separation of power among the three branches of government, in practice the executive branch of government (headed by the prime minister, who was also the leader of the majority party in Parliament) had the lion's share of the power, completely overshadowing the two other branches. In some ways, this system may be compared to Great Britain's prime-ministerial government.

When Papandreou rose to power after the 1981 general elections, he was supported by 48 percent of the popular vote. Through a system of weighted proportional representation, his party received a majority of seats in Parliament.

Papandreou, although a democrat by inclination, could be somewhat autocratic at times. Generally the leader of PASOK chose to ignore public opinion that expressed disapproval of his basic policies. In the latter half of the 1980s, Papandreou was besieged by spectacular allegations of moral and political corruption, which greatly weakened the respect accorded him as well as his popularity. The fact that, after numerous escapades, he left his wife and married a flight attendant young enough to be his daughter did not help.

MAJOR POLITICAL ISSUES

The first 7 years after the junta's demise proved a testing ground for the new Panhellenic Socialist Party. During the election campaign of 1981, it made foreign policy a central issue, claiming that all Greek postwar governments had in effect been "servants of foreign interests." Papandreou committed himself to radical changes and made *Allaghi* ("Change") his party's chief theme. The following sweeping changes were envisaged: 1) a withdrawal of Greece from the North Atlantic Treaty Organization; 2) the removal of U.S. military bases from Greek soil; and 3) a referendum on Greece's accession to the European Community (today known as the European Union, of which Greece had just become a full member).

However, virtually nothing was done with respect to these strident claims once PASOK had achieved victory and Papandreou had become prime minister. Greece remained a NATO member (for "national reasons"); the status of the American bases was renegotiated behind closed doors, or at least away from the glare of the media; and the promised referendum was never held. Nevertheless, the stark discrepancy between campaign promises and postelection performance did not cause the prime minister to tone down his anti–NATO and anti–U.S. rhetoric.

The difference between anti–NATO rhetoric and the implications of withdrawing from NATO had become painfully obvious to Greek governments. Once Greece withdrew somewhat halfheartedly—that is, only from the NATO command structure—steps were taken to put more emphasis on Turkish membership. The threat that Turkey might benefit from Greece's withdrawal provided a strong incentive for Greece to retain its membership.

The status of the U.S. bases in Greece (which naturally relates closely to the NATO issue, if only because NATO has always been identified with the United States) will surely remain on the governmental agenda for a long time to come. It involves specific terms, or periods: If an

agreement is about to expire, a new one will have to be negotiated or the bases removed. As for EU membership, that is no longer a serious issue, as it has become an asset rather than a liability. Indeed, Greece became a staunch supporter of the Treaty of Maastricht.

Greek foreign policy is greatly influenced by Turkey's immediate presence and the apprehensions that this presence evokes. Some of these sentiments may be traced back to centuries of cultural conflict, punctuated by a prolonged period of oppression. But even after the liquidation of the Ottoman Empire and the emergence of Greece as a modern nation-state, the adversarial relationship between Greece and Turkey lingered. Turkey was particularly aggrieved when a string of islands close to its coast was ceded to Greece after the Balkan Wars (1912–1913). And the Greeks still feel the slight of the Turkish invasion of Cyprus. Shortly after the invasion, Turkey added insult to injury by occupying 38 percent of the island. A great many Turks were then transported from Turkey into the occupied part of Cyprus. Undoubtedly this was done to strengthen any Turkish claim at future negotiations. It was a transparent ploy, but nothing was undertaken internationally to prevent it. And suddenly, in 1983, 9 years after the Turkish invasion, the Republic of Northern Cyprus was proclaimed, with much fanfare. Thus far, the United Nations has refused to consider its admission, and Turkey is the only country to have recognized it. To most countries—and the UN—it is obvious that such recognition would amount to taking sides in the Greco–Turkish conflict.

Another bitter dispute developed with respect to oil drilling in the Aegean Sea. Shortly after oil was discovered off the Greek island of Thasos, Turkey claimed the continental shelf east of the median line between the Greek and Turkish mainlands. Such a claim would have been in compliance with recent rules of international law, more specifically with the UN Conference on the Law of the Sea, were it not for the Greek islands, a stone's throw from the Turkish coastline. Future exploration and exploitation will thus be conducted from the Greek mainland and will be of no concern to Turkey.

Popular sentiments and governmental attitudes vis-à-vis Turkey tend to remain the same, regardless of what government happens to be in office. Since the fall of the first PASOK government, frictions between Greece and Turkey, particularly with respect to the Cyprus issue and the Aegean oil, have continued. And in August 1990, when Turkey developed into a staunch ally of the United States in the

A Greek revolution commences against the Ottoman Empire A.D. 1821	The boundaries of the modern Greek state are established (excepting the islands) 1827	King George I ascends to the throne and begins his 50-year rule of Greece 1863	Greece joins its Balkan neighbors in a war against the Ottoman Empire 1912	Greek expeditionary forces are defeated by Turks in Anatolia; all Greek residents in Turkey are resettled in Greece 1922	Germany occupies Greece; Greek resistance troops operate in the mountains 1941–1944

latter's conflict with Iraq, it seemed foreordained that Greece would reluctantly grant lukewarm support, in the context of the EU and NATO. On the other hand, it is entirely possible that Turkey might have refused to shut off the oil pipeline coming from Iraq had Greece immediately thrust itself into the fray.

CHURCH–STATE RELATIONS
The Greek Orthodox Church, to which 98 percent of the Greek people belong, has been an important social institution since the Byzantine era. Through centuries of subservience, Greece had lost its political institutions; but in those dark days, the Church played a critical role in the survival of the national spirit. Under Ottoman rule, the Church performed numerous quasi-political functions that customarily are undertaken by state agencies.

The Orthodox Church has deep roots in Greek society. It is also quite wealthy; the Socialist government asserted the right to expropriate Church property and to turn it over to "cooperative farming." The announcement of such measures evoked strong reactions on the part of the Church and its membership, endangering the traditional church–state harmony. The Orthodox hierarchy threatened to place itself within the fold of the Ecumenical Patriarchate of Istanbul, which would embarrass the PASOK administration. The strained relations between the Church and the government contributed to domestic tensions.

THE GREEK ECONOMY
Many scholarly and technical terms in our lexicon can be traced back to classical Greek. *Economy* is such a term, meaning "law of the house." Freely translated, *oikonomos* means "the way in which the house is customarily run," a phrase that perfectly describes the economies of extended families or of the smaller city-states that were politically independent and economically self-sufficient. The city-states came to be absorbed by the Macedonian Empire, after which Greece remained submerged in foreign empires for many centuries. A fully integrated, national Greek economy, therefore, is of relatively recent origin.

Another factor that may have hampered economic coordination and integration is the country's geography: the Hellenic Republic includes some 1,400 islands, about 170 of which are inhabited. Regular shipping services are maintained among them and with the mainland but, in spite of this network of connections, some island economies have remained largely separate.

The poor soil, on the mainland as well as on most of the islands, is another handicap. Greece nevertheless produces important crops, such as grains, rice, corn, cotton, tobacco, citrus fruits, figs, olives, and raisins. Although most of these are exported, the tendency toward a subsistence economy has persisted in some parts.

An industrial base was introduced into Greece in the mid-1950s. When PASOK gained office in 1981, industrialization was intensified. Attempts to shift the country's livelihood away from agriculture have met with some success; the Organization for European Cooperation and Development has designated Greece a "newly industrialized country."

Although Greece has been an intermittent source of labor for other countries, it has also found itself in the position of having to import foreign laborers. Sometimes these labor migrations have even proceeded simultaneously. However, unemployment is currently a troubling 10 percent.

Generally, the Greek economy is stagnant. The stagnation may be attributed in part to external factors: Greece shares in the European Union's overproduction of wine (a number of other Mediterranean members of the EU also produce wine). In addition, revenues from tourism have fluctuated in recent years, partly because of occasional fear of terrorism.

In contrast to general expectations, Papandreou refrained from massive nationalization of private enterprise. The Greek economy remains a mixture of privately owned and state-controlled enterprises. All major economic enterprises—banks, surface and air transportation, telecommunications, and so on—are state-owned. Shipping, an important source of hard currency, remained in private hands during the Papandreou administration of the 1980s. By the same token, PASOK's extensive nationalization record caused alarm among Greek ship owners, many of whom removed their vessels from Greek registry. Also, the Socialist government was blamed for creating a climate that discouraged foreign investment, thereby causing an outflow rather than an inflow of capital.

Whenever and wherever elections are held, the state of the economy is bound to be a factor of considerable moment. During the PASOK years in the 1980s, economic conditions fluctuated greatly, an urbanization-related phenomenon. To illustrate this, one may argue that, had the election been held in June 1988, PASOK might have won a third term. The countryside, where the Socialists were strongest, enjoyed unprecedented prosperity, if only because of the generous injection of EU funds. It had also been politically freed from right-wing hegemony, which often had proved stifling. The 2 years of stringent wage restraints were over, and real income was on the rise again. Finally, Prime Minister Papandreou himself had not yet been subject to smears and allegations. By June 1989, however, renewed stagnation and an increase in unemployment had weakened the PASOK position so much that Papandreou could no longer point to it with pride. He was forced to concentrate on noneconomic concerns, such as narrow nationalism and foreign issues.

THE RIGHT STRIKES BACK
Nevertheless, the result of the June 1989 election was difficult to predict. Papandreou turned out to be a shrewd strategist, able to render the sound and fury of his opponents to nothingness or even to make them counterproductive. Still, if 8 years earlier his campaign slogan had been "Change," the 1989 election was fought (and won) on the opponents' slogan of *Katharsis* ("Purge," or "Cleanup"). Although the charges may have been exaggerated, Papandreou's PASOK administration was marred by a degree of corruption and fraud.

Spirited campaigning—evading areas of public discontent—enabled the PASOK leader to capture 39 percent of the vote. The conservative New Democracy Party, led by Constantine Mitsotakis, won 44 percent. The balance was held by Harilaos Florakis, whose Communist-dominated Coalition of the Left won 13 percent of the vote. Florakis, who had called Papandreou an "untrustworthy partner" and PASOK a party that harbored "neo-Fascist tendencies," was unwilling to consider a union of the left. The alternative was a temporary government alliance of the major opposition parties, which, in spite of ideological differences, were prepared to collaborate in what they called a *katharsis* administration—

The returning
Greek
government,
aided by British
troops, faces
Communists in
powerful positions
1944

Civil war erupts
between
Communist
guerrillas and the
Greek
government
1946

Greece embarks
on the road to
industrialization
1950s

The Coup of
the Colonels
establishes a
military regime
1967

Civilian rule is
restored; the
monarchy is
abolished by
a referendum
1974

Andreas
Papandreou is
prime minister
1980s

PASOK is voted
out of power
1989

1990s

Papandreou's
successor,
Constantine
Mitsotakis, is
charged with
nepotism

PASOK and the
once-discredited
Papandreou are
elected again to
head the
government

Papandreou dies
in office;
Konstandinos
Stephanopoulis
becomes
president

what Papandreou called an "unholy alliance of nongovernment." However that may be, executive immunity no longer protected PASOK leadership; and Papandreou plus a handful of former PASOK ministers were indicted on charges of accepting bribes, involvement in a fraud against the European Union, and widespread telephone tapping.

Nevertheless, the interim government could not agree on sensitive issues. As soon as the worst excesses of PASOK rule had been investigated, a second election was held, on November 5, 1989. The major protagonists both increased their shares of the vote: The New Democracy Party got 46 percent and PASOK 40 percent. The loser in this election was the Left Coalition, whose share dropped to 11 percent.

After weeks of bargaining, the three party leaders decided to put aside their differences and to agree on a national-unity government until April 1990. Curiously, the negotiations stopped then and there, and no attempt was made to resolve the gridlock in the intervening period. When the April deadline arrived, the only decision made by the national-unity government was to replace the aged Xenophon Zolotas by another old hand, Tzanne Tzannetakis, who in turn yielded the office to Constantine Mitsotakis.

The latter felt (wrongly, as it turned out) confident enough to engage in nepotism. His daughter, Dora Bakoyannis, was made a junior cabinet minister in charge of coordinating government activities. It did not take Greeks long to complain that Prime Minister Mitsotakis's family was in charge. With his New Democracy Party holding but a two-seat majority in the 300-member Parliament, Mitsotakis could not afford to offend too many conservatives. Many ministers tendered their resignations. Only Antonis Samaras, the sole conservative with a continuously high approval rating,

seemed destined to remain in charge of foreign affairs.

Finally, however, friction erupted between Samaras and Mitsotakis over the Macedonian question. Yugoslavia, while crumbling, had yielded a new independent state that called itself "Macedonia." This also happens to be the name of a northern Greek province. Such a quasi-duplication would normally be taken in stride. (Belgium, for example, has a Province of Luxembourg, located quite close to the country of the same name.) But it became a major issue in Greece. While Prime Minister Mitsotakis was prepared to compromise and have the new state call itself "Slav Macedonia," Foreign Minister Samaras argued that the fledgling republic should choose a completely different name. Samaras was fired, but Mitsotakis soon adopted the foreign minister's stance in an attempt to appease public opinion. Eventually, a compromise was struck in that the area came to be called FYROM, the "Former Yugoslav Republic of Macedonia."

Meanwhile, Greece's relations with Albania, another country that had rid itself of a rigid Marxist regime and self-imposed isolation, degenerated into shooting incidents. Albania, fearing that Greece still had designs on the region known as Northern Epirus, refused to allow an ethnic Greek political party to take part in elections on March 22, 1991.

THE RETURN OF PASOK
It is not uncommon for political parties to the left and right to alternate in office, but the recent Greek case reveals a highly unusual picture. After the PASOK defeat in 1989, most analysts believed that it would take a long time for the Greek Socialist party to get on its feet again: PASOK's wily leader was in the hospital and seemed to have run out of tricks, and public opinion concerning him and his cabinet

had plummeted. Thus, political observers were surprised when PASOK and Papandreou were voted back into power (albeit narrowly) in October 1993. Possibly most voters were sick and tired of the *katharsis* that the right-wing parties had promised—but failed to deliver. However, Papandreou resigned from office early in 1996, due to illness (he died in June of that year). He was succeeded by Konstandinos Simitas of PASOK.

Greece has fared well economically in the subsequent years, although not well enough to be allowed to participate in the launch of the Euro in January 1999. It entered the exchange-rate mechanism—a requirement for European Monetary Union membership—in March 1998.

DEVELOPMENT

Greek merchant marines constitute more than 20% of the European Union's shipping capacity. While Greece's economy has improved over the past several years, its people still have one of the lowest per capita incomes in the EU, and aid from the EU accounts for about 4.5% of GDP.

FREEDOM

Greeks have defended their freedom of expression with a passion. About 70 dailies of various sizes of circulation are published, 16 of them in Athens alone. All major Western and Eastern newspapers are readily available.

HEALTH/WELFARE

All Greeks are covered by some form of medical insurance. Although the quality of health care is not comparable to that of many other Western European countries, it is at least readily available.

ACHIEVEMENTS

Greece boasts many outstanding literary figures, some of whom have been internationally recognized. George Seferis, Yannis Ritsos, Odyseus Elytis, Kostis Palamas, and Nikos Kazantzakis are considered giants of modern literature. Seferis and Elytis are recipients of the Nobel Prize in Literature.

The Holy See (State of the Vatican City)

GEOGRAPHY
Area in Square Miles (Kilometers): 0.17 (0.44) (about 0.7 time the size of the mall in Washington, D.C.)
Capital (Population): Vatican City (850)
Geographical Features: low hill; landlocked
Climate: temperate

PEOPLE

Population
Total: 860
Annual Growth Rate: 1.15%
Rural/Urban Population Ratio: 0/100
Major Languages: Latin; Italian; others
Ethnic Makeup: 85% Italian; 15% Swiss and others
Religion: 100% Roman Catholic

Education
Adult Literacy Rate: 100%

TRANSPORTATION
Highways in Miles (Kilometers): none
Railroads in Feet (Meters): 2,845 (862)
Usable Airfields: none

GOVERNMENT
Type: monarchical-sacerdotal state
Head of State/Government: Pope John Paul II; Secretary of State Archbishop Angelo Cardinal Sodano
Political Parties: none
Suffrage: limited to cardinals (under age 80) from all over the world

MILITARY
Military Expenditures (% of GDP): defense is the responsibility of Italy; the papal palace has traditionally been protected by Swiss guards; since an assassination attempt on the pope in 1981, security has been stringent
Current Disputes: none

ECONOMY*
Currency ($ U.S. Equivalent): 1,767.40 Vatican lire = $1 (at par with the Italian lira, which circulates freely)
Natural Resources: none
Agriculture: none
Industry: printing and production of a small amount of mosaics and staff uniforms; banking and finance

Note: Vatican City is supported financially by contributions from Roman Catholics worldwide; some income derives from the sale of Vatican postage stamps, tourist mementos, fees for admission to museums, and sale of publications.

http://www.vatican.va/
http://www.christusrex.org/www1/citta/0-Citta.html
http://portal.research.bell-labs.com/cgi-wald/dbaccess/411?key=107

The Congress of Vienna recognizes the existence of the Vatican as a world power
A.D. 1815

The papal states comprise thousands of square miles in area
1859

The territory of the papacy is confined
1871

The Lateran Pact
1929

Cardinal Karol Wojtyla is named pope and takes the name John Paul II
1978

A Turkish terrorist shoots and wounds Pope John Paul II in an assassination attempt
1981

A concordat replaces the Lateran Treaties
1985

1990s

Pope John Paul II continues official visits around the world

The Banco Ambrosiano implicates the Vatican bank in its scandal

The relationship of the Catholic Church with Nazi Germany comes under attack

THE HOLY SEE (VATICAN CITY)

The Holy See, often referred to as Vatican City or simply the Vatican, is the ruling center of the Roman Catholic Church. The pope has full governing powers in temporal matters as well. Electrical power and street access are provided by the city of Rome, within which the Vatican lies, and the Italian government is responsible for defense. Security concerns have grown enormously since an assassination attempt on Pope John Paul II in 1981. The government of Italy has promised that it will protect the pope as long as he is on Italian soil (technically this excludes the Vatican), but little can be done when he is globetrotting.

For several centuries, the Roman Empire was staunchly opposed to Christianity. Indeed, Christians were persecuted, often thrown to the lions for public entertainment. The year A.D. 312 marked a turning point, in that it witnessed Emperor Constantine's conversion to Christianity. Constantine made the Christian religion the official state religion. This ended the persecution, and Christian authorities were now allowed a foothold in Rome from which they could oversee and direct progress. They were no longer considered an exclusively spiritual force. According to Roman law, the Church was a "persona" that was able to act in worldly matters as well. Its legal existence implied that it could acquire worldly goods as well. Thus the Roman Empire had become a friend to the Church instead of a foe. By the time the Empire collapsed, 1½ centuries later, the Church had accumulated so much real estate that its leader, the bishop of Rome, was no longer viewed as merely a religious leader but also as "defender of the state." The so-called papal states gradually increased in size, largely because the empire as such had fallen apart.

The Reformation and the French Revolution constituted severe setbacks to papal power, from a worldly perspective. However, in Italy the Church was all-powerful.

After the Congress of Vienna (1815), which attempted to restore pre-Napoleonic Europe, the pope was again recognized not only as the leader of the Church but also as a chief of state.

The Risorgimento, an elite movement that sought to bring all of Italy back under one government, brought unity to Italy and also a sharp reduction in papal land. The Roman Catholic Church resented this nationalistic force. Nevertheless, the pope was forced to withdraw to the redoubt that the Church offered; that is, he became primarily a spiritual leader. The Lateran Treaties, concluded in 1929, ended the process of diminution of papal power definitively. The pope was to be sovereign in an area not exceeding 0.17 square mile. The Treaty of Conciliation was made part of the Constitution of Italy.

However, it could seem that the Kingdom of Italy, or at least Mussolini's Fascist government, was willing to compensate for the quantitative losses that the Lateran Treaties wrought, through qualitative increases in international power and prestige. A sovereign entity, the Santa Sede ("Holy See"), was created to that end, to be party in international negotiations and treaties. Ambassadors and other diplomats can be accredited to the Holy See, which in turn has its own emissaries, usually called *internuncios,* or *nuncios.* All this is bound to facilitate the contacts between the Vatican and the governments of more traditional nation-states.

The Lateran Treaties were replaced in 1985 by a concordat between Italy and the Vatican. The new accord abolished some privileges that the Church still had in Italy; notably, Roman Catholicism would no longer be regarded as Italy's state religion.

The Vatican's momentous decisions affect the lives of millions of people. Yet its decision making is far from democratic. It is not easy to identify the type of leadership in the Vatican. Even the professed papal infallibility does not render it a the-

ocracy. Maybe the term *oligarchy* would be most appropriate. But it is obvious that there are strong streaks of authoritarianism in the way in which the Vatican operates. In the past, this authoritarianism found expression in the well-known adage *Roma locuta, causa finita* (Latin for "Once Rome has spoken, the issue is settled"). The phrase still holds true in issues such as birth control, abortion, and women as priests, all of which the Church discourages. The pope has repeatedly denounced the so-called Liberation theologians in Latin America as Marxists who have no place in the Church. These theologians have activated here-and-now issues in that part of the world, which suffers from a poverty for which the Church has given no adequate solution.

The Santa Sede, of course, is not without human flaws. The involvement of the Vatican in the 1990s scandal of the Banco Ambrosiano reminds one that the Vatican is not entirely free of worldly concerns.

In March 1998, a Vatican committee released a document addressing the role and responsibilities of Europe's Roman Catholics regarding the Holocaust of World War II, in which approximately 6 million Jews and 5 million others were murdered in Europe. The document emerged from an 11-year probe encouraged by Pope John Paul. Entitled "We Remember: A Reflection on the Shoah [Holocaust]," the 16-page document acknowledged that many Catholics were guilty of falling in line with Nazi Germany's anti-Semitism—but it did not fully address the Church's responsibility as an institution. In evaluating the piece, many observers felt that the Church once again did too little, too late.

DEVELOPMENT

The Vatican City State relies on Italy for much of its infrastructure and defense. Though specific figures are not available, the incomes and living standards of lay people in the Holy See are thought to be comparable or superior to those of their counterparts in the city of Rome.

FREEDOM

Freedom is a limited concept as far as the Holy See is concerned. The Vatican is home to about 860 people, most of whom are Italians.

HEALTH/WELFARE

Through his pronouncements, the pope affects the health and welfare of millions of people throughout the world.

ACHIEVEMENTS

The Holy See was one of the parties involved in the prolonged negotiations that led to the Helsinki Accords, and it signed the Final Act in 1975. In 1994, the Vatican and Israel recognized each other.

Iceland (Republic of Iceland)

GEOGRAPHY
Area in Square Miles (Kilometers):
39,758 (103,000) (slightly
smaller than Kentucky)
Capital (Population): Reykjavik
(104,300)
Environmental Concerns: water
pollution; inadequate waste-
water treatment
Geographical Features: mostly
plateau interspersed with
mountain peaks, icefields;
coast is deeply indented by
bays and fiords
Climate: temperate; moderated
by North Atlantic Current

PEOPLE

Population
Total: 271,000
Annual Growth Rate: 0.52%
Rural/Urban Population Ratio: 8/92
Major Language: Icelandic
Ethnic Makeup: a homogeneous
blend of people of Nordic and
Celtic origin
Religions: 96% Lutheran; 4%
others or no affiliation

Health
Life Expectancy at Birth: 77
years (male); 81 years (female)
Infant Mortality Rate (Ratio):
5.3/1,000
Physicians Available (Ratio): 1/357

Education
Adult Literacy Rate: 100%
Compulsory (Ages): 6–16; free

COMMUNICATION
Telephones: 1 per 1.8 people
Daily Newspaper Circulation:
515 per 1,000 people
Televisions: 1 per 2.9 people

TRANSPORTATION
Highways in Miles (Kilometers):
7,406 (12,341)
Railroads in Miles (Kilometers): none
Usable Airfields: 90
Motor Vehicles in Use: 135,000

GOVERNMENT
Type: constitutional republic
Independence Date: June 17, 1944 (from
Denmark)
Head of State/Government: President
Olafur Ragnar Grimsson; Prime Minis-
ter David Oddsson
Political Parties: Independence Party; Pro-
gressive Party; Social Democratic Party;
People's Movement; Women's Party;
Socialists
Suffrage: universal at 18

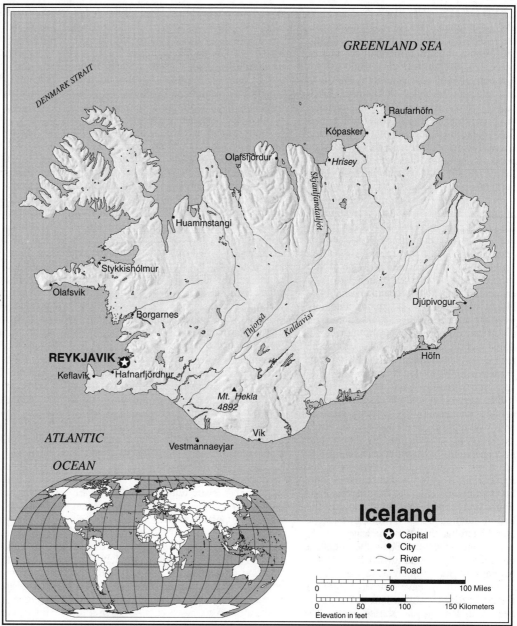

MILITARY
Military Expenditures (% of GDP): none
(Iceland's defense is provided by the
U.S.–Icelandic Defense Force)
Current Disputes: Rockall continental
shelf dispute with Denmark, Ireland,
and United Kingdom

ECONOMY
Currency ($ U.S. Equivalent): 68.3 kro-
nurs = $1
Per Capita Income/GDP: $21,000/$5.71
billion
GDP Growth Rate: 4.9%
Inflation Rate: 2.3%
Unemployment Rate: 3.8%
Labor Force: 131,000

Natural Resources: fish; hydropower; geo-
thermal power; diatomite
Agriculture: cattle; sheep; dairying; pota-
toes; turnips; fish
Industry: fish processing; aluminum smelt-
ing; ferrosilicon production; geothermal
power; tourism
Exports: $1.8 billion (primary partners
United Kingdom, Germany, United
States)
Imports: $2 billion (primary partners Ger-
many, Norway, United Kingdom)

 http://www.iceland.org/
http://www.odci.gov/cia/publications/
factbook/country-frame.html
http://portal.research.bell-labs.com/
cgi-wald/dbaccess/411?key=112

LAND OF ICE AND FIRE

Iceland, a lonely outpost on the northwestern fringe of Europe, halfway between the European and North American continents, is located just south of the Arctic Circle. It is actively volcanic, and both lava flows and glaciers meander through its landscape, which explains the graphic name bestowed on Iceland: "land of ice and fire." Nearly 10 percent of the land area is covered by glacial ice. This terrain appears so barren and desolate that those arriving by air may get the impression of landing on the moon.

One would not expect much in the way of human habitat in Iceland, and indeed the island appears not to have been inhabited before medieval times. For a considerable period, the unprepossessing area served merely as an orientation point and sometimes as a temporary shelter to fishermen braving the winds and waves of the North Atlantic. The first sparse settlements were established by Irish monks intent on dissociating themselves from the world. Some records describe these hermits in the mist of a half-mythical past, but it is not known what happened to them. They disappeared without a trace.

One of the first settlers was Ingolfur Arnarson, a chieftain from West Norway, who wanted to break away from royal authority. In A.D. 874, he, his family, and his dependents built settlements on the site of what is now the capital city of Reykjavik. Apparently this move stimulated a flow of settlers to the area that continued and increased in volume toward the end of the ninth century, probably because Harald Fairhair had become king of Norway around the year 885—the conquest of Norway by this king had been at the expense of many noblemen, who thereupon decided to leave Norway. Some of them left for the British Isles; others proceeded to Iceland and started a new life in these harsh surroundings. It is possible that Harald Fairhair's ascent to power served as a catalyst for the Age of Discovery, especially since Iceland was also used as a base for the discovery and subsequent settlement of Greenland. This achievement is largely attributed to Eric the Red, a Norwegian Viking. His son, Leifur Eriksson, one of the first persons to have been born and raised in Iceland, in turn led an expedition from Greenland to Vinland (often spelled Wineland), which must have been the northeastern part of North America. Over time, numerous items have been discovered that help to document the Viking Age. As recently as 1993, archaeological findings in the Vidgelmir Cave in western Iceland were traced to the Viking Age, thus contributing to our knowledge of the Vikings.

Conditions remained punishing in Iceland itself, its people eking out a living through fishing and farming. Sheep farming became an important livelihood. But whether the settlers had come as refugees or voluntarily, the laws that they took with them were fragmentary and often difficult to interpret and enforce. A new legal system that would reflect the situation seemed urgently needed. To that end, the various settlements started to institute local assemblies, which in turn led to the establishment of a Parliament (in Old Icelandic, the *Althing,* or "Whole Assembly"—the term indicates that all people were to participate in its proceedings; if the British Parliament is often nicknamed "the mother of parliaments," the Althing may be viewed as the grandmother of parliaments).

The Althing operated as a rule-making institution for some 3 centuries. Iceland was free from outside interference during that period, and since monarchical rule was absent, it could be classified as an independent republic of sorts. But in the late thirteenth century, the island lost its independence to Norway, not quite by force but, rather, as the result of a treaty. And a century later, both Iceland and Norway came under Danish rule.

The population on the island was fairly stable until the fifteenth century, when the plague arrived. Living conditions in Iceland generally remained extraordinarily austere and severe until the middle of the eighteenth century, past the time when other European countries had started to evidence some comfort. Icelandic health care was inferior, and recurrent pestilence took its toll, decimating the populace. The question of whether or not to resettle the survivors on the mainland was raised from time to time. The mainland authorities were hesitant to do so, however, since such a repatriation could mean the reintroduction of the plague in parts of Scandinavia.

INDEPENDENCE

But even if the social and health conditions left much to be desired, a great deal of progress was made in terms of political emancipation. Denmark still ruled supreme at the turn of this century, but it granted home rule (independent self-government in internal affairs) to Iceland in 1903. And during World War I, Denmark became serious about shedding all of its overseas holdings. It sold its Virgin Islands in the Caribbean to the United States, and it concluded a treaty with Iceland that recognized the island as an independent state under the king of Denmark. That treaty, which soon led to the so-called Act of Union, was concluded for a definite term—25 years—and Denmark was occupied by Nazi forces before it expired. The British, apprehensive that the fall of Denmark in April 1940 would be interpreted as implying the surrender of Iceland as well, took immediate steps to prevent a German occupation of the strategically located island.

The treaty with Denmark as well as the Act of Union may be said to have been canceled through circumstance, but during the British occupation (which subsequently became an Anglo–American occupation effort), the Althing continued to pass legislation meant to terminate the relationship that had existed with Denmark. Formally, Iceland became an independent republic on June 17, 1944, although it remained occupied, in view of the ongoing war.

In return for the cooperation rendered in wartime while emerging as an independent republic, Iceland received a share of U.S. Marshall Plan aid, even though it had not been damaged by the war. And a couple of years later, the island government was invited to help found the North Atlantic Treaty Organization. The United States by that time had become convinced of the strategic value of the small nation-state, which could not contribute armed forces since it had no army. Its major contribution thus became the air base at Keflavik.

Iceland's membership has occasionally caused the NATO leadership to resort to subterfuge. For example, when the Icelandic government included Communists or persons of a radical leftist persuasion, NATO excluded it from sharing its classified information and from deliberations concerning top-secret plans. The Icelandic government, however, has never taken offense, and Iceland has continued to be a member under these somewhat humiliating circumstances.

THE ECONOMY

Iceland was hit in the early 1990s by a severe recession. The adverse circumstances may have been due in part to Iceland's gradually changing economy. This was the subject of a study by Iceland's National Research Council. The Council concluded that the country was about to enter the postindustrial age, a time when skills, ability, and innovation are seen as more important than equipment and structures. In more recent years, the economy has rebounded impressively, with low inflation and unemployment and much improved per capita GDP incomes and growth rates. Iceland has made strides toward liberalizing its economy. And thanks to its membership in the European Eco-

(Iceland Tourist Board photo by Johan Henrik Piepgrass)

Fish and fish products constitute an important part—75 percent—of Iceland's total exports and involve employment of about 12 percent of the workforce. These fishing boats and trawlers are at port in Reykjavik.

nomic Area, Iceland can participate in the European Union's free-trade market (except in fish and food.)

In 1880, more than 73 percent of the working population were engaged in farming; by 1950, this proportion had declined to 30 percent. Currently, agriculture employs only about 4 percent of the workforce. These figures reflect the growing urbanization of the island, but it should also be taken into account that farmers are largely occupied with cattle and sheep breeding. (The amount of arable land is only 0.5 percent.)

Occupationally, agriculture and fishing, which both are forms of primary industry, have an interesting inverse relationship in Iceland, in that fishing increases as agriculture declines. So great has Iceland's dependence on fish and fish products become that its government, beginning in the mid-twentieth century, placed severe restrictions on foreign fishing vessels, which could deplete the waters that surround the island and thereby ruin its economy. A free-market economy predominates in Iceland, though government ownership of businesses has expanded by leaps and bounds, particularly in the fishing industry.

In 1952, Iceland extended the limits of its fisheries outward to a perimeter 4 miles from lines drawn between its longest promontories and between islets and rocks offshore, enclosing many fishing grounds previously open to foreign fishermen. Some fishing boats in violation of the new rule were detained. In retaliation, British trawler owners at Hull and Grimsby refused facilities to Icelandic vessels. However, this was only the beginning of what later came to be called the "Cod War," one

of the larger intra-NATO conflicts. One of the main reasons for extending Iceland's fishing rights in the northern Atlantic was the modern fish-harvesting technique being practiced, especially by the British fishing vessels. Gradually, step by step, Iceland continued to extend its own zone of fishing rights, by implication prohibiting foreign vessels from fishing in those waters. This was all done unilaterally, and occasionally without much advance notice. The International Court of Justice ruled in 1974 that the 50-mile limit that Iceland established in 1972 could not be imposed unilaterally. Iceland, however, rejected the ruling. Iceland's fishing rights eventually reached the 200-mile limit, which has now been universally accepted as the legacy of the United Nations Conference on the Law of the Sea.

The most recent partition has not removed the danger that some fish species may become extinct. It only means that the predator role has become monopolized. The Icelandic press reported that the exports of frozen seafood from Icelandic Freezing Plants Corporation reached a record of 91,500 tons, worth some $300 million, in 1993, as compared to 83,000 tons in the previous year.

Some 70 percent of all Iceland's exports are fish-related. Cod has traditionally been the most important species of the nation's fishing industry. The Marine Research Institute reported that by mid-1992, the lowest cod catch in half a century had been reached. It is a matter of course that fluctuations in fish catches will cause ups and downs in Iceland's economy. In addition, marketing and delivery have become momentous factors, and one wonders whether

Icelandic fish-auction markets can compete with their foreign counterparts. Modern telecommunications enable buyers to bid on fresh, unprocessed fish from virtually anywhere. As a result, the competition has become enormous.

The Issue of Whaling

Whaling is one of the more contentious subjects that a foreigner should avoid bringing up while visiting Iceland. Most Icelanders feel that whales are just fish, only bigger. Early Icelanders are said to have harpooned small whales from yawls, and Icelanders have always been quick to utilize beached whales. Indeed, the Icelandic word for a beached whale, *hvalreki,* has come to mean a "propitious windfall" or "godsend." Icelanders argue that their whaling record has undeservedly rendered them into pariahs in the international community. They believe that Iceland has done as much as, if not more than, other countries to protect the whale from extinction.

Whaling reached a peak at the turn of the century; by 1902, it had become clear that world whale stocks were on the decline. The Althing banned whaling in 1915, with the moratorium in place until 1935. However, the Althing's power extended only to Icelandic whaling, and many foreign whaling operations continued. In 1935, Icelandic whaling was resumed, but it stopped again when World War II started in 1939. After the war, Icelanders resumed whaling. In 1986, an international whaling ban was issued. Iceland, although a member of the International Whaling Commission (IWC), had never endorsed the international agitation on the ethical level, but it now pledged that it would fully abide by the new mandates. Finally, in 1992, after numerous recriminations concerning violations, Reykjavik decided to resign from the IWC. It was then that the Faeroe Islands, Greenland, Iceland, and Norway joined forces to found the North Atlantic Marine Mammal Committee (NAMMCO).

Benefits from Nature

No discussion of the Icelandic economy would be complete without mention of the extensive use that Iceland makes of its natural resources. It derives a large portion of its energy supply from hydropower and from thermal springs heated by molten lava. Thus, although the winters can be grueling, nature seems to compensate by providing thermal waters that can be used for heating systems. This low-cost energy is also used for the development of the aluminum-smelting industry. For its oil supply, the country has been largely dependent on deliveries from the former So-

The earliest Norse settlement in Iceland A.D. 874	The Althing meets for the first time 930	Christianity is introduced in Iceland 1000	Union with Norway 1264	Union with Denmark 1380	Recurrent pestilence 1400–1800	The Althing is abolished during the period of Danish absolutism 1800
●	●	●	●	●	●	●

viet Union, though it has started to acquire oil from the British-exploited North Sea fields as well.

SOCIAL POLICY

Iceland, in common with other Scandinavian countries, provides a comprehensive system of social welfare. More than half of the national budget goes to education, public-assistance programs, and health. Cost-free medical care supports one physician for every 357 people in the country. Iceland's rates of life expectancy for men and women are among the highest in the world. This good news, however, has serious implications for the future. With people living so long, Iceland will not be able to go on providing such a generous welfare system. Indeed, the government has begun trimming its largesse.

GOVERNMENT

Iceland is a constitutional republic. Like most Western European nations, it has a dual executive—a head of state, the president, who serves terms of 4 years; and a head of government, the prime minister. The president, in his or her largely ceremonial role, must appoint the prime minister, who presides over a government responsible to Parliament. Iceland's Parliament, which is still called the Althing, has 63 members, divided into upper and lower houses. The upper house consists of 22 members; they are elected by the Althing as a whole. The two houses have equal constitutional power.

There are half a dozen major political parties. They by and large fall into two groups: the Socialist bloc and the non-Socialist bloc. Since none of the political parties receives a majority vote, a government has to rely on coalitions. Interestingly, these coalitions often include political parties from both blocs. The conservative Independence Party invariably constitutes the bulk of such coalitions.

The Socialist bloc includes the Social Democratic party and the radical left, the People's Movement (in turn including the former Communist Party of Iceland). Both blocs suffer from increasing factionalism.

The early to mid-1990s witnessed a significant decline in government support. Public-opinion polls indicated that the government of Prime Minister David Oddsson had become less popular. But, perhaps reflecting the improved mood of the country with the return of good economic times, he remained prime minister when, in 1996, Olafur Ragnar Grimsson, a conservative, won the presidential election, succeeding Vigdis Finnbogadottir.

WOMEN

The woman's-liberation movement made vast strides in Iceland. This may be all the more remarkable because the *relative* improvement in the status of women has been so considerable. The status of women started at a low point in Iceland in contrast to the other Nordic countries and has always been inferior to that of men in sociopolitical respects. In 1976, Iceland enacted its Equal Rights Amendment. Until that time, 80 percent of Icelandic women employed outside the house had earned on the average about 40 percent less than their male counterparts.

Then, in 1980, Vigdis Finnbogadottir, director of the Reykjavik Theater, ran for the office of president. She was elected, a feat that provided an enormous stimulus to the women's movement. Encouraged, it put forward its first candidates in local elections in 1982. When they too were successful, the movement changed from a pressure group into a political party, the Women's Alliance, which in 1983 participated in national elections.

In the 1987 election, the Women's Alliance won 10.1 percent of the vote, which, under the proportional-representation system, translated into 6 seats. More important, the parliamentary role of the Women's Alliance became pivotal, since neither of the two blocs won a majority. As things stand, no government coalition can survive without the approval of what is today called the Women's Party. On the other hand, the party has a fairly narrow focus, being chiefly concerned with women's rights, particularly with equal employment opportunities. In 1984, the Women's Alliance ordered another women's general strike, which this time was honored by the president (who normally may not be identified with any party); she left her office for the day! A presidential election had been scheduled for June 26, 1992. However, the incumbent was the only person to register as a candidate. The election was therefore canceled, and President Vigdis embarked upon her fourth term of office on August 1. She subsequently announced that she would not seek a fifth term.

The inferior position that women traditionally held in Iceland is all the more remarkable because Iceland has followed Scandinavian social mores in many other respects. One may point to the patronymic tradition, for instance. Iceland has an unusual concept of family names; it pays more attention to first names. Often the first name of the father becomes the last name of the son or daughter. Thus, Jon's daughter Ragnihildur will be named, in full, Ragnihildur Jonsdottir. Also, in ancient sagas, the *Edda* (either of two Old Icelandic volumes of myths and poems compiled during the thirteenth century), and other poetic literature, the position of women is never portrayed as subordinate; rather, women are equal to men in valiance, courage, and other virtues. To most Icelanders, the ancient poetry is not pure imagery and myth. It is a living reality, and the heroes in, for example, the Eddaic verses are taken as historical persons and often as role models.

The events that take place in the sagas may not have occurred in reality, but Icelanders take it for granted that the *Edda* was more or less a realistic version of conditions and situations in the past. In part this is not an entirely inaccurate assumption; much of the ancient Scandinavian poetry was made in honor of kings of Norway, who often employed renowned poets (*skalds*) to conduct "public relations."

LANGUAGE

A factor that looms large in the popularity of ancient literature in Iceland is that its language has been preserved much better than in many continental European countries. Over many centuries, the language did not change to a great extent. Indeed, a study of source material over various centuries reveals a rigidity that most probably results from Iceland's isolation. Like the United States, Iceland started off as a colony of settlement; but, in sharp contrast to the United States, it was never a melting pot in any sense. Basically, all its immigrants arrived over a strictly limited period from Scandinavia—thus the same source in linguistic respect. (Danish, Norwegian, and Swedish differ only dialectically.) There has been an absence of other

The Althing is
restored as a
consultative body
1843

Home rule
1904

Act of Union;
Iceland becomes
Independent In a
personal union
with the Danish
crown
1918

British and U.S.
occupation
1940–1945

Iceland is
proclaimed a
republic; the
last ties with
Denmark are
severed
1944

The Cod War
1970s

Vigdis
Finnbogadottir
becomes the first
female president
of Iceland
1980

1990s

Iceland
experiences
economic
recession and
labor tensions
in the early
1990s, but the
economy
rebounds within
a few years

Iceland
strengthens
its
environmental
status but has
virtually no
relations with
the developing
world

Icelanders
debate the
merits of
joining the
European
Union and the
Euro—and
decline;
President
Finnbogadottir
is succeeded
by Olafur
Ragmar
Grimsson

outside influences. Thus, the fact that twentieth-century Icelanders are still able to enjoy the *Edda* and other sources of ancient literature may well be related to linguistic introversion.

THE INTERNATIONAL ARENA

Iceland has started to receive greater international recognition. This is especially the case with regard to global conferences and international organizations. Thus Prime Minister Oddsson could report to the Althing in June 1992 that Iceland had been invited to join the West European Alliance. Oddsson indicated that acceptance would prevent Iceland from having to choose between the two main pillars of NATO: Europe on the one hand, and the United States and Canada on the other. He added that the only alternative for Iceland would be to strengthen its ties with the United States while moving away from Europe. Such a course of action would neither serve the country's security interests nor be acceptable to its people as a European nation. In addition, the United States and Iceland reached a new 2-year agreement calling for a continued (though reduced) U.S. and NATO presence in Keflavik, in southwest Iceland. Today, Icelanders seem largely content with this arrangement.

Since the European economy in the early 1990s had started to absorb 80 percent of Iceland's exports, it was only natural that the idea to join the European Union started to take hold. However, resistance also gathered strength. By mid-1992, the press reported that 48.3 percent of Icelanders appeared to oppose the idea of Iceland becoming a member of the Union, 15.7 percent supported it, and an unusually large group of 34.5 percent had yet to make up their minds.

Iceland's foreign minister, Jon Baldvin Hannibalsson, was of two minds on this point. While he believed that the EU underestimated Iceland's defense role in a new Europe, he also thought that the European Economic Area would last longer as an intermediate phenomenon than many people were inclined to think. "The classical stumbling block to Icelandic membership," Hannibalsson stated in June 1992, "has been the [EU] Common Fisheries Policy, which would oblige Iceland to open its fishing grounds—the nation's only immediate resource—to the oversized European fleet." Thus, although participation in the EEA could well be viewed as a stepping stone to full membership in the European Union, it appeared unlikely that Iceland would become an EU member before the new millenium. (Iceland has for 3 decades been a member of the European Free Trade Association; most EFTA members have considered the EEA little more than a springboard to the EU.)

Outside the all-important economic field, Iceland also succeeded in gaining recognition for its ecological initiatives. During preparations for the 1992 Rio Summit, a world conference on issues pertaining to the environment and energy, Iceland's delegation in New York managed to achieve a reclassification of energy sources, to highlight which are environmentally safe and which are destructive. At the Rio meeting itself, Iceland became a distinctive force among Western nations for its unequivocal stand on environmental questions.

While some of the industrialized nations, particularly Great Britain and the United States, have consistently attempted to block effective restrictions on discharging and dumping at sea chemicals and even nuclear waste, and restrictions on nuclear submarine activity, Iceland has spoken out against them. This part of the

ecological debate provided an avenue to the whaling question. Here the Icelandic delegation argued that pollution of the seas by persistent organic substances posed a far more serious threat to whale and seal populations than a regulated hunt ever could.

DEVELOPMENT

Icelandic society has become considerably more urbanized since World War II. The industrial base continues to be small; fishery remains strong. Farming has declined, while tourism has increased tremendously.

FREEDOM

Plans to terminate the centuries-long rule by Denmark materialized at the end of World War I. Independence came during World War II, when Iceland was cut off from Denmark, which was occupied by the Germans.

HEALTH/WELFARE

Iceland has an excellent social-welfare system. Benefits cover maternity and child care, health care, education, unemployment compensation, and pensions. Iceland's quality-of-life indicators, including life expectancy, are among the highest in the world.

ACHIEVEMENTS

Iceland's unilateral extension of the limits of its fishing rights was accepted by other nations and eventually became universalized by the UN Conference on the Law of the Sea. Literacy is virtually total. Icelanders read and publish more books per capita than any other population. Even the ancient *Edda* is widely read.

Ireland (Eire)

GEOGRAPHY

Area in Square Miles (Kilometers): 27,135 (70,280) (slightly larger than West Virginia)

Capital (Population): Dublin (478,500)

Environmental Concerns: water pollution from agricultural runoff

Geographical Features: mostly level to rolling interior plain surrounded by rugged hills and low mountains; sea cliffs on west coast

Climate: temperate maritime

PEOPLE

Population

Total: 3,620,000

Annual Growth Rate: 0.36%

Rural/Urban Population Ratio: 42/58

Major Languages: English; Gaelic

Ethnic Makeup: Celtic; English minority

Religions: 93% Roman Catholic; 3% Anglican; 4% other

Health

Life Expectancy at Birth: 73 years (male); 79 years (female)

Infant Mortality Rate (Ratio): 6/1,000

Average Caloric Intake: 148% of FAO minimum

Physicians Available (Ratio): 1/681

Education

Adult Literacy Rate: 100%

Compulsory (Ages): 6–15

COMMUNICATION

Telephones: 1 per 2.7 people

Daily Newspaper Circulation: 170 per 1,000 people

Televisions: 1 per 3.3 people

TRANSPORTATION

Highways in Miles (Kilometers): 55,458 (92,430)

Railroads in Miles (Kilometers): 1,206 (1,947)

Usable Airfields: 44

Motor Vehicles in Use: 1,230,000

GOVERNMENT

Type: parliamentary republic

Independence Date: December 6, 1921 (from United Kingdom)

Head of State/Government: President Mary McAleese; Prime Minister Bertie Ahern

Political Parties: Fianna Fáil; Democratic Left Party; Labour Party; Fine Gael; Communist Party; Workers' Party; Sinn Fein; Progressive Democratic Party; Green Party

Suffrage: universal at 18

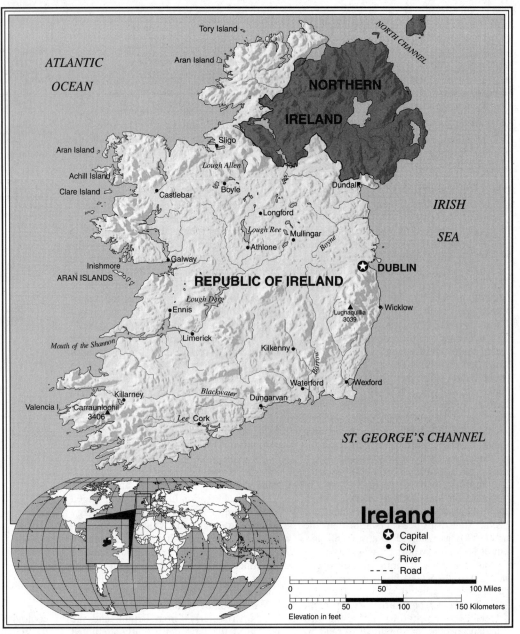

MILITARY

Military Expenditures (% of GDP): 1.3%

Current Disputes: Northern Ireland question with Britain; Rockall continental shelf dispute concerning Denmark, Iceland, and Britain

ECONOMY

Currency ($ U.S. Equivalent): 0.629 punt (Irish pound) = $1

Per Capita Income/GDP: $18,600/$59.9 billion

GDP Growth Rate: 6%

Inflation Rate: 1.6%

Unemployment Rate: 11.8%

Labor Force: 1,474,000

Natural Resources: zinc; lead; natural gas; petroleum; barite; copper; gypsum; limestone; dolomite; peat; silver

Agriculture: livestock and dairy products; turnips; barley; potatoes; sugar beets; wheat; fish

Industry: food products; brewing; textiles and clothing; chemicals; pharmaceuticals; machinery; transportation equipment; tourism; glass and crystal

Exports: $54.8 billion (primary partners EU countries, United States)

Imports: $44.9 billion (primary partners EU countries, United States)

 http://www.irlgov.ie/frmain.htm
http://www.odci.gov/cia/publications/factbook/country-frame.html

IRELAND (EIRE)

The large island immediately to the west of Britain, which came to be named Ireland, or Eire, has been inhabited for about 9,000 years. At the beginning of recorded history, a Celtic language was spoken in the area, a language closely related to Scottish, Welsh, Gaelic, and Breton. One may generally assume that Celtic tribes were not confined to Ireland but extended over parts of Britain and the European continent as well. These Celts had well-developed social and legal systems and a rich, orally transmitted culture.

Christianity was introduced on the island by the man who is now known as St. Patrick. He is still greatly revered by the Irish. The conversion from Druidism to Christianity took place in the fifth century A.D., and in the centuries that followed, Irish monks established centers of learning at home, in Britain, and in continental Europe. From 700 to 900, Viking raiders and settlers invaded parts of Britain, which caused some of the Celtic residents to flee westward and to seek refuge on the island. However, the raiders also conquered and colonized parts of Ireland itself.

Although British expansions may have started earlier, a massive transmigration took place in the sixteenth and seventeenth centuries, a time when religious warfare had started to make Britain very turbulent. The English swarmed all over the island, rendering it a colony, and brought over their aristocracy as landowners. Earlier, and smaller, groups of English people had become assimilated and in effect hardly distinguishable from the native inhabitants; but this had now become impossible, since the English took over government and governmental institutions. Another group settled in northern Ireland, different from the English in many ways: the Scots. They were very poor and very religious, adhering to the Presbyterian denomination. They too refused to mix with the native Irish, largely because the latter were universally Roman Catholic.

These invasions, which took away their land and government, naturally caused resentment among the Irish. In 1798, Wolf Tone and the United Irishmen, inspired by the American and French Revolutions, started a rebellion intended to terminate British rule. The rebellion, which was more an emotional reaction than a carefully calculated enterprise, was suppressed. The nineteenth century witnessed sporadic rebellions, but there was no sustained revolt, since the Irish people at that time lacked the wherewithal to rise against an infinitely stronger Britain. The potato famine of the 1840s proved devastating; more than 4 million Irish people died as a result of it. A great many others who survived this economic catastrophe emigrated to the United States.

In the early part of the twentieth century, not coincidentally at a time when Great Britain was immersed in World War I, the long-simmering conflict came to a head. An armed uprising (the Easter Rising) afforded a glimpse of Irish potential. It was put down by the British troops, the Black and Tan, but what the rebels failed to gain on the battlefield, they secured in the British election held in 1918. The Sinn Fein, a radical Irish party, won 73 seats, whereas the Unionists/Conservatives in the north won only 26 seats. After this victory, Sinn Fein proceeded to set itself up as an Irish Parliament, with Eamon deValera as its head. The members of the new Parliament as a matter of course refused to take their seats in the British Parliament.

THE ANGLO–IRISH WAR

Such defiance was not taken lightly by Britain, and after some skirmishes, the Anglo–Irish War broke out. The conflict (1919–1921) served as another catalyst to Irish independence, not so much because the British were superior in numbers and in strategy but, rather, because their (mostly mercenary) troops committed such atrocities on the Irish that public opinion in the United States and Great Britain was very adversely affected.

The changing climate of opinion forced the British to a truce and to the conference table. In December 1921, a treaty between Irish and British leaders brought into effect the Government of Ireland Act of 1920, which conceded British Commonwealth status and a parliament to 26 Irish counties (which jointly assumed the name Irish Free State) and kept six northern counties with a separate parliament within the United Kingdom.

However, if adversity had united the Irish, the treaty and its main product, the Irish Free State, caused bitter disputes in the ranks of the Sinn Fein. Some were prepared to accept the British concessions, believing that they were to lead to the ultimate ideal of complete independence of the entire island. Others, such as deValera, adamantly opposed what was being offered, certain that Great Britain was short-changing them. After losing the internal fight, deValera founded a new organization, the Fianna Fáil (which means "Warriors of Destiny"). By 1932, it was the dominant political party in Ireland; its leader then formed a government and embarked upon his long tenure as prime minister (1932–1959).

Although the terms of Irish independence were gradually strengthened, the British refused to make further concessions in regard to the six counties in the north. One may therefore say that deValera had made a turnabout by endorsing a system that he had initially rejected. By seeming prepared to wait for whatever time that could aid the Irish cause, deValera turned a turbulent situation into a stable one.

IRELAND'S NEW IDENTITY, HOME RULE, AND INDEPENDENCE

Since 1921, the Irish Republic has endeavored to pursue two broad goals simultaneously: On the one hand, it has wanted to convey the image of an independent nation; on the other, it has fervently aspired to resolve the border question and related issues. There can be little doubt that, for 7 decades, Eire has been enmeshed in a de facto triangular relationship with Northern Ireland and Britain.

This triangle has served as a persistent reminder that Ireland's jurisdiction is limited—that it does not cover the entire island, but only 26 out of 32 counties. The British presence, from which many generations have wanted to disentangle themselves, is in effect a frontispiece. It is right on their doorstep. One cannot study a map of the island without looking at a part of the United Kingdom (Northern Ireland). To Britain, the situation is certainly complicated, as irredentism usually is.

Ireland has built up a degree of hostility against the English. It has differed from Britain on four communal dimensions: language, ethnic origin, culture and tradition, and religion. And then there is the moral consideration: During the heyday of imperialism, Britain planted Scottish colonies in Northern Ireland. Here, too, the typical colonial picture prevailed; the Scottish vanguard became landowners at the expense of the Irish. Later tenants came from Scotland to strengthen the Protestant cause. Thus, a whole new society was created, entirely alien to the native Irish traditions in Ulster and completely different in character from every other part of Ireland. The Presbyterian Scots constituted a majority in the six northern counties; but if these counties would also be ceded to Ireland, their numbers would be so diluted that they would in effect constitute a minority. They would be a small Protestant fragment in a population that was almost universally Roman Catholic. For the British Conservative Party and some Liberals, giving Ireland any independence would not only engulf Protestants in a Catholic state ("Home rule was Rome rule") but also destroy the Constitution as defined by the empire that was built around Britain and Ireland.

Britain has certainly not always been led by ethical considerations in devising imperial policy. It is interesting to note that, when British India was about to gain independence, religious considerations were again instrumental in planning a dual solution (the creation of an additional, successor state). The Irish were convinced that the British concern with the Protestant cause in Northern Ireland was nothing but a hypocritical pretense and that the British wanted only to keep a foothold on the island that in the past had been theirs. For the same reason, the Irish Free State was inhibited by numerous restrictions after officially gaining independence. As a part of the Commonwealth, it was obliged to recognize the British Crown and a governor-general. It also had to subscribe to an oath of loyalty. It was obvious that the United Kingdom continued to block the further self-determination of the new state.

In 1937, the "colonial" Constitution was swept away by deValera and his government. But only when World War II broke out and the Irish government formally announced that Ireland would remain neutral did the Irish finally realize that they had at last attained a sovereignty that extended even to matters of foreign policy. Not joining the United Kingdom when the war broke out and making it face the music all by itself once France had fallen, amounted to a serious affront. Imperial powers have historically been little aware of injustices they have perpetrated. In Ireland's case, Irish neutrality was puzzling if not totally incomprehensible to the British. It did not take long for rumors to circulate to the effect that German submarines found refuge, and were even refueled and resupplied, in Irish ports. These rumors may have been groundless—it seems unlikely that Eire would have risked getting into a war with the United Kingdom—but they were nonetheless indicative of the British inability to appreciate Irish neutrality.

Did the British retaliate? It is possible that the United Kingdom had a hand in the delay that the Irish application for admission to the United Nations experienced. Ireland had been excluded from charter membership in large part because the UN was in effect an extension of the wartime alliance into peace, and since Ireland had emphasized its neutrality throughout the war, it did not qualify for charter membership. It finally became a member in 1955, together with such countries as Bulgaria, Cambodia, Jordan, and Laos.

So strained was the relationship between Ireland and Britain that the former abandoned the Commonwealth of Nations, a global organization that comprises Britain and all its dependencies and former dependencies. Apparently, deValera and his government found even this nonpolitical bond too restrictive, and as soon as this last tie with

the United Kingdom was severed, in 1948, Ireland proclaimed itself a republic.

By that time, the cold war had started to make itself felt; as a result, the North Atlantic Treaty Organization was established. This collective defense pact, sponsored by the United States, included practically all of Western Europe. Ireland nevertheless refused to become a NATO ally.

By the 1970s, some of these attitudes gave way to a more cooperative spirit, for in 1973, Ireland joined the European Union (at that time known as the European Economic Community)—ironically, at the same point in time as the United Kingdom.

GOVERNMENT

Ireland has adopted a system of parliamentary democracy that in many ways resembles the original model of parliamentary government created by Britain. Thus there is a dual executive; but since Ireland is a republic, its head of state is not a monarch but a president who is elected by direct vote of the people. The president has a fixed term of 7 years, and the position is largely ceremonial. The person who must make most major decisions, and who is pivotal in all other respects as well, is the prime minister. The prime minister heads a party or, more often than not, a coalition of parties that helps to execute a program. The prime minister is also elected by direct vote of the people, usually on the basis of his or her program.

The prime minister depends on majority support in *Oireachtas* (Parliament). There are two houses of Parliament, known respectively as *Dail* (House of Representatives) and *Seanad* (Senate). The Dail has 166 members and is the more important house. The Seanad has 60 members. It may initiate or amend legislation (the Dail has the power to reject any proposed legislation or amendments).

The five main political parties represented in the Dail are Fianna Fáil, Fine Gael, the Irish Labour Party, the Progressive Democrats, and the Workers' Party. Fianna Fáil, the party that deValera established about 65 years ago, has been in power the longest, although it has often depended on coalitions. It used to be a radical party but has over the course of time moderated its stand.

The current government is another coalition, again led by Fianna Fáil. The new Progressive Democratic Party is also a government party, and although the coalition has only a one-seat majority, it is unlikely that it will have to yield to another party or parties. Internally, changes are always possible. Following allegations of wiretapping of journalists by his party allies, with his knowledge, Prime Minister

Charles Haughey, who had survived many political crises, finally gave in and resigned on February 10, 1992. The main government party, Fianna Fáil, elected Albert Reynolds to succeed him. Reynolds tendered his resignation 2 years later. He was succeeded by John Bruton.

The office of president was created by the first fully republican Constitution (of 1937). It is a largely ceremonial post. For that reason, it is possible for the president and the prime minister to represent different parties, especially since the election dates can also differ. Currently both the president (Mary McAleese) and the prime minister (Bertie Ahern), who have been in office since 1997, are from the party Fianna Fáil, which is pro-labor.

Irish law is based on common law and legislation enacted by Parliament under the Constitution. The Constitution guarantees freedom of conscience and the free profession and practice of religion to all citizens. Regulations of the European Union have the force of law in Eire, as they do in all member states.

THE ECONOMY

Generally speaking, the late 1970s and early to mid-1980s were economically calamitous to Ireland. To some extent, the marked slump may have been induced by the type of budgeting that was in vogue. Then–prime minister Charles Haughey acknowledged as much when he declared that "deficit budgeting on the current side since 1973 has brought disaster." (Deficit budgeting in its crudest form means that, in the budget, the government expenditures exceed the revenues. In the early 1970s, deficit budgeting almost assumed the force of doctrine.) Haughey continued, "We intend to draw a line under that unhappy 20-year period and get back to balanced annual budgets."

By 1991, however, the Irish economy had experienced a complete turnaround, so much so that *Time* magazine praised the country as the "showpiece of the European [Union]." In part this was due to an economic pact, the so-called Program for National Recovery, which brought government spending under control and led to a lowering of inflation and interest rates. Average economic growth rates have steadily risen over the past decade and now stand at about 7 percent per year. In its trade with the rest of the European Union, Ireland is running a healthy surplus. Foreign companies (predominantly American), taking advantage of free access to the EU market, have also contributed to this picture of economic health. The government has actively courted foreign investors and, in the mid-1990s, created an

St. Patrick arrives to convert the Irish from Druidism to Christianity A.D. 432	Ireland is colonized by Viking raiders, who mostly operate from Wales 700–900	British groups enter Ireland in small colonies but soon assimilate into the main body politic 1200s	Large-scale transmigration from England, which soon assumes imperialistic overtones 1500s–1600s	The potato famine; more than 4 million die; many more emigrate 1840s	"The Troubles" start with the Easter Rebellion; violence and strife 1916–1919	Anglo–Irish War 1919–1921

industrial-development agency to assist small indigenous firms.

Yet against these positives, any objective economic assessment cannot ignore the weakest spot in Ireland's economy: unemployment. Indeed, the contrast between an overall solid economy and the huge unemployment has caused facetious observers to describe Ireland as "the country where the economy works but the people do not." Currently about 12 percent, it does not appear that the unemployment figures will decline soon. In 1979, Jack Lynch, then the prime minister, said that he would feel obliged to resign if unemployment started to exceed 100,000. Today, nearly twice that figure causes nobody to resign. The prime minister and the cabinet point as a matter of course to factors beyond their control; former prime minister Albert Reynolds called for a "consensus approach" to what he qualified as "the biggest unsolved problem facing Ireland today." (The search for a consensus is easily explained; in a parliamentary system, the government can be ousted by the opposition before it has completed its term. In Reynolds' case, he sought the cooperation of government, opposition politicians, labor unions, employers, and farm organizations, but these attempts to arrive at a degree of political harmony had precious little effect.)

Of all the members of the Organization of European Cooperation and Development, Ireland alone registered a net decline in jobs during the 1980s. To help the country, the EU Commission pledged $4.5 billion for national development, an amount to be roughly matched by infusions from the government and the private sector.

Ireland has an open economy that depends to a large extent on international trade. Industry now accounts for more than 80 percent of Ireland's total exports, 38 percent of Ireland's gross domestic product, and 26 percent of its total employment. The Irish industrial sector has developed rapidly over the last 20 years. Foreign investment, stimulated by tax exemptions, capital and training grants, as well as other means, has greatly contributed to the growth of the Irish economy. The main components of the manufacturing industry in Ireland are the food and drink and the mechanical-engineering sectors. The industrial sectors showing most rapid growth are electronics and pharma-

ceuticals, both of which have been aided by substantial foreign investment, especially on the part of the United States.

Labor unions have always been important elements in the Irish economy, and *the* factor that is bound to contribute to the upsurge or downfall of the economy is the attitude of the unions. In 1987, unions were persuaded to endorse the Program for National Recovery, which played a major role in Ireland's recovery by keeping wage increases and inflation below average EU levels. It has now been found that most of the sacrifices were in effect borne by the lower-paid and higher-taxed blue-collar workers. Subsequent signs of budding affluence have made the unions more determined to exact a tougher deal for the Program for National Recovery than the one that was negotiated in 1987, when the economy was in deep recession.

Agriculture is also a very important sector of the Irish economy. Approximately 11 percent of the workforce are employed directly in agriculture, which yields about 9 percent of the national income and about 25 percent of the total exports. Of the total land area of approximately 17 million acres, some 14 million acres are agricultural land (more than 82 percent of the total). Ireland's membership in the European Union has benefited the country's agriculture, if only because the EU provides a large market for its products.

Fishing has also gradually grown into an important part of the economy. Among the fish found in Irish waters are herring, cod, whiting, mackerel, plaice, and shellfish; Irish salmon is exported to many countries. Investment in fish processing is greatly encouraged by the government.

The Irish economy also benefits from mining operations. The country is the leading producer of zinc ores, and one of the world's largest zinc-lead deposits is located at Navan, County Meath. The principal mining activity is the quarrying of sand, gravel, and stone for the construction industry. There is also coal mining, though on a more limited scale. And in the Celtic Sea off the County Cork coast, a gas-production platform has been built.

The restoration of normal political conditions in Irish border areas would mean a welcome increase in tourism as well as an extension of a network of cross-border cooperation in economic and cultural sectors.

Ireland has adopted, like most industrialized democracies, a comprehensive welfare system. An Irish peculiarity is that the welfare system has no built-in controls. As a result, many persons draw from the system without really needing the benefits. (An unconfirmed story circulating some years ago had it that the person who won the Dublin marathon was a recipient of disability checks!)

A complete range of medical services is provided free of charge to lower-income groups. In addition, there is a social-insurance program, which entitles insured workers to free medical services. Generally, however, there has been some retrenchment in the benefits that the Irish welfare system provides.

SEARCH FOR COMPROMISE

Relentless terrorism and endless slaughter have as a matter of course generated considerable concern on both sides of the Ireland–Northern Ireland border. In 1983, a New Ireland Forum was established after political parties in both Eire and Northern Ireland had agreed on consultations about the manner in which lasting peace and stability can be achieved in a new Ireland through the democratic process. Participation was open to all democratic parties that had members elected or appointed to the Irish Parliament or the Northern Ireland Assembly.

Party leaders convened for the first time in Dublin in May 1983. The report of this first session, in which the four main nationalist parties, North and South, participated, was made public on May 2, 1984. The central operational conclusion of the report was that "the validity of both the Nationalist and Unionist identities in Ireland and the democratic rights of every citizen of this island must be accepted; both of these identities have equally satisfactory, secure and durable political, administrative and symbolic expression and protection."

If the establishment of the New Ireland Forum signaled a degree of progress in the meeting of minds, the Anglo–Irish Agreement of 1985 went even further. It had its roots in a meeting of the leaders of the Anglo–Irish Intergovernmental Council (AIIC), which enabled both parties to give institutional expression to the unique relationship between the two countries. On November 15, 1985, the historic meeting at Hillsborough was held (at the level of

The Government
of Ireland Act is
adopted, creating
a northern and
southern Ireland
1920

Eamon deValera
is prime minister
of the Irish Free
State
1932–1959

The new
Constitution is
ratified, changing
the nation's
name from Irish
Free State to Eire
1937

Ireland declares
itself an
independent
republic, no
longer part of the
British
Commonwealth
1939

Ireland is neutral
in World War II
1939–1945

Ireland refuses to
join NATO
1949

The Irish become
progressively
more resentful of
the British
presence in
Northern Ireland
1950–1980

Ireland becomes
a member of the
European Union
1973

The New Ireland
Forum; the
Anglo–Irish
Agreement
1980s

1990s

Economic
upswing is
nonetheless
accompanied
by high
unemployment

Irish voters
favor the
"closer union"
of the
Maastricht
Treaty

Ireland signs
the Northern
Ireland Peace
Agreement

heads of government). Here the prime minister of Ireland and the British prime minister signed the Anglo–Irish Agreement. It established an Intergovernmental Conference, which enabled the Irish government to express views and put forward proposals on various stated aspects of Northern Ireland affairs. Thus, for the first time, the Republic of Ireland would exercise some influence in matters relating strictly to Northern Ireland, the area that was withheld from Ireland when it embarked on the road to independence—an area that, in the words of one authority, is a "factory of grievances."

In 1998, history was made when Ireland, Northern Ireland, and Britain signed the Northern Ireland Peace Agreement, after years of discussion and negotiation. This "Multi Party Agreement" is designed to bring about a lasting peace on the island. Only time will tell if it can succeed.

IRELAND AND THE EU
June 2, 1992, was a dismal day for the European Union: Contrary to general expectations, a Danish referendum rejected the Treaty on European Union, better known as the Maastricht Treaty. Shortly afterward, it was Ireland's turn to take a stand and tell the world whether or not it accepted the treaty.

If the question had been put before a panel of authoritative analysts which country, Denmark or Ireland, would conduct a referendum that was to have a nega-

tive outcome, most would immediately have pointed to Ireland. It was obvious that the Irish referendum was dogged by emotional issues such as abortion and nationalism. In this overwhelmingly Roman Catholic society, abortion is viewed as a deeply religious issue. Less than a year before the referendum, the Irish Supreme Court had stirred public sentiments by decreeing that abortion could be legal in some circumstances; antiabortion activists now feared that a "yes" vote could reinforce that view.

The nationalists, on the other hand, rejected the pact because it was bound to compromise Ireland's independence and neutrality. What must have counted was the monetary argument: The government indicated that, although some sovereignty might have to be conceded under the treaty, Ireland would gain financially. According to government leaders, the union would yield about $10 billion over the next 5 years.

The turnout for the Irish referendum was 57.3 percent, which is not very high, considering that after the Danish referendum, the eyes of Europe, if not the world, were focused on this important contest. Another negative vote would almost certainly have jeopardized the entire Maastricht Treaty. However, in spite of intense discussions and debates that manifested a vociferous opposition to the ratification of the treaty, 69 percent voted in favor. Once the results were in, then–prime minister

Reynolds stated, "There is a lot of relief in the cabinets of Europe today." He added, "It is a great day for Ireland and a great day for Europe. . . . Our decision will give renewed momentum to the ratification of the treaty across Europe. . . . We have succeeded in putting European union back on the rails."

DEVELOPMENT

Great steps have been taken to overcome underdevelopment. In becoming an industrialized nation, Ireland has especially been aided by its inclusion in the European Union.

FREEDOM

Ireland is highly democratic. Although the country is overwhelmingly Roman Catholic, there is freedom of religion. While abortion is still illegal in Ireland, the Supreme Court has ruled that it is constitutional for physicians and clinics to provide women with addresses of foreign abortion clinics.

HEALTH/WELFARE

Ireland has an extensive and perhaps somewhat excessive welfare system, whose major defect is that it does not have a controlling mechanism to check whether or not recipients are really eligible for the benefits they receive.

ACHIEVEMENTS

Ireland's rich cultural heritage in literature, music, and dance has enjoyed a phenomenal resurgence of interest around the world in recent decades.

Italy (Italian Republic)

GEOGRAPHY

Area in Square Miles (Kilometers): 116,303 (301,255) (about the size of Arizona)

Capital (Population): Rome (2,688,000)

Environmental Concerns: air and water pollution; acid rain; waste treatment and disposal

Geographical Features: mostly rugged and mountainous; some plains and coastal lowlands

Climate: Mediterranean except north of the Po River, where it is temperate or Alpine

PEOPLE

Population

Total: 56,800,000

Annual Growth Rate: −0.08%

Rural/Urban Population Ratio: 33/67

Major Languages: Italian; French; German

Ethnic Makeup: Italian; with small German, French, Slovene, and Albanian minorities

Religions: 98% Roman Catholic; 2% others

Health

Life Expectancy at Birth: 75 years (male); 82 years (female)

Infant Mortality Rate (Ratio): 6.5/1,000

Physicians Available (Ratio): 1/193

Education

Adult Literacy Rate: 97%

Compulsory (Ages): 6–13; free

COMMUNICATION

Telephones: 1 per 2.3 people

Daily Newspaper Circulation: 105 per 1,000 people

Televisions: 1 per 2.3 people

TRANSPORTATION

Highways in Miles (Kilometers): 190,562 (305,388)

Railroads in Miles (Kilometers): 11,376 (18,961)

Usable Airfields: 136

Motor Vehicles in Use: 32,800,000

GOVERNMENT

Type: republic

Independence Date: March 17, 1861

Head of State/Government: President Oscar Luigi Scalfaro; Prime Minister Massimo D'Alema

Political Parties: Christian Democrats; Democratic Party of the Left; Italian Socialist Party; Forza Italia; Social Democratic Party; Italian Renewal; Italian Social Movement; National Alliance Party; others

Suffrage: universal at 18 (except in senatorial elections—minimum age 25)

MILITARY

Military Expenditures (% of GDP): 1.9%

Current Disputes: property and minority-rights issues with Slovenia and Croatia

ECONOMY

Currency ($ U.S. Equivalent): 1,767.4 lire = $1

Per Capita Income/GDP: $21,500/$1.24 trillion

GDP Growth Rate: 1.5%

Inflation Rate: 1.9%

Unemployment Rate: 12.2%

Labor Force: 22,851,000

Natural Resources: mercury; potash; marble; sulfur; dwindling natural-gas and crude-oil reserves; fish; coal

Agriculture: fruits; vegetables; meat and dairy products; fish

Industry: tourism; machinery; motor vehicles; iron and steel; chemicals; food processing; textiles; ceramics; footwear

Exports: $250 billion (primary partners EU countries, United States)

Imports: $190 billion (primary partners EU countries, OPEC countries)

THE REPUBLIC OF ITALY

Italy has from time to time been the target of highly unflattering characterizations. While it is true that the country did not exist yet when the Vienna Congress aimed at restoring pre-Napoleonic Europe, presiding Prince Metternich is reported to have exclaimed: "Italy is not a country; it is a geographical concept!"

In contemporary times, phrases such as "a difficult democracy," "a republic without a government," and "a stalemate society" have been used to describe Italy. Another stigma, referring generally to the character of Italian society, is described by "amoral familism." This particular term points to excessive emphasis on family relations, which to the Italian will always take precedence over public interests. Indeed, the interest in government and in governmental processes is notably low among Italians. But it is not the real government that solves problems and gets itself out of dilemmas. For such eventualities, the *sottogoverno* (literally, "under-government") exists. All sorts of unofficial wheelings and dealings take place, and the persons who provide these functions often are not even in government positions. Sottogoverno may be compared to a spare tire that comes into operation when all else fails—and such emergencies are not at all rare in Italy.

THE PROBLEM OF THE STATE

Italy's main handicap may be summarized as follows: It has neither a strong government nor an efficient civil service, nor, for that matter, a tradition of centralization. A number of historical factors accounts for these characteristics. First, unification and independence were late in coming. Also, the prolonged mix and overlap of church and state has to be taken into account—particularly in the 1870s, when the Roman Catholic Church subverted plans and processes for unification. In addition, regional disparities, which in Italy appear to be very pronounced, have, as a matter of course, been utterly dysfunctional to integrative policies.

The Resurgence Movement

As a Western European nation-state, Italy was a very late starter. For much of the period between the fall of the West Roman Empire in the fifth century A.D. and the *Risorgimento* (a movement toward liberation and unification in the nineteenth century), Italy was internally fragmented, consisting of numerous sovereign city-states and principalities of varying size. In addition, parts of Italy were dominated by foreign powers, particularly Austria.

As a result, the Risorgimento was narrowly based; it did not involve the bulk of Italian peoples. Indeed, the population at large was sometimes hostile, and at best indifferent, toward what poets and politicians perceived as the second birth of the Roman Empire, or the supreme achievement of Italy's destiny. Instead of a grass-roots movement, the Risorgimento was in essence an elitist endeavor, largely initiated by the Piedmontese monarchy and supported by the nobility elsewhere. Nor could a common means of communication help to resolve the problem of Italy's divisiveness. A variety of languages was spoken throughout nineteenth-century Italy; French was the language that served the Piedmontese court.

As was mentioned earlier, the Roman Catholic Church frustrated attempts at unification and independence. The Church's power had often been based on divide-and-rule precepts, and conditions in Italy facilitated the implementation of such directives. Since the variety of regimes prevailing in Italy were usually very weak, the Church had often assumed extra-ecclesiastical duties. Indeed, it had in effect become a quasi-governmental institution, taking care of people's needs in worldly matters as well. Now that a real government loomed with the Risorgimento movement, the papacy naturally feared that the competing system would take away tribute as well as loyalty normally owed to the Church. When in 1870 Italian troops entered Rome, the Vatican denounced the new state and called on Catholics not to participate in its politics. The Risorgimento—like the French Revolution a century or so earlier—thus abounded with anticlerical sentiments, its statesmen having become convinced the Vatican interference would always be the albatross around Italy's neck. They therefore proclaimed the separation of church and state as their central precept. But while in France the state proved sufficiently strong to dissociate itself from the Church and to become the dominant power in the land, for a long time the Church remained a rival force of legitimacy in Italy.

From Papal State to Vatican

The Roman Catholic Church has owned land since medieval times, exercising in effect sovereignty over extensive areas of Italy. These lands came to be called the papal states. Their area shrank considerably in the nineteenth century, particularly under the impact of Italy's gradual unification. Their size today is little more than the papal mansions—the living quarters of various cardinals and the Vatican offices in the heart of Rome, plus a summer palace in Castel Gandolfo, some 15 miles away.

The Holy See, or Vatican, is now a state by itself and is as such internationally recognized. In addition, there are millions of Roman Catholics all over the world who support the construction of a Vatican sovereignty—that is, a Church having secular sovereignty and worldly powers as well. The Fascist Italian dictator Benito Mussolini bought Vatican support by reaffirming this quintessence in the Lateran Treaties of 1929. These treaties between the Kingdom of Italy and the Vatican recognize the Holy See as a sovereign state. Mussolini may have regretted this concession, since it failed to end the political and secular influence that the Vatican enjoyed outside its own territory.

One may argue that, after World War II, the strife between church and state started to become less serious—certainly less intense—than it had been in the past. After all, the first 4 postwar decades witnessed a great deal of cooperation, if not symbiosis, between the Roman Catholic Church and the Christian Democrats (DC). Nevertheless, the DC lost some important battles that had the full backing of the Vatican, such as the referendum that concerned divorce in Italy and legislation regarding abortion.

A radical change came in 1994. It was then that the Christian Democrats—who, in spite of ups and downs, had been Italy's major power brokers for nearly half a century—lost a national election. This also meant that the Vatican lost much of its power to influence, let alone to manipulate, secular politics.

REGIONAL DISPARITIES

Regional disparities—that is, the divergence in cultures among the various parts of the country—have continued to be vast in Italy, much more so than in France or Britain. When territorial unification had finally been achieved to the extent that it invalidated Prince Metternich's cynical observation that Italy is a geographical concept, one of the Piedmontese unifiers reportedly exclaimed, "We have made Italy, now we must make Italians!"

Language, normally a major integrative factor, in Italy's case turned out to be a major obstacle. Italian, once spoken by only 2 percent of the population, became the country's lingua franca (common language), an imposition that forced a great many Italians to become bilingual. They now speak Italian in school, at work, and in other public places, but often use their own language or dialect at home or among themselves. Valle d'Aosta, a region in northwestern Italy close to the borders of

France and Switzerland, is French-speaking. A much larger area in the northeast that includes South Tirol, ceded to Italy by Austria after World War I, is German-speaking. (For some time it remained an Austrian irredenta, and even now, after having been part of Italy for several generations of rule, a resentful population often refuses to communicate in Italian.)

Although regionalism as a rule causes cultural and linguistic diversity, in Italy it appears to include developmental aspects as well. A north–south dichotomy, which some other countries also display, is very pronounced in Italy. The north is a well-developed, industrial area, inhabited by people who do not differ significantly in lifestyle from most other Western Europeans. The south is relatively undeveloped and rural, by contrast, inhabited by people almost universally involved in agricultural pursuits. So uneven has development been that some analysts consider Italy to consist

of two countries. It is difficult to explain this disparity satisfactorily. One may assume that northern Italy moved along with the rest of Western Europe, sharing its economic development and its cultural heritage. And since Rome has traditionally been the capital and trendsetter, a demarcation line north of the so-called Eternal City would have been impossible.

In the past quarter-century, the many Italian governments have made it a point to try to equalize the development of the two parts of the country by encouraging industry in the south. However, most governmental efforts have failed to produce the desired effect. To be sure, a number of industries moved south, but usually they left after a brief period of time. Their abandonment of the ill-fated industrial sites produced what came to be called "cathedrals in the desert": large, vacant buildings in the dismal context of rural poverty. Some economists have argued that the in-

frastructure of southern Italy is simply not there, or that it has at least not reached the take-off point that would render injections of money and capital equipment profitable.

A great many southern Italian villages and small towns have been demographically affected, in that their young people have often had to leave the area in search of work elsewhere. First they found employment in the north. When that area was saturated they went farther afield, settling in countries of the European Union. It is only a matter of course that these migrations have adversely affected the prospects of the south.

The weakness of the state, which in Italy manifests itself in regional disparities as well as in developmental discrepancies, is to some extent offset by a strong civil culture. This is evidenced by the lack of success that terrorist groups (on both the left and right) have had. It is clear that the Italian people have been firm in their condemnation of violence.

WORLD WAR II AND THE NEW ITALY

While in World War I Italy joined the Allies (a policy for which the country subsequently believed itself to have been poorly rewarded), in World War II it chose Adolf Hitler's side, becoming an Axis partner of Nazi Germany in June 1940. However, Italy fared poorly, soon losing *mare nostrum* (Latin for "our sea," meaning the Mediterranean) to the British, and fighting the ground war so dismally, first in North Africa and subsequently in Sicily, that its Axis partners had to come to the rescue. Massive German aid notwithstanding, Italy lost these areas. Once Sicily, the largest Mediterranean island, had been taken, the Anglo–American forces started their invasion of the Italian peninsula, a much more arduous task. This was, in effect, the "first second front." Here, they met with considerably more resistance than they had expected. Nevertheless, the Italian Fascist regime collapsed in 1943.

Although Italy then joined the Allies, officially declaring war on its former Axis partners, it could not immediately formalize the turnabout. In fact, many of the major changes had to await the end of the war. Since the king had compromised the monarchy by allowing Benito Mussolini and his fascism to gain a solid political foothold after the March on Rome in 1922, a referendum was conducted on the question of whether Italy should become a republic. By a majority of 54 percent, Italy rejected the continuance of the monarchy, and the Constituent Assembly that convened in 1948 embarked upon produc-

(Courtesy Embassy of Italy)

Much of the Roman heritage is still in evidence in Italy. It is not difficult to imagine what the Colosseum was like when the caesars ruled.

ing a constitution with a republican design. In this Constitution, two principles prevail that may help to explain why Italy has a "blocked" democracy: legislative supremacy and the multiparty system. The Constitution introduced legislative supremacy (which still prevails today). This allows the Legislature (the Chamber of Deputies) to oust a government through a vote of no-confidence. On important issues, various political parties in opposition team up against the government. Invariably, a few members of the government coalition abstain or join the vote of no-confidence. When a new government has been established, as a rule made up of members of the victorious parties, new confrontations may soon be initiated. This has been an ongoing process in Italy for half a century.

It would be wrong to think that the new cabinets are always made up of completely new ministers. Often there is a great deal of what in the political trade is called "replastering"—that is, the new ministers are recruited from the same set of politicians. When Aldo Moro was kidnapped and subsequently killed by the Red Brigades in 1978, he had been prime minister five times. Giulio Andreotti has

been in positions of power over a span of 4 decades, sometimes as defense minister, at other times as foreign minister or prime minister. On June 28, 1992, party leaders again compromised by electing a relatively young professor of constitutional law, Giuliano Amato, to the post of president of the Council of Ministers (prime minister).

Amato had been a deputy leader of the Socialist Party, and his name came up when the candidacy of Bettino Craxi, the party's leader, was rejected (the latter, who once had been prime minister, was implicated in a scandal). At that time, the Christian Democrats appeared to be riddled with corruption. That party, which has always been the dominant force in Italian politics, bases its platform on Roman Catholic Church dogma; its association with the Church is so close that it sometimes seems that the Vatican participates in Italian politics through the DC. (Another intermediary is afforded by Catholic Action, or AC, a large pressure group closely associated with both the Church and the DC.) Amato's reign did not last long, however; in April 1993, he was replaced as prime minister by Carlo Ciampi, who did not belong to any political party.

The multiparty system has contributed to the never-ending chaos in Italian party politics. The number of political parties in Italy competing for seats in the Chamber of Deputies or in the Senate invariably hovers around 20. It is a matter of course that none of them will receive a majority, which, in turn, implies that coalitions, often fragile, will have to be formed. That situation was still in full force during the 1994 elections.

By early 1994, Italy had used up more than 50 governments. A new election loomed in the spring. But now the "politics as usual" seemed to have come to an end. The man who wrought this change was not an average politician; indeed, he was not even a politician to begin with. Silvio Berlusconi started out as a businessman who, over the course of decades, had amassed a truly formidable fortune. Like Ross Perot, to whom he was often compared, Berlusconi was a billionnaire who was very unhappy about the way things were going in Italy. He thus thrust himself into the political arena, spending huge amounts of money in founding a new party, the Forza Italia, and in buying up the media to trumpet what the party stood for. The Forza Italia tilted strongly to the

(Courtesy United Nations photo/S. Jackson)

The canals of Venice are famous the world over. Boats like these have been used to transport people for hundreds of years.

| Italian troops enter Rome; the Risorgimento and the new Italian state are denounced by the papacy A.D. 1870 | Unification is achieved by the Risorgimento 1871 | The new Italian state becomes expansionist; attacks and conquers Somaliland and Eritrea 1889–1890 | Italy joins Great Britain and France in World War I 1914 | March on Rome; King Victor Umberto appoints Benito Mussolini as prime minister 1922 | Lateran Treaties; Mussolini buys off the Vatican 1929 | Mussolini attacks and conquers Ethiopia 1935 |

right, which was not surprising, considering the new political climate in Western Europe.

In May 1994, Berlusconi and 25 ministers from his right-wing coalition came to power, amidst fanfare of a new political era for Italy. But only 7 months later, on December 22, besieged by charges of corruption, Berlusconi submitted his resignation. The following month, Lamberto Dini, the treasury minister in the previous government, was named prime minister by president Oscar Luigi Scalfaro.

In subsequent years, Berlusconi has remained politically active despite a number of convictions for bribery and other wrongdoing (he contends that the charges are politically motivated).

ITALIAN PARTY POLITICS
The DC was always bound to garner the largest number of votes in an election, but only once did it avail itself of a majority. On all other occasions, it was necessary to enter into coalitions. These coalitions never included the second-largest party, the Italian Communist Party (PCI, which is now known as the Democratic Party on the Left, or PDS), although the PCI expressed a willingness in the late 1960s to cooperate with a "bourgeois" party. The "historic compromise," as the Communists labeled their olive branch, was never taken seriously by the Christian Democrats, although informal consultations between the DC and the PCI may well have amounted to the cooperation that the DC officially wanted to avoid. Since the DC was badly in need of coalition partners, it regularly included the Socialists.

The Socialist Party of Italy (PSI) had until 1956 been closely aligned with the Communists. From 1956 to 1963, the PSI was in a period of reassessment, and after 1963 it became receptive to the overtures of the Christian Democrats; this tendency on the part of the DC was nicknamed "the opening to the left." Cooperation between the DC and the PSI has in general been harmonious. On one occasion, the Christian Democrats allowed a Socialist to assume the prime ministership. That cabinet consisted largely of DC members, but it did make a difference in that Bettino Craxi, the Socialist prime minister, remained in office considerably longer (1983–1987) than most of his predecessors. However, it cannot be denied that the

Christian Democrats had a great deal of influence as a government party. But it was a "marriage of convenience," especially once the relations between the Socialists and the ex-Communists chilled, since they were in competition for the leadership of the left.

The Communists and Socialists
The old Communist Party reached the peak of its popularity when led by Enrico Berlinguer, who was a populist as well as an ideologue. When Berlinguer died, in 1984, the party started to suffer from a steady attrition, which accelerated after the collapse of the Soviet Union. At that point, the name change to the Democratic Party on the Left was effected.

The old PCI was an offshoot of the Socialist Party. The PCI had been banned in the mid-1920s, when Benito Mussolini's fascism became well established. One of the Communists' earliest leaders was an ideologue and writer named Antonio Gramsci. Although his works differ considerably from those of Marx, he has often been called the "Karl Marx of Italy." Mussolini, who had initially also been on the left end of the political spectrum, had Gramsci thrown in jail, where he eventually died. The PCI then moved underground and became extremely active in the Resistance. The enormous popularity that the party enjoyed immediately after World War II may in part be traced to the heroic conduct of Communists in the *Resistenza* ("Resistance").

While in prison, Gramsci laid the theoretical foundations for an international Communist system differing sharply from prevailing patterns. One of his major theses was that all nations had different cultures and that it would thus be dysfunctional to impose the same communism on all of them. While Gramsci remained a Marxist all his life, he steadily alienated himself from the Soviet Union. Palmiro Togliatti, who as one of Italy's Communist leaders had fled abroad when Mussolini started to persecute Communists, adopted some of Gramsci's earlier ideas upon his return to Italy, particularly those associated with the "Italian road to socialism."

Generations of political observers and analysts have argued that the DC and PCI (now the PDS) are in fact religious parties that have their roots in old Italy. The argument runs that, as modernization of the

economy and society continues, the Catholic and Marxist "faiths" will wither away.

This view was shared by Bettino Craxi. Italy's economic performance during his years as prime minister was very solid— no small accomplishment—but Craxi failed to create a third political bloc. The PSI was weak, with only around 12 percent of the vote, and it had a reputation for corruption at the local level. It could not claim with any plausibility to be the dominant force in a coalition that included the DC.

Political Parties and Factions
One of the more fascinating aspects of Italian politics is the kaleidoscopic nature of its political parties. Before the 1994 elections, there was a large array of political parties, headed by the Christian Democrats and, in second place, the Party of the Democratic Left. Under the circumstances, the DC had to rely on a coalition that involved two, three, and sometimes four other parties. If this external division was not enough, most political parties, but particularly the DC, were also highly multifactional—that is, they contained many factions that had a great deal of autonomy. To illustrate this, in Italy, factions have their own offices and their own newsletters or newspapers.

THE ECONOMY
The Italian economy expanded dramatically in the 1950s, when big companies such as Fiat and Olivetti drew thousands of southern workers to the northern cities of Turin and Milan. Growth was rapid but lopsided; labor relations were bitter. The 1960s were years of varying expansion. The early part represented an economic miracle almost on the scale of the West German experience; in the later part there was the "hot autumn" (1969), during which a wave of strikes and protests marred economic achievements. Then the dynamism of the economy was slowed by the oil crises of the early 1970s.

The strengths and weaknesses of Italy's economy are peculiar. The private sector has too few large companies, but these few are perfectly capable of competing in world markets. The state sector has fallen victim to Italian forms of bureaucracy, especially since the Christian Democrats expanded their clientelism. Nationalization is no longer viewed as a panacea, since

Italy enters World War II as an Axis partner
1940

Italy drops out of the war after heavy losses in manpower and territory
1943

A referendum on the monarchy: a majority favor a republic
1946

The first republican Constitution of Italy becomes effective
1948

Italy experiences an "economic miracle"
1958–1963

The "hot autumn" of strikes
1969

The divorce referendum, which the DC loses
1974

The abortion referendum, which the DC loses
1980s

1990s

The economy shows some signs of improvement

Despite financial problems, Italy manages to join the countries launching the Euro in 1999

Former prime minister Romano Prodi is named president of the European Commission

corporations often deteriorate when managed by the government. It is for that very reason that the PDS has voted against the nationalization of the Fiat autoworks. (A curious phenomenon—a Communist party voting against nationalization!)

Government spending in general is far too high, a factor that causes budget deficits and is bound to cut investments. (Italy's out-of-date banking system has greatly restrained investments anyway.) And if the bureaucracy can be burdensome, the legislation is certainly stifling. A maze of government regulations has descended on matters like hiring and firing, and this too will increase the inflexibility of the labor market. The black-market economy nevertheless flourishes, not merely in areas such as textiles and shoes but even in technologically advanced sectors like electronics.

During the 1980s, the south continued to lag behind, but the north witnessed a revival of its economy. Today, although unemployment remains very high—around 12 percent—exports have boomed, and Italy has overtaken Great Britain in gross domestic product. (To some extent, the Craxi government may take credit for that. It modified the system of wage indexation, which reduced inflation and labor costs. The Craxi administration also ran the public sector more rationally.) However, a greater impetus has come from the private sector, where Fiat (which has made a comeback after a poor performance during the 1970s), Olivetti, and Montedison are faring well. Small companies are also thriving, which has led experts to suggest that the weakness of the Italian state may be an advantage for the private sector. It can—so the argument goes—adapt and modernize, free from burdensome governmental regulations which the state can enact but not enforce. There could be some truth in this, but Italian industrialists generally argue that what they need is fewer but more sensible regulations. In this sense, the prob-lem of the state remains in spite of Italy's economic revival.

RECENT CONDITIONS
The persistent global recession that has plagued the industrialized nations of Western Europe has had its effects on the Italian economy. Unemployment is a particular concern. But Italy does not face the huge economic problems alone: It is an enthusiastic member of the European Union, which endeavors to find joint solutions, and is also one of the prestigious Group of Seven (G-7).

Another problem is the resurgence of the Mafia. On July 19, 1992, a car bomb exploded in central Palermo, killing the most prominent anti-Mafia judge, Paolo Borsellino. The blast had widespread ramifications. In Rome, it hindered the Amato government in its twin tasks of fighting the Mafia and restoring the battered economy. The government finally decided to move Mafia prisoners to an island off the coast of Tuscany. In Palermo, seven out of 16 deputy prosecutors resigned, one of them commenting that the job was "like standing in front of a firing squad." Other terrorists, such as the Red Brigade, have apparently dwindled in number.

Finally, Italy, which has for many years been a country of emigration, has again become a target of immigration. Nearby Albania is in a pitifully poor economic and political state; many Albanians are fleeing or trying to cross into Italy. Those who left Albania first were lucky: Their numbers were small, and the Italian government was prepared to allow them in. But they were followed by larger groups, literally thousands and thousands of people, and soon Italy made it known that economic refugees would no longer be welcome. The Italian Coast Guard was strengthened, and other measures were taken to prevent Albanians from crossing the Adriatic Sea. The continuing crises in the former Yugoslavia also remain of serious concern to Italy.

However, in the face of abundant problems, the Italian party system has collapsed, and it is now up to a few leaders to make things work. This was demonstrated when, during the elections of April 1996, Romano Prodi, certainly not a political veteran, came up with his center-left ULIVO ("Olive Tree") Alliance. This impromptu move made the day. The new alliance won, and Prodi became the 55th Italian prime minister since the end of World War II.

Prime Minister Prodi's avowed goal was to make Italy a "normal democracy." While he did not achieve that—to no one's surprise, as could Italian government ever be normal?—he did manage to cut public spending, to move ahead with privatization, and to get Italy included in the slate of European Union countries that launched the Euro. Perhaps most important, Italians began to get a sense of continuity in government in the course of his 2½-year stewardship.

However, the able manager's political steam ran out in the fall of 1998, and Prodi finally fell victim to a vigorous opposition (including the redoubtable Silvio Berlusconi) in October, when he narrowly lost his parliamentary majority in a vote of confidence. The prime ministership was then handed over to parliamentary leader Massimo D'Alema, an ex-Communist (a choice that has been sharply criticized by the Vatican). While D'Alema's stated goal was to provide more stability, his government was soon characterized by political maneuvering and bickering—not a promising sign for longevity.

DEVELOPMENT

Northern Italy (upward from Rome) is well developed, on a par with most Western European nations. The southern part is still very much unindustrialized, despite governmental efforts. Italy is a member of the Group of Seven, a prestigious global committee that reviews economic conditions on an annual basis.

FREEDOM

A 1984 antiterrorist law introduced search warrants by telephone. However, since the elimination of Fascist repression, Italy has bent over backward to maintain democracy. Certain areas that are culturally different have high degrees of autonomy.

HEALTH/WELFARE

Both men and women in Italy enjoy high life expectancy rates, and infant mortality is low. However, the country has thus far failed to develop a universal health-care system.

ACHIEVEMENTS

Italy's cultural brilliance has long been acknowledged. An achievement test that is not so well known is that fewer terrorists appear to be operating in contemporary Italy. The country has successfully walked the thin line between the strict surveillance that antiterrorism necessitates and a respect for freedoms and rights.

Liechtenstein (Principality of Liechtenstein)

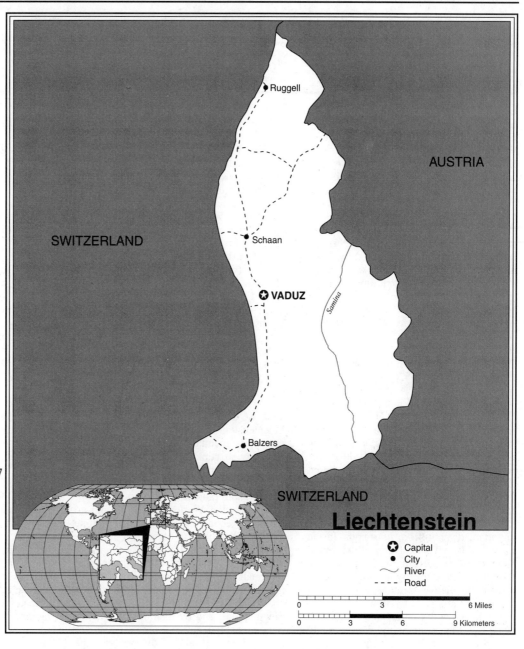

SWITZERLAND

AUSTRIA

Ruggell

Schaan

★ VADUZ

Samina

Balzers

SWITZERLAND

Liechtenstein

★ Capital
● City
∿ River
--- Road

| 0 | 3 | 6 Miles |
| 0 | 3 | 6 | 9 Kilometers |

GEOGRAPHY

Area in Square Miles (Kilometers): 62 (160) (about the size of Washington, D.C.)

Capital (Population): Vaduz (5,100)

Environmental Concerns: air pollution

Geographical Features: mostly mountainous (Alps) with Rhine Valley in western third; landlocked

Climate: temperate; continental

PEOPLE

Population
Total: 31,700

Annual Growth Rate: 1.05%

Rural/Urban Population Ratio: 79/21

Major Languages: German; Alemannic dialect

Ethnic Makeup: 88% Alemannic; 12% Italian, Turkish, and others

Religions: 80% Roman Catholic; 7% Protestant; 13% others and unknown

Health
Life Expectancy at Birth: 74 years (male); 80 years (female)

Infant Mortality Rate (Ratio): 5.3/1,000

Physicians Available (Ratio): 1/957

Education
Adult Literacy Rate: 100%

Compulsory (Ages): 7–16

COMMUNICATION
Telephones: 1 per 1.6 people

Daily Newspaper Circulation: 581 per 1,000 people

Televisions: 1 per 3 people

TRANSPORTATION
Highways—Miles (Kilometers): 150 (250)

Railroads—Miles (Kilometers): 11 (18)

Usable Airfields: none

GOVERNMENT
Type: hereditary constitutional monarchy

Independence Date: January 23, 1719

Head of State/Government: Prince Hans Adam II; Prime Minister Mario Frick

Political Parties: Fatherland Union; Progressive Citizen's Party; The Free List

Suffrage: universal at 20

MILITARY
Military Expenditures (% of GDP): none; defense is the responsibility of Switzerland

Current Disputes: Liechtenstein claims a portion of Czech territory confiscated in 1918

ECONOMY*
Currency ($ U.S. Equivalent): 1.43 Swiss francs = $1

Per Capita Income/GDP: $23,000/$713 million

Inflation Rate: 0.8%

Unemployment Rate: 1.1%

Labor Force: 22,200 (more than half are foreigners)

Natural Resources: hydropower potential

Agriculture: livestock; vegetables; corn; wheat; potatoes; grapes

Industry: electronics; metal manufacturing; textiles; ceramics; pharmaceuticals; food products; precision instruments; tourism

Exports: $2.14 billion (primary partners EU and EFTA countries, Switzerland)

Imports: $852.3 million (primary partners EU countries and Switzerland)

*Note: Liechtenstein is united with Switzerland in a customs and monetary union. It is represented by Switzerland in diplomatic matters.

 http://www.odci.gov/cia/publications/ factbook/country-frame.html

Liechtenstein becomes an imperial principality of the Holy Roman Empire
A.D. 1719

Liechtenstein is part of the Rhine Confederation
1806–1815

Independence is confirmed by the Congress of Vienna
1815

Liechtenstein is part of the Germanic Confederation
1815–1866

Customs union with Austria
1852–1918

Liechtenstein adopts the Swiss currency
1921

Customs union with Switzerland begins
1923

Crown Prince Hans Adam succeeds his father, Prince Francis-Joseph
1989

1990s

Social tensions result from the presence of foreign workers

Some refugees from Kosovo seek asylum in Liechtenstein

LIECHTENSTEIN

Liechtenstein is a small Alpine country sandwiched between the Austrian state of Vorarlberg and the Swiss cantons of St. Gallen and Graubunden. Liechtenstein is unique in that it is formally headed by the world's only surviving German-speaking monarchy. Its history dates back to May 3, 1342, when Count Hartmann III became the ruler of the country of Vaduz. As a result of subsequent acquisitions, it reached its current size (just 62 square miles) by 1434. Its relative inaccessibility and seclusion in a mountainous area enabled it to preserve a measure of independence. It was acquired by the House of Liechtenstein in 1712 and, 7 years later, it was officially granted political independence.

After Napoleon Bonaparte's defeat in 1815, Liechtenstein joined the Germanic Confederation. In 1852, it entered into a customs union with Austria, largely for economic reasons. When World War I caused the collapse of the Habsburg monarchy, Liechtenstein immediately turned to the other side—formally concluding its association with Austria, it looked for support from Switzerland. In 1921, it entered into a postal union with the Swiss. Although it adopted the Swiss currency, it continues to issue its own postage stamps. Like other mini-states, Liechtenstein earns important revenue from its stamps. In the early 1980s, sales of stamps contributed more than 10 percent of the total state revenues. Today the figure is closer to 3 percent, its relative importance diminished due to new sources of revenue.

The bonds with Switzerland culminated when the tiny principality was formally incorporated into the Swiss customs union. Liechtenstein remained neutral in World War II, along with Switzerland, and was spared German occupation. Since the war, the economic ties between Liechtenstein and Switzerland have grown increasingly close, with the latter remaining

responsible for the former's diplomatic representation abroad.

GOVERNMENT

Liechtenstein is a constitutional monarchy, which means that the princes of the House of Liechtenstein reign but do not rule. The current monarch, Prince Hans Adam II (born in 1945), is of a modern mind, leaving nearly all decisions to the head of government, Prime Minister Mario Frick. The 1921 Constitution provides for a unicameral *Tag* (German for *Diet,* or Parliament) of 25 (increased from 15 in 1988) members, elected for 4-year-terms. Elections follow the proportional-representation rules. A law is passed when it receives majority approval by the Tag and the prince's signed concurrence. The 11 communes (*Gemeinden*) are governed autonomously but under government supervision by mayors and councils elected every 3 years.

THE ECONOMY

Liechtenstein enjoys one of the highest per capita incomes in the world, and its economy sustains a very generous social-welfare system. The foundations of the country's current prosperity were laid during the rapid industrialization of the economy following World War II. Thanks to the rapid economic recovery in Europe and the liberalization of world commerce during the 1950s and 1960s, Liechtenstein was able to overcome the limitations of its small domestic market and lack of natural resources through specialization and trade. By importing food, energy, and raw materials and by manufacturing a variety of capital and consumer goods for export, Liechtenstein vastly increased the productivity of its workforce. Even in the 1980s, when most other European economies were experiencing a decline in the importance of the manufacturing sector, Liechtenstein still had more than 45 percent of its workforce in manufacturing.

Industrialization and specialization brought prosperity—but also problems. For one, Liechtenstein's dependence on foreign suppliers for food, raw materials, and energy has made it particularly vulnerable to supply shocks such as those caused by world oil crises. Liechtenstein has also been forced to import large numbers of foreign workers. At times, foreign workers constitute more than half of the labor force and fully one third of the entire population; they are supposed to leave the country when their work contracts expire. Their presence has created strains within Liechtenstein society.

Liechtenstein's economy has a free-enterprise orientation. The state's chief contributions to economic growth have been political stability and a stable macroeconomic environment. Liechtenstein has kept its budgets balanced and let the inflation-conscious Swiss regulate its money supply. In addition, the government's refusal to impose income or profit taxes has helped indigenous businesses and has attracted more than 70,000 foreign firms to Liechtenstein. Finally, the principality has its own external economic policies: It participates in the Swiss customs union, is a member of the European Free Trade Association and the European Economic Area, and has a special economic and diplomatic relationship with the European Union. Its export industries thus have increased access to major foreign markets. The government is working to harmonize its economic policies with those of an integrated Europe.

DEVELOPMENT

Due to its rapid industrialization after World War II and its appeal for foreign businesses, present-day Liechtenstein is a well-to-do country. In general, political stability and economic prosperity have been mutually reinforcing.

FREEDOM

Switzerland is responsible for Liechtenstein's defense and foreign relations. Like Switzerland, Liechtenstein ranks very high in human rights. Its democratic institutions have been effective at representing and promoting the various interests of its citizens.

HEALTH/WELFARE

Liechtenstein has a comprehensive social-welfare system, sustained by a variety of compulsory insurance schemes. Matters of public health are managed by a Committee of Public Health.

ACHIEVEMENTS

Women were finally given the right to vote in Liechtenstein's national elections in 1984. Recently, a university was established at Vaduz.

Luxembourg (Grand Duchy of Luxembourg)

GEOGRAPHY

Area in Square Miles (Kilometers): 1,034 (2,586) (about the size of Rhode Island)

Capital (Population): Luxembourg (76,400)

Environmental Concerns: urban air and water pollution

Geographical Features: mostly gently rolling uplands with broad shallow valleys; uplands to slightly mountainous in the north; steep slope down to moselle floodplain in the south; landlocked

Climate: modified continental with mild winters, cool summers

PEOPLE

Population
Total: 425,000
Annual Growth Rate: 1.02%
Rural/Urban Population Ratio: 10/90
Major Languages: Letzeburgesch; German; French; English
Ethnic Makeup: Celtic base, with French and German blend; about 25% foreigners (guestworkers)
Religions: 97% Roman Catholic; 3% Protestant and Jewish

Health
Life Expectancy at Birth: 74 years (male); 81 years (female)
Infant Mortality Rate (Ratio): 5.1/1,000
Average Caloric Intake: 154% of FAO minimum
Physicians Available (Ratio): 1/469

Education
Adult Literacy Rate: 100%
Education Compulsory (Ages): 6–15

COMMUNICATION
Telephones: 1 per 1.8 people
Daily Newspaper Circulation: 384 per 1,000 people
Televisions: 1 per 2.7 people

TRANSPORTATION
Highways in Miles (Kilometers): 5,108 (3,167)
Railroads in Miles (Kilometers): 165 (275)
Usable Airfields: 2
Motor Vehicles in Use: 249,000

GOVERNMENT
Type: constitutional monarchy
Independence Date: April 17, 1839
Head of State/Government: Grand Duke Jean; Prime Minister Jean-Claude Juncker

Political Parties: Christian Social People's Party; Luxembourg Socialist Workers' Party; Action Committee for Democracy and Pension Rights; Democratic Party; Green Alternative

Suffrage: universal and compulsory at 18

MILITARY
Military Expenditures (% of GDP): 0.8%
Current Disputes: none

ECONOMY
Currency ($ U.S. Equivalent): 31.5 Luxembourg francs = $1
Per Capita Income/GDP: $33,700/$13.48 billion
GDP Growth Rate: 3.7%
Inflation Rate: 2.3%
Unemployment Rate: 3.5%
Labor Force: 213,100 (one third foreigners)
Natural Resources: iron ore
Agriculture: barley; oats; potatoes; wheat; fruit; wine grapes; livestock
Industry: banking; iron and steel; food processing; chemicals; metal products; engineering; tires; tourism
Exports: $7.1 billion (primary partners Germany, France, Belgium)
Imports: $9.4 billion (primary partners Belgium, Germany, France)

http://www.odci.gov/cia/publications/factbook/country-frame.html

GERMANY

BELGIUM

Sure

Heiderscheid
Bettendorf
Sure
Reisdorf
Ettelbruck
Beaufort
Echtemach Rosport

Eisch

Syre
Moselle

Mamer Strassen

LUXEMBOURG

FRANCE

Mondorf

Luxembourg

★ Capital
● City
〜 River
--- Road

0 10 20 Miles

0 10 20 30 Kilometers

THE GRAND MINI-STATE

In the past few decades, the world has witnessed the birth of numerous "mini-states," countries characterized by populations of only a few thousand to a few hundred thousand. Most of them are small in area as well as geographically remote, economically weak, and/or of limited international, strategic, and political significance. As a result, they have customarily been ignored as significant political actors.

The Luxembourg case is altogether different. An ancient mini-state in the heart of Western Europe, it has, to a surprising degree, earned much favorable attention in the recent past for the successes of its economy; for its roles in European Union institutions; and, perhaps most dramatically, for the growth of a large international banking sector during the 1970s and 1980s.

At the center of a highly industrialized region where France, Germany, and Belgium meet, Luxembourg "sits on a mountain of iron," as a German industrialist, trying to persuade his government to annex the country a century or so ago, reported. Iron and steel have constituted the basis of Luxembourg's modern development, though the economy is becoming increasingly diversified. Of late, the country has been wooing computer and other high-tech companies to establish themselves within its borders. Nevertheless, agricultural production has also been important for generations, and Luxembourg wines have become known all over the world.

The iron-ore resources have become depleted over the years, but the country's international visibility and the substantial improvements in its standard of living have spurred progress in Luxembourg. National pride, revitalized in recent years, plays a large role. One may cite as an example the increased use of the vernacular—the popular Luxembourg language, Letzeburgesch, an ancient West Frankish dialect more closely related to German than to French. (Luxembourg has two other officially recognized languages—French and German—while English is taught in school and widely understood throughout the country.) The main characteristic of Letzeburgesch is that it is first and foremost a spoken language; there are hardly any written records in Letzeburgesch, and only in the last decade or so have linguists started to develop methods of transcription. Other sources of pride that deserve mention are the hard bargains that the country drove in the EU, the renegotiation of its treaty of economic unity with Belgium, and the fact that Jacques Santer, at that time the prime minister of Luxembourg, was selected to become the

successor of Jacques Delors, the president of the European Union, in 1994.

Such developments have helped to sustain a positive momentum in the face of a rapidly aging population and acute labor shortages. This is no small achievement, given that in recent years, the surrounding larger states in Western Europe have experienced severe deficits, foreign debts, high unemployment, cutbacks in social programs, and, in general, the politically troublesome consequences of being dependent on forces outside national control.

THE ROAD TO SOVEREIGNTY

Luxembourg was founded in A.D. 963 by Siegfried, the count of Ardennes, who made it into a fortress. For half a millennium, Luxembourg was a major actor in Central Europe and in the Holy Roman Empire. However, its defeat by Burgundy in 1443 signaled a decline; and from then onward, it was controlled by one or another of its larger neighbors, notably by Burgundy, Spain (which still had possessions in the Southern Netherlands), Austria, and France (during Napoleonic times). The 1815 Congress of Vienna, fearful that France might rise again to wreak havoc in Western Europe, ordained that Holland, Belgium, and Luxembourg were to constitute one country that could act as a buffer against such an eventuality. The measure revealed gross ignorance in regard to the incompatibility of the cultures concerned; when Belgium seceded from the Netherlands in 1830, Luxembourg eventually followed suit. However, it did not want to be part of Belgium either, and the Treaty of London, while granting independence to Belgium, provided some separate status to Luxembourg. The latter drifted into the so-called Germanic Confederation, which it left in 1866. The foundation of Germany in the next decade solidified Luxembourg's independence, since the two rivals, France and Germany, denied each other the possession of Luxembourg. Interestingly, when the Low Countries were overrun by the German war machine in 1940, Adolf Hitler made a distinction between Belgium and the Netherlands (which were viewed as occupied countries) and Luxembourg (which was considered to be reintegrated into Germany).

The Dutch flag and the Luxembourg flag are very similar, for good reason; indeed, for some time there was a personal union between the monarchies of the two countries. However, when King William III of the Netherlands (who was also king of Luxembourg) died in 1890 without a son, the union dissolved, since the Luxembourg Constitution did not allow fe-

males on the throne. Luxembourg then became a grand duchy, and all connection with the Netherlands—which for the previous half century had been minimal anyway—was severed.

EUROPEAN CONNECTIONS

Although Luxembourg has always prided itself on its independence, it realized that its interests would be promoted if it became a member of an economic union. As soon as the German *Zollverein* (customs union) was disbanded, Luxembourgers voted for an economic union with France. The latter held a dim view of Luxembourg's potential at that time and consequently rejected the offer. A union with the voters' distant second choice, Belgium, was concluded; in 1922, after prolonged negotiations, the Belgo–Luxembourgeois Economic Union (BLEU) was signed for 50 years. The arrangement included linkage of Luxembourg's currency to the Belgian franc, which in practice implies that one may pay in Belgian currency in Luxembourg, but not the other way around. BLEU had little regard for the fact that Luxembourg's economy may be smaller than that of Belgium, but it is in fact superior, in that when Belgium would decide to devalue its franc, Luxembourg would have to follow suit. Although a new BLEU surfaced in the early 1970s, this particular wrinkle had not been removed. When in the early 1980s Belgium decided to devalue its currency, Luxembourg reluctantly devalued the Luxembourg franc by 8.5 percent.

Key members of the governments of Belgium, the Netherlands, and Luxembourg fled into exile in London when Germany invaded their countries in 1940. The respective governments in exile agreed to form an economic union, to be called *Benelux*, once the war would be over. That union was formally launched in 1948, but the tasks of postwar recovery as well as the increasing politicization of their economies kept the three countries' policies little affected by the Benelux pact until the entire area had become submerged in what is now called the European Union. Paradoxically, it was only then that the Benelux started to operate: The three small countries saw an important advantage in a closer coordination of their policies within the new setting, in that it allowed them to obtain a measure of strength against the other three, much larger members (France, Italy, and West Germany).

Luxembourg in particular sought advantages through Benelux for its rapidly growing international monetary operation. Luxembourg now qualifies as one of Europe's few banking and tax havens, and

The founding of Luxembourg by Siegfried, Count of Ardennes A.D. 963	The conquest by the Duchy of Burgundy spells the beginning of more than 400 years of foreign domination 1443	The Congress of Vienna makes Belgium and Luxembourg parts of the Netherlands 1815	Independence as a result of the Belgian Revolution 1839	Separation from the Netherlands crown 1890	The end of the Zollverein; the beginning of the Belgo-Luxembourgeois Economic Union 1919–1922	Luxembourg becomes an international financial and banking center 1980s

1990s

Luxembourg is one of the first countries to enter the postindustrial era	Jean-Claude Juncker becomes prime minister	Luxembourg's voice in the European Union remains strong; the Euro is introduced

more than 180 banks have set up shop in the small country (indeed, it has one of the highest ratios of banks in terms of area as well as in terms of inhabitants). But high technology may one day replace banking as Luxembourg's key industry. In fact, the grand duchy has already become a European center for some of the world's leading blue-chip firms.

Luxembourg has thus far fared well as a member of the European Union. Although its voice is small in global and regional terms, it is much more influential than its share of either the population or the economy of the EU would seem to warrant. Several important EU agencies have been headquartered in Luxembourg for a considerable number of years, such as the European Court and the European Parliament. The EU's plans to create a single European market, which would naturally mean the harmonization of EU banking and tax laws, could mark an economic catastrophe for Luxembourg, but the mini-state started to hedge its bets through diversifying in other areas.

Traumatic experiences with the violations of its neutrality in both world wars made Luxembourg an eager charter member of the North Atlantic Treaty Organization. While the country is committed to the terms of NATO in general, an individual military contribution is not demanded from small Luxembourg.

In the years immediately following World War I, Luxembourg's constitutional monarchy moved rapidly toward a modern parliamentary democracy. The small size of the country, a thoroughly democratic political ethos, and a socially and economically heterogeneous populace combine to fragment the party system and to render it necessary for all governments to result from coalitions of two or more parties. The country has a unicameral Legis-

lature. Voting is compulsory, which is not unusual in Europe, but the electoral system is unique: Luxembourg allows a plural vote, which means that voters vote not only for the candidate of their choice but also for the party that they prefer. Part of the system's complexity has been modified in the face of the European elections, and there can be little doubt that more will fall by the wayside. It appears possible that the new minorities (Luxembourg has an unusually high proportion of "guest workers") will be enfranchised, which may mean the creation of new political parties. Currently, about half a dozen are contenders for power, with none approaching a majority.

Coalitions tend to be moderate, always slightly to the left or slightly to the right of center. They are committed to the development and maintenance of a comprehensive welfare state. The scope of coverage and the levels of benefits of social programs in Luxembourg rank at or near the top among all nations. Effective industrial policies, a smooth transition from manufacturing to the service sector in large portions of the economy, and limited pressure for new jobs have made the task of the government easier than that of governments in other industrialized countries.

One of the main difficulties is that the markedly aging population has created a chronic shortage of workers. In part this has been remedied by the steady introduction of guest workers as well as by automation. Unemployment has for a long time hovered between 1 and 4 percent. (The rate has remained low despite the recession.) About 25 percent of the workforce are foreigners, hailing mainly from Southern Europe. Indeed, the proportion of foreign residents in Luxembourg is among the highest of all countries in the world. However, their presence has posed

few problems to date, in contrast to what pluralistic societies normally experience.

THE FUTURE
As is the case with most Western industrialized democracies, the main challenge that Luxembourg faces today is to maintain the social and economic gains that it has achieved since World War II. Political stability and healthy industrial and service sectors, particularly in international financial transactions, bode well in this regard. Growth rates have slowed markedly since the early 1980s in Luxembourg, but no signs of economic danger are evident. The economy's openness to extraneous forces does make it subject, if not vulnerable, to international trends; but it is better positioned than most national economies to withstand the shocks and to minimize their effects.

DEVELOPMENT

From primary industries (agriculture and mining), Luxembourg's economy developed to secondary industry (manufacturing) and has now become a postindustrial society in which banking, finance, and other services play a predominant role in the economy. Luxembourg has become a financial center that emulates Switzerland. Banks maintain a high degree of secrecy.

FREEDOM

Luxembourg has a very favorable human-rights rating. There is a great deal of tolerance for foreigners, who comprise more than a quarter of the total population and about a third of the workforce.

HEALTH/WELFARE

Luxembourg, a very prosperous country, has high life expectancy rates, and a relatively low natural population growth. The state offers a comprehensive welfare system.

ACHIEVEMENTS

The University of Luxembourg, operating only during the summer, invites participants from all over the world to join in its Summer Seminars. These always focus on a particular theme, and the speakers are all experts in the fields selected.

Malta (Republic of Malta)

GEOGRAPHY

Area in Square Miles (Kilometers): 123 (320) (about twice the size of Washington, D.C.)

Capital (Population): Valletta (9,200)

Environmental Concerns: increasing reliance on desalination; recycling of solid waste

Geographical Features: mostly low, rocky, flat to dissected plains; many coastal cliffs; the country comprises an archipelago (only three of the islands—Malta, Gozo, and Comino—are inhabited); many good harbors

Climate: Mediterranean

PEOPLE

Population

Total: 380,000

Annual Growth Rate: 0.58%

Rural/Urban Population Ratio: na

Major Languages: Maltese; English; and an Arabic dialect

Ethnic Makeup: Maltese (descendants of ancient Carthaginians and Phoenicians, with strong elements of Italian and other Mediterranean stock), Italian

Religions: 98% Roman Catholic; 2% others

Health

Life Expectancy at Birth: 75 years (male); 80 years (female)

Infant Mortality Rate (Ratio): 7.7/1,000

Average Caloric Intake: 124% of FAO minimum

Physicians Available (Ratio): 1/444

Education

Adult Literacy Rate: 88%

Compulsory (Ages): 5–16

COMMUNICATION

Telephones: 1 per 1.9 people

Newspapers: 8 Maltese, 3 English

Televisions: 1 per 1.3 people

TRANSPORTATION

Highways in Miles (Kilometers): 949 (1,582)

Railroads in Miles (Kilometers): none

Usable Airfields: 1

Motor Vehicles in Use: 132,000

GOVERNMENT

Type: parliamentary democracy

Independence Date: September 21, 1964 (from United Kingdom)

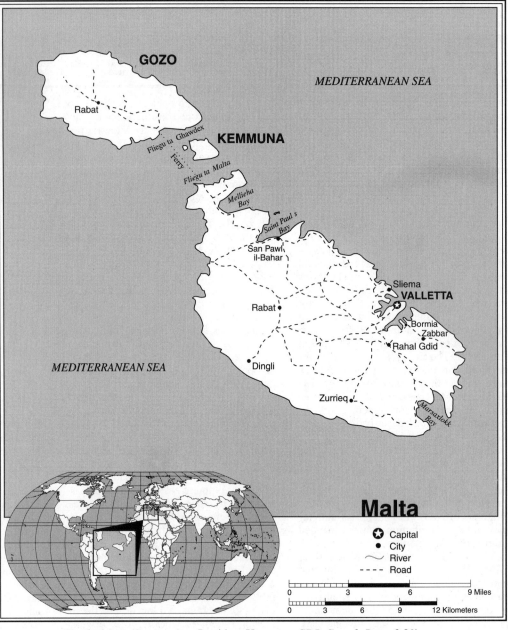

Malta

- ⊛ Capital
- ● City
- ∼ River
- --- Road

Head of State/Government: President Ugo Mifsud Bonnici; Prime Minister Alfred Sant

Political Parties: Nationalist Party; Malta Labour Party

Suffrage: universal at 18

MILITARY

Military Expenditures (% of GDP): 2.7%

Current Disputes: discussions with Tunisia regarding the commercial exploitation of the continental shelf between their countries

ECONOMY

Currency ($ U.S. Equivalent): 0.366 Maltese lire = $1

Per Capita Income/GDP: $12,900/$4.9 billion

GDP Growth Rate: 2.8%

Inflation Rate: 2.3%

Unemployment Rate: 3.7%

Labor Force: 149,000

Natural Resources: limestone; salt

Agriculture: fodder crops; potatoes; onions; beans; Mediterranean fruits and vegetables

Industry: tourism; electronics; ship building and repair; clothing; construction; food and beverages; textiles; footwear; tobacco

Exports: $1.7 billion (primary partners Italy, Germany, United Kingdom)

Imports: $3.0 billion (primary partners Italy, Germany, United Kingdom)

 http://searchmalta.com/

THE REPUBLIC OF MALTA
Malta, a group of rocky, low-lying Mediterranean islands, is poised at the crossroads of ancient seafaring nations. Not surprisingly, this exceptional location has made it a magnet to peoples for many centuries. The name *Malta* derives from a Phoenician term meaning "hiding place." Apostle Paul is said to have been shipwrecked there on his way to Rome in A.D. 60; after swimming ashore safely, he remained for a time to convert the inhabitants to Christianity.

Over the centuries, Malta has been conquered, colonized, occupied, or protected by Phoenicians, Carthaginians, Romans, Byzantine Greeks, Arabs, Normans, and a succession of modern peoples. In 1530, the Knights Hospitalers (also known as the Knights of St. John, a Roman Catholic religious and military order) made Malta their base, having been driven away from Rhodes by Turks. One of their most prominent leaders, Grandmaster Jean de la Valette, organized the Knights to resist the long siege by Turkish land and naval forces in 1565, thereby depriving the Turks of access to the western Mediterranean. La Valette supervised the construction of new fortifications, around which the capital city that now bears his name gradually grew.

In the 1790s, Malta was occupied for brief periods first by the Russians and subsequently by the French. Napoleon Bonaparte's preoccupation with large imperial conquests caused the French occupation to languish; and, in order to frustrate the proposed reinstatement of the Knights by the French emperor, the Maltese requested protection from the British in 1802. Malta thus became a British Crown colony, and for the next 150 years, British naval and military forces made it impossible for emerging Italy to follow the Romans in speaking of the Mediterranean as *mare nostrum* ("our sea"). Britain had finally started to realize the strategic importance of the three islands that jointly constitute Malta. Thus Lord Horatio Nelson, a British naval hero in the late eighteenth century, commented: "Malta is always in my thoughts."

The isles are located some 60 miles south of Sicily and 200 miles north of the coast of Libya. Thus, Malta's political, economic, and psychological orientation can be traced to Western Europe on the one hand and to the Arab world on the other. This mixture has strengthened over many centuries and remains part of contemporary Maltese politics and its people's worldview. The two worlds—the Arab and the Western European—seem to join in Malta's Semitic language, which is related to Arabic but written in Latin char-

acters and is strongly influenced by the Sicilian dialect of Italian.

During World War II, the Maltese experienced great stress; they were mercilessly bombed by the Germans and Italians. They endured the pressure of a siege that lasted for nearly 3 years (1940–1943) and resulted in 5,000 casualties. For their courage and endurance, the people of Malta were collectively awarded the George Cross, Great Britain's highest civilian decoration. This was the first time that the distinction was conferred on any part of the British Commonwealth. The emblem is displayed on their flag.

INDEPENDENCE
The British colony became self-governing in 1947. The debate on Malta's eventual emancipation found its small size and population to be major stumbling blocks. However, these criteria lost their validity in the decade that followed, and a referendum held in 1956 made clear that complete independence was preferred by a wide margin. Nevertheless, the Maltese political parties could not agree upon the method to achieve that goal. Finally, in 1964, the impasse was overcome, and a Conservative government led the island nation to independence.

Like most former British colonies, Malta opted to remain in the Commonwealth of Nations. In this political construction, Malta continued to recognize the sovereignty of the British Crown. In 1974, a Socialist government took the initiative to amend the Maltese Constitution so as to make Malta a republic, but without surrendering its membership in the Commonwealth. By then this had become a fairly well-known device in British macropolitics.

THE SYSTEM OF GOVERNMENT
The more than 160 years of British overlordship left the political heritage of a parliamentary form of government. Executive authority is exercised by a prime minister and a cabinet, who are responsible to the unicameral Legislature in Malta, the 75-member House of Representatives. Since independence, the two principal parties have been the (Conservative) Nationalist Party and the (Socialist) Labour Party.

The Nationalist Party is supported by business interests and a middle-class constituency, although it naturally also tries to appeal to broader cross-sections of the electorate. The party belongs to the European Christian democratic tradition and relies on the cooperation of the Roman Catholic hierarchy in Malta. Its foreign-policy orientation is decidedly pro-Western and European.

In contrast, the Labour Party, which regained power in October 1996, with Alfred Sant as prime minister, is closely associated with Malta's large and powerful trade-union movement. While in office from 1971 to 1987, the Labour government attempted to identify Malta's interests more closely with the developing world. Ideological links were forged between this island nation of devoutly Roman Catholic people and Libya (200 miles across the Mediterranean Sea to the south), North Korea, and other anti-Western states. The Labour Party's pronounced anticlericalism brought it into conflict with the Roman Catholic Church, which, in the 1960s, threatened supporters of the party with excommunication. The Labour Party nevertheless managed to gain office. Under Prime Minister Dom Mintoff, however, mutual hostility soon escalated, particularly when schools and hospitals that had been operated by religious orders were nationalized.

Mintoff, who remained prime minister until 1984, abrogated Malta's mutual-assistance security agreement with Great Britain almost immediately after assuming office. This action caused the departure of the Royal Navy, and the consequent loss of revenue could not easily be remedied. The Labour prime minister flirted with the Soviet Union, which had gained in prominence in the Mediterranean. At one point, he offered docking facilities for Soviet vessels in return for political and economic support.

However, even before the conditions had been spelled out in an agreement, the volatile prime minister turned to an anti-Western and anticapitalist country closer to home: Libya. Opponents of the Socialist Labour Party feared that Malta would become a satellite of the Qadhafi regime; and indeed, for some years, Malta sounded like Libya's echo. The same critics pointed to authoritarian streaks in Mintoff's political temperament. The prime minister used patronage openly to promote party loyalists in civil service, police, and state enterprises. He was also suspected of having gerrymandered Malta's system of electoral districts to perpetuate Labour Party rule. But it cannot be denied that Mintoff was a clever and skillful politician, managing to remain in power with a one-vote majority in Parliament during his first term of government. While in office, he succeeded in rendering Malta very visible in international circles, such as at the UN Conference on the Law of the Sea. Still, it is difficult to attribute the 1981 election results entirely to the vagaries of proportional representation: In that election, the Nationalists outpolled Labour, securing 54 percent of the vote,

Malta becomes a British Crown colony
A.D. 1802

The Maltese are besieged by the Germans and Italians during World War II
1940–1943

Malta becomes self-governing
1947

Independence within the Commonwealth of Nations
1964

The Labour Party and Prime Minister Dom Mintoff take office
1971

179 years of British military presence in Malta ends
1979

Prime Minister Edward Fenech Adami and his Nationalist Party come to power
1987

1990s

Tourism declines, then rebounds

Adami continues to urge stronger Maltese ties to Western Europe; President Ugo Mifsud Bonnici takes office

Alfred Sant of the Labour Party becomes prime minister; Malta's full membership in the EU continues to be a topic of conflict

but they failed to secure a parliamentary majority.

Six years later, in the 1987 election, the Nationalist Party finally succeeded in terminating Socialist control. Shortly after taking office, the new Nationalist Party prime minister, Edward Fenech Adami, pleaded with the Maltese people "to feel as one people" regardless of political party. The defeated Labour supporters, however, were reluctant to accept the decision of the electorate, taking their frustrations into the streets. The postelection rioting underscored the deep cleavages of class, ideology, and political traditions that divided the country.

Adami, who had won the election by a wafer-thin majority, pledged rapid shifts in foreign policy that would underscore Malta's solidarity with Western Europe. His government, for instance, wanted to apply for European Union membership. Indeed, this was one of the major planks in the Nationalist platform (the Labour Party saw fit to warn the electorate against integration into Europe because of that continent's AIDS cases!). However, with regard to Malta's position vis-à-vis the North Atlantic Treaty Organization, the two parties concluded a preelection agreement: They reached a consensus about Malta's status as a neutral country—a neutrality that specifically ruled out the long-term use of repair facilities in Maltese dockyards by warships from NATO fleets. But today, under Prime Minister Sant, the Maltese remain divided over the question of joining the EU.

MALTA AND THE EU
On July 16, 1990, Malta formally applied to join the EU, an initiative that was largely launched by the Nationalist Party. The opposition Labour Party would have preferred to maintain Malta's associate membership in the organization. Further steps toward full membership should, ac-

cording to the opposition, be a matter of "watching and waiting." The Nationalists, however, argued that such a hesitant skepticism was bound to dissipate, as events in the British Labour Party and PASOK (the Greek Socialist party) have shown. These two Socialist parties had initially opposed EU membership but had subsequently come to endorse the mergers, more or less enthusiastically.

THE ECONOMY
Economically, Malta is closely linked to the European Union; indeed, EU countries already account for about three quarters of Malta's imports and exports. Yet, as mentioned previously, many people in Malta are ambivalent with respect to full EU membership. The island's employers' federation, for instance, fears that becoming a full member will aggravate rather than solve Malta's economic problems. One should also bear in mind a visit by one of the EU's high officials who somewhat tactlessly argued that the membership of small states could ravage democratic aspects in the European Union's decision-making process unless such members would resign themselves to allowing others to conduct policy. On the other hand, Malta has more inhabitants than Luxembourg, and nobody can deny that the latter is part of the EU's decision making. The recent emphasis on subsidiarity, moreover, could appear to reduce the dangers of what extreme nationalists might qualify as "internal colonialism." (*Subsidiarity* means that the EU institutions will take care of policy matters only if the member states are unable to deal with them.) Although 38 percent of Malta's land surface is arable, most of its food supplies have to be imported. Malta's chief crops are potatoes, onions, and beans.

The biggest sources of income are the dockyards and tourism; 90 percent of the

vital tourist industry income derives from citizens of European Union countries. Tourism in Malta, however, experienced an alarming slump for several years. After reaching a saturation point in 1989, tourism declined the following year by 28 percent, in part due to conflict in the Persian Gulf region. But Mediterranean tourism has a volatile streak at even the best of times, and the number of alternatives to the rather fickle European public has grown of late. The island does not offer much in the way of camping; in addition, sightseeing opportunities are limited. It is an excellent resort for a somewhat sedate holidaymaker who likes to spend a week or two on the beach. For shorter vacations, however, the airfare to Malta can be prohibitive. Realizing that tourism is an important contributor to Malta's gross domestic product, the Maltese government has exerted itself to improve the conditions and the constraints under which the industry operates. A major constraint is ongoing conflicts in the Middle East, something that Malta cannot do much about, and the connection between Maltese tourism and tensions in the Middle East has been confirmed time and again. As soon as Kuwait had been reconquered in 1991, for example, and the tensions in that area subsided, tourism in Malta went up, and the following year, it reached an all-time high of 1 million visitors.

DEVELOPMENT

Most of Malta's trade is with EU countries. Malta is lacking in raw materials and must import its entire energy requirement. Unemployment—currently a low 3.7%—is believed to have occasionally soared to more than 20%—far more than the typical official estimate.

FREEDOM

Class divisions are sharp in Malta, as is the cleavage between devout Catholics and anticlerical elements identified with the Labour Party. Despite its rough-and-tumble history as an independent country, Malta has remained committed to political liberty and the protection of civil rights.

HEALTH/WELFARE

The Labour government's nationalization of Catholic schools and hospitals was an important issue in the 1987 election, bringing about its downfall. (Labour has since regained power.) Malta has a comprehensive state-supported welfare system. Improved health care has reduced infant mortality to a rate that is typical of the more developed countries.

ACHIEVEMENTS

Malta is a popular travel destination for Western Europeans, who go to the island to take advantage of its mild climate and attractive scenery. The government endeavors to make tourism less volatile as a source of revenue.

Monaco (Principality of Monaco)

GEOGRAPHY

Area in Square Miles (Kilometers):
0.7 (1.9) (about the size of
New York City's Central Park)
Capital district: Monaco-Ville
(31,900)
Environmental Concerns: issues
about pollution in the Mediterranean Sea
Geographical Features: hilly,
rugged, rocky
Climate: Mediterranean

PEOPLE

Population
Total: 32,000
Annual Growth Rate: 0.4%
Rural/Urban Population Ratio:
0/100
Major Languages: French; Eng-
lish; Italian; Monégasque
Ethnic Makeup: 47% French;
16% Monégasque; 16% Ital-
ian; 21% others
Religions: 95% Roman Catholic;
5% other or nonaffiliated

Health
Life Expectancy at Birth: 74
years (male); 82 years (female)
Infant Mortality Rate (Ratio):
6.7/1,000

Education
Adult Literacy Rate: 99%
Compulsory (Ages): 6–16

COMMUNICATION
Telephones: 1 per 2.1 people
Televisions: 1 per 1.3 people

TRANSPORTATION
Highways in Miles (Kilometers):
27 (44)
Railroads in Miles (Kilometers):
1.6 (1)
Usable Airfields: linked to airport in Nice, France, by helicopter service

GOVERNMENT
Type: constitutional monarchy
Independence Date: November 19, 1419
Head of State/Government: Prince Rainier
III; Minister of State Michel Leveque
Political Parties: National and Democratic
Union
Suffrage: universal at 21

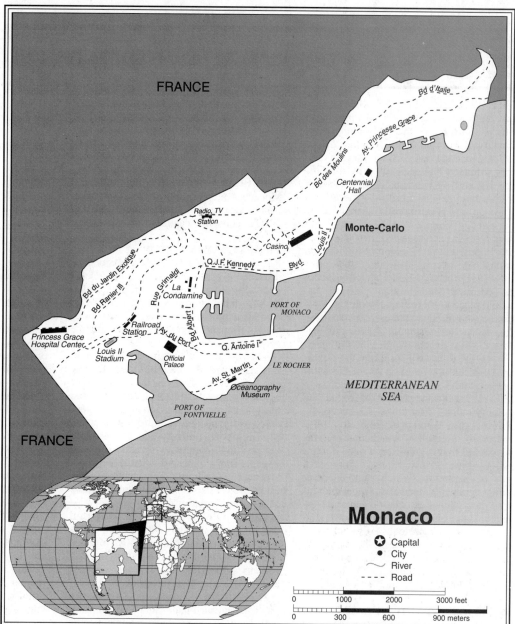

Monaco

- ★ Capital
- ● City
- ～ River
- --- Road

| 0 | | 1000 | | 2000 | | 3000 feet |
| 0 | | 300 | | 600 | | 900 meters |

MILITARY
Military Expenditures (% of GDP): de-
fense is the responsibility of France
Current Disputes: none

ECONOMY*
Currency ($ U.S. Equivalent): 5.60 French
francs = $1
Per Capita Income/GDP: $25,000/$800
million
Unemployment Rate: 3.1%
Labor Force: 30,500

Natural Resources: none
Agriculture: none
Industry: tourism; casinos; construction;
chemicals; food products; plastics; precision instruments; cosmetics; ceramics;
stamps

Note: Monaco has full customs integration with France.

 http://www.odci.gov/cia/publications/
factbook/country-frame.html

Monaco is ceded
to the House of
Grimaldi by
Genoa
A.D. 1297

The Grimaldis
are temporarily
deposed during
the French
Revolution
1793

Monaco is part of
France
1848–1861

The first
Constitution ends
absolute rule
1911

Prince Rainier
marries
American film
star Grace Kelly
1956

A new
Constitution
introduces
universal
suffrage
1962

Princess Grace
is killed in an
automobile
accident
1982

1990s

Prince
Albert is
groomed to
succeed
Prince
Rainier

Economic
diversification
takes shape

Monaco
becomes a
member of
the United
Nations

THE PRINCIPALITY OF MONACO

Located on the edge of the Mediterranean Sea in southeastern France, the tiny Principality of Monaco dates from the Middle Ages. Since the end of the thirteenth century, Monaco has been ruled by the Grimaldi family. Its independence, although tolerated somewhat fitfully by the French for centuries, was formally guaranteed by the Second Empire in 1861. After World War I, the French renewed their guarantee but imposed several major restrictions on Monaco's sovereignty—under the terms of a 1918 treaty, Monaco agreed to adopt no domestic and foreign policies that would be contrary to French political, economic, and military interests. A year later, the House of Grimaldi signed another treaty with the French, which granted France the right to incorporate the principality should the reigning prince die without an heir.

In 1911, Prince Albert approved the country's first Constitution. His successor, Prince Louis II, reigned from 1922 until his death in 1949, at which time he was succeeded by his grandson, Prince Rainier III. In 1962, Prince Rainier approved a new Constitution, which, among other things, granted universal suffrage, guaranteed the rights of association and trade unionism, abolished the death penalty, and provided for a more equal distribution of legislative power between the monarchy and the popularly elected National Council. This Constitution closely followed trends in France on a number of points.

POLITICS AND GOVERNMENT

Monaco is the second-smallest independent state in the world (after Vatican City State). In essence, Monaco has been a one-party state since 1962, when its two largest political parties, the National Union of Independents and the National Democratic

Entente, merged to form the National and Democratic Union (UND). The UND, which represents political interests most closely aligned with the policies of Prince Rainier, won all 18 seats in the National Council in 1968, 1978, and 1983. In the early 1970s, two new parties, the liberal Monaco Action and the leftist Democratic Union Movement, temporarily broke the UND's monopoly, capturing one seat each.

THE ECONOMY

Prior to World War II, Monaco's economy depended almost exclusively on two related industries: tourism and gambling. Revenues from the famous Monte Carlo Casino alone constituted more than 90 percent of the government's revenues. Meanwhile, the absence of income and estate taxes attracted wealthy foreigners wishing to avoid taxation elsewhere. By the time Prince Rainier came to power, however, the liabilities of Monaco's one-dimensional economy and the international reputation it had engendered were becoming painfully obvious. The European tourist trade had become increasingly competitive, and France's growing impatience with what it had come to view as the parasite on its southern flank threatened serious damage to French–Monégasque relations.

Prince Rainier launched a successful campaign to diversify the principality's economy. Since the late 1950s, Monaco has actively solicited light-manufacturing industries from abroad. It now produces and exports a number of products, including electronic components, automotive parts, pharmaceuticals, and beauty products. By 1986, more than 25 percent of its total workforce were employed in the industrial sector. In recent years, Monaco has also experienced rapid growth in some service industries, such as banking and commercial exchanges. Tourism still ac-

counts for an estimated 25 percent of Monaco's total income (official figures are not available); however, the state has also taken steps to diversify and stabilize this sector. While Monaco still has no income or estate tax, casino receipts probably account for less than 4 percent of government revenues. Most government revenues are now generated by value-added taxes on goods and services, including hotels and industry. The government's budget is thought to be in surplus as a result.

Though impressive to date, the economic transformation of Monaco has been heavily influenced, if not constrained, by the French. The French government's concern over lost tax revenues in the early 1960s forced Monaco to accede to the French demand that all corporations conducting less than 25 percent of their business in the principality come under the French financial system. Today, French citizens with fewer than 5 years' residence in Monaco are taxed at French rates. Monaco is completely integrated into the French monetary system and is therefore subject to extensive regulation and controls from Paris; this has clearly delayed the development of offshore banking in the principality. Monaco also participates in the European Union market system through its customs union with France. Thus, Monaco's economic future will continue to depend quite heavily on decisions made in Paris.

DEVELOPMENT

Prince Rainier has overseen a very successful diversification of Monaco's economy during his rule. No longer is the principality viewed solely as a tourist spot.

FREEDOM

Monaco rates high in civil liberties and political rights. With no defense forces of its own, the principality relies on France to guarantee its security. Monaco's foreign relations are for the most part directed from Paris.

HEALTH/WELFARE

Monaco has no income tax, and the Monégasque people have benefited from the diversifying economy. In fact, there is a fairly low unemployment rate in the city-state today.

ACHIEVEMENTS

In 1986, Monaco established a modern university that provides courses taught in English in business and business administration. The University of Southern Europe also conducts exchange programs with American and European universities.

The Netherlands (Kingdom of the Netherlands)

GEOGRAPHY
Area in Square Miles (Kilometers): 16,464 (37,330) (about twice the size of New Jersey)
Capital (Population): Amsterdam (722,000); The Hague (seat of government) (442,000)
Environmental Concerns: water and air pollution; acid rain
Geographical Features: mostly coastal lowland and reclaimed land; some hills in southeast
Climate: temperate; marine

PEOPLE

Population
Total: 15,731,000
Annual Growth Rate: 0.5%
Rural/Urban Population Ratio: 11/89
Major Languages: Dutch; Frisian
Ethnic Makeup: 96% Dutch; 4% Moroccans, Turks and others
Religions: 34% Roman Catholic; 25% Protestant; 3% Muslim; 2% others; 36% unaffiliated

Health
Life Expectancy at Birth: 75 years (male); 81 years (female)
Infant Mortality Rate (Ratio): 5.7/1,000
Average Caloric Intake: 131% of FAO minimum
Physicians Available (Ratio): 1/391

Education
Adult Literacy Rate: 100%
Compulsory (Ages): 5–18

COMMUNICATION
Telephones: 1 per 1.9 people
Daily Newspaper Circulation: 334 per 1,000 people
Televisions: 1 per 2 people

TRANSPORTATION
Highways in Miles (Kilometers): 76,200 (127,000)
Railroads in Miles (Kilometers): 1,675 (2,791)
Usable Airfields: 28
Motor Vehicles in Use: 6,257,000

GOVERNMENT
Type: constitutional monarchy
Independence Date: 1579 (from Spain)
Head of State/Government: Queen Beatrix; Prime Minister Wim Kok
Political Parties: Labor; Christian Democratic Appeal; Liberal; Democrats '66 (D'66); many minor parties
Suffrage: universal at 18

MILITARY
Military Expenditures (% of GDP): 2.1%
Current Disputes: none

ECONOMY
Currency ($ U.S. Equivalent): 2.03 guilders = $1
Per Capita Income/GDP: $22,000/$343.9 billion
GDP Growth Rate: 3.25%
Inflation Rate: 2%
Unemployment Rate: 6.9%
Labor Force: 6,600,000
Natural Resources: natural gas; petroleum; fertile soil
Agriculture: animal husbandry predominates; horticultural crops; grains; potatoes; sugar beets
Industry: food processing; metal and engineering products; electrical and electronic machinery and equipment; chemicals; petroleum products; natural gas; brewing
Exports: $203.1 billion (primary partners EU countries)
Imports: $1.791 trillion (primary partners EU countries)

http://portal.research.bell-labs.com/
cgi-wald/dbaccess/411?key=173
http://www.odci.gov/cia/publications/
factbook/country-frame.html
http://www.travel.org/nether.html

Netherlands

- ✪ Capital
- ● City
- ～ River
- --- Road

THE NETHERLANDS

The Netherlands (frequently referred to as "Holland," although that term in fact applies to the two oldest and most important provinces) is a small country with a glorious past. Once a European power ruling a large colonial empire, it still plays a greater role in international affairs than could be expected of a nation of its size and population.

About one third of the country's land area is actually below sea level, reclaimed by a complex system of dikes, polders, and drainage canals whose construction started as early as the thirteenth century and culminated in the execution of the so-called Delta Plan. The execution of the plan, which took more than a quarter of a century, was a reaction to a huge flood in 1953, which claimed nearly 2,000 lives. The twelfth province, which the Dutch recently added to their kingdom, is entirely made up of reclaimed land.

The Netherlands straddles the area where three large rivers—the Rhine, the Maas, and the Scheldt—flow into the North Sea. The fact that Rotterdam is now the world's busiest port is a twentieth-century reminder of a maritime tradition that began when William Beukelszoon discovered in 1384 how to cure herring with salt. This invention initiated a lively trade in cured fish, a trade that stretched from the Baltic to the Mediterranean Seas. In turn, this experience may have prepared Dutch seafarers for the lucrative trade in spices that they took over from the Portuguese two centuries later.

The Portuguese were the first Europeans to sail east to the almost mythical Spice Islands (the Moluccas, which are now part of Indonesia). Upon their return to Europe, they deposited their precious products in Lisbon, and the Dutch then distributed them all over Europe. However, the king of Spain became king of Portugal as well in 1580; since Spain was at war with the rising Netherlands, Dutch traders were no longer allowed to come to Lisbon. The Dutch then started to contemplate seriously getting the spices firsthand. Initially they believed that sailing through Arctic waters to the north of Scandinavia, Russia, and Siberia would yield a significant short cut. But such a voyage proved risky, as it led through areas that had never been charted. A Dutch ship got stuck at Nova Zembla, where the crew had to pass an unbearably harsh winter before returning to Holland the next spring.

The Dutch then decided to benefit from Portuguese explorations. However, they varied the customary Portuguese route considerably, no doubt because they wanted to minimize the contacts with the people who had become their enemies.

They thus first sailed to the Cape of Good Hope but did not go around it or go north along the African coast, as the Portuguese did. Instead, the Dutch went straight east, which carried them, after weeks and weeks, to western Australia. They then went north, finding their way to the Spice Islands. There they soon realized that, although it was possible to avoid other European explorers en route, it was impossible to ignore the Portuguese and Spaniards once they had arrived. Indeed, the Spaniards had by now also familiarized themselves with the route to the Indies.

The beginning of the sixteenth century witnessed the establishment of the United East India Company (better known by its Dutch initials VOC), which was granted a monopoly of the spice trade in the Moluccan Islands.

Dutch maritime activity also extended to the West; tobacco and sugar were carried from the New World to Europe, and Dutch seafarers took slaves from Africa to the British colonies in North America. By the mid-seventeenth century, the Netherlands had developed into a global commercial power, whose trade and prestige were protected by a powerful navy, the match of those of England and Spain. Amsterdam, the capital of the Netherlands, had grown into Europe's richest city, a center of commerce and finance. The great prosperity was enriched by a culture that highlighted art. Dutch painters, whose works currently sell for millions of dollars, lived in Amsterdam, Haarlem, and Leiden. Indeed, the Dutch refer to the seventeenth century as their "Golden Age."

It would, however, be wrong to think of the seventeenth century as a period in which peace prevailed in the Netherlands. In the decades preceding the Golden Age, the Reformation—a religious movement that led to the rejection of some Roman Catholic doctrine and the establishment of Protestant churches—had spread like wildfire. The Catholic king of Spain, to which the Netherlands belonged at that time, felt aggrieved about this and attempted to reverse the tide. King Philip II thus dispatched his armies to the Northern Netherlands, which had embraced the Calvinist faith. The year 1568 marked the beginning of the Dutch War of Independence, which was to last 80 years. Dutch grievances were partly political and partly economic, but the revolt typically focused on religious dissent. It was for all intents and purposes a Protestant war against King Philip II.

By the time the Eighty Years' War finally came to an end, at the Peace of Westphalia in 1648, the Netherlands had become a haven for Protestants and numerous other "dissidents." Jews fleeing from the Inquisition in Spain and Portugal, and Huguenots fleeing from France after the revocation of the Edict of Nantes, sought and found asylum in the Netherlands. Even the Pilgrims stayed in Leiden for some years before finding their way to the New World. (Interestingly, this latter group, though grateful for the asylum that was granted, wanted to start their westward trek as soon as possible, because they found Dutch children very ill-disciplined and feared that this might rub off on their own offspring!) The Eighty Years' War, which often epitomized religious intolerance, may have had an unexpected benefit, since it caused future generations in Holland to have a greater appreciation for religious and political freedoms.

THE RELIGIOUS DIMENSION

Religion has for a considerable time been a strong factor in Dutch politics and culture. Although the country has gone through a period of secularization, it is still possible to find evidence of the Calvinist religion, which reigned supreme during the Eighty Years' War and afterward. Even the monarchy, which can be traced back only to 1813, offers an example, as the Constitution decrees that members of the royal house may adhere only to the Dutch Reformed Church. When it appeared that one of the princesses had become Roman Catholic in order to marry a Spanish nobleman, she was immediately scratched as a member of the royal house, and her parents were not allowed to attend the wedding in Rome.

Nowadays, however, Dutch society is highly diverse, at least in the religious respect. The Roman Catholic Church has the largest following, though many are only nominally Roman Catholic. Also, the upper clergy of the Dutch Roman Catholic Church during the 1960s and 1970s openly rebelled against the Vatican, which strongly disapproved of the liberalizing tendency of the Dutch bishops and cardinals, fearing that it might erode established doctrine.

Although the Roman Catholics are now the largest religious denomination in the Netherlands, they were for a long time less accepted in Dutch society. Indeed, as indicated above, the tolerance that was so generously extended to religious refugees from other countries was not accorded to Catholic compatriots. But then, the Eighty Years' War was, after all, a religious war that was won by the Protestant cause; Roman Catholics were viewed as persons who had been, at best, indifferent to King Philip II's fight against the Protestants.

They had never been driven into churches that were then set on fire, as happened to the Protestants. The Catholics' lack of involvement caused them to be denied full civil rights, a condition that was to persist for 2 centuries. Until the mid-nineteenth century, Dutch Catholics were not even allowed to enter the public bureaucracy. The Constitution of 1848 started to change all this, but it was not until 1917 that all Dutch males, regardless of their religious beliefs, were enfranchised.

Protestantism in Holland may be less nominal than Catholicism, but it is certainly very diverse, ranging from free-thinkers and unitarians on the one hand to rigid fundamentalists on the other. The country is also becoming more secular: About one third of the Dutch population are unaffiliated with any religion, and this proportion is steadily growing.

The year 1917 was also significant in that it ended what the Dutch called the "School Struggle." All private schools (in large part denominational) were henceforth to receive governmental subsidies whose amounts closely correspond to the schools' enrollment sizes. Arend Lijphart, a well-known Dutch scholar, considers 1917 to be the beginning of what he has qualified as *consociationalism,* a political feature typical of the Netherlands. Dutch society, according to this political analyst, was in effect divided into three subsocietal segments: the Protestants, the Roman Catholics, and those unaffiliated with any religion (who were, rightly or wrongly, often referred to as "humanists"). So strong was the religious or humanistic orientation of these subsocietal groups that all their activities and associations revolved around their specific belief system. Educational facilities from kindergarten through university catered to members of the respective groups. There also were associations whose activities had no bearing on religion, such as stamp collecting and chess, that were either Protestant, Roman Catholic, or unaffiliated. It was therefore theoretically unnecessary to mix or even to meet with persons from the other groups.

The complete insulation of these three groups throughout one's entire life would naturally be utterly dysfunctional in a political system if it were not for their political elites. The elites of the segments communicated and negotiated with one another. They made compromises and generally conducted politics. Again, just as had been the case with the schools, the compromises were in large part based on numbers or, rather, proportions.

Lijphart asserts that the consociational system in the Netherlands came to an end

(Credit: U.N. Photo 186853/A. Brizzi)

The International Court of Justice is the principal judicial organ of the United Nations. Its seat is at the Peace Palace in the Hague, the Netherlands.

in 1967. By then, people had defected from their respective churches in large numbers and refused to be categorized in religious respect when it came to associations. Only politico–religious associations like political parties and trade unions remained more or less faithful to consociational patterns for another decade.

THE GOVERNMENT

The Netherlands is headed by a constitutional monarchy, which implies that the king or queen does not have any political power and is in effect "above" politics. The monarchy has been retained for ceremonial and symbolic purposes only. The king or queen (for more than a century, the Dutch have had a queen as head of state) may constitute a link in the process of government formation, may even seem involved in political rhetoric, but is nevertheless entirely apolitical.

The Netherlands has a multiparty system, and it frequently happens that 10 or more parties compete for seats in the Second Chamber, the lower house that functions as the main political arena. None of these parties receives majority support; as a result, coalitions have to be formed in order to establish a government. Frequently four or more parties participate in such a coalition; although parties that jointly constitute a cabinet are usually more or less like-minded, such governments tend to be fragile.

During the 1970s, the large religious parties merged into the Christian Democratic Appeal, an ecumenical power bloc that led the government for 2 decades, in conjunction with the Labor Party. Ideologically, the current government may be classified as center-left. The most formidable Socialist party was the Labor Party, which was established shortly after World War II and has often been part of the government. On the left, one also finds the D'66, a Social Democratic party founded in 1966, which represents a less doctrinaire type of socialism. The Communist Party, which shortly after World War II secured more than 10 percent of the vote, is no longer represented in Parliament.

In the Netherlands, voter support is translated into parliamentary seats through the proportional representation system. A party will generally be allocated the same proportion of seats in the lower house that it has secured of the total vote. Thus, while the Dutch system does not have a standard minimum limit expressed in percentages, there is an automatic threshold, in that, for each seat, a party has to gain the quotient of the total number of votes divided by 150 (the total number of seats in the Second Chamber).

The 1994 parliamentary election wrought havoc to the government coalition (consisting of the Christian Democrats and Labor). The former lost no fewer than 20 seats and was thus left with only 34 seats. Its coalition partner (the Labor Party), although currently enjoying a greater following than any other political party in the Netherlands, suffered a humiliating reduction—from 49 to 37 seats. The endangered coalition thus mastered a total of 71 seats, 5 less than a majority. Since minorities cannot govern, the coalition has to be enlarged, a measure that is bound to render the government more fragile. Most Dutch voters appear to favor enlarging the current center-left coalition with the Liberals (the VVD). However, a so-called purple coalition, which would consist of Labor, the Liberals, and the D'66, was believed to have more staying power.

POLARIZATION VS. PILLARIZATION

One may argue that the disintegration of the *verzuiling* (the term literally means "pillarization" and refers to the system of religious compartmentalization discussed earlier) was brought about by a strong decline in religious orientation during the late 1960s. Simultaneously, however, new lifestyles started to emerge in Western Europe in general and in the Netherlands in particular. Many young persons adopted a counterculture lifestyle; it did not take long for the capital city of Amsterdam to develop into the capital of the international hippie movement.

In matters of morality and sex, the Dutch witnessed the swing of the pendulum as well, having been very staid in the past. In the 1960s and 1970s, drugs started to be introduced into this part of Europe. Amsterdam came to succeed Marseilles as the drug capital of Western Europe. Some attempts were

made to legalize less harmful drugs. The experiment failed, however, because the governments of neighboring countries complained, finding that their young people had flocked to the Dutch distribution centers. Indeed, the drug traffic has become the crux in the negotiations concerning the opening of borders for the single market of the European Union.

THE WELFARE SYSTEM

A popular theory holds that attachment to religious values and economic prosperity relate inversely. In the Dutch case, it was certainly true that the decline of religious values was attended by an unprecedented prosperity.

The improved economy resulted in part from the discovery of natural gas in the northern province of Groningen. The subterranean gas bubble turned out to be so large that great quantities of natural gas were sold to neighboring countries that had no energy resources of their own. This steady income was a windfall for the Netherlands. Then, in the early 1970s, the world was struck by the energy crisis. The domestic use of natural gas, as well as the revenues from its sale to other countries, expanded enormously as a consequence of the three- to fourfold increase in energy prices in the period 1973–1976. However, the income that these new ventures generated was not used for capital investments but for consumption—that is, for the proliferation and enlargement of the already generous system of welfare benefits. The system fought the financial burdens resulting from unemployment, sickness, and disability.

In the Netherlands, welfare benefits are paid out for as long as they are needed by an individual. Until recently, they were even indexed so that they automatically matched the increases in wages in the private sector. The upgrading of the welfare system resulting from the economic prosperity of the 1970s caused more people to be eligible for benefits, while the established benefits grew in size. At one point, more than 25 percent of the workforce received some income from the government without working! The systemic generosity also extended to migratory workers, refugees, and the like.

The governmental service sector had already become top-heavy when, in the 1980s, energy prices started to plummet.

This, of course, had a disastrous effect on the revenues that the Dutch government received from its sale of natural gas. The shrinking budget forced the authorities into a retrenchment, and subsequently into a reversal, of the welfare system. The retrenchment, coming at a time when the Dutch workforce appeared to include 900,000 disabled persons, nearly caused a government crisis in 1993. The Dutch welfare system has now been trimmed. Many benefits that resulted from excessive paternalism have been revoked.

That the Dutch mindset and mentality have been profoundly affected by the welfare system is clear from the declining emigration numbers. In the first 2 postwar decades, fairly large numbers of young Dutch men and women left the country to seek new lives in Australia or Canada. In the 1980s, with the expansion of welfare, emigration diminished significantly.

ETHNICITY AND EQUALITY

The urgency to come to grips with the economy has in recent years raised questions about the extent to which social solidarity should apply to non-Dutch residents. A majority among them are Indonesians and Surinamese who came to the Netherlands as political and economic refugees when their homelands, former Dutch colonial possessions, gained independence. Among the Indonesians are the South Moluccans, who fought on the Dutch side during the Indonesian Revolution. During the late 1970s, they briefly engaged in terrorism.

In addition to the immigration waves clearly associated with its loss of empire, the Netherlands invited "guest workers" from the Mediterranean basin during periods of full employment. These people were scheduled to work in the manufacturing industry for 2 years. Yet their terms were renewed again and again—until unemployment made itself felt. They are now often called the "guest unemployed." Having paid into the unemployment and sickness funds while they were working, the foreign laborers are entitled to the same benefits in matters of unemployment or health as Dutch citizens. Although it is less prosperous than neighboring Germany, the Netherlands has also been a target for political or economic asylum-seekers, most of whom are not refugees in the orthodox sense of the word.

| The new Constitution eliminates the political role of the monarch and introduces direct elections to Parliament **1848** | The consociational approach in government, resulting from pillarization **1917–1967** | Five years of Nazi occupation leave the Dutch economy in ruins **1940–1945** | The Marshall Plan helps the Netherlands to get back on its feet **1947–1949** | Transfer of sovereignty to Indonesia; the Netherlands loses the cornerstone of its empire and joins NATO **1949** | The Netherlands joins the European Coal and Steel Community, a forerunner of the European Union **1958** | Queen Beatrix succeeds her mother, Juliana; a center-left coalition returns to office Prime Minister Ruud Lubbers **1980s** |

1990s

The Netherlands trims its welfare budget; the Netherlands presides over the European Council's deliberations on the Maastricht Treaty

Hundreds of thousands are temporarily evacuated as wintery floodwaters threaten to burst dikes

Prime Minister Wim Kok and his Labor Party meet with voters' approval in two parliamentary elections; the Netherland participates in the launch of the Euro

The Dutch tradition of tolerance has generally held up quite well in dealing with ethnic diversity. Indeed, the government has allowed the families of guest workers to come and join their relatives. Foreigners have even been permitted to participate in municipal elections and to run for local office. The great cultural differences have nevertheless imposed strains on Dutch society, strains that occasionally culminate in offensive graffiti or riots. The Dutch government has instituted programs to help these non-European immigrants assimilate. But then, not all appear to be interested in becoming assimilated.

THE FUTURE

In spite of its rigid adherence to certain principles (such as free trade, political liberty, human rights, and, in a sense, what remains of the Calvinist morality), Dutch society has manifested a remarkable flexibility, a willingness "to go with the flow." It has adapted well to changing circumstances.

The loss of empire (the factor that rendered the Netherlands global was its overseas empire) was soon followed by the country's integration into the North Atlantic Treaty Organization and the European Union. In both regional organizations, the Netherlands is small but not insignificant, loyal but vocal. The Dutch people strongly support European political and economic union. The Netherlands' influence in NATO was demonstrated when the United States insisted on the deployment of cruise missiles in the Netherlands. The majority of the Dutch initially disagreed. There were vociferous protests, demonstrations, rallies—in short, an uproar among the people. The government pleaded for more time, and for a brief period the Netherlands was the odd man out—that is, the

only country within NATO that had not yet accepted the new missiles. The Netherlands government indicated that it needed all that time to convince its opponents that the only alternative to accepting missile deployment would be to get out of NATO. Only a minority appeared to favor that solution. Finally, on November 1, 1985, Prime Minister Ruud Lubbers announced that the Netherlands had accepted deployment of the U.S. missiles.

In domestic matters, too, this mixture of principle and pragmatism has prevailed. When it was found that the 1980s decrease in energy prices had created huge liabilities for future generations, since a large part of the welfare system had been financed by the profits on natural gas, steps were taken to trim the welfare budget and to integrate it into the overall budget. The effective political response to this economic crisis has demonstrated again that the Dutch give their government authority to change policies that no longer work without abandoning the main premises that Dutch society holds dear.

Matters of family planning and birth control have also been tackled forthrightly in this country with a high population density. The prolonged debates on abortion have resulted in its conditional legalization.

For a considerable time, the Netherlands has been the only country in the world to discuss on the official level the legalization of euthanasia for the terminally ill. Finally, after more than 20 years of acrimonious debate, on February 9, 1993, Parliament produced a bill that gave physicians the green light to assist in suicide, under strict medical and ethical conditions. The carefully worded bill became law in 1994. It does in fact not legalize euthanasia but provides guidelines as to what doctors may do without risking

criminal prosecution. It allows a greater degree of control in this delicate area, and the Dutch government thus no longer turns a blind eye to a widely prevalent practice.

During the late 1980s and early 1990s, the Dutch economy spiralled downward. (It is obvious that the European Union does not provide any quick fixes.) While opening Parliament in September 1993, Queen Beatrix, in her Speech from the Throne, highlighted the "alarming" rate of unemployment and indicated that there was no light at the end of the tunnel. She noted that 1994 would provide a postwar record-high unemployment. Subsequent years have seen a measure of economic improvement, but unemployment remains high, at 6.9 percent.

DEVELOPMENT

The Netherlands is a highly developed country that has in effect entered the postindustrial era. About 89% of the total area is considered urban. The people have become very sensitive to concerns related to the environment.

FREEDOM

The Netherlands ranks very high among the world's countries in terms of freedom. Laws have recently allowed foreigners to vote or run for office in municipal elections. Holland is one of the few countries to allow physicians to assist in suicide.

HEALTH/WELFARE

Health indicators are generally good though funds for social welfare have been greatly lowered because the reduced revenues of natural gas have caused the funding to deteriorate.

ACHIEVEMENTS

One of the greatest achievements of recent times is the completion of the Delta Works, which protects the Netherlands from devastating floods, such as the ones that took place in 1953 and 1995.

Norway (Kingdom of Norway)

GEOGRAPHY

Area in Square Miles (Kilometers):
125,149 (324,220) (slightly
larger than New Mexico)

Capital (Population): Oslo (488,000)

Environmental Concerns: air
and water pollution; acid rain
damaging forests and lakes
and threatening fish stocks

Geographical Features: glaci-
ated; mostly high plateaus
and rugged mountains broken
by fertile valleys; small, scattered plains; coastline deeply indented by fjords; arctic tundra
in north; about 2/3 mountains

Climate: temperate along coast;
colder interior

PEOPLE

Population

Total: 4,420,000

Annual Growth Rate: 0.44%

Rural/Urban Population Ratio:
27/73

Major Languages: Norwegian;
Sami (Lapp); Finnish

Ethnic Makeup: 95% Germanic
(Nordic, Alpine, Baltic); a
minority of Sami (Lapp)

Religions: 88% Evangelical
Lutheran (state church); 4%
other Protestant and Roman
Catholic; 8% others

Health

Life Expectancy at Birth: 75
years (male); 81 years (female)

Infant Mortality Rate (Ratio):
5.1/1,000

Average Caloric Intake: 124%
of FAO minimum

Physicians Available (Ratio): 1/299

Education

Adult Literacy Rate: 99%

Compulsory (Ages:) 6–16

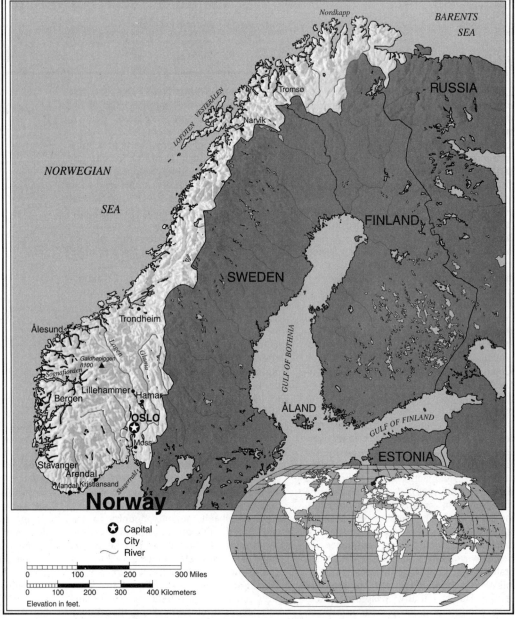

Norway

○ Capital
• City
～ River

0 ... 100 ... 200 ... 300 Miles
0 ... 100 ... 200 ... 300 ... 400 Kilometers
Elevation in feet.

COMMUNICATION

Telephones: 1 per 1.8 people

Daily Newspaper Circulation: 607 per
1,000 people

Televisions: 1 per 2.3 people

TRANSPORTATION

Highways in Miles (Kilometers): 54,157
(90,261)

Railroads in Miles (Kilometers): 2,512 (4,027)

Usable Airfields: 102

Motor Vehicles in Use: 2,082,000

GOVERNMENT

Type: constitutional monarchy

Independence Date: October 26, 1905

Head of State/Government: King Harald V;
Prime Minister Kjell Magne Bondevik

Political Parties: Christian Democrats; Labor Party; Conservative Party; Center
Party; Socialist Left; Norwegian Communist Party; Progressive Party; Liberal
Party; Left Party; Red Electoral Alliance

Suffrage: universal at 18

MILITARY

Military Expenditures (% of GDP): 2.9%

Current Disputes: territorial claim in Antarctica; maritime boundary dispute with Russia

ECONOMY

Currency ($ U.S. Equivalent): 6.56 kroner
(crowns) = $1

Per Capita Income/GDP: $27,400/$120.5
billion

GDP Growth Rate: 3.5%

Inflation Rate: 2%

Unemployment Rate: 2.6%

Labor Force: 2,130,000

Natural Resources: petroleum; copper;
natural gas; pyrites; nickel; iron ore;
zinc; lead; fish; timber; hydropower

Agriculture: animal husbandry predominates;
feed grains; potatoes; fruits; vegetables

Industry: oil and gas; tourism; food processing; shipbuilding; wood pulp; paper
products; metals; chemicals

Exports: $49.3 billion (primary partners
EU countries, United States)

Imports: $35.1 billion (primary partners
EU countries, United States)

LAND OF THE MIDNIGHT SUN

The Kingdom of Norway, often called the "Land of the Midnight Sun," is not a major world power. But it is affluent, its social problems are relatively few, and the quality of life is high for almost all its residents.

Norway lies on the Scandinavian peninsula and borders Sweden, Finland, and Russia. The distance from one end of the country to the other is about 1,100 miles—the same distance as from Oslo to Marseilles, France. There is a great deal of variation in Norway's climate, a result of the different degrees of latitude, differences in altitude, varying topography, the effectiveness of the prevailing westerly winds, and the effects of the Gulf Stream. Thus, even though Norway stretches as far north as Alaska and Siberia, its entire coast is open for shipping throughout the winter. Indeed, hay and potatoes grow in even the northernmost region of the country.

About half the land area is mountainous, and more than a quarter is covered with forest. Only 3 percent of the land is arable. Glaciers created many sharp mountain peaks and dug out numerous long valleys. The Norwegian coastline is punctuated by long, narrow fjords and thousands of islets. Most Norwegians live by the fjords or along the coast.

A QUEST FOR SOVEREIGNTY

The first recorded period in Norwegian history was the Viking Age, from approximately A.D. 800 to the mid-1000s. The unification of Norway took place during this era. This integrative phase culminated in the adoption of Europe's first national code of common law, in the 1270s. After that period, the Norse kings started to expand their control over the country, tightening their rule.

However, the so-called Black Death, moving across Europe, reached Norway in 1349 and killed off at least half the population. This catastrophe may well have caused the rapid loss of Norse influence. In 1397, Norway came under Danish rule; it remained a dependency of Denmark for more than 400 years.

In 1814, Denmark, which had followed Napoleon Bonaparte to defeat, tried to cede Norway to Sweden. The Norwegians protested, and a constitutional convention at Eidsvoll endeavored to reestablish Norway as an independent country. Negotiations with the Swedes resulted in a compromise among the neighboring countries later in the year. The Norwegians accepted the Swedish king as their own, but Norway was recognized as a separate country, and the democratic provisions of the Eidsvoll Constitution were preserved.

However, it is possible that, in the course of the nineteenth century, Norway lost some of the independence it had been given in the compromise following the Eidsvoll convention. Norwegian resentment toward the union grew, and the Norwegian government asserted greater autonomy. In 1905, under pressure from the Parliament, the Norwegian government abolished the union with the Swedish crown.

As soon as the personal union was dissolved and Norway had become independent, a Danish prince was invited to become king of Norway, taking the name Haakon VII. The current monarch, King Harald V, is the grandson of King Haakon VII. Like his father and grandfather, he adopted the motto "All for Norway." He was the first Norwegian prince to be born on Norwegian soil in 567 years.

THE SYSTEM OF GOVERNMENT

Norway is a constitutional and hereditary monarchy. Norway's founders had originally—that is, on May 17, 1814—decreed that royal succession would be possible only through male heirs. But this provision was changed as a result of subsequent amendments.

The Constitution vests legislative power in the *Storting* (the Norwegian Legislature, which has 165 seats). The king, as head of state, enjoys the so-called suspensive veto (a type of veto that can only delay but not annul legislation). Thus, the royal veto may be exercised; but if the same bill is passed by two successive Stortings (established by subsequent elections), it will become law without the assent of the sovereign. This type of veto is reminiscent of the power that England's House of Lords has in legislative matters. And indeed, since 1984, the Norwegian system of government has in many ways resembled that of Great Britain.

Formally, the king has the command of the land, sea, and air forces; and he also heads the government administration, which means that all appointments are made in his name. All branches of government are open to women, including positions within the state church.

In 1991, King Olav V, who had been a symbol of resistance to the German occupation of Norway during World War II, died, at age 83. He was succeeded by his son, who became the first King Harald since the Viking Age.

Norway's electoral system is based on proportional representation, which means that political parties receive the proportion of seats in Parliament that they have obtained of the votes in the election to the Storting. This encourages a multiparty system as well as splinter parties. Six par-

ties, for example, won seats in the 1985 election. All Norwegian citizens have the right to vote at age 18 (that is, about 75 percent of the population), and more than 80 percent of those eligible to vote do so at each election.

Norwegian politics are generally very stable. The Labor Party was in power virtually without interruption from 1935 to 1965, and it still remains the largest party, usually receiving about 40 percent of the vote. (In the parliamentary elections of September 1997, Labor garnered 65 of the 165 seats). Closely aligned to trade unions, it adheres to social-democratic principles.

The period following 1965 witnessed strong power shifts between the Labor Party and a coalition of non-Socialist parties. In 1985, the non-Socialist parties received a slight majority, but their coalition collapsed the very next year. Gro Harlem Brundtland, who in 1981 had become Norway's first female prime minister, was returned to office in 1986 as the head of a minority Labor government. The legislative elections that were held in 1989 again produced ambiguous results. Jan Peder Syse became prime minister of the government that then took office. Apparently it did not work out: Syse was forced to step down, and Gro Harlem Brundtland again became prime minister. It is thus obvious that, although left and right appear to match each other in Norway, most voters have a slight preference for a center-left government.

In the fall of 1996, Brundtland resigned as prime minister, and Thorbjørn Jagland was appointed to replace her. Jagland and the Labor Party retained power through the aforementioned parliamentary 1997 elections. He was succeeded by Kvell Magne Bondevik, a Lutheran priest of the Christian Democrat Party.

A central stated goal for the new government—a coalition between the Christian Democrats, the Center Party, and the Liberal Party—is to strengthen the welfare state, including more redistribution of wealth and a reduction in private consumption. The coalition is fragile, however, especially when it comes to debates over the merits and disadvantages of joining the European Union and the Euro zone—a source of heated dissension in Norway for years. Both between the coalition parties and within them, opinion remains sharply divided. And in the fall of 1998, Prime Minister Bondevik retired from the public scene for a month, claiming a "depressive reaction to overwork." Acting in his stead was Anne Enger Lahnstein, leader of the Center Party, whose environment-oriented party is virulently opposed to EU membership

An interesting character to have emerged in Norwegian politics in recent years is Carl I. Hagen of the rightest Progressive Party, a maverick who defies the Norwegian tradition of consensus (though he says he wants his party to be formally included in a ruling coalition). He has been snubbed by the country's mainstream parties because of his perceived hostility to immigrants, but in the last few years he and his party have become more prominent and popular.

THE WELFARE STATE

In Norway, taxes pay for a national insurance system, which tries to preserve the standard of living of those who cannot work because of old age, disability, illness, unemployment, or other reasons. The welfare system pays the full cost of hospitalization and most doctors' fees. Workers are paid regular wages when they are sick and receive 4 weeks of paid vacation each year. The government also subsidizes housing costs and provides for education. University students pay no tuition, and they may receive government loans for their living expenses.

Most newspapers get subsidies from the government, which also provides assistance to artists and writers as well as to most theaters and museums. Nevertheless, artists and the mass media do not feel inhibited about criticizing the government. A government corporation is responsible for radio and television broadcasts; no commercials are allowed.

Norwegian taxes are among the highest in the world, constituting almost half of the country's gross domestic product. Norwegians complain about the heavy tax burden, but so far they have not tolerated cutbacks in services.

A HOMOGENEOUS POPULATION

The Norwegian population is very homogeneous. The vast majority are Nordic and adhere to the Lutheran faith. The main minorities are the Sami (Lapps)—the 20,000 indigenous people of northern Scandinavia—and about 15,000 recent immigrants, mainly from developing countries. These peoples sometimes encounter a degree of hostility from the mainstream Norwegians.

Norwegians value their leisure time and spend much of it in the forests and mountains and along the fjords and coast. By international standards, the crime rate is low and drug problems are minimal, except for alcohol abuse. In Norway, driving under the influence is considered a serious offense that invariably results in the immediate and permanent revocation of one's license.

THE ECONOMY

The main goals of Norwegian economic policy have been to maximize employment and production value, maintain rural settlements, and achieve Norwegian control of natural resources and an equitable distribution of wealth and income. The government has been very successful in achieving these aims. (The unemployment rate reached 7.5 percent in 1993; but in 1998, it was only about 2.6 percent.) Only half the population live in cities of 10,000 or more people, and few countries have greater equality of income.

The traditional industries—farming, fishing, and forestry—are still important stimuli to boost economic patterns and self-sufficiency. However, they no longer employ many people or contribute much to the gross national product. Service industries, especially social and educational institutions, have become the main employers. The trade balance is very dependent on manufacturing, shipping, and petroleum exports. Most factories process Norwegian raw materials or exploit Norwegian energy sources. Norway primarily trades with European Union countries—although it still is not an EU member itself—and the United States.

Electric consumption per capita in Norway is the highest in the world, but hydropower from waterfalls and mountain lakes provides inexpensive energy from perpetually renewable sources for aluminum production and other manufacturing. Since 1975, Norway has also exported large amounts of oil and natural gas found in the North Sea. Norway shares these resources with Great Britain. Although certainly an asset, the exploitation renders the Norwegian economy dangerously dependent on the world market price of oil. Before oil prices suddenly plummeted in 1986, revenues from the "offshore" sector (that is, oil and natural gas production) constituted more than 20 percent of all government income. The sharp reduction in these revenues forced adjustments in the state budget and the introduction of an austerity program that could affect social services. In addition, inflation and high

(VG-FOTO/Tor Lindseth)

Gro Harlem Brundtland was first elected prime minister in 1981. She was returned to that post in 1986, in 1990, and again in 1993. She resigned in 1996. A medical doctor and master of public health, Dr. Brundtland became director-general of the World Health Organization (WHO) in 1998.

First unification of Norway **approximately** A.D. 885	Height of the Norwegian Empire: first attempts at the codification of national law **approximately** 1275	The Black Death kills half the population 1350	Union with Denmark 1397	End of Danish rule; Norwegian Constitution; union with Sweden 1814	Norwegian independence 1905	German occupation 1940–1945	Norway becomes a charter member of NATO 1949	Oil is discovered in the North Sea 1968	Gro Harlem Brundtland is elected as the first female prime minister 1981

1990s

Brundtland resigns in October 1996 and is replaced by Jagland, who is succeeded by Kvell Magne Bondevik	Norway hosts the 1994 Winter Olympic Games	Norwegian voters reject the Maastricht Treaty and opt to stay out of the European Union

wages are serious threats to the competitiveness of traditional Norwegian industries, such as shipbuilding and textiles.

The Norwegian government is heavily involved in the economy, since it owns corporations, extends subsidies to industry and agriculture, and regulates private firms. But the economy is in no sense socialist, and most Norwegian industry and commerce are privately owned and subject to market forces.

INTERNATIONAL RELATIONS

Although its landmass is considerable (Norway is larger than Italy), the country has a relatively small population, certainly as compared to its immediate neighbors. That condition causes its foreign policy to be somewhat subdued; apart from maintaining Norwegian sovereignty, it confines itself mainly to abstract targets such as promoting peace and reducing tensions. Norwegians are strong supporters of the principles embedded in the United Nations Charter. (The first secretary general of that organization, Trygve Lie, was a Norwegian.) Norway spends a higher percentage of its gross domestic product on aid to poor countries than any other state in the world.

In 1993, promoting peace and reducing tensions materialized in an exceptionally important initiative. Secret meetings were convened in a farmhouse near Oslo to which delegates of Israel and the Palestine Liberation Organization had been invited. There, outside the glare of the media, they met to work out a declaration of principles in September 1993—a document that was to lead to a peace agreement between the two parties, which had never ceased hostilities since the birth of the State of Israel in 1948.

To assure the Russians that no attack will come from Norwegian territory, Norway has allowed no foreign troops and no nuclear weapons to be based within its

borders, and no military training exercises are held close to the Russian border.

Military service is universal and compulsory. In peacetime, one may be drafted from ages 19 to 44. The training period in the Norwegian Army, Coastal Artillery, and Anti-Air Artillery is 12 months, and in the Air Force 15 months, with the possibility of refresher training afterward.

In the early 1970s, Norway and Denmark were scheduled to be admitted to the European Union (then called the European Economic Community). However, a public referendum held in Norway in 1972 made clear that a majority of Norwegians did not want admission to the organization. Denmark, with which Norway had very intricate economic relations, did become a member on January 1, 1973. Norway has been a member of the European Free Trade Association. In 1990, however, the government announced that it would prefer to join the EU. This is hardly surprising, since generally the institution of the European Economic Area is viewed as a preliminary to the complete dismantling of EFTA. Yet, as discussed earlier, there is still substantial division concerning whether or not to join the European Union. Many observers within Norway and abroad note that this reluctance is costly to Norway in terms of its international influence.

A remarkable initiative was taken by Prime Minister Brundtland in 1990. She intended to levy a tax on Norway's offshore oilfields. The money would be used to assist less wealthy countries in fighting global warming. In 1987, Brundtland had assisted in putting together the UN Report on the Environment. She firmly believed that economic development and environmental protection should be linked, her argument being that the rehabilitation of the European environment could be a test case of whether "we are capable of dealing with our common responsibilities." Norway is one of Europe's largest producers

of oil and gas, both hydrocarbon fuels that, when burned, produce carbon dioxide, a "greenhouse" gas that some people believe will cause a calamitous rise in global temperatures.

Other important foreign-policy issues of concern to Brundtland and her successors include expansion of Nordic cooperation, control of the Barents Sea around Svalbard, and protection of the North Sea petroleum installations. Somewhat uncharacteristically, in 1993, Brundtland announced that Norway would resume commercial catching of Minke whales. This decision provoked heated criticism from environmentalists around the world, followed by threats to boycott Norwegian exports. But so far, Norway has been unmoved.

THE FUTURE

There is fear that Norway's social harmony might dissipate, in that its people's consensus about values and goals could disintegrate. Norwegians are no longer used to suffering; a few serious mistakes by political or economic leaders could have devastating effects. In many respects, however, Norway can count on natural advantages. The country has numerous resources, and its people have accumulated considerable expertise in using them. There is a national tradition of honest and effective political leadership, of humanitarian solidarity, and of acceptance of the need for strong efforts. A high level of education is bound to help the Norwegians to deal with the problems that may come their way.

DEVELOPMENT

The drastic drop in energy prices in the 1980s cut revenues from North Sea oil production, decreasing revenues earmarked for maintaining the welfare state. Still, Norway has profited enormously from this resource. High labor costs have made Norway's traditional industries less competitive in world markets.

FREEDOM

Norway is a parliamentary democracy. Civil liberties are guaranteed in the Constitution, and the press enjoys considerable freedom.

HEALTH/WELFARE

Norway's welfare state is a costly, but comprehensive, cradle-to-grave system. The country has one of the highest life expectancy rates in the world as well as a high per capita income.

ACHIEVEMENTS

Norway has more than 300 art galleries, most of which are supported by public funds. A cultural fund guarantees the purchase of at least 1,000 copies of every work of Norwegian literature for circulation in the public library system. Nearly 1% of Norway's GDP goes toward helping developing countries, and Norway attempts to further democracy and human rights throughout the world.

Portugal (Portuguese Republic)

GEOGRAPHY
Area in Square Miles (Kilometers): 35,672 (92,391) (slightly smaller than Indiana)
Capital (Population): Lisbon (2,048,000)
Environmental Concerns: soil erosion; air pollution from industrial and vehicle emissions; water pollution
Geographical Features: mountainous north of the Tagus, rolling plains in south
Climate: maritime temperate; cool and rainy in north; warmer and drier in south

PEOPLE

Population
Total: 9,931,000
Annual Growth Rate: –0.01%
Rural/Urban Population Ratio: 64/36
Major Language: Portuguese
Ethnic Makeup: homogeneous Mediterranean stock with a small black African minority
Religions: 97% Roman Catholic; 1% Protestant; 2% others

Health
Life Expectancy at Birth: 72 years (male); 79 years (female)
Infant Mortality Rate (Ratio): 7.0/1,000
Average Caloric Intake: 128% of FAO minimum
Physicians Available (Ratio): 1/343

Education
Adult Literacy Rate: 85%
Compulsory (Ages): 6–15; free

COMMUNICATION
Telephones: 1 per 2.8 people
Daily Newspaper Circulation: 41 per 1,000 people
Televisions: 1 per 3.1 people

TRANSPORTATION
Highways in Miles (Kilometers): 41,239 (68,732)
Railroads in Miles (Kilometers): 1,914 (3,068)
Usable Airfields: 67
Motor Vehicles in Use: 3,480,000

GOVERNMENT
Type: parliamentary democracy
Independence Date: 1140; republic proclaimed October 5, 1910
Head of State/Government: President Jorge Sampaio; Prime Minister Antonio Manuel de Oliviera Guterres

Political Parties: Social Democratic Party; Portuguese Socialist Party; Portuguese Communist Party; Popular Party; National Solidarity Party; Center Democratic Party; United Democratic Coalition
Suffrage: universal at 18

MILITARY
Military Expenditures (% of GDP): 1.9%
Current Disputes: sovereignty over Timor Timur disputed with Indonesia

ECONOMY
Currency ($ U.S. Equivalent): 183 escudos = $1
Per Capita Income/GDP: $12,450/$122.1 billion
GDP Growth Rate: 2.5%
Inflation Rate: 3.4%
Unemployment Rate: 7.0%.
Labor Force: 4,530,000
Natural Resources: fish; forests; cork; tungsten; iron ore; uranium ore; marble
Agriculture: grains; potatoes; olives; grapes; other fruits
Industry: textiles; footwear; wood pulp; paper; cork; metalworking; oil refining; chemicals; fish canning; wine
Exports: $25.8 billion (primary partners EU countries and other developed countries)
Imports: $34.2 billion (primary partners EU countries and less developed countries)

PORTUGAL: WHERE CULTURES MEET

Modern Portuguese culture is a patchwork reflecting the influences of many different peoples, regions, and historical eras. Prehistoric cave painters left their decorations in Escural. The Romans left their mark in the township of Conimbriga and in the temple of Diana in Évora. Such southern towns as Olhão and Tavira exhibit the Moorish influence in their architecture. The Flemish, French, and Italian cultures have also enriched Portugal, and the voyages of the Portuguese discoverers opened the country to Asian influences. The opulence of the Baroque period owed much to the gold and diamonds of colonial Brazil. To visit Portugal is to travel backward in time and around the world within a single country.

Stretched along the westernmost part of the Iberian Peninsula, Portugal has played an important part in world history as well as in European history. Unlike Spain, the country that it borders on two sides, Portugal today has a homogeneous population—or, at least, no ethnic or linguistic minorities of any consequence. In the mid-1970s, when the Portuguese colonies in Africa attained independence, a large number of Portuguese whose forefathers had settled in Angola, Mozambique, and Guinea-Bissau in the early part of the century repatriated to Portugal. Surprisingly, however, these 700,000 "returnees" caused only temporary dislocations in a Portuguese society of barely 9 million. Among these *retornados* were many persons of mixed blood and about 100,000 blacks. A fairly large proportion of the returnees left for Brazil, a former Portuguese colony of great consequence.

HISTORY

The Iberian Peninsula was part of the Roman Empire for centuries, and the Roman presence left an indelible mark on the Portuguese culture and language. After the fall of the West Roman Empire in the fifth century A.D., Portugal was left to itself for a time (although it was, as were other parts of the Roman Empire, subject to interference on the part of the Visigoths). Little is known about this period; in the eighth century, however, Muslim invaders entered from the south. Coming from North Africa, they crossed the narrow body of water that came to be called the Strait of Gibraltar and brought Spain and Portugal under Muslim rule. Their occupation of the entire Iberian Peninsula lasted many centuries; the *Reconquista* ("Reconquest"), or reclamation, of the western (Portuguese) region proved to be a particularly arduous and intermittent process.

When the Reconquest of Portugal was finally completed, shortly before the fifteenth century, the country appeared to have assumed an identity of its own, an identity that differed markedly from that of its larger neighbor, Spain. It was only natural for the two countries to become rivals, since both excelled in seafaring and trade, exploits that almost inevitably led to commercial expansionism and a global presence. But whereas Portugal ventured south, Spain went west (severely underestimating the size of the globe!). The Portuguese, at least initially, viewed moving into Africa as a logical extension of the Reconquest: The Muslims had been driven back and expelled and now were to be fought on their own soil. It should be remembered that the Caliphate, expanding from the Arabian peninsula, had conquered the northern belt of Africa. Christianity, freed from its siege in Southern Europe, was to be carried into Africa.

Thus, at the end of the fifteenth century, Portugal became the first nation since the Roman Empire to "discover" and explore the African continent. Skilled Portuguese navigators sought to reduce the risk in seafaring by keeping the coastline in view; unlike the Spanish and, later, the English, they did not venture onto the open sea. When the elements conspired against them, they hurried toward some shelter along the coast, a bay or another inlet that would provide refuge. In this fashion they ventured farther and farther south, until, in 1488, Bartholomeu Diaz de Novaes rounded the Cape of Good Hope, eventually reaching the East African coast and the Indian Ocean.

This remarkable feat was a milestone soon to be overshadowed in importance by the news that Christopher Columbus, an Italian sailing for Spain, had (he assumed) found the way to the Indies by crossing the Atlantic in a westward direction. The serious rivalry that ensued between Europe's two top seafaring nations was somewhat reduced by the Treaty of Tordesillas (1494), which divided the world into Spanish and Portuguese areas of expansionism. (This treaty, sponsored by the pope, was not recognized by any nation other than Spain and Portugal.)

In 1580, however, the Portuguese throne was left without a homegrown successor, and Spain's King Philip II, whose wife was related to the Portuguese dynasty, "inherited" Portugal. The merger, which caused Portugal to be dominated by Spain, was to last some 6 decades.

Empire

Only in 1640 did Portugal regain its independence, under the leadership of the House of Braganca. However, the memories of the Spanish domination rendered Portugal, the smaller and less populous of the two nations, perpetually apprehensive of its neighbor's overtures. As a result, the country developed close commercial and political ties with England, which by that time had replaced Spain as an imperial rival.

The enormous empire that the Portuguese built and maintained for nearly half a millennium resulted from two different impulses. The first wave of expansionism was based on the spices that the almost legendary islands in the East produced—as well as on the gold that Brazil, far to the west of Portugal, was assumed to have. Some of these typically seventeenth-century operations had been either relinquished by Portugal or taken over by rival empires. The Dutch, for example, had done a great deal to destroy or at least reduce the Portuguese presence in the East Indies. That first wave included the conquest of Goa on the Indian subcontinent and of half of Timor, where Portuguese rule was maintained until 1975.

The second wave of Portuguese expansionism took place in the era of modern imperialism, a late-nineteenth-century phenomenon. Imperial powers, suddenly realizing that the world was finite and that this would be their last chance to enlarge their territories, divided all that was left. Modern imperialism initiated the scramble for Africa, since little had been done to that continent in terms of commercial colonialism. Traditions that dated back to early discoveries and explorations may well have revived Portuguese interests in Africa. It is surprising that small Portugal, a country by then much in decline, participated in this scramble on such a large scale. The three colonies in Africa that it managed to claim had a total area about 22 times the size of Portugal itself. To the west, Brazil, to which ancient Portuguese claims were reaffirmed, added a territory about 92 times as large as the mother country!

Brazil also provided a haven of refuge to the king of Portugal when Napoleon Bonaparte's armies invaded the Iberian Peninsula in 1808. During the occupation of Portugal, Brazil was the official seat of government. Upon its return to Portugal, the monarchy introduced various liberal innovations, which, however, did little to prevent political instability. The general restlessness increased steadily throughout the nineteenth century and finally came to a head in 1910, when a military revolt ousted King Manuel II. The Portuguese monarch managed to escape to Gibraltar. From there he went to England, where he died in exile many years later.

Political Disorder

Portugal's first experiments with a republican form of government were equally dismal. The parliamentary system that was adopted soon yielded the same legislative supremacy that supposedly democratic polities elsewhere in Western Europe experienced at different points in time. The parties not in power would team up against the government coalition, causing its downfall, and then would establish a new coalition government, which in turn would be subject to attacks.

During the endless succession of governments, the Portuguese economy steadily deteriorated. At one point, the military decided to appoint Antonio Oliveira de Salazar, a well-known economics professor, as minister of finance. He introduced a variety of austerity measures that enabled Portugal to get on its feet again. When elections were held a few years later, the post of prime minister went to Salazar, who embarked upon constitutional reform and a complete overhaul of the country's political institutions. The Constitution of 1933 outlined the *Estado Novo* ("New State"), a construction entirely based on Salazar's ultra-right-wing philosophy, which bore a remarkable resemblance to other Mediterranean varieties of fascism, such as those in Spain and Italy.

Salazar ruled with an iron hand for more than 3 decades. In 1968, he was felled by a stroke, and Marcello Caetano took over. Caetano seemed willing to introduce gradual changes into a system that had become ossified, but ultimately, every step forward was matched by a step backward. He thus proved unable, on the one hand, to maintain the structure that he had inherited and, on the other, to conceive meaningful reform. The sense of drift during these post-Salazar years provided the climate for the Revolution of 1974.

A major problem was Portuguese colonialism. Salazar's rigidity with respect to colonialism was what ultimately proved to be his regime's undoing. By the 1970s, all other colonial empires had been liquidated; yet Portugal's colonial empire was still intact, with the exception of the Portuguese possessions in India, which the Indians had retaken in 1961 after 14 years of fruitless negotiations.

As a result, during the 1960s, the United Nations largely concentrated its anticolonial rhetoric on Portugal. The Portuguese government, however, stubbornly insisted that there was no question of colonialism and that various amendments to the Constitution of 1933 clearly indicated that Portugal did not have "colonies" but only "overseas provinces." As could be expected, the subterfuge did not work, and the UN pressures continued. In fact, Portugal became an outcast in the family of nations. But its extremely rigid system of government failed to seal off the colonies, and finally the winds of change started to affect the peoples of Angola, Mozambique, and Guinea-Bissau. Rural rebellions proliferated, and urban uprisings were the order of the day. The Portuguese government, predictably, responded with force. Larger and larger troop contingents were sent to quell the insurrections.

The End at Last

These reactionary policies did not work either, and the situation in the colonies deteriorated rapidly. The African possessions, which had in the past been reasonably productive, became grave liabilities. In the early 1970s, Angola, Mozambique, and Guinea-Bissau constituted enormous drains on the metropolitan budget. This was particularly the case because the mere maintenance of the colonial system demanded prohibitive defense expenditures, which a small country lacking in resources could not possibly afford, as well as a rising toll

(Photo courtesy of Cornelia Warmenhoven)

Lisbon has a number of beautiful squares that echo their long history. The statue of Sedubal is located in the large, open area pictured above.

The Treaty of
Tordesillas
establishes the
demarcation
between
Portuguese
and Spanish
expansion
A.D. **1494**
●

Portugal comes
under the
Spanish Crown
1580
●

Portugal breaks
away from Spain;
the House of
Braganca
becomes
Portugal's ruling
monarchy
1640
●

Portugal moves
its seat of
government
to Brazil
1808
●

in lives. Also, Portugal, which had become an international pariah because of its stubborn colonialist attitudes, was denied developmental aid from UN agencies and other organizations. Military morale plummeted, and most Portuguese became convinced that even simple containment would be a hopeless task that could lead only to economic ruin.

In late 1973, a group of younger officers came together and established the Armed Forces Movement (MFA), initially intended as a pressure group. When conditions continued to worsen, some senior officers, including General Antonion de Spinola, joined the movement and, in April 1974, launched the coup that brought the Estado Novo down. De Spinola became interim president. Ultimately, the brutal jungle wars in Angola, Mozambique, and Guinea-Bissau determined the fate of the New State.

RETURN TO DEMOCRACY

The Estado Novo ended not with a bang but with a whimper. Considering that the die-hard regimes of Salazar and Caetano had been thoroughly entrenched for half a century, one might have expected a full-fledged revolution that would entail prolonged fighting. But there was no revolution, although many of the coup participants were inclined to view it as such. Some of the authorities of the *ancien regime* were put in protective custody; others were persuaded, if needed, to leave the country. A number went into exile once Brazil offered political asylum.

The army had come into power, for after the coup, the MFA could be seen as representative of the entire armed forces. However, it lacked ideological underpinnings, and at this point in time, political parties, which had been banned in Portugal for more than 50 years, resurfaced. Among them, the Portuguese Communist Party (PCP) was particularly active in competing for government power. Its initial success may well have been aided by the backlash that the PCP provided against the ultra-right positions and policies that had pervaded Portuguese politics for decades on end. But the possibility of prolonging the uneasy coalition between the military and the Communists receded quickly after a transitional phase.

Parliamentary elections, held in April 1975, must have given the Communists

the message that they were not viewed as the wave of the future: Non-Communist parties received more than 80 percent of the vote. Also, during the summer that followed, massive anti-Communist demonstrations were the order of the day, in cities as well as in rural areas. In August, another blow was delivered to the PCP, when non-Communist elements within the MFA forced the resignation of the pro-Communist prime minister, Colonel Vasco Goncalves.

In November 1975, Communist Party leaders, realizing that their power and popularity were slipping, staged a coup in a desperate attempt to reverse the tide. The coup was foiled, and its failure spelled the end of meaningful competition on the part of the PCP. It was then that massive purges were initiated within the armed forces. The removal of the Communists must have provided relief to the member states of what is today known as the European Union (then named the European Economic Community) and other Portugal-watchers, such as the United States. Still, the possibility that Portugal would experience a backlash to the right-wing dictatorship and turn Communist was very real for more than a year.

After 1975, Portuguese politics started to be characterized by competition among parties that were in varying degrees to the left of center but not Communist. The Socialist Party (PS) remained very important, although it failed to secure outright majorities in elections. Its main rival, the combination of the Popular Democratic and Social Democratic Parties (PPD/PSD) progressively increased its support. But, if the late 1970s were still marked by a measure of unpredictability, the decade of the 1980s revealed that the country had become fully committed to democratic principles, and that it had, as *The Economist* phrased it, "found its political center of gravity." The early 1980s also witnessed the preparation for the Treaty of Accession—that is, Portugal's admission to the European Union, which would never have been granted had any doubt lingered regarding Portuguese democracy. Portugal's membership in that important organization became effective on January 1, 1986.

By that time, a relatively young man named Anibal Cavaco Silva had become Portugal's man of the hour. His confi-

dence, enthusiasm, and powers of persuasion aided him in building up the Social Democrats, at the expense of the orthodox Socialists and in gaining the prime ministership.

THE ECONOMY

In the Portuguese economy, too, the legacy inherited from the Estado Novo was dismal. The authoritarian regime created by Salazar did not seek rapid modernization and industrialization for Portugal; indeed, it aimed at keeping Portugal self-sufficient, quiescent, and immune to pressures from outside. The results were mixed. On the one hand, Portugal remained a rural and basically underdeveloped country. On the other, since it could rely on its African colonies (particularly Angola) for raw materials and oil, it was not subject to the vagaries of the international economy. At the same time, Portugal expanded its trade relations with other European countries during the 1950s and 1960s, becoming a charter member of the European Free Trade Association and signing a preferential trade agreement with the European Union in 1972.

As soon as the repressive and debilitating structure of the Estado Novo had been removed, the new Portuguese leadership realized how far behind the government had gotten in economic matters. When the dust that the coup brought in its wake had settled, plans were conceived to modernize the economy.

The first step taken by the post–Estado Novo government was a very unfortunate one. In the spring of 1975, Marxist revolutionaries, who were still in de facto control, embarked upon a massive nationalization scheme. More than half of all fixed investments, or some 800 firms, were nationalized; their total value was estimated at $13.6 billion. In order to prevent undoing this measure, the nationalization was qualified in the new Constitution as an "irreversible conquest of the Revolution."

Next, in 1977 and again in 1978, contacts were made with several UN specialized agencies. The International Monetary Fund was willing to come to Portugal's rescue, but only on the condition that its government adopt an austerity program. A global recession had started to make itself felt, and the economic expansion in Portugal was therefore moderate. Nevertheless, the austerity program generally worked well.

| Portugal becomes a constitutional monarchy **1882** | King Manuel II is ousted; Portugal becomes a republic **1910** | Antonio Salazar becomes prime minister and establishes the Estado Novo **1932** | A new Constitution is adopted **1933** | Salazar, incapacitated, is succeeded by Marcello Caetano **1968** | The "Revolution of the Carnations" demolishes the Estado Novo; political parties resurface **1974** | Portugal becomes a member of the European Union **1986** | Portugal and China reach agreement over Macao's future **1987** |

1990s

| Portugal moves toward a free-market economy | The budget aims to reduce the deficit | The government explores ways to diversify and strengthen the economy |

In the early 1980s, the momentous decision was made to include Portugal in the European Union, although both the EU and Portugal realized that a number of stumbling blocks presented themselves. In the first place, Portugal requested free circulation of labor, in accordance with the terms in the Treaty of Rome. This would mean that Portuguese workers could settle and work wherever they wished within the EU. But the poor economic conditions in the Salazar period had caused a great many Portuguese workers to emigrate, not only to the African colonies but also to more economically advanced countries in Western Europe. In fact, 1 million to 2 million Portuguese laborers were working elsewhere in Europe, and the countries concerned did not want this number to increase. Another stumbling block toward accession was the huge discrepancy between Portugal's economy and the economies of the EU member states. The Portuguese economy in fact resembled that of a developing nation.

Specific problems that needed to be worked out concerned Portugal's inefficient farming methods and its antiquated fishing fleet. Little mechanization had been introduced on either front; two thirds of the fishing vessels even lacked engines. Generally, Portugal absorbed all the new measures very well. Indeed, when it came to becoming an EU member, a measure of impatience could be noted.

On June 1, 1989, the Portuguese Parliament approved a package of reforms that did away with the socialist economy and endeavored to reprivatize a large number of the firms that had been nationalized in 1975. This proved a giant step toward a free-market economy. However, a great deal of obstruction arose on the part of the former owners, who wished to be com-pensated. Compensation claims had been ignored at the time of the nationalization; small amounts had been paid many years later. It was now, according to the original owners, that the day of reckoning had come, especially since in most cases the firms had not been returned to them.

Among Portugal's chief industries are textiles, footwear, wine, chemicals, fish canning, paper, and cork (Portugal is one of the world's leading cork producers); its chief crops include grains, potatoes, rice, olives, grapes, and other fruits. The country also produces such minerals as tungsten, uranium, and iron. Its forests constitute a valuable resource as well. Although these resources appear very promising, the lack of capital may well be the greatest single obstacle to development in Portugal.

The Portuguese economy has made some strides since the turbulent days of the Revolution in the mid-1970s. This progress became more pronounced after the country became a member of the European Union. However, its recent economic history bristles with instances of social backslides. On August 4, 1993, for example, the minimum legal age of employment was moved back to 14. Although there was strong protest on the part of labor unions, which claimed that the measure violated the recommendations of the International Labour Organization, and public response in general was hostile, the Portuguese government did not reverse its decision.

COHABITATION IN PORTUGAL

France is not unique as far as *cohabitation* (a sharing of power between a president and a prime minister of different parties) is concerned: Portugal, like several other countries, has developed its own brand. While cohabitation is often considered highly dysfunctional in France, in Portu-gal, neither the general public nor the two main actors appear to have any objection to the contingency of a deadlock in decision making. The current administration, however, does not have to worry in any case. Prime Minister Antonio Manuel de Oliviera Guterres, in office since October 1995, is of the Socialist Party, as is Jorge Sampaio, who won the presidency in March 1996.

DEVELOPMENT

In June 1989, the Portuguese Parliament approved reforms that did away with a socialist economy. Since then, Portugal's economic development has been uneven.

FREEDOM

Since the harsh Salazar days, Portugal has made enormous progress in matters of human rights. While there is still a degree of child labor and one may be imprisoned for "insulting civil or military bodies," Portugal has nonetheless adapted itself in record time to democratic standards.

HEALTH/WELFARE

Health conditions are mixed in Portugal. Life expectancy is reasonable, but infant mortality rates are among the highest in Europe. Although Portugal has had Socialist governments since 1974, no major health-assistance scheme has been developed. Some 16% of Portuguese over 15 years of age are illiterate.

ACHIEVEMENTS

The country is well known for its *fados*— melancholic songs, usually about love. On several occasions, Portuguese *fado* singers have won prizes at European song festivals.

San Marino (Republic of San Marino)

GEOGRAPHY

Area in Square Miles (Kilometers): 24 (60) (about one third the size of Washington, D.C.)

Capital (Population): San Marino (4,600)

Geographical Features: rugged mountains

Climate: Mediterranean

PEOPLE

Population

Total: 24,900

Annual Growth Rate: 0.76%

Rural/Urban Population Ratio: 5/95

Major Language: Italian

Ethnic Makeup: 88% Sanmarinese; 12% Italian (however, ethnic differences are virtually nonexistent)

Religion: nearly 100% Roman Catholic

Health

Life Expectancy at Birth: 77 years (male); 85 years (female)

Infant Mortality Rate (Ratio): 5.5/1,000

Physicians Available (Ratio): 1/38

Education

Adult Literacy Rate: 96%

Compulsory (Ages): 6–14

COMMUNICATION

Telephones: 1 per 1.6 people

TRANSPORTATION

Highways in Miles (Kilometers): 132 (220)

Railroads in Miles (Kilometers): none

Usable Airfields: none

GOVERNMENT

Type: independent republic

Independence Date: 1600 (A.D. 301 by tradition)

Head of State/Government: co-regents are appointed every 6 months

Political Parties: Christian Democratic Party; Democratic Progressive Party; San Marino Socialist Party; Democratic Movement; Popular Alliance; Communist Refoundation

Suffrage: universal at 18

MILITARY

Military Expenditures (% of GDP): 1.0%

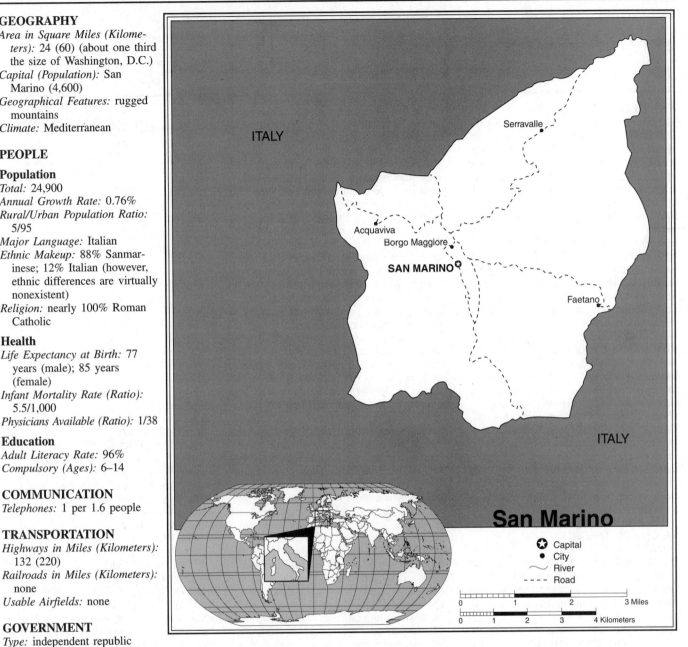

Current Disputes: none

ECONOMY*

Currency ($ U.S. Equivalent): 1,624.5 Italian lire = $1

Per Capita Income/GDP: $16,900/$408 million

GDP Growth Rate: 4.8%

Inflation Rate: 5.3%

Unemployment Rate: 3.6%

Labor Force: 15,600

Natural Resources: building stones

Agriculture: wheat and other grains; grapes and other fruits; maize; olives; vegetables; animal foodstuffs; cheese; livestock

Industry: tourism; textiles; banking; cement; ceramics; wine

Note: Trade data are included in statistics for Italy.

 http://inthenet.sm/rsm/intro.htm

| St. Marinus takes refuge on Monte Titano to escape religious persecution **A.D. 301** | A Constitution vests legislative power in a Grand Council **1600** | Italy guarantees San Marino's independence **1862** | Customs union with Italy **1939** | San Marino is ruled by a Communist-led coalition **1945–1957** | The Communist-dominated Government of Democratic Collaboration **1978–1986** | San Marino condemns U.S. policy toward Latin America **late 1980s** |

1990s

The admission of San Marino to the United Nations makes 1992 a year of historic importance for the Sammarinese

The European Union refuses to consider San Marino a full, independent member

San Marino continues to diversify its economy

THE OLDEST REPUBLIC

The world's oldest republic calls itself the Republic of San Marino. It is the sole survivor of a host of independent Italian city-states that existed prior to the unification of Italy in the early 1860s. Located on the slopes of Monte Titano in east-central Italy, the community of San Marino was first established by St. Marinus and a small contingent of fellow Christians seeking to escape religious persecution. This took place early in the fourth century A.D., at a time when Roman emperors ordered Christians to be thrown to the lions to entertain the public. In 1600, the self-governing community drafted a republican Constitution, that vested legislative power in a Grand Council composed of 60 men from San Marino's leading families. (Between the world wars, San Marino's Constitution was revised in order to render it more democratic.) The Sammarinese signed a treaty of friendship and cooperation with the new Italian state in 1862. Despite several revisions, this treaty still governs diplomatic relations between the two republics. In 1939, San Marino entered into a customs union with Italy and agreed to adopt the Italian currency as its own, in exchange for an annual subsidy from the Italian government.

SAN MARINO SINCE WORLD WAR II

During World War II, San Marino was largely left alone by Benito Mussolini's Fascist Italy, in spite of the fact that partisans used it as a hiding place. Since the end of the war, San Marino has had a series of coalition governments. Its multiple political parties closely correspond to their counterparts in the Italian political system. In 1945, the largest parties of the left—the Communists and the Socialists—joined forces to form a government that was to survive for more than a decade. They were defeated in 1957 by the Popular Alliance, a coalition of Christian Democrats, Social Democrats, and Republicans. The Popular Alliance remained in power until 1973, when the major coalition partners—the Christian Democrats and the Social Democrats—parted company over economic policy. As the political pendulum began to swing back to the left, the Socialists and the Christian Democrats formed a coalition government. However, divisions over economic policy once again brought down the government in 1977.

After months of unsuccessful attempts by the various parties to reconstruct a workable coalition, the Communists took the initiative in 1978 to form a "Government of Democratic Collaboration" with the Socialist and Socialist Unity Parties. As a result, San Marino became the only country in Western Europe with a Communist-dominated government. In 1982, the Social Democrats joined the all-left coalition. However, a year later, they rejoined the Christian Democrats in opposition, after charging their coalition partners with financial mismanagement. The coalition that the Communists had put together in 1978 was dissolved in 1986.

San Marino's people rely primarily on agriculture, light manufacturing, and tourism for their livelihood. The main exports include grains, wine, and olive oil as well as textiles, ceramics, and various handmade goods. The government generates more than 10 percent of its annual revenues from the sale of postage stamps, most of which are sold to foreign collectors.

Unemployment is low in this mountain republic, due to the constant emigration of its citizens, most of them to neighboring Italy. Since San Marino has an active full-employment policy, its government is committed to finding work for all those unemployed or to providing generous unemployment benefits. With revenues generated from the sale of postage stamps, sales and property taxes, and, since 1984, income taxes, as well as an annual subsidy from Italy, the Sammarinese have developed and sustained a comprehensive welfare state that is endorsed by both the right and the left.

San Marino's political independence, military security, and economic survival are guaranteed by a series of treaties with Italy; the tiny republic has no army of its own. Yet, despite its dependence on this somewhat imposing guardian, San Marino has sought to develop its own voice in international affairs. Without mentioning San Marino by name, former United Nations secretary-general Boutros Boutros-Ghali expressed sympathy with the independence of small countries of the world.

DEVELOPMENT

Despite its lack of natural resources, San Marino has developed a reasonably well-diversified economy based on light manufacturing, tourism, and agriculture. Italy is its major trading partner.

FREEDOM

San Marino, like its guardian neighbor Italy, rates very high in political rights and civil liberties. In recent years, San Marino has become more vociferous in international affairs.

HEALTH/WELFARE

The Sammarinese enjoy the benefits of a comprehensive welfare system and the government's active full-employment policy.

ACHIEVEMENTS

Stamps provide more than 10% of San Marino's annual revenues. San Marino's stamps rate very high in philatelic circles.

Spain (Kingdom of Spain)

GEOGRAPHY

Area in Square Miles (Kilometers): 195,988 (504,750) (about twice the size of Oregon)

Capital (Population): Madrid (4,072,000)

Environmental Concerns: pollution of the Mediterranean Sea; water quality and quantity; air pollution; deforestation; desertification

Geographical Features: large, flat to dissected plateau surrounded by rugged hills; Pyrenees in the north

Climate: temperate; more moderate along the coast

PEOPLE

Population

Total: 39,134,000

Annual Growth Rate: 0.08%

Rural/Urban Population Ratio: 23/77

Major Languages: Castilian Spanish; Catalán; Galician; Basque

Ethnic Makeup: Mediterranean and Nordic composite; Romani (Gypsies)

Religions: 99% Roman Catholic; 1% others

Health

Life Expectancy at Birth: 74 years (male); 82 years (female)

Infant Mortality Rate (Ratio): 6.5/1,000

Average Caloric Intake: 136% of FAO minimum

Physicians Available (Ratio): 1/246

Education

Adult Literacy Rate: 96%

Compulsory (Ages): 6–16; free

COMMUNICATION

Telephones: 1 per 2.5 people

Daily Newspaper Circulation: 104 per 1,000 people

Televisions: 1 per 2.6 people

TRANSPORTATION

Highways in Miles (Kilometers): 205,918 (343,197)

Railroads in Miles (Kilometers): 8,986 (14,400)

Usable Airfields: 96

Motor Vehicles in Use: 17,300,000

GOVERNMENT

Type: parliamentary monarchy

Independence Date: 1492 (expulsion of the Moors and unification)

Head of State/Government: King Juan Carlos I; President José Maria Aznar

Political Parties: People's (Popular) Party; Spanish Socialist Workers Party; Spanish Communist Party; United Left; others and regional parties

Suffrage: universal at 18

MILITARY

Military Expenditures (% of GDP): 1.4%

Current Disputes: dispute with Britain over Gibraltar; territorial disputes with Morocco over places of sovereignty

ECONOMY

Currency ($ U.S. Equivalent): 141.1 pesetas = $1

Per Capita Income/GDP: $16,400/$642.4 billion

GDP Growth Rate: 3.3%

Inflation Rate: 2.1%

Unemployment Rate: 22%

Labor Force: 16,200,000

Natural Resources: coal; lignite; iron ore; uranium; mercury; pyrites; fluorspar; gypsum; zinc; lead; tungsten; copper; kaolin; hydroelectric power; forests (cork)

Agriculture: grains; citrus fruits; vegetables; fish

Industry: textiles and apparel; footwear; food and beverages; metals and metal manufactures; chemicals; shipbuilding; automobiles; machine tools; tourism

Exports: $94.5 billion (primary partners EU countries, United States)

Imports: $118.3 billion (primary partners EU countries, United States)

Spain

★ Capital
● City
∿ River

0 50 100 150 200 250 Miles
0 50 100 150 200 250 300 Kilometers
Elevation in feet.

THE KINGDOM OF SPAIN

From a European perspective, Spain is a large country, comprising as it does 85 percent of the Iberian Peninsula, the Balearic Islands in the Mediterranean, the Canary Islands in the Atlantic Ocean, the enclave of Llivia in the Pyrenees, the African towns of Ceuta and Melilla, and several islands off the coast of Morocco. In terms of surface area, it is one of the largest countries on the European continent.

HISTORY

Spain is also one of the oldest nation-states in Europe. In its earliest history, successive waves of different peoples spread over the Iberian Peninsula, occasionally merging and mixing with previous settlers, but more often driving them into less habitable places. Early records mention the Iberians, whose presence (particularly in the eastern parts of the peninsula) was noted by colonizing Greeks and the omnipresent Romans. Celts, Phoenicians and their "subsidiaries," Carthagenians, Romans, Visigoths, and finally Arabs—all occupied Spanish territory at one time or another.

Spanish history became less blurred, or at least better recorded, when the West Roman Empire collapsed in the fifth century A.D. and the Visigoths began to drift into the peninsula, not massively but piecemeal over the course of a century.

In the eighth century, Muslims arrived from the increasingly Islamic lands of North Africa, crossing what has since come to be called the Strait of Gibraltar. Their forceful presence left an indelible mark on Spain. Even the derogatory name that they were given by the Spanish—Moors—entered the international vocabulary, as Shakespeare's "Moor of Venice," "Moorish architectural styles," and the "Moros," a religious minority in the Philippines, will attest. The Muslims ruled Spain for many centuries. The hostility between Muslim and Christian peoples (as well as Jews for that matter) during a large part of that period has been consistently overstated. Modern historians tend to consider the Muslim presence ultimately a civilizing and beneficial influence on the development of the Iberian Peninsula.

However, the arrival and departure of the invaders, the periods of conquest and reconquest respectively, were naturally marked by hostility and armed conflict. The *Reconquista* ("Reconquest") took an extraordinarily long time; it was finally completed when Granada fell in 1492—coincidentally, the same year in which Christopher Columbus, funded by Spain, sailed to what he believed to be the Indies. Spain, by then a monarchy, thus emerged

as a seafaring and early imperial nation as soon as Muslim rule came to an end. It was then that conquests were made, colonies founded; the conquistadores ("conquerors"), with a sword in one hand and the Bible in the other, embarked upon what in those days was viewed as a holy mission. Colonialism, particularly the Spanish and Portuguese variants, had strong missionary streaks.

Spanish Imperialism

Initially, Spain, like Portugal, appeared primarily interested in Southeast Asia, but its influence in those parts rapidly declined and ultimately remained confined to the Philippines. It is possible that Spain found the overheads too high, the voyages too time-consuming and costly. Such a conclusion is also warranted by the fact that the Philippines were administered not from Spain but from Mexico. Spanish interests thereupon shifted to Latin America and the Caribbean. In due time, Spain became dominant in South America (with the notable exception of Brazil), in Central America, and on many Caribbean islands, as well as in parts of North America. Even after Spain declined in importance as a European power, a process introduced by the defeat of the Spanish Armada in 1588 and highlighted by the Peace of Westphalia in 1648, it managed to retain a formidable imperial presence in the lands across the Atlantic.

However, the nineteenth century proved disastrous to the Spanish Empire: The Na-

poleonic Wars (a primarily European series of events) generated the beginnings of the decolonization process. If most of Latin America had been anxious to follow the example of independence set by the United States, the turmoil in Europe afforded the opportunity.

While Spain's holdings in Central and South America attained independence in the first half of the nineteenth century, armed conflict with the United States took care of numerous colonies elsewhere. A war of 3 months' duration triggered by the sinking of the *Maine* forced Spain, the loser, to cede the Philippines, Guam, Cuba, and Puerto Rico to the United States. On the other hand, Spain did gain a number of colonies in the latter part of the nineteenth century, the era of modern imperialism. Generally, however, it failed to acquire possessions of great value in the scramble for Africa. Also, when the time had come to liquidate its empire, Spain turned out to be considerably less reluctant than Portugal to grant its colonies independence. Indeed, in the case of the Spanish Sahara (a stretch of desert), Madrid decided simply to abandon the territory without further formality, its argument being that the nomadic peoples in the area did not qualify as a nationalist group to whom sovereignty might be transferred. However, since the Western Sahara is rich in phosphate, the Spanish withdrawal caused an armed conflict among various neighbors and claimants, such as Morocco, Mauritania, Algeria, and

(Photo courtesy Lisa Clyde)

Families display colorful, symbolic banners from the sides of buildings during a religious festival in Toledo.

a group of guerrilla fighters called themselves the Polisario. By the mid-1990s, it was evident that Morocco had prevailed, at least in the military struggle.

Gibraltar

Another anomaly is provided by Gibraltar, a spit of land that is little more than a rock at the tip of the Iberian Peninsula. It has been a British possession since the Treaty of Utrecht in 1713. This colonial leftover is a thorn in Spain's side. While Britain is not a Mediterranean country, it has always had an acute interest in the Mediterranean Sea (which in the past was also affirmed by its possession of Malta, Cyprus, and the Suez Canal). This special interest derived in large part from the much shorter voyage that the Mediterranean route afforded to the part of the empire generally called "East of Suez." And even now that the empire has been restructured into the Commonwealth, Great Britain is reluctant to cede Gibraltar to Spain.

In 1966, Spain pleaded with Britain to grant it "substantial sovereignty" of Gibraltar. When the plea fell on deaf ears, Spain instituted a partial blockade—that is, it cut Gibraltar off from its natural hinterland. The blockade was later lifted, but Anglo–Spanish relations remained very strained. At one point, the British proposed that a plebiscite decide the fate of Gibraltar. But to Spain's regret, the outcome of the plebiscite among the 30,000-odd residents of Gibraltar revealed a strong preference for the status quo, though the number of Spanish natives far exceeded the number who had come from Great Britain. The sensitive subject was again brought up when the British queen and her consort visited Spain in the late 1980s. In the early 1990s, Spain finally seemed resigned to reality, and the government decided to take away the Spanish guards who more or less surrounded Gibraltar. The fundamental dispute, however, still has not been resolved.

Ceuta and Melilla

If Spain views the Gibraltar situation clearly in terms of irredentism, it appears considerably less concerned about the continuance of colonialism when the shoe is on the other foot. Ceuta and Melilla are two towns in Morocco that had their origins in medieval times. They have been Spanish enclaves since 1580 and 1470, respectively. When France granted independence to Morocco, Spain might have surrendered these two tiny possessions, which had little strategic or economic value. But rather than granting them to Morocco, Spain chose to keep these towns under its rule, its main argument being

that the colonies had been in Spanish hands for so many centuries that they differed significantly from the Moroccan ambience. Spain has occasionally tightened its control, particularly when Moroccan nonresidents have attempted to settle in Ceuta and Melilla, which have a lower unemployment rate and a higher standard of living than Morocco.

Monarchy and Republicanism

Although Spain has strong monarchical traditions, it has not been without republican intervals. And remarkably, the transition from monarchy to republicanism was more often than not achieved without force or violence. Amadeo of Savoy ruled briefly in the third quarter of the nineteenth century and then decided to step down. Things were unsettled for a short period, but the military then determined that a monarchy was preferable to a republic and proclaimed Alfonso XII king of Spain.

His son and successor, Alfonso XIII, abdicated voluntarily, because in the municipal elections of 1931 the republican votes outnumbered those of monarchists. However, this time it took longer for the monarchy to be restored, if only because Alfonso XIII's abdication augured the prelude to the Spanish Civil War (1936–1939).

Franco

General Francisco Franco, upon becoming the head of state and the supreme commander of the armed forces in 1936, remained the undisputed central figure in the Civil War. The strict dictatorship that he created was Fascist in nature. Franco ruled with an iron hand for 40 years, during which time all political parties were banned except for his own, the Falange. Freedoms and democratic rights also fell by the wayside. Only during the last 5 years of his control did new trends manifest themselves.

Franco's approach toward the monarchy was somewhat ambivalent. He believed that, in general, Spanish monarchs had, as political symbols, helped to unify the nation. However, he certainly did not want to have a monarch as a top executive as long as *he* was head of state, since that would imply a competition for popular favor. His solution was simple: As long as he ruled, the institution of monarchy would continue to exist but would be, so to speak, on the back burner. Franco was well aware that his control would one day end, and although he wanted it to be followed by the reinstatement of the monarchy, he trusted that the Fascist state would survive, with all its authoritarian trappings intact. As to the question of who would be the future monarch, he made his choice

early. It would not be Alfonso XIII's son, who had offended him by his frequent criticism, but, rather, Alfonso XIII's grandson, Juan Carlos.

The old dictator died on November 20, 1975. Two days later, Spain had a monarch at its head: King Juan Carlos I.

A NEW ERA

Franco's death proved a watershed such as Spain had never known. Few people, least of all Franco himself, could have foreseen the profound and rapid changes that were to come. Juan Carlos had been born when the Civil War was about to end. He had been groomed in the dictator's shadow, which implied that his style had been authoritarian. Juan Carlos had been fed the daily diet of dictatorship; democracy was little more than an alien, theoretical concept to him.

Yet after Franco's death, King Juan Carlos wasted little time in rendering Spain a constitutional democracy, or, as the Spanish liked to call it, a "parliamentary democracy." Referenda were instituted as instruments of change; only a little more than a year after the dictator's demise, a referendum on political reform was held. Of course, being a constitutional monarch, Juan Carlos did not have a great deal of power, but he applied whatever influence he could to arrive at democratic structures. Demonstrating rare political skill and good judgment, he named a young reformist politician, Adolfo Suárez, to the premiership in 1976. Both men cherished similar ideals and took British democracy as a model.

Suárez was mainly responsible for the execution of what has been called the "Democratic Transition." Trade-union organizations, other pressure groups, political parties—in short, all the linkage mechanisms in a democracy—were allowed to come out of the woodwork. They had been banned and, more often than not, ruthlessly persecuted for nearly 4 decades. But now, even party leader Santiago Carrillo, who had been in exile for that period, was allowed to reorganize the Communist Party of Spain (PCE), which had been anathema in Franco's days. (This party and its leader, who subsequently designed the concept of Eurocommunism, were singularly unsuccessful in capturing public support.)

Basic liberties were recognized, and amnesty was granted for political offenses. The climax of these preparations for democracy was the parliamentary elections of June 15, 1977, the first elections held in Spain in 41 years. The *Cortés* (Parliament) was a necessary result of these elections. Shortly after its formal investiture, the Parliament started to work on a new constitution. After vigorous debate, it was approved in a referendum on December 6, 1978. Thus, only 3 years after Franco's death, a democratic Constitution became Spain's official guiding instrument. Its first article would make Franco turn in his grave; it reads:

Spain is hereby established as a social democratic State, subject to the rule of law, and advocating as higher values of its legal order, liberty, justice, equality and political pluralism. National sovereignty is vested in the Spanish people, from whom emanate the powers of the State. . . . The political form of the Spanish State is that of a Parliamentary Monarchy.

The Constitution proceeds to outline the Legislature (*Cortés Generales*) as consisting of two houses, a Congress of Deputies and a Senate. The government, headed by a prime minister and a deputy prime minister, is collectively accountable for its political management to the Congress of Deputies.

As in all parliamentary systems, the Congress of Deputies exercises control over the executive by its ability to withhold confidence from the government. In addition, it has the option of adopting a motion of censure, which has a similar effect. This lower house thus represents the Spanish people and exercises the legislative power of the state, approving budgets and supervising government actions in other respects as well. If the government is not made up of party leaders whose party enjoys a majority in the Congress of Deputies, coalitions will have to be established with other, preferably like-minded, parties.

The Senate is the house of territorial representation. Each province has four representatives. Autonomous communities also nominate one senator each, plus another for every 1 million inhabitants in their respective territories. Both senators and deputies have 4-year terms.

As compared to Franco's time, when only one party was allowed to operate, currently more than a dozen parties vie for seats in Parliament, including regional ones. Among them are extremely small splinter parties. Union organizations are considerably more limited in number, while pressure groups in general appear to be growing in numbers as well as in membership.

SOCIALIST RULE

Adolfo Suárez, having skillfully presided over the transition to democracy, stepped down in 1981. A brief interregnum by Leopoldo Calvo Sotelo followed, after which Felipe González Márquez was elected to the prime ministership. González led the Spanish Socialist Workers Party (PSOE), which in the parliamentary election of 1986 received a majority of seats in the Congress of Deputies. However, the late 1980s witnessed a drop in support for the Socialists. This soon turned out to be irreversible. At the general election in 1989, the PSOE lost its absolute majority, after which it declined further. In part this trend may be attributed to the fact that González deliberately freed the party from its doctrinaire positions. The prime minister was basically a technocrat and as such preferred the party to adopt some kind of technocratic neutrality, which did not sit well with the Socialists, still steeped in ideological causes. The real blow came in 1992 in Seville, the birthplace of the prime minister and a city that long had seemed the bedrock of socialism. Since the Expo '92 was held in that city, González granted it a great deal of extra money. How-

ever, the municipal elections, to everyone's surprise, turned the Socialist mayor out and voted a non-Socialist party leader in.

Nevertheless, the fact that 1992 happened to be Spain's big year may have slowed down the decline of the PSOE. The summer Olympic Games were held in Barcelona. Madrid was proclaimed the "Cultural Capital of Europe," and throughout Spain celebrations commemorated the 500th anniversary of Christopher Columbus's first voyage to the Americas.

Gradually Prime Minister González became more interested in the emerging Europe. He concentrated his attention on the European Union, particularly after Spain became an official member in 1986.

The domestic political initiatives pursued by the Socialist government were as a rule moderate in character. Legislation concerning abortion and divorce, as well as educational reform, was approved by the Parliament, but the government was careful not to risk too open a confrontation with the Roman Catholic Church. (Spanish legislation on abortion and divorce is among the most restrictive in Western Europe.) And in pursuing educational reform, the Socialist government did not question the right of private (primarily Catholic) schools to continue receiving state funds.

DEVOLUTION

The post-Franco government soon realized that political pluralism (as furthered by the Constitution) and ethnic diversity are different matters. Other referenda were conducted during González's tenure, such as the so-called autonomy referenda, which were to decide whether or not certain regions populated by ethnic minorities would be allowed to have some type of minor constitution. Spain's trend toward devolution—decentralization of power—appears to have muted minority-group dissatisfaction somewhat.

The Basques' Nationalist Quest: Elusive But Ending

The Basques are a very ancient people straddled across the Pyrenees, the population cut in two by the French–Spanish border. The Basques on French soil, numbering only about 200,000, have had quarrels with the French government, but there has been very little violence thus far. Spain, on the other hand, has about 2 million Basques, and while they possess the same culture, the same traditions, and the same language as their French counterparts, Spain has always experienced considerable Basque restlessness and violence. Indeed, it was here that the organization Basque Fatherland and Liberty (ETA) was estab-

(Courtesy Spanish Ministry of Tourism)

The fishing industry in Spain is supported by independent fishermen. This view is the Port of Sóller, on the island of Mallorca.

| The Reconquista is complete; Spain embarks on the road to discovery and empire A.D. 1492 | The Armada is defeated; Spain loses its place as the world's main imperial power 1588 | The Treaty of Westphalia 1648 | The Treaty of Utrecht formalizes the British occupation of the Rock of Gibraltar 1713 | The Spanish Civil War, won by the extreme right (the Franco Fascists) 1936–1939 | Franco dies; a new era in Spanish history begins 1975 | The text of the new (post-Franco) Constitution is adopted by universal suffrage 1978 | The Spanish and British governments negotiate on the problem of Gibraltar 1980s | Spain joins NATO; Spain joins the European Union as a full member |

1990s

| Economic adjustments to the EU and the increasingly global economy, but the economy falters | Spain hosts Expo '92 and the 1992 Summer Olympic Games; Spain participates in the launch of the Euro | The ETA declares a cease-fire, to end decades of Basque separatist violence |

lished. Inspired by radical nationalism, the ETA soon developed into a terrorist organization that has been responsible for a great many killings. A few years ago, French and Spanish authorities agreed that Spanish Basques may be extradited to Spain; this measure significantly weakened the ETA, since the group could no longer count on using France as a safe haven. The measure seems to have paid off, as in 1998 the ETA declared a cease-fire.

Other Groups

Basque separatism may have stimulated a similar stridency on the part of other ethnic minorities in Spain, such as the Cataláns, the Galicians, and the Andalusians. The Cataláns in particular are very proud of their heritage and language, which they do not wish to be confused with, much less identified as, those of Spain. Of the various regions, Catalonia has the second-largest population (approximately 6 million, as compared to Andalusia's 7 million).

Spain thus provides an interesting political paradox that is also being seen in many other European countries, such as Germany, France, and Britain. While it has come to terms with the drives that seek integration into a larger context, that is, the EU, it is internally challenged by the forces represented by various minority-group demands. The Spanish government's decision to use devolution to give its citizens a greater voice is proving to have resulted in a greater desire among the various regional groups to stick together rather than to fragment.

THE ECONOMY

More than 40 percent of the land in Spain is arable, and the climate is benign. For a long time Spain was predominantly agricultural, with its products geared largely toward the domestic market. After the end of World War II, Spain's position as an outcast among the European nations enhanced the tendency of economic introversion, of having as little trade and commerce with nations in the region as possible. For some time the Franco regime labeled this "self-reliance," but the situation suddenly changed in the 1960s, when Franco decided to diversify the economy. Apparently Franco had determined that the time had come to industrialize, or at least to expand Spain's very limited industrial base. The diversification was a remarkable success, in that the economy responded very favorably. In the economic history of Spain, the 1960s have come to be identified as an economic miracle—not perhaps of the same scope as that which took place in West Germany, but a miracle nevertheless. This feat helped Spain's image; it was no longer dismissed as a "backward" Southern European country. Some economic observers have even suggested that the powerful Group of Seven organization should be converted into a G-8, to include Spain.

In the late 1970s and early 1980s, exports started to increase, and, since the dictator had died and the new government appeared democratically inclined, the time had come to consider Spain's admission to the European Union. Both Iberian countries, Spain and Portugal, still had low levels of per capita income, but the Union was no longer so concerned about structural imbalances, believing that these wrinkles might be ironed out in time.

In the 1990s, on the economic front, the government has concentrated efforts on bringing inflation under control with mixed results. The rate today hovers between 6 and 7 percent, higher than the government would like. In matters of unemployment, the news is discouraging—at around 22 percent, Spain has the highest unemployment rate of the European Union members. And during the European currency crisis in 1993, the Spanish peseta had to be devalued by 5 percent. It has been devalued several times since—a boon to foreign tourists.

CHANGES IN GOVERNMENT

At the end of October 1992, González celebrated his 10 years of prime ministership. He vowed that he would run for reelection in 1993. Many observers were very surprised that, with an economy that had greatly deteriorated, he did manage to get reelected. But in early 1994, governmental corruption scandals erupted, with the interior minister convicted of running death squads to kill Basque terrorist sympathizers. González was implicated to the extent that his political ally, the leader of Catalonia's Convergence and Union coalition, warned the prime minister that he must deal with the scandals quickly or risk losing his support. However, the warning had come too late. González was forced to step down, and José Maria Aznar, of the People's, or Popular, Party (PP), became prime minister.

His government, described as the only purely right-wing government left in the European Union, has done rather well to date, even though Prime Minister Aznar himself is viewed as a rather dour individual—a potential problem (new elections are scheduled for mid-2000). The country's economic growth rate has rebounded, other economic indicators are up, and Spain was pleased to be among the first wave of countries to participate in the launch of the Euro in January 1999 (Aznar views the Euro as a catalyst in helping him bring about further economic change). Meanwhile, the Socialist Party remains in disarray.

DEVELOPMENT

Spain's transition from empire to nation has been remarkably smooth. However, it did take the country a long time to move away from its agricultural and rural base. Industrialization has progressed unevenly, with unemployment a persistent and serious problem.

FREEDOM

Freedom has increased progressively since Spain embarked upon the road to democracy after General Francisco Franco's death in 1975. Madrid has been the venue of a prolonged follow-up conference regarding human rights as outlined in the Helsinki Accords.

HEALTH/WELFARE

Health has greatly improved since Spain ceased to be an outcast in Europe and has begun participating in European medical conferences and other exchanges of medical science. Some cautious steps have been taken toward a welfare state.

ACHIEVEMENTS

On September 10, 1981, Picasso's *Guernica* arrived for permanent exhibition in Madrid. This famous painting, depicting the dismal destruction of a northern Spanish town by Fascist troops and planes, had been banned by the Franco regime.

Sweden (Kingdom of Sweden)

GEOGRAPHY

Area in Square Miles (Kilometers): 179,986 (449,964) (about the size of California)

Capital (Population): Stockholm (1,545,000)

Environmental Concerns: acid rain; pollution of the North Sea and the Baltic Sea

Geographical Features: mostly flat or gently rolling lowlands; mountains in west

Climate: temperate in south; subarctic in north

PEOPLE

Population

Total: 8,867,000

Annual Growth Rate: 0.26%

Rural/Urban Population Ratio: 17/83

Major Languages: Swedish; small Lapp- and Finnish-speaking minorities

Ethnic Makeup: a homogeneous Caucasian population; a small Sami (Lapp) minority; an estimated 12% are foreign-born or first-generation immigrants

Religions: 94% Evangelical Lutheran; 1% Roman Catholic; 5% others

Health

Life Expectancy at Birth: 77 years (male); 82 years (female)

Infant Mortality Rate (Ratio): 3.9/1,000

Average Caloric Intake: 119% of FAO minimum

Physicians Available (Ratio): 1/394

Education

Adult Literacy Rate: 99%

Compulsory (Ages): 6–15

COMMUNICATION

Telephones: 1 per 1.5 people

Daily Newspaper Circulation: 483 per 1,000 people

Televisions: 1 per 2.1 people

TRANSPORTATION

Highways in Miles (Kilometers): 81,740 (136,233)

Railroads in Miles (Kilometers): 7,574 (12,624)

Usable Airfields: 255

Motor Vehicles in Use: 3,922,000

GOVERNMENT

Type: constitutional monarchy

Independence Date: June 6, 1523

Head of State/Government: King Carl XVI Gustaf; Prime Minister Goran Persson

Political Parties: Conservative/New Democracy Party; Social Democratic Party; Moderate Party; Liberal Party; Center Party; Christian Democratic Party; Left Party; Communist Workers' Party; Green Party

Suffrage: universal at 18

MILITARY

Military Expenditures (% of GDP): 2.5%

Current Disputes: none

ECONOMY

Currency ($ U.S. Equivalent): 7.87 kronor = $1

Per Capita Income/GDP: $19,700/$176.2 billion

GDP Growth Rate: 2.5%

Inflation Rate: 2%

Labor Force: 4,552,000

Unemployment Rate: 6.6%, plus about 5% in training programs

Natural Resources: zinc; iron ore; lead; copper; silver; timber; uranium; hydropower potential

Agriculture: animal husbandry; grains; sugar beets; potatoes; fish

Industry: iron and steel; precision equipment; shipping and shipbuilding; wood pulp and paper products; processed foods; motor vehicles; tourism

Exports: $84.5 billion (primary partners EU countries, Norway, Finland)

Imports: $66.6 billion (primary partners EU countries, Finland, Norway)

 http://www.luth.se/luth/present/ sweden/
http://www.swedentrade.com/

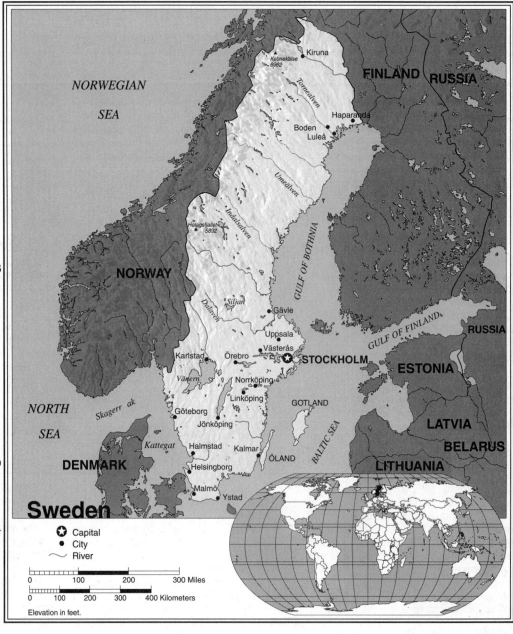

Sweden

- ⭐ Capital
- • City
- ⌇ River

0   100   200   300 Miles

0   100   200   300   400 Kilometers

Elevation in feet.

SWEDEN

Sweden is not only one of the oldest kingdoms in the world, it has also been one of the more significant countries in European history. With the largest population among the Nordic states, Sweden is a long country—indeed, the distance from Malmö, Sweden's most southern city, to the extreme north of Sweden equals that of Malmö to . . . Rome, Italy! As may be expected, the coastline is extensive—more than 1,500 miles.

Nordic history plays an important part in the Swedish world view. For some centuries Sweden was highly assertive in diplomacy and military matters. The beginning of modern Swedish history is usually associated with Gustav Vasa, who was elected king in A.D. 1523 after leading a revolt that terminated Sweden's century-long link with Denmark. It steadily rose in importance, becoming one of Europe's great powers during the seventeenth and eighteenth centuries. For a long time it waged war after war. In fact, between the thirteenth and early nineteenth centuries, Sweden fought Russia more than 40 times, usually in the role of aggressor. One of Sweden's greatest kings, Gustav Adolph II, was killed in a battle in southern Germany in 1632 while leading his army in the Thirty Years' War. Another king, Charles XII, was out of the country for more than 14 years in the early eighteenth century, warring in Poland and Russia.

But since the Napoleonic era ended, in 1814, a sharp reduction in its armed forces, its adoption of a policy of military/political neutrality, and its relative geographic isolation have all contributed to keeping Sweden out of war. Swedes pride themselves on having made that transition from a country frequently at war to a peaceful society, and they believe that they can help other nations, particularly those in the developing world, to do the same.

Sweden was one of the very few countries in Europe not to be engulfed by World War II. All postwar Swedish governments have studiously avoided becoming part of a collective defense pact. Thus, when the North Atlantic Treaty Organization emerged, the Swedish government indicated immediately that under no circumstances would it join.

In 1992, the question of Swedish neutrality came up again, possibly because the end of the cold war demanded some reassessment. But Margaret af-Ugglas, Sweden's foreign minister, simply reaffirmed that the policy would remain "nonparticipation in alliances in time of peace, aiming at neutrality in time of war." Sweden is a member of the Nordic Council, an organization that allows cooperation and consultation in many matters that have no bearing on war or violence.

RAPID DEVELOPMENT

Today, Sweden is one of the most prosperous, democratic, and highly developed nations in the world. It has certainly come a long way since the 1800s, when hundreds of thousands of Swedes emigrated to the United States, leaving behind them chronic poverty and shortages of economic opportunities. There were other reasons for leaving the country. Some simply wanted a new start in life; others believed that they had too little religious freedom in Sweden.

Swedes continued to emigrate to the United States in large numbers well into the twentieth century. Nearly every Swedish family now has a living relative in the United States; at one time, in fact, the second-largest community of Swedes in the world was located in Chicago.

Sweden entered the industrial age behind the vanguard of the Industrial Revolution: Great Britain and Germany. The early 1900s marked tremendous changes in the country. Industries started to mushroom, natural resources were utilized as never before, and many people left the land for the cities.

Most Swedes are only one or two generations removed from rural life. The relatively recent urbanization may in part explain the typical Swede's dream of owning a cabin in a little meadow by a lake. This bucolic ideal often conflicts with reality, which for many is a high-rise apartment in the suburbs. While there are no slums or ghettos, it is now recognized that the rapid buildup of concrete structures largely making up the "bedroom cities" is not without social consequences.

The "model" Swedish cities built in the 1960s are left as dreary monuments of a bygone era. Experiments on this scale

(Photo courtesy Lisa Clyde)

Stockholm, Sweden's largest city, was founded in the middle of the thirteenth century; it officially became the capital in 1436. The city is an attractive blend of old and new, with architecture represented from medieval times to the present. As pictured above, waterways and bridges are a prominent feature in the capital.

were possible in part because Sweden's entire population numbers less than that of New York City, spread out in an area the size of the state of California, and with a high per capita income. Sweden also has been able to organize and regulate its society in ways that more populous federated countries have not been able or willing to do.

THE RISE AND FALL OF SWEDISH POLITICAL PARTIES

In the nineteenth century, Sweden made the transition from authoritarian monarchy to parliamentary democracy, without revolution. Politics in Sweden has always been pragmatic and methodical—mob rule, corruption, and extremism have played little part in the country's history since the days of King Gustav III, whose assassination in 1792 is portrayed in Verdi's opera *Masked Ball*. Nothing similar occurred until 1986, when Prime Minister Olaf Palme was murdered as he walked home from a movie theater in downtown Stockholm. Swedes were stunned; their vision of Swedish insulation from the turmoil and violence of the outside world was shattered. (The killer has never been found.)

Ingvar Carlsson, who became prime minister after Palme's murder, was relatively unknown outside political circles, because he had always worked in Palme's shadow. A professional politician who rose from union organizer and youth leader to ministerial rank, Carlsson quickly established a profile of a quietly pragmatic leader. His style contrasted sharply with Palme's flamboyant image. Carlsson directed his attention more to social and economic problems than to foreign policy.

Sweden's parliamentary democracy is headed by a constitutional monarch. Thus the king, as the head of state, has an almost entirely ceremonial role, while the prime minister, as the head of government, exercises executive authority. The Parliament (the *Riksdag*), which since 1971 has consisted of a single chamber, has 349 seats, which are distributed in accordance with the proportion of votes that each individual party receives in the triennial elections. However, in order to prevent the fragmentation of the party system, a party must receive a minimum of 4 percent of the votes nationwide; or, alternatively, 12 percent of the votes in any of the 28 voting districts. A party that does not meet either requirement will not be seated in the Riksdag. This so-called quota rule was introduced in 1969.

Political power in Sweden rests with parties and other organizations, primarily labor unions and popular movements such as single-issue social groups. Voters cast their ballots for party lists, rather than for an individual, and it is the party leadership that determines the candidates and their positions on the lists.

For most of this century, the largest political party in Sweden has been the Social Democratic Party (SAP). In the past, the SAP was in the same unenviable position as the more conservative parties today: There was no absolute majority. Thus, it has often had to rely on the tacit support of a smaller party, such as the Left Party—formerly the Communist Party—in order to remain in power. The Communists, who generally receive a small percentage of the vote, do not vote against the SAP on most issues. This may explain the political longevity of various Social Democratic governments.

Sweden has four major non-Socialist parties: the Moderate Party (also known as the Conservative Party), the Center Party, the Liberal Party, and, since late 1990, the New Democracy Party. The Center and Liberal Parties coordinated their policies in an arrangement known as the "union of the middle." (It should be noted that the term *liberal* has no leftist connotation in Europe, as it does in the United States. Indeed, more often than not liberal parties in Europe are protagonists of big business; although somewhat centrist in orientation, the Liberal Party in Sweden is an example of just that.)

For the non-Socialists to form a government, they not only must win more votes but must also agree on a common purpose.

This is difficult, as the right and center in Sweden are typically much more divided among themselves than is the left, a phenomenon that was clearly evidenced in the years between 1976 and 1982.

Voter turnout in Sweden is normally very high—about 90 percent. Nevertheless, Swedish elections are usually decided by narrow margins. The Social Democrats sometimes have no more than a plurality in Parliament, amounting to just a few more seats than the next-largest party.

The parliamentary elections of September 1991 witnessed the defeat of Ingvar Carlsson and his Social Democratic government. This was a strong indication of popular disenchantment with the welfare state—or, rather, with the high taxes that the welfare state demands. In addition, the worldwide recession of the early 1990s was taking its toll on Sweden. Maintaining a high employment rate was considered the most important method of keeping the economy strong, so what to other countries may have seemed a relatively low unemployment rate of 3 percent was viewed in Sweden as unacceptable. Then there was the country's high inflation rate. Although it seemed to be improving, it contributed to the temporary downfall of the Social Democratic Party.

Elections in the fall of 1991 toppled Carlsson and brought Carl Bildt to power. Bildt was a non-Socialist whose views and policies were very much right-of-center. Still, his four-party coalition was unable to claim a majority in the Riksdag. Prime

(Photo courtesy Karin Badger)

Carl XVI Gustaf became king of Sweden in September 1973. Today, the role of the Swedish monarch is largely ceremonial. Members of the royalty are quite accessible in this highly egalitarian country, as can be seen in the above photograph, taken as the king and his wife, Queen Silvia, left a parliamentary function at Stockholm Cathedral in 1994.

Kalmar Union with Denmark and Norway A.D. 1397	First Parliament (Riksdag) at Arboga 1435	Gustav Vasa is elected king 1523	A coup takes place and King Gustav IV is deposed 1809	Norway is in a union with Sweden 1814
●	●	●	●	●

Minister Bildt thus needed to take into account, if not to consult with, the opposition parties on any great project.

Upon taking office, Bildt announced that the new government would work to complete four major tasks during its term: negotiating to bring Sweden into the European Union would be of the utmost importance (polls conducted in September 1992 evidenced that only 10 percent of Swedes opposed Sweden entering the EU); terminating the country's economic stagnation and reestablishing Sweden as a nation of growth and enterprise; initiating freedom of choice in welfare policy, thus enhancing welfare and social care; and shaping long-term environmental policies. Most of these programs were continued after the Bildt administration was voted out of office in 1994. The public brought Ingvar Carlsson, Bildt's predecessor, back to power. Meanwhile, the two party platforms had grown together. In 1996, after Carlsson resigned for personal reasons, Finance Minister Goran Persson, of the Social Democratic Party, won the prime ministership.

In the summer of 1998, opinion polls indicated nearly 40 percent of Swedes supporting the SDP, and indeed, Prime Minister Persson and his party were returned to office in the September 1998 elections. However, the Social Democrats did not have as strong a finish as in 1994. (Their decline in popularity may require the party to seek the support of a second party to form a stable government; the most likely partner is the Left party, which has left behind its Communist heritage). Although Carl Bildt and his Moderate Party did not win control of the government, they did give the Social Democrats a run for their money, and the SDP government must come to terms with the reasons for their popularity. The Moderates favor tax reductions, an overhaul of the welfare system, and more flexible labor-market regulations—policies that are in direct contrast to those proposed by the Social Democrats, who want to use the improved state of the public finances to increase spending on welfare, education, and health care.

FOREIGN POLICY
The Swedes make an interesting distinction between nonalignment (which they wish to pursue in peacetime) and neutral-ity (which is to prevail in a war in which they themselves are not involved). But the Swedes apparently reject the Danish solution of the pre–World War II era, when the Danes abolished their army: The Swedes want armed neutrality. They believe that a small, nonaligned nation can help to bridge differences and improve the dialogue in world politics. The Swedish political elite also assume that their country will not be attacked unless there is a general state of war in the world.

These assumptions made it difficult for Sweden to come to grips with submarine violations of Swedish territorial waters. Soviet submarines were discovered in sensitive areas, such as Sweden's naval bases. The Swedish government preferred to deal with these violations quietly, through diplomatic channels, and always hoped that the media would allow such a course.

Occasionally, however, its diplomacy vis-à-vis the Soviet Union was not so quiet. Sweden was the first country in 1986 to conclude that a major accident had taken place in Chernobyl's nuclear power installation. The Swedish government immediately alerted other European countries to the grave dangers that exposure to such high levels of radiation could cause.

Gradually over the year 1993, support for Sweden's membership in the European Union grew. By the end of the year, polls found that all the major political parties as well as the vast majority of business leaders backed the government in this endeavor. Sweden had already signed up for the preparatory stage that an agreement concerning the European Economic Area involved—that is, the free-trade agreement between the EU and the seven-nation European Free Trade Association, which was scheduled to take effect in 1994. EU membership would follow on January 1, 1995. (In June of that year, Carl Bildt became the EU's peace mediator in the former Yugoslavia.)

A difficult point that has recently loomed is to what extent it will be possible for Sweden to pursue nonalignment as a member of the European Union. Or, conversely, will the EU also have defense implications? One has only to think of the common foreign-policy ideals (such as that of political union) that have come out of various European Council meetings to realize that those risks exist.

CULTURE AND LIFESTYLE
Sweden has a rich cultural and intellectual history. August Strindberg, the playwright; Carl Larsson, the artist; and Ingmar Bergman, the film and stage director, are just a few of the Swedes known around the world. Students of botany learn Carl Linnaeus's classification system, and in this century, Sweden has also become known for the Nobel Prizes, annually awarded to top authors and scientists.

In the world of sport, too, Sweden has made its mark. Skiers watched Ingemar Stenmark dominate slalom events for nearly a decade. Bjorn Borg, Mats Wilander, and Stefan Edberg became tennis kings, and in 1987, Sweden's national hockey team won the World Cup.

Culture and quality of life go hand-in-hand with health and longevity. Life expectancy in Sweden is higher than in most countries.

Some stereotypes of Swedes, however, present less flattering images. Swedes are often thought by foreigners to be aloof, cold, preaching technocrats—a view that others vigorously refute. Swedish tourists are sometimes thought to overindulge in alcohol when abroad, perhaps because it is heavily taxed at home and thus expensive. Some authors, such as Roland Huntford, have even suggested sinister correlations between Sweden's high suicide rates and the welfare-state ideology of the Social Democratic Party.

The truth may lie somewhere in between the wholly positive and wholly negative images. The average Swede is a conformist who raises continuity to a virtue. Swedes generally follow the rules and expect others to do so as well—including foreigners. They believe that society should be fair and that, by and large, personal freedom and success should have limits. Swedish citizens are fond of their country and their flag, but many do not understand American-style patriotism.

The climate and geographic isolation help to shape the Swedish lifestyle. Winter in Sweden is usually less severe than winter in the American plains, but, due to its proximity to the polar circle, the winter months are dark. The capital city of Stockholm may receive only 4 hours of sunlight a day in midwinter, and overcast days can produce week after week of gray sameness. It is no surprise, then, that come

Jean Baptiste
Bernadotte
becomes king
and assumes the
name Karl Johan
1818

1.25 million
Swedes emigrate
to the United
States
1820–1930

The union with
Norway is
dissolved
1905

Universal
suffrage and a
democratic
political system
are introduced
1918–1921

The Social
Democrats come
to office;
introduction of
the "Swedish
model" welfare
system
1936

Prime Minister
Olaf Palme is
murdered
1986

1990s

Carl Bildt, of the
Moderate Party
temporarily
moves the Social
Democrats out of
power; the Social
Democratic party
regains control in
1996 and 1998

Sweden joins the
European Union
in 1995 but
declines to join
the launch of the
Euro in 1999

Sweden
confronts
challenges to its
neutrality during
World War II; it
joins forces with
the United States
and Britain to
teach about the
Holocaust

spring, the green of the countryside and the warm days bring Swedes outside, re-kindling ancient traditions. Midsummer, which occurs in the welcome soft light of 24-hour sunshine, is a holiday on the scale of the United States' Fourth of July. And in August, every Swede looks forward to a plate full of steamed crayfish and a shot of frozen akvavit to toast friends and the end of summer.

As could be expected, Sweden also has availed itself of that typically Scandinavian device, the ombudsman, a parliamentary commissioner who exercises a check on the government administration. The office of ombudsman was created to right wrongs that may have been perpetrated on members of the public by the government. In Sweden, the *Justitie-ombudsman* exerts supervision over all courts of law, the civil service, military laws, and the military services.

THE ECONOMY

Sweden has had Social Democratic governments for the bulk of more than half a century. One would thus expect its economy to be based on government-run or government-owned enterprises. However, the percentage of *private* enterprise has been over 90 percent during decades of Social Democratic administration. In the mid-1970s, it was reduced slightly, mainly because many of the private companies appeared to be languishing. Ironically, nationalizations took place during a 6-year period in which a non-Socialist government held office.

In the late 1970s, shortly after the nationalizations took place, the Swedish economy slumped. In fact, it eventually became so dismal that analysts started to refer to Sweden as the "sick man of Europe." Some attributed the poor performance at that time to the high ratio of

public spending (which reached 67 percent of the gross domestic product by 1982). Naturally, these critics were surprised to see Sweden recover within a decade, even though the role of the state in the economy was still very much larger than in other industrial economies.

Sweden established a huge State Company (*Statsföretag*), which serves as a type of umbrella organization for all the nationalized firms. Some 10 percent of the Swedish workforce is employed by state-run companies, which include post and telephone services, railroads, the iron-ore mining in Lapland, and a large part of the domestic energy production, mainly hydropower.

The Social Democratic Party prefers to leave the private character of the economy alone. The least that one can say is that there is no direct influence on the part of the government. Nevertheless, the SAP exerts tremendous influence on the economy, if only by taxing profits.

One of the major aspirations of SAP governments has been full employment. This ideal has not always been fulfilled in practice; most economies will, even in the best of times, be marked by pockets of unemployment, made up of people between jobs and people with no inclination to work. In the case of Sweden, the ambition to reach full employment has caused some cheating, in that the government has concealed unemployment by excluding those who registered for retraining programs as well as those who volunteered for emergency work (invariably on a temporary basis). However, it is obvious that these forms of "employment" actually are little more than waystations. But in those cases, there may be a psychological gain: Laid-off workers continue to be in contact with the labor market.

Curiously, inflation has never loomed large as a government concern. Occasion-

ally the inflation rate has soared while the government has done its utmost to fight unemployment (a highly stereotypical response of market forces). However, in general, the Swedish economy has surprised analysts, since there has been no inverse relation between inflation and unemployment.

Sweden has its primarily agricultural past long behind it. It endorsed industrialization wholeheartedly at the beginning of the Industrial Revolution and is now predominantly an industrial and service economy. Only 2 percent of the workforce engage in agricultural pursuits, but, since the farming equipment and methods are extremely modern, these individuals are able to supply the vast majority of the country's food needs.

Sweden has been exploring and exploiting nuclear energy more than any other nation in the world. Nuclear accidents such as occurred in Three Mile Island and Chernobyl generated mounting concerns as well as a commitment to close down all nuclear plants by the year 2010. However, the dilemma no longer dominates the Swedish political debates.

DEVELOPMENT

The Swedish economy is characterized by extensive cooperation among the state, private enterprises, and trade unions. About 90% of industrial output is accounted for by private enterprises. Sweden is heavily dependent on foreign trade for its prosperity. Sweden is one of the world's leading exporters of iron ore.

FREEDOM

Sweden is a constitutional monarchy and parliamentary democracy. It is an egalitarian society in which respect for individual rights is accorded top priority. This respect for individual rights has been enhanced by the institution of the ombudsman.

HEALTH/WELFARE

Health, welfare, pensions, social insurance, job training, and education are all covered by Sweden's cradle-to-grave system of benefits and services.

ACHIEVEMENTS

Sweden was the first country to institute the office of ombudsman, which is designed to protect the individual from the government. Cultural activities of all types are subsidized by the state, a fact that has contributed to Sweden's already rich culture.

Switzerland (Swiss Confederation)

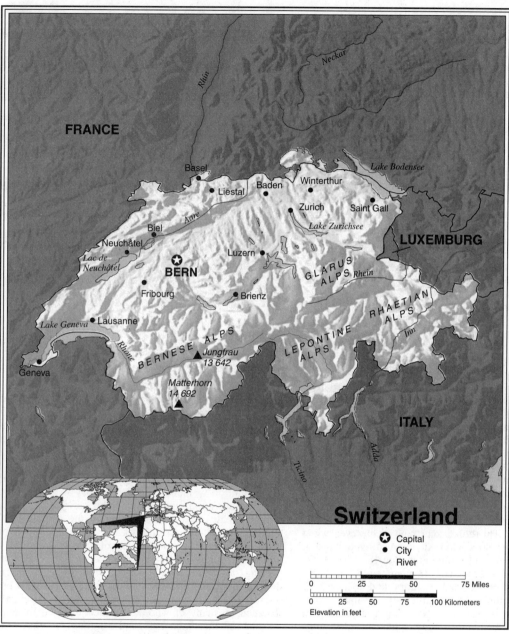

Switzerland

★ Capital
• City
〜 River

| 0 | 25 | 50 | 75 Miles |
| 0 | 25 | 50 | 75 | 100 Kilometers |

Elevation in feet

GEOGRAPHY

Area in Square Miles (Kilometers): 15,941 (41,288) (about twice the size of New Jersey)
Capital (Population): Bern (130,000)
Environmental Concerns: air and water pollution; acid rain; loss of biodiversity
Geographical Features: mostly mountains (Alps in south, Jura in northwest) with a central plateau of rolling hills, plains, and large lakes
Climate: temperate, but varies with altitude

PEOPLE

Population

Total: 7,260,500
Annual Growth Rate: 0.22%
Rural/Urban Population Ratio: 40/60
Major Languages: German; French; Italian; Romansch; others
Ethnic Makeup: 65% German Swiss; 18% French Swiss; 10% Italian; 7% Romansch and others
Religions: 47% Roman Catholic; 40% Protestant; 5% others; 8% unaffiliated or not indicated

Health

Life Expectancy at Birth: 76 years (male); 82 years (female)
Infant Mortality Rate (Ratio): 6.3/1,000
Average Caloric Intake: 135% of FAO minimum
Physicians Available (Ratio): 1/299

Education

Adult Literacy Rate: 99%
Compulsory (Ages): 7–16

COMMUNICATION

Telephones: 1 per 1.6 people
Daily Newspaper Circulation: 409 per 1,000 people
Televisions: 1 per 2.4 people

TRANSPORTATION

Highways in Miles (Kilometers): 44,378 (71,118)
Railroads in Miles (Kilometers): 3,596 (5,763)
Usable Airfields: 67
Motor Vehicles in Use: 3,500,000

GOVERNMENT

Type: federal republic
Independence Date: August 1, 1291
Head of State/Government: President Flavio Cotti is both head of state and head of government

Political Parties: Radical Free Democratic Party; Social Democratic Party; Christian Democratic People's Party; Swiss People's Party; Swiss Liberal Party; Green Party; many others
Suffrage: universal at 18

MILITARY

Military Expenditures (% of GDP): 1.2%
Current Disputes: none

ECONOMY

Currency ($ U.S. Equivalent): 1.42 Swiss francs = $1
Per Capita Income/GDP: $23,800/$172.4 billion
GDP Growth Rate: 0.4%
Inflation Rate: –0.1%
Unemployment Rate: 5%
Labor Force: 3,800,000
Natural Resources: hydropower potential; timber; salt
Agriculture: dairy farming; fruits; vegetables
Industry: banking; machinery; chemicals; watches; textiles; precision instruments; tourism
Exports: $99.2 billion (primary partners EU countries, United States, Japan)
Imports: $86.6 billion (primary partners EU countries, United States, Japan)

 http://www.admin.ch
http://www.odci.gov/cia/publications/
factbook/country-frame.html
http://portal.research.bell-labs.com/
cgi-wald/dbaccess/411?key=231

THE SWISS CONFEDERATION

Switzerland has a long history; its political origins can be traced back to medieval times. Indeed, the country's 700-year jubilee was celebrated not long ago. Thus, in 1291, three tribal chieftains from the areas that later came to be known as the cantons of Schwyz (from which the German name for Switzerland, *Schweiz*, derives), Uri, and Unterwalden, met and signed what might be called a collective defense treaty. By implication, this treaty amounted to a proclamation of independence from the Habsburg Empire, which hitherto had taken care of security in its own fashion. Lucerne, a pretty town not far from the meadow where the pristine ceremony took place, was invited 2 decades later to join in the growing (but still loose) confederation. The centuries that followed did not bring peace to the new structure, or even constant goodwill among its inhabitants.

Although it is exceptionally beautiful, the country has very few natural resources—so few, in fact, that for several centuries a great many Swiss men found a livelihood by leaving the country and hiring themselves out as mercenaries. Europe always had plenty of wars, and it was not hard to become a soldier or even an officer in a foreign army. It is said that the Swiss guards in the papal palaces in the Vatican constitute a relic of what used to be a widespread practice. However that may be, each canton guarded its independence fiercely and refused to surrender any of its sovereignty to a more centralized, intercantonal authority.

This condition changed, however, when the Swiss Confederation suffered defeat at the hands of the French in 1515. The Confederation states then agreed to coordinate their external relations and to pursue a common objective of optimal independence from other European states. An effective guarantee of the Confederation's independence was achieved as early as 1521, when members signed a treaty with France. In this accord, which was to survive until the French Revolution, the Swiss states promised to provide soldiers and arms for the French king; in return, they were to receive the protection of the French Army as well as free access to French markets.

Whereas defeat in battle had produced greater unity in the area of foreign policy, the Reformation of the sixteenth century tore the Swiss Confederation apart. Switzerland, notably Geneva, became a haven for Protestant refugees, while at the same time its inhabitants largely remained Roman Catholic. After more than a decade of religious violence, pitting the Catholic

(Photo courtesy Cornelia Warmenhoven)

Switzerland has a long and colorful history. Often the country is remembered for its famous, some would say infamous, banking laws. The country, however, has many magnificent cities and towns. Pictured above is a bridge over the River Aare in the capital city of Bern.

rural cantons against their Protestant urban counterparts, the Peace of Kappel in 1531 forged a settlement that divided the country into Protestant and Catholic cantons. All citizens of a canton were to share the same faith. Cantons in which the denominations were equally represented were cut into halves.

In addition to identifying the country–city faultline as a religious divide, the Reformation also dramatically altered the ethnolinguistic composition of the Swiss Confederation. The immigration of thousands of French Protestants (Huguenots) fleeing persecution in Catholic France helped to transform Swiss society from a mono- to a multiethnic one. Moreover, the Huguenots, many of whom were accomplished merchants, bankers, and manufacturers, helped to transform the economic base of the Confederation, enabling it to pioneer the Industrial Revolution on the European continent.

The year 1648 provided an important milestone, in that the Peace of Westphalia decreed that the Swiss Confederation would henceforth be independent of the Holy Roman Empire. The next major transformation in Switzerland's political organization resulted from the French Revolution and its aftermath. During the Napoleonic Wars, the Confederation was temporarily absorbed into the French empire. However, the brief humiliation of French occupation was more than compensated for by the territorial gains and constitutional innovations enjoyed by the Swiss Confederation under

Napoleon Bonaparte's sovereignty. The French emperor virtually doubled the territory of the confederation by adding six new cantons: one French-speaking, one Italian-speaking, three German-speaking, and one Romansch-speaking.

Napoleon unsuccessfully tried to mold the Confederation into a highly centralized republic and then decided to provide the Swiss with the foundations for a federal democratic constitution, with the Act of Mediation in 1803. This act was in effect a new charter, inspired by the U.S. Constitution. It combined federalism, popular sovereignty, the separation of powers, and a bill of rights with a central government in charge of foreign policy.

Napoleon was defeated in 1815, and the Congress of Vienna, which had suspended its activities during the brief comeback of the emperor, devoted comparatively little time to the position of Switzerland. Nevertheless, some of its decisions were of great significance. The Congress recognized Switzerland's military/political neutrality, which has since been a tradition. More important, it completed the Swiss Confederation's territorial expansion by adding two more French cantons to its jurisdiction. In 1848, on the eve of the autocratic retrenchment throughout most of Europe, Swiss advocates of a democratic national constitution finally gained control of sufficient cantons to transform the cantonal military alliance into a unified nation-state with an official federal Constitution and institutions.

Although significantly revised in 1874, in order to delineate and constrain the powers of the federal government vis-à-vis the cantons, Switzerland's democratic Constitution and institutions demonstrated considerable resilience in peacetime as well as during the two world wars in the twentieth century. Armed neutrality during the wars prevented not only Switzerland's occupation and destruction from without but also averted a potentially suicidal conflict among the country's French, German, and Italian ethnic groups. The period between the world wars presented the Swiss democracy with its most serious test, as extreme right- and left-wing political movements manifested themselves. However, democratic institutions were able to weather the storm in Switzerland, which was not the case in neighboring Germany, Italy, and Austria.

During World War II, the warring parties may well have benefited from having a neutral haven—Switzerland—in their midst, as a venue that could be used for secret negotiations. (In recent years, it has become clear that Switzerland itself benefited from the money, artworks, and other treasures that had been deposited in Switzerland for safekeeping—most of which have never been returned by the banks to the real owners, such as the Jews of Germany.) Following the war, Switzerland retained its neutral stance. Since the United Nations was founded by the victorious nations, Switzerland refused for many decades to join that organization. Indeed, a few years ago, Swiss voters rejected a parliamentary proposal to join the United Nations, in the belief that membership would subvert the country's policy of neutrality.

Its neutrality, political stability, and, particularly, economic prosperity have made the country the envy of the Western world. Part of its prosperity derives from Switzerland's expertise in international finance and banking.

A UNIQUE BRAND OF FEDERALISM

As this brief overview of Switzerland's political history indicates, the transformation of the loose cantonal alliance into a unified nation-state was a long, drawn-out process. The national Constitutions of 1848 and 1874 committed all cantons to the principles of democracy and conceded the new federal authority jurisdiction over defense, trade, and many legal questions. The cantons, nevertheless, made certain that any and all powers not expressly granted to the national government by the Constitutions remained in their own hands (which is also the tenor of the Tenth Amendment of the U.S. Constitution). Further-

more, the cantons ensured that national institutions were organized in such a manner that any further encroachment on cantonal autonomy by the central government would be prevented.

Following World War II, Switzerland was unable to completely escape the global trend toward increased intervention by central governments in the management of social and economic life, an intervention that manifested itself naturally more strongly in unitary systems. However, the Swiss have been more successful than other Western democracies at keeping that trend in check. Today, as was the case 50 or 100 years ago, the true loci of Swiss political loyalty and activity remain the canton and the commune; thus, the focus is on the state and local levels. As a result, the Swiss national political institutions are extraordinarily underdeveloped and weak for a modern democratic state.

Switzerland is composed of 20 cantons and six half-cantons, which, in turn, are made up of some 3,000 communes (townships). Both the cantons and their constituent communes enjoy extraordinary independence from the central government, seated in Bern. Each canton and half-canton has its own constitution and is free to choose its own form of government and electoral system, as long as these are consistent with democratic principles and the federal Constitution. In 1978, the voters in the French-speaking part of canton Bern voted in favor of self-government. As a result, the canton of Jura was established in 1979.

Currently, all cantons are governed by a directly elected, unicameral legislature with a collegial executive. While most cantons have instituted similar electoral systems, which extend the vote to all citizens above the age of majority, one half-canton, Appenzell Outer Rhodes, enfranchised women only as recently as 1991. Women had been allowed to vote in national elections by a national law passed in 1972. (Thus, in the intervening 20 years, the odd situation prevailed in this particular canton that women could vote in national elections but not in cantonal elections!) To be sure, the powers and responsibilities of the cantons are considerable. Each canton has its own taxing authority, law-enforcement facilities, and independent school system.

The communes' right to self-government is also guaranteed by the federal Constitution. However, they must submit to cantonal supervision in a number of areas. Like the cantons, each commune can choose its own form of government and electoral system, as long as they are compatible with the federal or cantonal constitutions. Communes are responsible for administering utilities, roads, schools, and

fire and police forces, among other things. Perhaps even more noteworthy is the exclusive power of communes to grant Swiss citizenship. In other federally structured countries, questions of nationality and citizenship are resolved by the national government.

FEDERAL INSTITUTIONS

The organization of the national government also provides the cantons with an effective check on the centralization of political power. The national Legislature is called the Federal Assembly. Its lower house, the National Council, is made up of 200 members directly elected to 4-year terms in national elections, according to a system of proportional representation. The National Council's federal aspirations, however, are effectively contained by the upper house, the Council of States. Modeled on the U.S. Senate, the Council of States is comprised of 46 representatives—two from each canton and one from each half-canton.

Cantons vary in size from about 35,000 to more than 1 million inhabitants. Since both houses must approve all bills before they become law, the Council of States can block legislation that it considers inconsistent with the interests of a majority of cantons. The conservative bias of the upper house is reinforced by the fact that the more rural, less densely populated cantons have a disproportionately large political voice in it. Yet another check on federal excess is the legal requirement that constitutional amendments be approved by a "double-majority"—a majority of voters in a national referendum and a majority of the cantons.

The executive branch of the federal government, the Federal Council, is a collegial body with seven councillors, who are elected by the Federal Assembly (both houses) for 4-year terms. Since 1959, when four leading political parties entered into a grand coalition, the seven Council posts have been distributed according to a formula that reflects the relative strength of the four parties in Parliament, while ensuring that the country's French and Italian ethnic minorities are represented. (In 1988, the only female member of the Federal Council—who was to have become vice president in 1989 and president in 1990—resigned, citing political pressures.)

To outsiders, Swiss foreign policy can seem somewhat erratic at times. An example of this is Switzerland's sudden denunciation of the so-called European Economic Area. While Switzerland had applied for membership in the European Union (albeit far less enthusiastically than neighboring Austria), a referendum suddenly indicated that a majority of Swiss did not want to recognize the EEA, which was understood

(UN photo by M. Vanappelghem)

Switzerland has often needed to import labor in order for Swiss manufacturers to expand. Companies that elect to remain in Switzerland rather than setting up operations in other countries must often use so-called guest workers, such as those pictured here, to stay in business.

to be some kind of transitional phase between the coexistence of the European Union and the European Free Trade Association on the one hand and, on the other, a considerably expanded Union. It is possible, of course, that most of those who participated in the referendum were not aware of the intricacies of the issue.

Decision making within the executive body, as in most other branches of Swiss federal, cantonal, and communal government, is a collective process characterized by compromise and consensus building. The Federal Council is not responsible to Parliament; that is, it cannot be disbanded or voted out of office in mid-term. However, its powers are quite limited.

THE PARTY SYSTEM

The weakness of national political institutions is also demonstrated by the Swiss party system. While political parties are relatively effective at channeling and representing the public will at the cantonal and communal levels, they are loosely organized and lack discipline at the national level. Moreover, the major national parties, which serve as umbrella organizations for their cantonal affiliates, have essentially been captured by the country's major organized economic interest groups (labor, business, agriculture, etc.).

One explanation for the weakness of Swiss political parties is the fact that the multiple divisions within the society (religious, ethnic, class, and regional) cut across and mute one another and thus have tended to de-ideologize the electorate. Other factors working to undermine party politics include the consensual style of Swiss politics and a distinct reliance on direct democracy through referendum at the national and cantonal levels, while, on exceptional occasions, there is also some public decision making at the *Landesgemeinde* level. (The Landesgemeinde is *the* typical example of direct democracy. Just as in the New England township, people come together to decide jointly on issues. There is no representation.)

A look at party interaction at the national level reveals why most Swiss citizens are not really interested in what goes on in the country's capital, Bern. Since 1959, the four largest Swiss parties, all of them moderate, have collaborated to dominate both houses of Parliament and the Federal Council. The largest of these, the Radical Free Democratic Party (FDP), usually wins about a quarter of the vote in parliamentary elections. At the center of the political spectrum, the FDP is a status-quo party with close ties to industry, finance, and the media. Two other coalition parties, the Christian Democratic People's Party (CVS) and the Social Democratic Party (SPS), also control large blocks of seats in Parliament. The former is slightly left of the FDP, drawing most of its support from Swiss Catholics. The latter, traditionally the party of the working class, is further to the left but has essentially abandoned the Socialist platform of its founders. The smallest member of the coalition is the Swiss People's Party (SVP). It has traditionally represented the more conservative elements of Swiss society, including small-business people, farmers, and artisans.

Since forming the grand coalition, the four member parties have all but converged along the political spectrum. Their combined share of the national vote has never fallen below 79 percent. They have, therefore, never experienced serious opposition in Parliament. A smattering of smaller parties—some moderate, some more extreme—have occasionally generated excitement on the national political stage. Nonetheless, with only 21 percent of the vote combined, the smaller parties are unlikely to alter the political status quo. While the overwhelming majority of the center parties has been good for consensus politics, their convergence has had a debilitating effect on national political life. As a result, voter turnout for national elections has fallen to extremely low levels in recent years. (Generally, Switzerland is known for its low voter turnout, thereby defying the often-made claim that low voter turnouts tend to destabilize political systems.)

INTEREST GROUPS

The extreme federalism of the Swiss political system has been quite effective at reinforcing the bonds of community at the cantonal level as well as defusing and containing intercantonal disputes. Moreover, a distinct reliance on plebicitary democracy through frequent referenda at the national level has lent considerable legitimacy to the Swiss political system. Yet, in view of the anemic nature of Swiss parties and political institutions at the national level, one may assume that the Swiss will find it difficult to act decisively on important national policy issues, other than those regarding foreign policy and defense of cantonal rights. In fact, a national consensus does exist concerning a wide range of political, economic, and social issues on an essentially federal level. Moreover, the Swiss have proven that they are quite capable of formulating and instituting effective national economic and social policies.

To explain the paradox of strong federal governance without a strong state or strong political parties, one must pay attention to Switzerland's highly organized system of interest-group representation. Moving into the political vacuum at the federal level, a number of nationally or-ganized interest groups have assumed many of the powers and responsibilities usually associated with national political parties and central government.

The most influential of Swiss interest groups are those that represent economi-cally defined national constituencies, such as labor, business, agriculture, and fi-nance. Their power derives from the fact that they have a monopoly of repre-sentation within their economic sector, en-compass a broad section of Swiss society, are hierarchically organized and hence relatively disciplined, and are granted quasi-governmental status by the federal Constitution. It stipulates that they must be consulted by the government and the major political parties on all legislation concerning their interests.

In practice, however, the influence of these private interest groups on policy making and policy implementation is much greater than the Constitution would suggest. Their penetration into the na-tional political parties has assured the ma-jor interest groups de facto representation in Parliament. Furthermore, the con-straints placed on the central government by the Constitution and the size of the fed-eral bureaucracy have allowed the private interest groups to assume many of the functions of national government.

For the most part, organized labor, busi-ness, and finance regulate themselves. They have also collaborated with one another to develop a private social-welfare system on the national level. This system has included, among other things, unemployment insur-ance, health insurance, and private-pension schemes for the Swiss workforce.

ECONOMIC FOUNDATIONS OF THE POLITICAL CONSENSUS
The result of Swiss political and industrial stability has been an economic prosperity envied for many years throughout much of Western Europe. The fact that Switzer-land was able to stay out of World War II granted the country a head start. Blessed with peaceful industrial relations, a skilled workforce, and abundant capital, the Swiss economy grew at a rapid rate for the first 2 decades after the war. Inflation was low and unemployment virtually non-existent.

During the 1970s and early 1980s, how-ever, Switzerland's main economic indica-tors turned sour, along with those of much of the rest of industrialized Europe. After the second oil shock in 1979, economic growth stagnated and inflation rose to nearly 7 percent. By the mid-1980s, how-ever, things had begun to turn around again. Economic growth resumed, albeit

at a lower rate, and inflation began to fall. Switzerland's economic growth rates be-gan to compare favorably to those of most of its Western European neighbors.

The pillars of the Swiss economy are a large international banking and financial-services sector and a highly competitive and diversified industrial sector. Favorable banking laws with strict secrecy require-ments, a stable currency, and a minimum of government regulation have allowed Switzerland to develop into one of the world's leading centers of international banking and insurance.

In regard to the renowned secrecy, one must note that the Swiss Supreme Court ruled in 1971 that Swiss banks must show U.S. tax officials their records of U.S. citi-zens suspected of tax fraud, a ruling that in large part negates a 1934 law that could seem to prohibit any bank disclosures. Se-crecy was further compromised when the drug trade started to become rampant throughout Europe.

Swiss industry has prospered since World War II, thanks to well-developed domestic capital markets, a relatively docile yet highly skilled labor force, and virtually unlimited access to the prosperous markets of Europe and North America. Precision engineering and timing devices have long been Swiss strengths; other important export industries include chemicals, pharmaceuticals, and heavy engineering. (The famed Swiss watch industry experienced a brief recession when it refused to comply with the trend of pro-ducing digital watches in the 1970s. How-ever, the fad faded, and the industry is fully back in business.)

Due to a limited domestic market, trade has played a particularly important role in Swiss industrial growth. The government has been aggressive at negotiating bilat-eral trade treaties and other agreements designed to open markets to Swiss exports. Switzerland was a founding member of the European Free Trade Association in the late 1950s, and, though not yet a mem-ber of the European Union, it has cultivated extensive commercial relations with EU member countries. Today, Switzerland ex-ports nearly 40 percent of its gross national product—most of it to the advanced indus-trialized economies of the European Union.

The most serious constraint on Swiss industrial development has been the coun-try's perennially limited supply of labor. In order to expand, Swiss manufacturers have either had to import foreign labor or locate more and more of their production facilities abroad. Since the late 1950s, the number of foreign "guest workers" in Swit-zerland (mostly from Southern Europe) has expanded rapidly. At the same time, Swiss industry has been in a good position

to pursue multinational strategies of direct foreign investment abroad. Swiss multina-tional corporate giants like Nestlé, Brown Boveri, Ciba-Geigy, and Hoffman-LaRoche now employ more than 75 percent of their workforces and sell between 65 and 90 per-cent of their products outside Switzerland.

Overalienization
The multinationalization of Swiss industry accelerated during the 1980s, after the government took steps to reduce the in-flow of foreign workers. Some of these measures were caused by public apprehen-sion concerning the phenomenon of *Uber-fremdung*—a German term that may be translated as "overalienization." Switzer-land is a small country, with a population of only about 7.2 million. In 1945, for-eigners made up only 5 percent of the resi-dent population; within a few decades, this proportion had climbed to 17 percent.

Taking into account that Switzerland has not just one homogeneous culture but, rather, several different cultures, it was feared that these proportionally large waves of foreigners would overwhelm, or at least seriously dilute, all that was typi-cally Swiss. The Swiss have thus availed themselves of the referendum as an im-portant decision-making instrument at the supracantonal level. (Here the Swiss Con-stitution differs from that of the United States, which allows only subnational units to organize referenda.)

The referenda that were prepared were aimed at obstructing the influx of aliens and at permitting the forcible removal of those whose work contracts had expired. Although the most far-reaching referenda were ultimately rejected, many Swiss have remained more than a little sensitive on this point. (The stormy protest movement, it should be noted, was most virulent in Switzerland's German-speaking areas.)

The Swiss government feared that the country might eventually be stigmatized as racist by the outside world, which would know little of the intrinsic merits of the case, and endeavored to regulate the foreign inflow in such a way that refer-enda might be preempted. During the eco-nomic depression of 1974–1976, tens of thousands of foreign workers had to leave for their homelands. In spite of these mas-sive departures, apprehension continued, and in 1981 another referendum was held, this time against a law that was to improve the legal status of the foreign worker. That too was defeated.

In spite of these upheavals, Switzerland has made the transition from an industrial to a postindustrial society. The rural areas have lost population; urbanization has pro-ceeded steadily. Only a little more than

Switzerland emerges as an "oath association" of three cantons A.D. **1291**	A treaty with France guarantees Swiss independence **1521**	The Peace of Kappel divides Switzerland into Roman Catholic and Protestant cantons **1531**	The Peace of Westfalia; Switzerland becomes officially independent from the Holy Roman Empire **1648**	Switzerland is absorbed by the French Empire; Napoleon decides to enlarge the Swiss territory **1799–1804**	A democratic national Constitution, endeavoring to counter centralization, gives major power to the cantons **1874**	Switzerland manages to remain neutral during two world wars **1914–1918; 1939–1945**	The first referendum dealing with the future of foreigners in Switzerland **1970**	Women are accorded the vote in national elections **1972**	East–West arms-control talks are based in Switzerland **1980s**

1990s

The Swiss reject the European Economic Area in a referendum	Scandal explodes over Swiss banks' ties to Nazi Germany	Allegations surface regarding labor camps for Jews in Switzerland during World War II

half a century ago, in 1941, the agricultural sector accounted for 21 percent of those in employment, but by 1970, that proportion had sunk to 8 percent. It is now under 3 percent. The number of persons employed in industry and services rose markedly, although some 200,000 jobs were lost in the recession years, predominantly in industry. The proportion of individuals employed in services started to exceed 50 percent (today that percentage is more than 66 percent), and Switzerland thus became a postindustrial society.

Currently only about 31 percent of the Swiss workforce are employed in industry; most people are engaged in services, including banking, finance, and marketing. The shift from industrialism to postindustrialism has been accelerated by the migration in recent years of more and more Swiss manufacturing into other countries as well as by the rapid growth of the country's financial sector.

INTERNATIONAL RELATIONS

Domestically, Switzerland could appear to be the very epitome of law and order. There are rarely protest meetings, demonstrations, rallies, or the like. Even during national elections, the country exudes a measure of placidity. It is possible that the country's noninvolvement in foreign affairs has contributed to what could seem apathy. Since World War II, Switzerland has continued to adhere strictly to the precepts of armed neutrality. All male Swiss citizens must perform a year of compulsory military service. Thereafter, each soldier becomes part of the country's large citizens' militia (or military reserve force) and participates in periodic refresher training exercises. In accordance with absolute political neutrality, the Swiss are committed to maintaining diplomatic and economic relations with all countries of the world, regardless of the type of political regime they have or the foreign policies they conduct. Thus, though clearly of a Western economic and political orienta-

tion, Switzerland has refused to participate in any regional or international organization that might require it to take sides in international disputes.

In spite of the fact that many specialized agencies of the United Nations have had their headquarters on Swiss soil, particularly in Geneva, the Swiss government, as has been mentioned, long refused to join the world organization, an attitude that contrasted sharply with the country's prominence in the League of Nations. Only after several referenda had been held on becoming a UN member did Switzerland finally join the organization, in the late 1980s. It has become a donor country (but not a member) of the International Monetary Fund and the World Bank. Switzerland has also started to become increasingly involved in European Union matters, albeit in a strictly nonpolitical manner.

Nonetheless, Swiss neutralism has not led to the country's disengagement from the international system. On the contrary, it has allowed the small nation to play an important mediator role in world politics. Switzerland hosts a number of international organizations, including several specialized agencies of the UN, the General Agreement on Tariffs and Trade, and others. It has also hosted numerous international conferences, most notably East–West arms control talks.

The Swiss diplomatic service also frequently offers its "good offices" to nations that are estranged from one another or simply lack diplomatic representation of their own in certain parts of the world. Thus, the image that Switzerland has increasingly projected has been one of prosperity, neutrality, and international nonpolitical involvement.

Switzerland has sometimes been a source of irritation to other European countries. In the mid-1980s, for example, a large pharmaceutical company spilled toxic waste into the Rhine River. The pollution killed thousands of fish, and West Germany and the Netherlands, which were grievously affected, embarked upon lengthy lawsuits,

which ultimately were settled out of court. Also, banking practices do not always incur approval, particularly if the customers happen to be unscrupulous dictators who have obviously enriched themselves through kleptocracy.

In the mid-1990s, it was revealed that billions of dollars in assets had never been returned by Swiss banks to Jewish Holocaust survivors and their families—an issue that has yet to be explored fully and resolved satisfactorily. As the scandal blossomed, other aspects of Switzerland's relationship with Nazi Germany were scrutinized on the world stage, and the country's once pristine reputation was further tarnished. In 1997, a British television documentary revealed that some of Switzerland's most famous ski resorts were the sites of forced-labor camps for Jewish refugees during World War II. Switzerland had always denied that any of the approximately 25,000 Jewish refugees who were permitted to enter the country during the war, along with other non-Swiss Jews, some of whom had lived in Switzerland for years, were subjected to forced labor. But the mounting body of evidence, supported by recently released official documents and backed by victims' statements, has swept away any lingering doubts. It is now known that a network of more than 100 work camps was established by an official decree on March 12, 1940. Those who were interned do not equate the Swiss labor camps with the Nazi concentration and death camps, but they do say that Jews were held, against their will, in harsh conditions.

DEVELOPMENT

Switzerland has made a rapid transition from an agricultural society to a postindustrial society. Its glowing worldwide reputation has been tarnished by revelations of its bank ties and other connections to Nazi Germany.

FREEDOM

In spite of the cultural differences within Swiss society, there is little overt discrimination. It has a very favorable human-rights rating.

HEALTH/WELFARE

Switzerland has high life expectancy and literacy rates, and its welfare system is sound.

ACHIEVEMENTS

Switzerland plays an inordinately prominent role in foreign affairs, often assisting in mediating efforts. It hosts numerous international organizations, conferences, meetings, and summit talks.

United Kingdom
(United Kingdom of Great Britain and Northern Ireland)

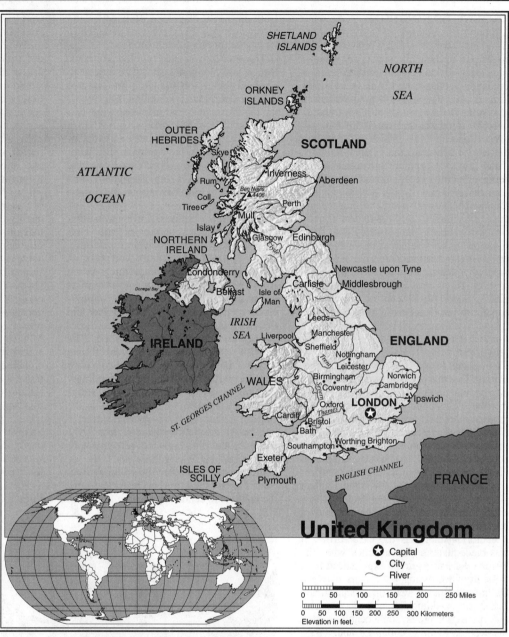

GEOGRAPHY

Area in Square Miles (Kilometers): 94,251 (244,111) (slightly smaller than Oregon)
Capital (Population): London (7,640,000)
Environmental Concerns: air and water pollution
Geographical Features: mostly rugged hills and low mountains; level to rolling plains in east and southeast
Climate: temperate

PEOPLE

Population
Total: 57,592,000
Annual Growth Rate: 0.24%
Rural/Urban Population Ratio: 9/89
Major Languages: English; Welsh; Scottish
Ethnic Makeup: 81.5% English; 9.6% Scottish; 2.4% Irish; 1.9% Welsh; 4.6% others
Religions: 76% Anglican; 14% Roman Catholic; 5.5% Presbyterian; 2.5% Methodist; 2% Jewish and others

Health
Life Expectancy at Birth: 75 years (male); 80 years (female)
Infant Mortality Rate (Ratio): 6.0/1,000
Average Caloric Intake: 132% of FAO minimum
Physicians Available (Ratio): 1/629

Education
Adult Literacy Rate: 99%
Compulsory (Ages): 5–16

COMMUNICATION
Telephones: 1 per 2 people
Daily Newspaper Circulation: 351 per 1,000 people
Televisions: 1 per 2.3 people

TRANSPORTATION
Highways in Miles (Kilometers): 233,299 (388,831)
Railroads in Miles (Kilometers): 10,537 (17,561)
Usable Airfields: 387
Motor Vehicles in Use: 27,900,000

GOVERNMENT
Type: constitutional monarchy
Independence Date: January 1, 1801 (the United Kingdom established)
Head of State/Government: Queen Elizabeth II; Prime Minister Tony Blair
Political Parties: Labour Party; Conservative and Unionist Party; Liberal Democrats; Welsh National Party; Scottish National Party; Ulster Unionist Party; Democratic Unionist Party; Social Democratic and Labour Party; Sinn Fein; Alliance Party
Suffrage: universal at 18

MILITARY
Military Expenditures (% of GDP): 3.1%
Current Disputes: Northern Ireland question; dispute with Spain over Gibraltar; other territorial disputes with Argentina, Mauritius, and Antarctica; Rockall continental shelf dispute

ECONOMY
Currency ($ U.S. Equivalent): 0.61 pound = $1
Per Capita Income/GDP: $20,400/$1.19 trillion
GDP Growth Rate: 2.4%
Inflation Rate: 2.6%
Unemployment Rate: 6.7%
Labor Force: 28,100,000
Natural Resources: coal; petroleum; natural gas; tin; limestone; iron ore; salt; clay; chalk; gypsum; lead; silica
Agriculture: wheat; barley; potatoes; vegetables; livestock; poultry; fish
Industry: machinery and transport equipment; metals; food processing; paper and paper products; textiles; chemicals; clothing; motor vehicles; tourism
Exports: $240.4 billion (primary partners EU countries and the United States)
Imports: $258.8 billion (primary partners EU countries and the United States)

THE UNITED KINGDOM

Although this country is variously called "England" (which in fact refers only to the larger part of the main island) or "Britain" and "Great Britain" (the combined area of England, Scotland, and Wales), today its official designation is "United Kingdom of Great Britain and Northern Ireland" (which includes that part of Ireland that was retained by the British). Nearby are the Isle of Man and the Channel Islands, which enjoy a separate territorial status, being governed by lieutenant-governors on behalf of the British sovereign. The Channel Islands are closer to France, and their inhabitants speak a dialect that is closer to French than to English. Their situation appears reminiscent of the days when England reigned supreme in parts of France, which lasted until the seventeenth century. The islands were the only area officially under British control that was occupied by the Germans during World War II.

HISTORY

Throughout its rich and eventful history, Britain has enjoyed the strategic advantage of being an island. The natural barrier that the seas around it afford constitutes a protection against invasions. However, the barrier has also generated a degree of insularity that has often led to blatant ethnocentric attitudes. A classic example of this is the headline in the British press reporting a dense fog all over the English Channel, noting "Continent Isolated."

It is interesting that the natural barrier has proved much more effective in the last 2 centuries than was the case earlier. It was inadequate in Roman times, when the Roman general Agricola experienced little difficulty in crossing the waters between Gallia (as France was then called) and Britain, thus adding England to a vast empire in A.D. 43. When, some centuries later, the Roman Empire collapsed and its armies withdrew from the island, northern Germanic tribes, known as the Jutes, Angles, and Saxons, embarked upon large-scale invasions.

Then it was the turn of yet another group, the Vikings, who not only periodically raided the coastal areas but also established settlements. Indeed, for some time a large part of England served as an extension of Viking bases in Scandinavia. In the ninth century, a tribute known as *Danegeld* had to be paid to these usurpers.

Finally, in 1066, William the Conqueror led the Norman Invasion. He too experienced no difficulty in crossing the English Channel, and he defeated King Harold in Hastings. However, this turned out to be the last successful invasion of Britain.

Both France's Napoleon Bonaparte and Germany's Adolf Hitler were frustrated in their attempts to subdue England.

The early invasions (by the Romans, Danes, and Normans) proved beneficial to England, with the blending of cultures proving enormously enriching. Shortly after the Norman Invasion, there were two cultures: that of the Anglo-Saxons (in a way the original inhabitants) and that of the new overlords, the Normans. The latter had by that time developed certain societal refinements, such as an aristocracy, and they tended to look down upon the rugged Anglo-Saxons.

After a few centuries, however, the distinction between conquerors and conquered faded and a new nation was born, which, in the Hundred Years' War, became quite powerful. This war, which lasted from 1337 until 1453 (thus longer than its name suggests), resulted from the complicated relationship between England and France, whose royal dynasties were closely related, if not intertwined. The English claim to the French throne sparked the hostilities. The war consisted in large part of fervent attempts, notably by King Henry V, to make English kings rule the kingdoms on both sides of the English Channel, a concept that came to be known as dual monarchy. Ironically, the war had the opposite effect, establishing two rival kingdoms that were in conflict with each other for prolonged periods. These conditions were to last until the eighteenth century, by which time both

countries had built large empires. The Hundred Years' War itself also provided a measure of irony: Although England came out triumphant, it lost sizable territories across the Channel. However, England would retain numerous holdings on the European continent until the seventeenth century. By then, the contours of the current nation-state had become visible.

Britain experienced religious persecution from time to time as well. Although one might have expected that the establishment of its own state church would result in religious independence, a climate of tolerance was absent. But the overall quality of life in England was superior to that of continental Europe. There can be little doubt that the English royalty greatly contributed to these superior conditions. In particular, the powerful Tudor Dynasty (1485–1603) introduced a distinct English civilization. During that period, England became successful in trade; it became prosperous as a result, and, immediately following the vanguard in explorations and discoveries (Portugal and Spain), it embarked upon expansion. Whereas continental Europe remained bogged down in religious warfare (caused by the Reformation and its aftermath), England was relatively peaceful, especially after the Spanish Armada had been defeated. Indeed, the Elizabethan Age (1558–1603) was a period in which a very rich culture, most notably in literature, flourished.

The seventeenth century witnessed political difficulties. The monarchy was set

(Photo courtesy Lisa Clyde)

Stonehenge is at the center of one of the richest prehistoric landscapes in the world. It is generally considered to have been a place of worship. Over the millennia, it has gone through three distinct stages of evolution, the first taking place around 3000 B.C., the second in roughly 2000 B.C., and the third in approximately 1500 B.C. Ongoing archaeological investigations continue to seek its meaning.

aside, and Britain experienced republican rule for a brief time. After the Restoration by Charles II in 1660 and the subsequent ouster of his brother, James II, in 1688, resulting from the so-called Glorious Revolution, a foreign king, William III of Orange, was invited to sit on the British throne. This episode weakened the power of the monarchy and, conversely, strengthened the sovereignty of the British Parliament, which became even stronger in the eighteenth century. A notable event at the end of that century was the secession of the American colonies.

However, in 1815, England defeated Napoleon, and the entire nineteenth century may be called "the century of Britain." During this period, the ascendance of the British Empire was truly spectacular. Even before the scramble among various European countries for territories in Africa, the extensive British possessions were referred to as an empire "where the sun never sets." Britain ruled the waves, commerce and trade prospered, and the Pax Britannica was a global concept. Although the French language may have retained its supremacy as a diplomatic language, England was indisputably the most powerful nation in the world from the Congress of Vienna in 1815 until World War I. That era has been called "a century of peace." It may not have been peaceful all over Europe, but at least there was no conflict engulfing numerous nations in the period from 1815 to 1914. Apparently the Vienna Congress had succeeded in establishing a balance of power, and Britain had become the main balancer. World War I (1914–1918) is often termed "the Great War," and once it ended, another nation, which for a century had expanded under the aegis of its self-proclaimed Manifest Destiny, arose as a major world power: the United States of America.

The period between the two world wars witnessed a steady diminution of British power, and the liquidation of the British Empire after World War II further weakened the United Kingdom. As if to offset this trend, Great Britain had started to move into the postindustrial era.

THE TWO MAINSTREAMS OF DEMOCRACY

The political cultures of the United States and the United Kingdom have a great deal in common. In spite of the American Revolutionary War, it is possible to speak of a sizable heritage, in that values, visions, perspectives, and other cultural facets of the colonial power were inherited by the successor government. After all, there were no substantial linguistic or ethnic differences between the United States

and Great Britain. However, whereas the United States became the first country to possess a modern constitution, thereby putting itself in the vanguard of democratic ideology, its British counterpart is not only considerably older but in large part unwritten. The British Constitution cannot be traced back to an assembly of historic proportions such as the Constitutional Convention in Philadelphia. Instead, it consists of customs, traditions, and conventions that have evolved over the centuries. But it is not entirely unwritten either: Important laws such as the Magna Carta, the Habeas Corpus Act, various reform bills, and other major pieces of legislation have in the course of time gained constitutional validity.

If this amounts to a difference in format, there are also differences in substance between the two Constitutions. Thus, in the United Kingdom, the judiciary lacks judicial review, which has been a principle of constitutional validity in the United States since the early nineteenth century. In Britain, parliamentary sovereignty prevails, to the point that the judiciary cannot declare legislation unconstitutional; in other words, an act of Parliament can be overturned only by a subsequent act of Parliament.

The principal difference between the presidential and the parliamentary systems into which the two mainstreams of democracy have eventually materialized is that the presidential system has an explicit separation of powers: The branches of government are independent of one another. Such a separation may be somewhat mitigated by the typically American system of checks and balances, but it still contrasts with the fusion of the executive and legislative branches of government, which has in effect been the hallmark of the British system of governance.

In the United Kingdom, the executive branch of government is seated in the House of Commons. In fact, the British prime minister and his or her cabinet ministers *are* members of Parliament and are elected as such. At the same time, the highest judicial organ is part of the House of Lords. The Law Lords, who constitute a committee in Britain's upper chamber, exercise functions similar to those of the U.S. Supreme Court.

An additional contrast between the presidential and parliamentary systems involves the tenure system. In the United States, all branches of government have a fixed tenure (e.g., the presidency, 4 years; the Senate, 6 years; the House of Representatives, 2 years). In the British parliamentary system, there is no fixed tenure. It is obviously absent in the House of Lords, since that chamber depends on he-

reditary succession. In the House of Commons, the rule prevails (a rule that as a matter of course also applies to the executive) that an election should take place within 5 years after the last election. But both the government and the opposition can call an election at any time either of them deems fit. The year 1974, for example, was marked by two national elections. Subsequently, there were no elections for 5 years; and it was then, in 1979, that the leader of the Conservative Party, Margaret Thatcher, submitted a vote of no-confidence. This forced an election that ousted the Labour government from power and made Thatcher prime minister.

The governments of the United States and the United Kingdom also differ as far as the executive structure is concerned. Great Britain has a dual executive, whereas the United States has a single chief executive, the president (the vice president does not count, since the U.S. Constitution does not assign him or her any statutory responsibilities). In the United Kingdom, the post of the chief of state is taken by the monarch, who in effect has no formal powers and who serves the country as a symbol. The monarch is, of course, not elected, but succeeds to the throne on the basis of heredity. He or she must be "above" politics and in fact may not make any political utterances in public. (The Speech from the Throne, comparable to the U.S. State of the Union or State of the World address, does not constitute a violation of that principle, since it is prepared by the prime minister and his or her cabinet. The monarch, in effect, acts only as a mouthpiece of the government.)

The prime minister is the most powerful person in the British system. Some political analysts, when comparing the U.S. president and the British prime minister, believe the prime minister to be more powerful in his or her context. Indeed, some people have suggested substituting the term "prime ministerial system" for the customary phrase "parliamentary system" or "parliamentary-cabinet system."

The British Parliament offers one more anomaly: It is bicameral only in a strictly formal sense. The House of Lords has lost so much of its power and influence that it no longer plays a role of any significance in British politics. It has, in effect, become a debating club. The House of Commons is where the action is; it is the hub of British politics.

HURDLES AND HIGHLIGHTS

British trends and tendencies have nearly always been marked by extreme gradualism (that is, approaching a desired end in gradual stages). A strong resistance to

NORTHERN IRELAND: AN INTEGRAL PART OF THE UNITED KINGDOM OF GREAT BRITAIN AND NORTHERN IRELAND

"Home rule is Rome rule." "A Protestant Parliament for a Protestant people." "Ulster will fight; Ulster will be right." Each of these phrases portrays the intensity of feelings of the Protestant community in Northern Ireland regarding the creation of an Irish state, with its government in Dublin, in the period 1870–1920. These same slogans have been heard in modern times, in response to both the terrorist tactics of the Irish Republican Army (IRA) and the decidedly more peaceful meetings between the prime ministers of the Irish Republic and Britain.

The history of this rather small region (less than 17 percent of the island from which it has been carved) has not differed markedly from that of the remainder of the island—that is, the Republic of Ireland, or Eire. Since there was no boundary or other type of demarcation, the vicissitudes of the two parts were very similar, at least until an accident of history caused Northern Ireland to remain an extension of Britain.

In the distant past, this British foothold was—like the entire island, other British isles, and various areas on the continent—inhabited by Celts, whose presence in Western Europe has generated a great deal of speculation. Their religion, which is identified as Druidism, seems to have included human sacrifice. However, in A.D. 432, Patrick, who subsequently became the patron saint of Ireland, arrived and embarked upon the conversion of Celts to Christianity, a labor of love that was completed by his successors.

Danish invasions took place a few centuries later. While these raids produced few permanent settlers (as they had in England, where Danelaw became the system of government), the eastern part of the island continued to be colonized from south Wales, an Anglo–Norman stronghold.

It being closer to the European continent, England was much more subject to population waves than was Ireland, both before and after the year 1066 (the time of the Norman Invasion). Furthermore, the differences between the two regions became more pronounced after the Reformation made itself felt throughout Europe. In England, the Reformation met with a degree of success even before King Henry VIII created the Church of England, a Protestant denomination whose creed became the official state religion. However, Ireland's relative isolation caused it to remain unaffected by the Reformation; it remained almost universally Roman Catholic. By that time, the island had come under English domination, but the English overlordship was fairly tolerant with regard to differences in religion.

But early in the seventeenth century, a large plantation, consisting of nine counties in the north jointly called Ulster, was opened to Presbyterian Scots and other Protestant groups in northern England. Most of these people had been eking out a living in the generally barren parts of northern England and northeastern Ireland, so it appeared to grant them new opportunities. However, as time went on, the Ulster plantation gradually became an enclave and its society a distinct minority. In religious respect, the Ulster settlers were surrounded by Roman Catholics. This may have caused them to be on the defensive, to adopt what has been called a "fragment mentality"—a stridency that derives from being vastly outnumbered.

As might be expected, relations between the Protestants and the Roman Catholics were already poor during the time when the greater part of Western Europe was embroiled in religious warfare. But since the Protestants had been imported and were in effect part of the occupation, they remained under the protection of the British.

As if religious segregation was not enough of an irritant, class distinctions emerged, with the Protestants being better off on the occupational and social scales. They made no attempts to assimilate or to integrate, and when, in the nineteenth century, relations between the British and the Irish steadily deteriorated, the "Unionists" (a label referring to their union with Britain) remained staunchly pro-British. The Anglo–Irish War (1919–1921) tested the loyalty of the Ulster plantation. At no point did the Unionists involve themselves with the revolutionary action that the Irish had initiated. Nevertheless, they started to experience considerable apprehension lest Britain should abandon them. To guard against that eventuality, they established their own Constitution and made elaborate plans for a government of their own, a government that would be protected by loyal military forces. If necessary, Ireland would also have revolted against British constitutional authority in order to safeguard its right to self-determination.

BRITAIN GUARANTEES THE UNION

In the face of so much loyalty to the imperial cause, it would have been difficult for Britain to ignore the Northern Irish claims. The pressures exerted by the mobilized Unionists translated into the Government of Ireland Act, which explicitly excluded the northeastern part of the island from the new political entity, the Irish Free State. Naturally, now that the self-determination of the Irish was at hand, borders needed to be drawn.

Of Ulster's nine counties, three were heavily populated by Roman Catholics; these three were allocated to the new state. Their elimination caused the remaining six counties to tilt very heavily to Protestantism. Thus, the enclave that was left to the Unionists may have had a smaller area, but it was at least cohesive in religion.

From that point on, Britain affirmed its guarantees to Northern Ireland with every step that the Irish Free State (subsequently, Eire) took to dissociate itself further from Britain and the Commonwealth. When in 1939 Ireland declared that it would remain neutral in World War II, the British immediately mobilized Northern Ireland. British military strategists considered it highly fortunate that part of the island to the west of Britain was still in British hands: It shortened the risky route of the ships carrying supplies from the United States to the United Kingdom.

When Ireland decided to leave the British Commonwealth after the war, the British Parliament passed the Ireland Act of 1949, which guaranteed that Northern Ireland was to remain part of the United Kingdom unless its own Parliament voted otherwise. That Parliament was dissolved in 1972, and the successive assemblies that followed proved so ineffective that they had to be suspended. Since it would be difficult to rely on a parliamentary vote in these circumstances, the British government decreed that the status of Northern Ireland could be changed only through a popular referendum.

Referenda being fairly alien to British politics, it was an unusual suggestion. But it might well work, since it is seemed obvious that the Protestant majority would not vote itself out of its union with the United Kingdom.

EXERCISES IN STALEMATE

For a considerable period, the United Kingdom practiced "salutary neglect" in Northern Ireland—it allowed Northern Irish institutions to administer the area. In due time, however, it became clear that the Unionist government harbored inherent biases against the Catholics in Northern Ireland and that tensions and clashes between the Protestants and the Roman Catholics were more often than not provoked by the former. Also, measures that the Northern Irish government took were often directed against the Roman Catholic minority. Britain thus decided to dissolve the Parliament in Belfast (in which the Roman Catholics had disproportionately little representation) and to terminate salutary neglect. Subsequently, Northern Ireland was directly ruled. Local government was largely left alone.

Law and order became precarious, as the security forces, largely identified with the Protestant government, were unable to maintain civil order. Therefore, the United Kingdom stationed several thousand British troops in Northern Ireland beginning in 1969, the year in which massive sectarian violence erupted. A large part of this violence was aimed at Catholic civil-rights activists.

At first the Catholic community welcomed the British troops, naïvely assuming them to be neutral, or at least more objective, in their approach than the Royal Ulster Constabulary (the only armed police force in the United Kingdom) and the auxiliary part-time Special Force (a vigilante organization established by the Protestants). But it did not take long for the Catholic community to conclude that the British troops had been dispatched to restore and maintain law and order—that is, the law and order of the Union. While essentially protecting the status quo of the Northern Irish territory, these troops were, as a matter of course, more supportive of British and Northern Irish interests. The introduction of British Army units amounted to an escalation, which was matched by the re-activation of the Irish Republic Army (IRA), a paramilitary organization that had been semidormant for nearly 15 years. The early 1970s thus witnessed a restoration of the balance of power.

The IRA initially merely protected Catholic areas from attacks by armed Protestants before British troops could respond. However, it soon split into two factions: A Socialist faction, basically ideological and almost nonviolent, and a Provisional faction, dedicated to the use of total force to "rid the island of the British." But since the British Army was numerically and technically superior, "total force" implied terrorism. Other similarly militant groups subsequently came into being on both sides, often extending terrorist activities into Eire and England.

PEACE INITIATIVES

Warlike conditions ("The Troubles") have prevailed in Northern Ireland since the late 1960s. Some initiatives seem to bear fruit, such as the so-called Peace Lines, which crisscross working-class Belfast, separating the Protestants from the Catholics and creating a sectarian map that has no relation to the city as it appears in official atlases.

The New Ireland Forum was established in 1983. Participation was open to all democratic parties that rejected violence and that had members elected or appointed to the Irish Parliament or the resurrected Northern Ireland Assembly. Its first session was held in Dublin in 1983. The Forum published various reports, with one central operational conclusion: "The validity of both the Nationalist and Unionist identities in Ireland and the democratic rights of every citizen of this island must be accepted; both of these identities must have equally satisfactory, secure and durable, political, administrative and symbolic expression and protection."

At the highest level, an Anglo–Irish Agreement was established after long and painstaking negotiations between the governments of the United Kingdom and Eire. Here a new element was added: an Intergovernmental Conference, meant to enable the Irish government to express views and put forward proposals on various stated aspects of Northern Ireland affairs. The Conference intended to make determined efforts to resolve any differences between the two governments. It also hoped to improve cooperation in ending terrorism. Yet the validity of these and other peace initiatives are still in question. The fighting in Northern Ireland continues, and the IRA has remained very active. There have been repeated bomb attacks in London. In March 1991, terrorists succeeded in firing three mortar rounds at the very heart of the British government, 10 Downing Street, where the prime minister and his cabinet were discussing the Persian Gulf War.

In 1993, the IRA called a cease-fire in order to begin peace talks concerning the rule of Northern Ireland; Sinn Féin, an influential Northern Irish political party, was to be included in these talks. February 1995 witnessed the issue of a "Framework Document," which proposed a basis for negotiations. Predictably, it met with mixed reactions. On February 9, 1996, the IRA, out of frustration because it was not included in the peace talks, called an end to the cease-fire by bombing the Canary Wharf in London. In response, both the Nationalists and the Loyalists in Northern Ireland marched onto the streets to show their support for a resumption of the peace process.

At the end of February, the governments accounted that all-party talks would begin in June and be open to all parties disavowing violence. In May 1996, elections were held to determine participation in the talks. Sinn Fein won nearly 16 percent of the vote, but the party was turned away from the negotiations when they began on June 10 because of IRA's continued campaign of violence.

Through early 1997, the negotiations made little progress. The May 1997 election of Tony Blair and the Labour Party government, however, re-energized the process and led to increasing pressure on the IRA to restore the cease-fire. After some negotiation, the IRA restored its cease-fire in July 1997, and Sinn Fein was admitted to the talks process in September 1997.

In a final marathon push in April 1998, which included the personal intervention of President Clinton, all parties, on April 10, signed an agreement. The "Good Friday Agreement" (April 10 was Good Friday) was put to a vote, and strong majorities in Northern Ireland and Ireland approved it in simultaneous referenda on May 22. The agreement provided for a 108-member Northern Ireland elected Assembly, to be overseen by a 12-minister Executive Committee in which Unionists and Nationalists would share responsibility for governing. The agreement would institutionalize cross-border cooperation with Ireland and would create mechanisms to guarantee the rights of all.

Finally, it seemed that there would be a true, sustained peace. Two major players, David Trimble (leader of the Ulster Unionists) and John Hume (the Catholic Nationalist leader), were even awarded the 1998 Nobel Peace Prize for their part in the peace process. (This was the second Nobel Peace Prize offered in the Northern Ireland question. The first, in 1976, was awarded to two Northern Irish women—Mairead Corrigan and Betty Williams—who led the Northern Ireland peace movement.)

Bitter disillusionment set in beginning in August 1998, however, when the self-styled "Real IRA," a breakaway group opposed to the Good Friday Agreement, set off a blast in Omagh, Northern Ireland, in a crowded market, killing 28 and injuring 220. It was the worst single terrorist incident in Northern Ireland's history.

For a time it seemed that the terrible event would actually strengthen the peace process, as all of Ireland—North and South, Nationalist and Unionist, Irish Republican and Ulster Loyalist—was appalled. But additional scattered terrorist incidents since then have underscored a sure breakdown in the peace process. By March 1999, the blockage was acknowledged when the deadline for devolution of power to a new power-sharing administration in Northern Ireland, originally set for March 10, was formally postponed.

change—no doubt enhanced by British insularity, which withstood outside influences—has always predominated.

British society is often qualified as deferential, since class distinctions are fairly large and conspicuous. It is interesting that class *distinctions* prevail as opposed to class *conflict*. Karl Marx, who lived in London for many years, frequently despaired of the possibility that the British proletariat would ever allow itself to be mobilized into a revolution.

However that may be, Britain has, in spite of its penchant for gradualism, often been in the forefront of spiritual movements and in the vanguard of material innovations. One of these concerns the Industrial Revolution, beginning in the early nineteenth century. It may be said that that era constituted the watershed between the traditional, predominantly rural life and the fast pace of an industrialized, technological society. Britain has never been self-sufficient in agriculture. This shortage in agricultural production was offset by an unparalleled commerce and trade in early times and, subsequently, by the sale of new industrial products.

Almost a century after the start of the Industrial Revolution, the United Kingdom again had to adapt to bewildering changes, this time brought about by decolonization. During World War II, but before the United States became a participant in that conflict, U.S. president Franklin D. Roosevelt and British prime minister Winston Churchill jointly issued the Atlantic Charter. This document was a series of highly ambiguous statements concerning self-determination, which, according to Churchill, referred to the victims of recent Nazi aggression: There could be no doubt that the war was also fought to help them to regain self-deter-

mination. However, Roosevelt clarified that it referred to colonies as well—in fact, to all non-self-governing territories. The positions of the two leaders were antithetical, and Churchill once declared that he had not become His Majesty's prime minister to preside over the liquidation of his empire. But that liquidation came inexorably after the war and, contrary to British trends, it did not proceed gradually. Yet, even today, Great Britain still has a number of colonies, including Bermuda, Gibraltar, the Falkland Islands, and some less important territories. Hong Kong reverted to China in 1997.

THE COMMONWEALTH

Despite the avalanche of change in imperial matters, the British people have been able to cope and compromise. In part, this flexibility may have been aided by the "substitute" that British statesmen provided for the British Empire: the Commonwealth of Nations. The Commonwealth is a large and global organization, formally headed by the British sovereign. But this hierarchical apex has little significance. The British monarch has, after all, little or no power in the domestic context, and there is no political supremacy on the part of the United Kingdom either. The Commonwealth thus concentrates on the commercial and trading advantages that accrue to its members. Membership is entirely voluntary and usually is offered as soon as a colony gains its independence. Very few countries have refused to join. One such exception is Burma (currently called Myanmar), which in 1948 feared that its nonalignment policy would be compromised by joining an organization sponsored and led by its former imperial overlord. And South Africa was thrown out as a result of its apartheid and other

racist policies; it was allowed to return to the fold when Nelson Mandela came to power. Fiji, a small group of islands in the Pacific, was expelled in 1987 because the Fijians themselves (who ironically constituted a minority) usurped power after staging a coup.

It is interesting to note that, after World War II, a number of members of the Commonwealth demonstrated a desire to become republics within the organization. Before the war, the colonies of settlement (such as Canada, Australia, and New Zealand) had attained a larger degree of autonomy within the British Empire/Commonwealth. But they were so attached to Britain that they refused to surrender the "God, King, and country" ideal that had characterized their relationship in the past. (Naturally, such sentiments of loyalty were absent in the colonies that had suffered exploitation.)

But these colonies, when the question of whether they wanted to join the British Commonwealth was raised on the eve of their independence, almost universally agreed to continue the link with Great Britain. However, they added that they nevertheless wanted to become republics. Since the British sovereign is the head of the Commonwealth, this was an unusual request, but Britain showed itself to be remarkably flexible in not resisting such an anomalous structure. In part, that flexibility may also have been promoted by the absence of political affinity between the United Kingdom and some of its former colonies: Britain's traditional political model (the so-called Westminster model) has never taken root in those countries that became independent after World War II. It is true that there are some superficial resemblances in parliamentary procedure, but the ex-colonies have never been able to commit themselves fully to democratic ideals.

The Commonwealth meets on an annual basis, rotating the venue among the capitals of members. A permanent secretariat has been established in London (which is logical, since the British sovereign is, after all, its ex officio head). Commonwealth matters assume an important place in British policy making. They are usually dealt with at the cabinet level and are considered closely related to foreign affairs. Indeed, departmentally they have been assigned to the minister of foreign affairs, whose full title is "Secretary of State for Foreign and Commonwealth Affairs and Minister of Overseas Development."

THE ECONOMY

One hurdle that Great Britain has always faced, since it started to mature into a modern nation-state, is the extreme vulnerability of its economy, resulting from its lack of self-sufficiency in food production. Enemies have naturally attempted to capitalize on this weakness, trying to starve the British by cutting off their supplies.

Napoleon's so-called Continental System, which outlawed all trade between Britain and the European mainland, represented such an attempt. And after the fall of France, in 1940, Adolf Hitler not only tried to bomb England into submission— he also cut the supply lines on which the United Kingdom depended. A great many supply ships were sunk on their way to Britain by Germany's U-boats.

Modern wars, therefore, have been extraordinarily hard on the United Kingdom, even if it managed to win them. The two world wars were devastating to the country; both struggles consumed so much of Britain's strength that it finally ceased to be a major world power.

Ironically, the powers vanquished in World War II, Japan and Germany, managed to rebuild their economies in a relatively short period of time, whereas the European Recovery Plan, better known as the Marshall Plan, launched by the United States, proved an inadequate remedy for the exhausted British economy. Admittedly, the United Kingdom was very heavily bombed during the war and its capital equipment was, in many cases, damaged beyond repair. But Germany and Japan suffered massive destruction, too. The question thus remains: Why couldn't Britain recover?

Some analysts have suggested that the loss of empire should rank high among the factors that contributed to Britain's decline. This argument, however, is not very convincing, since, in a few cases, former

(Photo courtesy Lisa Clyde)

About 80 miles southwest of London is the town of Salisbury. A dominant presence in the history of the town and in its skyline is the Cathedral of St. Mary, construction of which began in 1220 and ended in 1258. Its spire is 404 feet tall, the highest church spire in England.

colonial powers (such as the Netherlands and Portugal) were able to improve their economies after the ties with colonies had been severed.

Other analysts conclude that the extensive welfare program that Britain embarked on shortly after World War II was its undoing. Was this not a luxury that it could ill afford? But again, this theory is weak: Welfare systems had become a general trend among industrialized democracies in Western Europe. The Scandinavian countries, Ireland, and other nations at that time viewed welfarism as a top priority, but none of them was as adversely affected as the United Kingdom.

The rapid deterioration of the British economy became a matter of international record when the British government requested that the United States take over certain responsibilities in the eastern Mediterranean. Washington was prepared to do so (a measure that was to lead to the Truman Doctrine). Nevertheless, the

British economy remained dismal throughout the 1950s and sank to an even lower level in the 1960s.

THE EUROPEAN UNION

Before it finally joined the European Union in 1973, the United Kingdom's application for admission had been rejected twice. French president Charles de Gaulle was in the vanguard of the opposition to British membership during the 1960s. Most analysts believed that de Gaulle's negative attitude vis-à-vis the United Kingdom stemmed from the strong bias that he had developed against the Anglo–American coalition during the war years. However, the French president officially based his rejection of the British application on the backwardness of Britain's industrial capacity. In his view, the United Kingdom lagged behind "Little Europe," as the European Union was nicknamed in those days. According to de Gaulle, the capital equipment that was to be part of the British contribution to the organization was obsolete. Plants that had been bombed during the war had not been properly repaired or replaced. In his mind, there could be no doubt that, if admitted, the United Kingdom would drag the EU to lower levels of competitiveness and output.

A few years after de Gaulle left the scene, the British admission was renegotiated. This time, the application met with success. The United Kingdom was admitted in 1973, along with Ireland and Denmark. For the British, this was a historic moment—it was, in fact, the first time that the country in a sense became an integral part of Europe.

Winston Churchill had many years earlier explained British affiliations in terms of circles. The first circle, the one closest to the United Kingdom, constituted its imperial legacy, the Commonwealth, at that time dominated by former settlement colonies such as Canada, Australia, New Zealand, and South Africa, whose affinity to "King and country" was unquestionable. The second circle had reference to the strong bonds with the United States. These ties had been strengthened as a result of a common culture as well as a common front in wartime. Their alliance related to heritage and morality rather than to explicit treaties. The third, and outer, circle referred to Europe, of which the United Kingdom had always been a part, in a strictly geographical sense. The country had always interfered in European politics through balances of power, but it had never participated in a joint endeavor. Many Britons realized that, whatever the bonds with the United States would be,

the Commonwealth had lost out against the European Union. Nevertheless, a belated referendum (held in 1975, 2 years after the British admission became official) indicated that a majority of Britons favored the step.

However, the integration of the British economy into the EU did not stem the negative trends. Inflation and unemployment were extraordinarily high in comparison to those of its fellow members. Throughout the 1970s, the United Kingdom was often called the "sick man" in the European Union.

THE THATCHER ERA

After World War II, the two major British parties—the Conservative Party and the Labour Party—alternated in power without offering significant changes in their economic policies. True, there was a degree of discontinuity, in that a Conservative administration might denationalize, or privatize, large industries that had been nationalized by Labour governments. But the welfare system was considered sacrosanct. No Conservative administration would tamper with it, for fear of incurring public indignation.

In 1979, the Conservative Party assumed office, and the Thatcher era started. Margaret Thatcher was the first British postwar prime minister to introduce major changes in the economy. Her government made cuts in the costly National Health Assistance System and in other welfare projects, in an attempt to come to grips with the wages and prices spiral.

To that end, Thatcher had to tackle the trade unions, whose influence in economic matters had often been very decisive, yet at times dysfunctional. The methods that Prime Minister Thatcher used in the realm of trade-union reform reduced union influence in the economy to a minimum. She also proved highly innovative when it came to coining names for controversial concepts that aimed to boost the economy, such as "People's Capitalism" and the "enterprise revolution" (an economic shake-up that was to generate an "enterprise culture"). A relatively strict monetary policy and freedom from exchange-rate controls were introduced. Finally, Thatcher aimed for lower taxation rates. There was thus a definite departure from the past, which was marked by what is known as the Social Democratic/Keynesian consensus. One of her chief goals was to make the middle class large and confident again. The term "Thatcher revolution" is often used in this context. In some ways, Thatcher's revolutionary policies ran parallel to Reaganomics, another set of controversial

policies that was initiated on the other side of the Atlantic during the same period.

In her attempts to get the economy on its feet again, the British prime minister was aided by three factors. First, during the early part of her administration, North Sea oil exploitation started to pay off. Not only did the United Kingdom become self-sufficient in oil (a fact that naturally translated into savings), but there was enough surplus to sell to other countries, thus generating revenues. Second, as in many other countries in the West, the public mood experienced a distinct shift to the right; socialism and welfarism had oversold themselves. What emerged, possibly as a result of welfare abuses, was what some analysts identified as "compassion fatigue." Finally, the Conservative Party had little to fear from the opposition. The British Labour Party, traditionally factionalized, had become more fragmented than ever, as a result of ultra-leftist penetrations.

Thatcher's economic policies met with some success. Inflation and unemployment rates slowed down and appeared to stabilize, and exports went up, in spite of the strengthening of the British currency. Also, the exploitation of oil fields proved a windfall that was only partly offset by the worldwide oil glut. By 1986, the United Kingdom was no longer the "sick man" in the European Union. In 1988, however, the economy became a victim of its recovery, since its strong growth had led to renewed inflation and record trade deficits (resulting from consumer demand).

The prime minister also fought hard in the EU, believing her country to be shortchanged from time to time. She insisted that the United Kingdom should get as much out of the European Union as it put in; she occasionally threatened to withdraw Great Britain's membership. These threats were conceivably part of a hard bargain by the "Iron Lady," who would have realized that the British withdrawal would harm Britain more than the Union. However, the membership issue was still very much alive in the United Kingdom even a decade after the referendum. Indeed, the Labour Party had indicated that it favored withdrawal and that it would effect a cancellation of British membership as soon as it would come to power.

Margaret Thatcher possessed a great deal of political acumen, if not cunning. She had become prime minister in 1979 as the result of a successful no-confidence motion. Elections would normally have been due in 1984. However, the decisive victory of the British forces in the Falkland Islands crisis added greatly to her popularity. (In 1982, Argentina had suddenly taken this group of British islands off its coast; Thatcher's immediate response was to send an expeditionary force, which reconquered the islands in a matter of weeks). Thatcher thus decided to advance the parliamentary elections by a full year, and in June 1983, she increased her party's majority in the House of Commons. The next elections witnessed the same procedure—they were held not in 1988 but a full year earlier, the prime minister's reasoning being that the economy had favorably responded to a series of government measures.

Again Thatcher did very well. But, by the same token, it soon became apparent that she had reached the apogee of her popularity. Her rating in public-opinion polls started to decline, first gradually, and then in a somewhat precipitous fashion. Some observers believe that the so-called community charge, popularly known as the poll tax, ultimately proved her undoing. For Thatcher, this type of government revenue was integral to her philosophy. But it was clear that it enhanced inequality in an already highly deferential society. If the community charge was a matter of substance, her style too had become increasingly irritating; a large part of the public had become tired of the self-congratulatory attitudes and the sanctimonious tone that Thatcher adopted when discussing her causes. Her European policies, and particularly the negative views she projected of an eventual political union, had started to cause concern. She reiterated her belief that the European Union promoted socialism in an insidious manner. She wanted no part of the direction in which the Union was heading; indeed, even if monetary unification would result in a single European currency, Great Britain would lose part of its sovereignty, if only because it would no longer be completely free to put its own budget together. Still, amazingly, in spite of all her criticism of the monetary measures within the "ever closer union," Margaret Thatcher, on October 4, 1990—that is, shortly before her loss of power—did allow Britain to enter the EU's Exchange Rate Mechanism. But this U-turn had come too late.

When the end came, it was not the opposition that forced Thatcher to step down, but her own party. The only face-saving gesture that the Conservative Party was prepared to make in the fateful days of November 1990 was that her successor would be a transitional figure, and not someone whose policies would contrast with hers. John Major seemed to fit that description to a nicety.

Margaret Thatcher will occupy a unique place in the pantheon of British prime ministers. Without irony, one must note that, her Euro-phobia notwithstanding, her prime ministership witnessed the completion of the basic work on the Chunnel, the tunnel under the English Channel that connects Great Britain with continental Europe.

POLITICAL PARTIES

A party system is usually regarded as a two-party system if the two largest parties secure 75 to 80 percent of the total vote. The British party system consequently has always been regarded as a two-party system, since its two largest parties (first the Conservatives and the Liberals; and after the turn of the century, the Conservatives and Labour) traditionally received the qualified majority vote. However, in 1981, the new Social Democratic Party emerged as an offshoot of the Labour Party. It was the first new major party in Great Britain in 80 years. Although its manifesto differed considerably from that of the Liberal Party, an agreement was made that it would run on the same ticket. The coalition, intended only as an electoral device, was named the Alliance. The Alliance, however, evaporated as soon as an election was over; that is, in the House of Commons, one would find only SDP members and Liberal members. The Alliance worked to the advantage of these two small parties, which jointly received more than a quarter of the total vote in 1983. The party disbanded in the late 1980s.

The British Labour Party has very close ties with the various trade unions, in particular the Trade Union Congress (TUC), the British equivalent of the American AFL-CIO. During the Industrial Revolution, the trade unions were the only organizations to counter capitalistic excesses. But the unions acted from the outside and lacked direct influence in Parliament and its proceedings. After a time, labor believed that it should also be represented by a political party that participated in elections and competed for seats in Parliament. Thus the British Labour Party was born, and it made rapid strides in parliamentary politics, increasing its voting totals at the expense of the Liberal Party.

THE ELECTORAL SYSTEM

The British electoral system, although attempting to reflect democracy, has through the centuries included certain anomalies. Universal suffrage has come only gradually (which, of course, is also the case in other democratic countries). Some reform acts in the nineteenth century greatly extended the electorate. Sir Walter Bagehot, the famous author and commentator on the English Constitution, called this process "the most silent of revolutions." Women over age 30 were allowed to vote in 1918, and in 1928, women over age 21 won suffrage.

In addition, the United Kingdom became known for its plural vote, meaning that one person could have more than one vote. University graduates, for example, could have an additional ballot at their alma mater. Businesspeople could vote on behalf of their businesses. Thus, some persons were able to avail themselves of three or four votes. Only as late as 1948 was the principle of "one man, one vote" fully adopted.

A discussion of electoral anomalies would not be complete without mention of the so-called rotten boroughs, which existed in the past. No census was taken for the purpose of elections in earlier years, and consequently the boundaries of electoral districts were never redrawn. As a result of mobility and other factors, it could happen that a member of Parliament represented a very small number of persons. Interestingly, in this modern age, the British have become very generous with respect to voting rights and even granted them to de jure foreigners. Not only may citizens of Commonwealth nations who happen to reside in Britain (Indians, Nigerians, Malaysians, Ghanaians, and others) vote in British elections, but this right is also accorded to citizens of the Republic of Ireland who live in the United Kingdom. (In 1984, Ireland reciprocated, granting the right to vote in Irish elections to British citizens residing in Ireland.)

One of the most controversial issues surrounding British elections is the method according to which votes translate into parliamentary seats (one political wag speaks of a system of "*dis*proportional representation"). To win an election to Parliament, a candidate need not gain an absolute majority of the votes. The system, based on the "first-past-the-post" concept, grants victory to the candidate who secures a plurality of votes (more votes than any other candidate, but not necessarily a majority). This electoral system has made possible incredible discrepancies and distortions. A party may achieve the largest number of votes and still end up with fewer seats than its rivals. (This happened, for instance, in 1951, when the Labour Party secured 235 seats for its 13,948,605 votes, whereas the Conservative Party obtained 321 seats for its 13,717,538 votes.) While either of the bigger parties may on occasion benefit from the first-past-the-post rule, it inevitably operates to the disadvantage of the smaller parties. In 1983, the Alliance received

The Norman Invasion; Battle of Hastings A.D. 1066	The Magna Carta; noblemen wring concessions from King John 1215	The Hundred Years' War 1337–1453	The Spanish Armada is defeated; supremacy over the known world shifts from Spain to England 1588	Civil war; establishment of a republic 1642–1649	The Bill of Rights 1689	Loss of the American colonies 1776	Britain's role in the defeat of Napoleon strengthens its position as a world power 1815	Extensions of the franchise 1832, 1867	The Anglo–Boer War in South Africa 1899–1902

more than a quarter of the total votes, but it was accorded only 23 seats. There has been a great deal of debate on the electoral formulae that prevail, but so far there has been no proposal to change the system. The parties that have the largest stake in a change are those that are smaller and weaker and consequently least able to propose, let alone to effect, legal adjustments.

THE POST-THATCHER YEARS

If in the late 1980s Margaret Thatcher never minced words with regard to what she liked, and even more to what she disliked, about the European Union, her rhetoric had become tiresome to many. Having been invited to speak at the European College in Bruges, she delivered a scathing attack on both the EU and its president, an avowed Socialist. In this speech, she showed herself very critical of a federated Europe; elaborating on the theme of federation, she made reference to what she called the "hated F-word." The prime minister cleverly played on the nationalist sentiments of her audience at home. The Bruges speech was widely publicized and increased her popularity among extremists in the Conservative Party, some of whom saw fit to found a society that called itself "the Bruges Group," an association that apparently aims at enshrining the celebrated ideas and thoughts of the revered former prime minister. In addition, an anti-EU European Reform Group was established. For a brief period, it seemed that Britain was preparing a breakaway from the Union. But, in the end, Thatcher's hostility vis-à-vis the EU caught up with her.

Her downfall came in November 1990, resulting from causes mentioned above. The Conservative Party's main fear was that Thatcher would be a liability rather than an asset in the upcoming election. An internal ballot seemed the best solution to determine who should face that election as prime minister. After several inconclusive attempts, a solution emerged that was to reconcile the party, since the person selected was also favored by the outgoing prime minister. To be Thatcher's choice as well as the party's made the conditions extraordinarily difficult for John Major. The obvious question would be whether or not he was the "Son of Thatcher," as some suggested.

However, it did not take long to find out that Major was his own man. It is true that, in general, he endeavored to follow the broad outlines of Thatcherism, most of which amounted to the interpretation and formulation of the right wing of the Conservative Party. John Major's crucible came in December 1991, when the European Council (as the summit meetings of EU's prime ministers and foreign ministers are called) met in Maastricht, the Netherlands, to discuss the Treaty of Political and Economic Union.

Since Britain was known to object to and reject some of the principal points in this treaty, a couple of pre-Council meetings had been convened to give Britain the chance to explain its position. The EU found itself in an awkward position. On the one hand, unanimity was required. On the other, the Union's leadership did not want the draft treaty to founder on the legacy of Thatcher. In the end, it was decided to accord Britain the right of opting out, at least temporarily. The device simply implied that the United Kingdom did not yet need to sign those parts of the draft that it objected to. Approval could wait until the British Parliament had determined the political will of the British people. There was thus no need for Britain to dissociate itself from the EU altogether. Major handled the complexities of the situation well, displaying expert diplomatic skills.

Domestically, too, he did not fare badly, although the British economy remained weak. In 1992, elections were held. Although the incumbents were at a grave disadvantage as a result of the poor economy, Major's astute and suave handling of problems and conflicts helped to prolong the Conservative leadership of Britain in spite of the recession.

It is true that slips were made both before the general elections and thereafter, but they were of no consequence. Neil Kinnock, for example, having retired from the office of leader of Her Majesty's Loyal Opposition, aspired to fill the post of EU commissioner in Brussels. Major had apparently at one point promised to submit Kinnock's name to that end. Before the promise had been honored, the press got to know of Kinnock's still largely speculative plans. As is customary in these cases, the former Opposition leader immediately made light of this particular ambi-

tion and, through his words, made it impossible to pursue it further.

Then there was the coal-mine situation. Margaret Thatcher had scored a victory over the miners and their union in the mid-1980s. But this was a far cry from a permanent victory, especially since mining was gradually becoming too costly. The majority of the British mines are old, if not obsolete, and most of their operations, particularly deep mining, had become prohibitively expensive. In an attempt to cut government expense, Major decided in October 1992 to close all mines. The proposal caused an uproar, since a great many people work in the mines, and it seemed doubtful that other work could be found for them in a time of high unemployment. As a result, numerous rallies and protest meetings were organized to denounce the measure. Articulating their grievances in the regional accents of Yorkshire, Lancashire, and Durham, all heavily hit areas, the miners handed "Coal not dole" stickers to passersby. Women carried placards that said, "30,000 jobs to go. Today the miners, tomorrow you!"

Major's popularity subsequently plummeted to the lowest level ever for a British leader, with only 16 percent of the British public expressing confidence in him. The prime minister quickly put a revised plan to the test, which in effect would allow a majority of the mines to remain open. This plan was passed by the House of Commons after the opposition motion had just been narrowly defeated.

LABOUR TAKES THE REINS

However, Major was unable to stave off the rising popularity of the Labour Party and the party's leader, Tony Blair. As the May 1, 1997, elections date approached, it became apparent that Major and the Conservative Party were in big trouble. After the votes were tallied, the Conservative Tories experienced their worst performance since 1906. Nineteen years of conservative control was ended as Labour won a clear mandate, with just over 43 percent of the vote. Tony Blair was confirmed as the new prime minister. At age 43, he was the youngest to hold that post since 1812.

The new prime minister's center-left government took the reins of power during a complicated economic and political era. He has stated that the bulk of his time is

World War I 1914–1918	The first minority Labour government 1924	The Battle of Britain; the Nazi air force attempts to bomb England into submission 1940	Election of the first majority Labour government 1945	British India, the cornerstone of the British Empire, becomes independent (India and Pakistan) 1947	The United Kingdom and France decide to invade Egypt to secure the Suez Canal; compelled to withdraw 1956	The United Kingdom becomes a member of the European Union 1973	Margaret Thatcher is elected as the first female prime minister 1979	Britain defeats Argentine forces in the Falkland Islands War 1982

1990s

taken up with dealing with the Northern Ireland problem. But he has also had to deal with persistent economic concerns, including high unemployment and underemployment, and continued pressures to trim the social-welfare budget while retaining services and the "safety net"; difficult social issues, such as increasing single motherhood and rising crime and truancy in poorer urban neighborhoods; the political challenges stemming from the steady rise of nationalism in Scotland and Wales, both of which voted in September 1997 referenda for increased political autonomy; and his desire to assert British political and economic authority in the European Union.

Prime Minister Blair's national as well as global stature was heightened enormously in August 1997, when he provided leadership during Britain's shock and intense grieving period following the death of Princess Diana in a car accident in Paris. His energy and charm, as well as boyish good looks and glamour, have stood him well during his tenure in office,

Labour's Tony Blair becomes the new prime minister; in referenda, both Scotland and Wales win greater autonomy

Resolving the Northern Ireland problem remains the leading political issue in Britain

The Euro is launched successfully under Britain's EU presidency

but he still needs to clarify what his Labour government truly stands for and where it is going.

(British Information Service)

A rare photograph of the Chamber of the House of Commons in session, and the first to feature John Major's government. Shown to the right are Opposition Members of Parliament (MPs), to the left the government, and in the center, the speaker (in this photo Betty Boothroyd, the first woman speaker).

DEVELOPMENT

Britain was the first country to enter the Industrial Revolution. Britain's industrial output is still very large, although much of its capital equipment has become outdated.

FREEDOM

Britain was the first European country to create democratic conditions within its borders. Today the United Kingdom rates high in human rights.

HEALTH/WELFARE

The Labour government, coming into office immediately after World War II, introduced the welfare system. The cornerstone of this system is the National Health Service.

ACHIEVEMENTS

The exploitation of North Sea oil has been a success. Britain is self-supporting in the realm of energy and is able to export and sell some of the surplus to neighbors. In 1994, the Channel Tunnel opened between Britain and France.

Articles from the World Press

Annotated Table of Contents for Articles

Topic Guide to Articles

TOPIC AREA	TREATED IN	TOPIC AREA	TREATED IN
Human Rights	7. Migration Challenge: Europe's Crisis in Historical Perspective 16. Survey of the Nordic Countries	**Politics**	1. Hope for Europe 2. Europe United, but Who Runs It? 3. Euro Era Begins: European Central Bank Makes Its Debut 4. Europe Needs an Ethical Union, Not a Monetary Union 5. Shifting Tide in Europe: 'Conservative' Socialists Move to the Fore 11. Arresting the Decline of Europe 13. What Is France's Long-Term Strategy? Jospin Pursues Ambitious Controversial Agenda 15. Irish Ayes Are Smiling: Ireland Votes for Peace
Immigration	7. Migration Challenge: Europe's Crisis in Historical Perspective 10. Europe's Crowded Lifeboat: A Flood of Immigrants *and* The Kurds: An Endless Exodus		
Integration	1. Hope for Europe 2. Europe United, But Who Runs It? 7. Migration Challenge: Europe's Crisis in Historical Perspective		
International Relations	1. Hope for Europe 4. Europe Needs an Ethical Union, Not a Monetary Union 6. Putting Ethics at the Heart of Europe	**Race Relations**	7. Migration Challenge: Europe's Crisis in Historical Perspective 10. Europe's Crowded Lifeboat: A Flood of Immigrants *and* The Kurds: An Endless Exodus
Labor	10. Europe's Crowded Lifeboat: A Flood of Immigrants *and* The Kurds: An Endless Exodus	**Social Unrest**	7. Migration Challenge: Europe's Crisis in Historical Perspective 10. Europe's Crowded Lifeboat: A Flood of Immigrants *and* The Kurds: An Endless Exodus 15. Irish Ayes Are Smiling: Ireland Votes for Peace
Language	14. Pilgrim's Search for Relics of the Once and Future King		
Monetary Issues	2. Europe United, but Who Runs It? 3. Euro Era Begins: European Central Bank Makes Its Debut	**Social Welfare**	10. Europe's Crowded Lifeboat: A Flood of Immigrants *and* The Kurds: An Endless Exodus 17. Spain's Bright Future: Economy Continues to Grow
Morality	1. Hope for Europe		
Nationalism	4. Europe Needs an Ethical Union, Not a Monetary Union 7. Migration Challenge: Europe's Crisis in Historical Perspective 14. Pilgrim's Search for Relics of the Once and Future King	**Standard of Living**	17. Spain's Bright Future: Economy Continues to Grow
		Tourism	14. Pilgrim's Search for Relics of the Once and Future King
North Atlantic Treaty Organization (NATO)	8. NATO: The Dilemmas of Expansion	**Unemployment**	10. Europe's Crowded Lifeboat: A Flood of Immigrants *and* The Kurds: An Endless Exodus 17. Spain's Bright Future: Economy Continues to Grow
Nordic Countries	16. Survey of the Nordic Countries		

Article 1

The New York Review of Books, June 20, 1996

The Hope for Europe

Václav Havel

President Havel gave the following address in Aachen on May 15, 1996.

1.

Recently, when I looked into how Europe got its name, I was surprised to discover that many see its primeval roots in the Akkadian word *erebu*, which means twilight or sunset. Asia, on the other hand, is believed to have derived its name from Akkadian *asu* meaning sunrise.

At first sight this discovery does not seem very auspicious. In our minds the word twilight has been traditionally linked with notions of end, extinction, defeat, ruin, or approaching death. In certain respects, the conventional connection makes sense: twilight is indeed the end of something. At the very least the end of one day and the hustle and bustle that filled it. But it does not mean defeat, doom, or the end of time. Far from it: it is merely a punctuation mark in the eternal cycle of nature and life, in which one thing ends simply in order that something else may begin.

For people this may mean that the time of work, which is largely physical and directed toward the world around us, has come to an end, to give way to a time of quiet contemplation, reflection, evaluation, introspection—in other words, of inwardly directed endeavor. From time immemorial people have taken the evening to reflect on what they have done during the day. They have paused to look at things in perspective, to gain strength and resolve for the day to come. In somewhat simplified terms, one may say that dawn and daylight are a time of hands, while twilight is a time of the mind.

The somewhat melancholy associations we tend to attach to the word twilight may be the typical consequence of the modern cult of beginnings, openings, advances, discoveries, growth, and prosperity, of a cult of industriousness, outward activity, expansion, and energy, that is, of the characteristically modern blind faith in quantitative indices. Dawn, daybreak, sunrise, "the morning of nations," and similar words, phrases, or metaphors are popular these days, while notions like sunset, stillness, or nightfall carry for us, unjustly, only connotations of stagnation, decline, disintegration, or emptiness.

We are unjust to twilight. We are unjust to the phenomenon that may have given Europe its name.

It is true that a particular phase in the history of Europe appears to be drawing to a close. The extraordinarily fortunate amalgamation of classical antiquity, Jewish religiosity, and Christianity, combined with the fresh energy of the so-called barbarian tribes, led eventually to unprecedented progress in Europe, and in the end has brought humanity countless gifts and left its stamp on the entire planetary civilization of our time. Europe seems to have introduced into human life the categories of time and historicity, to have discovered the idea of development, and ultimately what we call progress as well.

Centuries from now, all European history may seem to have been no more than a single day filled with vigorous activity, magnificent human endeavor, great discoveries of the human mind, the release of enormous energies and the ethos of expansion related to it. From the secrets of Being and salvation to the secrets of matter, from the discovery of treasures hidden on faraway continents to political achievements like the recognition of human dignity and liberty, the rule of law, and the idea of equality before the law—these are all remarkable European discoveries which Europe has then spread further, often to the benefit of the world as a whole, often to its detriment as well.

The history of Europe has not only been a history of the spread of the ideals of salvation, freedom, progress, and humanity: it has also meant the brutal suppression of other cultures. It has meant conquest, plunder, colonization, and some highly dubious exports, of which I may mention only one, dangerous in the extreme, the effects of which I have experienced personally: communist ideology. And if the world in part owes beneficial and useful things such as democracy and the idea of human rights or the invention of television and the computer to the European spirit of progress and endless searching, it also has that same European spirit to thank for many of its huge social inequities, its arrogant anthropocentric treatment of the planet, the cult of consumerism, as well as the enormous stockpiles of unbelievably destructive weapons that often end up in the hands of highly suspect regimes. This double-edged European expansionism reached its sad climax this century in two wars into which our continent dragged the whole world.

The various benefits deriving from the European notion of progress have long since been adopted by other parts of the world as well. Many have embraced them so completely that they now surpass Europe precisely in areas where Europe once claimed lasting predominance. Europe has ceased to be the center of colonial power or the control room of the world, and it no longer decides the world's fate.

It seems to me the time has come for us to pause and reflect upon ourselves. I believe we are facing a great historical challenge, a challenge to grasp and put into practice at last what is implied in the word twilight. We should stop thinking of the present state of Europe as the sunset of its energy and recognize it instead as a time of contemplation when the work of the day ceases for a while and, as the sun goes down, the rule of thought sets in. This does not mean we need be estranged from ourselves and the world we live in. It simply means taking a calm look back at what we have accomplished, assessing the meaning and the consequences of our efforts and making a few resolutions for the day to come.

At no time in its modern history, I think, has Europe had a better opportunity to do so than now, and it would be a serious mistake for us not to grasp it. With your permission, I shall try to outline a few subjects to which we should give serious thought if we are to make the best use of this time of evening meditation. This time should not be an occasion for exhausted slumber after work, or nostalgia for the achievements of long ago, but rather a time to articulate Europe's task for the twenty-first century.

The term Europe has essentially three meanings. The first one is purely geographical, determined by the lines on the map on the wall of every elementary schoolroom, and in every atlas.

The second meaning of the term Europe refers to those countries in Europe that were spared the experience of communism, and that are now, for the most part, members of the European Union. It thus embraces the part of Europe that has been able, over the past decades, to cultivate a democratic political system and a civil society that is relatively stable politically, that enjoys economic prosperity, and has step by step become integrated into a single large political and economic league. This Europe is certainly attractive to everyone else,

and it is no coincidence that the slogan "Return to Europe" is reiterated, often to a tiresome degree, in many countries that do not belong to this group. The phrase essentially means admission to the club of those nations historically fortunate enough to have been on the other side of the Iron Curtain.

Europe in this sense of the word, however—and let us be frank here—shows relatively little concern for the challenge I have just mentioned, that is, the challenge of rising above its daily labors and undertaking a profound examination of its role in our civilization. Stretching the point a little, we might say that this Europe is far more preoccupied with transfer payments from Brussels or the export of beef from cattle suspected of madness. For all the fine words it offers us from time to time, it is still a rather self-centered Europe, concerned more for its immediate economic interests than for global philosophical considerations.

But there is also a third meaning of the word Europe. This Europe represents a common destiny, a common, complex history, common values, and a common culture and way of life. More than that, it is also, in a sense, a region characterized by particular forms of behavior, a particular quality of will, a particular understanding of responsibility. As a consequence, the borders of this Europe may at times seem fuzzy or variable: it cannot be defined by looking at a school atlas or studying a list of member states of the European Union or of countries that could join should they wish, such as Norway, Switzerland, or Iceland. This is why any discussion of this third Europe is more difficult, and occurs less often. Yet this is precisely where all debates about Europe and its future should begin.

It seems to me, in other words, that the starting point of all our twilight meditations should be a discussion about Europe as a place of shared values, about European spiritual and intellectual identity or—of you like—European soul: about what Europe once was and what it believed in, what it is and believes in now, what it should be or could be, and what role it could play in the future.

Don't worry: I shall not try to answer these questions here. Others are better equipped to do so, and countless books have already been written on the subject. I shall simply mention a few aspects of Europe that I think deserve our attention at this moment.

The first of these is that Europe, in the third meaning of the term, has always been and still is a single indivisible political entity, however immensely diverse and intricately structured it may be. This is not just a consequence of geography, that is, of the fact that many loosely related peoples are concentrated on a relatively small peninsula and its immediate vicinity. What is more important is that the millennia of common history shared by its peoples, who often lived in differently constituted multinational empires, have molded Europe into a single intellectual unit or sphere of civilization, interwoven by so many political connections that severing any of them might, in certain cases, lead to its total disintegration.

This apparently banal fact, however, has important political consequences. It means that unless the future order of Europe is founded on a clear awareness of this interconnectedness, it will ultimately bring no benefit to anyone. We simply cannot imagine a Europe that continues to be divided, not only by the Iron Curtain this time, but economically, into a part that is prosperous and increasingly united, and another part that is less stable, less prosperous, and disunited. Just as one half of a room cannot remain forever warm while the other half is cold, it is equally unthinkable that two different Europes could forever live side by side without detriment to both. And the more stable and prosperous one would pay the higher price.

So it is not true that the united part of Europe would suffer if it expanded. On the contrary: in the long run, it would suffer only if it failed to expand. In fact Europe, as a phenomenon of civilization, now has an historically unprecedented opportunity: it can remake itself on the principles of agreement among all those concerned, the principles of equality and peaceful and democratic cooperation. If it squanders this opportunity in the name of short-term, particular, or even exclusively economic interests, it will have to pay for it. It would open the door, in both of its halves, to all those who prefer confrontation to dialogue, who would rather define themselves in opposition to others than as neighbors. It is no good pretending that people of this type no longer exist. To put it another way: if democrats do not soon begin to reconstruct Europe as a single political entity, others will start structuring it their own way, and the democrats will have nothing left but their tears. The demons that have so fatally tormented European history—most disastrously of all in the twentieth century—are merely biding their time. It would be a tragic mistake to ignore them because of technical preoccupations with transfer funds, quotas, or tariffs.

The European Union is an unprecedented attempt to create of Europe a single region held together by a sense of solidarity. I know that neither the European Union nor the North Atlantic Alliance can open its doors overnight to all those who aspire to join them. What both most assuredly can do—and what they should do before it is too late—is to give the whole of Europe, seen as a sphere of common values, the clear assurance that they are not closed clubs. They should formulate a clear and detailed policy of gradual enlargement that not only contains a timetable but also explains the logic of that timetable. Six long years have passed since the Iron Curtain came down, and it makes no sense to deny that—despite certain promising halfway steps—little has actually happened to bring this larger unity about.

2.

Let us now turn from these rather external matters to the fundamental ones.

One of the great European traditions—a tradition that Europe increasingly forgot in the first half of the twentieth century—is the idea of the free citizen as the source of all power. After World War II, having learned a lesson from the horrors inflicted by fanatical nationalism, the free part of Europe rededicated itself to this tradition and made it the foundation of reconciliation and cooperation. And although European integration began primarily as economic integration, it was nevertheless obvious what its political points of departure and its political objectives were. The hope was to bring about a great renaissance of the civic principle as the only possible basis for truly peaceful cooperation among nations. The point was not to suppress national identity or national consciousness, which is one of the dimensions of human identity, but rather to free human beings from the bondage of ethnic collectivism—that source of all strife and enslaver of human individuality.

As paradoxical as it may sound, European unification has never meant limiting freedom in the sense that particular civil rights are expropriated by a power that is increasingly remote from the citizen. Quite the contrary—it has been a process of enhancing people's freedom not only by liberating them from the fear of others but also by offering them more latitude to fulfill themselves as citizens. It seems to me that only now, with the European Union launching a new round of talks on its future (which among other things involves a discussion of its common foreign and security policy) are Europeans and European politicans beginning to recognize this deeply political dimension of the unification process. And I wonder whether some of them are not a little daunted by the magnitude of the task they have undertaken, now that its profound significance is becoming so clear. If it exists, such discouragement is all the more dangerous now, just when Europe has the opportunity I have just mentioned—the opportunity to establish itself on democratic principles as a whole entity for the first time in its history.

How can we counter this loss of heart? Where can we find the courage to pursue truly broad-minded solutions? How can we look beyond our immediate and particular interests to seek a better future for the entire continent?

In my view relatively little is needed. We need only to remind ourselves of the anthem of the European Union. Does not Schiller's "Ode to Joy" offer an answer to this question? When it points out that life in the sacred circle of freedom requires giving allegiance and commitment to "the judge above the stars"? What else can this mean but that freedom and responsibility are two sides of the same coin and that freedom is thinkable only when it is based on a sense of responsibility toward an authority that transcends us?

The concept of a metaphysically anchored sense of responsibility has been a cornerstone of the values that underlie the European tradition. And it seems to me that the time of twilight, taken as an opportunity for self-reflection, is a direct invitation to rededicate ourselves to this European tradition and to admit clearly that there are values transcending our immediate interest, that we are not accountable solely to our party, our electorate, our lobby, or our state, but to the whole of humanity, including those who come after us, and that the ultimate worth of our deeds will be decided somewhere beyond the circle of mortals who surround us. In the language of today's world, this means nothing more and nothing less than to heed the voice that calls to us from the depths of our conscience.

In a somewhat exalted fashion we might say that the task of Europe today is to rediscover its conscience and its responsibility, in the deepest sense. That means not just responsibility for its own political architecture, but also for the world as a whole.

We are all familiar with the threats that hang over the world today. We all know that the planet's resources are limited and that sooner or later the idea of constant growth will clash with these limitations. We all know about the deepening abyss between the rapidly increasing population of the poor and the stagnating population of the increasingly rich. We all know we are damaging nature, the air, and the waters around us. We all know what conflicts lie dormant within humanity, now that a single global civilization is pushing people from different spheres of culture ever closer together, thus inevitably arousing their determination to defend their identity against this pressure toward uniformity.

But what are we doing to avert these dangers or to confront them? Very little, I'm afraid. We withdraw into our shells, assuring ourselves that none of this is our affair, as if we had entirely forgotten the "judge above the stars" of whom the European anthem reminds us. It is as if, while constantly talking about Europe, we have entirely ignored one of the pillars of the European tradition—universalism, the commandment to think of everyone, to act as everyone should act, and to look for universally acceptable solutions.

Humanity is entering an era of multipolar and multicultural civilization. Europe is no longer the conductor of the global orchestra, but this does not mean it has nothing more to say to the world. A new task now presents itself, and with it a new meaning to Europe's very existence.

That task will no longer be to spread—violently or nonviolently—its own religion, its own civilization, its own inventions, or its own power. Nor will it be to preach the rule of law, democracy, human rights, or justice to the rest of the world.

If Europe wishes, it can do something else, something more modest yet more beneficial. It can become a model for how different peoples can work together in peace without sacrificing any of their identity; it can demonstrate that it is possible to treat our planet considerately, with future generations in mind; it can demonstrate that it is possible to live together in peace with other cultures, without people or countries having to deny themselves and their truth in the process. Moreover, Europe has one final possibility, if it so desires: it can reclaim its finest spiritual and intellectual traditions, and go back to the roots of those traditions and look for what they have in common with other cultures and other spheres of civilization, and join forces with them in a search for the common moral minimum necessary to guide us all so that we may live side by side on one planet and confront jointly whatever threatens our lives together.

Europe's task is no longer, nor will it ever be again, to rule the world, to disseminate by force its own concepts of welfare and what is good, to impose its own culture upon the world or to instruct it in its proper course. The only meaningful task for the Europe of the next century is to be the best it can possibly be—that is, to revivify its best spiritual and intellectual traditions and thus help to create a new global pattern of coexistence. We shall do most for the world if we simply do as we are bidden by our consciences, that is, if we act as we believe everyone should act. Perhaps we will inspire others: perhaps we won't. But we should not act in the expectation of that outcome. It may be hard to abandon the belief that it makes no sense to live by an imperative from above as long as others do not live by it or are not prepared to do so. But it can be done. And it is not impossible that this is, in fact, the best thing Europe can do for itself, for the restoration of its identity, for its own new dawning.

Europe will only be able to bear the cross of this world, and thus follow the example of Him in whom it has believed for two thousand years, and in whose name it has committed so much evil, if it first pauses and reflects upon itself, when—in the best sense of the word—it lives up to the potential inherent in the twilight to which it owes its name.

—translated from the Czech by Alexandra Bravcová and Paul Wilson

Article 2   *The Christian Science Monitor*, January 13, 1999

Europe united, but who runs it?

By Peter Ford
Staff writer of The Christian Science Monitor

STRASBOURG, FRANCE—When a European citizen is angry about a European Union policy, where does he or she go to complain?

With the recent launch of the single European currency, the euro, highlighting the way in which EU decisions reach into every corner of daily life, the question is more than theoretical.

And the lack of a clear answer highlights a glaring anomaly in the shape of an increasingly unified continent. An economic and financial giant, the European Union is a political dwarf, where democracy is an alien concept.

But a dramatic showdown this week in the European Parliament here may mark a first step toward accountability. In a debate echoing the US Senate's impeachment of President Clinton, Parliament will vote Jan. 14 on a motion of censure that could fire the entire 20-member European Commission, the union's executive body, over allegations of fraud and cronyism.

Such an outcome would throw the European Union into chaos, paralyzing the 15-nation organization just as it prepares a package of far-reaching reforms.

That prospect alone will probably be enough to scare the Parliament away from the "nuclear option," as the censure procedure is known, making it unlikely to muster the two-thirds majority needed. But the debate itself is an important milestone in Parliament's efforts to win more control over the secretive and byzantine workings of EU headquarters in Brussels.

"The censure motion has had the unforeseen consequence of bringing to public attention in our countries issues that had previously been dealt with behind closed doors," said Joaquim Miranda, leader of the United Left group in the Parliament, as debate opened Jan. 11.

"This is about the ambience, the ethos of secrecy, patronage, nepotism, and obstructionism which appears to surround the Commission," added Pauline Green, leader of the Socialists, the largest parliamentary group, who submitted the motion.

The crisis erupted last year when Parliament used one of its few real powers and refused to sign off on the EU's 1996 budget, citing reports by the union's own auditing body of financial mismanagement and abuse in the $100 billion spending program.

Commission president Jacques Santer dared Parliament to follow up with a vote of no confidence. With European par-

liamentary elections due in June, Parliament took up the challenge in a bid to boost its influence.

Although the 626-member Parliament is the European Union's only elected body, turnout in elections tends to be low by European standards: Only 56 percent of voters bothered to cast a ballot in the last poll in 1994.

"Parliament is caught in a vicious circle," says Anand Menon, a lecturer in European politics at Oxford University in England. "It has no powers so it doesn't have an electorate, and if it has no electorate, why should it be given more power?"

The EU launched the euro. Now a governing body must grapple with corruption and lack of accountability.

The fight over the corruption scandal "is a profile-raising exercise," he adds. "A big turnout at the elections in June would be ammunition backing demands for more power."

The European Commission, meanwhile, comprising 17,000 bureaucrats headed by 20 national commissioners (named by their national governments) is the most powerful unelected body in the world. It alone has the authority to initiate European legislation (Parliament can only amend its texts), which overrides national law in member states and now accounts for 80 percent of economic and social legislation in Europe.

The commission also administers the EU budget, dispensing $35 billion a year in aid to poorer regions. It manages the largest foreign-aid budget in the world, and it is the driving force behind the whole project of European integration.

It can boast considerable success, building a single seamless market from Portugal to the Polish border, and launching a single currency. But in the process it has also built a reputation as an arrogant, secretive, and unaccountable organization, even among supporters of the European project.

Mr. Santer, chastened by the storm of criticism the corruption scandal has provoked, appeared before the Parliament with his 19 fellow commissioners on Jan. 11 to promise greater openness and new codes of conduct. But he is powerless to change the fundamental way in which the European Union fashions its policies, which is through closed-door negotiations between civil servants and ministers from the 15 member states.

"The real obstacle" to greater democracy in European policymaking, says Dr. Menon, "is member-state governments, who use the European Union to bypass the democratic constraints tying them at home. "This increases policymaking efficiency because it insulates governments from public opinion" and allows them to blame unpopular decisions on Brussels, he suggests.

That style of governance, however, leaves European citizens out in the cold. European parliamentary elections do not lead to the creation of a government and voters often use them simply to cast a protest vote against national governments.

Thus far along the road to a united Europe, ordinary citizens have reacted to being ignored simply by being apathetic about the whole idea.

But if things go badly wrong in the future on the economic and financial front, warns Menon, the lack of any broad popular involvement and support and the absence of democratic political foundations mean that "potentially, you have a very big problem."

Article 3   *Europe*, February 1999

Euro Era Begins
European Central Bank Makes Its Debut

By Bruce Barnard

It was set up less than eight months ago and only began its job at the beginning of the year but already the European Central Bank is soaring up the learning curve.

The world's second most powerful bank after the US Federal Reserve has no track record, made its debut in a volatile economic environment, and is almost certain to face major battles within months as it attempts to stamp its identity on the global financial markets.

The ECB was buoyed by the trouble free launch of the euro into the world's financial system on January 1, but the going will get tougher as the market tests the new bank's resolve.

If the bank keeps its nerve it will play a pivotal role in gluing Europe's fragmented national markets into an economic superpower. If it loses its way, Europe's bid to create a single market to challenge the United States will be doomed.

The bank faces two major problems, one economic, the other political.

First, it must set a single interest rate that will suit all eleven members that have adopted the single currency, the euro, from the EU's economic giants France and Germany to its poorer members Spain and Portugal. Two years ago, most commentators thought the ECB would be dealing with a euro zone consisting of a small manageable core of countries with currencies that had successfully tracked the mighty deutschemark. Now they are talking about up to four more members, including Greece, joining within three years.

Second, the ECB faces the uncomfortable fact that the center-right politicians who engineered monetary union in the early 1990s have been largely replaced by center-left leaders with a markedly different agenda.

> Mr. Duisenberg, bloodied in earlier clashes with the politicians, has warned the ECB won't buckle. Monetary policy shouldn't be used as "a scapegoat for not delivering what people want most, which is a job and goods."

The ECB won the first bout with the politicians—but only on points. It fiercely resisted calls to cut interest rates to stimulate economic growth in late 1998. Then after winning its spurs in the markets, it ordered eleven central banks to cut rates together. It wrong-footed the pundits, but there was more than

The Euro
EUROPEAN INVESTMENT BANK

Europe's "other" bank, the European Investment Bank, the world's biggest non-government borrower and multilateral lender, is as old as the European Union itself, created by the Treaty of Rome in 1958 to finance capital investment in the member states.

The EIB's low profile, compared to the European Central Bank, belies its pivotal role in pump priming major infrastructure projects in the EU and more recently in Central and Eastern Europe and developing countries linked to the EU through the Lomé convention.

The EIB is a major financier, lending some 29 billion ecus, or $34 billion in 1998, a figure that's likely to be overtaken this year and denominated in euros.

Owned by the fifteen EU member states, the Luxembourg-based EIB raises the bulk of its funds on the capital markets where its bond issues are consistently graded AAA, the best credit rating. This means the bank can raise funds at the lowest rates and then lend at advantageous rates to governments, or projects, in developing nations or Central and East European countries that would pay higher market rates.

The EIB's lending priorities have changed over the past forty years, reflecting the evolution of the six-nation European Coal and Steel Community into the fifteen-member EU that is negotiating to accept five Central and Eastern European states and Cyprus.

Initially, the bank concentrated on strengthening the weaker regions of the EU, but its brief has since expanded to financing projects outside the EU under the bloc's cooperation policy toward other countries.

During 1998–99 loans totaling 5.5 billion euros ($6.5 billion) will be funneled to projects in ten Central and East European countries seeking EU membership.

The EU however remains the major recipient of EIB funds, getting some $26 billion of total loans of nearly $30 billion in 1997.

The EIB doesn't just lend to poor regions. Its investments stretch across the EU to develop trans-European transportation, telecommunications, and energy networks. Often it will step in where private financing is reluctant to invest because of long pay-back periods. Most recently, the bank's president, Sir Brian Unwin, said the EIB is prepared to lend substantial amounts to finance the construction of a sixty-eight-mile rail link between the Channel Tunnel—which links the United Kingdom and France—and London and the modernization of the London subway network.

In 1997, the EIB was asked by its shareholder governments to provide risk capital to innovative small and medium-sized firms and, for the first time, to invest in the labor-intensive education and health care sectors as part of an EU-wide campaign to create jobs. That program "roared ahead" in the past twelve months, according to Mr. Unwin as the EIB approved more than $3 billion in loans.

The ECB will grab the headlines in the coming months, but the EIB will play an equally important role in creating the new Europe.

—Bruce Barnard

---

a whiff of suspicion that its action was, in fact, a belated face-saving response to the political pressure.

The ECB knows it has to earn its credibility not just with the politicians and the markets but also with the European public. Wim Duisenberg, the chain-smoking Dutch president of the ECB, has said the world regards him as "ambassador for the euro" and that he must be a "consistent and credible defender" of the new money.

The ECB will be judged against the track record of the bank on which it is based and whose powers it has usurped—the Bundesbank, Germany's former central bank. It's a hard act to follow. As Jacques Delors, the former European Commission president and one of the architects of the euro, put it, "Not all Germans believe in God. But they all believe in the Bundesbank."

Germans revered the Bundesbank because its obsession with inflation, its pride in its independence, and its instinctive distrust of politicians made it the perfect guardian of their hard-earned money.

On paper, the ECB is probably the most independent central bank in the world. A treaty established it; its leaders are free of political influence and can only serve one term; and it cannot bail out insolvent governments. The seventeen members of the ECB's decision-making council—six executive board members in Frankfurt and the eleven central bank governors from euro countries—cannot be fired unless they are grossly incompetent or display symptoms of mental breakdown. Moreover, only by revising its founding Maastricht Treaty, which requires unanimity of all fifteen EU countries, can the members change the statutes of the ECB.

Like the Bundesbank, the ECB has a single goal—price stability—that it must pursue to the exclusion of other objectives. It alone defines price stability and the means of attaining it.

Moreover, the ECB's pursuit of this "mission statement," laid down in the Maastricht Treaty, will put it into conflict with EU governments—and ordinary Europeans—if economic growth falters and the jobless rolls rise during 1999. Central bank independence enjoyed wide political and popular support in Germany but not in most other euro zone countries, "Thus, the willingness to defend the ECB's independence will be weaker in these countries," warned Paul de Grauwe, a professor of economics at the University of Leuven and a member of the Belgian parliament.

Mr. Duisenberg, bloodied in earlier clashes with the politicians, has warned the ECB won't buckle. Monetary policy shouldn't be used as "a scapegoat for not delivering what people want most, which is a job and goods." It isn't the ECB's responsibility to cut Europe's 11 percent unemployment level

EUROPEAN BANK FOR RECONSTRUCTION AND DEVELOPMENT

The European Bank for Reconstruction and Development (EBRD) has experienced more drama and controversy in its eight years of existence than most other banks have in an entire century.

The EBRD, created in response to a proposal by then President of France François Mitterrand for an institution to promote economic restructuring and liberalization in the former communist nations, opened the doors of its London headquarters in 1991.

The EBRD has sixty shareholders: fifty-eight countries, the European Investment Bank, and the European Union. EU members have a controlling 51 percent stake but the largest single shareholder is the United States (10 percent) followed by Japan (8.5 percent).

The bank hit the headlines in its early years when it was discovered it had spent more on its headquarters than in loans to Central and Eastern Europe. This scandal led to the resignation of its first president, Jacques Attali in 1993, delivering a body blow to the bank's credibility.

The EBRD has since largely reestablished its credentials as a significant contributor to the economic development of the former communist nations.

The EBRD is a "political" bank in that it can only lend to countries "committed to applying the principles of multiparty democracy, pluralism, and market economics." Moreover, at least 60 percent of its lending in each country must be for private sector projects.

The bank's task became much more complicated when the disintegration of the Soviet Union and Yugoslavia greatly expanded its client base, which now spans countries that are well down the road to a market economy, such as Poland and Hungary, impoverished Albania, and distant Moldova and Turkmenistan.

The EBRD's loans are relatively modest—totaling some $1.9 billion for sixty-five projects in the first nine months of 1998 compared with $1.4 billion for forty-five projects in the year earlier period. But they have a disproportionate impact in jump-starting ventures that otherwise would stall for lack of financing.

The EBRD also plays an invaluable role in tracking the progress of some twenty-six countries toward a market economy. Its annual *Transition Report* is the bankers' bible for the region. Russia's financial crisis hit the EBRD hard, being largely responsible for a surge in provisions for the first nine months of 1998 to $842 million, or 13 percent of its outstanding loans and share investments. Nevertheless, the bank says it is strongly capitalized and its financial viability isn't at risk.

However, the EBRD faces a tough 1999 as its customers grapple with recession. A recent EBRD statement summed up the bank's challenges: "Progress in transition has been slower and more erratic than in any year since the fall of the Berlin Wall."

—Bruce Barnard

but that of the politicians who must reform the continent's inflexible labor markets.

The next few months will show whether the ECB will be all-powerful or whether it will play a secondary role to its eleven participating central banks. The ECB has a staff of approximately 600, while the central banks' payrolls top 60,000. Moreover, the central bank governors have a built-in majority over the ECB's executive board that will grow as more countries adopt the euro.

There are fears that ECB could become a toothless secretariat taking orders from the central banks, which might themselves be swayed by national politicians. There are genuine fears the central banks will wield too much power in the ECB. Hans Tietmeyer, president of the Bundesbank, reckons the ECB system of national banks will be much more decentralized than the German system.

There are parallels with the US Fed, which was set up as a very decentralized central bank in 1913 and spent the first twenty years of its existence dogged by power struggles between the Federal Reserve Board in Washington and the Federal Reserve Banks and between the banks themselves. This infighting was partly to blame for the bank collapses that led to the depression of the 1930s when the Federal Reserve Board couldn't act as a lender of last resort.

The parallel should not be stretched too far, but the International Monetary Fund has expressed concern that neither the ECB nor the participating central banks have a role as lenders of last resort.

The ECB is bracing for a barrage of criticism in the coming months for its lack of accountability and transparency as it sets its "one size fits all" monetary policy for Euroland. Critics allege it is immune from political oversight and will conduct all its proceedings in secret—minutes of meetings will not be published for sixteen years. Politicians are calling for more openness. Viktor Klima, the Austrian chancellor, says the US Fed publishes its minutes, and there is no reason why the ECB should not do the same.

Mr. Duisenberg insists the minutes must remain confidential to protect the eleven central bank governors from political pressure, and he is not going to give way to his critics.

Nobody doubts the ECB will face a tough year establishing its credentials with the international money markets as its every move is dissected and analyzed. However, the smart money is riding on success.

Bruce Barnard is a EUROPE contributing editor and a Brussels correspondent for the Journal of Commerce.

Article 4   *New Perspectives Quarterly*, Fall 1997

Europe Needs an Ethical Union, Not a Monetary Union

ANDRÉ GLUCKSMAN, ONE OF FRANCE'S ACCLAIMED "NOUVELLE PHILOSOPHES" WHEN THEY EMERGED 20 YEARS AGO, HAS STIRRED UP A CONTROVERSY RECENTLY BY ARGUING IN HIS BOOK, *Le Bien et le Mal,* THAT, THOUGH HEADED TOWARD A COMMON CURRENCY, FRANCE AND GERMANY REMAIN CULTURALLY DISTANT FROM EACH OTHER AND THEREFORE TOO OFTEN POLITICALLY PARALYZE THE EUROPEAN UNION.

PARIS—For 40 years after the Second World War, France and Germany got along quite well, both economically and politically. They seemed to understand each other. It was easy because America made all the big decisions about the European order.

Since the end of the Cold War and the fall of the Berlin Wall, France and Germany have had to make important decisions by themselves, most notably on the issue of Bosnia and the former Yugoslavia. This new situation revealed just how little France and Germany actually understood each other; it revealed how little they saw eye to eye on Europe's common destiny. Just as in the old Europe before the Second World War, France supported the Serbs and Germany supported the Croats. This split showed that the main partners of the European Union not only disagreed on a positive vision of Europe, but also on the main danger to Europe—a revival of division, nationalism and ethnic strife.

Because France and Germany do not share a common idea of Europe, we had four years of war in the former Yugoslavia. Two hundred thousand people were killed. Europe was completely incapacitated and unable to intervene.

> # The French live happily on in their cafes, oblivious to the dangers that exist on the other side of the fallen wall.

At the time, Francois Mitterrand said that the flowering of understanding between France and Germany meant that war in Sarajevo would not degenerate into war along the Rhine. One is compelled to answer that if peace between France and Germany along the Rhine requires so many dead in Bosnia, then it is not a very quiet peace.

Once again, it was up to the United States to step in and stop Europe from devouring itself. Unable to build a common Europe themselves, France and Germany, in effect, had to invite America back in to do the job it had been doing for four decades.

The return of the Americans is very paradoxical, especially in light of the fact that in 1999 the Europeans are preparing to launch a common currency, the euro. Both economically and militarily, France and Germany certainly possess the wherewithal to rise to challenges such as Bosnia. But they lack the mentality—the shared cultural ground—required for a common political agenda.

The problem is not a technical one of transaction costs, exchange rates or economic mechanisms. It is a problem of culture. In this sense, the policy of Jacques Delors and others to bring about Europe through the back door of economic integration, instead of the front door of political unity, has been a failure. Without the kind of deep dialogue and controversy an agenda of "political unity first" would have generated, a cultural consensus has not been achieved.

AFTER THE EURO, WHAT? Nonetheless, the euro will arrive as scheduled and we will have a common currency. But then what? If there is any kind of crisis in the world—economically, politically or strategically—what will happen? To defend the euro, France and Germany must have the same analysis and the same criteria of what is important, what is critical and what is peripheral. They will have to agree on what is to be done, and what is not to be done.

That means that they will have to agree in some measure on the good and the bad, on what they want and what they don't want, on the vision they hope to achieve, the mistakes they must avoid and the threats against which they must defend themselves.

These are not idle questions. East Europe is mired in post-Communist chaos. Who knows what will happen in Russia, in two weeks, in two years or in 20 years? What would happen if the mafia-types secured a hold on power? With all that wealth, won't they corrupt Western Europe too? Where are Russia's nuclear weapons and its scientists? Whom are they working for? What will happen south of Europe, in North Africa? Today, we see the extremely bloody Islamic terrorists taking their toll. What if they come to power in Algeria?

When Western Europe was in chaos after the Second World War, the US formulated and implemented the Marshall Plan. That was a cogent policy based on an assessment of what

Europe needed in that moment. It was designed to stabilize Europe so prosperity could arise again, thus bolstering democracy and short-circuiting any chance for the renewal of fascism. Western Europe needs something similar today for its new frontier in the East.

The strategy of integrating through the euro, a good thing in itself, was conceived as a project for "*this side*" of Europe when the Wall came down in 1989. It didn't then, and doesn't now, take into account either the eastern or southern frontiers of that part of Europe tied together by a common currency. For 10 years we have spoken of the euro without elaborating some strategy that takes into account the changed historical circumstances and the new challenge.

A CULTURE OF MEMORY This challenge must be met on the cultural level. So far, the requisite cultural dialogue has happened only between Germany on the one hand and the former GDR, the Czech Republic, Poland and Hungary on the other. The old GDR, of course, has been wholly absorbed into a unified Germany. And the Czech philosopher-president, Vaclav Havel, like his counterparts in Poland and Hungary, has actively sought to return to the cultural heart of Europe. Why? Because they all have the historical memory of the catastrophe chaos can bring to Europe.

By way of example, in September of this year, Havel and German President Roman Herzog hosted a performance of Verdi's "Requiem," played by the Czech Philharmonic, at the Terzen concentration camp outside Prague where Czech Jews were imprisoned before they were sent to be exterminated. Together, they remembered.

In contrast, the French live happily on in their cafes, oblivious to the dangers that exist on the other side of the fallen wall. Worried about economic competition and immigrants, they instead seek to put up new walls, not just around France but around Western Europe as a whole. Rather than remembering catastrophe, the French only remember the dream of victory over fascism. And it is a dream because—despite the fact that Charles de Gaulle gave them the right to dream—the victory was not theirs, but that of the US, England and the Soviet Union.

Since the collapse of the Soviet empire all Europeans have asked themselves silently what to do. Instinctively there is a sense that we need to forge an ethical community, a shared set of values upon which to base action. But everyone has his own idea of the Good. There are too many ways to different paradises, many kinds of left heavens, or right ideals, of Catholic, Reformed, Jewish, Muslim or atheistic preachings on how to behave.

The only way of building an ethical community is thus a negative way through a common reflection upon the bad experiences of the past, through a common appreciation of the devils that surround and inhabit the prosperous and democratic western part of Europe.

> The requisite cultural dialogue has only happened between Germany on the one hand and the former GDR and the Czech Republic, Poland and Hungary on the other.

It would be presumptuous to believe that young Europeans today are more fond of elementary human rights and democratic procedures than their grandfathers because they are better people. No. It is because there is an echo of memory concerning what happens in the absence of such principles.

Today, the Polish, German, French and Spanish people don't like dictatorship because they remember Hitler and Stalin. To the extent the British and French are awake at all, it is because they know the price of false dreams embodied in the Treaty of Munich and the Maginot Line.

History is a severe master. And actuality refreshes memories daily with the genocide of the Tutsis in Rwanda, religious terrorism in Algeria, war against civilians in the former Yugoslavia and the post-Communist mafias that wreak havoc in Russia.

Common European action presupposes opening our eyes to the community of dangers and closing the door on them before catastrophe strikes again.

The conception of danger and promise is, after all, fundamentally a cultural construct. The reality of a unified Europe will not take hold in the world until there is a cultural consensus between France and Germany, an ethical community that actively resists the replay of the past we know too well.

In short, Europe, to endure, needs a common idea more than it needs a common economy. France and Germany must therefore become more than enemies no longer. They need to become friends and, as they say in America, "soulmates."

Article 5 *Europe*, October 1998

A Shifting Tide in Europe

'Conservative' Socialists move to the fore

By Martin Walker

When Europe's fifteen heads of government gathered in Cardiff in June for the European Union summit, only two of their number had been present at the last summit under a United Kingdom presidency, at Edinburgh in December 1992. Jean-Luc Dehaene of Belgium was still in place and, at that time, so was then German Chancellor Helmut Kohl. Jacques Santer, who had attended the Edinburgh summit as prime minister of Luxembourg, returned to Cardiff as president of the European Commission. But through elections or retirement, all of the other government leaders had changed. It was a striking example of the pace and variety of political change in Europe. In the United States by contrast, President-elect Bill Clinton of 1992 was still in the White House six years later.

In Germany, Social Democrat leader Gerhard Schröder finally brought the Kohl era to an end after sixteen extraordinary years in power, longer than Konrad Adenauer. However, the recession, which took German unemployment in 1998 to its highest point since the Great Depression of the early 1930s, was a heavy political burden for the Kohl administration. It will be remembered, with German reunification as its high point, as the most significant political reign in Germany's postwar history.

In Belgium, beset with political scandals and the long-running crisis in law enforcement, which followed a series of pedophile murders, the government looks ill-placed to win the next elections, which must be held within the year.

These changes in Europe's political landscape were not and will not be limited to personnel. A distinct shift from a broadly center-right Europe to a broadly center-left array of governments has taken place. This did not attract much attention

outside Europe until two years ago, when the United Kingdom's Tony Blair won his landslide election victory. In 1996, Italy voted its center-left coalition led by Romano Prodi into power. In France, Lionel Jospin's Socialists, with Communist support, won their majority in the National Assembly the following year.

However, the shift of the political tide had begun much earlier, largely in response to the stubborn economic recession of the early 1990s. Greece was the first to turn to the Left, in 1993. Within twelve months, the Netherlands had rejected the Christian Democrats, who had been continuously in power since 1918 (with a brief break for World War II), and installed a Social Democrat-Liberal coalition. Finland and Portugal elected their Social Democrat governments in 1995. Now, with the Social Democrats returning to power this autumn in Germany, Europe's turn leftward is almost complete, with only Spain's conservative government standing against the tide.

This broad agreement of Europe's voters that it was time to give the center-left a chance at governing is relatively unusual and suggests to some optimists that at last a Europe-wide political sensibility is emerging. This impression is reinforced by the degree to which Europe's Social Democrats have changed. Rather like President Clinton's decision in the US to campaign as a "New Democrat," the center-left in Europe has abandoned much of the old ideological rigidity and has embraced free markets and free trade.

Spurred by the need to cut budget deficits, which was a requirement to qualify for the new single currency, the center-left governments have ruled with classic economic orthodoxy. Spending has been cut and taxes raised—despite double-digit un-

employment—with a watchful eye on the judgements of the international financial markets. The traditional links with the trade unions have been weakened, and banks, national airlines, and public utilities have been privatized, and whole industries—from telecommunications to financial services—have been deregulated to increase competition in Europe's single market.

The EU's special jobs summit in Luxembourg in 1997 agreed to a coordinated Europe-wide effort to bring down unemployment. But instead of adopting the traditional Keynesian remedies of deficit spending to create jobs through public works, they instead followed the supply-side agenda pioneered by Ronald Reagan and Margaret Thatcher in the 1980s, pledging to cut payroll taxes and promote small businesses and entrepreneurs and create a venture capital industry. Labor market flexibility, rather than jobs for life, became the watchword. In the UK, where Tony Blair was elected under the banner of "New Labor," even the party's traditional name was changed to symbolize the distance from the statist and interventionist past.

It is not yet clear whether this tendency toward a broad policy consensus in Europe represents the arrival of a genuinely Europe-wide political sensibility, or whether it is part of a global conversion to the free market system. The real test will come next year, in the first elections for the European Parliament since the 1997 Amsterdam Treaty significantly increased the Parliament's constitutional powers. Long the weakest link in the EU's tripartite system of the Council where the national governments meet, the Commission, which proposes and implements EU policies, the Parliament was not even elected until 1979.

Parliament's powers have grown slowly since then, but the Amsterdam Treaty grants it wide powers of co-decision with the Council and an effective veto over the next Commission president. The Parliament showed this year, during its US Congress-style hearings into the proposed board for the new European Central Bank, that it now sees itself as an equal player in the European

process with the Commission and the Council.

Europe's political parties seem to agree that the new Parliament must be taken seriously and have pressed strongly for the party system to grow from the nation states into a European system. On the eve of the Cardiff summit, at a meeting of the socialist and social democratic heads of governments

and opposition leaders, Tony Blair won unanimous approval to establish a new working group to make the PES (Party of European Socialists) something more than the current coalition of convenience within the European Parliament. The goal is to hammer out a common ideology, dubbed by Mr. Blair "the Third Way," which formalizes their move toward the electable center and which is

POLITICS '98

A Guide to Europe's Governments

AUSTRIA	BELGIUM	DENMARK	FINLAND	FRANCE
FORM OF GOVERNMENT: republic	**FORM OF GOVERNMENT:** constitutional monarchy	**FORM OF GOVERNMENT:** constitutional monarchy	**FORM OF GOVERNMENT:** republic	**FORM OF GOVERNMENT:** republic
HEAD OF STATE: President Thomas Klestil	**HEAD OF STATE:** King Albert II	**HEAD OF STATE:** Queen Margrethe II	**HEAD OF STATE:** President Martti Ahtisaari	**HEAD OF STATE:** President Jacques Chirac
LEGISLATIVE SYSTEM: bicameral, Bundesrat and Nationalrat	**LEGISLATIVE SYSTEM:** bicameral, Senate and Chamber of Deputies	**LEGISLATIVE SYSTEM:** unicameral, Folketing	**LEGISLATIVE SYSTEM:** unicameral, Eduskunta	**LEGISLATIVE SYSTEM:** bicameral, Senate and National Assembly
CURRENT GOVERNMENT: Social Democratic and People's Party coalition	**CURRENT GOVERNMENT:** center-left coalition	**CURRENT GOVERNMENT:** left of center coalition	**CURRENT GOVERNMENT:** center-left-green coalition	**CURRENT GOVERNMENT:** Socialist-Communist coalition
LEADER OF GOVERNMENT: Chancellor Viktor Klima (above), Social Democrat	**LEADER OF GOVERNMENT:** Prime Minister Jean-Luc Dehaene (above), Christian Democrat	**LEADER OF GOVERNMENT:** Prime Minister Poul Nyrup Rasmussen (above), Social Democrat	**LEADER OF GOVERNMENT:** Prime Minister Paavo Lipponen (above), Social Democrat	**LEADER OF GOVERNMENT:** Prime Minister Lionel Jospin (above), Socialist
LAST ELECTION: December 1995	**LAST ELECTION:** May 1995	**LAST ELECTION:** March 1998	**LAST ELECTION:** March 1995	**LAST PARLIAMENTARY ELECTION:** June 1997
NEXT ELECTION: by September 1999	**NEXT ELECTION:** by May 1999	**NEXT ELECTION:** March 2002	**NEXT ELECTION:** March 1999	**NEXT PARLIAMENTARY ELECTION:** by March 2002
SYSTEM OF ELECTION: proportional representation	**SYSTEM OF ELECTION:** proportional representation	**SYSTEM OF ELECTION:** proportional representation	**SYSTEM OF ELECTION:** proportional representation	**SYSTEM OF ELECTION:** single member constituencies, direct election

also intended to strengthen ties with the US Democratic Party.

Europe's conservatives have also been preparing for this new politics of Europe-wide parties. Their own EPP (European People's Party) has hitherto been a very loose grouping within the Parliament, used mainly as a way to maximize influence in the process of selecting the Parliament's committee chairmen. The UK's Conservatives were not even full members. However, on the eve of the Cardiff summit, the EU's conservative heads of government and parties also met and took the controversial step of bringing Silvio Berlusconi's Forza Italia into their ranks.

Dutch and Belgian Christian Democrats opposed this bitterly, claiming that Forza Italia were populists of dubious

democratic credentials. They were overruled, thanks to the influence of Spain's prime minister, Jose Maria Aznar, Germany's Helmut Kohl, and the British Conservative Party leader William Hague, the first leader of his party to attend one of these conservative summit gatherings. Their motive was to add the twenty votes of the Forza Italia MEPs to the EPP numbers, in the hope of winning an EPP majority in the European Parliament next year.

In short, the Parliament is now taken seriously by the parties as a political force. Moreover, influential Europeans appear to agree. France's Jacques Delors, who preceded Jacques Santer as president of the European Commission, has proposed that Europe's political parties should each put forward their own candidate to be the next Commission president as part of their

election campaign. He argues that this would give a powerful democratic le-

---

> # A distinct shift from a broadly center-right Europe to a broadly center-left array of governments has taken place.

GERMANY

FORM OF GOVERNMENT:
republic
HEAD OF STATE:
President Roman Herzog
LEGISLATIVE SYSTEM:
bicameral, Bundesrat and Bundestag
CURRENT GOVERNMENT:
center-left coalition
LEADER OF GOVERNMENT:
Chancellor Gerhard Schröder (above), Social Democrat
LAST PARLIAMENTARY ELECTION:
September 1998
NEXT PARLIAMENTARY ELECTION:
September 2002
SYSTEM OF ELECTION:
mixed proportional and direct election

GREECE

FORM OF GOVERNMENT:
republic
HEAD OF STATE:
President Costis Stephanopoulos
LEGISLATIVE SYSTEM:
unicameral, Vouli
CURRENT GOVERNMENT:
Socialist
LEADER OF GOVERNMENT:
Prime Minister Costas Simitis (above), Socialist
LAST PARLIAMENTARY ELECTION:
October 1993
NEXT ELECTION:
by October 2000
SYSTEM OF ELECTION:
direct election

IRELAND

FORM OF GOVERNMENT:
republic
HEAD OF STATE:
President Mary McAleese
LEGISLATIVE SYSTEM:
bicameral, Senate and Dail
CURRENT GOVERNMENT:
center-right coalition
LEADER OF GOVERNMENT:
Taoiseach Bertie Ahern (above), Fianna Fail
LAST PARLIAMENTARY ELECTION:
June 1997
NEXT PARLIAMENTARY ELECTION:
by June 2002
SYSTEM OF ELECTION:
proportional representation, single transferable vote

ITALY

FORM OF GOVERNMENT:
republic
HEAD OF STATE:
President Oscar Luigi Scalfaro
LEGISLATIVE SYSTEM:
bicameral, Senate and Chamber of Deputies
CURRENT GOVERNMENT:
left-center coalition
LEADER OF GOVERNMENT:
Prime Minister Romano Prodi (above)
LAST ELECTION:
April 1996
NEXT ELECTION:
April 2001
SYSTEM OF ELECTION:
proportional and majority representation

LUXEMBOURG

FORM OF GOVERNMENT:
constitutional monarchy
HEAD OF STATE:
Grand Duke Jean
LEGISLATIVE SYSTEM:
unicameral, Chamber of Deputies
CURRENT GOVERNMENT:
Christian Democrat-Socialist coalition
LEADER OF GOVERNMENT:
Prime Minister Jean-Claude Juncker (above), Christian Socialist
LAST ELECTION:
June 1994
NEXT ELECTION:
June 1998
SYSTEM OF ELECTION:
proportional representation

gitimacy to the new 'Mr. Europe', and would also intensify this process of Europeanizing party politics. This suggestion may be premature, and the member states do not like the idea of giving up their own current power to nominate the next Commission president. Nevertheless, the Delors plan underlines this growing trend to define common EU policies.

It is important not to overestimate this trend. Even though the Social Democrats won this year's election in Germany, it is far from certain that their ideological colleagues in Austria, Belgium, Finland, and Portugal can maintain power in the spate of elections that will take place within the next eighteen months. Europe remains a political entity in embryo, still marked by distinc-

tive national features and political traditions.

Think of an America in which California, Texas and Ohio were constitutional monarchies, like the UK, Sweden, the Netherlands, Denmark, and Spain. Think of Rhode Island being a Grand Duchy, like Luxembourg. Consider a political system in which Florida and Pennsylvania used their own distinctive election system, based on the kind of proportional representation used in Germany. Also, ponder the implications of Michigan being governed like Italy, by a coalition whose largest single party was only recently converted from communism and whose previous government coalition included a party that traced its roots back to Mussolini's fascists. One of the few familiar contours

of the European landscape to an American, familiar with power being shared between White House and Congress, is the French system. An elected and powerful president, the center-right Jacques Chirac, finds himself governing in opposition to an elected Socialist prime minister.

But the complexity does not stop there. Consider further an America with a different currency in each state, and of a California that drags its feet over the attempt to forge a new single currency, and constantly harks back to its 'special relationship' with Japan across the ocean. Ponder an America in which the second and third-richest states, Texas and New York, possessed nuclear weapons, but the richest, California, did not. Add to this confusion a Texas that in-

NETHERLANDS

FORM OF GOVERNMENT: constitutional monarchy
HEAD OF STATE: Queen Beatrix
LEGISLATIVE SYSTEM: bicameral, two chambers of States-General
CURRENT GOVERNMENT: center-left and liberal coalition
LEADER OF GOVERNMENT: Prime Minister Wim Kok (above), PvdA
LAST ELECTION: May 1998
NEXT ELECTION: by May 2002
SYSTEM OF ELECTION: proportional representation

PORTUGAL

FORM OF GOVERNMENT: republic
HEAD OF STATE: President Jorge Sampaio
LEGISLATIVE SYSTEM: unicameral, Assembly of the Republic
CURRENT GOVERNMENT: Social Democratic
LEADER OF GOVERNMENT: Prime Minister Antonio Guterres (above), Social Democrat
LAST ELECTION: October 1995
NEXT ELECTION: by October 1999
SYSTEM OF ELECTION: proportional representation

SPAIN

FORM OF GOVERNMENT: constitutional monarchy
HEAD OF STATE: King Juan Carlos
LEGISLATIVE SYSTEM: bicameral, Senate and Congress of Deputies
CURRENT GOVERNMENT: conservative coalition
LEADER OF GOVERNMENT: Prime Minister Jose Maria Aznar (above), Popular Party
LAST ELECTION: March 1996
NEXT ELECTION: by March 2000
SYSTEM OF ELECTION: proportional representation

SWEDEN

FORM OF GOVERNMENT: constitutional monarchy
HEAD OF STATE: King Carl XVI Gustaf
LEGISLATIVE SYSTEM: unicameral, Riksdag
CURRENT GOVERNMENT: Social Democratic coalition
LEADER OF GOVERNMENT: Prime Minister Goran Persson (above), Social Democrat
LAST ELECTION: September 1998
NEXT ELECTION: September 2002
SYSTEM OF ELECTION: proportional representation

UNITED KINGDOM

FORM OF GOVERNMENT: constitutional monarchy
HEAD OF STATE: Queen Elizabeth II
LEGISLATIVE SYSTEM: bicameral, House of Commons and House of Lords
CURRENT GOVERNMENT: Labor (social democratic)
LEADER OF GOVERNMENT: Prime Minister Tony Blair (above), Labor
LAST ELECTION: April 1997
NEXT ELECTION: by May 2002
SYSTEM OF ELECTION: single member constituencies, the most votes wins

sisted that the main force of economic and political gravity lay with relations to the poor and populous south, while New York and Michigan insisted that the real issue was a menacing and unstable neighbor to the north.

All these differences argue that a United States of Europe is still far distant, even should it ever emerge. Moreover, one of the most striking features of the new politics of Europe is that the traditionally most pro-federalist country, Germany, is starting to resemble the reluctant United Kingdom. Former Chancellor Helmut Kohl demanded a new budget arrangement to limit the net payments Germany makes to the EU budget, just as Mrs. Thatcher did fifteen years ago. Mr. Kohl was far more polite about it, but he and other German politicians insist that their country can no longer afford to continue paying 60 percent of the net payments to the budget. Germany pays 30 percent of the entire $90 billion budget, but gets in return only 15 percent of EU spending.

The traditional links with the trade unions have been weakened, and banks, national airlines, and public utilities have been privatized .

Moreover, on the eve of the Cardiff summit, then Chancellor Kohl and President Chirac sent to their summit host, Prime Minister Blair, a joint letter which stressed that "it cannot be the goal of European policy to establish a central Europe state." The letter also echoed traditional British concerns about bringing Europe closer to its people. The two leaders stressed the need for more 'subsidiarity,' the principle that decisions should be taken whenever possible at national or local level, rather than in Brussels.

That explains why Margaret Thatcher would have enjoyed the Cardiff summit. But so would Charles de Gaulle. Those twin advocates of a Europe of nation states jealously guarding their traditional grandeur and their constitutional prerogatives against the federalist tide could claim to have won the argument. A mass conversion seems to have taken place among Europe's heads of government. They all now preach subsidiarity, clawing back the decision-making power from Brussels. And they all now echo Tony Blair in talking of a Europe that moves "closer to its people," and what they all seem to mean is strengthening the role of national governments.

There is an inherent tension between the European political system, which is coalescing in the European Parliament, and this determination by the national governments to keep the reins of power in their own hands. Looking at the way the US Constitution is designed to maintain just such a tension in the deliberate balance of powers between Congress, White House, Supreme Court, and the individual states, this need be no bad thing.

But these countervailing new currents in Europe are not flowing in a vacuum. They move in a political and economic context transformed by the two dramatic changes that will govern Europe's future. The first is the coming of the single currency. From January of next year, eleven of the EU's fifteen members will conduct a common monetary policy through the European Central Bank, and their own banks and shops and bills and paychecks will start running their accounts in the euro alongside each national currency. In January 2002, the new euro notes and coins come into use, and the likelihood is that by then the UK, Sweden, Denmark, and Greece will be poised to join the euro system.

Europe's heads of government all now preach subsidiarity, clawing back the decision-making power from Brussels.

But even as that change is being absorbed, Europe itself will be redefined by the enlargement process. At some point in the coming decade, the fifteen member states are scheduled to be joined by five and perhaps seven new ones. Detailed accession negotiations are underway with Poland, Hungary, the Czech Republic, Slovenia, Estonia, and Cyprus. This will take the current EU population of 372 million to 436 million. After its latest elections, the island of Malta resumed its application, and after a series of negotiations on problems of transport and the free movement of labor, the final hurdles to Swiss membership are being cleared away.

Such a Europe of twenty-two nations will not be the limit. Negotiations for entry are proceeding at a slower pace with Lithuania, Latvia, Romania, Bulgaria, and Slovakia. Once they join, the population of the EU will be within a whisker of 500 million, almost double that of the United States. So the political landscape of Europe today is but a snapshot, a single frame of a long-running film the outcome of which we still cannot know. However, the main themes of the unfolding drama, the tension between the familiar nation states and their traditional prerogatives, and the forces that seem destined to evolve a common European politics to match its common currency, are already well established.

Martin Walker, based in Brussels, is a EUROPE *contributing editor and the European editor of The Guardian.*

Article 6

The World Today, March 1998

PUTTING ETHICS at the HEART OF EUROPE

Hazel Smith

Does Europe have a foreign policy? The British Foreign Secretary, Robin Cook, equipped with a new ethical approach, clearly hopes it does. As president of the European Union, he's tussling with the carnage in Algeria, which continues to claim innocent lives. Mr Cook may have chosen an issue which allows him to use a powerful tool of Union policy: inter-regional cooperation.

THE COMMON BELIEF IS THAT a serious or effective foreign policy for the European Union is unattainable. The Common Foreign and Security Policy (CFSP), established by the Maastricht Treaty in 1993, has proved insubstantial, resulting at best in well-meaning démarches (policy statements)

HAZEL SMITH is Director of the University of Kent's London Centre of International Relations. The author of *European Union Foreign Policy and Central America* (Macmillan, 1995), she is completing *The Foreign Policy of the European Union* for Macmillan.

on issues of international concern—ex-Yugoslavia, the Middle East or Somalia—or, at worst, irrelevance.

This interpretation argues that the lack of a military force and the inability to make decisions that can override national interest are permanent constraints on effective EU action. This is tied to the idea that no Union body is sovereign and, as only sovereign bodies carry out foreign policy, the EU is not—and never will be—a foreign policy actor.

There are enormous problems with this conventional interpretation of EU foreign policy. Firstly, to take the three areas of crisis already mentioned, Brus-

sels is the major aid donor and is also helping to create post-conflict structures to enable peace to be made and hopefully kept.

In former-Yugoslavia, the EU has administered the divided Croat-Muslim city of Mostar, supervised the Western European Union provided police force, and has been an active participant in the post-Dayton Peace Implementation Council.

In the Middle East it has provided financial and technical support for the electoral process and the training of Palestinian police and has initiated and is financing a Mediterranean-wide political and economic dialogue designed to support the Middle East peace process.

In Somalia, among other things, it is directly helping to create a new constitution with a decentralised system organised as far as possible along functional cooperation lines.

None of these statements imply that the EU is the major or most significant external player, although in Somalia it might well claim to be so, or that the Union achieves all objectives in all circumstances—what state, including the United States does? They do, however, belie the myth of an EU foreign policy that is entirely procedural and solely based on insouciant statements from Brussels divorced from practical involvement in current conflicts.

NO ARMY, NO POLICY

The second problem with the conventional understanding of EU foreign policy is the conceptual contradiction at its core. If the EU cannot be a foreign policy actor because it does not have effective use of military force then many, if not most, states could not possess meaningful foreign policies.

Costa Rica has not had an army since 1948 and many small nations, including EU states such as Belgium, Ireland, Luxembourg and the Netherlands, do not realistically expect to achieve foreign policy objectives through military force.

In terms of the lack of centralised decision-making capacity, it is arguable whether, given the fragmentation of power between Congress, the Presidency and the Supreme Court, US foreign policy decision-making is any easier than within the institutionally fragmented EU. Yet this has not stopped the United States becoming the world's most powerful state.

As for the view that the EU is not sovereign and therefore cannot have a foreign policy, this ignores two important issues. Firstly the evidence suggests that member states have not had any qualms about 'signing away' their sovereignty on significant aspects of foreign relations—for instance, on external trade, a fundamental part of foreign policy in this era of globalisation.

Secondly, such an argument denies the possibility of the pooling of sovereignty, that foreign policy competencies

can be shared by member states working both bilaterally and nationally, and collectively and multilaterally with other members.

COMPLIMENTARY POLICY POSSIBILITIES

The EU has developed an extensive foreign policy since the early 1970s. This was first made possible in the late 1960s by the common external tariff which enabled the then European Community (EC) to pursue shared economic interests abroad and to utilise collective economic instruments—including economic sanctions—to achieve political ends. One of the earliest examples was the Commission's suspension of aid to Greece in 1967 after the military coup.

Union foreign policy has not replaced member-state's foreign policy but created a complementary network of policy possibilities. It has neither evolved as a mere instrument of member-states nor as a Commission-led independent foreign policy.

None of the three major institutions—the Council, Commission or Parliament—has a monopoly on any aspect of foreign policy decision-making, and increasingly all of them, including the Parliament—conventionally (mis)understood as a toothless watchdog—have some say. This gives member-states a very strong input—being directly represented in the Council and indirectly through the national and party affiliation of European Parliament members.

GLOBAL PLAYER

European Union foreign policy is global in scope and multidimensional in nature and functions. An illustration of the global reach is that by 1993, 157 non-member states had established diplomatic missions in Brussels, precisely because of the importance for them of EU foreign policy.

Although EU policy is variegated in terms of the issues with which it is concerned, it reflects—as would foreign policy in any state—the evolution and nature of the Union's domestic concerns. Security and defence (in the broadest sense, including democracy and human rights) provide an important focus—as do external trade, develop-

ment and inter-regional cooperation and enlargement. Monetary relations are not yet on the Union's foreign policy agenda but they will become an important issue with European Monetary Union.

The inter-regional approach is the most distinctive aspect of EU foreign policy. The Union has expanded inter-regional links so that it now has a global network with regional and sub-regional organisations in Asia, Latin America, the Middle East, Africa and Europe. This addresses four interrelated objectives of Union foreign policy.

Firstly, the EU encourages both the development of regional integration between its partners for economic reasons—economies of scale, larger markets, etc—and political reasons—the idea that peace between neighbours is more likely if they assume the 'habit of cooperation' within technocratic, politically neutral, economic institutions.

USEFUL AMBIGUITY

Secondly, the EU prefers to negotiate trade and political agreements with multilateral partners since it can encourage trade-offs between states and use ambiguities of diplomatic phrasing to achieve agreements that might otherwise have been 'difficult to sell' at home or to partners.

In this way Brussels can promote conflict resolution with disparate partners in multilateral groupings—for instance in its dealings with Central America in the 1980s when it supported the peace process by encouraging region to region diplomacy.

In this case, the approach on human rights, peace and democratisation was general enough for European Social Democrats to argue that it was directed at the right in Central America—and the European Christian Democrats and the right could argue that it primarily had the left wing Nicaraguan Sandinistas in its sights. This rhetorical ambiguity allowed the development of an uneasy coalition across Central America and Europe that eventually succeeded in making peace—inter-regional diplomacy developing an ethical foreign policy.

Thirdly the EU uses inter-regional diplomacy as collective security mechanism. Partner states which sign agreements including human rights, rule of law and de-

Two Algerian children who lost their family in a massacre in January

(Associated Press)

mocratisation clauses, are both persuaded to adhere to those commitments by promises of aid and coerced into maintaining them by threats of sanctions.

Although this type of approach can only work with poorer dependent states, it has a semi-global application since it is the basis of the EU's treaty relationships with the 71 states of the African, Caribbean and Pacific (ACP) grouping. In 1994, for instance, eight ACP states—Gambia, Equatorial Guinea, Liberia, Nigeria, Somalia, Sudan, Togo and Zaire—had aid suspended or restricted for political or security reasons.

Fourthly, the EU uses inter-regional diplomacy to provide fora in which it can develop relationships it would otherwise have some difficulty justifying. This particularly applies to states with obnoxious human rights regimes—but with which the EU conducts relations because of strategic and/or economic interests. The best example of this is Brussels' relationship with the Gulf Cooperation Council (GCC) which allows it to negotiate with Saudi Arabia, the GCC's dominant power, more or less unfettered by European public opinion.

INTEREST AND ETHICS

The first, second and third of these objectives combine both interest and ethics. The pursuit of conflict resolution encourages political stability which in turn creates a safer, more predictable environment for trade and minimises domestic fall-out from external conflicts. Containing conflict abroad can mean less pressure on the EU, in terms of migration for instance, and it also reduces the possibility of external conflicts being fought on the streets of Paris or London. The fourth objective is entirely directed by strategic and economic interest.

The major failure of the EU's inter-regional policy has been in the attempt to sustain a multilateral arrangement with the north African states of Algeria, Libya, Mauritania, Morocco and Tunisia—which since 1989 have been collectively organised within the Arab Maghreb Union (AMU).

There have been at least four attempts to create inter-regional cooperation with the five Maghreb states. The AMU and its members have been very keen to develop such cooperation and

met EU officials several times in the early 1990s to try to further links.

BETWEEN 60,000 AND 80,000 PEOPLE HAVE BEEN KILLED IN ALGERIA SINCE 1991 IN A CONTINUING BLOODY, PRIMITIVE AND INHUMAN BARBARISM.

Also in 1990/91 France, Italy and Spain proposed a Conference on Security and Cooperation in the Mediterranean

183

(CSCM) and again in 1990 and 1991, President Francois Mitterand tried to establish a 'Five plus Five' arrangement which would have included France, Italy, Portugal, Spain and Malta as well as the AMU states.

These efforts foundered because of British and United States opposition to any move that would have included Libya in a multilateral arrangement and given diplomatic credibility and legitimacy to the Ghadaffi regime.

The only multilateral initiative left to the EU is the 'Barcelona process'—a loose link of north and south Mediterranean states, established in 1995 and designed to support the Madrid peace process through the promotion of free trade, transfers of development aid and support for democratisation.

This approach is hopelessly inappropriate as a framework for policy towards north Africa—partly because two of the five Maghrebi states are not participants. Mauritania's organised links with the EU are through ACP treaties and Libya is excluded because of United States and British insistence that it continue to be treated as a 'pariah' state.

Tunisia and Morocco have negotiated bilateral agreements in the context of the Barcelona approach but it would be difficult for Brussels to establish such an agreement with Algeria, given that European public opinion seems likely to demand visible and discernible improvements in the most basic of human rights—the right of children, women and men not to be massacred.

Between 60,000 and 80,000 people have been killed in Algeria since 1991 in a continuing bloody, primitive and inhuman barbarism. The Algerian state—the military, the bureaucracy and the government—are complicit in that they are not preventing the carnage. The Algerian government's claim not to be directly involved is irrelevant as, even if it were true, the absolute lack of activity designed to stop the violence is justification enough to charge it with criminal negligence.

Algeria continues to receive substantial financial benefits from EU aid—partly from general funds through the Barcelona process and partly from emergency and food aid budgets. The Union is anxious not to exclude Algeria from benefits and keen to maintain good diplomatic relations because it has very direct economic and political links in the Maghreb.

In 1991 Libya and Algeria were respectively the fifteenth and seventeenth most important sources of the EC's imports. Algerian gas is supplied directly by pipeline through Tunisia to Italy, and construction is under way to allow the same direct access by way of Morocco for Spain and Portugal.

FORCING CHANGE

If the EU and Britain seriously want to engage in Algeria, however, there is a way to formulate and implement policy. They can resurrect the EU-AMU dialogue and start to develop a policy which can do trade offs across and between the two regions.

Not all the mechanisms of inter-regional cooperation could be used to produce change in Algeria. For instance Algeria is not a particularly poor country in global terms—the 1997 World Bank reports puts it 69th in world development terms—just above Jordan and Jamaica and just below El Salvador and the Ukraine.

Brussels has much less financial leverage than it would have on say Mauritania. But at the same time Algeria does want to maintain and expand trade links with the Union and even its government must now realise that long term internal political instability will not benefit domestic or international political credibility.

The EU's inter-regional approach could deliver the goods for British foreign policy given its track record of managing ethics and interest. But it would mean that the foreign secretary would have to be tough enough to diverge from the United States in a change of tack towards Libya. Given some imagination a new approach might help sort out two problems at once—Libya and Algeria.

We have yet to see whether Britain's new foreign policy can deliver—not just or primarily to test its credibility—but for a much more important reason: to help protect the safety, security and lives of tens of thousands of innocents in Algeria.

Article 7   *Harvard International Review*, Summer 1994

The Migration Challenge

Europe's Crisis in Historical Perspective

James F. Hollifield

James F. Hollifield is Assistant Professor of Political Science at Auburn University.

Few issues have had a greater impact on the politics and society of contemporary Western Europe than immigration. The variety of national responses to the migration crisis would seem to indicate that each state is designing its own policy, and that there is little to link one national experience with another. Moreover, a majority of West European governments and elites have rejected any comparisons with the American experience, arguing that the United States is a nation of immigrants, with much greater territory and a political culture that is more tolerant of ethnic and cultural differences. In recent years, the American "model" of a multicultural and immigrant society has been deemed by many political and intellectual elites in Western Europe a bad model, which can only lead to greater social and political conflict—such critics point to the 1992 riots in Los Angeles. Yet the problems of immigration control (and ultimately the assimilation of foreign populations) in Europe are much the same as in the United States, for two reasons.

First, the global economic dynamic which underlies the migration crisis is similar in the two regions. The great postwar migrations to Western Europe and the United States began, for the most part, in response to the demand for cheap labor and the pull of high-growth economies, which in the 1950s and 1960s literally sucked labor from poorer countries of the periphery, especially Mexico, the Caribbean, southern Europe, North Africa and Turkey. These labor migrations (and *demand-pull* forces) were subsequently legitimized by the receiving states through what came to be known as guestworker and bracero policies. This economically beneficial movement of labor was consistent with the liberal spirit of the emerging global economy.

But what started as an efficient transfer of labor from poor countries of the South to the North, rapidly became a social and political liability in the 1970s, when growth rates in the OECD countries slowed in the aftermath of the first big postwar recession of 1973–74. The recession led to major policy shifts in Western Europe to stop immigration or, at least, to stop the recruitment of foreign workers. At the same time, however, demand-pull forces were rapidly giving way to *supply-push* forces, as the populations of poorer, peripheral coun-

tries began to grow at a rapid pace and their economies weakened. Informational and kinship networks had been established between immigrants and their home countries (via families and villages). These networks helped to spur immigration, despite the increasingly desperate attempts by receiving states in Western Europe to stop all forms of immigration.

Global economic (push-pull) forces provide the necessary conditions for international migration, especially the continuation of immigration in Western Europe after the implementation of restrictionist policies in the 1970s. But to understand fully the crisis of immigration control in the 1980s and 1990s, we must look beyond economics to liberal political developments in the major receiving states. The struggle to win civil and social *rights* for marginal groups, including ethnic minorities and foreigners, and the institutionalization of these rights in the jurisprudence of liberal states provide the sufficient conditions for continued immigration. Therefore, to get a complete picture of the migration crisis we must look at the degree of institutionalization of rights-based politics in the countries of Western Europe and at the struggle to redefine citizenship and nationhood in states such as France, Britain and Germany.

The migration tides of the 1950s and 1960s created new and reluctant lands of immigration in Western Europe and brought to the fore questions of citizenship, the rights of minorities and multiculturalism. The migration crisis also led to the rise of anti-immigrant, right-wing parties opposed to the extension of rights to non-citizens, ethnic minorities and asylum seekers. These right-wing political and social movements amounted to a populist/nativist backlash tinged with neo-fascism and opposed to rights-based, liberal politics. But the migration crisis also demonstrated the extent to which new civil and social rights for foreign and ethnic minorities had become embedded in the jurisprudence, institutions and political processes of the West European states since 1945. A new sensitivity to the rights of minorities and refugees grew out of the experiences of the Second World War and the Cold War, making it difficult for states simply to expel or deport unwanted migrants, as was done in earlier periods.

Origins of the Migration Crisis

The origins of the migration crisis in Western Europe can be traced to three historical developments, each of which contributed to the political-economic dynamic described above. First is the crisis of *decolonization* which led to an unsettled period of mass migrations from roughly 1945 to 1962–63. The political and economic significance of these movements of populations early in the postwar period should not be underestimated, for it was the aftermath of war and decolonization that created new ethnic cleavages and a new ethnic consciousness in these societies and, thereby, laid the groundwork for the rise of extremist, populist and nativist movements such as the *Front National* in France and the *Republikaner* in Germany.

The second and perhaps most important wellspring of the migration crisis in Western Europe is the set of public policies known as guestworker (*Gastarbeiter*) or rotation policies. These policies for recruiting ostensibly temporary foreign workers began as early as 1945 in Switzerland, whose policy came to be viewed as the model for guestworker programs in other West European countries. The central feature of these policies was the concept of rotation, whereby foreign unmarried male workers could be brought into the labor market for a specified, contractual period and sent back at the end of this period. They could be replaced by new workers as needed. This was a rather neat macroeconomic formula for solving what was shaping up to be one of the principal obstacles to continued high rates of non-inflationary growth in the 1950s and 1960s. In fact, it seemed to be working so well in the Swiss case that the newly reorganized Organization for Economic Cooperation and Development (OECD) recommended the policy to European states that were experiencing manpower shortages. The Bonn government forged a consensus in 1959–60 among business and labor groups to opt for a policy of importing labor rather than taking industry, capital and jobs offshore in search of lower labor costs, as was being done in the United States. This was the beginning of the largest guestworker program in Western Europe, which would eventually bring millions of Turks, Yugoslavs and Greeks to work in German industry.

Two fateful turning points in the history of the German guestworker program are of interest. The first came in 1967–68, following the shallow recession of 1966. It was at this point that the Grand Coalition government (1966–69) successfully stopped Turks and other guestworkers from entering the labor market, and sent many of them home. This operation was so successful that there was little resistance to bringing the guestworkers back in 1969–70, when the West European economies were heating up again. The second fateful turning point in the history of the *Gastarbeiter* program in Germany came in 1973 when the attempt was made to stop all recruitment of foreign workers, to repatriate them and to prevent family reunification. It was at this point that the relatively new liberal features of the German state came fully to the fore to prevent the government and administrative authorities from stopping immigration (especially family reunification) and deporting unwanted migrants.

France is often mentioned as a European country that pursued guestworker-type policies, a somewhat misleading conception. The Provisional or Tripartite Government under General Charles de Gaulle (1945–46), as well as the first governments of the Fourth Republic, did put in place policies for recruiting foreign labor. But the new workers were defined from the outset as *travailleurs immigrés* (immigrant workers). Policies of Fourth Republic governments encouraged foreign workers to settle permanently because immigration was part and parcel of population policy, which was itself a reflection of pronatalist sentiments among the political elites.

As the French economy boomed in the 1960s, authorities rapidly lost all control over immigration. But instead of sucking more labor from culturally compatible neighboring countries, such as Italy and Spain (which were beginning to develop in their own right), the French economy was supplied principally by the newly independent states of North Africa (Algeria, Morocco and Tunisia). By the end of the 1960s, Algerians were rapidly becoming the most numerous immigrant group. Their special post-colonial status gave them virtual freedom of movement into and out of the former *metropole* of France. The principal "mode of immigration" during this period was immigration "from within," whereby foreigners would enter the country (often having been recruited by business), take a job and then have a request be made on their behalf by the firm for an adjustment of status.

By the early 1970s, the rapid increase in North African immigration convinced the Pompidou government that something had to be done to regain control of immigration. The deep recession of 1973–74, which brought an abrupt end to the postwar boom, simply confirmed this judgment. The new government under Valery Giscard d'Estaing took fairly dramatic steps to close the immigration valve, using heavy-handed statist and administrative measures to try to stop immigration, repatriate immigrants and deny "rights" of family reunification. Thus, the French followed much the same logic as the Germans in attempting to use foreign workers, on one hand, as a kind of industrial reserve army and, on the other, as shock absorbers to solve social and economic problems associated wish recession—especially unemployment. Other labor-importing states in Western Europe followed the same guestworker logic in changing from policies of recruitment to suspension.

The migration crisis in Western Europe in the 1980s and 1990s cannot be fully understood apart from the history of the guestworker programs. These programs created the illusion of temporary migration, leading some states (especially Germany) to avoid or postpone a national debate over immigration and assimilation policy. This problem was compounded by the statist attempts in 1973–74 to stop immigration and repatriate foreigners, which furthered the "myth of return" and heightened public expectations that governments could simply reverse the migratory process. Also, taking such a strong, statist stance against further immigration made it virtually impossible for French and German governments in the 1980s and 1990s even to discuss an "American-style," legal immigration policy. Instead, immigration became a highly charged partisan issue, leading to soul-searching debates about national identity and citizenship. The more practical questions—which an American policymaker or politician might ask—of "how many, from where, and in what status," simply could not be asked. The result of trying to slam shut the "front door" of legal immigration led to the opening of side doors and windows (for family members and seasonal workers). Most importantly, the "back door" was left wide open (especially in Germany) for refugees and asylum-seekers. Not surprisingly, many would-be legal and illegal immigrants (as well as legitimate asylum-seekers and others) flooded through the back door in the 1980s and 1990s.

The third historical development in the migration crisis is the influx of *refugees* and *asylum-seekers,* which is causally related to colonialism and to the failed guestworker policies. Large-scale refugee migrations began in Europe in the aftermath of the Second World War and with the advent of the Cold War. In practice, flight from a communist regime was sufficient grounds for the extension of political asylum in most of the countries of Western Europe. The famous Article 16 of the West German Basic Law, which granted an almost unconditional right to asylum for any individual fleeing persecution, was written with refugees from the East in mind, especially ethnic German refugees.

Refugee and asylum policies in Western Europe functioned rather well for almost three decades from roughly 1950 to 1980 (during most of the Cold War), but with the closing of front-door immigration policies in the 1970s, political asylum became an increasingly attractive mode of entry for unwanted migrants who would come to be labeled "economic refugees." As governments across Western Europe struggled to redefine their immigration and refugee policies in the wake of severe economic recessions and rising unemployment, the pace of refugee migrations increased. The first efforts to address this new movement of populations came at the level of the European Community, where it was thought that national governments could simultaneously reassert control over refugee movements and avoid the painful moral and political dilemmas involved in limiting the right to asylum. The Single European Act of 1985 set in motion a new round of European economic integration, which included the goal of "free movement of goods, persons, services and capital"—in effect, the establishment of a border-free Europe. It quickly became clear, however, that achieving this goal would require European states to agree upon common visa and asylum policies.

Toward this end, five states (France, Germany, and the Benelux countries) met in the Dutch town of Schengen, and in 1985 unveiled the Schengen Agreement as a prototype for a border-free Europe. The Agreement called for the elimination of internal borders, the harmonization of visa and asylum policies and the coordinated policing of external borders, leading

to the construction of a symbolic "ring fence" around the common territory. Schengen, which was enlarged to include Italy, Spain and Portugal, was followed in 1990 by the Dublin Agreement, which established the principle that refugees must apply for asylum in the first EC member state in which they arrive. But no sooner had the states of Western Europe begun to focus on a common policy for dealing with the refugee and asylum issue, than had the entire international system in Europe changed with the collapse of communist regimes in East-Central Europe and, finally, the collapse of the Soviet Union itself.

The euphoria associated with the "triumph of liberalism" over communism did contribute, at least briefly, to a surge of refugee migration. That surge lasted for about four years, from 1989 to 1993. Governments were forced to reconsider and rewrite sweeping constitutional provisions, which guaranteed the right to asylum, at the same time that new irredentist movements swept the Balkans, Transcaucasia and other formerly communist territories, leading to civil wars and new refugee migrations.

How have the states of Western Europe and the EC responded to the migration crisis? The responses can be identified at three levels. The first is political, in the sense that politicians, especially on the right, have exploited the migration crisis for political gain. The second is a policy-level response, which has lurched from one extreme to another. Liberal and assimilationist policies of amnesty (for illegals) have been followed by harsh crackdowns on asylum-seekers and attempts to make naturalization more difficult. Finally, emerging from this cauldron of political and policy debates is a search for national "models" of immigration, which range from tempered pluralism in Britain to stringent assimilation in France.

The Search for a National Model

France was the first state in Western Europe to feel the full political force of the migration crisis, in part because of the stunning victory of the left in the presidential and parliamentary elections of 1981. The socialists won the elections partly on a liberal platform, which promised to improve civil rights for immigrants by giving them a more firm legal standing. To carry out these promises, the first socialist government of Pierre Mauroy enacted a conditional amnesty, which led to the legalization of well over 100,000 undocumented immigrants. Other measures also were taken to limit the arbitrary powers of the police to carry out identity checks, to grant long-term (10-year) resident permits to foreigners and to guarantee the rights of association for immigrant groups. These liberal policies, carried out in the wake of the left's electoral breakthrough and with the right in a state of temporary disarray, provided an opening for a little-known populist and neo-fascist candidate, Jean-Marie Le Pen, and the *Front National* (FN). The early 1980s was also a period of recession, rising unemployment and general insecurity, especially among workers. Le Pen and his group seized the moment and won what seemed to be a small victory (16.7 percent of the vote) in the town of Dreux, near Paris. But this was the beginning of an intense period of immigration politics, as the right struggled to regain power and Le Pen, under the banner of *La France aux français,* garnered more support from an extremely volatile electorate.

The traditional parties of the right, *Rassemblement pour la République* (RPR) and *Union pour la Démocratie Française* (UDF), under the leadership of Jacques Chirac, Mayor of Paris, began to attack the socialists' handling of the immigration issue. The socialists responded by defending liberal and republican principles of naturalization and assimilation, holding out the prospect of voting rights for resident aliens in local elections, while promising to enforce labor laws (employer sanctions) in order to crack down on illegal immigration. In the parliamentary elections of 1985, which were fought under new rules of proportional representation, the right won a narrow victory. The FN won over 30 seats in the new parliament, giving Le Pen a forum in which to pursue his anti-immigrant, populist, nativist agenda. The Minister of the Interior in the government of *cohabitation* (headed by Chirac), Charles Pasqua, launched a series of initiatives and bills, which came to be known as *la loi Pasqua.* They intended to give greater power to the police to arrest and deport undocumented migrants, and to deny entry to asylum-seekers, who would not be allowed to appeal their cases to the office for protection of refugees (OFPRA).

Immigrant rights groups, such as *SOS-racisme, France Plus,* MRAP and the GISTI, organized protests and legal appeals to stop the reform. Thousands marched in the streets under banners that read *ne touche pas mon pote* (don't touch my buddy) and the French Council of State was called upon to review the legality (and constitutionality) of the government's immigration policy. In the end, the government made a decision to appoint a special commission composed of leading intellectual and political figures. The commission held public hearings and wrote a long report, concluding that French republican principles of universalism and the right of foreigners born in France to naturalize (*jus soli*) should be upheld. At the same time, the commission stressed the importance of maintaining the assimilationist, republican principles, inherent in French immigration law and practice. The right lost the presidential and parliamentary elections of 1988, essentially failing to capitalize on the immigration issue, while Jean-Marie Le Pen succeeded in gaining 14.5 percent of the vote on the first ballot of the presidential elections. But the FN received only one seat in the new parliament, which was elected according to the old two-round, single member district rules used throughout the history of the Fifth Republic until 1985. Le Pen cried foul, arguing that the voices of a significant proportion of the French electorate were not being heard, and opinion polls, which showed that over a third of the voters supported the positions of the FN, seemed to bear him out.

The socialist government of François Mitterrand and Michel Rocard continued to defend rights of foreigners, but also launched a campaign for tougher enforcement of labor laws and set up a new council for integration (*Haut Conseil à l'Intégration*) to study ways of bringing immigrants into the mainstream of French social, economic and political life.

French Immigration Policy in the 1990s

Immigration in France continued during this period of the 1980s at a rate of about 100,000 annually, and refugee migrations picked up to about 25,000 annually. As the country slipped slowly into recession in 1991–92, the left began to lose its nearly decade-long grip on power. The parliamentary elections of 1993 were fought in part over the issue of immigration control, with the right feeling little compulsion to restrain anti-immigrant, populist and nativist sentiments among the public. In fact, the decision was made to try to steal the thunder of Le Pen and the FN by proposing harsh measures for dealing with illegal immigration and asylum seekers. The badly divided socialist party suffered a crushing defeat in March 1993, and the reinvigorated right (RPR-UDF), under the new leadership of Edouard Balladur wasted little time in implementing draconian measures (by French standards) to stop immigration. Once again, Pasqua was named to head the Interior Ministry, and with the right controlling nearly 80 percent of the seats in the National Assembly, he proposed a series of bills to reform immigration, naturalization and refugee law (*la loi Pasqua II*). These measures amounted to a broadside attack on the civil and social rights of foreigners. They sought to undermine key aspects of the republican model, as spelled out in the *Ordonnances* of 1945, especially residency requirements for naturalization, the principle of *jus soli* and the guarantee of due process for asylum-seekers.

La loi Pasqua II also included a bill designed to prevent illegal immigrants from benefiting from French social security, particularly health care. This legislation immediately opened a rift in the new French cabinet between the hard-line Minister of Interior and Regional Development, Pasqua, and the more liberal-republican Minister of Social, Health and Urban Affairs, Simone Veil, who argued successfully that emergency medical care should not be denied to foreigners. *Pasqua II* also sought to limit the civil rights of immigrants and asylumseekers, by increasing the powers of the police and the administration to detain and deport unwanted migrants. Under the new policy, the police are given sweeping powers to check the identity of "suspicious persons." Race is not supposed to be sufficient grounds for stopping an individual, but any immigrant (legal or otherwise) who threatens "public order" can be arrested and deported. Immigrant workers and students are obliged to wait two years, rather than one, before being allowed to bring their families to join them in France, and illegal immigrants cannot be legalized simply by marrying a French citizen. Finally *Pasqua II* resurrected the Chirac government's proposal to reform French nationality law (1986), which requires the children of foreigners born in France to file a formal request for naturalization between the ages of 16 and 21, rather than automatically attributing French citizenship to them at age 18.

These repressive measures, which were designed specifically to roll back the rights of foreigners, immigrants and asylum seekers, immediately drew fire from those institutions of the liberal and republican state that were created to protect the rights of individuals. The Council of State, as it had done several times before, warned the government that it was on shaky legal ground, especially with respect to the "rights" of family reunification and political asylum. But the rulings of the Council of State are advisory; no matter how much moral, political and legal weight they may carry, the government can choose to ignore them. The rulings, however, can presage binding decisions of the Constitutional Council, which has limited powers of judicial review. This is precisely what happened in August 1993, as the Constitutional Council found several provisions of the new policy (*Pasqua II*) to be unconstitutional.

All this political and legal maneuvering in 1993 has led inexorably to a full constitutional debate over immigration and refugee policy in France. French President François Mitterrand, who has considerable constitutional responsibilities and political and moral authority, has stayed for the most part on the sidelines. The Minister of the Interior, Pasqua, has continued doggedly to pursue more restrictionist immigration and naturalization policies, at the levels of both symbolic and electoral politics. Any political victories on this front would seem to come at the expense of the principal rivals of the RPR-UDF, namely the FN on the right and the Socialist Party on the left.

These policy and political responses to the migration crisis in France constitute a tacit recognition that there is only so much any state can do to alter push-pull forces, and that a "roll back" of civil and social rights is the most effective way to control or stop immigration. But in France, as in the US and Germany, administrative and executive authorities are confronted with a range of constitutional obstacles associated with the liberal and republican state. The republican model, with its universalistic and egalitarian principles, remains essentially intact, despite repeated assaults from the French right. France still has the most expansive naturalization policies of any state in Western Europe and it has preserved the principles of *jus soli*, as well as due process, equality before the law and the right to asylum. Whether the republican model will survive the current assault and whether it can serve as a broader European model remains to be seen.

The German Response

Until recently, debates over immigration and refugee policy in Germany were confined to policy and administrative elites or academic and intellectual circles. But in the late 1980s, and especially since unification, politicians have seized on the immigration and refugee issue. A full-blown national debate has erupted, with politicians vying for mass support and various social movements on the left and the right seeking to influence policymaking. Unlike France, Germany does not have an established "national model" around which to organize this debate. Debates over immigration, naturalization and refugee law are not, however, devoid of ethno-nationalist or ethno-cultural arguments. The current German nationality law dates from 1913; there are clear historical and national overtones in the debate. But the experience of the Holocaust and the defeat suffered in World War II make it difficult for German authorities to appeal to the past as a way of coping with immigration. Until 1989, a consensus existed among political and policy elites simply to avoid debates over immigration, naturalization and citizenship issues. Foreigners were granted social and civil rights, but barriers to naturalization remained high and the politically explosive issue of reforming the nationality code was avoided.

> The sufficient conditions for immigration . . . are likely to persist, even if they are weakened by attacks from the extreme right and lack of popular support.

This ostrich-like approach to immigration policy and the elite's consensus not to raise the issue simply fell apart under the pressure of events in the 1980s. Decades of repressed nationalism have come bubbling to the surface in contemporary party politics. Polls, which showed rising opposition to immigration, encouraged politicians to take up the issue. When Helmut Kohl was chosen to head the new government of the right in 1982, he introduced a new *Ausländerpolitik*, but in the election campaign of 1982–83, the issue simply disappeared from the national agenda. In effect, policy and political elites decided to return to the earlier consensus of silence. Also strong was an appeal to the founding (economic) myth of the Federal Republic, or *Wirtschaftswunder*, that seemingly intractable social, economic and even political problems could be solved by another German economic miracle. But this economic solution proved insufficient to solve the problems of immigration control and assimilation, especially with rising unemployment rates and severe housing shortages. By the mid- to late-1980s, foreigners were increasingly being blamed for taking jobs, housing and public services away from German citizens.

In the Bavarian *Landtag* elections of 1986, the CSU raised the issue of immigration control, in part to counter the breakaway of a small faction of the party, under the leadership of a former talk show host, Franz Schonhuber. This faction became the *Republikaner* party and gained 3 percent of the vote. In the following years the *Republikaner* continued to make inroads at the level of state and local politics. With the collapse of the German Democratic Republic and the unification of Germany in 1989–90, it appeared that the *Republikaner* had lost its appeal. It received only 2.1 percent of the vote in the first all-German, federal election in 1990. But its fortunes were to improve in the early 1990s. Clearly, with the collapse of Communism and the end of the Cold War, some of the restraints on overt expressions of German nationalism were removed and the immigration issue was no longer taboo. A new anti-foreigner slogan, *Ausländer raus,* became the rallying cry of far-right, skinhead and neo-Nazi groups. The massive influx of asylum seekers from 1989–93 contributed to the atmosphere of crisis, placing more pressure on the government to act, and making it easier for politicians (of the right) to use the immigration and asylum issue to get votes.

In 1990, the newly reelected government of Kohl faced two problems: how to facilitate the integration and naturalization of the large foreign population, without alienating more of the right-wing electorate, and how to build a consensus for changing Article 16 of the German Constitution to stem the rising tide of asylum seekers, while keeping the front door open to ethnic German refugees from the East. The first task was at least partially accomplished by rushing a bill through parliament to facilitate naturalization of second-generation immigrants, thereby solidifying the rights of resident aliens, and removing some of the legal ambiguities concerning residency, work permits and family reunification. This was done quietly in the midst of the social and political euphoria following unification.

Reform of immigration and refugee policy was given a new urgency in 1992 and 1993 by a series of much-publicized racist attacks against foreigners, including a firebombing by skinheads in the town of Solingen resulting in the death of five Turks who were permanent residents of the Federal Republic. More racist attacks occurred, however, just weeks after the Christian-Liberal government and the Social Democrats agreed in May 1993 to amend Article 16 of the Constitution. Although the language of the new asylum law, which states that "those politically persecuted enjoy the right to asylum," is consistent with the Geneva Convention, in practice the new law allows the German government to turn back asylum-seekers who arrive through a safe country. Since about 80 percent of refugees enter through Poland and the Czech Republic, an agreement had to be reached with these states to allow for the *refoulement* of asylum-seekers. Since the new policy was instituted, the

number of migrants apprehended trying to enter the country illegally has skyrocketed.

Despite a great deal of rhetoric following racial violence and fatal attacks on foreigners in 1993 and 1994, the Kohl government was unable to change German nationality law, which dates from 1913 and rests on the principle of *jus sanguinis* (blood, rather than soil or place of birth). The German law also does not allow dual citizenship. Hence, millions of foreign residents have been granted some civil and social rights, but without naturalization. They remain outsiders without full political rights, even though in many cases they have been born, reared and educated in Germany.

The Immigration Issue in Southern Europe

The countries of southern Europe—Italy, Spain, Greece and Portugal—are still far from developing national models for immigration control and assimilation. As the traditional receiving states in northern Europe tried to close their borders to new immigration in the 1970s and 1980s, more unwanted migrants (especially from Africa) began to enter the EC via the soft underbelly of Italy, Spain and Greece. Political change (democratization in Greece, Spain and Portugal) together with high levels of economic growth contributed to the influx of unwanted migrants. Policy responses have lurched from one extreme to another, in the face of a growing political backlash against foreigners, especially in northern Italy where the anti-immigrant Northern League has been capturing about one fifth of the vote in recent elections. Amnesty was extended to illegal immigrants in Spain (1985) and Italy (1987) in the hopes of bringing marginal groups and ethnic minorities into the mainstream of society by offering protections under the rubric of social welfare. But the push to establish a border-free Europe, as a result of the Single European Act, the Schengen Agreement and, finally, the Maastricht Treaty (which holds out the prospect of a kind of European citizenship in the next century), has forced the states of southern Europe to reformulate their immigration and refugee policies. To be a part of a border-free Europe, they must demonstrate a capacity for controlling their borders and stopping illegal immigration.

The perceived failure of national policies and the lack of a dominant national model for dealing with the migration crisis have led many governments in Western Europe to look for a Europe-wide solution to the problem of immigration control. The hope here is that the states of the European Union will be able to accomplish together what they have been unable to accomplish alone: stop immigration.

A European Solution to a Global Problem?

From the Treaty of Rome (1957) to the Maastricht Treaty, the logic of European integration has driven the states of Western Europe to cooperate on border control issues. The logic is one of both inclusion (free movement of goods, services, capital and *people*) and exclusion (a common tariff policy, an economic and monetary union and common visa and asylum policies). But common visa and asylum policies have proved illusive. The prospect of a truly border-free Europe places enormous pressure on member states to cooperate in the policing of external borders.

Control over population and territory are key aspects of national sovereignty that strike at the heart of notions of citizenship and national identity. Since ceding this aspect of sovereignty to a supranational organization such as the EU is a potentially explosive political issue, member states, as well as the European Council and the Commission, have proceeded with great caution. In Dublin in 1990, the European Council established the principle that refugees can apply for political asylum in only one member state. Shortly thereafter, the Schengen Group, which had been enlarged from the original five (France, Germany and Benelux) to include Italy, Spain and Portugal, met to sign the Convention that set in motion a process for lifting all border controls among these states. Britain, as an island-nation, steadfastly refused to get involved in the Schengen process for fear of losing its natural advantage in border control. Still, the inclusionary and exclusionary logic of Schengen seems to be taking hold in post–cold war Europe, as other states and regions have scrambled to join the border-free club. Only Switzerland and Denmark have been reluctant to jump on this bandwagon.

How will "Europe" respond to the global migration crisis? We can learn some things by looking at the recent past, especially the liberal dynamic of *markets* (demand-pull and supply-push) and *rights* (civil, social and political) described above. We must also compare the European and American experiences, because the EU and the United States will be the pacesetters in searching for an international solution to the global migration crisis. Will there be separate American and European models for coping with migration, or will the two models converge? The liberal dynamic and the recent past point to convergence. With the end of the Cold War, all OECD states have experienced an upsurge in migration because (happily) people are freer to move, and because (sadly) ethnic and nationalist forces have been unleashed, causing a wave of refugee migration. The liberal logic of interdependence and economic integration has reinforced the propensity of people to move, in search of higher wages and a better way of life.

Supply-push remains strong, but demand-pull is weak. Most of the OECD states are in (or just emerging from) recession. Nevertheless, with slower population growth (especially in Western Europe and Japan) and higher levels of economic growth, demand for immigrant labor is likely to increase as we move closer to the turn of the century. The necessary economic conditions for immigration are present and likely to strengthen, hence all OECD states will be forced to deal with this reality. But what will political conditions, which are the sufficient conditions for immigration, be like in the receiving states?

At present, it would appear that the politics of xenophobia, nativism and restrictionism prevail and that each state is defining immigration and refugee policies in idiosyncratic and nationalistic terms. The rights of immigrants and refugees have been restricted and infringed in Europe and the United States, as governments (freed from the bipolar constraints of the Cold War) have sought to roll back some of the liberal political developments (especially in the area of civil rights) of the past forty years. But liberal-republican institutions and laws are quite resilient. It seems unlikely that what have come to be defined as basic human or civil rights will simply be suspended for non-citizens. Therefore, the sufficient conditions for immigration, which are closely linked to the institutions and laws of the liberal-republican state, are likely to persist, even if they are weakened by attacks from the extreme right and lack of popular support. It is also unlikely that liberal-republicanism will be abandoned or overridden by supranational institutions, such as the EU. The same institutional and legal checks found at the level of the nation-state are evident at the European level.

Since immigration is likely to continue, pressure will mount for states to cooperate in controlling and managing the flow. The states of Western Europe already have taken several steps in this direction at the level of the European Union. But no national or regional model for integration of the large and growing foreign populations has emerged. Policies for controlling the doors of entry (front, side and back) will emerge, barring some unforeseen international catastrophe. Redefining citizenship and nationhood in the older states of Western Europe, however, will be a much longer and more painful process. It remains to be seen which states are best equipped, politically and culturally, to face this challenge.

Article 8   *The National Interest,* Fall 1998

NATO: The Dilemmas of Expansion

Zbigniew Brzezinski

THE FIFTIETH anniversary of NATO, which falls next April, will mark the conclusion of the first enlargement of the Alliance undertaken since the peaceful end of the Cold War. It is also certain to give rise to a new debate as to whether the Alliance should continue to expand. It is therefore not too early to ponder the several ramifications of that issue. They involve such broad geostrategic matters as the nature of the long-term relationship of America to Europe, the proper scope of the Euroatlantic alliance, its connection to the also ongoing expansion of the European Union, the relationship of Russia to the expanded Euroatlantic and European structures—as well as the more immediate policy choices that may need to be made regarding the specific timing of any further expansion, its geographical direction, and its depth.

In brief, *whether,* and if so, *why, when, where,* and *how much* next to expand, and eventually where to stop, are the questions that need to be addressed and aired.

Europe is Unfinished Business

THE BASIC LESSON of the last five decades is that European security is the basis for European reconciliation. Without NATO, France would not have felt secure enough to reconcile with Germany, and both France and Britain would have even more actively opposed Germany's reunification. It is enough to recall here the last-ditch maneuvers by both Thatcher and Mitterrand to delay (and thus even prevent) the reunification of Germany in order to appreciate the extent to which NATO has helped pacify the persisting European fears of a powerful and potentially dominant Germany, its good democratic and European postwar record notwithstanding.

Moreover, without NATO, it is most unlikely—for the same reasons—that the EC and now the EU would have ever come into being. Similarly, the ongoing reconciliation between Germany and Poland would not have been possible without the American presence in Germany and the related sense of security that Poland's prospective membership in NATO has fostered in Poland. The same is true of the Czech Republic and Germany, Hungary and Romania, Romania and Ukraine; and the desire to get into NATO is also having a similar influence on Slovenia's attitude toward Italy and Lithuania's toward Poland.

In the foreseeable future, the evolving reconciliation between Poland and Russia is also likely to become more marked. The Poles, once in NATO, will fear less that a fraternal embrace by their more powerful neighbor will become again a stifling yoke. And once the Russians realize that Central Europe is no longer a geopolitical vacuum, their definition of their sphere of influence will become less ambitious. Given the fact that all of Russia's western neighbors—rightly or wrongly—fear its aspirations, greater regional security thus will be to the benefit of all of Europe, Russia included.

This point—that security breeds reconciliation—deserves reiteration, given the recent debates over NATO's expansion. Even a cursory review of the arguments made by the principal opponents of that expansion indicates how dramatically wrong have been their diagnoses. In fact, it would be positively unkind to list serially and identify all the apocalyptic predictions made by various scholars, ex-ambassadors, and editorialists regarding Russia's likely behavior in the wake of NATO's expansion. They simply failed to draw the most elementary lessons from Europe's recent history.

Moreover, the construction and expansion both of the EU and of NATO are clearly long-term historical processes that are still far from finished. Even if at this stage it may be premature to draw a demarcating line—and perhaps it should *never* be drawn with any degree of finality, given the contingent nature of historical processes—it is certainly evident that neither the EU nor NATO can be viewed as having reached its ultimate limits. Both institutions are committed publicly to further expansion, and even a glance at a map indicates why their present scope cannot be considered as final.

The expansion of the EU and of NATO are also mutually reinforcing processes. Each tends to facilitate the other, and the overlap between the two creates also the reality of greater political interdependence. That enhances the sense of shared security and even further binds Europe and America together. The two processes also leapfrog each other. At any point in time, expansion of one may be ahead of the other. Poland will be in NATO before it is in the EU. Estonia is likely to be in the EU before it is in NATO. But the overlap between most of the EU and most of NATO creates a sense of common geopolitical space that collectively reassures all involved in the two frameworks.

For NATO, however, the commitment to expansion does raise the more specific and fundamental question of the degree to which the organization should remain primarily an integrated political-military alliance and to what degree it should evolve into a regional security system. In the former case, collective defense has to be the central concern; in the latter, more emphasis can be assigned to peacekeeping. Again, in the former case, additional members should be judged primarily by the degree to which they may enhance the Alliance's political-military potential; in the latter, by the extent to which they increase the scope of political stability. The former argues for greater selectivity in admission; the latter for less discrimination.

Ultimately, neither formula can be seen as iron-clad, and expansion cannot be guided mechanically by either criterion. Nonetheless, the distinction should be kept in mind, in order to make certain that any additional expansion does contribute tangibly to collective security, and that it does not produce a watered-down NATO that gradually loses its political-military cohesion and its capacity for united and effective action. Concern for the preservation of the primacy of collective defense should also guide—and restrain any excessive enthusiasm in codifying—the formulation of NATO's new strategic doctrine and the assumption by NATO of new "out-of-area" roles and mission. By seeking to take on too much, one could run the risk of undermining the magnetic core of the Alliance.

Hence, gradual and measured expansion—one that provides time for the integration of new members, one that carefully meets the objective criteria of membership, and one that is derived from the subjectively voluntary desire of a given nation to join—is both desirable and even necessary. Halting the process would be arbitrary, demoralizing for those left out, and

pernicious to Europe's security. A significant gap between the eventual scope of the EU and of NATO could create tensions in the American-European connection, breed misunderstandings, and perhaps in some cases even tempt external challenges. A proclaimed or even de facto halt in NATO's expansion would also be a denial of everything that has lately been affirmed by all the top NATO leaders. It would thus fundamentally damage Euroatlantic credibility while perhaps unintentionally signaling that what is beyond NATO may be up for grabs.

When, Where, and How Much?

THE THREE NEW members—Poland, the Czech Republic, and Hungary—will be admitted early in 1999, either before or during the Alliance's fiftieth anniversary. At that point, some overt confirmation of the Alliance's oft-stated commitment to a continuing process ("open door policy") will be necessary, lest the impression be created that the first enlargement has been the last. One can anticipate that Russia will pursue that objective and might even condition President Yeltsin's attendance at the Washington fête—presumably much desired by the Clinton administration and justified by the existence of the NATO-Russia Council—on a promise that the issue of enlargement be ignored or muted, and that formal enlargement not even take place on that occasion.

Yet silence and inaction on the issue could prove as counterproductive as excessive emphasis on immediate and substantial follow-on enlargement. The Alliance is hardly ready to take on promptly a large second wave of members. It must absorb the newly admitted members, while Russia must accustom itself to the non-threatening reality of a gradually expanding alliance. That will require several years, and it is no

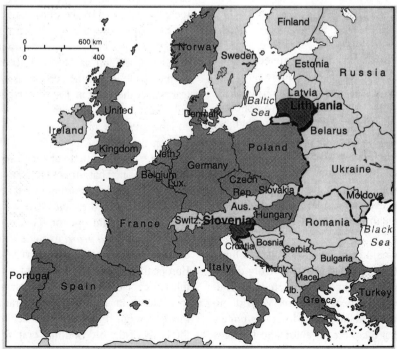

- - - the border of the old
Soviet Union (the "red line")

betrayal to acknowledge this reality. But silence or only a token enlargement limited to a single geopolitically insignificant and thus non-controversial new candidate would be tantamount to a message that further expansion has been relegated to *ad calendas grecas*. For reasons already stated, such a price should not be paid, even for a spectacular American-Russian public relations success at the 1999 NATO summit.

Accordingly, given these conflicting considerations, the best course of action should involve coupling a ceremonious welcome to the new members in April with a collective statement that the foreign and defense ministers of the Alliance are being charged with the task of identifying at a December 1999 ministerial the next potential candidates for membership. Negotiations with these candidates regarding the matter could subsequently begin, pointing perhaps to eventual admission a year or so later, depending on their respective states of readiness. This would give everyone concerned time to learn that gradual expansion enhances European reconciliation, while avoiding an ego contest at the April 1999 summit among the heads of state regarding the selection of any new candidates.

The foregoing would thus reconfirm that expansion is a continuing historical process, related to the construction of a new Europe and to the progressive redefinition of the scope and role of the Euroatlantic alliance. But doing so would necessitate also making a prudent choice regarding the direction and the depth of the second wave of enlargement. Expansion to the southeast of Europe would pose fewer problems with Russia, and probably hardly any if it were limited to Slovenia; expansion to the northeast, namely the Baltic states, would involve a wide crossing of Russia's declared "red line" and thus reignite the controversies that took place during the first enlargement. The southeast involves an area of greater instability but lesser external threat; the opposite is the case with the northeast. What follows from that fact in so far as NATO's interests are involved?

It has already been noted that expansion confined to only one and very non-controversial state would be more an act of evasion than of fidelity to oft-stated commitments. Yet selecting several states in one direction only could also prompt complications. To pick the Baltic states in one bite would be, indeed, to invite a quarrel with Russia that could be divisive both for Europe and for the Alliance itself. Yet to go deep exclusively in the southeast direction runs the risk, not only of selecting candidates who might not be quite ready for membership and thus actually weakening the Alliance's cohesion, but also of legitimating through the passage of time Russia's unilaterally drawn "red line."

Perhaps the best choice would be to remain faithful to three principles: first, that only qualified candidates who truly desire and are ready for membership should be considered; second, that in keeping with the solemn declaration of Madrid, no qualified European state can be excluded by Moscow's unilateral "red line"; and third, that there are no automatic linkages or clusters of states that have to be admitted together, either in

the southeast or the northeast. Just as the EU did not hesitate to select Estonia ahead of the other Baltic states, so NATO should not feel compelled to consider states in some special clusters.

Accordingly, it might be appropriate and constructive to examine the possibility of a limited expansion *both* to the southeast and to the northeast, involving no more than two or so states, depending on the degree to which they satisfy respectively the criteria of membership, and demonstrating thereby—but on a prudent basis—that no democratic state of Europe can be arbitrarily blackballed by a non-member from participation in the Euroatlantic alliance.

At the present time, in the southeast, Slovenia and perhaps also Romania seem to be most advanced in their preparations; and in the northeast that is the case with Lithuania. A decision in favor of Slovenia and Lithuania would have the advantage of enhancing the Alliance's geographical cohesion (and of establishing a direct land connection with Hungary), and both Italy and Denmark would be especially gratified. In the event that Lithuania were to be the northeastern choice, and given Estonia's advanced status in negotiations with the EU, it might also be wise to make concurrent efforts to facilitate Latvia's entrance into the WTO and to open a NATO information office in Riga (such offices exist in Moscow and Kyiv), in order to reassure Latvia that it was not being permanently left behind the "red line."

The Issue of Russia

A PROPERLY PACED process of enlargement should be one that neither over-stretches the Alliance's cohesion and capabilities nor unnecessarily delays Russia's liberation from its imperial nostalgia. Hence, Russia cannot, and should not, be excluded from the process of constructing a larger Europe securely embraced by the Euroatlantic alliance. But Russia cannot be allowed to exercise a veto on the free choice of individual European states and, even worse, to justify doing so on the basis that some of them had formerly been part of the Soviet Union. To the Baltic states, the additional fact that Russia still formally insists that they had in 1940 joined the Soviet Union *voluntarily* only adds insult to insecurity.

However, the process of expansion must be pursued in a fashion that gives Russia time to digest the new realities and to learn from them that enhanced security breeds more genuine reconciliation. That process has already started in Russian-Polish relations. It is important that it be matched by reconciliation with the Baltic states and also with Ukraine. At some point, Ukraine too might opt for a closer link with NATO, and NATO certainly cannot *a priori* exclude Ukraine simply because Moscow might disapprove. Moreover, Russia, if it is to be a truly European national state and not a nostalgic craver of empire, must accept the fact that democratic European states do wish to coalesce in a joint security framework with America, and that sovereign right cannot be denied to them. Lines drawn on the basis of the old Stalinist empire can only serve to separate Russia from Europe.

By the same token, Russia cannot be asked to accept the expansion of NATO if it is at the same time seen as excluded forever from a deepening association with it. The creation of the Joint NATO-Russian Council is a good beginning in forging a new relationship, and that step too should be viewed as a continuing and evolving process. If President Yeltsin were to attend the Washington NATO summit, he should hear there not only a reaffirmation of NATO's commitment to growth—in keeping with the voluntary desire of democratic European nations—but also a more explicit affirmation of the principle that, in tandem with the expansion of Europe, NATO's doors will remain open to all European states—Russia included—that subjectively desire membership and objectively meet the requirements of that membership.

In politics, one should never use the words "never" or "end." One simply does not know where Europe will "end", say, fifty years from now, and hence one cannot also postulate that Russia should "never" be considered for membership. No one ever dreamed a hundred years ago of a Euroatlantic community and no one can stipulate categorically what that community of values and interests will encompass a century from now. The key issue is to keep the historical process of growth open, to sustain it with prudence and deliberation, and to be clearheaded about the shared values it implies.

Zbigniew Brzezinski, former national security advisor to the president of the United States, is author of *The Grand Chessboard: American Primacy and its Geostrategic Imperatives* (1997).

Article 9

Environment, January/February 1998

EU
Environmental Policy
at 25

The Politics of Multinational Governance

By Andrew Jordan

On 22 November 1998, environmental policy in the European Union (EU) will be 25 years old. Although a few ad hoc environmental measures were enacted earlier, it was on that date in 1973 that the European Economic Community (a predecessor to the EU) first adopted an action program giving environmental policy a sound political and intellectual platform from which to develop. Over the years, that policy has succeeded in garnering widespread support from a public that is generally suspicious of EU institutions and unsure about the long-term implications of integrating sovereign states into a common institutional framework. Even now, when there is growing resistance to

faster and deeper integration, many people in EU countries have more faith in that body's environmental institutions than they do in those of their own governments. This article charts the transformation of environmental policy in the EU from a series of "incidental measures"[1] to a far-reaching multilevel governance system. It then identifies the challenges—some old, some new—that remain to be tackled in the next 25 years.

The European Union

The European Union is a consortium of 15 Western European nations that endeavors to formulate joint policies in ar-

eas of common interest. Though nominally of recent origin (it was formed in 1993 with the ratification of the Maastricht Treaty), it is actually the latest in a series of supranational bodies that began with the European Economic Community (formed by the Treaty of Rome in 1957). The European Economic Community was an attempt to create a common market among six countries—France, Germany, Italy, Belgium, the Netherlands, and Luxembourg. By eliminating internal tariffs and removing other barriers to trade, these countries hoped to form an "ever closer union among the peoples of Europe . . . to ensure economic and social progress by common action to eliminate the barriers

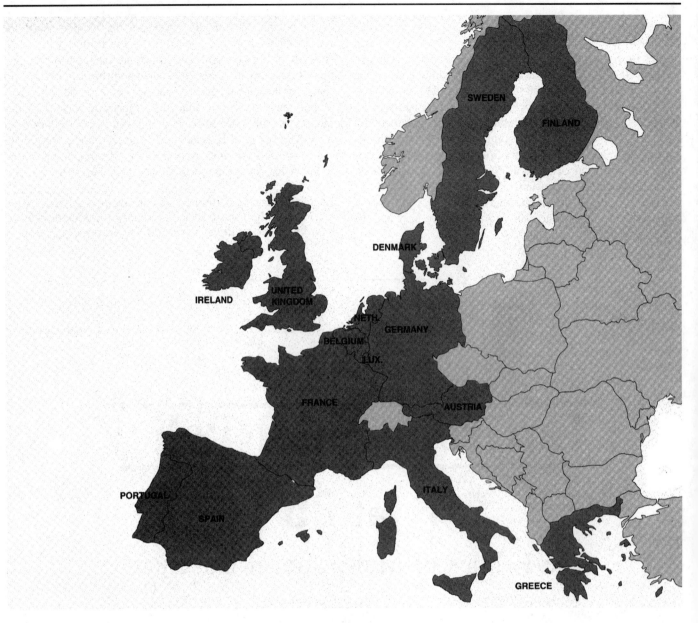

which divide Europe." Over time, both the number of countries involved and the scope of the issues addressed have grown. Denmark, Ireland, the United Kingdom, Greece, Portugal, Spain, Austria, Finland, and Sweden have become members of the European Union (see map), and other countries have applied for admission. Economic integration now includes the unrestricted movement of capital and labor between member countries, and monetary integration (in the form of a common currency—the European currency unit, or ECU—and a central bank) is scheduled to begin in January 1999. Furthermore, noneconomic issues such as environmental concerns have begun to appear on the negotiating table.[2]

Institutional Structure

The actual governance of the EU is shared by several different bodies. The *European Commission* is the EU's executive body, which is responsible for seeing that EU laws are fully implemented. In addition, the Commission enjoys the sole right of proposing new legislation. Operationally, the Commission is divided into 23 *directorates general* (DGs), with environmental matters being the responsibility of DG XI. The main decisionmaking body is the *Council of Ministers,* which has the authority to adopt or reject the Commission's proposals after consulting with the *European Parliament.* Although the Council of Min-

isters is nominally one entity, the complexity of the issues with which it deals has led to the creation of more than 20 subcouncils, including the Environment Council. These councils have traditionally made decisions by consensus, which is the usual practice in international organizations. In 1987, however, a treaty change known as the Single European Act allowed decisions in most policy areas to be made by qualified majority voting. Under this system, a large country can block a measure to which it is opposed by obtaining the support of two or three small countries. In practice, however, only a minority of issues are put to a formal vote because countries still prefer to operate on the basis of consensus.

AUSTRIA

BELGIUM

DENMARK

The European Parliament has 626 members who are chosen by European-wide elections every five years. In the past, the Parliament had few powers and its role in policymaking was limited to offering opinions on proposals before the Council of Ministers. Concern about the elitist nature of EU institutions has gradually led to its receiving greater powers, however. First, the Single European Act introduced the cooperation procedure, which required that members of the European Parliament cooperate fully in policy decisions. Second, the Maastricht Treaty gave the Parliament the authority to veto (by an absolute majority) any policy measure on which the Council of Ministers cannot reach an agreement. These changes have led to more consensual decision-making in the EU and greatly diminished the collective control that governments had exercised through the Council of Ministers.

In addition to the above bodies, there is the *European Court of Justice,* which is the final arbiter of compliance with EU legislation. Unlike with most international agreements, the rulings of this court are immediately binding on member states. Finally, there is the *European Council* (not to be confused with the Council of Ministers), which is the name given to the biannual meetings of heads of state at which matters of strategy are discussed.

Internal Tensions

Even though the nations of Western Europe have been moving toward greater integration for some time, there has always been controversy over how far this should go. *Maximalists,* a group that includes the Commission, most members of the European Parliament, and the original member states, have tended to favor much closer cooperation, giving the EU greater responsibility in such sensitive areas as foreign and monetary policy. *Minimalists* such as Britain and Denmark, on the other hand, have traditionally fought to preserve national autonomy in many areas and prefer limiting integration to a much lower level of political cooperation.

The ambivalence toward further integration is clearly reflected in the EU's governing structure. While entities such as the Commission, the European Parliament, and the European Court of Justice try to subsume the individual interests of the member states within the broader pursuit of the common good, the Council of Ministers stands as the guardian of those interests. The same ambivalence is also apparent in the different degrees of authority that are conferred on the EU in different policy areas. In areas such as trade and agriculture, for example, the EU governs much like a federal government, with key decisions being made by in-dependent supranational bodies. In areas such as foreign policy, on the other hand, decisions are usually reached only after bargaining between governments and, as is often the case in international organizations, require complete unanimity. Given the EU's "split personality," it has been well described as "neither a federation nor an international organisation."[3]

EU Environmental Policy, 1973–98

At its founding in 1957, the EU had no environmental policy. In fact, the environment was not even mentioned in the Treaty of Rome, which stated that the primary objective of European integration was the promotion of "a harmonious development of economic activities." At that time, there was little recognition that there might be environmental limits to growth. It was only after the surge of environmental awareness in the late 1960s and early 1970s, which culminated in the United Nations Conference on the Human Environment in Stockholm in 1972, that the EU started to deal purposively with the environmental repercussions of integration. At first, because the EU's governance structure was relatively immature, environmental policy developed in an ad hoc and largely incremental fashion. To be adopted, each statute had to secure the support of every state in the Council of Ministers; the European Parliament's role was extremely limited, and environmental pressure groups had only a very minor presence. To all intents and purposes, policymaking was a closed and techno cratic affair dominated by experts with very little input from the public and governments at lower levels. This was no accident: The Commission deliberately concentrated on "technical" issues like environmental standards and avoided political debates about surrendering national sovereignty in order to

> **After the surge of environmental awareness in the late 1960s and early 1970s the EU started to deal purposively with the environmental repercussions of integration.**

FINLAND

FRANCE

GERMANY

firmly establish supranational environmental institutions. Nonetheless, maximalists feared that lack of an explicit environmental provision in the Treaty of Rome would make the Commission hesitant about making ambitious proposals.

This fear proved to be largely unwarranted, however, because the Commission's approach was highly successful in creating a body of environmental law in the EU. During the 1980s, in fact, EU environmental policy underwent a rapid and profound transformation. By 1987, the organization had adopted more than 200 pieces of environmental legislation and four action programs of steadily increasing complexity and scope. Early measures on the classification, labeling, and packaging of hazardous substances were clearly justified as part of the development of a common market. But those relating to seals, natural habitats, genetically modified organisms, and climate change went "beyond any conceivable standards that would be strictly necessitated by a concern to ensure a single functioning market."[4]

Subsequent amendments to the Treaty of Rome, namely the Single European Act of 1987 and the Maastricht Treaty (formally the Treaty on European Union) of 1993, gave environmental protection a firm legal basis and enunciated principles to guide the EU in enacting new legislation. The Single European Act enhanced DG XI's position in the Commission by stipulating that environmental protection was to be a component of the EU's other policies. It also introduced the polluter-pays principle and eased the adoption of environmental standards by introducing qualified majority voting in the Council of Ministers for environmental measures linked to the single market. The Maastricht Treaty extended qualified majority voting to most areas of environmental policy, made sustainable growth one of the EU's main goals, and called for all environmental policies to be based on the precautionary principle. Along the same lines, the introduction of cooperation

and codecision procedures greatly enhanced the role of the European Parliament's Environment Committee.[5]

The EU now has more than 400 pieces of legislation relating to environmental protection, and until recently the environment was one of the fastest growing areas of policy. Between 1989 and 1991, for example, the Environment Council adopted more environmental policies than it had in the previous 20 years. The EU has also created a European Environment Agency and appropriated a modest amount of funds under the LIFE (*L'instrument financier pour*

Between 1989 and 1991 the Environmental Council adopted more environmental policies than it had in the previous 20 years.

l'environnement) program to support waste reduction and habitat conservation measures in member states. Moreover, in the last 25 years the EU has acquired a significant international profile by signing many important international conventions.[6] According to one expert on environmental matters, these legal and political developments have culminated in a "*federal* system with more than one legislature, but where the higher level of government is not itself a nation state (emphasis added)"[7]—in other words, in what political scientists generally call a "multilevel governance structure."

It is doubtful that anyone in the early 1970s could have envisioned the vast role that the EU would eventually play with respect to the environment. How then did this extraordinary transformation come about? Why have so many policy actions been taken despite the

need to accommodate the varying interests of member states, supranational bodies, and pressure groups?

One analyst suggests that the answer lies in the fact that the most important political division in the environmental field is green-brown rather than maximalist-minimalist.[8] She believes that the competitive dynamic between "leader" countries like Germany and the Netherlands (who have often pressed the EU to adopt their own high standards to ensure that their industries are not placed at a competitive disadvantage) and poorer, less environmentally progressive countries like Spain and Italy is the main engine of EU environmental policy. She shows that while not every legislative proposal has been adopted by the Council of Ministers, enough have been to get the "laggard" states to go further than they would have otherwise. The adoption of a directive on large combustion plants in 1988 is a good case in point. It stemmed largely from the efforts of Germany—the most populous and economically powerful state in the EU—which had adopted an ambitious policy to combat acid rain earlier that decade. The Germans and the Dutch were also instrumental in developing policies on water quality (in the 1970s) and automobile emission standards (in the 1980s). Similarly, the adoption of a far-reaching directive on packaging waste in 1994 stemmed directly from pressure by Germany. At a very basic level, then, the EU can be visualized as

GREECE

 IRELAND

 ITALY

a complex institutional forum in which member states compete to get their own policy approaches adopted at the European level.

But this is only part of the story, as other factors have also played a role in setting environmental standards that are higher than the least common denominator of member state preferences. These factors include:

The mechanics of negotiation. The national environment ministers who meet biannually in the Environment Council to adopt policy do so in secret and as a result are somewhat insulated from pressures by their industry and commerce departments. A veteran of many such meetings describes the extra leverage that this gives them in this way:

Although the attitudes and balance of forces between the different Member States and the Commission change from time to time, the general ethos of [the Environment] Council is strongly pro-environment, and several Member States are thereby encouraged to make better progress than they would do by themselves. . . . The Council . . . has its strong impetus to make environmental progress, but can be at risk of going beyond the collective readiness of each Member State to undertake the necessary measures and bear the necessary costs. [In contrast, t]he Cabinet of Ministers in each Member State has a much greater ability to balance the claims of the environment against other priorities, but is always at some risk of short-termism and therefore of giving insufficient weight to the longer-term concerns which are at the heart of the sustainable development imperative.[9]

Package dealing. States will often compromise on a particular issue in the expectation of gains in other areas. It is said, for example, that Spain and Greece accepted high environmental standards in the 1980s in exchange for financial assistance channeled through an environmental "cohesion" fund. Package dealing is a proven technique that the

Commission has used to advance integration.

Supranational activism. The supranational character of EU institutions has given them the ability to extend their jurisdictions (or "competence") in the environmental area. The Commission, for instance, has often acted like a "purposeful opportunist,"[10] working with other maximalists such as the European Court of Justice to remove bottlenecks in the policy process and extend EU authority to new domains. Once rules are adopted, the area in question comes under the Court's jurisdiction and member states can no longer formulate their own rules. Landmark rulings by the Court have underlined the binding nature of directives and supported the Commission's efforts to promote higher environmental standards. Environmentalists have also made good use of the European Parliament to raise important issues and draw attention to failures in compliance. More recently, observers have noted the increasing (but still contingent) influence of the Parliament's

> ## States will often compromise on a particular issue in the expectation of gains in other areas

own Environment Committee, particularly at the agenda setting and decision-making stages.[11]

Short-termism. Politicians tend to have a very short time horizon, normally not extending beyond the next election. As a result, they frequently agree to policies (particularly those with great symbolic value) whose costs will not come due until a later administration. Bureaucrats in the Commission, by contrast, are not directly elected and can thus afford to be more strategic in their

thinking. As a result, they can avoid the unintended consequences that short-term thinking leads to and that governments often have to struggle to correct.

Lack of opposition. Many of the early environmental directives sailed through the policymaking process because none of those affected thought that they were very important. In the 1970s, for instance, the directorates that represent industrial interests regarded DG XI (and its predecessor) as weak and paid little attention to them or to environmental affairs generally. Similarly, government officials in the various member states did not treat Commission proposals that seriously, and even national legal experts regarded directives as no more than broad "statements of intent" rather than binding obligations. Now, of course, the situation is very different.

Expectations of poor compliance. Because the Commission has only limited power to enforce its directives and until recently made little effort to see that member states were actually complying with existing laws, states tended to agree to policies they had little intention of implementing.

Green pressure. Although green parties are still poorly represented in the European Parliament, environmental groups like Greenpeace and the World Wide Fund for Nature are much larger, better organized, and better able to exploit the new lobbying opportunities afforded by the EU's more open and pluralistic governance structure. At present, the points of greatest leverage are the Environment Committee of the Par-

LUXEMBOURG   NETHERLANDS   PORTUGAL

THE STRUGGLE TO REVISE WATER QUALITY STANDARDS IN THE EU

Improving water quality is arguably one of the most ambitious parts of the EU's environmental strategy. It is also proving to be one of the most expensive and—judging by the number of noncompliance cases brought before the European Court of Justice—one of the toughest to implement. EU regulation in this area is becoming increasingly unpopular in countries like the United Kingdom and France, who believe that the standards are unnecessarily strict, that they lack internal consistency, and that they will lead to a serious misallocation of resources.[1] In 1993, these two countries gave the European Commission a "hit list" of legislation that they wanted repealed or revised, which included the bathing and drinking water directives. After consulting with various interest groups, the Commission proposed standards that are actually stricter than those they are meant to replace.[2] Some parties, notably construction firms, stand to benefit financially from stricter standards. Others, such as Britain's water companies, have invested large sums of money to attain the current standards and would be dismayed if they were weakened. The estimated cost of implementing the Commission's proposals is many billions of European currency units. The sharp divergence of opinions over standards has prevented the adoption of revised directives in this area. This episode reveals that European integration is a path-dependent process: Once institutional rules are in place, the various parties adapt to them, often making substantial investments in the process. Reversing those investments is costly, so the multilevel governance structure gradually becomes "locked in."

---

1. See A. J. Jordan, N. Ward, and H. Buller, "Surf, Sea, Sand, and . . . Sewage: The Implementation of European Bathing Water Policy in Britain and France," *Environment and Planning A* (forthcoming).
2. See A. J. Jordan, *EC Water Standards: Locked In or Watered Down?*, CSERGE Working Paper WM 1 (Norwich and London: Centre for Social and Economic Research on the Global Environment, forthcoming).

liament and the policy networks surrounding the Commission's directorates general, although pressure groups continue to lobby their own national governments.[12]

Drawing these factors together, one can say that the EU's environmental regulation is determined by three main elements: competition between the governments of the different member states; the pro-environment agenda of supranational entities and pressure groups; and the ability of national and subnational actors to make modifications at the implementation stage.[13] The result is an extremely complicated and constantly evolving multilevel governance structure that even large states and powerful national lobbies find hard to control. The uncertainty this entails has been aptly described by one analyst as follows: "[O]nce inside . . . , any issue is subject to capture by other actors, so that what emerges at the other end may contain elements uncongenial to its original proponents."[14] (For an illustration of the intricacies and unpredictability of environmental policymaking in the EU, see the box on this page, which discusses recent attempts to revise the standards for bathing and drinking water.) Two questions that require much more detailed investigation are when and why unforeseen consequences arise and how supranational and subnational actors manage to extend the scope of

EU competence despite opposition from the member states.

Progress to Date

How far has the EU come in its efforts to promote sustainable development? Given that it started from such a low base, the answer is very far indeed, especially in the last 10 years. The Fourth Action Program (1987–92) in particular marked an important turning point in the EU's environmental strategy. Whereas the previous three programs formulated policies on a sector-by-sector basis and paid little attention to implementation, the fourth underlined the need to integrate environmental considerations into all policy areas and ensure that policies are fully implemented. These themes were even more prominent in the Fifth Action Program (1992 to the present), which has emphasized the fact that sustainability must involve all sectors of society, that it must use a wider array of policy tools than legislation alone, and that it must address environmental problems at their root—that is, in the daily patterns of resource consumption—rather than at the end of the pipe.

Over time, the EU's principles and practices have become embedded in the member states themselves. In the view of one distinguished commentator, it is now virtually impossible to understand the environmental policy of any member state without referring to the EU's own policy stance.[15] Even "awkward" countries such as the United Kingdom, which have fought doggedly to preserve their own traditions and policy approaches, have come around to a large extent. In its report on the implementation of Agenda 21, the U.K. government explained that "[e]nvironmental policy in the UK is now inextricably bound up with EC policy. . . . Much of the UK's environmental protection legislation is now developed in common with other . . . member states."[16] The same is probably true for the other EU members.

SPAIN

SWEDEN

U.K.

Notwithstanding these positive developments, there are indications that the EU's environmental policies have not been overly effective. In fact, the authors of the Fifth Action Program concluded that there has been "a slow but relentless

In recent years, environmental regulation in the EU has lost a good deal of momentum.

deterioration of the environment" of member countries. Among the most "disquieting trends" that they noted are increases in energy and water use, car ownership, and the production of wastes.[17] Along the same lines, in 1995 the European Environment Agency released an assessment of the Fifth Action Program saying that the EU was not implementing the program fast enough and citing transportation as a key problem. A companion volume acknowledged the EU's progress during the last 25 years but warned that it was not enough "to improve the general quality of the environment and even less to progress towards sustainability."[18]

In recent years, environmental regulation in the EU has lost a good deal of momentum. This is connected to a more general sense of disillusionment with attempts to step up the pace of integration and extend the EU into the former Eastern bloc—feelings that came bursting out in the long and difficult process of ratifying the Maastricht Treaty. The Danish people's decision to reject that treaty was a particularly strong sign that European institutions were not democratic enough, that they were preoccupied with technical issues like monetary union, and that they were dangerously out of touch with public opinion. The changing public mood, in turn, stemmed largely from worsening economic con-

ditions in Europe, particularly in the larger countries like France and Germany that until recently have led the drive towards greater integration. Reflecting the new attitude toward the EU, in the early 1990s Britain and France tried to repatriate some especially costly pieces of legislation back to the national level under the banner of subsidiarity—an emerging principle of EU law that requires that policy decisions be made at the lowest appropriate level. Later, when Jacques Delors, then the president of the European Commission, expressed his willingness to sacrifice environmental goals to save that of deeper political integration, the way seemed clear for a root-and-branch reform of EU activities.

The debates about competitiveness, subsidiarity, and democracy that were unleashed by the Maastricht Treaty have undoubtedly slowed the pace of EU regulatory activity considerably. The Commission, for instance, has significantly trimmed its environmental work program and withdrawn a number of proposals dating back as far as 1975. It has also begun to explore the possibility of substituting voluntary agreements with industry for more traditional command-and-control regulation. But there has not been the wholesale repeal of green laws that some environmentalists feared. Rather, events have shown that environmental concerns have a power of their own that will be difficult to dislodge. Significantly, the demand for greater subsidiarity has not entirely stemmed the tide of EU regulation. In recent years, the organization has adopted directives on ambient air quality, pollution from stationary

sources, packaging waste, and habitat preservation; created a program to finance environmental improvement projects in member countries and elsewhere; implemented a product labeling scheme; and discussed proposals for new directives on landfills and water quality. Gone, however, is the belief that supranational governance is necessarily better than that of the member states themselves. In the future, therefore, the Commission will be under much more pressure to justify taking action at the European level than it has been until now.

Persistent Problems

Environmental policy in the EU suffers from two significant "gaps": an implementation gap—the failure of member states to put its mandates into action—and an integration gap—the failure to incorporate environmental considerations into decision-making at all levels. Both of these gaps are exacerbated by the unique multilevel governance structure of the EU. As political commentators like Giandomenico Majone have persuasively argued, the Treaty of Rome gave the Commission such limited authority that DG XI had little option but to spawn a lot of legislation to expand its political power base.[19] Commission officials soon learned that the chance of getting a proposal adopted was much greater if they did not point out its full implications to member states (even when they knew those implications).[20] Majone argues that over time the EU evolved into a hyperactive "regulatory state" that is extremely good at setting standards and timetables but not greatly concerned about their implementation.

The Implementation Gap

Until relatively recently, neither EU institutions nor member states paid much attention to whether or not rules formulated to protect the environment were actually being followed. In the

AUSTRIA

BELGIUM

DENMARK

early years, the Commission concentrated on creating a legal framework of principles and laws—an understandable focus given that environmental policy had only tenuous links to the Treaty of Rome. The Third Action Program (1982–86), for example, dealt with the whole issue of enforcement in just three lines and early textbooks on EU environmental law and policy gave it scant coverage. The institutional structure of the EU is largely to blame for the implementation gap. It is often said that the need for unanimity in the Council of Ministers in the 1970s and 1980s led to poor lawmaking. Many directives from this period are peppered with vague phrases and contradictory objectives. More importantly, the Commission—the body that initiates legislation in the EU—has little responsibility for its implementation. This allows it to engage in green symbolism knowing that any costs involved will be borne by the member states.

Starting in the mid-1980s, however, a number of factors helped to put enforcement at the top of the EU's environmental agenda.[21] One of the most important was business's growing awareness of the need for comparable

enforcement as part of the single-market program. Poor enforcement, it was felt, would give non-compliant countries a competitive advantage over more honest ones. Another important factor was the disappearance of several drums of toxic waste from a chemical plant in Seveso, Italy, which led to a highly critical investigation by the European Parliament. Other factors include landmark rulings by the European Court of Justice asserting the supremacy of EU legislation over member states' own laws; a rising number of complaints from individuals and pressure groups about states' lack of compliance with EU laws; greater academic interest in policy implementation; and intensified lobbying by environmental groups such as Friends of the Earth in the United Kingdom.[22]

A damning report by the EU's own Court of Auditors in 1992, which concluded that environmental directives were "being implemented slowly" and that there was a "significant gap between the set of rules in force and their actual application," followed high-level discussions in the Council of Ministers and a series of ministerial announcements stressing the urgent need to deal with implementation.[23] Research

shows that many governments still do not inform the Commission what they are doing to incorporate EU directives into their own laws, and some are deliberately obstructive. As part of a series of responses, since 1984 the Commission has presented an annual report to the European Parliament on the application of EU law. DG XI made implementation an explicit theme of the Fourth and Fifth Action Programs and in the late 1980s initiated a series of high-profile legal proceedings against noncompliant states (see Table 1). It currently takes the most egregious cases to the European Court of Justice, which, by virtue of the Maastricht Treaty, now has the authority to fine states that persist in flouting its rulings.

According to one analyst, there are significant structural reasons why implementation is such an enduring problem in the EU.[24] Unlike a federal state such as the United States, the EU lacks political parties operating at both levels of government as well as a high degree of economic, natural, and cultural homogeneity. And unlike the bodies responsible for economic affairs (e.g., competition, mergers, and the protection of fisheries), DG XI enjoys no direct powers of enforcement and has no agents to carry out its policies. This means that in the very places where environmental policy really needs to "bite"—factories, river banks, beaches, and so on—it has little or no direct presence. It certainly cannot compel national or subnational actors (either public or private) to comply with its policies. Even where they are utilized, enforcement proceedings are slow, secretive, inflexible, complex, and almost exclusively between member states and the Commission. Individuals and pressure groups have limited means of redress, being unable to take public interest cases against noncompliant states before the European Court of Justice. The Commission knows full well that the environment will probably be damaged irreparably by the time the Court issues a ruling, so wherever possible it

Table 1. Number of infringement proceedings in the European Union, 1982–90

| Year | Infringement category | | | Year total |
	Partial compliance	Non-notification	Poor application	
1982	1	15	0	16
1983	10	23	2	35
1984	15	48	2	65
1985	10	58	1	69
1986	32	84	9	125
1987	30	68	58	156
1988	24	36	30	90
1989	17	46	37	100
1990	24	131	62	217
Total	**163**	**509**	**201**	**873**

SOURCE: A. J. Jordan, "Post-Decisional Politics in the EU: The Implementation of EC Environmental Policy in the UK" (Ph.D. diss., University of East Anglia, Norwich, U.K., 1997).

 FINLAND

 FRANCE

 GERMANY

tries to work with states directly and uses legal proceedings only as a last resort.

A wide variety of solutions to the implementation gap have been proposed, including creating a centralized environmental inspectorate with the power to investigate alleged breaches of the law and levy fines; allowing the Commission to institute proceedings against local officials and other subnational actors; devolving the handling of non-compliance cases to the national courts; improving the legal and technical drafting of directives; extending the application of qualified majority voting (land-use planning, fiscal measures, and energy and water management are currently exempt); and providing more funds to the poorer states in the EU. Clearly, many of these proposals are at odds with the *realpolitik* of the EU, which, despite all the evidence of greater supranationality and multilevel governance, still consists of 15 very different countries, each with its own political culture, legal traditions, administrative practices, economic structure, and environmental circumstances. Given these differences, slow or at least differential implementation is probably inevitable.

Since the ratification of the Maastricht Treaty, DG XI has taken a decidedly more pragmatic line, stressing "soft" measures that are consonant with the principle of subsidiarity, such as improved consultations with national-level officials, better environmental reporting at the national level, and more collaboration with national inspectorates. As Ludwig Krämer, the former head of DG XI's enforcement unit, concedes, efforts to strengthen the Commission's powers of intervention "would increase the powers of Community institutions and [are] thus resisted by member states.[25] But it will become ever more difficult for member states to oppose such moves if they continue failing to report promptly to the Commission, to monitor

compliance honestly, and to enforce EU law evenly and comprehensively.

The Integration Gap

Although the EU has done much to improve the environmental performance of its members, its own environmental record has been less impressive. Although the requirement that environmental considerations be factored into all policy decisions was implicit in the First Action Program, it only became a formal principle of EU law in 1987 with the passage of the Single European Act. In the past, in fact, the EU has been strongly criticized for promoting policies that directly harm the environment. Its common agricultural policy, for example, subsidizes intensive farming that has led to the pollution of waterways by nitrates and phosphates from fertilizer. Similarly, its efforts to improve transportation links between member states have destroyed important wildlife habitat and boosted motor vehicle emissions.

Not surprisingly, DG XI has come under strong pressure from environmental groups to address these failings.[26] The Tagus Bridge project (a bold plan to improve road connections across a major river near Lisbon) because a *cause célèbre* when an alliance of Portugese and European environmental groups used it to expose the environmental failings of EU cohesion policies. Part of the problem is that, like most bureaucracies, the Commission is divided into different units, each fighting

furiously to defend its turf.[27] Contrary to popular opinion, DG XI is a tiny organization, comprising only 2 to 3 percent of the Commission's total workforce. As one analyst has cogently observed, it has a mere 15 officials to deal with hazardous chemicals, compared with 500 in the U.S. Environmental Protection Agency.[28] Because DG XI has no formal power over the other directorates, it has to rely upon informal coordinating mechanisms to promote greater integration.[29] These include creating a network of green officials spanning all the directorates in the Commission, forming an Integration Unit within itself to improve coordination and promote the best practice, and publishing a code of conduct. DG XI continues to campaign for more formal, "top-down" controls but faces resistance from other directorates and member states.

New Challenges

The EU's long-term political strategy is to broaden its membership by including countries from the former Eastern

> It is highly unlikely that the new entrants will be able to conform to the EU's current environmental requirements in the short term.

bloc. Such an expansion, which could lead to an organization with 30 or so members by 2010, has enormous environmental implications for both the existing members and the new entrants. In July 1997, the Commission presented its ideas about the process of enlargement to the European Parliament in a document entitled *Agenda 2000*. Running to more than 2,000 pages, it details the changes that will have to be made to the

GREECE

 IRELAND

 ITALY

existing decisionmaking procedures and policies, particularly the common agricultural policy and the various structural funds. (These funds were created to provide assistance to the poorer members of the EU. Now totaling some $100 billion per year, they are politically and economically vital to the recipient counties.) Due to considerable uncertainty about the political and legal complexion

It is highly unlikely that the new entrants will be able to conform to the EU's current environmental requirements in the short term. Indeed, the difficult task of determining how long this will take them has hardly begun. As a practical matter, bringing these countries' water and air quality up to current standards will require a huge investment in infrastructure. The new entrants' own

ity. Although the Commission talks (in the abstract) about the need for a "new development model," it has yet to come up with one. Significantly, in a recent Council of Ministers white paper entitled *Growth, Competitiveness, and the Environment,* the discussion of ways to meld development and environmental goals was banished to the conclusion.[33] Surely, if the Commission were really serious about sustainable development, it would have made environmental factors a guiding feature of every chapter.

> States were so consumed with grand issues that the environment came close to being ignored despite frantic lobbying by European environmental groups and DG XI.

of a new Europe, there have been intense disagreements over many important institutional matters such as representation on the Council of Ministers. Contrary to popular opinion, small states are currently over-represented on the Council, and a way needs to be found to achieve a better balance between voting power and population. (Maximalists like France fear that decisionmaking will grind to a halt if the principle of unanimity is retained in a body with 20 to 30 members instead of being replaced by majority voting.) Such questions are extremely important because they will affect the delicate balance of power between small and large states and, by implication, between environmental leaders and laggards in an enlarged union. The structural funds are another live political issue. *Agenda 2000* recommends that all states be required to help contain costs by accepting reductions, but countries like Spain say they will block expansion of the EU unless the current budget is substantially increased.

budgets will not be able to bear the sort of sums currently under discussion,[30] and current members will doubtless resist any major assistance. When compared with the enormous challenge of cleaning up highly polluted countries like the Czech Republic, Hungary, and the Baltic states, the successes that the EU has achieved over the last 25 years start to look rather modest.[31]

Environmental groups feel that the debate over expansion has not yet fully acknowledged the scale of the challenges that expansion entails. The Commission admits that incorporating existing EU legislation into the new entrants' legal systems will be a huge problem and that implementing it will be more complicated still.[32] But, say the environmental groups, there is no indication that any of the proposals for expansion have been tested against the principle of sustainability. Certainly, there is little evidence that current members are prepared to fundamentally revise their plans for a unified economic and political system to promote the goal of sustainabil-

History shows that when the EU makes important strategic decisions, environmental considerations tend to get pushed aside by weightier matters like greater material wealth, jobs, and inflation. A good example is the EU's single-market initiative of the 1980s, which aimed at removing the remaining impediments to the free flow of goods and services, capital, and labor among member states by 1992. According to two analysts who have studied this initiative, there are important political, intellectual, and organizational reasons why the environment got such short shrift. DG XI was too weak compared to the trade and industry directorates in the Commission and too poorly represented on key panels like the Cecchini committee.[34] Like the drive eastwards, the single-market program was designed to reinvigorate the EU, bring skeptical states like Britain more into the fold, and improve the ability of European businesses to compete in world markets. These were geopolitical considerations against which the environment could not hope to compete. In the end, environmental arguments were relegated to an ancillary status because there was "simply too much weight pushing in the opposite direction."[35] Of course, environmental policy in the mid-1980s was neither as politically nor as legally established as it is today. The big question now is whether principles like integration, precaution, and sustainability can hold their own against the powerful economic forces pressing for enlargement.

LUXEMBOURG   NETHERLANDS   PORTUGAL

The Amsterdam Summit

Some indication of how the environment currently ranks came when leaders of the member states sat down in Amsterdam in June 1997 to agree on further revisions to the founding treaties. This meeting was the culmination of a year-long intergovernmental conference process involving Commission officials, members of the European Parliament, member states' foreign secretaries, and national negotiating teams. The purpose of the meeting was to change EU institutions to reflect the introduction of a single European currency and the entry of new members. As it happened, states were so consumed with these grand issues that the environment came close to being ignored altogether despite frantic lobbying by European environmental groups and DG XI. None of the "big three" states (France, Germany, and the United Kingdom) listed the environment as a priority in their opening submissions, and it might have slipped from the agenda entirely had there not been a strong push from recent entrants like Sweden and Finland.

Although the final text of the meeting (which must still be ratified by member states' own parliaments) sounds some positive notes, it also underlines the powerful impediments to a complete transition to sustainability in the EU. The major environmental developments occur in six areas:

Sustainable development. In the revised treaty, sustainable development becomes a fundamental objective of the EU, enshrined in Article 2 and mentioned in the preamble. In a sense, this change completes the job begun by the Maastricht Treaty, which altered the purpose of the EU from simple economic growth to "sustainable and non-inflationary growth respecting the environment." Supporters of this particular amendment say that it underlines the importance of protecting the environment by removing the ambiguous reference to the word *sustainable*. It will also give

legal weight to the principle of integration, although, significantly, there will be no new institutional machinery to enforce it. Real change will depend on DG XI's ability to win key battles with other directorates.

Policy integration. A new Article 3D stipulates that "environmental protection requirements must be integrated into the definition and implementation of Com-

> The difficulty that the EU has in implementing environmental policy symbolizes the conflicting forces and contradictions that have characterized the organization since its inception.

munity policies and activities . . . , in particular with a view to promoting sustainable development." Like the article on subsidiarity, this amendment is intended to apply across the full range of EU activities. (Until now, integration has been tucked away in the environmental section of the treaty (Article 130R) and its scope has been somewhat ambiguous.) In a political declaration attached to the final draft, the Commission promised to prepare environmental impact assessments when making proposals with significant environmental ramifications. However modest, this particular change is likely to be warmly welcomed by DG XI as it tries to gain leverage over the trade and industry directorates.

The European Parliament. Changes to Article 189 will extend codecision-making to all environmental quality decisions (rather than just a few), possibly opening the way to stricter and more wide-ranging environmental standards. Under the proposed procedure, which is extremely complicated, when the Euro-

pean Parliament and the Council of Ministers cannot agree on a proposal, a conciliation committee made up of representatives from each body will have to be convened. This measure, which considerably enhances the power of the Parliament, is one of the EU's responses to the perceived "democratic deficit" in the current decisionmaking process. To date, the conciliation procedure (which has been available since late 1993 in areas like the single market) has worked well, only once failing to produce an agreement.

Access to information. A new Article 191A confers on every citizen of an EU member state the right of access to documents held by the Council of Ministers, the Commission, or the European Parliament (subject to certain exemptions). Each body will have to decide on specific rules for disclosure. Of all the proposed changes, this could be the most far-reaching. It could, for example, preclude secret votes in the Council of Ministers and put an end to the custom of attaching unpublished "interpretative minutes" to directives.

There were, however, some significant setbacks for those seeking a further greening of the EU:

Voting procedures. Environmentalists failed in their bid to extend qualified majority voting to all aspects of environmental policy. The Danish government, environmental groups, and DG XI were particularly eager to remove fiscal

SPAIN

SWEDEN

U.K.

measures from the four exempt areas in order to introduce environmental tax reforms, but careful consensus building could conceivably have led to qualified majority voting in all four areas. It seems, however, that the proponents of this proposal tried to move too quickly and thereby engendered fierce resistance from the Germans.

Public access to justice. EU law has always been largely intergovernmental in nature. That is, it mainly governs relations between member states; individuals and environmental groups cannot sue those states in the European Court of Justice, even on public interest grounds. The revised treaty would not change this, although the Commission is known to be actively considering the idea of improving access to environmental justice at the national level.

Conclusion

Against all odds, environmental policy in the EU has come a very long way since 1973—in fact, on current issues like climate change and ozone-depleting chemicals, Europe even leads the industrialized world. The first 25 years were spent creating an environmental governance structure for Western Europe. The challenge now is to integrate environmental concerns with the region's wider political and economic development priorities. The Fifth Action Program was an intellectual turning point in this respect, but many significant barriers remain. Some of them can be surmounted by the Commission, but removing the others will require sustained collaboration among affected parties. Some of the most powerful barriers reflect member states' deeply rooted unwillingness to surrender powers to supranational agencies or to compromise on national economic priorities. It is common for politicians at the national level to use EU institutions as scapegoats for their failure to solve problems (like the environmental repercussions of the common agricultural policy) that those institu-

tions simply cannot solve without assistance from the states. The EU is also routinely blamed for enacting laws that were in fact adopted by the states. It is all part of an old but unproductive political game.

The difficulty that the EU has experienced in implementing environmental policy symbolizes the conflicting forces and contradictions that have characterized the organization since its inception. These include the need for unity within diversity, the competition between national priorities and supranational imperatives, and the distribution of powers among different organizations at different levels of government. The EU is getting better at coping with these problems, however. The days of pumping out as much environmental legislation as possible without regard to its quality and consistency appear to have passed. This is largely because the multilevel governance structure of the EU is institutionally "thicker" and more mature than it was in the 1970s and 1980s. But it is also because the other directorates now realize the importance of environmental rules and make sure their views are known. Overall, the process of adopting legislation is much more protracted and complicated than it ever was in the past simply because many more stakeholders are now involved. But few would disagree that this is a fair price to pay if the resulting legislation is better thought out, reflects the best available scientific and technical understanding, and is thoroughly and openly debated.

Andrew Jordan is a senior research associate at the Centre for Social and Economic Research on the Global Environment, which is jointly located at the University of East Anglia, Norwich, and University College London. This article stems from a long-term study of the ways in which business and governmental institutions are responding to global environmental issues. The author wishes to thank Timothy O'Riordan and Heather Voisey for helpful comments on earlier drafts. He may be

contacted at the School of Environmental Sciences, University of East Anglia, Norwich NR4 7TJ, United Kingdom (telephone: 011–44–603–593176; e-mail: a.jordan@uea.ac.uk).

Notes

1. This term comes from P. Hildebrand, "The EC's Environmental Policy, 1957 to 1992," *Environmental Politics* 1, no. 4 (1992): 13.

2. The Maastricht Treaty created a new institutional structure with three separate "pillars." The most important by far is the European Community, which handles most of the EU's business, including environmental protection. The other two pillars (namely, Common and Foreign Security Policy and Cooperation on Justice and Home Affairs) operate more like conventional intergovernmental organizations, with limited input from supranational bodies. To simplify terminology, this article will refer to the European Community and its predecessors as the European Union.

3. W. Wallace, "Less than a Federation, More than a Regime," in H. Wallace, W. Wallace, and C. Webb, eds., *Policy Making in the European Community* (London: John Wiley, 1983). At any given time, there are numerous struggles going on among the various entities involved, and these struggles determine not only which policies and laws are adopted but also the delicate balance between maximalism and minimalism. To complicate matters, decision rules and policy processes change over time as a result of these struggles and alterations to the Treaty of Rome. And, as Albert Weale has noted, many disputes are not just about the rules of the policy process but also about the rules for making those rules. See A. Weale, *European Environmental Governance: Towards an Ever Closer Ecological Union?* (Oxford, U.K.: Oxford University Press, forthcoming).

4. A. Weale, "Environmental Rules and Rule-Making in the European Union," *Journal of European Public Policy* 3, no. 4 (1996): 598.

5. See D. Judge, D. Earnshaw, and N. Cowan, "Ripples or Waves: The European Parliament in the European Community Policy Process," *Journal of European Public Policy* 1, no. 1 (1994): 27.

6. A. Sbragia, "Institution Building from Above and Below: The EC in Global Environmental Politics" (paper presented at the ECSA [U.S. European Community Studies Association] Biennial Conference, Seattle, Washington, May 1997).

7. N. Haigh, "The European Community and International Environmental Policy," in A. Hurrell and B. Kingsbury, eds., *The International Politics of the Environment* (Oxford, U.K.: Oxford University Press, 1992), 233.

AUSTRIA

BELGIUM

DENMARK

8. A. Sbragia, "Environmental Policy," in H. Wallace and W. Wallace, eds., *Policy-Making in the European Union* (Oxford, U.K.: Oxford University Press, 1996).

9. D. Osborn, "Some Reflections on U.K. Environmental Policy, 1970–1995," *Journal of Environmental Law* 9, no. 1 (1997): 15–16.

10. L. Cram, "The European Commission as a Multi-Organisation," *Journal of European Public Policy* 1, no. 2 (1994): 195. In the same vein, it is argued that the Commission has used "subterfuge" to extend the EU's environmental competence into new areas. In the 1970s and 1980s, for instance, DG XI used Article 235 of the Treaty of Rome (which provides for common action where the powers necessary to attain an EU objective are not specified by the treaty) as a legal basis for issuing environmental directives. See A. Héritier, "Policy Making by Subterfuge," *Journal of European Public Policy* 4, no. 2 (1997): 171.

11. C. Hubschmid and P. Moser, "The Co-operation Procedure in the EU," *Journal of Common Market Studies* 35, no. 2 (1997): 226.

12. S. Mazey and J. J. Richardson, *Lobbying in the EC* (Oxford, U.K.: Oxford University Press, 1993).

13. A. J. Jordan, " 'Overcoming the Divide' between International Relations and Comparative Politics Approaches to the EC: What Role for 'Postdecisional' Politics?" *West European Politics* 20, no. 4 (1997): 43.

14. Weale, note 4 above, page 607.

15. N. Haigh, *Manual of Environmental Policy* (Harlow, U.K.: Longman, 1992), v.

16. H. M. Government, *Sustainable Development: The UK Strategy,* Command 2426 (London, 1994), 190. See also A. J. Jordan, "Post-decisional Politics in the EU: The Implementation of EC Environmental Policy in the UK" (Ph.D. diss., University of East Anglia, Norwich, U.K., 1997); and A. J. Jordan, "The Impact of UK Environmental Administration," in P.

Lowe and S. Ward, eds. *British Environmental Policy and Europe: From a National to a European Perspective* (London: Routledge, 1997).

17. *Official Journal* C138 17–5–92, 11, 24–25.

18. European Environment Agency, *Europe's Environment: The Dobris Assessment* (London: Earthscan, 1995); and European Environment Agency, *Environment in the European Union: 1995* (Copenhagen, 1995).

19. See G. Majone, *Regulating Europe* (London: Routledge, 1996).

20. EU officials tended to withhold information even in the relatively rare cases in which they had conducted compliance cost assessments.

21. Jordan, "Post-decisional Politics in the EU: The Implementation of EC Environmental Policy in the UK," note 16 above.

22. A. J. Jordan, N. Ward, and H. Buller, "Surf, Sea, Sand, and . . . Sewage: The Implementation of European Bathing Water Policy in Britain and France," *Environment and Planning A* (forthcoming).

23. *Official Journal* C245, 23–9–92, 1.

24. See F. Scharpf, "Community and Autonomy: Multi-Level Policy Making in the EU," *Journal of European Public Policy* 1, no. 2 (1994): 219.

25. L. Krämer, *EC Treaty and Environmental Law* (London: Sweet and Maxwell, 1995), 2e.

26. See A. Lenschow, *Greening the EC Regional and Cohesion Funds,* EUI Working Paper RSC No. 97–13 (Florence, Italy: European University Institute, 1997).

27. L. Cram, *Policy-Making in the EU* (London: Routledge, 1997), 157.

28. Sbragia, note 8 above, page 244.

29. D. Wilkinson, "Towards Sustainability in the EU," *Environmental Politics* 6, no. 1 (1997): 153.

30. The Commission estimates that bringing 10 candidate countries into compliance with 90 major EU statutes will cost from 120 billion to 180 billion European currency units (approximately $103 billion to $155 billion). See "Environment

Looked at in Terms of Eastern Enlargement," *Europe Environment* 506 (1997): 12.

31. At present, most EU members favor a "selective" approach to expansion, that is, opening the door to the most economically advanced countries first and leaving the rest until later. But a significant minority are pressing the Commission to invite all potential entrants to join at the same time (as in a boat race) so as not to undermine efforts to promote democracy, human rights, and environmental protection in those countries where they are most needed. Critics of the "flotilla" approach claim that the EU's finances and decisionmaking structures simply cannot cope with so many poor countries at the same time. The stage is thus set for some complicated bargaining.

32. Commission of the European Communities, *White Paper on the Preparation of the Associated Countries of Central and Eastern Europe for Integration into the Internal Market of the Union* (Brussels, 1995), 1.

33. COM (93) 700 final.

34. The Cecchini committee, chaired by Paolo Cecchini (a senior Commission official), was responsible for identifying impediments to free trade among EU countries, such as different national standards and bureaucratic practices. It reported that such impediments cost the EU the equivalent of 5 percent of members' gross domestic product each year and predicted that their removal would increase growth and create 5 million jobs. Although the report did not address environmental matters, environmentalists nonetheless claimed that the externalities resulting from the growth in trade (e.g., more exhaust fumes and greater waste) would greatly reduce the economic benefits of a single market.

35. See A. Weale and A. Williams, "Between Economy and Ecology? The Single Market and the Integration of Environmental Policy," *Environmental Politics* 1, no. 4 (1992): 45. The quotation appears on page 58.

FINLAND

FRANCE

Article 10   *World Press Review*, April 1998

Europe's crowded lifeboat

A Flood of Immigrants

The **European**

G erd Türk's eye is immediately caught by the Croatian license plate. The 34-year-old Bavarian police officer taps his partner's shoulder, accelerates, and overtakes the suspect vehicle. Seconds later, three Croatians are being questioned on the shoulder of the Munich-Stuttgart motorway.

They could have been Kurds, fleeing from state persecution in Turkey. They could have been North Africans, desperate to escape the slaughter in Algeria. They could have been Poles or Bosnians or Romanians, even West Africans—almost any nationality seeking an end to suffering or just a better life. Their problems have become Europe's.

"High-minded intentions are rapidly foundering."

The problem is getting worse. According to Sadako Ogata, the United Nations high commissioner for refugees, half a million Algerians have opted for refugee status since the conflict started in their country six years ago, joining an even larger number of Kurds—most of them hoping to win asylum status in Northern Europe, especially Germany. Humanitarian good intentions are rapidly foundering as the European dream of an affluent ship on stormy international waters becomes an overcrowded lifeboat.

In March, 1995, when seven European Union (EU) governments abolished internal frontiers under the Schengen Agreement, it was thought that the problem of clandestine immigration—at that time mainly from the former communist countries of Easter Europe—was past its peak and under control. Such confidence was misplaced. Right from the start, Schengen has provoked a string of crises.

Germany is indignant that its generous social welfare and employment provisions, already under strain from the aftereffects of unification, should be stretched to the limit and beyond by illegal immigrants. Bonn is painfully aware that it cannot be seen to take an overtly hard line on the subject. Memories of Jews in cattle trucks are still too fresh in the collective memory. Yet with racial attacks growing, and with even moderate politicians struggling to contain their resentment, it is clear that something must be done.

Happily, from the German point of view, the rotating EU presidency is currently held by Britain. London shuns Schengen and argues passionately for the right of nation-states to monitor and police their own frontiers. France, in its heart, agrees; any deal on immigration brokered by Britain, with German support, would command the approval of Paris, in spite of much high-minded rhetoric on human rights. French checks remain in place on France's border with the Netherlands and with Belgium.

But it is from the south that the danger of a major breakdown in Schengen looms. The spark was the Rome government's accession to Schengen last October. Italy now has control-free air routes and, along with Austria (another late signatory), was due to abolish its land controls on borders with other Schengen countries in March. Under the agreement, police are permitted to stop a sampling of entrants just inside national boundaries. Meanwhile, Italy is sending out signals that run directly contrary to the agreed policy of tight external controls. President Oscar Luigi Scalfaro went so far as to announce that the nation's arms were "wide open" to genuine refugees. And since passport-free travel is guaranteed within the Schengen zone, migrants who reach one country, legally or otherwise, are entitled to travel unchecked throughout the Schengen area.

At the beginning of February, the German interior minister, Manfred Kanther, called on Italy to tighten border controls. In Kanther's view, that means keeping out the thousands of Kurds who have arrived on Italy's coasts since early December, hoping to join their compatriots in Germany. Last year, thousands of Albanians poured into the southern ports of Italy, and fears are growing that the worsening violence in Algeria could send another wave of refugees scrambling across the Mediterranean.

Germany blames Italy for failing to apply rigorous standards. Italy responds that it has a humanitarian duty to refugees and that its critics have exaggerated both the numbers and the scale of the problem. Italy insists there are just over a million foreigners registered for residence in Italy—under 2 percent of the Italian population. What can only be guessed at is the number of *clandestini*.

In theory, the Amsterdam Treaty, negotiated at the EU's June, 1997, summit, is supposed to have yielded a solution to the influx of immigrants. It was agreed that member states, apart from Britain, which maintains the right to control its own immigration policy, should move toward common asylum, immigration, and visa policies by 2004. What remains unclear is whether all EU countries will accept that these policies should be decided by majority voting.

One other important step agreed to at a recent meeting of EU interior ministers was an undertaking by Italy to fingerprint every refugee and asylum seeker arriving on Italian shores. At present, would-be immigrants can adopt aliases, thus dodging a requirement that immigrants cannot apply for asylum in more than one EU member state.

No one denies the need for action. The latest figures show that 16,900 Kurdish refugees arrived in Germany from Turkey last year, of whom only 11.5 percent were deemed eligible for asylum even though Germany has one of the most liberal asy-

lum laws in Europe. In total, Germany received 117,000 applications for political asylum in 1996 compared with Italy's 700. This was more than the total for the United States, and twice that of the rest of the EU combined.

Whatever plans the EU puts forward to solve the problem, the pressures on its borders are likely to worsen. Greece becomes a full member of Schengen next year. Sweden, Norway, and Finland also are on the road to full membership, raising the specter of a porous route from the East. Should officials in London manage to come up with proposals that safeguard German interests while not offending either French or Italian sensibilities, they will have done themselves and the EU a signal favor. They will also have performed a miracle.

—Walter Ellis, Robert Fox, and Ian Mather, "The European" (centrist weekly), London, Feb. 2–8, 1998.

The Kurds: An Endless Exodus

stern

The Italian coast guard was not aware of their presence until they heard the screams in the dark. The freighter *Ararat* was bobbing, without a captain, off the coast of Calabria in southern Italy. On the morning of December 27, 835 exhausted, scared, and disoriented people were hanging from its rails. They were Kurds from Turkey, Iran, and Iraq who had made it to Istanbul by train or bus, then met Turkish smugglers who took them to the port of Mersin and stuffed them into the hold of the *Ararat.*

The *Ararat* was the seventh large ship to beach itself on the Italian coast last year. Four days later, another freighter— the *Cometa*—ended up in Ontranto in Apulia, having set sail from Turkey with 386 people on board.

The Italians expect more ships. At the beginning of the year, more than 5,000 Kurdish refugees were waiting in Istanbul and Izmir for passage, according to the National Liberation Front of Kurdistan. They were fleeing oppression, economic misery, and the operations of the Turkish army. And Gerhard Hoppe, head of the border police in Bavaria, reports that 10,000 Iraqi Kurds on the south coast of Turkey also are preparing to set off for Italy. It is an exodus without end.

Although these "boat people" can, as recognized refugees from a war, ask for asylum in Italy, almost all of them try to get a *foglio di via,* an identification paper that will permit them to leave Italy within 15 days. For the Kurds want to go on north—to Holland, Belgium, or Scandinavia, but, above all, to Germany, where they have friends and relatives. Unlike Italy, Germany gives welfare benefits to people applying for political asylum.

[According to an analysis of the Kurdish influx by Christian Hoche in the magazine *Marianne* of Paris, Germany already

has Western Europe's largest Kurdish community—500,000— and the new Kurdish exodus shows little sign of dwindling. Everything conspires to increase it.

[Turkey's government, resentful at having been left out of the next stage of negotiation on the expansion of the European Union, is thought to be deliberately encouraging the Kurdish exodus. Safa Haeri, a specialist in the region's problems, believes that "in a country where the police and army are everywhere, it seems virtually impossible that boatloads of refugees should be able to leave the Bosphorous under the very nose of Turkish customs without the government's complicity." To what end? "To destabilize Europe through underground immigration," Haeri replies. And as Kendal Nezan, chairman of the Kurdish Institute of Paris, said in an interview with *Le Monde,* Ankara must be saying to itself, "the fewer Kurds there are, the better off we are."—WPR]

Almost all of the Kurds who survive their voyages to Italy end up at the town of Ventimiglia, on the French border near Monaco. They wait for the signal that they can go on, and then disappear. Some cross into France on the beach, while some attempt the *passo della morte,* the dangerous trip over the mountains. Those who make it to France head to the French-German border in Baden-Württemburg.

Every year, tens of thousands of foreigners try to enter Germany. For illegals, the important thing is get through the 18.6-mile-wide "security zone" at the German border as quickly as possible. Those lingering in the area risk being picked up and immediately deported back to where they came from. Almost 15,400 illegals were caught in Germany in the first half of 1997 by the border police. The number who actually make it across and then go underground in Germany can only be estimated: It may be 1.2 million people since 1990, and the figure keeps growing.

Those who make it past the security zone file for asylum—and even if the request is eventually denied, they can still stay for at least a year or simply go underground. Then they are quickly absorbed into their ethnic communities.

To get to Germany, most of these refugees entrust their fates to professional smugglers. And some of them pay horrendous sums: $27,500 to be smuggled out of China, for example, $1,650 to get out of Turkey, and up to $275 to be hidden in the false bottom of a truck leaving Poland or Chechnya.

"More than 60 percent of the refugees are brought to their countries of destination by professional criminals," says Manfred Kanther, Germany's minister of the interior. These gangs accept the death of their clients as part of the cost of doing business. Dozens of dead emigrants wash up each year on Italy's coasts and on the south coast of Spain, near Gibraltar.

"Smuggling people is more profitable than smuggling drugs," says Erich Scheidl of the Bavarian border police, "so it is hard to imagine that the Mafia would pass up such a source of income."

The service has put a top priority on arresting the smugglers and, if possible, the people behind them. In 1996, 2,215 were arrested—almost all from the Czech Republic, Poland, the former Yugoslavia, and Turkey. Most are small-time operators, but Muhlis Pinarbasi, a Turk, is estimated to have brought 90,000 Kurds into Germany illegally since the mid-1980s. He got four years in prison.

The Italian authorities are now after the powers behind the ships full of Kurdish refugees. Five crew members from the *Ararat* are already under arrest. The police are looking for their bosses. One clue: In mid-December, the *Ararat,* a former cement freighter, was sold for $165,000 in Turkey. "We believe that Turkish and Russian gangs were behind it," says anti-Mafia prosecutor Alberto Maritati.

In the cases of the *Ararat* and *Cometa,* anti-Mafia prosecutors believe that they recognize the fingerprint of the 'Ndrangheta, the Calabrian Mafia. The Italian authorities estimate that the gangs made more than $2 million for arranging the *Ararat*'s voyage.

— Werner Mathes, "Stern," (liberal newsmagazine),
Hamburg, Jan. 8, 1998.

Article 11

World Policy Journal, Winter 1997–1998

Arresting the Decline of Europe

Roger C. Altman and Charles A. Kupchan

Roger C. Altman, *an investment banker and founder of Evercore Partners, served in the Treasury Department during the first Clinton administration.* Charles A. Kupchan, *a professor of international relations at Georgetown University and a senior fellow at the Council on Foreign Relations, served on the National Security Council during the first Clinton administration.*

The Atlantic Alliance is now in a steady decline that will not be reversed by NATO's impending enlargement. Europe itself is in the midst of prolonged economic and political stagnation. The United States is meanwhile turning its attention from the Atlantic to the Pacific, drawn by the inexorable rise of Asia.

The erosion of the Atlantic link began when the Soviet Union disintegrated, which ended the urgent need for the Western democracies to band together against communism and allowed economic considerations to loom larger in setting U.S. priorities. But it speeded up with the arrival of the Clinton administration and its decision to elevate trade liberalization and export promotion to the top of America's foreign policy agenda.

America's new focus on economics does not augur well for the Atlantic link. Trade across the Pacific is already outpacing commerce across the Atlantic.[1] Despite the recent turmoil in a number of East Asia's economies, the region is poised to enjoy strong growth for the foreseeable future. And to the extent that strategic challenges still inform U.S. priorities, Asia again trumps Europe. Deep political and ideological fault lines divide Asia's major powers, requiring a vigilant American military presence to keep the peace. In contrast, Europe's major powers are at peace and the main purpose of a U.S. presence is to provide reassurance. These economic and strategic realities necessarily mean an American tilt toward Asia.

The American gravitation toward the Pacific is therefore understandable, but global stability will be undermined if the Atlantic link withers as a result. The European Union's futile attempt to bring peace to Bosnia made clear that the EU is not ready to manage continental security on its own. A U.S.-European partnership has also been behind the main successes of the decade—countering Iraq, bringing peace to the Balkans, and liberalizing international trade. For the foreseeable future, no Asian coalition will replace America's European allies in constructing an international order based on liberal multilateralism. If the Atlantic Alliance fades, the United States will find the world a far more lonely and difficult place.

Reviving the Atlantic community even as America tilts toward the Pacific requires three principal tasks. First, Europe must take a series of bold steps to restore its economic vitality and competitiveness. Doing so entails implementation of painful structural reforms. Deregulating the European economy, scaling back the welfare state, and lowering labor costs top the list. Second, the European Union must become a more coherent political actor, enabling it to share with the United States the role of global leadership. To do so, the Franco-German coalition must become Europe's political core, not just its economic engine. Finally, the Atlantic community needs to open its doors to Russia. Instead of compensating Moscow for its exclusion from Europe, the United States should press for Russia's integration into NATO and the European Union. For the sake of Russian reform, European stability and prosperity, and the vitality of the Western alliance, the Atlantic democracies have to embrace Russia as it moves down the path of political and economic reform.

The Stagnation of Europe

The EU is stuck in a prolonged recession, with lagging growth rates and towering unemployment levels.[2] The introduction of a single currency will help matters by inducing fiscal discipline, shrinking budget deficits, and lowering transaction costs. But Europe's preoccupation with monetary union is diverting political capital from the pursuit of far more important economic tasks. Corporatist industrial structures and an overextended welfare system, not too many currencies, are at the heart of Europe's economic stagnation. Tackling these structural constraints is essential if Europe is to compete effectively in the global market.

Europe's economic doldrums notwithstanding, the United States continues to have a huge stake in trade and investment across the Atlantic. American companies still have more employees in Europe than in any other region outside the United States. But America's Eurocentrism will not outlast Asia's ascendance. East Asia's projected growth rates are almost twice those of Europe's, and its savings and investment rates—the key to long-term growth—are 50 percent higher.[3] America's private sector has already taken notice. Over the past decade, American companies have steadily increased their personnel in Asia while decreasing their workforces in Europe. These trends will only pick up speed in coming years, making more pronounced a shift in American priorities from the Atlantic to the Pacific.[4]

America's attention will also drift from the Atlantic because Europe is at peace. U.S. forces are likely to remain in Europe for the foreseeable future, but mainly to help with peacekeeping and to guide NATO's evolution, not to preserve a balance among states competing for primacy. In contrast, American forces in East Asia remain critical to preventing conflict on the Korean peninsula and to dampening competitive jockeying between Japan and China. The importance of America's role as an offshore balancer will only increase as China's military and economic might grows.

Europe's failure to forge a more active and coherent foreign and defense policy also takes a toll on its strategic partnership with the United States. Despite all the talk of a new European defense identity, the Western European Union remains little more than a hollow shell. Whether in Asia, Africa, or the Middle East, the European Union shares America's broader objectives but often leaves it to Washington to expend the effort and resources needed to bring these objectives to fruition. Without European willingness to shoulder greater defense burdens, the United States will find the Atlantic link of declining relevance to the new strategic landscape.

America's increasing involvement in East Asia need not come at the expense of its engagement in Europe; there will be no one-to-one trade-off. But the resources America devotes to foreign affairs are limited and, in fact, declining. Defense spending has fallen by 30 percent during the 1990s. The foreign aid budget is under siege and the State Department under pressure to downsize. As Asia rises and America's appetite for foreign engagement diminishes, ensuring that the Atlantic link remains vital will be a Herculean task.

The Western alliance will continue to erode without a dramatic change of course. The Atlantic community must therefore devote itself to three main tasks: (1) promoting Europe's economic growth and competitiveness; (2) overcoming Europe's fear of itself and deepening Franco-German leadership; and (3) locating Russia in a new Atlantic construction.

How to Modernize

Continental Europe practices an outmoded brand of capitalism. Europe's more centralized and corporatist structures rest on interlocking compacts between labor, management, finance, and the state. These less-than-arms-length relationships have dampened competition and produced systemic rigidities within labor and capital markets that impede innovation and growth. If measured in terms of economic performance, European capitalism compares unfavorably with America's brand of laissez-faire capitalism and Asia's investment-driven brand. (Finance, industry, and the state also maintain close linkages in many East Asian countries. But East Asian economies benefit from much higher savings and investment rates than in Europe and do not bear the costs of an extensive welfare system.)

Europeans maintain that their economic structures give them a comparative advantage in capital-intensive sectors requiring skilled labor—such as the production of machinery and tools. But even if company/bank ties and labor/management compacts still give Europe an edge in some types of manufacturing, these strengths are eroding as the service and high-technology sectors rise. And labor costs in Europe are so high that many of its industries face the prospect of either losing market share or exporting jobs. In Germany, for example, labor costs in manufacturing are nearly twice those of the

United States, causing even the most competitive companies to move production abroad. Siemens expects that the majority of its 379,000 employees will be foreigners by 1999. Foreigners already comprise almost one-half of the work force of Hoechst AG, Germany's leading chemical company.

Like most of Europe's economic problems, high labor costs stem from structural rigidities—in this case, from labor/management/state compacts and the costs of the welfare system. In Europe, workweeks are shorter, vacations longer, and benefits higher than in the United States or Japan. Despite the objections of Britain, the EU recently passed legislation mandating a maximum workweek of 48 hours and a minimum vacation of four weeks. These rules add to already burdensome national regulations, such as sick-pay rates in Germany that are 100 percent of basic wage rates.

Europe also suffers from insufficient venture capital funding and inadequate corporate debt and equity markets. Even Germany, the engine of the European economy, has a thin and inactive stock market, fostering excessive dependence on a cautious banking sector for capital. The lack of capital for start-up companies contributes to a shortage of entreprenurialism. And European companies lack the accountability and discipline that accompanies greater attention to enhancing shareholder value. U.S. capital markets are gargantuan in comparison with those of Europe, with venture capital placements and initial public offerings alone providing more than $80 billion to support new companies in 1996. And in Asia, extraordinary levels of savings and investment finance industrial development as well as public infrastructure.

Restoring Europe's economic vitality necessitates, first, scaling back the state's role in the economy and accelerating privatization. Globalization and competition, not state intervention, will modernize European industry. Across the European Union, enterprises owned or controlled by the state are running up huge losses. In contrast, those sold off are becoming profitable and creating jobs. State-controlled Renault, for example, is still in the red, while the performance of British Airways has soared since the company was privatized.

Second, Europe's remaining protectionist barriers must be eliminated if its core industries are to remain competitive. The French and Italian automobile makers, for example, have relied on protection to dominate their home markets—but at the expense of their international competitiveness. In a globalized auto industry, only manufacturers with sufficient economies of scale will prosper. Europe's system of agricultural subsidies must also be dismantled, both to free up EU expenditures for more productive purposes and to open the door to a new round of global liberalization.

Negotiation of a transatlantic free trade area would help provide the political momentum needed to overcome the entrenched interests that continue to favor protectionism. Support for protection against non-EU imports will only increase in coming years, as West European producers face an influx of goods from Central and Eastern Europe. A new round of trans-

atlantic liberalization would not just drive forward structural adjustment within the European Union but also ensure that Europe does not drift from integration into the global economy.

Third, deeper and less regulated capital markets are required to fuel growth and innovation. A corporate fixed-income market did begin to develop during the course of 1997, but it may be only a temporary result of the enormous liquidity in global capital markets. Accordingly, Europe must move ahead with the deregulation of the banking and securities industries in order to foster more competition and attract foreign portfolio investors. The ties between banks and industry should also be loosened, permitting other sources of financing to develop. Regulatory steps to promote more active trading, deeper equity markets, and longer-term bond markets are especially important. Without the vibrant capital markets of the United States or the high internal savings rates that finance investment in Asia, Europe will only fall further behind.

Fourth, Europe must share more fully in the benefits of the information revolution. The EU's high-tech sector remains weak and, despite domestic protection, suffers from insufficient demand. One-third of American households own a personal computer, compared to only one of every seven households in France and Germany. Among white-collar workers, over 90 percent of Americans use computers in their offices, while only 55 percent of Europeans do so. In 1996, use of the Internet in the United States grew by 12.4 percent, as compared with 2.5 percent in Germany and 1.8 percent in France. A large part of the problem is Europe's entrenched telecommunications monopolies, which make the cost of transmitting data over three times more expensive than in the United States.

Europe is just now beginning to deregulate and privatize its telecommunications sector—in keeping with the World Trade Organization's telecommunications agreement signed last March. A rapid and thorough restructuring of the industry is required not just to lower the costs of doing business in Europe but also to increase labor productivity through the introduction of new information technology.

Finally, Europe must revamp its social welfare and corporate benefits programs. The goal is not just to reduce labor costs and alleviate structural unemployment. As Europe's population ages and the ratio of workers to pensioners approaches parity—as it will do in Germany around 2020—reform of the welfare system is essential to ensure the solvency of the state. Europe may well want to find a middle road between its current system and the minimalist American variant. But scaling back the welfare state must be a centerpiece of any efforts to restore the long-term health of the European economy.

The Backlash against Austerity

The recent Socialist victory in France raises vexing questions about the public's willingness to ride out the dislocation that will accompany economic reform. The left benefited from a backlash against austerity and Prime Minister Lionel Jospin's promise to give job creation precedence over deficit reduction and privatization. Europe badly needs jobs—but by stimulating growth in the private sector, not by expanding an already bloated state sector. Fortunately for France and for Europe, Jospin has yet to fulfill his promises and abandon the discipline introduced by the previous government. Nevertheless, the French election illuminates the political obstacles standing in the way of structural reform and underscores the difficulties that Europe's leaders will face as they seek to recast the European economy and welfare state.

Europe's Fear of Its Past

Europeans continue to believe that the greatest threat they face is Europe's own past. The image of the 1930s remains the driving force behind European integration, and avoiding the repetition of this history is the objective against which the European Union's success is measured.

Although fear of its own past has served Europe well by dampening national rivalries and encouraging Germany to confront openly the darker moments in its history, this fear also lies at the heart of the European Union's paralysis in the realm of security policy. Stalemate prevails whenever individual members disagree about how to deal with specific strategic challenges. If the past is Europe's greatest threat, the logic goes, it is better for the EU to do nothing than risk internal splits and the reemergence of national rivalries. Allowing imagined threats to override real ones, however, leaves Europe's periphery neglected and unstable. It relegates major powers such as Russia and Turkey to second-class status, leaving them to wonder where they fit into Europe. And it leaves the United States frustrated that its main partner so often finds itself unable to muster deeper engagement in meeting shared challenges.

Overcoming this fear of the past entails addressing both ideological and political obstacles. On the ideological front, Europe's leaders must launch a public education campaign explicitly intended to move popular attitudes beyond the historical legacies of the 1930s. Instead of casting integration as a question of war and peace—as Chancellor Helmut Kohl continues to do—elites must forge a new ideological foundation for Europe. Adaptation to global economic change, Europe's ascendance as a vigorous international actor, and the construction of a new political space that allows the national state to exist comfortably alongside a supranational union must now provide the impetus behind integration. The past should remain a warning but should no longer act as a check on Europe's willingness and ability to shoulder increased global responsibilities.

On the political front, the EU should abandon its quest for a union-wide foreign policy and instead rely on the Franco-German partnership to serve as the catalyst of ad hoc coalitions. Europeans do not like to admit it, but key decisions

about Europe's future are already made in Bonn and Paris, not Brussels. Strengthening the coalition's guidance on matters of foreign policy would extend into the political realm the influence it now wields over economic policy. Germany will have to assume greater defense responsibilities, something that its neighbors should welcome so long as it occurs in a multilateral context. The involvement of German troops in NATO's peacekeeping mission in Bosnia is a step in the right direction. The broader and more important question is whether the Franco-German coalition will continue to cohere and deepen even as Germany comes on line as a normal power and Europe's border moves east.

France and Germany must confront three daunting challenges if Europe's core is to strengthen and provide political leadership: continued economic duress, generational change, and their incompatible visions of Europe's future. Because Europe's economy will, under the best of circumstances, be slow to revive, France and Germany need to prevent economic austerity and the run-up to monetary union from splitting the coalition. The efforts of France's new Socialist government to renegotiate the terms for monetary union have already produced strains between Paris and Bonn. As austerity continues and squabbling intensifies over preparations for the single currency, the temptation will only increase for French and German elites to blame each other—or the European enterprise—for any setbacks. Unless both sides agree to resist this temptation, monetary union, which is intended to lock in the Franco-German coalition, will have precisely the opposite effect.

Generational change will also pose increasing problems for the Franco-German coupling. Chancellor Kohl and his generation remain the engine behind integration, fueled by a visceral aversion to the national state and the conviction that the European Union is Europe's best guarantee against the reemergence of national rivalry. But the next generation of European leaders will have lived through neither the horrors of the Second World War nor the formidable task of patching together a Europe at peace. Younger Germans, including Bundestag members from Kohl's own party, are more at ease with the national state and less intent on sublimating Germany inside a broader Europe. Younger Frenchmen are less fearful of rivalry with Germany and thus less intent on holding their neighbors in a tight embrace.

Europe's current leaders thus have a special burden. They must pass on to the next generation an abiding appreciation of the importance of the Franco-German coalition. And they must generate new arguments to do so, constructing an ideological foundation for integration rooted in the 1990s, not the 1930s. But it will not be enough just to update the arguments used to justify the European enterprise. The Germans and the French also need to arrive at a common vision of where the EU is headed.

Incompatible Visions

French and German leaders in fact hold incompatible conceptions of the ultimate objectives and character of the union.

These different visions not only cause strains in the coalition but also contribute to Europe's failure to forge a more coherent foreign policy. For Germany, Europe is a construct for moderating and managing power—for ensuring that the continent never again falls prey to the destructive forces of national rivalry. This perspective is not just a reaction against the Second World War. It has deep roots in the Holy Roman Empire, which aimed to dampen ambition and diffuse power in Europe. For France, the EU is about amassing and projecting power, aggregating the union's military and economic resources so that it can assert itself as a global player. The EU is to do for Europe what the national state is no longer strong enough to do for France. This perspective, too, has deep historical roots that trace back to Napoleonic and Jacobin conceptions of France's destiny as a great power.

Melding these competing visions of Europe will require compromise by both parties. Germans will need to become comfortable with a Europe that is more engaged and active in global affairs. Frenchmen will have to stop pursuing an independent course with the sole objective of challenging U.S. leadership, seeking instead to strengthen Europe's ability to share defense burdens more equitably with the United States.

Ironically, the Labour Party's recent victory in Britain raises the novel possibility that London might be able to help Paris and Bonn forge a compromise vision. Prime Minister Tony Blair shows signs of trying to push Britain toward much deeper engagement in the EU. The first trip abroad of Blair's foreign minister, Robin Cook, was to Paris and Bonn, not Brussels or Washington. And the new government is far more receptive than its predecessor to Britain's participation in monetary union, if not in 1999, soon after. It is at least conceivable that Britain will not only cease being Europe's naysayer but will also take on a guiding role in the evolution of the EU. The British share Germany's perception of the EU as an instrument for binding and managing power but at the same time appreciate the importance of projecting influence beyond Europe. Britain could therefore help define a middle road between Germany's desire to sacrifice national sovereignty for a deeper union and France's Gaullist insistence on preserving a strong national state. It would indeed be a strange twist of fate should Britain become part of Europe's core and provide a vision of the EU that ultimately carries the day.

Russia in No-Man's-Land

Russia is falling into a geopolitical no-man's-land. To its east is a rising China and a Pacific Rim economy that grows increasingly dynamic and integrated. To its west is an Atlantic community that is expanding to Russia's borders. Western leaders are seeking to placate Moscow through various means, such as the new NATO-Russia consultative council. But the rhetoric of a united Europe aside, current plans for EU and NATO enlargement promise to leave Russia alone in the heart of Eurasia. Moscow is already reacting by tightening control over its former republics and strengthening its ties to China, Iran, and India. And the Russian Duma is showing signs of opposing further advances on nuclear arms control.

In the aftermath of NATO's decision to move ahead with enlargement, the West must therefore move with purposeful speed not just to placate Yeltsin but to pave Russia's way into a broader Europe—as long as its transition to stable democracy continues apace. By proceeding with its expansion, the United States is making NATO the centerpiece of a new Atlantic security order. Russia's ultimate inclusion in NATO and the EU is now a logical necessity and a strategic imperative for four main reasons.

First, building a new Europe that excludes Russia simply makes no strategic sense. Russia has long been and will again become one of Europe's great powers. The central determinant of European stability in coming decades will be whether Russia exercises its power in a benign or malign manner. During this critical period in Russia's transition, the West should therefore do all it can to lock in democratic reform and to expose Russians to the norms and attitudes that underpin the responsible conduct of foreign policy.

Making clear in deed as well as rhetoric that the West's doors will be open to Russia cannot wait until the very end of the enlargement process; time is running out on the current strategy of offering consultations and pledges of good will to ease Moscow's sense of isolation. Russia has thus far played along with such measures of compensation because it has had little choice and because it has faced only the prospect, not yet the reality, of Central Europe's entry into NATO.

But when the first wave of new entrants is celebrating admission to NATO on the alliance's fiftieth anniversary and the next wave is waiting impatiently at the gate, Russian restraint will be in short supply. And it will become increasingly difficult for U.S. officials to keep asserting that the enlargement of the alliance erases Europe's dividing lines as NATO's new members erect formidable defenses on their eastern borders.

Second, integrating Russia into NATO will help avoid the emergence of a new gray zone in the heart of Europe. Those states that will lie between an enlarged NATO and Russia—the Baltics, Romania, Bulgaria, Moldova, Belarus, Ukraine—are already Europe's most fragile and vulnerable countries. NATO enlargement promises only to exacerbate their security predicament by leaving them in strategic limbo. They face the prospect of ending up on the wrong side of not just NATO's new border. EU enlargement is proceeding with excruciating slowness and is not intended to extend beyond Central Europe. And monetary union and the *de jure* differentiation it will cause *within* the EU reinforces the sense that Europe's less fortunate states are being left behind. The current course presents a potent risk of dividing Europe into a wealthy inner core and a poor and fragmenting periphery.

The Clinton administration plans successive waves of NATO enlargement to eliminate this gray zone and ensure that centrifugal force continues to pull Europe's periphery toward its center. But admitting Central Europe's new democracies into NATO sequentially from west to east will surely drive Moscow into a dangerous and lonely corner. Russia will not stand idly by as every country on its western flank is absorbed into an opposing military bloc. The only solution is to expedite Russia's own inclusion in NATO, thereby enabling Europe's gray zone to enter the West without steadily moving a new dividing line closer to Russia.

Third, Russia's entry into NATO and the EU would give the United States and its allies far more influence over developments in the former Soviet space. And it is in Europe's east, not its center, that the key challenges of the coming decades lie. At stake are Russia's relationship with China, the independence and stability of Ukraine, access to Caspian oil—interests that warrant deep Western engagement. In addition, Russia's relationship with its smaller neighbors would be subject to the restraining effects of NATO's rules and habits of cooperation, helping to eliminate the residue of imperial ambition.

Fourth, drawing Russia and its immediate neighbors into NATO and the EU would help stimulate economic growth across Europe. As Russia's economy improves, it will constitute a huge market for European producers. And Russia's highly skilled and educated workforce would strengthen Europe's economy. Competition from low-wage countries in Eastern Europe would also help drive forward the restructuring in Western Europe essential to the EU's economic renewal. Including Russia in Europe would thus raise Europe's economic as well as strategic value to the United States, strengthening the Atlantic link.

Bringing Russia into NATO and the EU would no doubt change the essential character of these institutions. NATO would have to give up the pretense of being a traditional military alliance focused on repelling external enemies and instead work to integrate all of Europe's democracies into a cooperative security community. And the EU would have to abandon, at least for now, its federal aspirations, working to build a wider, even if looser, union. But as Russian democracy deepens and the need to hedge against the return of imperial ambition disappears, this transformation is precisely what will be required to make NATO and the EU relevant to the new European landscape.

Whereas putting Europe's economic and political house in order is largely the responsibility of the Europeans themselves, drawing Russia into Western institutions is principally America's job. If left up to the EU, the West's border would stop at the Poland-Belarus frontier—a cultural and historical dividing line between Western and Orthodox Christianity. Enlargement further eastward would also require a more extensive dilution of the EU's institutions than Europeans are currently willing to contemplate. It is therefore up to Washington to provide the geopolitical vision and the political momentum needed to ensure that the Atlantic community fully opens its doors to Russia.

An Atlantic Bargain

The Western alliance is in much worse shape than conventional wisdom admits. Its members must recognize Europe's increasing marginalization and take compensatory steps before it is too late. Europe must overcome, at long last, the deep structural impediments that straitjacket its economy. It must shake loose of the ideological and institutional constraints that limit its global role, relying on the Franco-German coalition, with or without Britain's participation, to take the lead in forging ad hoc coalitions. And Europe must rethink its approach to core-periphery relations and recast its vision of how far east Europe should extend. Otherwise, Europe's fragmentation, not its unification, will result.

America's end of the bargain is to take the lead in enlarging the Atlantic community, ensuring that the door is open to Russia and to those countries soon to be left in limbo in Europe's new gray zone. American policymakers must come to their senses and realize that Yalta has already has been reversed: Central Europe is free and clear. It is securing democracy and liberty further east that is the pressing issue of the day.

The United States should also do what it can to help Europe tackle the painful challenges of economic and political renewal. To this end, a transatlantic free trade area should be high on the agenda, in no small part because it will give elected officials leverage in overcoming the domestic political obstacles that stand in the way of Europe's economic renewal.

On the political front, Washington can make a novel contribution to the deepening of Europe's core by dealing with France and Germany collectively rather than individually. A Paris-Bonn-Washington dialogue should be maintained through regular ministerial meetings, providing added impetus for the countries comprising Europe's core to harmonize their short-term policies as well as their long-term visions. Should Tony Blair continue to move Britain closer to the EU, London should be included as well.

The EU's smaller powers would no doubt object to the loss of influence that would accompany an exclusive, high-level dialogue between the United States and Europe's power brokers. But all of Europe would be the beneficiary if Europe's core is thereby strengthened and ultimately provides the leadership needed to make the EU a more coherent and effective actor.

The future of the Atlantic Alliance rests on Europe's capacity to bring about its own renewal and the West's willingness to open fully its doors to the east. The alternative is the erosion of the very partnerships and principles that Americans and Europeans worked so hard to make the anchor of global order.

Notes

The authors gratefully acknowledge the research assistance of Delphine Park and Samuel Na, and the thoughtful comments of the W. Averell Harriman Study Group at the Council on Foreign Relations.

1. In 1995, trade between the United States and East Asia totaled roughly $465 billion, while U.S.-European Union trade totaled $360 billion (International Monetary Fund, *Direction of Trade Statistics 1996* [Washington, D.C.: IMF, 1996], pp. 445–47).

2. Projected growth rates for 1997 are as follows: European Union, 2.4 percent; United States, 3 percent; and East Asia, 4.2 percent. Projected unemployment levels are: European Union, 11.3 percent; United States, 5.5 percent; and East Asia, less than 3 percent (International Monetary Fund, *World Economic Outlook* [Washington, D.C.: IMF, 1997], pp. 131, 135; and U.S. Treasury Department).

3. Savings and investment rates (as a percentage of GDP) are roughly 20 percent in Europe and 30 percent in East Asia (IMF, *World Economic Outlook,* pp. 200–201).

4. The slowdown of the Japanese economy during the 1990s as well as the recent volatility in the currencies and stock markets of a number of East Asia's "tigers" have raised the possibility that the region's period of robust growth is coming to an end. Many analysts agree, however, that the economic fundamentals in the region as a whole are solid and that strong growth will continue well into the next century. The recent turmoil resulted more from mismanagement and overconfidence than from structural problems (Joseph Stiglitz, "How to Fix the Asian Economies," *New York Times,* October 31, 1997; and David Hale, "Is Asia's High Growth Era Over?" *The National Interest* [spring 1997]).

Article 12

Foreign Affairs, May/June 1998

The Trouble with France

Dominique Moïsi

A ROTTEN MOOD

TO AMERICANS, France is a beautiful country, home to that most elegant of cities, Paris, the seductive tones of the French language, and some of the world's finest wines, which makes it all the more difficult for them to understand how such a charming nation could be so irritating an ally. The French always seem to be opposing the United States on some issue or other, whether it is in the realm of international diplomacy, where between the lines of France's carefully worded diplomatic statements one can discern a distinct distaste for America's oft-proclaimed sole-superpower status, or on matters of culture, where France is always the first to denounce American "cultural imperialism." Lately, Franco-American friction has manifested itself most visibly in the Persian Gulf, where France's interests—in Iraq and Iran—seem to clash with America's security needs. Many Americans ascribe France's prickliness to the legacy of "Gaullism," the conservative, nationalist inheritance bequeathed by that country's greatest twentieth-century leader. But in France nobody even knows what Gaullism means anymore, apart from being able to say no to the United States.

In fact, the annoying behavior coming out of Paris is best explained by the fact that the country is, quite simply, in a bad mood, unsure of its place and status in a new world. The less confident France is, the more difficult it is to deal with. On the eve of the 21st century, France faces four major challenges, which are together the source of its melancholy. The first is globalization, which is often blamed for the erosion of France's culture and its depressingly high levels of unemployment. (Last year, one of Paris' biggest bestsellers was a tract titled *The Economic Horror*—a bitter philippic against globalization's ills.) The second is the unipolar nature of the international system, in which the United States leads and a once-proud France is grudgingly forced to follow. The third is the merger of Europe, which threatens to drown out France's voice. The fourth, and by far the toughest, challenge is France itself. The nation must overcome its economic, social, political, moral, and cultural shortcomings if it is to successfully face its other challenges. The rise of Jean-Marie LePen's extreme right National Front is symptomatic of France's internal difficulties. To combat them, France must, in essence, transcend itself.

IT'S NOT EASY BEING MEDIUM

ALL MEN ARE equal, but some are more equal than others. In the age of globalization, size matters. If small is beautiful and big is powerful, then medium is problematic. The Internet, information technology, and other trappings of the global economy can reinforce the centrality of the United States or multiply the strength of a small city-state like Singapore, but

DOMINIQUE MOÏSI is Deputy Director of the French Institute for International Relations and Editor in Chief of *Politique étrangère.*

they often penalize middle-size countries like France. France's special strengths are its culture and its heritage, and these are being worn away, replaced by a "universal culture" that looks strangely American. If France were a young state, less set in its ways, less burdened by the weight of old traditions or images from the past, it might be able to adapt. But France is an ancient country. It cannot forget its history, and in trying to reconcile it with elements of the modern world ends up merely superimposing it upon them, creating a hodgepodge that is true to neither. Tellingly, France's most popular computer game today is not a high-tech, outer space adventure, but a thriller called "Versailles," which takes place amid the grandeur of the court of Louis XIV.

Consider the difference between France and the United States. America is not only big and young; it is, above all, open. French society remains closed and rigid—incapable of attracting the best talent from other countries while unwittingly supplying its own to America. For example, Dr. Luc Montagnier, codiscoverer of the AIDS virus, now teaches and conducts research in the United States because he reached mandatory retirement age at the Institut Pasteur. Contrast the essential message of Hollywood—if you want to make a difference you can—with the classical archetype of the French movie: A loves B, who loves C, who loves D, all of whom end up in despair. America's flexibility can be seen in the success of its melting pot, which, in an age of globalization, is exported worldwide. Today, the sounds of the world are essentially African-American, everybody eats Italian-American pizza at least once a week, and children the world over delight in films by an Eastern European, Jewish American named Steven Spielberg. The American-accented brand of English is the closest thing we have to a universal language, while the French, obsessed with defending "Francophonie" and dreaming of a world united by their tongue, erect protective linguistic barriers, not understanding that this isolates them instead of preserving their culture. What France should seek to preserve—once it has conceded defeat in the language battle—is the context and originality of its message, not its medium.

France's dream of challenging the United States is the rest of Europe's nightmare.

France's struggle with globalization is complicated by its people's high quality of life. Most of the French feel they have little to gain and much to lose from globalization—the space and beautiful diversity of their countryside, the quality of their food and wine, and the respect for tradition. Why risk all these unique pleasures for the sake of an uncertain competition in a global world? The temptation for many Frenchmen is to retreat into the protective bubble of the good life.

TOPPLING THE GIANT

THE END OF the Cold War only reinforced French envy of America. They resent the global reach of America's power and Washington's presumption to speak in the name of the international community. Unlike the pragmatic British or the historically guilt-ridden Germans, the French feel that they, like the United States, carry a universal message. Remember that France, like the United States, is the font of ideas about "the rights of man," liberty, equality, and fraternity. French frustrations are exacerbated by the mixture of benign neglect, sheer indifference, and mild irritation with which Washington considers Paris' initiatives. In the absence of the unifying threat posed by the Soviet Union, Franco-American tensions can be eased only by shared interests. In the short run, France's jealousy of America will be muted by the political constraints imposed on it by a united Europe, the other members of which do not share France's feelings. The French know all too well that their secret dream—to build a Europe that will challenge the United States—is the nightmare of their continental partners. By openly expressing its differences with America, over the Middle East for example, Paris more often than not isolates itself from London and Bonn, not to mention the rest of the European Union. There are, however, subtle issues on which France can tilt Europe against America. If France is alone in supporting Iraq, for example, on Iran the rest of Europe is on its side and against the United States.

On security matters, Paris and Washington are at once allies and competitors. France's ambition to create a genuine European foreign and security policy, although formally welcomed by Washington, clashes with the United States' inclination to take the lead. France well knows that its long-term European ambitions will require it to rejoin NATO and give up on trying to attain some special status. France understands that more Europe tomorrow means more NATO today—a bitter pill, since expanding the alliance could reinforce the U.S. monopoly on security. But there is no alternative, since Europe lacks the political will to take on such a large commitment alone. In fact, the French have come to see any expansion of NATO without a corresponding widening of the European Union as an American attempt to preclude any specifically European initiatives in the security field.

In Paris, the peaceful end to the most recent crisis in the Persian Gulf was considered a triumph of French diplomacy over American belligerence. But it was a cosmetic victory, since Saddam Hussein's receptiveness to diplomacy was certainly the result of his fear of being bombed by America. The neat division of labor that France and the United States enjoyed in the Middle East in the 1970s—France in Baghdad, America in Tehran—did not exist this time around. U.S. and French policies over Iraq are antithetical—the French eschew military options, and the Americans show little faith in diplomacy. This essential difference will not disappear and could rebound at the first opportunity—most probably when Saddam takes his next adventure.

Exploiting its position as a permanent member of the U.N. Security Council, France can present itself as an alternative Western voice to the nations of the Third World. In the Middle East, for example, Benjamin Netanyahu's election and the resulting stall in the peace process has given a new legitimacy to Europe's and in particular France's role as an honest broker between Arabs and Israelis. Not content with merely bankrolling a peace process led by others, France intends to play a more active role, political as well as economic, complementing the United States but not replacing it. But the French cannot afford to balance America's pro-Israeli position simply by being pro-Arab. France must demonstrate that it is serious about peace. It has certain advantages: unlike the United States, it is not a prisoner of domestic politics. If Paris cannot make peace, it can at least facilitate it.

On the African continent, the French must admit that they need Washington's clout, just as Washington must admit that it needs France's experience and presence. Africa brings out the best and the worst in the French. France is per capita the largest donor of foreign aid in the world after Japan, and well ahead of most European countries. But French money has gone more to regimes and leaders than to the African people. Rivals in economic terms, Paris and Washington are necessary geopolitical partners in this area. The United States has been keen to reassure the French that America has no secret agenda, no ambition to become Africa's gendarme. In fact, the French are starting to realize that their views on the continent's future converge with those of the Americans. Both fear regional destablization, as in the new Democratic Republic of the Congo, formerly Zaire.

LOST IN THE CROWD

ALTHOUGH "EUROPE" does not yet exist in security and diplomatic terms, it is very real in economic and commercial terms, an actor whose power and influence will be strengthened by the coming of the euro. This is the only hope for the Europeans to balance America—only in the monetary field does a new bipolarity seem within reach. There is an irony here: The only card with which France can challenge American hegemony is Europe, and to play it, Paris must abandon much of its sovereignty.

A united Europe will allow France to multiply its influence.

For the Germans, European unification has been, together with their participation in NATO, the way to sever their links with their Nazi past, to erase the grim legacy of that dark period. For the Italians, always in search of domestic stability and a way to overcome their low self-esteem, Europe provides legitimacy, allowing them to triumph over their doubts about themselves and the credibility of their nation-state. For France, however, Europe—in its various forms, from the confederal model favored by de Gaulle to the federal one preferred by François Mitterrand—has been at the very heart of the French nationalist project, a way to pursue France's past glory and power by multiplying its influence. For France to remain France, it must become Europe. Leaders of the left and the right, once in power, have strictly adhered to the European credo. France's allegiance to the cause of Europe is now focused on the achievement of a common currency. To create a common European identity, to strengthen the voice of Europe in the world, to forge a new economic power, there is only one answer: the euro.

Yet for all of France's devotion to the European ideal, one can sense its apprehensions. Beyond their fear of having created a technocratic monster, too intrusive for some, too impotent for others, the French worry about their country's place within this new and enlarged Europe. In 1992, the debate about the Maastricht referendum was really a debate about Germany. Did the treaty offer the best guarantee against the potential threat of a reunited and powerful Germany, or would it lead to German supremacy in Europe? Does France run the danger of being squeezed between an economically dynamic Britain and an ever more powerful Germany? The city of London has recovered its old financial power, bursting with energy and activity. Berlin, once torn, will soon become not just the capital of the new Germany, but the capital of the new Europe. But Paris, some French fear, is in danger of becoming a new Rome, a pleasant and beautiful metropolis but one that is mainly a museum of its own past.

For now it seems that France's best option is to continue to pay lip service to a united Europe and promote the euro, while taking advantage of the lack of a diplomatic and military "Europe" to pursue an independent French foreign policy. This is the kind of Janus-faced exercise for which France certainly has the cunning and skill but which could prove dangerous for the future of Europe—if France were to be imitated by the Germans, for example.

Hesitant about their influence within an enlarged Europe, with a strong Germany at its center, the French are also anxious about the applicability of France's model of state centralization to the requirements of a new Europe. There is a nagging fear in France that Britain's laissez-faire economic model, built by Margaret Thatcher and largely preserved by Tony Blair's new Labour, and Germany's form of decentralized government are more modern than France's old-fashioned statist recipe—a fear bolstered by the number of young French who are heading to Britain to find jobs in that dynamic economy. The state, once the pride of France, is now the main obstacle to adjustment and change.

L'ÉTAT, C'EST LA FRANCE

THE FRENCH behave toward their state the same way that adolescents behave toward their parents: with a mixture of rebellion and submission. They criticize its heavy-handedness and inefficiency, but they appreciate its reassuring presence and protection. The spring 1997 legislative elections, which brought the Socialists to power, perfectly demonstrated this contradictory attitude. Socialist leader Lionel Jospin's triumph showed that, on a moral and political level, the majority of the French want a less corrupt and more accountable government. At the same time, the electorate wants the state to protect the weakest, poorest elements of society and regulate the effects of the market. For example, Jospin's plan to cut the maximum working week from 39 to 35 hours, against the wishes of many employers, may not make sense economically but is in tune with the feelings of most Frenchmen, who want to be protected by the state from long working hours. It does not matter to them if the idea that governments can create jobs better than market forces is outdated. France is a conservative society—its majority clings to the status quo.

The centrality of the French state is compounded by the society's rigidity. France's work force, for example, is decidedly less mobile than Britain's. Too many people prefer to remain unemployed instead of moving to new towns or villages to fill jobs. This may contribute to family stability or the harmony of social life—which means that French families can always have Sunday lunch at grandma's—but certainly not to the dynamism of the economy.

Criticisms of the state extend to those who incarnate it at the highest levels. The prestigious but stiflingly conformist civil service training school, the National School of Administration, is the focus of most complaints about the administration and political class, since its graduates have long monopolized the corridors of power. The French often accuse their civil servants of knowing neither the importance of social dialogue nor the way to govern in a genuinely democratic environment in which all citizens expect to be treated as equal. These attacks are almost reminiscent of their ancestors' challenge to the nobility at the end of the ancien régime. If those who embody the state at the highest level cannot find an answer to unemployment and social injustice, the French ask, why should these mandarins enjoy virtual immunity from accountability?

France is a country forced into revolution by its inability to reform.

Since the days of Alexis de Tocqueville, France has been described as a country forced into revolution by its inability

to reform. Although today's France is not about to revolt, it is suffering from a lack of hope for the future, which in large part explains the success of rightist groups like the National Front. The French economy is actually doing far better than the unemployment figures suggest: French industry is increasingly competitive, the trade balance is positive, inflation is down, and the franc is strong. Nevertheless, the French are morose. Their country is slowly and painfully transforming itself from a welfare state into a modern one, learning to live within its means. France has not chosen the easiest path to its goals and certainly not the most direct one.

IN SEARCH OF IDENTITY

EUROPE'S ATTEMPT to transcend its fratricidal quarrels by integrating its resources, economies, currencies, and political institutions into a quasi-federal state will serve it well in the global era. Regionalization is the best way to meet the challenges of globalization, because it makes states bigger, and bigger is better. But globalization reinforces the likelihood of fragmentation. Today, the need to express one's difference in a global world leads to a desperate search for identity that can end in peaceful divorce between some nation-states and jingoistic tensions and bloody conflicts between others.

France is a perfect example of this identity dilemma. For decades the French have oscillated between celebrating their exceptionalism and proclaiming its end. Today France is torn more than ever between the desire to be a modern, normal country and the reflex to cling to the belief that France is not like other nations. The first choice presupposes openness, flexibility, and a secure sense of one' identity. The second opposes globalization, is wary of a more unified Europe, and embraces anti-Americanism. But the second choice is no choice at all; protectionism would lead to isolation and decay.

France is probably sicker politically than is generally thought. The fact that large numbers of the French have thrown their support behind LePen's National Front, which is highly represented in the country's regional assemblies, indicates that the people of France have reached the end of their tether. Gripped by despair over their country's high unemployment rate and declining importance in the world, they have begun to cast their lot with the exceptionalists, in a wistful but dangerous attempt to recapture France's past glory. The moderate right is falling by the wayside, incapable of producing a message that will resonate with the masses like LePen's and increasingly co-opted by it. The left and the Socialists, though in power, must contend with the fragility of their own coalitions. Corruption—and the threat that it will be exposed—hangs like the sword of Damocles over the heads of politicians on both sides. All of this combines to coarsen France's political life and plunge the country further into its depression.

Yet despite the weaknesses, there is hope for France. The exceptionalists may be making gains, but for the time being, they are in the minority. Indeed, the National Front has lost its only seat in Parliament. And the more successfully France's internal problems, particularly its unemployment, are tackled, the less political and social discontent men like LePen will have to exploit.

France has surmounted crises worse than this current crisis of confidence. Its long history will ultimately guarantee its stability. The land of Liberté, Egalité, Fraternité will not soon cede all of that for an imaginary kingdom of French suprem-

acy, for its citizens know the despair that would bring. The French will come to realize that globalization, that most feared bogeyman on the streets of Paris, will not bring France's demise but rather force it to hone its skills and refurbish its message. A more unified Europe will not smother it but in fact give it new purpose, allowing it to determine its own destiny in the world far better than it could do alone. The depression will subside. In the end, France will endure.

Article 13

Europe, May 1998

What is France's Long-Term Strategy?

Jospin Pursues Ambitious Controversial Agenda

"People here want a prime minister who works for them. Jospin fills that role. I see him as France's next president."

—*Mario Florentin, Paris taxi driver, formerly a sales executive.*

By Axel Krause

That comment made in Paris en route to a Socialist Party rally in March was deliberately upbeat. But it summed up much of the prevailing, complex reaction in France to Lionel Jospin, completing ten months as prime minister.

Despite many obstacles, the sixty-year old Jospin is actively pursuing an ambitious, controversial, and frequently misunderstood reform program, amid uncertainties about France's position in Europe and with regard to its long-time ally, the United States.

At the Paris rally, flanked by Communists, ecologists, and other allied leftists, including Dominique Strauss-Kahn, his close friend and finance minister, Jospin told some 5,000 enthusiastic supporters, "We are turned to the twenty-

first century, committed to greater economic growth, democracy, equality, and reorienting European policy." More familiar rhetoric on the eve of key, regional elections?

In a way, yes. But several weeks later, Jospin's Socialist-led government scored an important victory by not only wresting control of regional and local councils long-dominated by conservatives, but he avoided an expected voter backlash in the government's first popularity test since taking office last June.

"This [election result] is encouragement for what are doing," declared Martine Aubry, who, as Jospin's powerful minister of employment and solidarity, is leading the drive to significantly reduce not only France's chronic unemployment, now in excess of 3 million,

but to improve the lives of several million "working poor," 200,000 of whom lack any form of health insurance.

How Jospin's "new-Socialist realism" fares in reducing record joblessness and creeping poverty will, in the view of most observers, make or break the government and, possibly, him. As he approaches his first anniversary in office, his popularity rating remains a steady 60 percent of those polled.

The intense, austere prime minister has lots going for him—fresh approaches to old problems, a strong personality, a widely respected cabinet led by Strauss-Kahn and Aubry, and a very non-French style. In many ways, he more closely resembles President Bill Clinton and British Prime Minister Tony Blair than most contemporary French

Cohabitation

France is unique in that the constitution of the Fifth Republic, which was designed by President Charles de Gaulle as a vehicle to consolidate his personal power after the democratic chaos of the Fourth Republic, gives the country two official foreign policies. The strategic direction of foreign policy is entrusted to the president and his staff in the Elysée Palace. But the administration of French diplomacy is the business of the foreign minister, who is a member of the cabinet and responsible to the prime minister at his office in the Hôtel Matignon.

When the president and prime minister come from the same political grouping, the differences are minor. But just as American voters have for all but four of the past twenty-six years required the president of one party to govern with a Congress dominated by a rival party, so France has grown accustomed to cohabitation. President Jacques Chirac, of the center-right, governs alongside Lionel Jospin, the Socialist prime minister, whose majority in the National Assembly depends on the support of Communist Party delegates. At least an American president can choose his secretary of state, although he must be confirmed by the Senate. But a French president can find himself trying to work with a foreign minister with widely different political views.

Direct clashes have usually been avoided, thanks to the broad consensus on a French foreign policy that cleaves to its alliance with Germany, its future in the European Union, and its insistence on freedom of action from the US-led NATO alliance. But President Mitterrand's discreet support for the Atlantic alliance in the 1980s and President Chirac's hopes of returning France to full NATO membership, both met considerable internal opposition.
—*Martin Walker*

leaders. "He is calm, credible, avoids plunging into things," said forty-five-year-old cab driver Mario Florentin, "and people don't mind his austerity . . . it's arrogance they can't stand."

Born into a modest, Protestant family in suburban Paris, his father, a teacher and Socialist pacifist, his mother a mid-

wife, Jospin played tennis, rugby, basketball, and boxed throughout his studies, even while preparing for the stiff entrance exams for France's elite ENA, the Ecole Nationale d'Administration for civil servants. Friends recall that as a student, he firmly believed the political Left was good, the Right bad, and that his future would be in teaching or politics. He did well in both fields, while rising rapidly within the Socialist Party, which he joined in 1971, helping shape its policies with regard to education, developing countries, and foreign policy.

Under Socialist President Mitterrand, whom he both admired and criticized, Jospin served as education minister before becoming first secretary of the party. He held that influential post until his unsuccessful bid for the presidency as Mitterrand's successor in 1995 against Gaullist Jacques Chirac. Since then, and particularly since his spectacular victory in last year's parliamentary election that swept him to power, Jospin has been lucky.

The economy is recovering with GNP growth expected to reach 3 percent this year, double the 1996 rate. The Paris Bourse is booming, as leading private and government-controlled companies and banks report high earnings. Jobs are being created, mainly in the public sector. Chirac, whose term runs until 2002, shares power under a constitutional arrangement known as "cohabitation" but agrees with much of what Jospin is doing. Meantime, Chirac's conservative allies are in bitter disarray over alliances with the extreme-right National Front party, which scored 15.5 percent of the votes cast in the regional elections.

What is Jospin's long-term strategy? How does he view the EU and the Commission? Does he relate to Tony Blair and Britain? Is he anti-American? He addressed these questions in an interview with *EUROPE,* but doubts remained, notably among President Clinton's advisors preparing for Jospin's visit to Washington scheduled for late June. Observers trying to assess his personality and role agree it's a difficult task.

Insider Dominique Merchez, who has worked on Jospin's staff since 1985, including as spokesman, describes the prime minister as "complex but not complicated" to understand. Consider the following words used by many in an attempt to describe him: austere, solemn,

primeval, rigorous, methodical, slow, energetic, rebellious, generous, sensitive, Blairish, escape artist, loner, plodding, brilliant, classy, disciplined, athletic, severe, proud, dignified, builder, stubborn, bon vivant.

The first and only Jospin biography published in 1996, *L'Héritier Rebelle* [The Rebellious Heir] cites two particularly revealing incidents.

Several years after graduating from ENA (twenty-third out of ninety) and then from a Harvard University seminar taught by Henry Kissinger, the rising young diplomat Jospin told startled friends and family that diplomacy was not for him. Deeply affected by France's leftist-led May 1968 upheavals and strikes and opposed to General De Gaulle's conservative domestic—but not his nationalistic foreign—policies, Jospin declared it would be impossible to pursue a political career as a diplomat. "Can you imagine me serving little cakes or escorting duchesses to the London Opera?" he laughingly asked a colleague.

In 1993, the Socialists soundly defeated by conservatives, a tired, depressed Jospin, out of a job, returned to the foreign ministry seeking an assignment, possibly as ambassador. Most observers predicted his political career was over; his second wife, Sylviane, told biographer-journalists Gerard Leclerc and Florence Muracciole that "I sensed him [at that time] capable of giving everything up." Shortly afterward, Gaullist Foreign Minister Alain Juppé told him there were no openings. It doesn't matter, a hurt Jospin replied to the man he would succeed as prime minister, "I have a role to play on the national scene." Strauss-Kahn then helped convince him to return to politics.

The two events, twenty-five years apart, illustrate how Jospin's mix of leftist and Gaullist approaches were being formulated early on and that he stuck to his basic convictions. In a 1981 interview with the French weekly *L'Express,* he predicted that within a decade France will have become a "mixed society" in which workers' rights would be far better protected, unemployment reduced, and the work week reduced to thirty-five hours from thirty-nine hours without cutting pay. The latter proposal, then in the Socialist Party program but barely noticed, has emerged as the centerpiece of the Jospin government's plan to create as many as 1 million jobs that will apply to all French workers by the year 2002.

The controversial hiring plan, already approved by the leftist-dominated National Assembly, would be implemented by offering employers new, eased labor regulations and lower charges and taxes. Yet, the plan is still vigorously opposed by many business leaders, including the powerful employers confederation, le Patronat, whose new president Ernest Antoine described it as "precipitous, costly, and archaic." In the interview with *EUROPE,* Jospin brushed off

criticism as being ideologically motivated and vowed to implement the compulsory plan.

Not everything is going well for Jospin. Labor unrest over reforms continue to simmer amid protests by the jobless and poor. Tax levels remain high, discouraging investments. Teenage crime, particularly in the suburbs, is spreading. Young, talented French men and women, many in their twenties, are flocking to Britain to find jobs. Allegations of corruption involving top political and business executives have shaken public confidence in national leadership.

France, along with ten of its EU neighbors, will enter unchartered financial territory as it abandons its cherished franc in favor of the new European single currency, the euro. Now that France's parliament has voted in favor of the new European currency, both Chirac and Jospin insist that France will still keep its identity and establish its own national policies, even after the launch of the euro.

Axel Krause is a EUROPE *contributing editor based in Paris.*

Article 14

Smithsonian, February 1996

A Pilgrim's Search for Relics of the Once and Future King

Ancient stones and much-loved stories yield both hints and guesses about Arthur and his Camelot

Caroline Alexander

The author published The Way to Xanadu *in 1994. Her latest book,* Battles' End: a Seminole Football Team Revisited, *has just been released by Knopf.*

Hidden in a thicket, I drew my coat around me and peered into the darkness. It was Christmas Eve. The night was clear and still and without moonlight. I had positioned myself beside a muddy bridle path that winds down a hill between the trees and was quietly awaiting the thunder of hoofbeats. The hill behind me is known as Cadbury Castle, for centuries regarded as the most likely site of King Arthur's Camelot. According to legend, on Christmas Eve the ghosts of Arthur and his knights gallop out of the castle's fallen gates on silver-footed horses.

Cadbury Castle is in Somerset just outside the village of South Cadbury, in southwest England. In daylight, the open grassy summit is brilliant green, rising above an encircling band of forest. From the top, you can look down on flocks grazing the clipped pasturage at the base of the hill. Northward lies the whole width of Glastonbury plain. The first recorded identification of Cadbury Castle as Camelot was made by the antiquarian John Leland in 1542. But it wasn't until the 1960s that parts of the hill's many layers of former settlements were

finally excavated, revealing that it had been occupied off and on since at least early Neolithic times. More important, ruins from the Arthurian period were well represented, with evidence of former ramparts, a fortified gate-tower and a sizable timber structure thought to have been a great hall.

I had expected to share my vigil on Christmas Eve with any number of other faithful (or gullible) pilgrims. But when I trudged across the frosty fields to my thicket, I was very much alone. The whirring wings of a disturbed wood pigeon made the only sound I heard all night. At last I reluctantly gave up my post and trudged back down through the fields. The once and future king had failed to appear.

How to account for the spell that Camelot has cast over the world's imagination? In scores of languages and shaped to all sorts of storytelling genres, from medieval epic to modern musical, tales of Arthur and his knights have been enthralling people for more than a thousand years. On plot alone, the legend is hard to resist: the undistinguished boy, Arthur, pulling the sword from the stone to become king of England; his marriage to beautiful Guinevere; the brotherhood of the chivalrous Round Table knights; the quest for that elusive object, the Holy

Grail; the disastrous passion between Lancelot and the queen; evil Mordred's treachery; the ultimate destruction of Arthur's realm; the banishment of loyalty, piety and righteousness from the land.

But the emotional pull of Camelot is greater than its captivating storybook romance. Arthur's loss of his Round Table, though set in the worldly realm of kings and counselors, jousting tourneys, swashbuckling knights and bewitching ladies, is a replay of mankind's fall from grace in the Garden of Eden. It ends in treason and civil war, with brother against brother, father against son. It has become part of the geography of our collective imagination. Today, that "fleeting wisp of glory called Camelot" stirs an overwhelming sense of loss—a nostalgic yearning for a better-ordered and more-spiritual age that we long to believe once existed.

A Magic World of Profound Melancholy

I have spent years more or less in thrall to the Camelot story. Walt Disney's film *The Sword in the Stone* set me on the path, imparting beyond the comedy and magic a sense of something grave and wondrously tragic. Based on T. H. White's *The Once and Future King,* it opened up Arthur's whole life and world, a medieval land full of hawking and archery and imagined fighting described in whimsical detail yet marked by overwhelming melancholy. Later, Thomas Malory's unwieldy but masterful epic poem *Le Morte d'Arthur* worked for me at a more profound level of regret and grown-up loss, its archaic language evoking images of armored footsteps receding down deserted flinty halls. But it was through Tennyson's epic *Idylls of the King* that all the "Arthurian" emotions—loyalty and loss and the impotent regret of wisdom learned too late—became entirely personal.

Like many pilgrims, then, I had come to England hoping to find something that might allow me to believe that Camelot was "real." And indeed, the West Country of England is shaped by Arthurian associations. At Tintagel, where Arthur supposedly was conceived, a ruined castle still clings to the dark, sea-beaten cliffs guarding the Cornish coast. A few miles inland, on the willow-fringed banks of the unprepossessing river Camel, is Slaughter Bridge, a village so nondescript that I drove right through it before realizing it is supposed to be the site of the Battle of Camlann, where Arthur and Mordred meet in mortal combat.

From here, so the story goes, the grievously wounded king was carried inland by faithful Sir Bedivere to the heart of brooding Bodmin Moor. One evening I walked the moor toward a pond called Dozmary Pool, near whose waters Arthur's wounded body was laid and into which he thrice commanded the reluctant Bedivere to hurl his sword, Excalibur. Reflecting an evening of vivid sunset, the pool's shallow waters turned blood red. Perhaps it was after seeing such an apocalyptic sight that Tennyson described an astonishing arm: "Clothed in white samite, mystic, wonderful," rising from the water to catch, to

thrice brandish and finally sink forever beneath its surface with the world's most famous sword.

A hundred miles or so west from Dozmary Pool in the town of Amesbury, I visited a pretty cruciform church where the repentant Guinevere is said to have retreated to the spacious grounds of an early abbey, now a ruin. A pub and some shops have claimed a good deal of the old abbey land, but behind the church is a gently flowing river where a black swan stretched its neck among a crowd of ducks.

Arthur, an old soldier after all, never really dies but fades away—to the enchanted Isle of Avalon, which, since the late 12th century, has been associated with Glastonbury. The extraordinary hill, known as Glastonbury Tor, that juts abruptly from the plain just outside the modern town was formerly surrounded by marsh and may once have had the appearance of a misty, enchanted island. In 1191, the grave of Arthur and his queen was "discovered" in Glastonbury Abbey—a find that launched a lucrative pilgrimage industry and enabled the canny monks to rebuild their abbey, which had burned to the ground in 1184.

In each of these places I caught a glimpse of the kind of romantic "truth" I was seeking. Amesbury was the most evocative, perhaps because it was so easy to imagine the grieving queen pacing the riverbank on a winter's morning, or perhaps because for me the end of Camelot, especially in *Idylls of the King,* has always been most irrevocably signaled by the final parting between Arthur and Guinevere. In the end, however, all these towns and castles failed me. In part this was due to modern realities, such as the King Arthur tourist shops dominating Tintagel, that kept crowding my vision. In larger part, though, it was because I knew before I arrived that the few historical facts known about Arthur cannot be squared with any of these places.

The shadowy figure who became the Arthur of legend first appeared, if he appeared at all, not in medieval England but in the afterglow of the Roman occupation of Britain. The native Britons were "Celts" (SMITHSONIAN, May 1993)—a term used to define a linguistic and cultural group rather than a race. But from Emperor Claudius' invasion in A.D. 43 until the departure of the last legions in 410, Roman culture shaped the island. From the late fourth century on, Roman garrisons in Britain were reduced in order to strengthen the waning empire on the continent then being overrun by Germanic tribes. It is unclear how rapidly the social fabric created by the long Roman occupation unraveled in Britain after the Romans' departure. With the central government gone, local authority was fought over by powerful local rivals. From the 430s onward, fierce Anglos and Saxons, intent on making settlements of their own, streamed across the North Sea into the east and south of Britain. In the north of Britain, skirmishes with Picts and Scots, old enemies, were renewed. In response to this last threat, the Britons made a fatal mistake: they hired Anglos and Saxons as mercenaries. Sometime around 450, these paid allies turned against their British hosts, and the south and east of Britain fell entirely under Anglo-Saxon rule.

The only surviving near-contemporary account of this period, by a West Country monk named Gildas, reports that these invaders pursued a "scorched-earth" policy: fire "burned almost the whole surface of the island and was licking the western ocean with its fierce red tongue." In the still-unconquered west, Anglo-Saxon and British forces fought a series of battles, culminating, sometime around 500, in a decisive victory for the British at a place called Mons Badonicus, or Badon Hill. The Briton responsible for this landmark victory, as we are told by the very few extant documents pertaining to the period, was a warrior called Arthur.

Badon Hill has been cautiously identified as a long, barrow-shaped hill-fort called Liddington Castle in the Thames Valley, north of Salisbury Plain in a region full of ancient earthworks, stone circles and other prehistoric enigmas. Now in pursuit of history rather than legend, I clambered up its rain-slick slopes on a blustering winter's day, crossed the moatlike ditch that once defended the summit and stumbled upon a herd of grazing cows. A valuable tactical lesson: clearly a squadron of cavalry could have occupied Badon Hill and gone undetected from below.

The victory at Badon Hill temporarily halted the Saxon progress in the Thames Valley and bought the British in this region some 40 years of respite. Nothing much is known about the battle, but general knowledge of military practices of the period suggests that Arthur's men fought from horseback, making repeated passes at the enemy, rather than in a unified cavalry charge. Spears, javelins and long-bladed Roman cavalry swords were the weapons of choice. Most warriors carried oval or round whitewashed shields. A warrior chief of Arthur's standing probably wore battle dress modeled on that of a high-ranking Roman general: a knee-length leather tunic, perhaps with leather breeches and rudimentary armor.

In general, though, the sum of our knowledge about Arthur (or Artorius, his probable Roman name) is that he fought 13 battles, 12 victorious and one mortal, the great majority of which are associated with now unidentifiable places. The earliest account, Gildas' *The Ruin and Conquest of Britain,* dating between A.D. 530 and 540, describes the battle of Badon Hill, but it does not make a single mention of Arthur. His name first makes its appearance about three centuries later in *History of the Britons,* a sometimes specious historical miscellany attributed to a man named Nennius who states, matter-of-factly, that "Arthur fought against [the Saxons] in those days with the kings of the Britons, but he himself was leader of battles." A dozen successful campaigns are then listed, concluding with Badon Hill.

The most exciting source is *The Annales Cambriae,* a manuscript kept in the British Museum. Beginning in an unspecified year, apparently about A.D. 450, it contains sequentially numbered years next to which significant events are recorded. Gently turning its thick parchment pages, I read the following Latin entries: "Year 72. Battle of Badon in which Arthur carried the cross of Our Lord Jesus Christ on his shoulders [on his shield] for three days and nights and the Britons were victorious." "Year 93. The battle at Camlann in which Arthur and Medraut were killed." These brief lines preserve something of the later legend: the Christian warrior-king in a final showdown with the treacherous knight Mordred. Although the chronological format inspires confidence, the annals were in fact compiled about 500 years later from material preserved in monastic records. Even so, nothing in the intrinsic nature of the annals warrants their being dismissed out of hand. The surest facts about Arthur, then, seem to be the sites of his greatest victory and his death.

Despite fierce British resistance in the west, the Anglo-Saxon conquest and appropriation of Britain rolled on. Many Celts fled overseas to kinsmen in what is now Brittany (then called Amorica) or to Wales or Cornwall, which held out against the Anglo-Saxon invaders until 848. The Domesday Book (SMITHSONIAN, July 1986), commissioned by William the Conqueror in 1086, suggests that the population of the island at the time was less than half what it had been under the Romans, an eloquent indication that British displacement had been drastic. Some Britons, of course, had to remain, but the fact that the Old English word characterizing them—*Wealh* (Welshman, Briton)—came to mean "slave" says a good deal about their condition.

So much for historic Arthur. What of archaeological Camelot, the court and headquarters of the legendary king? The 1966–70 excavators of Cadbury Castle discovered remains of earthworks and defenses dating to the critical Arthurian period. Combining features typical of both Roman and British fortifications at the time, they greatly strengthened the site's centuries-old identification with Camelot. Excavations at other sites, however, showed that repossession of Iron Age hill-forts in the fifth century A.D. was common all over southwest England—so there is nothing conclusive about Cadbury's archaeological record. In all likelihood the identification with Camelot arose from the evocative names of the nearby villages: Queen Camel and West Camel.

Nonetheless, the whereabouts and, perhaps more important, the character of the warrior-hero's headquarters were issues that early Welsh bards who embroidered on the Arthur story had to address. And the only truly imposing structures they had by way of models were those built and left by the Romans. The luxurious villas with atrium gardens, central heating, running water and mosaic floors; the great towns at Colchester, Silchester, Wroxeter, with public baths, basilicas, temples, theaters, marketplaces and forums; the ubiquitous self-contained fortresses: to later generations these must have seemed the stuff of dreams. That even the conquering Anglo-Saxons were not insensible to these monuments of past glory is evident from an eighth-century Anglo-Saxon poem, "The Ruin": "Bright were its palaces, its many bathing-halls, / Its wealth of tall pinnacles, its tumult of warriors, / Many a mead-hall filled with festive life, / Until mighty fate overturned all."

And if resonant for the Anglo-Saxons, how much more so for the Britons, for whom such relics had once been part of a life now all but destroyed. To many Romano-Britons, the fragmentation of Roman order must have indeed signaled the arrival of a dark age, the banishment of loyalty, piety and righteousness from the land; perhaps it is their centuries-old nostalgic despair that finds its voice in the legend of Camelot.

One raw day I took a look at the remains of Viroconium, once the fourth-largest city in Roman Britain, now lying outside the village of Wroxeter in Shropshire. The fog was so thick that even the great brick wall of the town's old baths, the most intact relic, vanished from sight at a distance of 20 feet. Spiderwebs spanning the plum-colored masonry had frozen into rigid lacework. The fallen walls looked like so many piles of rubble but, as I realized when I touched them, were stoutly rooted in their position for all eternity—truly Roman handiwork. Remarkably, after several centuries of decline, this town underwent reconstruction until as late as the end of the fifth century and was apparently used in some capacity until the mid-seventh, thus overlapping Arthur's lifetime. Anglo-Saxon and Briton alike would not see anything to match it for centuries to come. It is reasonable to think that the memory of such unimaginable splendor sparked the earliest description of Arthur's court; if so, Camelot was, in fact, a Roman town.

Ultimately, though, it is not from any pieced-together history or Arthurian tourist sites but from literature, from the magic of storytelling, that what we mean by "Camelot" seems most real. Some glamour now lost to us, some ineffable charisma must have clung to the historical war hero Arthur, slipping through the cracks of the bare surviving facts, because Welsh legends about him began appearing in the ninth century and were doubtless sung as early as the late sixth century.

From the great mass of romancing about the king of Camelot, the works of two authors stand out, one British and one French. The first, Geoffrey of Monmouth's *The History of the Kings of Britain,* written in Latin and completed in 1136, became an international bestseller. Geoffrey combined all the loose-ended and free-floating Arthurian lore up to his time, producing a coherent if improbable narrative suffused with Celtic glamour and unfolded against an otherworldly backdrop of dragons, wizards, visions and prophecies. The familiar outline is laid forth: Merlin's prophecy and Uther Pendragon's deceitful seduction of another man's wife, resulting in the conception of Arthur; the adultery of Guinevere; the final battle between Arthur and Mordred on the river "Camblam"; the wounded king's departure to the mysterious Isle of Avalon.

The authoritative, straightforward tone of Geoffrey's pseudohistory put Arthur on the map, so to speak. But the legend of Arthur was permanently embellished by the unashamedly romantic work of Chrétien de Troyes. A late 12th-century French poet, Chrétien often wrote under the patronage of Marie, Countess of Champagne, so that his series of Arthurian romances reflects the refined and feminized tastes of her court in Troyes. Five romances survive. In often titillating detail they tell of the adventures, both amorous and martial, of various Round Table knights. Feasts, tourneys and assemblages of court are featured—and inordinate attention is paid to the dress of both knights and damsels.

Chrétien was not, as is sometimes claimed, the father of Arthurian romance. Behind him, as behind Geoffrey, lies a rich and virtually lost tradition of singing and storytelling. In Wales, for instance, the increasingly elaborate memory of the British war hero's deeds was kept alive in popular folklore and by professional bards, fragments of whose work survive. On the continent Arthur's fame was spread by Breton bards and minstrels who took the stories and songs of their ancestral hero to aristocratic French courts. For a professional storyteller, the entertainment value afforded by an entire company of colorful, chivalrous knights, many amorously linked with some fair lady, was considerable. The relatively advanced status of women in the French courts meant that feminine tastes and the tradition of courtly love already exercised influence. To this increasingly significant audience the story of King Arthur and his court doubtless afforded welcome relief from the other great poetic themes of the day, the unremitting battles of Charlemagne and Alexander the Great. More than a few of the characteristics of today's paperback romances were insinuated into the Christian warrior-king's saga.

The evolution of the "Matter of Britain," as the Arthurian romances were called, spans centuries and cultures, absorbing the characteristics of each passing age. Consider the successive renderings of the name of Arthur's sword: in Irish, it is called Caladbolg; in Welsh, Caledvwlch; Latinized in Geoffrey's *History* it comes out Caliburnus; in French it is Calibourc; and finally, in English, Excalibur.

Similar is the development of one quintessential Arthurian theme, the fellowship of the Round Table. The Round Table is first mentioned in a paraphrase of Geoffrey of Monmouth's *History,* written in French verse by the Norman poet Maistre Wace in 1155. According to Wace, Arthur "made the Round Table, of which the Bretons tell so many a tale," as a way of settling a dispute among his knights about the order of precedence of their seating. Subsequent romances have the table variously seating 13 or 250 or 1,600 warriors.

The bond of loyalty between the Germanic lord and his retainers, famous even in Tacitus' day and heroically dramatized in the Anglo-Saxon epic *Beowulf* also left its mark on the knights of Camelot. From it came the ideal of a brotherhood of aristocratic warriors equal in their service to their lord. In the poems of Chrétien de Troyes, chivalry tended to be measured by a knight's prowess in the coy game of courtly love, but later narratives introduced a religious dimension. In the *Quest for the Holy Grail,* apparently written by a 13th-century Cistercian monk, a new asceticism crept in: for Chrétien, the ideal knight was an ardent but faithful lover of his lady, but the Grail saga offers total chastity as an ideal in itself. It is the virgin Galahad, not the adulterous Lancelot, who is the one to actually see the Grail.

No worldly quest for Arthur is complete without a visit to the medieval Great Hall of Winchester Castle, which, with its cobbled yard and lofty tie-beamed roof and solemn doors, is of all places in England most like my vision of Camelot. A 2,400-pound circular oak table measuring some 18 feet in diameter hangs on one of the flint-and-rubble walls. On it, a portrait shows Arthur as a white-bearded patriarch surrounded by the names of 24 of his knights. To his left, Galahad holds pride of place in the Siege Perilous, the name of the seat reserved for the most pure and blameless knight; "Sir Mordrede," the traitor, is seated to Arthur's right.

For centuries, the Winchester table was venerated as *the* Round Table. Alas, when it was restored in 1976, carbon dating revealed that far from being a sixth-century artifact, the table had been made between 1250 and 1280, during the reigns of Henry III and Edward I. The painting, it appears, was added in the 16th century, probably at the behest of Henry VIII, to whom the portrait of Arthur bears a more than passing resemblance. The table's prosaic origin illustrates how deeply entrenched in history, as opposed to legend, Arthur had become: Henry VIII clearly saw a political advantage in publicizing his royal "descent" from so famous a king.

Despite its many French refinements, the Camelot story's most memorable versions came from England. Thomas Malory's *Le Morte d'Arthur* was published by William Caxton in 1485. Malory was a Warwickshire soldier-rebel who, as a political prisoner of Edward IV's, whiled away the last of several stints in prison producing his mournful version of King Arthur and his knights. Perhaps it was his sobering experience of contemporary politics that gave Malory his melancholy vision of even the most high-minded government. Shedding the charming, country fairy tales of Chrétien, he concentrated on the fateful triangle of Arthur, Guinevere and Lancelot, and wrote an epic. Malory represents the downfall of each as the result of weakness and conflicting loyalties. Though still picturesque, the quasi-medieval world of Malory's creation is harsh and wintry, fraught with darkness and danger. The stakes Malory's characters play for are fatally high. Lancelot returns from his failed quest for the Grail not glamorously disheveled but mortally harrowed. Guinevere, Lancelot and the strangely passive Arthur are destroyed not by potions and magic spells but by more-insidious and more-deadly foes, the passions of their own humanity.

Malory's work inspired Tennyson, whose *Idylls of the King* (published intermittently between 1859 and 1885) brought Arthur to the affectionate awareness of a broad English public. Having inherited the essentially medieval content of the Arthurian tales, Tennyson gave them their final autumnal coloring. He was a master of the elegiac tone, and it is his own sorrow for Arthur's loss that is the poet's most haunting contribution.

Toward the end of *Idylls of the King,* Arthur pays one last visit to his fallen queen, now doing penance with the nuns at Almesbury. As Guinevere lies repentant at his feet, Arthur bluntly tells her: "Thou hast not made my life so sweet to me, / That I the King should greatly care to live; / For thou hast

spoilt the purpose of my life." Yet he cannot keep from wondering aloud, "But how to take last leave of all I loved?"

Powerfully taken by the spell of such a scene, it is hard for a reader to remember that every detail—the misty, vaporous night; the "sad nuns" standing with flaming torches outside the cold walls of the abbey; the golden-haired Guinevere, groveling on the floor; the stern and brokenhearted king in armor; the emotional finality—is utter fiction. None of this ever happened; none of this ever existed. It is a marvel that some mix of collective need and artistic imagination, which over the long and fickle centuries fabricated the legend of Arthur down to the last bright rivet of armor and thread of gold embroidery, had, at the end of the day, integrity enough to preserve the essential truth of irrevocable loss that lies at its deeply buried core.

It is here in the works of these two very different men that I like to feel the real Arthur—the Romano-British Artorius fighting for his life against barbaric forces—at last received a fitting characterization and tribute. Although the victory of Badon Hill bought borrowed time, the overall cause of this obscure warrior was doomed, and whoever he was, he lost a world.

The curt, unadorned style of the references to the Battle of Camlann in *The Annales Cambriae* has convinced many experts that this entry, at least, is genuine. Some scholars believe that Camlann itself may be a late form of Camboglanna, the name of the largest Roman fort built near the western end of Hadrian's Wall (SMITHSONIAN, April 1985), which runs from Newcastle upon Tyne to the Irish Sea. This would place Arthur's last battle not in the Celtic West Country, where legend and logic, as well as Tennyson and others, have placed it, but in the north of Britain, on the Northumbrian border far from where I had originally sought it. Intriguingly, the very few tentatively identifiable battle sites named in Nennius' list of 12 are also in the north. But if it is true, as many believe, that Camboglanna represents the most hard and certain fact in the whole tissue of Arthurian lore, then Arthur did not die fighting his Anglo-Saxon enemies but in an internecine border war with another British faction.

Eventually I walked an outline of fallen stones, all that now remains of Camboglanna. To the east and to the west, the Roman wall—already centuries old by Arthur's time—stretches to the horizon across rolling pasturage, green even in midwinter. Arthur may have died fighting for this fort, or he may have fallen somewhere beyond, in the perpetually green fields. A dramatic loop of the Irthing River flows through a glen below the fort, and it may be that he was finally lost in its swift, dark waters. It says much about the power of the Camelot myth—and my own romantic susceptibility—that even at the end of this quest I continued to believe some tangible proof of its reality had eluded me only because I looked in the wrong places. Now, at what may be the site of that "last, dim, weird battle," I couldn't help but think that if it was ghosts I was after, it was here and not at Cadbury Castle that I should have kept my midnight vigil for the once and future king.

Article 15   *In These Times,* June 28, 1998

IRISH AYES ARE SMILING

Ireland Votes for Peace

By Kelly Candaele

BELFAST, NORTHERN IRELAND

It's great to be in Belfast during a week when history is being made," said Bono, leader of the Irish rock band U2 and the best known Irishman in the world, when he came to Belfast for a three-song rock concert and media event a few days before the May 22 vote on the Irish Peace Agreement. Before launching into a particularly heartfelt rendition of John Lennon's "Don't Let Me Down," he brought two men on stage who, he said, "had taken a leap of faith out of the past and into the future."

From opposite ends of the stage came John Hume, leader of the Social Democratic and Labour Party (SDLP), the largest nationalist party in Northern Ireland, and David Trimble, head of the dominant unionist group, the Ulster Unionist Party. Hume and Trimble—with Bono between them—shook hands and left without saying a word. The following day, this gesture of reconciliation between political and ideological opponents was plastered across the front page of every newspaper in Ireland and Great Britain, giving a much needed boost to a faltering "Yes" campaign.

Hume and Trimble had been campaigning for weeks in favor of ratifying the "Good Friday" peace agreement, which was negotiated for eight months under the watch of former Maine Sen. George Mitchell and signed April 10. But the concert was the first time the two leaders had appeared together in any forum—a testament to both the caution of the "Yes" campaign and the delicate balancing act that is essential for political survival in Northern Ireland. Here, getting too close to the "other side" can be lethal.

The resulting "Yes" vote of just over 71 percent in Northern Ireland was welcomed as a historic step forward by most political leaders in the North and South—the first step in what will be an ongoing and contentious effort to consolidate peace. The vote sets up a new democratic assembly in the North as well as a "North/South Ministerial Council" that will enhance the role of the Dublin government in certain Northern Irish affairs—a crucial demand of the Northern nationalists. A Council of the Isles will also be established, comprising representatives from the British and Irish governments as well as Northern Ireland, Scotland and Wales. In a simultaneous vote in the Irish Republic, 94 percent of voters agreed to surrender the South's territorial claim on the six northern counties. The principle of consent has been established in both the North and South, assuring unionists that the status of Northern Ireland will change only with the approval of a majority of voters.

Elections to establish the new political assembly will take place on June 25. The assembly, which will legislate on domestic matters such as education and agriculture, will consist of 108 members elected by proportional representation. All major decisions in the assembly will be made on a cross-community, consensus basis—not a simple majority vote—to keep the unionists from dominating the assembly as they did the previous one before it disbanded in 1972. Since then, the government of Northern Ireland has been run from London, which retains the power to enact justice and security legislation under the new agreement.

A divided Protestant vote on the peace agreement—only 51 percent voted in favor of the referendum—reveals deep fissures that could threaten the stability of the new political body in the North. Unionists, the supporters of continued political union with Great Britain, have a wealth of experience saying no to change in Northern Ireland. In the '70s and '80s, attempts to create political structures that offered a modicum of accommodation to nationalist aspirations succumbed to violent unionist intransigence. In 1974, a power-sharing assembly, set up after the so-called "Sunningdale Agreement," was brought down when the Protestant Ulster Workers Council paralyzed the country with a general strike.

This time it was different. Trimble's Ulster Unionist Party—which generally receives the largest percentage of votes in the North—was on board, and the major Protestant paramilitary groups endorsed the peace agreement. Opinion polls three weeks before election day indicated that only 15 percent of Protestant voters in the North were adamantly opposed, a very small percentage in light of their historical fear of change. But in Northern Ireland, the past clings to the present and won't let go.

Part of that past is embodied in the Rev. Ian Paisley—a Bob-Jones-University-educated evangelical preacher who often confuses his political constituents with his Protestant congregation. One Irish wit has suggested that Paisley is an "immigrant into the 20th century," a comment that would be funnier were it not for Paisley's destructive political influence. His focus on Protestant historical grievances and a keen understanding of Protestant political insecurity generates a voter base that often surprises both his unionist and nationalist opponents. Considered by some observers to be a political anachronism, the 72-year-old Paisley heads up the Democratic Unionist Party and has generated broad populist support in times of political crisis. And for many unionists, this referendum was a big-time crisis.

Four days before the election, Paisley met in Omagh with the local Orange Order, a Protestant fraternal organization best known for its provocative parades through Catholic neighborhoods during the summer "marching season." His speech was vintage Paisley—a bellowing Talmudic dissection of the peace document, which he had no part in creating since his Democratic Unionist Party sat out the "all party" talks. He argued that the document was "stamped with the words of murderers and liars" and suggested to the supportive crowd that they were being "sold like cattle on the hoof to the enemies of Ulster." An "enemy," as far as Paisley is concerned, is anyone who would disturb the status quo.

President Clinton, who played a crucial role in pushing the negotiators forward in the last hours, took a beating as well. In a comment Paisley repeated at virtually every stop in his campaign against the agreement, he said, to the prurient amusement of the audience, "If Clinton comes here we will have to lock up all of our women." Clinton was in Birmingham, England, at the G-8 economic summit but stayed away from Northern Ireland for fear of antagonizing an already insecure electorate.

At an anti-referendum march in Lurgan, a Protestant stronghold south of Belfast, several marchers also made clear their disdain for Clinton and distrust of American "interference" in Northern Irish affairs. "Clinton would not be welcome here," said Grahme Jardin, a 24-year-old student, "because he only listens to Ted Kennedy and that lot."

British Prime Minister Tony Blair traveled to Northern Ireland three times in the two weeks before the election to reassure unionists that the link with Great Britain was safe as long as the majority of people in Northern Ireland desired it. He also said he would initiate legislation in parliament to strengthen provisions in the agreement to keep anyone associated with paramilitary activity out of the new assembly.

While Trimble tried to explain at campaign stops how arcane "constitutional changes in the agreement secured the union with Great Britain," the "No" campaign held the advantage of a simple and visceral message: "Keep terrorists out of government." They were referring, of course, to Sinn Fein, the political party aligned with the Irish Republican Army (IRA), and its leaders, Gerry Adams and Martin McGuinness.

It is likely that Adams and McGuinness will become ministers in the Northern Irish Executive Committee after the June 25 elections. The thought of Adams running part of the government makes a substantial number of unionists apoplectic.

But the alternative to a broad-based political solution is continued war. At a polling station in East Belfast, a self-described unionist voter said, "Ian Paisley doesn't speak for all Protestants here, and when it comes right down to it, he doesn't offer a real alternative."

Whatever Adams' tactical missteps, it is clear that he has brought Sinn Fein, and by extension the IRA, out of the political cold with consummate political skill. Sinn Fein will now compete with Hume's SDLP for seats in the Northern Assembly and will attempt to broaden its support in the South, where it holds only one seat in parliament.

Sinn Fein did not even campaign for the referendum, yet 95 percent of Catholic voters in the North voted yes. Sinn Fein was officially "neutral" on the referendum, but at a special conference called on the eve of the referendum, Sinn Fein leaders changed the party's constitution to allow their candidates to enter the new assembly if elected. Entering the assembly, unthinkable to many Sinn Fein activists, was a key victory for Adams and McGuinness.

Over beers at the Telstar pub in working-class Derry, several Sinn Fein supporters reflected on the vote. Gary Donnelly, a young construction worker and veteran of the notorious Maze prison, said he voted no. "This agreement does not face up to the core issue," he said. "There is no declaration of British intent to withdraw. The war will not be over until the British are gone."

At an election-day press conference, Adams said that it was "time to push forward an equality agenda that is essential for pushing the peace process forward." He had to shout to reporters as a British Army helicopter hovered overhead virtually drowning out his voice. It was an appropriate metaphor for the challenge Adams faces in the new assembly. Sinn Fein's "voice" must be heard for dramatic "changes on the ground" to take place, which would further legitimize Sinn Fein's drift into parliamentary politics. At the same time, Sinn Fein has to deliver economic and political gains to a deeply skeptical membership base. Catholics in Northern Ireland are twice as likely to be unemployed as their Protestant counterparts. In addition, most Catholics consider the Royal Ulster Constabulary, a 95-percent-Protestant police force, an oppressive presence in their communities. Adams welcomed the strong "vote for peace" but added that the political status of the north was still "in limbo," a delicate way of saying that he will continue to push for major reforms. But for the vast majority of people, North and South, limbo is greatly preferable to the war of attrition that has claimed more than 3,000 lives in the past 30 years.

For Hume of the SDLP, the referendum is the culmination of 30 years of tireless, nonviolent political work. With a political base in the Catholic middle class, the SDLP generally takes more than 60 percent of the Catholic vote, a point often overlooked by the American media's focus on Sinn Fein. A "safer" nationalist than Adams, Hume will be the primary intermediary with the unionists. But he must also help keep

Adams and McGuinness close to power as they adapt to the world of high politics.

There are critical issues that were left ambiguous in the peace document and will now have to be dealt with. Trimble, the likely first minister in the new government, has said that decommissioning of arms must take place prior to the establishment of the Executive Committee of Ministers, a gesture of surrender that Sinn Fein and the IRA will never accept without the commensurate demilitarization of the Royal Ulster Constabulary and the British Army. Prisoner releases, scheduled to take place within two years, are another highly contentious issue that Trimble is attempting to link to arms surrender.

The June 25 elections could be the most hard-fought and bitter of any in the history of Northern Ireland. Paisley and other anti-treaty unionists have declared war on Trimble and his supporters. If enough Paisley supporters are elected they will attempt to undermine any cooperation with the nationalist community. Then, in early July, the unionist "marching season" begins, characterized by Orange Order parades though Catholic areas. It will be the first crucial test of whether new political arrangements can ameliorate this annual ritualized street conflict.

It's difficult to say whether Northern Ireland has wrenched itself away from the recalcitrant clutch of its bitter history. Previous attempts at reconciliation would always break down somehow. But it's clear that most of the people in Northern Ireland are willing to give this peace a chance.

Kelly Candaele *has written about Ireland for several national publications. He lives in Los Angeles.*

Article 16   *The Economist*, January 23, 1999

A SURVEY OF THE
NORDIC COUNTRIES

Happy family?

IS THERE a Nordic block, complete with a Nordic economic model and a special kind of Nordic welfare? Nordic collective security? Nordic values, Nordic sex, Nordic gloom? Undeniably the Nordic countries—the Scandinavian trio of Sweden, Denmark and Norway, plus Finland on the eastern flank and Iceland for north-west in the Atlantic—have a great many things in common. And undeniably the lure of the European Union has been drawing all the Nordics, even stand-offish Norway and Iceland, into an ever tighter embrace of rules and regulations that are bound to have an economically unifying effect. In a generation or so, perhaps, the Nordic five will come more closely together in one big European family. But, this survey will argue, for the next few years they are as likely to stay apart, as they have done since the end of the cold war. Each of them has been following its own particular path. Nordic solidarity? For the moment, forget it.

That may seem surprising. After all, the five have a lot in common. Start with their entwined history. For the best part of four centuries, the Danes controlled Norway, as well as, for more than a century, a large chunk of southern Sweden. In 1814, having allied themselves with Napoleon, the Danes lost Norway to the Swedes, who held on to it until 1905. For long stretches the Swedes also owned Finland, most recently until 1809, after which it came under the sway of Russia until 1918. The Icelanders started out as Norwegian seafarers who, more than a millennium ago, found their own patch of freedom by heading rebelliously west. But for many centuries they too came under the Danish crown, winning independence only in 1944. So, at one time or another, every Nordic country has been joined with, or under the thumb of, another.

It helps, too, that their languages are close enough for Norwegian, Swedish and Danish to be mutually intelligible though people from the Scandinavian trio cannot quite decipher Icelandic. Finnish has different roots (shared with Estonian and Hungarian), but 6% of Finns are ethnic Swedes, and their country is officially bilingual. Moreover, virtually all Nordics who went to school after the second world war speak excellent English. Its use in international business, computers and now

the Internet, along with pop music, television soaps, CNN and undubbed Hollywood films, ensure that it is constantly practised. One way or another, the Nordics can easily communicate with each other.

The five Nordic countries remain defiantly different from the rest of Europe—and from each other. Xan Smiley explains

Then there is religion—and Martin Luther, whose reforming creed swept across the entire Nordic zone in the 16th century, leaving a powerful cultural and ethical imprint These days, few Nordics are devout believers; under 5% attend church regularly, a smaller proportion than anywhere else in the culturally Christian world. Lutheran priests often seem like just another lot of social workers. But the moral legacy of Luther remains strong. Nordics tend to be suspicious of Catholicism, which may heighten their scepticism towards what they see as the Catholic-driven European Union.

Instead, the Nordics believe in nature, greenery and the gods of reason, science and material well-being. They adore their countries' great expanses of forest and lake, the fjords, mountains and lonely islands, and the pristine emptiness of the Arctic. Most urban Nordics keep their family connections with villages at the back of beyond. This helps to explain the lingering strength of political parties rooted in communities of small farmers and fishermen, even though these days no more than 3% of Nordic people make their living that way.

Lutheranism may also be responsible for a swathe of shared Nordic traits which casual Anglo-Saxons and carefree Latins alike find admirable but sometimes disconcerting. Nordics tend to be modest, punctual, honest, hard-working and highminded. They do not, on the whole, like ostentation. Rich people generally dress, eat and travel in the same style as the prosperous middle classes. To be ten minutes late for a meeting is considered unprofessional, even rude. Honesty, both in personal and public life, is particularly valued. Financial peccadillos that would be shrugged off in many parts of Europe are fiercely frowned upon up north.

Overdoing it

There is a downside to such an enviable set of values. Public discourse can seem ploddingly priggish, and schemes to help the poor, both at home and abroad, can sometimes look smug and goody-goody (only the mainland Nordics and the Dutch meet the UN-urged figure of 0.7% of national income spent on development aid). Keeping an eye on the neighbours can degenerate into nosiness, sometimes under the guise of "transparency" and "the citizens' right to know". In most Nordic countries, for instance, everybody's tax returns can be held up to public scrutiny.

A darker, more dangerous side to Nordic nannying was revealed two years ago when the Swedish government admitted that some 4,500 mental patients had been forced to undergo lobotomies under officially encouraged eugenics programmes, starting in the 1920s and continuing until the 1970s. Over the same period, some 60,000 Swedish women were forcibly sterilised, sometimes for reasons such as "unmistakable gypsy features". All four main Nordic countries owned up to similar selective breeding programmes. Experiments with radiation on mentally retarded Norwegians went on until 1994.

The end which was supposed to justify such means was the deep Nordic desire for equality. In no other part of the rich world is this idea so zealously upheld—to the point of sometimes being confused with sameness. Except in Sweden and Denmark, where a thin and now insignificant layer of nobility has survived, there were no great class schisms either before or during the industrial revolution.

The Nordics' social cohesion has been helped, too, by a striking ethnic homogeneity, compared with other European countries. Except in the biggest cities of Sweden and Denmark there are few immigrants, yet those few meet with growing hostility from the indigenous population. Especially in Norway and Denmark race-tinged populism is growing. Likewise, relations with the reindeer herding Sami (or Lapps), of whom about 65,000 live in the northern reaches of the three northern Nordics, are ambivalent, caught between an acceptance of the Sami's cultural rights and the desire to make them more "modern".

Underpinning this general Nordic yen for equality is a commendable openness. Most public documents are genuinely in the public domain. Important people are much less likely to hide behind secretaries and bureaucrats than further south in Europe. Ordinary citizens in Sweden have the right to see the prime minister's official mail, and often exercise that right.

For another illustration of the Nordic drive for equality, take a look at the relationship between the sexes. The proportion of women in most Nordic parliaments and governments is much higher than anywhere else (see chart 1), except in Iceland—and that country had a female president for i6 years. Across the Nordic zone, women have headed, or are heading, serious political parties, including the former communists and the Greens in Finland and Sweden, and the most right-wing party in Denmark's parliament. Sweden has followed Denmark's (much earlier) example in changing the law so that the monarch's first-born child, regardless of sex, inherits the throne. The present king's elder daughter, Princess Victoria, not his son, will succeed him.

But the most striking manifestation of the push for equality is the Nordic welfare state. Poverty, although not quite abolished, has been reduced to near-invisibility: nowhere else are the unfortunate and the feckless so generously treated. Nowhere else are public services so extensive, nor do they eat up such a big share of the national cake. Perhaps the most distinctive feature of Nordic welfare is the day-care system for all young children up to primary-school age, which provides good-quality, heavily subsidised nurseries and kindergartens so that mothers can get back to work. A typically Nordic row (if that is not too strong a word for the polite exchange of firmly held views) has been going on in Norway, where a Christian Democratic-led government wants to offer new mothers financial incentives to encourage them to stay at home with their babies. The Labour opposition has been fighting the idea, arguing that it goes against the grain of gender equality.

Inevitably, the price of the Nordics' generous welfare system has been sky-high taxes. Income-tax rates in the four mainland countries are near the top of the world league, with the highest rate exceeding 60%, and kicking in at quite low income levels. In Denmark, for instance, the 60% band starts at earnings of less than $38,000 a year. Yet in the interest of "social cohesion", most Nordics seem willing to keep paying up as long as high standards in public services are maintained. It is plain, though, that the number of grumblers is increasing.

The business end

Is there a Nordic way of doing business? Only up to a point. True, the Nordics have always put greater stress on partnership and co-operation between employer (never "boss") and worker than most other European economies. Across the Nordic sweep, thrifty, hardworking, efficient, well-educated people have created exceptionally successful, export-oriented economies. They have been preeminent in paper and pulp, strong in engineering and pharmaceuticals, clever at medicine, good at building ships and cars and weapons and furniture. More recently the Nordics were quick to develop high-tech skills. Computer literacy is much higher than in most other European countries. It is no accident that Europe's two leading telecoms manufacturing companies, accounting for 45% of all mobile phones in the world, are Swedish and Finnish respectively: Ericsson and Nokia.

Since the oil-price explosion of the 1970s, however, Nordic prosperity has seemed a little more fragile. All the Nordic countries, at various times, have undergone cycles of recession. Several have seen unemployment rates rise above the 10% mark; in the early 1990S, 20% Of Finnish workers were out of a job. Today, the real unemployment rate in Sweden, including those on make-work schemes, is around 11%.

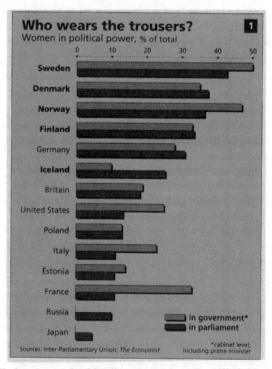

Who wears the trousers?
Women in political power, % of total

- Sweden
- Denmark
- Norway
- Finland
- Germany
- Iceland
- Britain
- United States
- Poland
- Italy
- Estonia
- France
- Russia
- Japan

- ■ in government*
- ■ in parliament

Sources: Inter-Parliamentary Union; *The Economist*
*cabinet level, including prime minister

All the same, the Nordic economies are still ticking over nicely. All bar Sweden's have been growing faster than the EU average over the past three years. But over the past 20 years some, most strikingly Sweden's, have slipped badly in the various league tables ranking countries by income per head.

The golden days, anyway, are over. Whatever the Nordic growth rate, over the past decade the taxman's share has been rising even faster, eroding disposable incomes. At the same time, governments have been trimming, sometimes even slashing, the welfare state. People are living longer, building up a pensions time-bomb that may explode in two or three decades unless something drastic is done. All the Nordic countries agree that in future they will not be able to go on providing a welfare system as generous as in the past.

Parties across the political spectrum, including even the former communists, have acknowledged, too, that labour markets need loosening up and economies deregulating. All the Nordic countries have endorsed a measure of privatisation. All agree that liberalisation is the way to go—including Norway and Iceland, which have stayed outside the EU but are part of the European Economic Area (EAA), which confers virtually all the trading rights and obligations that go with full EU membership, bar those for farming and fishing. All accept that if welfare is too generous, it may discourage work and foster a culture of dependency among those at the bottom of the heap. And all know in their hearts that their economies must become leaner and fitter to cope with global competition and open markets.

Yet in Nordic politics, as in business, consensus is still the watchword. Political systems of pure proportional representation, which require a share of only 4% of the total vote (and only 2% in Denmark) before a party can win seats in parliament, might be expected to produce coalition governments unwilling and/or unable to come up with radical policies. Surprisingly, some such coalitions have forced harsh medicine down reluctant Nordic throats. The three Nordic EU members, for instance, achieved a broad consensus to meet the tough Maastricht criteria for membership of Europe's single currency, even though two of them decided against applying in the first wave. (Finland did ask, and was thrilled to get in.) Finland and Denmark show that broadbased coalitions and sometimes minority ones can do better at shoving through nasty but necessary reforms than ideologically narrower governments.

Drawing together

The end of the cold war and the dropping of neutrality by some Nordics has further helped pep up Nordic co-operation. So did the entry in 1995 of Finland and Sweden into the EU, alongside Denmark, which had joined along with Britain in 1973. Big companies in the Nordic market are realising that they must consolidate to compete with much bigger German, British and French firms. This has produced a spate of Nordic bank and business mergers in the past two years. Merita of Finland, the country's biggest bank (and itself the product of a recent merger), has teamed up with Sweden's Nordbanken. Sweden's SE-Banken has gobbled up Trygg-Hansa, the country's second-biggest insurer. Den Danske Bank has embraced a big provincial bank in Sweden's south and is close to swallowing Fokús a large Norwegian one. In like vein, Stockholm's stock exchange has agreed to a joint equities-trading system with its counterpart in Copenhagen, to be called Norex.

A number of big Nordic industrial companies have also merged. In the past year or so, Stora, a vast Swedish forestry concern, has joined up with Enso, a Finnish rival. Nordic arms companies, too, have been seeking to co-operate. Finns, Swedes and Norwegians are planning to produce ammunition together. Finns and Swedes are jointly making gunpowder. A British company, Alvis, has bought Hagglunds, a Swedish one that makes military vehicles. And 35% of Saab Aerospace has been sold to British Aerospace. All four main Nordics have been discussing a joint purchase of helicopters and, Finland excluded, submarines. Such mergers, takeovers or joint procurement plans would have been unthinkable for Finns and Swedes during the cold war.

There has been ado, too, about a Nordic or North European security zone. Next summer, when Finland is due to take the EU president's chair, there will be much talk about the "northern dimension". The main idea is to find ways of helping Russia settle down and prosper in the region under a kindly Nordic eye. All the Nordics are especially keen to welcome the Baltic trio into the Nordic family. Finland has turned Estonia, the most successful of the post-Soviet countries, into its own backyard. The Danes have singled out Lithuania as their special Baltic friend, while urging all the Nordic countries to pile into the Baltic area with every sort of economic and military aid.

Denmark sees itself as something of a dynamo for a resurgent Baltic and Nordic zone. It sets much store by the redevelopment of Copenhagen's Kastrup Airport as a hub for north European aviation. And, in June 2000, a new bridge-cum-tunnel 16km (10 miles) long will link Copenhagen and the Swedish city of Malmo across the Oresund, creating the most vital region in the Nordic area (or so its enthusiasts say). If the economies on both sides are to grow together, Danes and Swedes will have to find ways of harmonising labour, tax and social policies. The Oresund region, its architects claim, could become a laboratory of transnational regional co-operation within the EU.

The Danes are both geographically and psychologically best placed to shift the overall gravity of the Nordic countries. What with the Oresund bridge-tunnel link and the likelihood that, after Finland, Denmark will be the next Nordic to join the single currency, Denmark can be expected gradually to pull towards the centre of the continent—and Sweden and even Norway may feel a consequent tug in the same direction. Denmark is the Nordics' hub country. The hub is edging south.

Nordic integrationists see European and Nordic fusion proceeding in parallel. The EEA, they say, already binds Norway and Iceland much more tightly into the big European scheme than their governments let on to their wary voters. The stay-outside pair already do the EU's bidding on almost everything to do with the free flow of trade, capital, labour and services. Moreover, they have had a joint passport and customs regime for more than four decades. Norway and Iceland are being woven into the EU's Schengen agreement that seeks to dissolve border controls.

All this seems to suggest a Nordic identity that is alive and well. But only up to a point. There are a host of reasons, some of them more powerful now than before, why the Nordics should not be considered a cohesive, let alone uniform, block. These days, for all that they have in common, it is the differences among them that are most compelling.

Variety show

MEASURED by a global yardstick, all the Nordic countries are prosperous and efficient democracies with a strong sense of civic responsibility, underpinned by similar political systems and parties. But look more closely, and the differences come into sharp focus.

For every feature that binds the Nordic quintet together, there is another pulling it asunder

For a start, their economies are strikingly dissimilar. Sweden's is the only one with a broad industrial base, making cars and aircraft as well as a range of other heavy-engineering products. That sort of economy is not easy to reshape. Certainly the Swedes are doing worst among the Nordics at getting in trim. The Finns make many of the same things, but have admirably managed to swing their economy round: high-tech electronics have now become their chief export, ahead of timber and paper products. In the past half-decade, Finland has been the Nordics' biggest economic success.

Denmark has for more medium-sized and small firms, more of a service economy, and a host of impressive companies and producer-owned co-operatives processing and selling food. Norway, measured by purchasing power per head, is the richest of the lot (see chart 2), but relies too heavily on its oil, and needs to diversify. Peripheral Iceland's handful of people live on fish, fish, fish—and, these days, an impressive little bit of high-tech. Far-flung in lonely Atlantic isolation, it has done brilliantly.

An excess of welfare

All the Nordics are trying to slim their welfare budgets, but here too the differences stick out. Once again, the Swedes are most at risk by trying to keep up a degree of welfare they cannot afford. Once again, the Danes have done better, over the past decade or so, in tackling the welfare state's excesses. The other Nordics have also shown more determination than the Swedes to reform their systems.

But perhaps the biggest thing keeping the Nordics apart is their different approach to Europe and its Union. True, all five

Nordics must together abide by the rules of the EEA agreement. But beyond that, each of them follows a quite distinctive European agenda. "There is no such thing as a Nordic block," says a senior Danish minister. "It isn't a healthy notion at all, inside the EU". His words are echoed inside the Finnish government. It is perhaps symptomatic of Sweden's current edginess about the EU that it is the Swedes who most often invoke Nordic solidarity—but with little substance to their words.

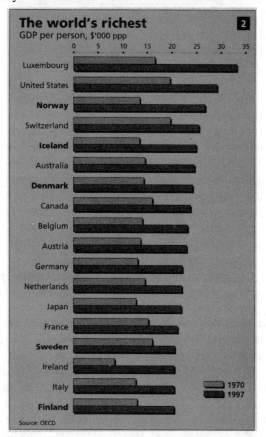

The world's richest 2
GDP per person, $'000 ppp

Source: OECD
1970
1997

The Nordic Council, in which MPS from all the Nordic countries occasionally gather, and the (technically separate) Nordic Council of Ministers are both resolutely "soft-issue" talking shops. Carl Bildt, Sweden's cosmopolitan former prime minister who now leads the Moderate (ie, right-wing) opposition, happily confesses he has never read a Nordic Council paper, conceding only that the sessions are useful meeting-points. A leading Danish editor breezily comments: "Basically we're not as interested in each other as people outside expect."

The Finns are today's biggest enthusiasts for Europe. They feel triumphant at having manoeuvred their markka into the euro in the first round, and proudly point to its stability during the past few months' global financial turmoil, when other Nordic currencies received a buffeting: early evidence, they say, that their euro-decision was wise. They want the other Nordics to enter the euro zone too.

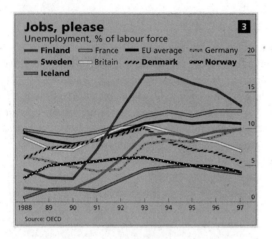

Jobs, please
Unemployment, % of labour force

Finland — France — EU average — Germany
Sweden — Britain — Denmark — Norway
Iceland

Source: OECD

Although Denmark has become the Nordics' swing country and is the longest-standing Nordic member of the EU, it also has the most distinctive and *nuancé* attitude to the Union—more so even than Britain. It has won a record four "opt-outs" from various bits of EU policy, including permission not to join the euro. But it is strikingly adept at playing the EU game, earning a reputation as one of the Union's trickiest customers. It fights tenaciously for its own interests, subjecting its ministers to the strictest parliamentary control of any member country when they go to EU council meetings. All the mainstream Danish party leaders are minded in principle to join the euro, but are waiting until they can convince their public. Most also say openly that if Britain joins, they are likely to follow suit; "within minutes", as one puts it.

It is the Swedes who are in the biggest muddle about the EU. The minority Social Democratic government is itself divided over the euro, and many leading figures in the two parties on whose votes it depends in parliament, the former communists and the Greens, are against EU membership altogether. As in most of the Nordic countries, the right, broadly speaking, is keen on "Europe", whereas the left is tepid or against. But in Sweden there are wrinkles right across the spectrum. Whereas Mr Bildt wants Sweden to join the euro, some of his Moderate allies have been arguing against it. Sweden's prime minister, Goran Persson, is loth even to declare an intention in principle to join. A couple of years ago the government commissioned a Swedish economist, Lars Calmfors, to weigh up the euro's pros and cons. Wait and see, he advised.

The Norwegians, for their part, show no interest at all in joining the EU in the near future, let alone taking the euro-plunge. True, the Norwegian krone has dropped by more than 10% since last May, but the country's second vote in 1994 to stay out of the Union (albeit with only 52% against) has dis-

couraged pro-EU politicians from trying again. With oil and gas still gushing, self-exclusion from the EU brings no sense of impending economic doom.

In Iceland there is even less appetite. Of the six parties in parliament, only one—the Social Democrats—wants to join. According to the prime minister, David Oddsson, "It's just not on the agenda."

Some more neutral than others

Away from Europe, the old question of Nordic neutrality remains fraught, too. Although the Swedes and Finns have been able to slide away from their previous rigorous abstention from all collective security matters (except for peace-keeping under United Nations auspices), neither country has found it easy to contemplate joining any alliance. A few Finns in government have dared to suggest a discussion of the merits of joining NATO. Some say that if Russia becomes still more chaotic, the case for Finland joining NATO might harden, but not for a few years yet.

Sweden has not even got as far as debating the merits of eventually joining NATO. When the present deputy prime minister, Lena Hjelm-Wallen, was foreign minister, she told Mr Bildt, who thinks Sweden should join, that even raising the issue was "dangerous". Like all the Nordics, Sweden is keen to help the Baltic countries by drawing them into Baltic peace-keeping tasks and by encouraging Russia to take part in NATO's Partnership for Peace programmes. But it still shrinks from any muscular idea of Nordic joint security.

Denmark, once viewed by the United States as NATO's most wimpish and disloyal member, is now viewed across the Atlantic as a bit of a star. It has been first in line to bring the Balts in from the cold, it has forged trilateral military links with Germany and Poland, and it is always urging Sweden and Finland to join every sort of Nordic and European military scheme as they gradually peep out of their once neutral bunkers.

Norway and Iceland also make polite noises about bringing the Baltic countries into the Nordic embrace, but both really prefer to look the other way—out into the Atlantic, towards the United States and Britain, and north to the Barents Sea. Both are keen to involve Canada, as well as Russia, in discussions about the Arctic and Barents regions.

Iceland is much more enthusiastic about NATO than about any other possible security alliance. As well as having a NATO airbase on its soil, it also has a bilateral arrangement with the United States. Ten years ago this was controversial; now it is applauded by just about everyone on the island. The Icelandic prime minister has also struck up an informal Atlantic relationship with the Faroes and with Greenland, both of which are looking for greater independence from Denmark. No marks there for Nordic solidarity.

The Norwegians greatly cherish their membership of NATO. Most of them dislike the idea of a European defence identity separate from the Alliance, and are dismissive about the Western European Union, the EU's fledgling (and so far unpromising) defence arm. Even more than other Nordics, they dislike what they consider to be France's designs to foster a non-American defence alliance. The French ambassador to Oslo complains that whenever France is mentioned by the Norwegian media, it is prefixed by the adjective "arrogant".

Not a lot of love lost

In sum, the Nordics are a long way from forming anything like a real strategic block, let alone a military alliance. When you get down to it, they are not as friendly to each other as the outside world often assumes. History has a lot to do with it. Despite—or perhaps because of—the periods when they shared national boundaries, most of them are intensely nationalistic.

If there is one Nordic country all the others love to denigrate, it is undoubtedly Sweden. One old joke has representatives of the Nordic quintet sharing the gondola of a hot-air balloon. An emergency requires one of the five to be ejected. The luckless Swede is unanimously chosen by the other four, who chorus "Long live Nordic solidarity!" as he plummets. In another old joke, a spokesman for each of the five is asked which of the Nordic nationalities he likes best. All dutifully choose a neighbouring Nordic nation—except the Dane, who chooses Denmark.

The Danes are regarded as tough, a bit more worldly than their fellow Norsemen, a bit less tidy, and perhaps even slightly unscrupulous by highminded Nordic standards. "Danes are really Germans pretending to be British," is one old northern Nordic saw. It is natural for the Danes to be preoccupied by their relations with Germany. After all, the northern outskirts of Hamburg once came under the Danish crown, and the bit-

terness of occupation by the Germans in the second world war is not entirely forgotten. One reason why Denmark demanded, and won, an opt-out from EU plans for joint policing was that many Danes found the idea of German police on Danish soil too much to bear.

Most Nordics, especially the older generation in Norway and Denmark, both occupied by the Nazis, still resent Sweden's war-time neutrality, which tilted in favour of Germany. In many Nordic minds, memories of that period still lie uncomfortably with Sweden's post-war tone of lofty morality.

Finnish nationalism is still kicking, too. Finns treasure their own attempts, during the second world war, to fight the Russian monster on their doorstep, even though they lost a substantial hunk of land in the south-east. That they were briefly, as a result, allied with Nazi Germany gives them no great cause for shame. But coming out from under the shadow of Russia at the end of the cold war has been a huge morale-booster—at least after the initial economic shock from the loss of Soviet trade. Finland's success in bonding with little Estonia, just across the water from Helsinki, has been another boon. And now, being accepted into the club of early euro-joiners is yet another mighty uplift.

And on the western flank, the Norwegians are no less nationalistic—and even more inclined than the Finns to scoff at the Swedes. These days, having a Swedish maid or driver is something of a Norwegian status symbol; a hundred years ago, it was the Swedes who employed servants from other Nordic countries. Poor Sweden: it has been on its best behaviour for nearly two centuries, not bashing anybody, and yet its Nordic neighbours seem singularly disinclined to love it.

Too good to be true

SWEDEN is the most troubled of the Nordic countries. Over two decades it has slithered down the OECD's league of GDP per head at purchasing-power parity, to 15th place from fifth. Some 11% of its people, if you include those who are on state make-work and training schemes, are out of a job. The country's fabled welfare system just does not look affordable in the long term, and Sweden's much-vaunted third way is now heading into a cul-de-sac. The Social Democrats, who have been in charge since 1932 with only brief interruptions, are back after a spell of centre-right government during 1991–94, but the coalition they lead is weak and swings between complacency and angst.

This is quite a come-down for a country which in the 1950s and 1960s became one of the richest in the world. It built up a raft of world-class industrial companies, such as Volvo, Saab Automobile, Scania and Asea (now ABB, a Swedish-Swiss company) in cars, trucks and engineering; Astra (now merging with Zeneca, a British company) in pharmaceuticals; Tetra Pak in packaging; Stora in paper; Ericsson in telecoms; and IKEA

in furniture. Sweden also created a vast, generous and generally efficient welfare state, underpinned by a rock-solid tradition of consensus, both in business and in politics. The country seemed to epitomise the rule of reason and a kindly, yet practical, social democratic ethos.

Several of its well-known companies are marking time or declining, and Sweden's welfare spending plainly needs cutting back. Yet there is no sense of urgency, no hint of anything radical afoot. The welfare state, the Social Democrats imply, must be gently adjusted, not drastically shaken up. "There is still a yearning for times past, a suspension of belief [that things may get worse]," says a foreign diplomat. In essence, the cosy, corporatist, high-spending credo is still intact.

Redistributing the cake

Goran Persson, the prime minister, in his budget speech last October promised lots more welfare, but provided little detail of how it would be paid for. "The entire discussion [during

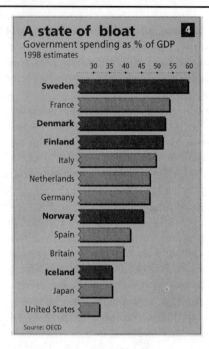

A state of bloat `4`
Government spending as % of GDP
1998 estimates

Sweden · France · Denmark · Finland · Italy · Netherlands · Germany · Norway · Spain · Britain · Iceland · Japan · United States

Source: OECD

or seven years down the road there will either be massive cutbacks or massive increases in taxes," says Mr Bildt.

The trade unions, which still have 90% of all workers under their wing, remain resolutely stuck in the past, insistent on such practices as "last in, first out" when workers have to be shed. An ageing population and slowing growth are both bound to put more pressure on Swedish welfare. Moreover, freer trade and capital movements could further erode the country's tax base.

The old understanding between the Social Democrats and big business has worn thin. Many large companies have talked of moving their headquarters out of the country. Ericsson, for example, is planning to move key parts of its head office to London, which will also be home to the merged AstraZeneca's main board. When Store merged with its Finnish rival, Enso, the joint headquarters went to Helsinki. So did Merita Nordbanken's.

Many of the big names are under pressure, including several in the vast Wallenberg empire, whose holding company, Investor, still controls companies making up an astonishing 40% of the Stockholm bourse by value. But several Investor-controlled companies, such as SKF, a ball-bearings mammoth, look a bit sickly. SEB, an Investor-linked bank, has been badly hit by its exposure to Russia. Astra has depended too heavily on the ulcer remedy Losec, the world's best-selling prescription drug.

last autumn's election campaign] was about redistribution, not growth," recalls Lena Mellin, a columnist on *Aftonbladet,* a leading leftish newspaper. A leading sociologist, Ake Daun, explains that: "There is still a belief that the rest of Europe is less advanced," and that Swedes must accept ever higher taxes as the price of maintaining their cherished welfare state.

Sweden's third way has turned out to be a cul-de-sac

In last autumn's general election, the Social Democrats scored their lowest share of the vote for 78 years. Although they easily remained the biggest party, they had to seek allies further to the left, relying on former communists and Greens to keep them afloat. This has moved pro-market reforms even further out of range. The former communists, for example, want a 30-hour week, and the Greens are demanding new energy taxes and a speedier fulfilment of a previous Social Democratic promise to close all the country's nuclear power stations.

Carl Bildt's right-of-centre Moderates, who tried gamely but without much success to revamp Sweden between 1991 and 1994, seem destined to play second fiddle to the Social Democrats. In Sweden's big cities, including Stockholm, and among young voters, Mr Bildt's lot won the largest share of the vote. But some 60% of the voters depend on the state for work or welfare, so the Social Democrats have a big built-in bonus. Unless there is an unexpected economic upswing, "six

Where in the world?

In foreign policy, too, muddle prevails, mainly because neither the government nor the Swedish people can decide what kind of EU member they want Sweden to be. In a recent editorial, the *Frankfurter Allgemeine,* an influential German newspaper, complained that nobody knows what Sweden is or where it is going, and called it "a dwarf that has become so small it is no longer visible".

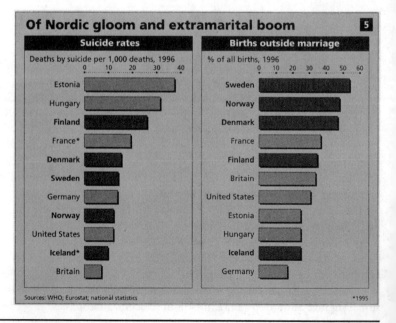

Of Nordic gloom and extramarital boom `5`

Suicide rates	Births outside marriage
Deaths by suicide per 1,000 deaths, 1996	% of all births, 1996

Estonia, Hungary, Finland, France*, Denmark, Sweden, Germany, Norway, United States, Iceland*, Britain

Sweden, Norway, Denmark, France, Finland, Britain, United States, Estonia, Hungary, Iceland, Germany

Sources: WHO; Eurostat; national statistics   *1995

The nervous hostility towards the EU that infuses the centre and the left is striking. Mr Persson himself is tepidly pro-Europe and agnostic-to-doubtful on the euro; his party is utterly divided on both questions. The two junior parties backing it in parliament only grudgingly accept the fact of EU membership, and are hostile to the euro; some leading members want to get out of the Union altogether. Virtually everyone on the left pillories the EU as undemocratic, opaque and bureaucratic.

Only Mr Bildt's party, along with the limping Liberals, is fully signed up to speedier EU integration, and even some of his supporters remain queasy about the euro. Swedish businessmen often look across enviously at Denmark's mix of economic pragmatism and diplomatic savoir-faire within the EU. "The Danes have been much cleverer than us," says a top Swedish banker.

In another corner of Sweden's foreign-policy jungle, all that do-gooding in poor countries looks sadly less effective than it should have been, though old-school Social Democrats show remarkably little contrition for having spent billions of taxpayers' kronor propping up dodgy economic systems and even dodgier leaders. But gone are the days when a Social Democratic minister (who, as it happens, is still in the government, in charge of aid) could smugly declare: "We are a moral superpower."

But not everything in Sweden is gloom and doom. Annual growth of barely 2% over the past three years has been respectable, if unexciting. Inflation last year was less than 1%. Unemployment has been coming down. The government seems determined to consolidate public finances, and is aiming for a budget surplus this year.

These days Mr Persson rarely mentions socialism. Instead, he praises markets. He is squeezing social spending, particularly on health and education. Sick pay has become less readily available: the average number of days each worker takes off "sick" has dropped from 25 a year in the late 1980s to 11 now. Some local councils have privatised such services as care for the old. And businessmen are pleased that two genuine free-marketeers, Mona Sahlin and Bjorn Rosengren, have been promoted to run a "superministry" for economic growth.

Since 1989, finance has been drastically liberalised. "Till then, Sweden was really a little pond," says a leading banker. Banks, which suffered a crisis in the early 1990s, and a number of big businesses have been getting together to compete more effectively against their bigger cousins further south. EU membership, which Sweden took up in 1995, has helped open up the economy.

Meanwhile, back on the home front, things could be much worse. Health and social services, and particularly subsidised child day-care, are excellent. The environment is fiercely cherished. Equal treatment for women and men is strongly encouraged. Sports facilities are superb (witness all those tennis stars). Most public services—buses, trains, street cleaning—seem to work better than in less regulated countries.

It would be grossly unfair to suggest that Sweden is a grim, grubby or coldly sterile place. Nor is it true, as is often asserted, that Swedes are especially suicide-prone: they come about half-way down the European league table (see chart 5). True, as the sheen of welfare-cushioned achievement has worn off, ordinary life looks less rosy. Divorce rates are high, and the conventional family is on the decline: 52% of all babies are now born out of wedlock.

Still, much the same applies in other Nordic countries. Sweden is still a remarkably comfortable, steady, decent, peaceful and egalitarian sort of country. But it needs a salutary jolt.

Comeback kids

IF THE Swedes are down, the Finns are up. Finland has gone through an extraordinary transformation. Fifty years ago 70% of Finns worked on the land; now the figure is nearer 6%. Fifty years ago Finland's GDP per head was a third below Sweden's. Now, in terms of purchasing-power parity, Finland is just about level: no small feat for a vast backwater of lake and forest in a colder and remote part of the world. More recently, Finland took a terrible knock when its main market dried up with the collapse of the Soviet Union, throwing one Finn in five out of work; but for the past five years the Finnish economy has grown by an average of about 5% a year. The Finns are immensely proud that they, alone among the Nordics, have joined Europe's single currency. "Suddenly, somehow, we Finnish bumpkins think we have become the most sophisticated of all the Nordics," says a Finnish writer.

Nokia, Finland's biggest high-tech company, epitomises the country's recent transformation. Founded in 1865 around a wood-pulp mill in a small town of the same name, the company until 15 years ago made rubber, cables and paper. Since then it has reinvented itself to become one of the world's most successful companies, accounting for nearly a quarter of the global market for mobile telephones (which make up around half its business). Sales—almost all of them outside Finland—have been rising by around 25% in each of the past few years. Nokia's current stockmarket value is about $70 billion.

Finland has come out from under

One big factor in Nokia's success was the speed at which it spotted the huge new markets that the demise of state telecoms monopolies would open up. Another was to grasp, in its

Northern light

A TRIP to a little town not far south of the Arctic circle gives a clue to how the Finns have got ahead. Till the second world war, Oulu produced tar and timber and not a lot else. It was little more than a big village in the forest near the Gulf of Bothnia. Now it is probably the most northerly high-tech success story in the world. How did it do it?

A generation or so ago, the Finns realised that if they wanted to become richer without losing their natural heritage, they had to do two things. First, stem the flow of people from the rural reaches of the north to the more urban south and along the coastal strip. Second, embrace high technology.

Oulu was chosen as a suitable northern outpost, later to host what has become one of the best universities in the Nordic countries. Some 13,000 students now flock to take advantage of its superb academic offerings. Booming science parks, dedicated to electronics, medicine, biotechnology and "green business", funded with a mixture of private and public money, have pulled in more than 10,000 boffins and entrepreneurs. Oulu's population, which has multiplied several times over in barely a generation and now musters 115,000 souls, has every facility imaginable: an international airport, a magnificent sports stadium, a symphony orchestra complete with composer-in-residence, and a fine newspaper with extensive international coverage. The atmosphere of get-up-and-go is palpable.

Internet connections and mobile phones are everywhere. Children in local schools teach parents how to work computers. A growing number of older people do their shopping electronically, and order books from public libraries through the Internet. "Distance working" via computer for people in outlying villages is becoming more common. "These days Finns trust computers, telecoms and technology," says Pertti Huuskonen, who runs Technopolis, the town's prime scientific business park.

But it has not all been plain sailing for Oulu. The brutal Finnish recession of the early 1990s left its mark. The local council (the usual Finnish rainbow coalition of left, right and centre) has had to shed 700 of its 8,500 public-service workers, from teachers to rubbish collectors. And life in the villages outside Oulu is still hard. One in three people there is unemployed, and many gravitate towards the town. But some 17% of Oulu's own people are jobless too, and drink and drugs are a problem. Those winter nights, even in model Oulu, are awfully long.

own small domestic market, that people would take to mobile phones in droves. Having found its niche, it has constantly upgraded its technology, investing vast resources into R&D, and extended its markets. It cannily outsources much of its production to low-cost countries such as Estonia, just across the water. Recently, Nokia's shares have strongly outperformed those of its Swedish rival, Ericsson.

It may be unwise to cite Nokia as a parable for Finland's success. In such a competitive field, fortunes can swing around frighteningly fast. And Finland still suffers from Nordic shortcomings that hurt all its companies, especially its gummed-up labour market and high wage and social costs. But things are getting better. The powerful trade unions have agreed with employers to freeze wages until 2000. Plans are afoot to decentralise wage bargaining so that pay and terms of employment can vary by enterprise and region. Short-term contracts and flexible working are becoming easier to arrange. And high income-tax rates, under which rich Finns had to hand over two-thirds of their income to the state, have been creeping down a little, by 1% a year for the past four years.

Unemployment remains high, at around 10% of the labour force, but Finland's government, unlike Sweden's, gives the impression of knowing where it is going. Paavo Lipponen, the Social Democratic prime minister, is solidly in charge of a rainbow coalition (again, a much wider one than Sweden's) that includes Conservatives on the right as well as Greens and ex-communists on the left. He vaunts the fiscal rigour that enabled Finland to join the euro zone in the first wave. He is rightly proud, too, of the economy's diversification, which has made the share of high-tech (mainly electronic) products as a percentage of GDP jump fivefold in ten years.

Accounting for only 2% of exports in 1970, they are now Finland's largest export sector, providing more than a quarter of exports, ahead of paper and pulp (23%), and machinery and metal products (19%).

But, like most Nordics, Mr Lipponen says he is determined to keep a generous welfare system. "We can finance our welfare state if we reform the labour market and change our economic structure," he says. There is no question of dismantling it. That view is shared at both ends of the ideological spectrum: the current finance minister is from the Conservative Party. The main opposition leader, Esko Aho of the rural-based Centre Party, who preceded Mr Lipponen as prime minister, has nothing radical to propose instead. While mildly jibbing at the government from the right, Mr Aho admires Britain's Tony Blair as a European politician to be emulated. Mr Aho says he wants to revamp the tax system, yet sounds reluctant to cut taxes or spending much faster than the present government or to allow wage differentials to widen. "We must keep our social balance," he says warily.

Opinion polls suggest that Mr Aho's Centrists have a chance of winning the most seats in the general election due in March; last time, in 1995, they came second to the Social Democrats, with 20% against 28% of the votes. But even if Mr Aho were to win, as he did in 1991, he would still have to seek out a broad coalition—rather like the one now in power. He is more sceptical than the government about foreign involvement in the Finnish economy, and says he is nervous about the effects on Finland of the single European currency. But his policies would probably not turn out very different from Mr Lipponen's.

Most Finns seem keen on further European integration. Food prices, note Finnish Euro-enthusiasts, have come down a bit since Finland joined the EU four years ago. Some businessmen say it is easier now to break into European markets. And Finns have thrown themselves with unFinnish gusto into the whirl of European politics.

"The European Union has internationalised Finland enormously," says Martti Ahtisaari, Finland's non-executive (but by no means ceremonial) president, at the same time noting the "tremendous boost" Finland's outlying regions have received from EU regional funds. "It's as if we've marched ten years on in four years." Undoubtedly, membership of the club has wrought a huge change in Finnish attitudes. The country has come out from under Russia's shadow. It has unFinlandised itself.

Awkward squad

T HE Danes' attitude to Europe is the trickiest among the Nordics to categorise. They are in the club all right, belligerently so; but they are deliberately awkward, sometimes even bloody-minded. In 1992, they nearly scuppered the entire Maastricht treaty by voting narrowly against it. After various amendments, they only narrowly endorsed it a year later.

How the Danes have become the Nordic pivot

Still, the Danes count They are the link, both geographically and psychologically, between the Nordics and the rest of Europe. Like the Swedes, they are conscious that they once had an empire that poked its way along the southern reaches of the Baltic. They can claim to have founded the Estonian capital, Tallinn. For centuries they owned the fertile southern slab of Sweden. They still have the world's largest island, Greenland, which lost the then European Community half of its territory (and a population now running to 56,000 people, plus a lot of polar bears) when its home-rule government pulled out of the European club in 1985. The Danes also still, perhaps tenuously, have the Faroes, whose recalcitrant 43,000 people are muttering about independence too, though the is-

landers probably could not survive without their fat hand-outs from the mainland. In short, the Danes like to punch above their weight.

It is hard to say whether they are twitchier in dealing with Germans or Swedes, their ancient rivals for Nordic supremacy. The main thing, these days, is that Danes look south, not north. Yet they have opted out of the single European currency for the time being, as well as from parts of the EU's defence, asylum and law-and-order policies. "We are not ardent integrationists," says their foreign minister, Niels Helveg Petersen.

Some of Denmark's opt-outs are prompted by anti-German feeling, more than half a century after occupation by the Nazis. Or perhaps that antipathy goes back even further, to 1864, when Denmark lost a third of its land and half its citizens to Germany. Even so, engaging effectively with the whole of Europe to its south, including Germany, is far more important to the Danes than nurturing some kind of special relationship with Sweden, let alone with other Nordics. "We welcome the new Germany—under a European flag," declared Denmark's then prime minister when the two Germanies joined up. Danes often compare themselves to the Dutch, rather than with their Nordic cousins. And Danish satisfaction at Sweden's economic and foreign-policy travails is barely disguised. "We've been working out how to deal with Brussels for a generation," says a leading Danish businessman. "The Swedes don't know where to begin."

Denmark, which during much of the cold war was a pretty tepid member of NATO, has become more gung-ho about it. It has also encouraged the Baltic countries, for which NATO membership is not on the cards for the moment, to join in every other sort of western military arrangement, such as NATO's Partnership for Peace, peace-keeping in the Balkans and training schemes with all and sundry. Denmark also helped make sure that NATO's door is not irrevocably slammed in the Balts' faces.

It is keen, too, along with the Finns, to foster a "northern dimension" to Europe, which would embrace Russia. According to Denmark's go-ahead defence minister, Hans Haekkerup, "The trick is to develop sub-regional structures." Hence, as well as making special links with Lithuania, Denmark now also has a special three-way military

A sceptical lot　　　　　　　　　　　　　6

% support for euro

% support for EU membership

EU average

Denmark　　Finland

Sweden

1995　　96　　97　　98

Denmark

Finland　　EU average

Sweden

1995　　96　　97　　98

Source: Eurobarometer

link with Germany and Poland. And it has pushed "Baltbatt", a joint Baltic peacekeeping battalion, parts of which have been serving in Bosnia. Danes ignore the WEU, the EU's defence arm. It is superfluous; NATO is good enough," says a prime ministerial adviser.

The Danes see themselves as the northern hub of Europe—a link between the central core of the EU, the other Nordics, the Balts, and perhaps even western Russia and the region around St Petersburg. The tunnel-and-bridge between Copenhagen and the southern Swedish town of Malmo should dramatically strengthen the hub (see map). Many Swedes, by contrast, are a bit nervous about the link, fearing that the Danish capital will become a magnet for a new Nordic super-region.

Keeping in shape for the euro

Even though Denmark has opted out of first-wave membership of the single currency, it wants to be ready for early entry if need be. Were Britain to join, the pressure on Denmark (and indeed Sweden) to follow suit would become hard to resist. Meanwhile, unlike Britain and Sweden, Denmark has returned to the EU's mark-two exchange-rate mechanism, agreeing to keep the krone in a band within 2.25% of the euro from the beginning of this year.

But there is very little support, even among pro-European Danes, for a "United States of Europe". Most Danes are prickly about sovereignty and critical of the Brussels bureaucracy, yet fairly rude about Europe's own parliament in Strasbourg. Still, they are more businesslike and pragmatic in their approach to "Europe" than the Swedes. And unlike Sweden's political elite, Denmark's very largely favours the euro. Only the former communists and most of the Socialist People's Party, to the left of the ruling Social Democrats, are dead against. The prime minister, Poul Nyrup Rasmussen, is merely waiting for the Danish public to come round—and hopes it will say yes in a referendum, perhaps in 2001.

Meanwhile, though Denmark still needs to sharpen up its economy, it is in fair shape, thanks partly to a string of tough reforms during the so-called "potato-diet" days of Poul Schlouter, an economically liberal conservative who ran the government for

most of the 1980s. In Denmark the welfare state has undergone a steady squeeze, whereas in Sweden the more dominant Social Democrats have managed to protect it. Moreover, Denmark, unlike Sweden, has managed to build a broad cross-party consensus about the need for painful adjustments.

Denmark still suffers from the usual Nordic vices of high taxes plus high labour costs, but has at least started to tackle them. Its labour market has become more flexible, hiring and firing is fairly easy, pension reform has begun and, amid fury that Mr Nyrup Rasmussen has broken an election promise, the age at which Danes can benefit from a much-loved early-retirement scheme has gone up from 60 to 62. Training programmes, which have helped to bring the official unemployment rate down to around 5.5%, will be supervised more rigorously. A plan by a right-wing local council north of Copenhagen to sell off day-care centres and water-treatment plants has stirred controversy.

Small and medium-sized companies do better in Denmark than elsewhere in the north, and family companies such as Lego continue to perform well—though a striking number of them (like Lego) set up factories abroad. Agri-business is a continuing success story. All told, Denmark looks craftily poised as it watches its European neighbours embark on their euro adventure. When the time comes, it will be ready to jump in fast.

Well-oiled independence

ON THE face of it, the Norwegians have not the slightest reason to regret spurning the EU, first in 1972 and then again in 1994. Despite falling oil prices, their economy has gone on growing at an average of more than 4% over the past five years. Instead of splurging out, they dutifully put much of their oil cash into a special savings pot for a rainy day: it now tots up to nearly $16 billion. Norway has the lowest unemployment rate in mainland Europe (bar Luxembourg),

at 3%. Its GDP per head at purchasing-power parity is third-highest in the world, ahead of all the other Nordics.

Nobody knows when the oil will run out. It could start flowing less freely in about ten years, but enormous reserves of offshore gas (which currently accounts for about 15% of Norway's combined oil-and-gas income) will go some way towards offsetting lower oil revenues. By any standards, Norway is exceptionally rich.

Like other Nordics, Norwegians attach enormous importance to social equality and a generous social-security net. But the drop in oil prices over the past year has persuaded all the main political parties that a bit of thrift is in order. The budget for this year has been revised downwards. Already over the past few years sickness, disability and unemployment benefits, as well as support for single mothers, have begun to flow a little less freely. Besides, Norway's welfare state has always been rather less lavish than those of the other main Nordic countries, its public sector smaller, its overall tax burden appreciably less heavy.

Norway can afford to do its own thing

But some shadows are darkening this sunlit picture. Norway has failed to diversify enough. True, it has created superbly efficient fish farms—but no serious industrial or manufacturing base. It still has 10%, in tonnage, of the world's commercial fleet, but its shipping is in the doldrums. "Shipping is dead," declares one of Norway's leading entrepreneurs, whose family once drew its wealth from ships. In banking and financial services, the country has been slower to liberalise and consolidate than its Nordic rivals. Several of Norway's political parties are tinged with protectionism.

Moreover, high social costs and restrictions on hiring and firing make it hard for small and medium-sized businesses to get going. Less money than in other Nordic countries goes into research and development. "No one in their right mind would set up a factory in Norway," says the editor of a leading financial newspaper. "We capitalists have been crowded out by bureaucrats from the state-owned banks and oil companies," says the entrepreneur from the shipping family.

Political leadership has been in short supply of late. A minority government of the centre-right is hanging on, with a mere 42 seats out of 165 in parliament In a Nordic tale of consensus politics and secular piety, the prime minister, Kjell Magne Bondevik, a Lutheran priest from the Christian Democratic Party, last autumn .disappeared from view for nearly four weeks, claiming a "depressive reaction to overwork". Nobody seemed much to mind. The rather colourless leader of the opposition Labour Party, Thorbjorn Jagland, declared primly: "One must be allowed to be sick in this country? The press left Mr Bondevik alone, awarding him brownie points for his "openness".

The Labour Party, as Norway's social democrats are called, had been the natural party of government for decades until it lost power in 1997. It seems in no hurry to take back the reins—and has no drastically different policies on offer, though it has been kicking up a big fuss over the Christian Democrats'

proposal to offer mothers cash to stay at home and look after their children.

The continuing rise to prominence of Carl I. Hagen gives Norwegian politics a more intriguing twist. Mr Hagen is a maverick of the libertarian and populist right who defies the Nordic tradition of consensus, though even he forbore to snipe at Mr Bondevik for his walk in the woods. Mr Hagen and his Progressive Party have—until now—been given the cold shoulder by the mainstream parties because of his perceived hostility to immigrants, of whom Norway has a small but rising number. More broadly, he calls for lower taxes but also higher spending on such causes as old people, computers in schools, and shortening hospital waiting-lists. To pay for them, he naughtily suggests dipping into the oil-gotten national savings pot.

In the 1997 general election Mr Hagen garnered the second-biggest share of the vote, with 15% to Labour's 35%. He seems well on the way to establishing his party as Norway's leading force on the mainstream right. Mr Bondevik's centre-right lot has been depending on Progressive Party support for such matters as passing the budget and getting the child-care voucher scheme through. But, unNordic as he is, Mr Hagen says he now wants his party to be formally included in a ruling coalition.

Don't mention it

What makes Norway the mainland Nordics' oddest man out is its extreme awkwardness towards the EU. The question of membership is off the current agenda, but Norwegians are not united in their view of Europe. They are at one only in a shared reluctance to reopen an acrimonious debate—which cannot, however, be put off for ever.

The fragile ruling coalition is utterly divided. Mr Bondevik's party voted against joining in 1994, but the prime minister has apparently changed his, if not his party's, mind. The Centre Party, led by the redoubtable Anne Enger Lahnstein, who stood in as prime minister when Mr Bondevik was out of action, is virulently against. Her Centrists stand for the farmers and the fishermen, the countryside against the cities, the wild north against the softer south. Mrs Lahnstein is against even being part of the EEA. The EU, she has said, is "good for multinationals but bad for our farmers, our small companies, our poor, our environment and the third world". The third party in the coalition, the Liberals, is in favour of joining the Union.

The Labour Party is no more united over Europe. Mr Jagland and most of his party bigwigs want to join, the rank and file are two-thirds in favour, the trade unions evenly split and the old socialist left and most of the young hotly against.

As for Mr Hagen, unlike far-right leaders in other Nordic countries and elsewhere in Europe, he has broadly favoured joining, but has recently begun to equivocate. On euro membership, he, along with most Norwegians, is doubtful to hostile.

EU enthusiasts point to high interest rates and the Norwegian krone's wobbliness during the recent international financial turmoil, whereas the Finnish markka, even before it entered the euro, stood firm. But those Norwegians who want to stay out of both the currency club and the entire Union point out that membership of the EEA provides almost all the advantages of Union membership. The downside is that Norway has to abide by a large majority of EU rules, yet has no say in making them.

More broadly, too, and especially in foreign policy, Norway is increasingly left out of the loop. "It really has been marginalised," says a senior Swedish minister. Many Norwegian diplomats admit privately that they are finding it harder to gain a hearing from their foreign counterparts.

Not that Norway is altogether detached. It is, after all, a zealous member of NATO, making much of being the Alliance's only country to share a border with Russia, and it holds the rotating presidency of the Organisation for Security and Co-operation in Europe. It is also keen on every sort of collaboration in the Arctic region and in the Barents Sea, with the United States, Canada, Russia and other Europeans. It feels a special affinity for Britain and the United States, and a special disapproval for French attempts to create a European foreign policy.

Norway can also cut a dash mediating in such troubled places as Myanmar, Colombia, Guatemala and the Middle East. It was in Oslo in 1994, remember, that the then Norwegian foreign minister, the late Johan Jorgen Holst, got Israelis and Palestinians to agree in principle to peace. Note, too, that Norway still shells out a higher percentage of its GDP than any other country, 0.88% at last count, in aid to the world's poor countries.

From Norway's point of view, much depends on who prevails in Europe: those who seek to create a new European foreign policy, or those who want to keep NATO as Europe's strategic cornerstone. But Norwegians tend to be wary of "unions": they have too often found themselves at the wrong end of them. It was no fun being subservient to Denmark from 1536 to 1814, to Sweden from then until 1905, and to Nazi Germany (and Vidkun Quisling) in the second world war. No wonder the Norwegians win the Nordic prize for nationalistic prickliness.

Happily afloat

IF THEIR Norwegian cousins have proved reluctant to join Europe's Union, the Icelanders, all 279,000 of them, are even more firmly set on staying out. They are doing remarkably well on their own, thanks to their fish and their own sturdy common sense. Quite simply, they do not want to share their catch with other European fishermen, nor let others decide how much or what should be fished. With a 200-mile marine boundary around them, and their fish stocks ably managed, why fix a system which, for them, ain't broke? "We look on the ocean as other nations look on their land, their forests, their gardens," says the foreign minister, Halldor Asgrimsson, himself from a fishing family.

Iceland prefers its own company

The Icelandic economy has been growing by more than 5% a year for the past three years. Barely 2% of the labour force are out of work; indeed, the island has had to import labour: Poles, Filipinos, Thais. The prime minister, David Oddsson, who in his spare time is a comic playwright, points to the OECD's league table putting Iceland fifth in the world, measured by what you can buy for your buck. When Iceland won independence from Denmark in 1944, "Many people said it was a nonsense: we couldn't survive". How wrong they were.

But Icelanders are far from insular or backward looking. They speak English as fluently as their fellow Nordics. They publish more books per person than any other country in the world. They are avid Internet users. They are cultured, sporty, nature-loving. They are imaginative architects. And with volcanoes punctuating their island moonscape, they are at the forefront of geothermal science.

Like the other Nordics, they also have a generous welfare system, but one more modest than on the Nordic mainland—and they have recently been trimming it back. They have gone further, too, in making people pay for a good whack of their own pensions. And they have decided that people should have longer working lives too: the official retirement age for men and women, now 67, may go up to 70. Like most other Nordics, they subsidise their farmers. But such largesse may start to wither.

Icelanders look as much to the United States and Britain as they do to their fellow Nordics. America is easily the favourite destination for students going abroad, followed by Britain, Germany and Denmark. As well as being a NATO member (though lacking an army of its own), Iceland has a separate defence treaty with America. Both arrangements have ceased to be controversial. Icelanders are also keen to co-operate with Russia, Canada, and Norway in the Barents Sea and in the Arctic region. In five years or so, an undersea cable may carry electricity, of which Iceland has much, to the Scottish mainland 825km (550 miles) away.

The islanders enjoy tweaking the noses of the big powers. They were the first to recognise Estonian independence in 1991; they were unafraid to scrap vigorously with Britain over cod in the 1970s; they are arguing fiercely with Norway over fishing waters off Spitsbergen now. They also like to do the decent thing—for instance, sending a medical team to Bosnia, development aid to Namibia, Malawi and Mozambique, and food via the Red Cross to hungry Russians around Murmansk.

The biggest change in the past few years has been the march of economic liberalisation, much of it thanks to membership of the EEA, which bonds Iceland into the EU's free-trade market, bar fish and food. "It has done us a lot of good," says Geir Haarde, the youthful finance minister, who studied in Boston, Washington and Minneapolis. Capital controls have been lifted; shares in Iceland's handful of state banks are being sold off. Telecoms will also be freed after the next general election, due in May, assuming that the ruling centre-right coalition is returned as expected. The trickiest decision is whether to free the allocation of fishing quotas too—within the Icelandic family.

There is one small splodge on this charming canvas. Two clusters of interlocking companies, which crabbier Icelanders nickname "the octopus and the squid", have stitched up an awful lot of the island's business between them. They are informally tied to the two main parties in the ruling coalition. Might Mr Oddsson let a few new crustaceans get their claws into Iceland's action?

A future apart?

WHETHER the Nordics come cosily together or stay crossly apart depends on three main things: money, guns and butter.

The first item is all about the European Union and about whether, now that most of its members (but only a lone Nordic one) are using a single currency, it will prove so attractive that the other Nordics cannot resist being swept into its embrace.

That will not happen soon. After the Finns, only the Danes look poised to plump for the single currency within the next few years. Most Nordics will continue to treat the EU with suspicion. They lack that sense of shared historical grief and idealism that impel most of the Union's central continental countries to huddle around the French-German axis. For the Nordics, "ever closer union" within Europe is not, as it was for Germany's former chancellor, Helmut Kohl, a "matter of war and peace".

Never mind solidarity; prosperity will do

In assessing the power and role of the Union, most Nordics sound more like the British. They are practical, free of historical baggage, suspicious of bureaucracy and generally loth to get involved in the subtle high diplomacy of Bonn, Paris or Brussels. They resent putting more into the EU budget than they take out. They are largely indifferent to the Mediterranean countries on the southern edge of the EU: they think that the Iberian pair and Greece have different values, nurtured by the strong memory of life under a dictatorship. The Mediterraneans are grateful to the EU for helping them to become modern and democratic. The Nordics reckon they have no need for such help.

The Finns are risking quite a lot by jumping into the euroboat. Like Ireland, they may prove more vulnerable than countries nearer the heart of Europe to asymmetrical economic shocks. What, for instance, if the Russian market dried up completely? Finns depend much less on it now than they used to, but it still accounts for 7% of their trade. Or what if Nokia went wrong? What if a recession pushed Finnish unemployment back up towards 20% again? What, too, if Britain, Sweden and Denmark, which together make up nearly half of Finnish trade, not only stayed out of the euro but devalued against it? And with only some Nordics in the EU, even fewer in euro membership, and some staying out of everything, the idea of Nordic economic togetherness would look silly.

Eastward ho!

The second big question affecting the Nordics' fate is a matter of strategy. Russia is still a massive, worrying presence on the edge of the Nordic world. Will it become prosperous, let alone democratic? Its economic, political and military development will vastly influence the way the Nordics place themselves in a new strategic setting. If Russia comes good, the rich Nordics will be at the heart of an expanding new Nordic-Baltic zone. The old worries about neutrality and security will fade as St Petersburg, as well as Tallinn and Riga, become part of the family. But if Russia goes bad, the old neutrality-inducing ghosts will return, dividing Nordics into tough guys and feeblings, isolationists and joiners: the opposite, indeed, of Nordic solidarity.

The third issue, welfare, is the great Nordic enigma that has long puzzled outsiders. Rich though the Nordic countries are, they cannot afford to go on lavishing such generosity on their poor, as well as their not-so-poor. They must either trim quite, drastically or brace themselves to pay a lot more taxes. And unless they trim fast, they will surely become poorer. Either way, they look set to become less comfortable places as the wind of globalisation sweeps through. In this respect, the Swedes are most vulnerable, the Finns and Danes look sturdier if still a bit wobbly, whereas the Norwegians and Icelanders are sheltered, for now, by oil and fish.

Yet it would be wrong to assume that continuing bloated welfare across the Nordic countries must spell impending doom, though in Sweden, especially, the figures are heading the wrong way. Most people in the Nordic countries still cherish their welfare states. So far they have voted to sustain them—even as average real income is starting to slip against the rest of the world. The state may have to exact an ever fatter slice of incomes to keep welfare generous. Will the Nordics remain willing to pay that price? So far, they have done so. Maybe they will go on doing so. But unless growth is a lot perkier than is likely, they may become less keen.

Meanwhile it would be wrong to imagine that the Nordics are a gloomily humourless bunch, their spark snuffed out by soft living and that pious ethos of equality. The Nordics still live extraordinarily well, and happily. They manage themselves with remarkable efficiency, as well as humanity. In all this, they are quite similar to each other. But in their response to the trio of big issues listed above, their calculations are very different.

Article 17

Europe, October 1998

Spain

Spain's Bright Future
Economy continues to grow

"Spain is doing well," is perhaps Prime Minister Jose Maria Aznar's favorite, and most famous, phrase and since he first uttered it at a press conference last year the words have entered the national consciousness.

By Benjamin Jones

And it's largely true. The Spanish economy is one of the fastest growing in Europe, the country will be among the first tier of nations to join the euro currency regime, unemployment is dropping, Spain is gaining more respect internationally, and while the country's soccer team disappeared from the World Cup rather quickly, this year the men's and women's tennis titles at the French Open were both taken by Spanish players. Meanwhile, the new Guggenheim Museum Bilbao, located on the banks of the Nervion River, has created a stir in the international art world. The titanium-clad museum opened its doors a year ago and was hailed by the *New York Times* as a burst of "optimism."

Aznar's catch phrase is directed most of all at the economy, and in its two years at the helm, the center-right government's team has managed to steer a prudent course while preparing Spain for entry into the single currency through cutting the budget deficit to some 2.2 percent of the GDP, lowering interest rates and putting a cap on public spending.

Predicted economic growth of 3.7 percent is expected to continue into next year, according to the secretary of state for the economy, Cristobal Montoro. "We're assured of a growth cycle of between 3.5 percent and 4 percent for 1999," he claims. There is even room, he argues, for further lowering the current interest rate of around 4 percent.

In the first six months of this year, business profits were up an average of 13 percent over the same period in 1997, and foreign investment in the first quarter more than doubled to $4.3 billion compared to last year, the economy ministry proudly announced.

Spaniards are having a ball. Lower interest rates mean big ticket items like homes and cars are cheaper, and the increased prosperity translates into packed shops and restaurants, exotic vacations for middle-class families, and tonier schools for those being privately educated. The painful days of the recession in the early 1990s, which came hard on the boom years triggered by Spain's 1986 entry into the European Union, are fading from memory.

Unemployment, at 19 percent, is still the highest in the EU, although it is showing signs of falling for the first time in many years, and Spain now generates jobs faster than the rest of its European partners. But a recent report by the Organization for Economic Co-operation and Development said the government could do even more to reduce the jobless rate by freeing up the labor market and getting rid of the red tape involved in starting up a new business.

Politically, things are just rubbing along for Aznar. Halfway through his four-year term, the former tax inspector has clearly grown into the job and has lost much of the stiffness in public that critics made much fun of in his early days as prime minister.

But he still has problems connecting with the people. A recent poll in the leading Madrid daily *El Pais* found that, on a scale of one to ten, the majority of those questioned rated Aznar a so-so five, dead even with his predecessor Socialist Felipe Gonzalez. Even more disconcerting, Aznar's score was lower than those given to his team members—Interior Minister Jaime Mayor Oreja, Economy Minister Rodrigo Rato, and Foreign Minister Abel Matutes.

In parliament, his ruling Popular Party's (PP) shaky coalition with the regional Basque and Catalan parties is under constant strain. There have been some embarrassing charges that PP appointees act like ideological bullies in some government agencies, and there was a feeling that Aznar's team needed to perhaps position itself more to the center of the Spanish political spectrum.

Against this backdrop, Aznar fired his chief spokesman, Miguel Angel Rodriguez, in July, his first cabinet-level change since coming to office. Although the latter claimed he was leaving of his own free will, it was understood that Aznar and other senior ministers were tired of Rodriguez' constant sniping at the Catalans and his inability to "sell" successfully the image the government wanted to present. So they pushed him out.

The main opposition to Aznar's government remains the Socialists. In April,

they chose charismatic former public works minister Jose Borrell as their candidate for the next elections. The move was not only a snub to Gonzalez' handpicked successor as party secretary general, Joaquin Almunia, it also turned the Socialists leftward.

Borrell, a trained aeronautical engineer from Catalonia, is a firm advocate of state meddling in the economy and greater social justice. With his boyish good looks, active demeanor, and polished speaking skills, he could give Aznar a run for his money in the next general elections. Recent opinion polls indicate the two parties are running just about even in popular support.

When might these elections be? They are not scheduled until the year 2000, but many believe Aznar could call an early vote to take advantage of the feel-good factor and economic good times and try for a true parliamentary majority instead of the uneasy alliance with the regional parties on which he must now rely.

The only real dark cloud on Spain's—and Aznar's—domestic horizon is the northern Basque region and the decades of terrorism there. This year the terrorist Basque separatist group ETA marked the thirtieth anniversary of its first killing. The organization has murdered almost 800 people, mostly members of the Spanish security forces, during its campaign for an independent Basque homeland.

> The only real dark cloud on Spain's—and Aznar's—domestic horizon is the northern Basque region and the decades of terrorism there.

Over the past year, the violence has gotten particularly nasty with Aznar's ruling party clearly in the terrorists' sights. ETA shocked Spain and the world in July 1997, when it kidnapped a young, Basque Popular Party town councilman and threatened to kill him unless authorities moved ETA prisoners to jails closer to their homes in the Basque region. After the government refused, the politician was found in a forest with two gunshot wounds to his head and died soon after.

Millions poured into the streets across the country to protest the death and demand that ETA stop the slaughter but to no avail. Since then, the gunmen have killed five more local Popular Party councilmen.

Moreover, the war on ETA made other headlines. In August, a former interior minister in the Gonzalez administration and his deputy were found guilty of charges related to a shadowy, government-run death squad that targeted suspected ETA members in the mid-1980s and was responsible for killing twenty-eight people.

Outraged at the verdict by the Spanish Supreme Court, which tried the case, Gonzalez defended the innocence of his former underlings, put himself back on the registry of practicing lawyers, and signed the pair's motion to appeal.

Analysts said that Gonzalez, who some tip to be the next European Commission president, was not only endangering his own reputation, but also that of the entire Socialist Party.

Internationally, Spain is respected as a thoroughly engaged member of the EU, NATO, and other partnerships. Spaniards now head NATO, UNESCO, and the International Olympic Committee, and another, Carlos Westendorp, is the chief international troubleshooter in Bosnia.

"It's a long way from the Franco years when Spain was isolated internationally and almost wasn't mentioned in polite company," says a senior Western envoy in Madrid. "Now you can't visit Geneva, Brussels, or any of those diplomatic entrepots without tripping over a Spaniard."

Benjamin Jones is EUROPE's *Madrid correspondent.*

Credits

Sources for Statistical Reports

U.S. State Department, *Background Notes* (1998).

C.I.A. *World Factbook* (1997–1998).

World Bank, *World Development Report* (1998).

UN *Population and Vital Statistics Report* (January 1998).

World Statistics in Brief (1998).

The Statesman's Yearbook (1998–1999).

Population Reference Bureau, *World Population Data Sheet* (1998).

World Almanac (1998).

Glossary of Terms and Abbreviations

Allies   A coalition of countries during World War II, headed by the United States, Great Britain, the Soviet Union, and China.

Anschluss   German term denoting "union" or "joining," usually applied as a euphemism for the annexation of Austria by Nazi Germany in 1938.

Atlantic Charter   An agreement concluded between Franklin D. Roosevelt and Winston Churchill "somewhere on the Atlantic" on August 15, 1941. Although the United States was officially neutral at that time, it provided assistance to a beleaguered Britain, which was fighting World War II on its own.

Axis   A term generally used to denote the coalition of Germany and Italy during World War II that would, it was said, steamroll over Europe like an axis. Later the term came to include Japan when it, after Pearl Harbor, started to fight on the same side.

Basic Law   The name for the West German Constitution when the Federal Republic of Germany arose in 1949. It was not called a constitution, since the West German leaders wanted to wait to promulgate a constitution until elections would have been held in a unified Germany. At that time, it was expected that such a unification would take place in the foreseeable future; the cold war made the phase last until 1990. Contrary to all expectations, the unification did not provide a new beginning, and the reunited Germany still relied on the Basic Law of 1949.

Basques   An ancient (pre-Indo-European) people who for a long time have lived in and alongside the Pyrenees. The French Basques number about 200,000 people. Their Spanish counterparts number approximately 2 million.

Benelux   An acronym formed from *Bel*gium, the *Nether*lands, and *Lux*embourg, having particular reference to the toll union among these countries, planned in London by their governments-in-exile in 1944 and materialized in 1948. Neither the term nor the concept itself was ever popular.

Bicameral   Refers to a legislature that has two chambers.

BLEU   A term that refers to the economic union between Belgium and Luxembourg, established in the 1920s, which had important financial implications, in that the currencies of these two countries became inseparably linked.

Canton   A term used in Switzerland to refer to an entity that in the United States would be called a state. The Swiss confederation has 20 full and six half cantons. In many cases, the cantonal borders coincide with cultural frontiers.

Cohabitation   A sharing of power between a president and a prime minister of different parties. The term originated in France.

Cold War   A sharp deterioration of Soviet–American relations following their alliance during World War II; caused by political and ideological rivalry. It lasted from 1947 to 1989.

Common Market   *See* European Economic Community.

Commonwealth of Nations   A voluntary association of the United Kingdom, its dependencies and associated states, and most of its former dependencies. As a successor of the British Empire, the Commonwealth has primarily trade and commercial implications. In a purely formal sense, the British sovereign heads the Commonwealth.

Communism   An ideology whose followers seek to overthrow capitalism through revolution in order to establish an ideal classless society that eschews individual ownership of the means of production, including real property. The first officially Communist nation was the Soviet Union, founded in 1919. After World War II, other nations in Central/Eastern Europe and elsewhere followed. Communism was discredited as an operational construct in most countries (excepting China and Cuba) in the 1990s, as a result of its tendencies toward overbureaucratization and totalitarianism.

Congress of Vienna   An international conference that shortly after the Napoleonic Wars (1814–1815) attempted to restore Europe to what it had been before those wars.

Consociational Democracy   A political system in which the large cleavages (in ethnic or religious respect) that divide a society are purposely segregated by rigorous vertical organization. Only the top segments are politically interacting with each other. Arend Lijphart, who coined the term, believed the Netherlands to be a clear example from 1917 to 1967.

Council of the European Union   The main decision-making body of the Eruopean Union, made up of ministers from all member states.

Danelaw   The law in force in the part of England held by the Danes before the Norman conquest; also, the area of England in which the Danelaw had been imposed.

Détente   Relaxation of tensions between the Soviet Union and its allies and the Western countries. A decline in intensity of the cold war.

Dirigisme   One of the major bases of the French economy. It reflects an emphasis on mercantilism. The government "directs" the economy, i.e., is very involved in what products will be grown, what projects will be entertained, etc.

Enosis   A Greek term meaning "induction." Refers to a policy to render Cyprus part of Greece.

Estado Novo   Portuguese for "new state," a political system that Antonio Salazar designed. It amounted to fascism and was outlined in the Portuguese Constitution of 1933.

Euro   The integrated currency of the European Union, launched January 1, 1999. It will replace participating countries' national currencies, beginning in 2002.

Eurocommunism   A movement emerging in Western Europe in the 1970s that announced national models of communism. The Italian, French, and Spanish Communist Parties made it clear that they would not follow the Moscow line if elected into power. They would also allow themselves to be voted out of power in democratic elections.

European Atomic Energy Community (Euratom)
Founded by a Treaty of Rome at the same time (1957) that
another such treaty established the European Economic Community. Euratom sought to develop the nuclear-energy resources of the six charter states, but as no solution was
provided for the nuclear-waste problem, the body became
progressively more obscure.

European Coal and Steel Community (ECSC) The
first of the three Communities. It was established by the
Treaty of Paris (1951) and was initially intended to pool
French and German coal and steel resources. However, between its announcement and its establishment, Italy and the
Benelux countries joined in the venture. Its aim, to create
unified products and labor markets, proved such a success
that the two other Communities (the EEC and Euratom) were
established in March 1957.

European Community A name referring to the economic integration of Europe. *See* European Economic Community.

European Economic Community (EEC) Known as the
Common Market; established by the Treaty of Rome in
March 1957 to promote the integration of Western European
economies through the removal of trade barriers. Initially,
there were three distinct Communities; but, after the
Merger Treaty of the mid-1960s, the three Communities
were viewed as one organization. The qualification "Eco-
nomic" gradually was dropped, to "European Community."
The Maastricht Treaty (1992) changed the name officially to
"European Union."

European Free Trade Association (EFTA) A trading
bloc established in Stockholm in 1960, largely at the instigation of the United Kingdom. Since it operates on premises
entirely different from those of the original European Economic Community, the membership of these two organizations has been mutually exclusive. As the EEC expanded, the
EFTA correspondingly dwindled. The two blocs have agreed
on a merger of their respective areas, which was defined as
the European Economic Area (EEA).

European Monetary Union (EMU) European economic integration formalized by the Maastricht Treaty of
1992.

European Recovery Plan *See* Marshall Plan.

European Union The term most recently applied to the
process of economic and political integration in Europe. Used
broadly in this volume for ease of understanding. *See also*
European Economic Community.

Fascism An ultra-right ideology that glorifies the state at
the expense of the individual and opposes democratic and
socialist movements. It became dominant after the March on
Rome in 1922. Although initially not racist, fascism started to
evidence a strong racist orientation as a result of the Italo–
German alliance.

Fifth Republic Refers to France since 1958 when the
Fifth Constitution was introduced and Charles de Gaulle

came to power. The French give ordinal numbers to their
constitutions and their republics. In reality, the number of
constitutions that have been proposed and occasionally
adopted has been much larger.

**Franco–German Non-Aggression Pact and Friendship
Treaty** To end the intermittent hostility between Germany
and France, this 1963 treaty prescribed semiannual consultations between the chief executives of France and Germany
and listed a range of issues for further collaboration.

Free French Consisted largely of French civilians and
military who managed to escape from France shortly before
or during the German occupation, in the period 1940 through
1944. Headed by Charles de Gaulle, it assisted in the Normandy invasion (June 1944) and the liberation of Paris (August 1944). Although it cooperated closely with the French
resistance, that collaboration was marked by rivalry when the
war was about to end.

Führer Both Benito Mussolini and Adolf Hitler revealed a bias against the term *prime minister* or *chancellor.*
They came up with the alternatives of *duce* (Italian for
"leader") and *führer* (German for "leader") once they gained
power.

Gastarbeiter A German term meaning "guest worker."
When the Western European and particularly the West German economy started to expand in the late 1950s and early
1960s, the decision was made to import laborers from the
Mediterranean basin. These laborers concluded contracts
with Western European employers usually for 2 or 3 years.
Rather than returning home once their contracts had expired,
most preferred to renew the contracts. These renewed contracts also allowed the workers to have their families join
them. As a result, a new subclass was born that became a
permanent minority.

General Agreement on Tariffs and Trade (GATT) An
important UN agency, established in 1958, that seeks to
promote a global economy through reducing tariffs and eliminating other barriers to trade. At the Uruguay Round (1990–
1992), huge obstacles surfaced. These were finally overcome
in 1994.

Gross Domestic Product (GDP) The total value of all
goods and services in a country in a given year.

Holocaust The name later given to the period (1933–
1945) of ruthless persecution and extermination of European
Jews by Nazi Germany. Nearly 5 million other people were
also murdered.

Industrial Revolution Refers to the dramatic social and
economic changes in the late eighteenth and early nineteenth
centuries that marked the transition from a stable agricultural
and commercial society to a modern industrial society.

International Atomic Energy Agency (IAEA) A UN
agency, established in 1957, that aimed at promoting the
peaceful use of atomic energy. It lapsed into oblivion as a
result of insurmountable difficulties with regard to the disposal of nuclear waste.

International Bank for Reconstruction and Development (IBRD) Commonly known as the World Bank, it constitutes a UN agency, established in 1945, that endeavors to promote economic development through guaranteed loans and technical assistance.

International Monetary Fund (IMF) A UN agency that endeavors to promote international cooperation and development. It issues moneys (either as gifts or as so-called soft loans) to less developed countries that have designed multi-year development projects.

Keynesian Economics The body of macroeconomic policies that derive from the British economist John Maynard Keynes, who believed that the governments of industrial democracies were able, and in fact were obliged, to involve themselves in their economies. Keynesian policies reigned supreme for half a century, from the Wall Street crash in 1929 until the late 1970s.

Lager A German term meaning "camp." It is often used with reference to Austrian politics, where it has come to stand for a subculture.

Laissez-Faire Originally, *laissez-faire, laissez aller*, meaning "leave them alone." A concept of nonintervention developed by eighteenth-century French physiocrats in reaction against mercantilism. The concept became better known as a result of the classical economic writings of Adam Smith.

Lateran Treaties of 1929 Often referred to as the Concordat, these treaties were concluded between the Holy See and Italy and confirmed the sovereignty of Vatican City. They also recognized Roman Catholicism as the state religion of Italy. The late 1970s spelled a revision of the clauses dealing with Roman Catholicism as the state religion and with the requirement of religious instruction at public schools.

League of Nations A peacekeeping organization established after World War I, considerably smaller than its successor, the United Nations. Although de facto no longer a political force when World War II broke out, it was officially dissolved in 1946.

Low Countries Belgium, Luxembourg, and the Netherlands.

Magna Carta A charter, issued by King John in 1215, which curbed absolutism in England. Considered the most famous document in British constitutional history, it clearly reveals the viability of opposition to the arbitrary use of power. It is always cited as an example of the "written part" of the British constitution.

Marshall Plan Officially known as the European Recovery Program (ERP). Nicknamed the Marshall Plan after George Marshall, the secretary of state in the Truman administration, who designed and in 1947 announced the plan. It consisted of a massive transfer of goods and moneys from the United States to a war-devastated Europe. Almost all Western European countries were beneficiaries. The ERP dispensed more than $12 billion in loans and goods from 1948 to 1952 to be used for the industrial recovery of Europe.

Nazi The official name of the party that assumed power once Adolf Hitler had been made chancellor was the National Socialist German Workers' Party. Its members soon came to be called Nazis.

North Atlantic Treaty Organization (NATO) A collective-defense organization, founded in 1949 by the United States, Canada, and numerous Western European nations. Although its Central/Eastern European counterpart, the Warsaw Pact, was officially dissolved in 1990, NATO continues to exist. Some amendments were made to NATO's charter, which made the organization come to life as an anti-Communist organization. Since the maintenance of NATO is extremely expensive, it is possible that the organization, which currently lacks a focus, will in the future aim at cultural cooperation among its membership. NATO's hesitancy during the Bosnian crisis has contributed to doubts concerning its validity and legitimacy.

Organization for Economic Cooperation and Development (OECD) An international organization established in 1961 to supersede the OEEC, promoting economic growth, aiding developing nations, and working to expand world trade.

Organization for European Economic Cooperation (OEEC) When announcing the European Recovery Program, the United States indicated that it did not want to deal with Western European countries on an individual basis. It wanted to deliver all the aid, goods, and moneys to one central point in Western Europe from whence the internal distribution could take place. The OEEC, headquartered in Paris, became responsible for the receipt and distribution of all Marshall Plan aid.

Organization of Petroleum Exporting Countries (OPEC) An organization established in 1960 to set oil prices and coordinate the global oil policies of its members. It reached its apogee of power in the early 1970s, when it started to use oil distribution as a political weapon. After the mid-1970s, it was riddled with rifts and divisions, and it ceased to be a political force in world politics.

Ostpolitik A term that originated with Chancellor Otto von Bismarck, who did not want the new Germany (1871) to have overseas colonies. Instead he wanted the country to expand overland in an eastward direction. The drive toward the East is a theme that may be compared to the American Manifest Destiny. Ultimately, Bismarck succumbed to the pressures for a "place in the sun," as colonialism was called in those days. As chancellor of West Germany, Willy Brandt recycled the term. It now came to mean the reestablishment of diplomatic relations between West Germany and all the countries to its east.

Paysantisme One of the two major strands upon which the French economy is based; the term points to the close relationship of the French with the soil, a relationship that has continued through times of industrialization.

Postindustrial Era This is the phase that many Western countries have attained in which manufacturing has to some extent been replaced by service industries.

Prime Ministerial System A species of the parliamentary system in which the prime minister is no longer regarded as the *primus inter pares* (first among equals) but is considered far superior in power to the other members of the cabinet. In addition to the United Kingdom, Germany with its Chancellor's Democracy may serve as an example.

Proportional Democracy A system whereby public appointments, from the cabinet level down, are distributed the various political parties in proportion to their representation in the legislature.

Proportional Representation An electoral system that allows each party to have the proportion of seats in the legislature that it achieved in votes vis-à-vis the total vote. Put simply: a party that gets 10 percent of the total vote is entitled to 10 percent of the available seats in the legislature.

Reconquista Spanish for "reconquest," the term has come to refer to the reconquest of territory held by the Moors in Spain. The Reconquista ended with the fall of Granada in 1492, a year that provides a watershed as the Age of Discovery then attained new heights.

Reformation Although the term may appear very general, it usually applies to religion, notably the religious revolution that engulfed large parts of Europe in the early sixteenth century. Martin Luther became one of the foremost leaders of Protestantism, which resulted from his reformation efforts.

Renaissance Literally "rebirth," this term refers to the rich period of Western European civilization marking the transition from the Dark Ages to modern times. The Renaissance shifted the emphasis from God and religion to man and individuality. It also emphasized worldly experience and produced brilliant accomplishments in scholarship, literature, science, and the arts.

Risorgimento An Italian term, meaning "resurgence," that refers particularly to the liberation and unification of Italy in the nineteenth century. It was by no means a popular movement but, rather, the aim and ambition of aristocratic circles in an Italy that was still greatly fragmented.

Scandinavia A term used to describe the Nordic countries: Sweden, Finland, Denmark, and Norway.

Social Democratic Party of Germany (SDP) The only political party emerging in West Germany in 1949 that had pre–World War II roots. Its program was considerably diluted at the 1959 Bad Godesberg Convention. This was done to expand its constituency. The SPD, like many other socialist parties, suffered losses in the 1990s as a result of a negative coattail effect. While it was communism that came to be publicly discredited, socialism often shared its fate.

Socialism A political and economic theory that aims at collective or government ownership and management of the means of production and distribution of goods.

Sottogoverno An Italian term meaning "subgovernment" and referring to nonofficial sources of power. In Italy, politics often faces gridlocks that can be resolved only by sottogoverno, an outside force bent on compromise and reconciliation.

Thatcherism A style of rigid right-wing governance, exemplified by Margaret Thatcher during the long period of her prime ministership (1979–1990). She exhibited a strong bias against compromise. The unions were soon muzzled. In domestic policy, she became known for her monetarist policies. In foreign policy, Thatcher repeatedly revealed suspicions that the EU bristled with socialistic endeavors.

Third Reich The official name of Germany during the period of Adolf Hitler's dictatorship (1933–1945).

Trade Union Congress (TUC) A British umbrella organization comprising most, if not all, trade unions in the United Kingdom. There is a connection between the TUC and the British Labour Party, in that the membership fees for the latter are reduced if one is a member of the former.

Truman Doctrine A foreign-policy doctrine conceived and issued by President Harry S. Truman that made it clear that the United States would come to the aid of legitimate governments troubled by insurrections that were aided from the outside. The doctrine appeared to point to the multitude of liberation fronts that emerged all over the world and were often aided by the Soviet Union. Initially it applied to Greece and Turkey.

Unicameral Refers to a legislature that has only one chamber.

United Nations (UN) The term was initially used to denote the Allies. At various war conferences, plans were made to create a successor organization to the League of Nations. Hardly had World War II ended in Europe than a large conference was held at San Francisco to establish the United Nations as an organization. The United Nations endeavors to resolve conflict and maintain peace and security as well as to achieve international cooperation in international economic, social, cultural, and humanitarian problems.

United Nations Conference on Trade and Development (UNCTAD) Convened as a special trade conference in 1964 (122 nations attended). That same year, the UN General Assembly granted it permanent status. It applies pressure on the advanced industrial states to lower their trade barriers so as to expand trade in primary commodities.

Value-Added Tax (VAT) A tax imposed on all goods and services at every stage of their production, based on the increase in value of that good or service. The VAT started out in England but is now rapidly spreading through the European Community.

Vichy France When Germany defeated France in 1940, it did not want to occupy the entire area of France. It created the *Etat Français,* a satellite that closely collaborated with the neighboring Nazis. Officially it was the successor of the Third Republic and was therefore responsible for the colonies as well. Vichy was dissolved when the Allied troops approached its area.

Vote of Confidence Refers particularly to British politics. When a government feels that, in spite of reverses, it still has the support of the majority of the House of Commons, it can demand a vote of confidence, which will indicate that it still has the backing of the majority. Votes of confidence are always undertaken by the government.

Vote of No-Confidence This refers to the traditional instrument of the opposition to oust the government. It is undertaken only when the opposition feels that the time has come to bring down the government on an important piece of legislation.

Weimar Republic The German federal system that emerged after Germany as the successor of the Wilhelmine Empire. When Germany lost World War I, it needed a new constitution. The Weimar Constitution proved highly democratic, so much so that it rendered the position of government very precarious. The 1920s, moreover, were a time of extremist agitation, unemployment, depression, and severe inflation. The Weimar Republic was succeeded by the Third Reich.

Zollverein A customs union established in nineteenth-century Germany to eliminate tariffs among the various states, principalities, and other political units. The Zollverein preceded the emergence of a unified Germany in 1871.

Bibliography

NATIONAL HISTORIES AND ANALYSES

Andorra

Barry Taylor, *Andorra* (Oxford; Santa Barbara: Clio Press, 1993).

Austria

Karen Barkey and Mark Von Hagen, *After Empire: Multiethnic Societies and Nation-Building: The Soviet Union and Russian, Ottoman and Habsburg Empires* (Boulder: Westview Press, 1997).

Gunter Bishof and Anton Pelinka, eds., *Austria in the New Europe* (New Brunswick: Transaction Publishers, 1993).

Sheldon Gardner and Gwendolyn Stevens, *Red Vienna and the Golden Age of Psychology, 1918–1938* (New York: Praeger, 1992).

Alan Levy, *The Wiesenthal File* (London: Constable, 1993).

Dagmar C. G. Lorenz and Gabriele Weinberger, eds., *Insiders and Outsiders: Jewish and Gentile Culture in Germany and Austria* (Detroit: Wayne State University Press, 1994).

Bruce F. Pauley, *From Prejudice to Persecution: A History of Austrian Anti-Semitism* (Chapel Hill: University of North Carolina Press, 1992).

Anton Pelinka, *Austria* (Boulder: Westview Press, 1997).

Harald von Riekhoff and Hanspeter Neuhold, eds., *Unequal Partners: A Comparative Analysis of Relations Between Austria and the Federal Republic of Germany and Between Canada and the United States* (Boulder: Westview Press, 1993).

Belgium

John Fitzmaurice, *The Politics of Belgium: Crisis Compromise in a Plural Society* (London: Hurst & Co., 1996).

Lisbet Hooghe, *A Leap in the Dark: Nationalist Conflict and Federal Reform in Belgium* (Ithaca: Cornell University Press, 1991).

Ann Owen, "Belgium: Slimmer SHAPE," *Lancet* (North American ed.), 340: 1342–3, November 28, 1992.

M. A. G. van Meerhaeghe, ed., *Belgium and EC Membership Evaluated* (London: Pinter Publishers; New York: St. Martin's Press, 1992).

Cyprus

Vassos Argyrou, *Tradition and Modernity in the Mediterranean* (New York: Cambridge University Press, 1996).

Tozun Bahcheli, *Greek-Turkish Relations since 1955* (Boulder: Westview Press, 1990).

Dan Hofstadter, *Goldberg's Angel: An Adventure in the Antiquities Trade* (New York: Farrar, Straus and Giroux, 1994).

Zaim M. Nedjatigil, *The Cyprus Question and the Turkish Position in International Law* (Oxford; New York: Oxford University Press, 1989).

John Reddaway, *Burdened with Cyprus: The British Connection* (London: Weidenfeld & Nicholson, 1986).

Rodney Wilson, *Cyprus and the International Economy* (New York: St. Martin's Press, 1992).

Denmark

Jens Henrik Haarh, *Looking to Europe: The EC Policies of the British Labour Party and the Danish Social Democrats* (Aarhus: Aarhus University Press, 1993).

Gunnar Viby Mogensen, *Danes and Their Politicians: A Summary of the Findings of a Research Project on Political Credibility in Denmark* (Aarhus: Aarhus University Press, 1993).

Morten Strange, *Culture Shock! Denmark* (Portland, Oregon: Graphic Arts Center Publishing, 1996).

Finland

Christian Bordes-Marcilloux, *Three Assessments of Finland's Economic Crisis and Economic Policy* (Helsinki: Bank of Finland, 1993).

Jyrki Kakonen, ed., *Politics and Sustainable Growth in the Arctic* (Aldershot; Brookfield, VT: Dartmouth, 1993).

Kimmo Kiljunen, *Finland and the New International Division of Labour* (Houndmills, Basingstoke, Hampshire: Macmillan Press, 1992).

Vojtech Mastny, *The Helsinki Process and the Reintegration of Europe, 1986–1991: Analysis and Documentation* (New York: New York University Press, 1992).

Risto E. J. Penttila, *Finland's Search for Security through Defence, 1944–1989* (New York: St. Martin's Press, 1991).

H. M. Tillotson, *Finland at Peace and War, 1918–1993* (Wilby, Norwich: Michael Russell, 1993).

France

Robert Aldrich, *France's Overseas Frontier: Departements et Territoires d'Outre-mer* (Cambridge; New York: Cambridge University Press, 1992).

Richard Bernstein, *Fragile Glory: A Portrait of France and the French* (New York: Knopf, 1990).

Frank Costigliola, *France and the United States: The Cold Alliance since World War II* (New York: Twayne Publishers; Toronto: Maxwell Macmillan, Canada; New York: Maxwell Macmillan International, 1992).

Jill Forbes and Michael Kelly, *French Cultural Studies: An Introduction* (Asheville: Outcomes Unlimited Press, 1966).

Julius Weis Friend, *Seven Years in France: François Mitterrand and the Unintended Revolution* (Boulder: Westview Press, 1989).

Steven Philip Kramer, *Does France Still Count? The French Role in the New Europe* (The Washington Papers, 1964; Westport: Praeger, 1994).

Herbert R. Lottman, *The Fall of Paris: June 1940* (New York: HarperCollins Publisher, 1992).

Cheryl MacLachlan, *Bringing France Home* (New York: Crown Publishing Group, 1995).

Peter Morris, *French Politics Today* (Manchester: Manchester University Press; New York: Distributed by St. Martin's Press, 1994).

Jean-Claude Scheid and Peter Walton, *France* (London; New York: Routledge in association with the Institute of Chartered Accountants in England and Wales, 1992).

Paul Stillwell, ed., *Assault on Normandy: First-Person Accounts from the Sea Services* (Annapolis: Naval Institute Press, 1994).

Germany

John Borneman, *Belonging in the Two Berlins: Kin, State, Nation.* Cambridge; New York: Cambridge University Press, 1992).

Robert Burns, ed., *German Cultural Studies: An Introduction* (Oxford: Oxford University Press, 1995).

Marilyn Shevin Coetzee, *The German Army League: Popular Nationalism in Wilhelmine Germany* (New York: Oxford University Press, 1990).

Robin Cross, *Fallen Eagle: The Last Days of the Third Reich* (New York: Wiley, 1996).

Marc Fisher, *After the Wall: Germany, the Germans, and the Burdens of History* (New York: Simon & Schuster, 1995).

Gene E. Frankland, *Between Protest and Power: The Green Party in Germany* (Boulder: Westview Press, 1992).

Mary Fulbrook, *The Divided Nation: A History of Germany, 1918–1990* (standard title: *Fontana History of Germany, 1918–1990*) (New York: Oxford University Press, 1992).

Herbert Giersch, *The Fading Miracle: Four Decades of Market Economy in Germany* (Cambridge; New York: Cambridge University Press, 1992).

John Gimbel, *Science, Technology and Reparations: Exploitation and Plunder in Postwar Germany* (Stanford: Stanford University Press, 1990).

Ullrich Heilemann, *Christmas in July? The Political Economy of German Reunification Reconsidered* (Washington, D.C.: Brookings Institution, 1993).

David M. Keithly, *The Collapse of East German Communism: The Year the Wall Came Down* (Westport: Praeger, 1992).

Raymond A. Kennedy, *The Bitterest Age* (New York: Ticknor & Fields, 1994).

Emil J. Kirchner and James Sperling, *The Federal Republic and NATO: 40 Years After* (New York: St. Martin's Press, 1992).

John J. Kulczycki, *The Foreign Worker and the German Labor Movement: Xenophobia and Solidarity in the Coal Fields of the Ruhr, 1871–1914* (Oxford; Providence, RI: Berg Publishers, 1994).

Rand C. Lewis, *The Neo-Nazi and German Unification* (Westport: Greenwood Publishing, 1996).

Stephen Padgett, ed., *Adenauer to Kohl: The Development of the German Chancellorship* (Washington, DC: Georgetown University Press, 1994).

William E. Paterson and David Southern, *Governing Germany* (New York; London: W. W. Norton & Co., 1991).

Ernest D. Plock, *East German–West German Relations and the Fall of the GDR* (Boulder: Westview Press, 1993).

Gordon Smith et al., eds., *Developments in German Politics* (Durham: Duke University Press, 1992).

W. R. Smyser, *The Economy of United Germany: Colossus at the Crossroads* (New York: St. Martin's Press, 1991).

Gregory F. Treverton, *America, Germany and the Future of Europe* (Princeton: Princeton University Press, 1992).

Paul J. J. Welfens, ed., *Economic Aspects of German Unification: National and International Perspectives* (Berlin; New York: Springer Verlag, 1992).

Greece

David Close, *The Origins of the Greek Civil War* (London; New York: Longman, 1995).

Kevin Featherstone and Dimitrios K. Kasoudas, eds., *Political Change in Greece: Before and After the Colonels* (London: Croom Helm, 1987).

Robert Frazier, *Anglo-American Relations with Greece: The Coming of the Cold War, 1942–47* (New York: St. Martin's Press, 1991).

Nicholas Gage, *Hellas: A Portrait of Greece* (New York: Villard Books, 1987).

Michael Grant, *A Social History of Greece and Rome* (New York: Scribner: Maxwell Macmillan International, 1992).

Nicholas Stavrou, ed., *Greece Under Socialism: A NATO Ally Adrift* (New Rochelle: A. D. Caratzas, 1988).

Iceland

E. Paul Durrenberger and Gisli Palsson, eds., *Images of Contemporary Iceland: Everyday Lives and Global Contexts* (Iowa City: University of Iowa Press, 1996).

Gudmundur Gunnarsson, *The Economic Growth in Iceland, 1910–1980* (Stockholm, Sweden: Almqvist & Wiksell International, 1990).

John J. Horton, *Iceland* (Oxford; Santa Barbara: Clio Press, 1983).

Donald Edwin Nuechterlein, *Iceland, Reluctant Ally* (Westport: Greenwood Press, 1975, 1961).

Richard F. Tomasson, *Iceland: The First New Society* (Minneapolis: University of Minnesota Press, 1980).

Ireland

J. Bowyer Bell, *The Gun in Politics: An Analysis of Irish Political Conflict* (New Brunswick: Transaction Books, 1987).

George D. Boyce, *Making Modern Irish History* (New York: Routledge, 1996).

Niamh Brennan, *Ireland* (London; New York: Routledge in Association with the Institute of Chartered Accountants in England and Wales, 1992).

Sean Byrne, *Third Parties in Northern Ireland: Exacerbation or Amelioration?* (St. Louis: University of Missouri, Center for International Studies, 1994).

Neil Collins, *Irish Politics Today,* 2nd ed. (Manchester; New York: Manchester University Press; distributed exclusively in the United States and Canada by St. Martin's Press, 1992).

John E. Finn, *Constitutions in Crisis: Political Violence and the Rule of Law* (New York: Oxford University Press, 1991).

John Hume, *A New Ireland: Politics, Peace, and Reconciliation* (Niwot, Colorado: Robert Rinehart, 1996).

Independent Study Group, *Ulster After the Ceasefire* (London: Alliance Publishers, Ltd., for the Institute for the European Defence and Strategic Studies, 1994).

Richard T. Vann, *Friends in Life and Death: The British and Irish Quakers in the Demographic Transition* (Cambridge; New York: Cambridge University Press, 1992).

Italy

Percy Allum, *Chronicle of a Death Foretold: The First Italian Republic* (Reading: Department of Politics, University of Reading, 1993).

Christopher Duggan, *A Concise History of Italy* (New York: Cambridge University Press, 1994).

Francesco Francioni, ed., *Italy and EC Membership Evaluated* (New York: St. Martin's Press, 1992).

Mark Gilbert, *The Italian Revolution: The End of Politics Italian Style?* (Boulder: Westview Press, 1994).

Cheryl Maclachlin, *Bringing Italy Home* (New York, Crown Publishing Group, 1995).

Ray Porter and Mikulas Tiech, eds., *The Renaissance in National Context* (Cambridge; New York: Cambridge University Press, 1992).

Robert D. Putnam, *Making Democracy Work: Civic Traditions in Modern Italy* (Princeton: Princeton University Press, 1993).

Nico Randeraad, *Authority in Search of Liberty: The Prefects of Liberal Italy* (Amsterdam: Thesis Publishers, 1993).

Frederic Spots and Theodore Wieser, *Italy: A Difficult Democracy* (Cambridge: Cambridge University Press, 1986).

Randolph Stern, *Arts of Power: Three Halls of State in Italy 1300–1600* (Berkeley: University of California Press, 1992).

James Walston, *The Mafia and Clientelism: Roads to Rome in Post-War Calabria* (London; New York: Routledge, 1988).

Leonard B. Weinberg and William Lee Eubank, *The Rise and Fall of Italian Terrorism* (Boulder: Westview Press, 1987).

Liechtenstein

Wolfgang F. Danspeckgruber, ed., *Emerging Dimensions of European Security Policy* (Boulder: Westview Press, 1991).

Regula A. Meier, *Liechtenstein* (Oxford; Santa Barbara: Clio Press, 1993).

Luxembourg

Ed Needham, *The Countries of Benelux* (London: Gloucester Press, 1994).

Timothy M. Smeeding, Michael O'Higgins, and Lee Rainwater, eds., *Poverty, Inequality and Income Distribution in Comparative Perspective: The Luxembourg Income Study (LIS)* (Washington, DC: Urban Institute Press: Lanham: Distributed by the University Press of America, 1990).

Malta

Salvino Busuttil, *The Future of the Mediterranean* (Valetta: University of Malta, 1995).

Desmond Gregory, *Malta, Britain, and the European Powers, 1793–1875* (Madison: Fairleigh Dickerson University Press, 1996).

Adrianus Koster, *Prelates and Politicians in Malta: Changing Power Balances between Church and State in a Mediterranean Island Fortress, 1800–1976* (Assen: van Gorcum, 1984).

Christopher F. Shores, *Malta: The Hurricane Years: 1940–41* (London: Grub Street, 1987).

Mario Vassallo, *From Lordship to Stewardship: Religion and Social Change in Malta* (The Hague; New York: Mouton, 1979).

Barry York, *Malta, a Nonaligned Democracy in the Mediterranean* (Sydney: A Friend of Malta publication, 1987).

Monaco

Raymond de Vos, *History of the Monies, Medals, and Tokens of Monaco* (Long Island City: Sanford J. Durst, 1978).

Anne Edwards, *The Grimaldis of Monaco* (New York: Morrow, 1992).

The Netherlands

Herman Bakvis, *Catholic Power in the Netherlands* (Kingston, Ontario: McGill-Queen's University Press, 1981).

Frans M. Dieleman and Sako Musterd, *The Randstad: A Research and Policy Laboratory* (Dordrecht; Boston: Kluwer Academic Publishers, 1992).

H. Entzinger, *Immigrant Ethnic Minorities in the Dutch Labor Market* (Amsterdam: Thesis Publishers, 1994).

Ph. P. Everts, ed., *Controversies at Home: Domestic Factors in the Foreign Policy of the Netherlands* (Dordrecht; Boston: M. Nijhoff, 1985).

Fernando Garrido, *EC and National Regulations on Environment and Agriculture in Denmark, the Netherlands and Spain* (Esbjerg: South Jutland University Press, 1994).

Simon Shama, *The Embarrassment of Riches: An Interpretation of Dutch Culture in the Golden Age* (New York: Knopf, 1987).

Theo Verbeek, *Descartes and the Dutch: Early Reactions to Cartesian Philosophy, 1637–1650* (Carbondale: Southern Illinois Press, 1992).

Norway

Christian Hiorth Aall, *Footprints in the Sund: An Autobiography* (Combloux, France: Starvan Montage, 1991).

W. Timothy Coombs, *A Comparative Analysis of International Public Relations Practices, Phase Two: Interpretations of Differences and Similarities between Professionalization in Austria, Norway and the U.S.* (1992).

Sherwood S. Cordier, *The Defense of NATO's Northern Front and US Military Policy* (Lanham: University Press of America, 1989).

Erik Damman, *Revolution in the Affluent Society* (London: Heretic Books, 1984), translated by Louis Mackay.

Kurt Feldbakken, *The Honeymoon* (New York: St. Martin's Press, 1987).

Anne Coshen Kiel, ed., *Continuity and Change: Aspects of Contemporary Norway* (Oslo: Scandanavian University Press, 1993).

Arne Selbyg, *Norway Today: An Introduction to Modern Norwegian Society* (Oslo: Norwegian University Press, 1986).

Portugal

Enrique A. Baloyra, ed., *Comparing New Democracies: Transition and Consolidation in Mediterranean Europe and the Southern Cone* (Boulder: Westview Press, 1987).

Lawrence S. Graham and Douglas Wheeler, *In Search of Modern Portugal* (Madison: University of Wisconsin Press, 1983).

Kimberley A. Hamilton, *Lusophone Africa, Portugal and the United States: Possibilities for More Effective Cooperation* (Lisbon Luso-American Development Foundation; Washington, DC: Center for Strategic and International Studies, 1992).

Ulrike Liebert and Maurizio Cotta, eds., *Parliament and Democratic Consolidation in Southern Europe: Greece, Italy, Portugal, Spain, and Turkey* (London; New York: Pinter Publishers, 1990).

Walter C. Opello, *Portugal's Political Development: A Comparative Approach* (Boulder: Westview Press, 1985).

____, *Portugal: From Monarchy to Pluralist Democracy* (Boulder: Westview Press, 1991).

Eric Solsten, ed., *Portugal: A Country Study* (Washington, DC: Library of Congress, 1993).

Spain

Rodrigo Botero, *Reflections on the Modernization of Spain* (San Francisco: ICS Press, 1992).

Luis Costa et al., eds., *German and International Perspectives on the Spanish Civil War: The Aesthetics of Partisanship* (Columbia: Camden House, 1992).

J. H. Elliott, *The Hispanic World: Civilization and Empire* (London: Thames and Hudson, 1991).

James D. Fernandez, *Apology to Apostrophe: The Autobiography and the Rhetoric of Self-Representation in Spain* (Durham: Duke University Press, 1992).

Richard A. Fletcher, *Moorish Spain* (New York: H. Holt, 1992).

Jeffrey R. Franks, *Explaining Unemployment in Spain: Structural Exchange, Cyclical Fluctuations, and Labor Market Rigidities* (Washington, DC: International Monetary Fund, 1994).

José A. Gonzalo, *Spain* (London; New York: Routledge, 1992).

Richard Gunther, ed., *Politics, Society, and Democracy. The Case of Spain* (Boulder: Westview Press, 1992).

Thomas D. Lancaster, *Political Stability and Democratic Change: Energy in Spain's Transition* (University Park: The Pennsylvania State University Press, 1989).

D. S. Morris, *Britain, Spain and Gibraltar, 1945–1990: The Eternal Triangle* (London; New York: Routledge, 1992).

Edward Moxon-Browne, *Political Change in Spain* (London; New York: Routledge, 1989).

Mary Elizabeth Perry and Anne J. Cruz, *Cultural Encounters: The Impact of the Inquisition in Spain and the New World* (Berkeley: University of California Press, 1991).

Robin L. Rosenberg, *Spain and Central America: Democracy and Foreign Policy* (New York: Greenwood Press, 1992).

Sweden

Ebba Dohlman, *National Welfare and Economic Interdependence: The Case of Sweden's Foreign Trade Policy* (Oxford: Clarendon Press; New York: Oxford University Press, 1989).

Lars Engwall, ed., *Economics in Sweden: An Evaluation of Swedish Research in Economics* (London; New York: Routledge, 1992).

Jonas Frykman and Orvar Lofgren, *Culture Builders: A Historical Anthropology of Middle Class Life* (New Brunswick: Rutgers University Press, 1987), translated by Alan Crozier.

Lars Hultkrantz, *Chernobyl Effects on Domestic and Inbound Tourism in Sweden: A Time Series Analysis* (Umea: University of Umea, 1994).

Michael Maccoby, ed., *Sweden at the Edge: Lessons for American and Swedish Managers* (Philadelphia: University of Pennsylvania Press, 1991).

Michele Micheletti, *Civil Society and State Relations in Sweden* (Brookfield, VT: Ashgate Publishing Co., 1995).

Militarhistoriska Forlaget, *The Swedish Armed Forces and Foreign Influences, 1870–1945* (Stockholm: 1992).

Jonas Pontusson, *The Limits of Social Democracy: Investment Politics in Sweden* (Ithaca: Cornell University Press, 1992).

Bo Rothstein, *The Social Democratic State: The Swedish Model and the Bureaucratic Problem of Social Reform* (Pittsburgh, PA: University of Pittsburgh Press, 1996).

Switzerland

Janet E. Hilowitz, ed., *Switzerland in Perspective* (New York: Greenwood Press, 1990).

Kenneth D. McRae, *Conflict and Compromise in Multilingual Societies* (Waterloo, Ontario: Wilfrid Laurier University Press, 1983).

Rene Schwok, *Switzerland and the European Common Market* (New York: Praeger, 1991).

Ralph Segelman, *The Swiss Way of Welfare: Lessons for the Western World* (New York: Praeger Publishers, 1986).

Donald Arthur Waters, *Hitler's Secret Ally, Switzerland* (La Mesa: Pertinent Publications, 1992).

The United Kingdom

Anderson Consulting, *The Future of European Health Care* (London: Burston Marsteller, 1993).

David George Boyce, *The Irish Question and British Politics, 1868–1986* (Basingstoke: Macmillan Education, 1988).

Avta Brah, *Cartographies of Diaspora: Contesting Identities* (New York: Routledge, 1996).

Simon Bulmer, Stephen George, and Andrew Scott, eds., *The United Kingdom and EC Membership Evaluated* (New York: St. Martin's Press, 1992).

Ernest E. Cashmore, *United Kingdom: Class, Race and Gender Since the War* (London; Boston: Unwin Hyman, 1989).

Richard Critchfield, *An American Looks at Britain* (New York: Anchor Books/Doubleday, 1990).

Nelson Antonio Da Costa, *An Impossible Meeting of the Minds: A Rhetorical Analysis of the 1982 Falkland (Malvinas) Conflict Between Argentina and the United Kingdom* (Lawrence: University of Kansas, Communication Studies, 1994).

Rudi Dornbusch and Richard Layard, eds., *The Performance of the British Economy* (New York: Oxford University Press, 1988).

John Greenaway, Steve Smith, and John Street, *Deciding Factors in British Politics: A Case-Studies Approach* (London; New York: Routledge, 1992).

Alfred F. Havighurst, *Britain in Transition: The Twentieth Century* (Chicago: University of Chicago Press, 1985).

Bill Jones and Lynton J. Robins, eds., *Two Decades in British Politics: Essays to Mark Twenty-One Years of the Politics Association, 1969–1990* (Manchester; New York: St. Martin's Press [distributor], 1992).

Dennis Kavanagh, *British Politics: Continuities and Change* (Oxford; New York: Oxford University Press, 1990).

_____, *Thatcherism and British Politics: The End of Consensus?* 2nd ed. (New York: Oxford University Press, 1990).

Dennis Kavanagh and Anthony Selden, *The Thatcher Effect* (Oxford: Clarendon Press; New York: Oxford University Press, 1989).

Brian Lapping, *End of Empire* (New York: St. Martin's Press, 1985).

William Roger Louis, ed., *Adventures with Britannia: Personalities, Politics, and Culture in Britain* (London: I. B. Tauris, 1995).

Kenneth MacKinnon, *The Politics of Popular Representation: Reagan, Thatcher, AIDS, and the Movies* (Rutherford: Fairleigh Dickenson University Press; London; Cranbury: Associated University Presses, 1992).

Dawn Oliver, *Government in the United Kingdom: The Search for Accountability, Effectiveness and Citizenship* (Milton Keynes; Philadelphia: Open University Press, 1991).

James S. Olsen, et al., *Historical Dictionary of the British Empire* (Westport: Greenwood Publishers, 1996).

Orde, *The Eclipse of Great Britain* (New York: St. Martins, 1996).

Peter Orton, *UK Health Care: The Facts* (Dordrecht; Boston: Kluwer Academic Publishers, 1994).

Michael Stephen Partridge, *Military Planning for the Defense of the United Kingdom, 1814–1870* (New York: Greenwood Press, 1989).

Giles Radice, *Labour's Path to Power: The New Revisionism* (New York: St. Martin's Press, 1989).

Peter Riddell, *Thatcher Decade: How Britain Has Changed during the 1980s* (Oxford: Basil Blackwell, 1989).

_____, *The Thatcher Era and Its Legacy* (Oxford; Cambridge: B. Blackwell, 1991).

Anita Inder Singh, *The Limits of British Influence: South Asia & the Anglo-American Relationship* (New York: St. Martin, 1993).

Steve Smith et al., eds., *British Foreign Policy: Tradition, Change, and Transformation* (Winchester: Unwin Hyman, 1988).

Vatican City

Louis F. Aiello, *Time and History in the Ecclesiology of Vatican II: Theological Investigation of the Concept "People of God"* (unpublished manuscript, 1986).

Owen Chadwick, *Britain and the Vatican during the Second World War* (Cambridge; New York: Cambridge University Press, 1986).

Malachi Martin, *Vatican* (New York: Harper & Row, 1986).

Francesco Papafava, ed., *The Vatican* (Firenze: Scala Books; New York: Distributed by Harper & Row, 1984).

Thomas Reese, *Inside the Vatican: The Politics and Organization of the Catholic Church* (Cambridge, MA: Harvard University Press, 1996).

SOURCES WITH A GENERAL OR REGIONAL PERSPECTIVE

Guido Baglioni and Colin Crouch, eds., *European Industrial Relations: The Challenge of Flexibility* (London; Newbury Park: Sage Publications, 1990).

Richard Batley and Gerry Stoker, eds., *Local Government in Europe: Trends and Development* (New York: St. Martin's Press, 1991).

Patrick Birkinshaw with Ian Harden and Norma Lewis, *Government by Moonlight: The Hybrid Parts of the State* (London; Boston: Unwin Hyman, 1990).

Gillian Bottomley, *From Another Place: Migration and the Politics of Culture* (Cambridge; New York: Cambridge University Press, 1992).

Luciano Cheles, Ronnie Ferguson, and Michalina Vaughan, eds., *Neofascism in Europe* (London; New York: Longman, 1991).

John Coakley, *Social Origins of Nationalistic Movements: The Contemporary European Experience* (Sage Publications, 1991).

John E. Finn, *Constitutions in Crisis: Political Violence and the Rule of Law* (New York: Oxford University Press, 1991).

Michael Grant, *The Social History of Greece and Rome,* 1st American ed. (New York: Scribner: Maxwell Macmillan International, 1992).

Vilho Harle, ed., *European Values in International Relations* (London; New York: Pinter Publishers, 1990).

Voitech Mastny, *The Helsinki Process and the Reintegration of Europe, 1986–1991: Analysis and Documentation* (New York: New York University Press, 1990).

Hans J. Michelmann and Panayotis Soldatos, eds., *Federalism and International Relations: The Role of Subnational Units* (Oxford: Clarendon Press; New York: Oxford University Press, 1990).

Organisation for Economic Cooperation and Development. *Nuclear Legislation: Analytical Study: Regulatory and Institutional Framework for Nuclear Activities* (Paris: Nuclear Energy Agency, Organisation for Economic Cooperation and Development; Washington, DC: Sales agents, OECD Publications and Information Center, 1983–1984).

Geoffrey Pridham, ed., *Encouraging Democracy: The International Context of Regime Transition in Southern Europe* (New York: St. Martin's Press, 1991).

Paul Anthony Rahe, *Republics Ancient and Modern: Classical Republicanism and the American Revolution* (Chapel Hill: University of North Carolina Press, 1992).

Stephen Salter and John Stevenson, eds., *The Working Class and Politics in Europe and America, 1929–1945* (London; New York: Longman, 1990).

Josep Miquel Sobrer, ed. and translator, *Catalonia, A Self-Portrait* (Bloomington: Indiana University Press, 1992).

Gregory F. Treverton, *America and the Future of Europe* (Princeton: Princeton University Press, 1992).

Tibor Vasko, ed., *Problems of Economic Transition: Regional Development in Central and Eastern Europe* (Aldershot: Avebury; Brookfield: Ashgate Publishing Company, 1992).

K. Steven Vincent, *Between Marxism and Anarchism: Benoit Malon and French Reformist Socialism* (Berkeley: University of California Press, 1992).

Helen Wallace, ed., *The Wider Western Europe: Reshaping the EC/EFTA Relationship* (London; New York: Pinter Publishers for the Royal Institute of International Affairs, London, 1991).

PERIODICALS AND CURRENT EVENTS

The Christian Science Monitor
One Norway Street
Boston, MA 02115
This newspaper is published 5 days per week, with news coverage, articles, and specific features on world events.

Commonweal
Commonweal Publishing Co., Inc.
232 Madison Avenue
New York, NY 10016
This biweekly publication reviews literature, current events, religion, and the arts.

Current History, A World Affairs Journal
Provides focus on geopolitical regions throughout the world.

The Economist
125 St. James's St.
London, England
This periodical presents world events from a British perspective.

The German Tribune—A Weekly Review of the German Press
Collects the most important articles in the German press and translates them into English.

Le Monde (weekly edition, in English)
7 Rue des Italiens
Paris, France
A summary of the previous week's news, with separate sections on various geographical regions.

Multinational Monitor
Ralph Nader's Corporate Accountability Research Group
1346 Connecticut Avenue, NW
Washington, DC 20006
This monthly periodical offers editorials and articles on world events and current issues.

The New Republic
The New Republic, Inc.
1220 19th Street, NW, Suite 200
Washington, DC 20036
Weekly coverage of politics, literature, and world events.

The New York Times
The New York Times Co.
229 West 43rd Street

New York, NY 10036

A daily newspaper that covers world news through articles and editorials.

Newsweek

Newsweek, Inc.

444 Madison Avenue

New York, NY 10022

A weekly publication with news and commentary on the week's developments in the nation and the world. Articles cover national and international affairs, science, sports, business, medicine, religion, entertainment, and the arts.

Time

Time, Inc.

Time and Life Building, Rockefeller Center

New York, NY 10020

A weekly magazine offering national and international news organized by departments—including art, behavior, books, business, cinema, education, environment, law, modern living, music, nation, press, religion, theater, and world. Each issue includes an in-depth examination of a significant situation or personality and essays dealing with issues and ideas.

UNESCO Courier

Place de Fontenoy

Paris, France

Published by the UN, the magazine presents extensive treatment of world events by devoting each monthly issue to a specific topic.

The Wall Street Journal

Dow Jones Books

Box 300

Princeton, NJ 08540

Presents broad daily coverage of world news through articles and editorials.

World Press Review

The Stanley Foundation

230 Park Avenue

New York, NY 10169

Each month this publication presents foreign magazine and newspaper stories on political, social, and economic affairs.

Index